C000066691

1,000,000 Books

are available to read at

orgotten ooks

—◆—

www.ForgottenBooks.com

—◆—

Read online
Download PDF
Purchase in print

ISBN 978-0-266-05852-6
PIBN 10952717

This book is a reproduction of an important historical work. Forgotten Books uses
state-of-the-art technology to digitally reconstruct the work, preserving the original format
whilst repairing imperfections present in the aged copy. In rare cases, an imperfection in
the original, such as a blemish or missing page, may be replicated in our edition. We do,
however, repair the vast majority of imperfections successfully; any imperfections that
remain are intentionally left to preserve the state of such historical works.

Forgotten Books is a registered trademark of FB &c Ltd.
Copyright © 2018 FB &c Ltd.
FB &c Ltd, Dalton House, 60 Windsor Avenue, London, SW19 2RR.
Company number 08720141. Registered in England and Wales.

For support please visit www.forgottenbooks.com

1 MONTH OF
FREE
READING

at

www.ForgottenBooks.com

By purchasing this book you are eligible for one month membership to ForgottenBooks.com, giving you unlimited access to our entire collection of over 1,000,000 titles via our web site and mobile apps.

To claim your free month visit:

www.forgottenbooks.com/free952717

* Offer is valid for 45 days from date of purchase. Terms and conditions apply.

English
Français
Deutsche
Italiano
Español
Português

www.forgottenbooks.com

Mythology Photography **Fiction**
Fishing Christianity **Art** Cooking
Essays Buddhism Freemasonry
Medicine **Biology** Music **Ancient**
Egypt Evolution Carpentry Physics
Dance Geology **Mathematics** Fitness
Shakespeare **Folklore** Yoga Marketing
Confidence Immortality Biographies
Poetry **Psychology** Witchcraft
Electronics Chemistry History **Law**
Accounting **Philosophy** Anthropology
Alchemy Drama Quantum Mechanics
Atheism Sexual Health **Ancient History**
Entrepreneurship Languages Sport
Paleontology Needlework Islam
Metaphysics Investment Archaeology
Parenting Statistics Criminology
Motivational

PUBLIC DOCUMENT. No. 27.

FORTY-EIGHTH ANNUAL REPORT

OF

THE TRUSTEES

OF THE

PERKINS INSTITUTION

AND

Massachusetts School for the Blind,

FOR THE YEAR ENDING

SEPTEMBER 30, 1879.

BOSTON:

Rand, Avery, & Co., Printers to the Commonwealth,

117 FRANKLIN STREET.

1880.

TABLE OF CONTENTS.

70378

Commonwealth of Massachusetts.

PERKINS INSTITUTION AND MASS. SCHOOL FOR THE BLIND,
So. BOSTON, Oct. 17, 1879.

To the Hon. HENRY B. PEIRCE, *Secretary of State.*

DEAR SIR, — I have the honor to transmit to you, for the use of the Legislature, a copy of the Forty-Eighth Annual Report of the Trustees of this Institution to the Corporation thereof, together with the usual accompanying documents.

Respectfully,

M. ANAGNOS,

Secretary.

OFFICERS OF THE CORPORATION.

1879-80.

SAMUEL ELIOT, *President.*
JOHN CUMMINGS, *Vice-President.*
HENRY ENDICOTT, *Treasurer.*
M. ANAGNOS, *Secretary.*

BOARD OF TRUSTEES.

ROBERT E. APTHORP.
JOHN S. DWIGHT.
JOSEPH B. GLOVER.
J. THEODORE HEARD, M.D.
HENRY LEE HIGGINSON.
JAMES H MEANS, D.D.

ANDREW P. PEABODY, D.D.
EDWARD N. PERKINS.
JOSIAH QUINCY.
SAMUEL G. SNELLING.
JAMES STURGIS.
GEORGE W. WALES.

STANDING COMMITTEES.
Monthly Visiting Committee,
Whose duty it is to visit and inspect the Institution at least once in each month.

1880. January . . . R. E. APTHORP.
February . . J. S. DWIGHT.
March . . . . J. B. GLOVER.
April. . . . . J. T. HEARD.
May . . . . . H. L. HIGGINSON.
June . . . . . J. H. MEANS.

1880. July . . . . . A. P. PEABODY.
August . . . E. N. PERKINS.
September . JOSIAH QUINCY.
October . . . S. G. SNELLING.
November. . JAMES STURGIS.
December . . GEO. W. WALES.

Committee on Education.
J. S. DWIGHT.
A. P. PEABODY.
JOSIAH QUINCY.

House Committee.
E. N. PERKINS.
G. W. WALES.
J. H. MEANS.

Committee of Finance.
R. E. APTHORP.
J. B. GLOVER.
JAMES STURGIS.

Committee on Health.
J. THEODORE HEARD.
E. N. PERKINS.
H. L. HIGGINSON.

Auditors of Accounts.
ROBERT E. APTHORP.
SAMUEL G. SNELLING.

OFFICERS OF THE INSTITUTION.

DIRECTOR.
M. ANAGNOS.

MEDICAL INSPECTOR.
JOHN HOMANS, M.D.

LITERARY DEPARTMENT.

Miss M. L. P. Shattuck.
Miss J. R. Gilman.
Miss Julia Boylan.

Miss Della Bennett.
Miss S. L. Bennett.
Miss S. E. C. Hatheway.

Miss Mary Moore.

MUSICAL DEPARTMENT.

Resident Teachers.
Thomas Reeves.
Frank H Kilbourne.
Miss Freda Black.
Miss Lizzie Riley.
Miss Lucy Hammond.

Assistant.
Henry T. Bray.

Non-Resident Teachers.
Mrs. Kate Rametti.
Henry C. Brown.
C. H. Higgins.

Music Readers.
Miss Allie S. Knapp.
Miss K. M. Plummer.
Miss Katie P. Miller.

TUNING DEPARTMENT.

J. W. Smith, *Instructor and Manager.*

INDUSTRIAL DEPARTMENT.

Workshops for Juveniles.
J. H. Wright, *Work Master.*
Miss A. J. Dillingham, *Work Mistress.*
Thomas Carroll, *Assistant.*
Miss H. Kellier, *Assistant.*

Workshop for Adults.
A. W. Bowden, *Manager.*
P. Morrill, *Foreman.*
Miss M. A. Dwelly, *Forewoman.*
Miss E. M. Whittier, *Clerk.*

DOMESTIC DEPARTMENT.

Steward.
A. W. Bowden.

Matron.
Miss M. C Moulton.
Miss A. F. Cram, *Assistant.*

Housekeepers in the Cottages.
Mrs. M. A. Knowlton.
Miss A. J. Dillingham.
Miss Bessie Wood.
Miss Lizzie N. Smith.

Miss E. B. Webster, *Book-keeper.*

MEMBERS OF THE CORPORATION.

ALL persons who have contributed twenty-five dollars to the funds of the Institution, all who have served as trustees or treasurer, and all who have been elected by special vote, are members.

Agassiz, Alexander, Cambridge.
Alger, Rev. William R., Boston.
Amory, James S., Boston.
Amory, William, Boston.
Appleton, T. G., Boston.
Apthorp, Robert E., Boston.
Atkinson, Edward, Boston.
Atkinson, William, Boston.
Austin, Edward, Boston.
Barrows, Rev. S. J., Dorchester.
Beard, Hon. Alanson W., Boston.
Bigelow, E. B., Boston.
Blake, G. Baty, Boston.
Bouvé, Thomas T., Boston.
Bowditch, J. I., Boston.
Bradlee, F. H., Boston.
Brewer, Thomas M., M.D., Boston.
Brewster, Osmyn, Boston.
Brimmer, Hon. Martin, Boston.
Brooks, Francis, Boston.
Brooks, P. C., Boston.
Bullard, W. S., Boston.
Chandler, P. W., Boston.
Chandler, Theophilus P., Brookline.
Childs, Alfred A., Boston.
Claflin, Hon. William, Boston.
Clapp, William W., Boston.
Coolidge, Dr. A., Boston.
Crosby, Joseph B., Boston.
Cummings, Charles A., Boston.
Cummings, Hon. John, Woburn.
Dalton, C. H., Boston.
Davis, James, Boston.
Dix, J. H., M.D., Boston.
Downer, Samuel, Dorchester.

Dwight, John S., Boston.
Eliot, Dr. Samuel, Boston.
Emerson, George B., Boston.
Emery, Francis F., Boston.
Emery, Isaac, Boston.
Emmons, Mrs. Nath'l H., Boston.
Endicott, Henry, Boston.
Endicott, William, jun., Boston.
Fisk, Rev. Photius, Boston.
Folsom, Charles T., M.D., Boston.
Forbes, J. M., Milton.
Galloupe, C. W., Boston.
Gardiner, Charles P., Boston.
Gardner, George A., Boston.
Glover, J. B., Boston.
Goddard, Benjamin, Brookline.
Goddard, Delano A., Boston.
Gray, Mrs. Horace, Boston.
Gray, John C., Boston.
Greenleaf, R. C., Boston.
Hale, George S., Boston.
Hardy, Alpheus, Brookline.
Haskell, Edwin B., Auburndale.
Higginson, George, Boston.
Higginson, Henry Lee, Boston.
Hill, Hon. Hamilton A., Boston.
Hilton, William, Boston.
Hogg, John, Boston.
Hooper, E. W., Boston.
Hooper, R. W., M.D., Boston.
Hovey, William A., Brookline.
Howe, Mrs. Julia Ward, Boston.
Houghton, Hon. H. O., Cambridge.
Hunnewell, H. H., Boston.
Hyatt, Alpheus, Cambridge.

Jackson, Patrick T., Boston.
Jackson, Mrs. Sarah, Boston.
Jarvis, Edward, M.D., Dorchester.
Jones, J. M., Boston.
Kendall, C. S., Boston.
Kennard, Martin P., Brookline.
Kidder, H. P., Boston.
Kinsley, E. W., Boston.
Lawrence, Amos A., Longwood.
Lincoln, L. J. B., Hingham.
Lodge, Mrs. J. E., Boston.
Lord, Melvin, Boston.
Lothrop, John, Auburndale.
Lowell, Augustus, Boston.
Lowell, John A., Boston.
Lyman, George W., Boston.
Mack, Thomas, Boston.
May, Miss Abby, Boston.
May, F. W. G., Dorchester.
Means, Rev. J. H., D.D., Dorchester.
Merriam, Caroline, Boston.
Minot, William, Boston.
Montgomery, Hugh, Boston.
Morton, Edwin, Boston.
Motley, Edward, Boston.
Mudge, Hon. E. R., Boston.
Nickerson, Joseph, Jamaica Plain.
Nickerson, S. D., Boston.
Noyes, Hon. Charles J., Boston.
Osborn, John T., Boston.
Parker, H. D., Boston.
Parkman, Francis, Boston.
Parkman, George F., Boston.
Parkman, Rev. John, Boston.
Parsons, Thomas, Chelsea.
Payson, S. R., Boston.
Peabody, Rev. A. P., D.D., Camb'ge.
Peabody, F. H., Boston.
Perkins, Edward N., Jamaica Plain.
Perkins, William, Boston.
Peters, Edward D., Boston.
Pickman, W. D., Boston.
Pierce, Hon. H. L., Boston.
Phillips, John C., Boston.
Preston, Jonathan, Boston.
Quincy, Hon. Josiah, Wollaston.
Quincy, Samuel M., Wollaston.
Rice, Hon. A. H., Boston.

Robeson, W. R., Boston.
Robinson, Henry, Reading.
Rogers, Jacob C., Boston.
Ropes, J. S., Jamaica Plain.
Rotch, Benjamin S., Boston.
Russell, Mrs. S. S., Boston.
Saltonstall, H., Boston.
Saltonstall, Leverett, Newton.
Sanborn, Frank B., Concord.
Schlesinger, Sebastian, Boston.
Sears, David, Boston.
Sears, W. T., Boston.
Shimmin, C. F., Boston.
Shippen, Rev. Rush R., Jamaica Pl.
Slack, C. W., Boston.
Snelling, Samuel G., Boston.
Stone, Joseph L., Boston.
Sturgis, Francis S., Jamaica Plain.
Sturgis, James, Jamaica Plain.
Taggard, B. W., Boston.
Taggard, Mrs. B. W., Boston.
Thaxter, Joseph B., Hingham.
Thayer, Rev. George A., Boston.
Thayer, Nathaniel, Boston.
Thorndike, S. Lothrop, Cambridge.
Tucker, Alanson, Boston.
Tucker, W. W., Boston.
Upton, George B., Boston.
Wales, George W., Boston.
Wales, Miss Mary Ann, Boston.
Wales, Thomas B., Boston.
Ware, Charles E., M.D., Boston.
Washburn, Hon. J. D., Worcester.
Weld, W. G., Boston.
Wheelwright, John W., Boston.
Wigglesworth, Edw., M.D., Boston.
Wigglesworth, Miss Mary, Boston.
Wigglesworth, Thomas, Boston.
Wilder, Hon. Marshall P., Dorch.
Winslow, Mrs. George, Roxbury.
Winsor, J. B., Providence, R.I.
Winthrop, Hon. Robert C., Boston.
Wolcott, J. H., Boston.
Wolcott, Mrs. J. H., Boston.
Woods, Henry, Paris, France.
Worthington, Roland, Roxbury.
Young, Charles L., Boston.

Commonwealth of Massachusetts.

REPORT OF THE TRUSTEES.

PERKINS INSTITUTION AND MASS. SCHOOL FOR THE BLIND.
SOUTH BOSTON, Sept. 30, 1879.

To THE MEMBERS OF THE CORPORATION.

Gentlemen, — In compliance with the regulation which requires our board to lay before you, and, through you, before the legislature, our annual account of the condition and operations of the institution, we have the honor to present the following report for the year ending Sept. 30, 1879 : —

It affords us great pleasure to state at the outset that the general management of the affairs of the establishment has been good, and its administration efficient and successful.

The total number of blind persons immediately connected with the institution in all its departments — as pupils, instructors, and work men and women, — is 162.

The health of the pupils has been remarkably good ; their industry commendable ; their advancement in their studies and occupations steady, and in many cases rapid ;

their habits cleanly and regular; their disposition generally cheerful; and their deportment satisfactory.

The institution has fully maintained the high opinion which the public has formed of it, and the march of progress can be easily noticed in all its departments. It has never been more complete in its corps of instructors, or supplied with finer facilities for the work of education, than it is to-day. Its teachers and officers are heartily in sympathy with its aims and purposes. They are thoroughly imbued with its system of instruction and training, its traditions, and the noble spirit breathed into its organization by its great founder, and fully able and determined to carry it to the highest possible point of excellence and usefulness.

In the management of the affairs of the establishment our constant aim is to enable the blind to help themselves, and so to render them independent on the one hand, and, on the other, to lighten as much as possible the burden which their infirmity imposes upon the community.

There has been but one change in the corps of teachers and officers; and the same persons have as heretofore directed the intellectual and moral training of the pupils, and have supplied their wants, and ministered to their comfort.

The members of our board have given personal attention to the educational, financial, hygienic, and all other interests of the institution. In the visits which we have made either as committees or individually, we have found ample evidence of the cleanliness and good order which reign throughout the establishment, and the judicious management of all things relating to the welfare

of the pupils, and the care and skill bestowed upon
their bringing up.

SUPERVISION AND TRAINING OF THE PUPILS.

The internal arrangements of the school are such as
to make supervision easy and effective, and the facilities
for a thorough classification according to peculiarities of
mind and character are excellent.   In the place of
those general rules and inflexible regulations necessary
where large numbers are to be directed, we have less
of perceptible government, and more of parental oversight.

The highest objects of the school are constantly kept
in view ; and we endeavor to secure and retain the services of accomplished and zealous teachers and officers ;
to provide improved appliances, and sufficient apparatus
for the pupils ; to surround them with healthy influences,
so that their morals and deportment may be carefully
nurtured ; to give them opportunities for associating and
commingling with intelligent and discreet seeing persons ; to discipline their minds, and not only to furnish
them with useful knowledge, but to awaken the love of
all good learning ; and to set before them the highest
aims, which shall act as stimulus throughout life.

Of the efficiency of our methods, and of our success
in carrying them out, we must leave you and the friends
of the school to judge by the results of the past year, as
well as of its predecessors.

MORAL AND SOCIAL ELEVATION OF THE BLIND.

In order to understand and appreciate the value of
the work accomplished by this institution during the

past forty-eight years, and to show the fruit borne by the system of instruction and training arranged by our late director, and adopted by all kindred establishments in the country, let us turn back a few pages of history, and compare the present condition of the blind with that of the past.

In all ages and in all countries, blindness has been considered as the greatest of human misfortunes, and has been associated with dependence and pauperism. There prevailed everywhere a common notion that man's capacity for usefulness ceased to exist with the extinction of vision. When Belisarius became blind, the hand that had upheld a falling empire was stretched out for alms. Sympathy and material aid were generously and even lavishly bestowed upon sightless persons; but their ability for work was denied. They were promptly allowed to occupy the beggar's post in the churchyards and streets of the large cities of Europe; but they were excluded from all the benefits of schools and academies. They were considered as incapacitated, and utterly helpless.

This popular opinion was cruelly unjust to the blind, and gratuitously added a vast amount of anguish to their sore calamity. It segregated them from the industrious classes of society. It prevented them from participating in the activities of life, and from enjoying the benefits of labor. It condemned them to idleness and intellectual darkness, and rendered them mere objects of pity and charity.

One of the most effective means which could assist the blind to rise above the clouds of ignorance and prejudice, to assert their human attributes, and to rest

calmly in the great realities of existence, was education, __
and education alone. But no one thought it feasible and
practicable in their case ; and they received none until
the year 1784, when the fruit-seeds were sowed by the
great apostle of their cause, the celebrated Abbé Valen-
tine Haüy, first in Paris, where he established the
Institution des Jeunes Aveugles, and afterward in St.
Petersburg and Berlin. Most of these seeds were
planted in fertile and genial soil, and they have multiplied, until all the principal countries of Europe have
their special institutions for the instruction of the blind
in the rudiments of learning, in music, and in the mechanical arts. , These establishments have greatly contributed to the intellectual and moral development of
the blind, and have laid the foundation for their social
elevation. But it was not until the work was taken
up in this country, and carried on under the vitalizing)
influence of pure democratic principles, that their right '
to a full share of the means of education accorded by !
the state to all the young was asserted, and that the :
barriers to social equality and happiness were removed.

It is to the credit of Massachusetts that she has led
the way in this, as in so many other benevolent and
philanthropic enterprises. Having acknowledged that
sightless children have even stronger claims than seeing
ones to systematic and thorough instruction, because they
start at a disadvantage in the race of life, because they
carry a heavy burden in their infirmity, and because,
without special intellectual and professional or mechanical training, they are not only doomed to mental as well
as bodily darkness, but to certain poverty and dependence, she has adopted the policy of providing liberally

for the education of the blind, and has kept her institution in the front rank of kindred establishments in the world. The blessed results of this provision are shown in scores and hundreds of blind persons scattered all over New England, many of them skilled and eminent as music-teachers and tuners of piano-fortes, all getting a good living, aspiring to independence, and eager to accept and assume the responsibilities of life under the same conditions as their more fortunate brethren.

May we not hope that the school which has accomplished so much in the field of justice and humanity, and has proved to be the most important agency in the social and moral elevation of the blind of New England directly, and of those of the whole continent indirectly, may be aided to advance yet further in the march of progress and enlightenment, to increase its appliances and apparatus, and to extend the circle of its usefulness, until it shall stand like a guiding beacon all ablaze with the light of knowledge and improvement for those who are under the cloud of physical darkness?

FINANCES.

The report of the treasurer, Mr. Henry Endicott, herewith presented, sets forth in a clear and comprehensive manner the receipts of money from all sources, and the disbursements made during the year, and shows the finances of the institution to be in a satisfactory condition.

This exhibit may be summarized as follows : —

Cash on hand Oct. 1, 1878   .   . $2,649 67
Total receipts during the year   .   . 97,359 57*
———————— $100,009 24
Total expenditures 99,430 03*

Cash balance in the treasury $579 21

The report of the treasurer is accompanied by the usual analysis of the steward's accounts, which gives specific information in regard to the principal articles consumed, their amount and cost, and by which both the ordinary and extraordinary expenses and resources of the income may be understood at a glance.

In the management of the financial affairs of the institution a system of strict accountability has been observed. All the funds are received by the treasurer, who pays out money as it is wanted only upon the presentation of an order from the auditors. The director controls the disbursements; but his accounts are examined monthly, and vouchers are required for every item of expense.

The account of expenditure has been rigid and exact; and the funds of the institution have been applied with the strictest economy consistent with the best results and the greatest efficiency of the school. The policy of the trustees has always been to spend nothing upon ornamental architecture or outward display, to be frugal as regards expensive furniture and internal luxuries, but to be liberal in increasing the means, and improving the appliances necessary for thorough instruction and systematic training of the pupils.

The auditors have performed their duty with regu-

* Of this amount $32,000 belong to the permanent fund of the institution, and were merely changed from one investment to another.

larity, promptness, and diligence ; and they certify that the accounts are properly and correctly kept, and that all entries are authenticated by vouchers.

The books are open to the inspection of the members of the corporation, and the most careful examination is solicited.

NEED OF FUNDS.

The income of the institution from state appropriations and from all ordinary sources is barely sufficient for the pressing wants of the year. Applied with prudence and with the strictest economy, it enables us to carry out the general purpose of educating the blind. But, in order to extend the operations and influence of the establishment, and to render it a perennial fountain of blessing, an exhaustless source of intellectual and moral light, an instrument of good and happiness to its beneficiaries, additional funds are greatly needed. For these we place entire reliance upon the contributions of individuals who are blessed with the means, and thrice blessed with a disposition to aid in works of benevolence. Without this assistance, the value of the school as an agency in developing and diversifying the powers of the blind, and in raising them to the rank of industrious and productive members of society, cannot be maintained, and its usefulness would be sadly circumscribed.

The prevailing idea that the institution is richly endowed and well provided for is utterly groundless ; and we doubt not that a knowledge of its real condition and wants, and of its mission, will obtain for it a share of the gifts and bequests which are so numerous in our community.

To the generosity and sense of justice of the citizens of Massachusetts in general, and of those of Boston in particular, belongs the honor of having kindled in America the Promethean fire of enlightenment for the blind, and of raising them in the scale of humanity and social equality; and to them we must continue to look for aid in the furtherance of our work.

Repairs and Improvements.

Some of the most urgently needed repairs and improvements have been made during the past year, with a view to keeping the buildings in good condition, and increasing the general efficiency of the establishment. The principal of these are as follows: —

The main building has been thoroughly and tastefully painted outside, and, while its general appearance has been greatly improved, the preservation of those portions liable to decay has been secured. The fences around it have also been painted.

The music-hall has been entirely renovated, and put in excellent condition. A new stage has been built; the gallery has been raised higher than before, and its capacity doubled; the floors have been relaid with southern hard pine; the ceiling and the walls neatly repainted in fresco; the heating apparatus has been remodelled; and new hard-wood settees have replaced the old ones.

The large room under the music-hall, formerly used as a printing-office, has been transformed into a commodious library. The walls and ceiling have been replastered and repainted, and the latter has been refrescoed, the floor relaid with southern hard pine, and the whole of the wood-work repaired and repainted. Black-walnut cases for books, minerals, and various models, and convenient accommodations for all kinds of specimens and educational apparatus, have been amply provided.

The old library has been changed into a spacious schoolroom, supplied with the best kind of furniture for young children, with complete sets of both dissected and wall maps, and with the necessary facilities for kindergarten and object classes.

The floors of the corridors of the third and fourth stories, and of several of the rooms, have been relaid with southern pine; and staircases have been built at both ends of the north side of the latter, leading to the attic, so that, in case of fire, there are abundant means of exit.

A new boiler has been made to order, and placed in the underground vault built for the purpose last year.

Many other alterations and improvements of a minor character have been made during the year. They consist in paving the drive-way on the south side of the main building with concrete; in rebuilding both the staircases leading to the music-hall; in taking off the paper from the walls of the corridors and of seven rooms, and painting them over; in increasing and perfecting the means of ventilation; replacing the old composition roof on the west side of the building, and the slate roofs of the piazzas, by tin ones; renewing the sashes of eighty-five windows; thoroughly repairing the piazzas, copper gutters, and fences; and putting the premises generally in as good condition as the means at our disposal have allowed us to do.

These repairs and improvements have been both extensive and expensive, and we were aware that they would drain our treasury entirely; but, as they were obviously needed for the preservation of the buildings and for the good of the institution, they have been undertaken without hesitation. They are of a permanent character, supplying urgent wants, and calculated to promote the tone of the school. Whatever tends to increase the comfort, convenience, pleasantness, neatness, and orderly appearance of such an establishment, serves also a high moral purpose.

The building has stood forty-three years in a very exposed situation, and naturally subjected to rough usage by its young inmates, and there is an absolute necessity for the continuance of this process of renovation until its interior is put in excellent condition. Worn floors, decayed window-frames, shaky sashes, loose plastering, soiled wall-paper, impaired graining and painting, all will have to be replaced or repaired, and made sound. An extra appropriation is sorely needed for this purpose; but, as circumstances do not seem auspicious for asking for one, we shall depend upon the friends of the blind for assistance, and shall exercise rigid economy in the expenditure of the annual income of the institution, so that we may be able to carry on the work of reconstruction.

EMBOSSING BOOKS FOR THE BLIND.

During the past year our press has been constantly at work, and a new edition of Milton's " Paradise Lost " has been printed. According to the uniform testimony of experts, this edition is, in point of legibility and me-

chanical execution, by far the best work issued in the
line character. As soon as it was completed, Higginson's "Young Folks' History of the United States,"
specially revised and adapted for our purposes by the
author himself, was printed and electrotyped at the
expense of one of the kind and generous friends and
benefactors of the blind, with the condition that his
name should be withheld. May others imitate his
benevolent liberality until intellectual light and knowledge shall be within the reach of every blind person in
our land!

The plan of furnishing the blind of America with a
choice library in raised characters originated in this institution; and all the real and substantial improvements
made on Haüy's invention of embossing books, and on
the modes of constructing apparatus adapted to the
sense of touch, were instituted and carried out here.
This enterprise engaged the attention, and absorbed the
thoughts of the great founder of the school, as soon as
the establishment was organized in 1832, and it remained the object nearest to his heart through life.

Dr. Howe commenced the work without aid or encouragement from any direction, and pursued it with all
the energy and ardent enthusiasm which characterized
him in all his philanthropic undertakings. He advanced
the money for the first experiments, and never asked
remuneration. The means at his command were very
limited, and the obstacles often disheartening; but his
faith in the beneficent effects of the enterprise was so
strong, that it inspired him with courage and hopefulness in the midst of difficulties. There was nothing
that went so against the grain of his chivalrous nature

as asking favors. For his own benefit, he could never do it. But, having determined not to rest until a library of select books was provided for the blind, he went on toiling for this object to the last of his life. In all his conceptions and plans on this as well as on any other subject, his motto was " *semper aliquid melius;* " and his unremitting efforts met with remarkable success.

Our printing-office was removed last spring to its new quarters, and has been entirely renovated in all its appliances and machinery.

Type of both the Boston and Braille characters, cases, tables, steam-engine, and various fixtures, have all been made new; and an improved platen-press, planned by the officers of the institution, and manufactured by Mr. Francis Meisel of South Boston, has replaced the old one. Thus our printing-establishment is now in perfect order, well supplied with extensive and costly apparatus, and we are very desirous that the work of embossing books for the blind should be carried on uninterruptedly and vigorously where it originated and has been developed to maturity.

For the continuance of this truly great undertaking, and for the multiplication of books in raised characters, we earnestly call for the aid of the benevolent. The appeal is a strong one, and, were it well considered by humane persons, it would be irresistible; for it is a call of the blind to the seeing for light which they can give. It cannot be difficult for feeling hearts to conceive the rapture of a sightless person on finding that means are provided by which he can cheer his solitude, and pass pleasantly and usefully the hours which before were wont to drag their slow length along in sadness and listlessness.

WORK DEPARTMENT FOR ADULTS.

This department has been kept steadily in operation, and supplied with a fair amount of work, during the past year.

The receipts from all sources amount to $12,371.24, exceeding by $343.50 those of the previous twelve months. The expenses for all purposes have been $14,378.86 ; so that the balance against the department has been increased to $1,890.47, whereas $1,711.74 were paid out of the treasury of the institution the previous year.

There have been twenty blind persons employed to do the work, and the amount of wages paid to them was $3,136.31..

That the condition of our trade is somewhat improved is sufficiently shown by our books. They indicate plainly the growth of the business during the past five months as compared with the transactions of the same period in the preceding year. But the fact that the work department is a losing concern, entailing a heavy burden upon the limited means of the institution, remains still unaltered. This state of things cannot go on indefinitely, and unless relief is afforded, either by the increase of patronage, or in the form of a permanent fund, — the income of which may be sufficient to pay the rent of a store and the salaries of its employés, — the existence of the workshop must become doubtful, and the continuance of its blessings to so many active and respectable persons problematic.

The industrial department has never been, nor is it intended to be, a source of gain to the institution: on the contrary, large sums of money have at various times been paid out of the treasury of the latter for its improvements and support. It is wholly maintained for the benefit of those who work there. Through its agency many sightless persons have been enabled, not only to become self-supporting, but to secure for themselves, by diligence and thrift, the comforts of home and the inestimable enjoyments of domestic life.

It is highly desirable to prevent a class of our fellow-men from being deprived of such a boon, and most of them from being thrown into the poor-houses; and we would improve this opportunity to make known the importance of our industrial department, and to earnestly solicit the patronage of the public for it. We warrant that our work is thoroughly and faithfully done, and put at the lowest possible market-prices, and that the materials are carefully selected, and are of the best quality. Those who make their purchases at our store may be sure that the authorities of the institution feel under obligation to give in return the full value of the money they receive, and that they are assisting in the most appropriate way meritorious persons who are striving by industry to obtain an honest subsistence.

Prompt attention will be given to the execution of all orders, which may be left at the salesrooms of the institution, No. 37 Avon street, for new mattresses, comforters, bolsters, pillows, and feather-beds; for dressing, cleansing, and re-upholstering all kinds of parlor furniture; for reseating cane-bottomed chairs; for supplying churches and vessels with cushions; for brooms, brushes, door-mats, and the like. Orders for all these articles, as well as for tuning piano-fortes, will be wel-

come, and will help to sustain an establishment, the
existence of which is of immense practical value to
the industrious blind directly, and to the community
itself indirectly.

RECOGNITION OF THE WORK OF THE INSTITUTION.

The bestowal of those marks of approbation which
are awarded at the great world festivals, or international expositions, is a subject of congratulation to the
friends of the institution.   These awards not only draw
popular attention to the work which the establishment
aims at carrying on, but also (which is far more important) testify to the success of our endeavors and to
the excellence of their results.   Premiums have been
decreed to this institution by the juries of every one
of the great expositions thus far held in London, Paris,
Vienna, and Philadelphia.   The medal last received
from Europe was that granted by the French exposition of 1878, and was awarded for embossed books,
tangible apparatus, and pupils' fancy work.   Three
medals were also received at the mechanics' fair held
in this city last year, — one of gold, for embossed books,
maps, and tangible appliances for the use of the blind ;
one of silver, for mattresses, bolsters, and upholstery
work ; and one of bronze, for a horse-shoe invented by
Mr. Dennis A. Reardon, formerly a pupil, and now an
employé, of the institution.   Mr. Reardon is a man of
rare mechanical ability.   His inventions bear the stamp
of originality and the evidences of a powerful mind.
His talents are found to be of great service everywhere
in our establishment, but most especially in our print-

ing-office, of which he has a general supervision. In the words of the director, " His mechanical genius, power of putting perfection into the minutest details, and love of the simple and beautiful, are remarkable mental characteristics, and are of great use in the planning and execution of our improvements in the best and most economical manner. It is a striking instance of the power of the mind to overleap outward barriers, that, where experienced workmen have been baffled by mechanical difficulties and unforeseen obstructions, his keen insight and correct judgment have invariably found a way out of every dilemma."

The system of electric bells which are placed in different parts of the establishment, and rung simultaneously by a clock, is not the least of Mr. Reardon's inventions ; and the perfection of our new press, in the planning of which he has had a prominent part, is another proof of his mechanical genius.

General Remarks.

It is a source of no small gratification to be able to assure the friends and patrons of the institution of its continued prosperity and usefulness, and of the satisfactory results of its labors.

Every year bears fresh testimony to the fact that the establishment meets an important need in our educational system, and that it holds its place worthily among the public schools, which stand like monuments to the intelligence and the generous and humane spirit which abound in our community.

It has been our aim and effort at all times to keep

pace with the advance of science in education, and to obtain every thing which may tend to increase the efficiency of the school, and add to the comfort and happiness of the household.

We earnestly invite the members of the legislative bodies of Massachusetts and of the other New-England states, the executive and other public officers, and all citizens interested in the cause of education in general, and in the welfare of the blind in particular, to visit the institution, and satisfy themselves by personal examination of the results of its work. They will be pleased to see how successful have been the means conceived by benevolence, developed by study, and perfected by science, to alleviate calamity, and render the path of life smooth to those who walk in darkness. They will not find a flourish of trumpets, or any parade of grand results, or pompous show of magnificent achievements; but they will perceive that with calm and silent potency the work is gradually but certainly carried forward.

For the continuance of the support and prosperity of the institution, for the increase of its usefulness, and for the full realization of its highest aims and purposes, we trust in the goodness of the cause it represents, in the fairness of the representatives of the people, the liberality of those who have the stewardship of riches, and the humanity and benevolence of the public.

In conclusion, the trustees refer you to the report of the director, which is hereto appended, and which gives an account of the present condition of the various departments of the institution, of the work that has been accomplished or inaugurated during the year, and the results which are being attained in this most interesting field of human culture.

All which is respectfully submitted by

ROBERT E. APTHORP,
JOHN S. DWIGHT,
JOSEPH B. GLOVER,
J. THEODORE HEARD,
HENRY LEE HIGGINSON,
JAMES H. MEANS,
ANDREW P. PEABODY,
EDWARD N. PERKINS,
JOSIAH QUINCY,
SAMUEL G. SNELLING,
JAMES STURGIS,
GEORGE W. WALES,

Trustees.

SOUTH BOSTON, Oct. 8, 1879.

At the annual meeting of the corporation, summoned according to the by-laws, and held this day at the institution, the foregoing was adopted, and ordered to be printed, together with the reports of the director and treasurer and the usual accompanying documents; and the officers for the ensuing year were elected.

M. ANAGNOS, *Secretary.*

THE REPORT OF THE DIRECTOR.

To the Trustees.

Gentlemen, — It has again become my duty to submit to your consideration the report of the director for the last twelve months. It contains a brief statement of the history and present condition of the institution and of its wants and prospects, and touches upon such subjects as are germane to the education of the blind.

The period covered by this report has been one of general prosperity. The great objects for which the school was founded have been steadily and successfully pursued, and no untoward incident has occurred to interrupt the flow of its beneficence, or to call for special remarks.

The various departments of the institution have been carried on with regularity and efficiency, and all the teachers and officers have performed their duties cheerfully and faithfully.

The scholars have been obedient, orderly, dutiful, and industrious. The recitations have been conducted with intelligence, zeal, and profit. The spirit of true politeness and civility has been carefully cultivated and generally practised, and the moral training has occupied as prominent a place as the intellectual. There has been no weariness on the part of teachers and officers in instilling into the minds of the pupils such principles as will render them happy and useful beings.

The fruits of the labors of the past year in the field of instruction and training are as gratifying as those of any of its predecessors, and the progress made by our pupils is as satisfactory as ever. Their daily advancement may not be perceptible; yet, as weeks and months succeed each other, we have sufficient evidence that their progress is substantial and real. This is seen in the gradual lightening up of the countenance, in the awakened love of knowledge, and especially in the increased ability to express their thoughts with fluency and clearness.

Whatever changes mature experience has suggested in the methods of instruction and training have been promptly adopted, and expedients have been constantly devised for reaching more surely and rapidly the desired results.

Our educational means and appliances have been multiplied, new apparatus of various kinds have been obtained, and the collections of models and specimens have been extended; and the institution is at present in a fair condition to carry out in most respects the plans and desires of its great founder, who labored assiduously and enthusiastically for nearly half a century in shaping its policy, and placing its activity upon a broad and permanent basis.

During the past year the school has been visited by thousands of citizens from Boston and the neighboring towns, from the New-England states, and from all parts of the country. It has also been the subject of several newspaper and magazine articles from the pen of well-

known writers, one of the latter being illustrated by
artists of real merit. This attention furnishes ample
evidence that the establishment has a permanent hold
on the affections of the public, and stimulates those who
carry on its beneficent work to increased efforts for the
instruction and social and moral elevation of that portion of the children of New England who cannot be educated in the common schools.

NUMBER OF INMATES.

The total number of blind persons connected with the
institution at the beginning of the past year as pupils,
teachers, employés, and work men and women, was 158.
There have since been admitted 26 ; 22 have been discharged, making the present total number 162. Of
these, 142 are in the school proper, and 20 in the work-
department for adults.

The first class includes 130 boys and girls enrolled as
pupils, 8 teachers, and 4 domestics. Of the pupils
there are now 67 boys and 47 girls in attendance, 9 of
the former and 7 of the latter being absent on account
of physical disability, or from other causes.

The second class comprises 17 men and 3 women
employed in the workshop for adult blind persons.

The number of the inmates is slowly but surely
increasing. No applicant of the proper age, of good
moral character, and of ordinary intelligence, is refused
admission : on the contrary, all who seem to be fit subjects for the school are promptly received on probation,
and retained or discharged after a fair and patient trial.
With the repairs and improvements of the last two
years, the capacity of our buildings has been sufficiently

increased to accommodate the blind children from
Massachusetts and the neighboring states for many
years to come, and no one will be refused admittance
for want of room.

SUCCESS OF GRADUATES.

The result of the work of the institution can be seen
in a widely extended substratum of solid character and
intelligence among its beneficiaries.   It has been to
them a nursery of usefulness, happiness, and good citizenship, tending as it does, by means of the most healthful influences, to remove the obstacles and obliterate the
effects flowing from the loss of sight.   It has raised
most of them to positions of trust and profit from which
they must otherwise have been excluded ; and it is very
gratifying to receive from time to time favorable accounts of hundreds of our former pupils scattered over
all parts of New England, industrious, intelligent, respected members of society, bright examples of the
extent to which so sad an affliction can be relieved, and
of the priceless blessing which the school has already
conferred upon the class of people for whose good it
was established.

SANITARY CONDITION.

The health of the pupils has been remarkably good,
considering that some are afflicted with hereditary disease, and not a few constitutionally weak and delicate.

No epidemic of any kind has prevailed, and no cases
of death or severe illness have occurred at the institution
itself.   Edward O'Neil of South Boston was taken sick
with brain-fever on the day of the commencement of

the term, and died soon after, lamented by all who knew him; but he was not a member of our household. He was a day scholar, living at home, under the care of his relatives, and coming to school for his lessons as ordinary children do.

This enjoyment of uninterrupted health is mainly due to our system of training and our dietary, coupled with proper hygienic regulations, and sustained by sanitary surroundings. No one object receives more attention in this institution than that of carefully and wisely guarding against any and all influences that would impair or endanger the health of the household. If there are not more cases of pale faces, sallow cheeks, drowsy minds, and languid bodies, it is simply because the officers and teachers have a watchful care over the habits of the pupils. They prevent imprudent and thoughtless exposure, insist upon regular hours of sleep, recreation, and work, interdict inflammatory reading, and impress most tenderly and judiciously, yet candidly and forcibly, warnings against secret vices.

The sanitary measures of an institution of learning constitute the foundation upon which is raised the structure of its educational system, and the reasons for this are obvious. For any kind of intellectual work it is indispensable that the mind should be alive, awake, fresh, in full force and exercise. But mental vigor and activity depend wholly upon physical health. The brain — which is the material instrument of the mind, and which gives rise to all the intellectual, emotional, and voluntary activities of mankind — obeys the same laws of nourishment, growth, exercise, and rest, as the other organs of the body. It is developed gradually.

It cannot arrive at healthy maturity, or acquire an increased susceptibility of action and the power of sustaining it, without the assistance of a good supply of pure blood; and this is only the legitimate product of wholesome food, fresh air, and regular exercise. Hence a well-nourished and vigorous body is the proper basis for mental discipline and intellectual culture. It is a source of pleasure and a factor of happiness. It is a perennial fountain of soul-lifting cheerfulness, which makes the mind clear, gives tone to thought, adds grace and beauty to the countenance, lifts the clouds of sorrow, lightens the burdens of misfortune, and lights up the intellectual horizon of those who are not permitted to look upon the beauties and grandeur of surrounding nature.

It is obvious from the above remarks that health is the greatest blessing that can be bestowed upon the inmates of an educational establishment, and that its conservation merits the perpetual and increasing attention which it receives here.

Statistics concerning Blindness.

Of the twenty-six inmates admitted during the past year to this institution, six lost their sight by accident, two by whooping-cough, two by scarlet-fever, four by cataract, two by the effects of a severe cold, one by water on the brain during infancy, two by measles, one by paralysis of the optic nerve, one by granulated lids, one by ophthalmia neonatorum, and four were either born blind, or with impaired vision and a tendency to its gradual loss. Thus in six cases blindness had been caused by accident, in ten by disease, and in ten it was hereditary or organic, that is to say, was the visible effect of some latent general physical disorder.

Although the main object of an institution like ours is to educate the blind, and prepare them effectually for the struggle of life, it is also very important to carry on those lines of investigation and research for which a school of the kind affords such ample scope and material. In our own establishment this object has always been considered of great value, and we continue to keep a concise record of the history, parentage, antecedents, mental and moral calibre, hereditary taints, physical weaknesses, and peculiarities of character and disposition of each case, and to gather and file away as many facts concerning blindness and its effects as we can obtain.

These materials, added to the accumulation of past and successive experience elsewhere, and reduced to proper scientific form by comparison, classification, deduction, verification, and generalization, will be of great service in two ways: —

First, they will bring to light the nature and character of some of the prolific causes of blindness, and suggest the means which may be employed to guard against these causes effectually.

Secondly, they will call attention to the best agencies for ameliorating the condition of the blind, and indicate the laws which should regulate their education.

The value of these statistics will be enhanced in proportion to the extent of the territory where they are gathered. The wider the range, the more trustworthy are the results of comparison. The different phases of social life, the tendency to intermarriage, the homoge-

neous or heterogeneous nature of the population, the
segregation or intermixture of dissimilar races, the moral
and intellectual status of divers communities, and the
climatic influences of various countries, all have more
or less direct bearing upon the degree of soundness or
defectiveness of the people; and the field of research
must be vastly extended in order to ascertain the real
strength of each factor, and to reach correct and weighty
conclusions.

For these reasons, it is highly desirable that there
should be adopted by all the institutions for the blind in
this and all other countries a general system of collect-
ing and recording facts concerning blindness and its
physiological and psychological effects, and that a synop-
sis of these statistics, arranged in a tabular form, should
be published in their reports.

MEANS AND EFFECTS OF THE EDUCATION OF THE BLIND.

The system of education and training for the blind
adopted in this institution, although far from being perfect, is as complete as can be attained by the means at
our command.   It is broad in its scope, and comprehensive in its purposes.   It is methodically arranged, and
embraces an ascending chain of exercises.   It provides
for the gradual development of the mental faculties in
their natural order, for the improvement of the moral
character by all possible incentives to well-doing, for
æsthetic culture which shall nurture taste, and lead to
the appreciation, if not the creation, of the beautiful,
for physical growth and well-being by means of careful exercise of the muscles of the body and by special
training of the hand to dexterity.

The noble founder of this institution was a great believer in the influences of education and in man's capacity for improvement. His conception of the *beau-ideal* of human nature was that of a being whose intellectual faculties were active and enlightened, his sentiments dignified and firm, and his physical formation healthy and beautiful; and he devoted his genius and his rare qualities of head and heart to the organization of a system of instruction and training for the blind which should bring them as near as possible to this ideal, and should enable them to utilize all those sources of happiness which nature supplies, to find out how to use their faculties to the greatest advantage to themselves and others, and to learn how to live completely. In order to accomplish his purpose, Dr. Howe never ceased, as long as life lasted, diving into the sea of observation, and gathering flowers from the blooming fields of experience with the fondness of a devotee; and though he could not avoid bringing up occasionally pebbles with pearls, and picking straws with the violets, the treasures obtained were of great importance, and they will prove to be the most valuable contributions to the erection of that magnificent temple in which the science of the education of the blind is to be permanently enshrined and preserved.

But, however marvellously successful were his efforts in behalf of the blind, the stand-point which they now take in American society imposes absolutely new conditions upon their education. It requires not only better, higher school-culture for the improvement of the understanding in the usual sense, but also the development of a certain degree of individual creativeness or intellectual productivity.   Upon that which the blind are to become depend their future happiness and welfare far more than upon that which they have already attained. Society itself will never reach the proper point of equity and perfection, unless it provide for all its members, be they sound or defective in mind or in body, sufficient means for thorough cultivation and training, so as to develop in them that individual force and native energy which radiate from within outwards, and which triumph over external conditions and surrounding difficulties. To nurture the powers of all children without distinction, and to awaken in them insight and creative ability, is alike the duty and the interest of the community; and education then, and only then, will achieve its greatest practical success, when it meets all new conditions, and when, in the words of the poet, —

> " Earth's universal frame shall feel the effects,
> Even till the smallest habitable rock,
> Beaten by lonely billows, hear the songs
> Of humanized society, and bloom
> With civil arts that send their fragrance forth
> A grateful tribute to all-ruling Heaven.
> From culture unexclusively bestowed
> Expect these mighty issues; from the pain
> And faithful care of unambitious schools,
> Instructing simple childhood's ready ear,
> Thence look for these magnificent results."

This prophetic strain may be a vision of a poet's brain, which is, perhaps, unattainable to its fullest extent; but it indicates sufficiently the effects of culture, and beautifully illustrates its aim.   If the principles of true education are scientifically educed, and accurately defined, and its objects faithfully pursued, its legitimate processes will undoubtedly operate like the genial agencies of nature, quietly, almost imperceptibly, yet with unerring certainty attaining their proper ends. Montaigne's statement, that the most important difficulty of human science is the education of children, is perfectly true ; and the difficulty becomes vastly greater when the recipients of instruction are deprived of one of the most important avenues of sense. Nevertheless the attempts at the culture and training of the blind are no longer regarded as an experiment of doubtful results : on the contrary, the fruitfulness of past endeavors in their behalf promises a full success in the future. The seed has already been abundantly laid in the bosom of the earth ; and the dew, the rain, and the vivifying light and air, are all working together slowly, but surely, to produce the golden harvest.

THE VARIOUS DEPARTMENTS OF THE INSTITUTION.

Of the work of the institution as carried on in its various departments, a brief account will be hereafter given. Its educational methods and exercises, compared with those employed in the schools for seeing children, need to be as much more varied and comprehensive, as the peculiarities and obstacles in the way of teaching are greater in the one case than in the other.

The day is divided between instruction in the schoolroom and study, lessons and practice in instrumental and vocal music and in tuning piano-fortes, training in some simple mechanical occupation (in order to give manual dexterity, and prepare the children for a trade, if such is to be their calling), and physical exercise both under shelter and in the open air. Moreover, the moral

law reigns supreme, and the pupils are surrounded by
an atmosphere which makes conscience the guide and
judicial power in all their acts. High moral character
is the one thing which bridges over all distinctions
arising from physical imperfections, and is esteemed
indispensable in preparing the blind to constitute an
integral and not a distinct part of human society. Rectitude, veracity, integrity, purity, kindness, uprightness,
and virtue are instilled by precept and example. No
man prospers, no life succeeds, without these: any departure from them is a flaw in our armor, an organic
weakness in the forces employed in fighting ignorance
and vice. If the blind are what they ought to be in
moral weight and fibre, in intellectual power, in physical vigor, and in indomitable energy, surely they need
not fear lest they shall find good and ample scope for
those qualities, in spite of their infirmity. With an
enlightened mind, with self-respect born of intellectual
development, with proper views of the dignity of labor,
with habits of industry and application, with a good
character, and with a determination not to be a burden upon others, they can go out into the world well
equipped to make a successful struggle with the odds
that are against them, and will grapple resolutely with
the difficulties opposing their advancement to independence, and, if they have friends to give them a helping
hand at the outset, will finally walk firmly alone.

Of all the agencies requisite for compassing this end
none is more important than a judicious division of
labor based upon sound principles, and conscientiously
carried out in every department and every detail.

LITERARY DEPARTMENT.

"That training which teaches how to make
money, or aims at the development of mere physical strength, or the communication of skill in any
mechanical business or common art, without *intellectual culture* and a sense of right, does not
deserve the name of education." — *Plato.*

This department is the basis of our system of education, and the importance of its work is strikingly set forth
in the language of the most luminous star in the firmament of philosophy.   It exercises great influence in developing the mental powers and the æsthetic faculties
of the pupils, in the increase of their capacity, and in
the formation of their character.   It constitutes the solid
foundation upon which the superstructure can be
securely reared, broad and high, beautiful and substantial.   It represents a sort of intellectual and moral
gymnasium, preparatory for the great struggle in the
arena of life.

During the past year the intellectual department has
received all the attention which its vast scope merits,
and its present condition is exceedingly satisfactory.
Its concerns have been so administered as to secure for
the largest possible number the highest possible results,
and to enable them to use to the best advantage those
talents with which they are endowed.

The organic forces and mechanical means necessary
for the advancement and efficiency of the school have
been increased, and the facilities for thorough and systematic instruction are excellent.   Not that we possess
costly apparatus, expensive appliances, or luxurious

accommodations ; but what we have is admirably suited
to its purpose, and includes all that is absolutely necessary.

The pupils have been faithfully taught, and have
diligently improved their opportunities; and the range
and quality of their acquirements are creditable both
to themselves and to their instructors.   There is a noble
spirit manifested among them, which is most gratifying
and commendable.   This is evinced by a real interest in
their studies, by a respect and cheerful deference to the
wishes of those in authority, by an ambition to excel in
their classes, and by a general demeanor worthy of all
praise.

The teachers have endeavored to give clear and
correct instruction, with careful explanations of words
and principles.   Their prominent aim has been to direct
the scholars how to study, and to encourage them to
surmount difficulties.   They have led them to get a
distinct and accurate understanding of the subjects
under consideration, and required them to express their
thoughts and views in their own language.   They have
stimulated as far as possible their aptitude for invention,
and have sought to inspire them with confidence in their
own powers and resources.   All who have witnessed
the efforts of our instructors, and watched them atten-
tively, are impressed with the thoroughness of their
work, their skilful probing of the pupils' knowledge,
their manifest love for their vocation, and their simple
and interesting manner of unfolding facts and principles.
As a general rule, they prepare every lesson before
crossing the threshold of the schoolroom.   They are
methodical in their arrangements, definite in their plans,

succinct in their teaching, and invincibly patient in the
pursuit of a fixed end. This quality is indispensable
for securing satisfactory results in any undertaking;
for patience is nothing else but common sense intensified. John Foster named it "the faculty of lighting
one's own fire;" and Buffon pronounced it the true
touchstone of genius. The man or woman who is
patient, and keeps a calm temper, no matter how accurately the difficulties before him are estimated, and how
keenly the disappointments felt, will have vastly greater
power to accomplish good and to correct evil than those
who become impatient, and fall into a sour mood. A
sweet spirit, like the fragrant flower, has a perfume to
cast upon the path of every one who passes by: it has
also for itself a rare life of love, which every one ad-
mires.

The course of study pursued here has been so often
detailed in former reports, that it need not be rehearsed
again. Suffice it to say that its scale has been enlarged
and extended, and is calculated to bestow that practical
knowledge and breadth of culture which are necessary
to the highest success. The objects with which the
pupils are brought into daily contact, the phenomena
which constantly appear before the mental vision, the
facts of nature and of consciousness upon which all
science and philosophy are based, receive careful and
systematic attention.

The subject-matter of the lessons given in the classes
is not of a fragmentary or disconnected character, but
shows distinctly the relations of one thing to another,
and while it arouses the attention, and trains the powers
of observation, also presents that connected chain of

thought necessary to the development of the reasoning faculties. The operation of the higher powers of the mind in solving the problems of thought and in arriving at just conclusions depends upon the faithfulness with which perception has been cultivated.

There has been a marked improvement in the modes of imparting instruction. Much more time than formerly has been given to oral and object teaching, and has been attended with most encouraging results. The rational method, in contradistinction to the mere mechanical, has been applied to various branches ordinarily taught to children, but not carried beyond the boundaries prescribed by reason and wisdom. Nature has been our guide; and instead of attempting to overrule her, and substitute our senseless wishes and designs for her unalterable and imperative enactments, we anxiously study and implicitly obey them. To do otherwise would be to labor for an impossible result.

"Naturam expelles furca, tamen usque recurret."

Our instructors are enjoined to study the special aptitude of every pupil, and to adapt their mode of teaching to the wants of each individual. The inequality of different minds in imbibing instruction under precisely identical circumstances is a glaring fact, and is one of the obstacles encountered in teaching numbers together, that is, in classes. Hence the adaptation of class work to individual capacity must of necessity form the basis of the whole system of instruction.

Attention has been given to the principles which govern every intelligent effort to impart instruction. Mountains of learned verbalism, and clouds of mere

formulæ of words, have not been allowed to stand
between the mental vision of the pupils and the object;
and clearness in thought, and distinctness in the representation of ideas have been considered of more moment
than linguistic exercises, for perspicuity of expression
follows definiteness in thinking.   Combe's educational
motto, "*Res, non verba, quaeso*," has been the guide in
our school, because "*dum res maneant verba fingant.*"
The learning of words is a noisy process; whereas the
virtue of things steals into the intellect with noiseless
step, and is ever working in the thoughts of the pupils
most when they perceive it least.   It does not confine
itself to the surface of the mind, rustling in its fringes,
and roaring in its outskirts, but reaches its vital springs,
and feeds its native vigor.   It is as silent as the growing
of the plants, as unconscious as the assimilation of the
food and the vitalizing work of the blood.

Accuracy and thoroughness in whatever is studied,
with the frequent application of principles to the duties
and affairs of life, is of the first importance.   A smat-
tering of letters, scraps of grammar, odds and ends of
history, crumbs of the abstract sciences, are of little use
to the blind; and, instead of being thankful for them,
they are more likely to say, with the shoemaker in
Martial,—

"At me literulas stulti docuere parentes."

What they especially need is the cultivation of spontaneous intellectual energy, and a thorough mental discipline, including the habits of observation, of quick and
accurate perception, of steady attention, and of close
and patient reasoning.

More stress is laid upon principles and leading

thoughts than upon the quantity of details and facts.
This is as it should be; for mere accumulation of knowledge, without fostering and promoting the activity of
the intellectual faculties, is not education.   It occu-
pies, but does not enrich, the mind.   It imparts a stimulus for the time, and produces a sort of intellectual
keenness and cleverness; but, without an implanted
purpose and a higher object than mere pleasure, it does
not call forth any conscious effort of ratiocination, and
will bring with it no solid advantage.   In such cases,
knowledge produces but a passing impression, — a sensation, but no more.   It is in fact the merest epicurism
of intelligence, — sensuous, but certainly not intellectual.
Locke, throughout the whole of his treatise on education,
reiterates the necessity of simplicity in subject; of training and method, rather than variety and amount.   The
tendency to put a higher value upon the quantity of
knowledge acquired than upon the mental discipline
derived from school-life develops an opinionative self-
sufficiency, not a real intellectual activity.   It should be
continually borne in mind, that it is not the amount of
information which our pupils carry from the school that
constitutes a criterion of their capacity, and opens to
them the gates of usefulness, but the ability to learn, the
appetite for good knowledge, and the habits of thought
into which the mind has settled in acquiring it, the skill
in applying what they know to practical business, and the
vigor of health that gives aptitude for its use.

Endeavors to expand the intellect by the introduction
of mechanically compressed facts have been avoided
among us, not only as futile, but as positively injurious.
The pupils are trained to perceive, think, investigate,

reason, and discover for themselves, to a very great extent. We make a point of awakening the energy, quickening the intellectual activity and moral power, clearing the mind by driving away pretentions and shams and illusions, and giving tone and tension to the thought of the day.

The mind of a child is not a passive recipient, but an active principle, constantly developing, expanding, and tending to maturity. It is therefore important that it should be nourished with the aliment best fitted for its growth; not with dry facts, wordy formulas, scientific definitions, and tables of chronology, but with something that addresses the ideality, awakens the observation, pleases the perceptive faculties, gives play to conception, and stimulates ratiocination. On the other hand, the attempt to bring into active and unceasing exercise the reasoning powers of youth of a very early age is very injurious; for minute analyses and consecutive trains of argumentative and demonstrative thought task the brain more severely than any other intellectual process, and hinder its normal growth and expansion. In educational matters the pendulum of error often oscillates from senseless, stupefying repetition, and learning by rote, on the one hand, to continuous analyzing and reasoning on the other. To keep a just balance between the two is alike pointed out by common sense, and demanded by the interests of the children. The first and most fundamental principle in the work of any school is, that the instruction be simple and well adapted to each stage of mental capacity, directly tending to prepare the next step of development, and that the intellectual faculties be properly fed and developed.

Process of Mental Development.

The development of the mental powers should be systematic and perfectly proportioned in order to form a complete individuality. No undue attention should be bestowed on any one of them to the neglect of the others. No colossal overshadowing tree should be raised in the midst of sapling faculties, intercepting the sun from their leaves, or covering the ground of the organism with roots, and sapping the nutriment from the vital centres. They should be unfolded in that definite order which is pointed out by the laws of nature, and prescribed by science.

The dawn of active intelligence in the mind of a child passes rapidly and beautifully from mere sensation to observation, and from this to the recognition of persons and objects formerly beheld, or of sounds previously heard passively. In this manner, conception is brought into play, the mind receives ideas, the memory retains and recalls them by the wonderful principle of association, words are acquired and connected with them in an indissoluble manner by the process of assimilation, and talking and thinking move on together. Then follows the comparison of objects and ideas after which the mind passes to a recognition of abstract qualities; then logical thought, or ratiocination. This, with judgment and imagination, are developed slowly, and in their highest exercise belong to the last stage of mental growth. It is thus that the foundation of the whole intellectual character is laid by conception, aided by the law of association, which Rogers has so graphically described, —

" Lulled in the countless chambers of the brain,
 Our thoughts are linked by many a hidden chain.
 Awake but one, and, lo, what myriads rise !
 Each stamps its image as the other flies.''

The laws which govern the growth and operations of
the human mind are as definite, and as universal in
their application, as those which control the material
world.   Hence education in general must take cognizance of the fact, and shape its course accordingly.
But, in the training of the blind, particular attention
needs to be paid to the peculiar nature of the difficulties
arising from their infirmity. The long night of their
life knows no morning. The ever varying, ever beautiful face of nature is to them a blank ; and not only so,
but all modes of expression founded upon the countless
changes of light and shade so numerous in all languages are to them of vague and uncertain import.
Then there are many forms of existence so obvious, that
no one considers it necessary to describe them to seeing children, — things which the simplest books do not
explain. Who would think, for instance, of telling his
pupils that a mule had four legs, and a hen but two ;
that an ox had horns, and a horse had not ? Yet how
is the sightless child to know these particulars, unless
he feel of the animals themselves, or of their tangible
representations ? It is here that the blind are cramped,
and it is the province of the schools established for
their special benefit to provide them with ample means
for the exercise of their senses, and to bring them as
far as may be into direct communication with the multifarious objects of external nature. It will readily be
seen that teaching of this kind is indispensable for

training the physical and intellectual powers of the blind, for building up their whole character, and for raising them as near as possible to the social and moral standard of the community.

Object-Teaching and Illustrative Apparatus.

During the past year the facilities afforded by the institution for object-teaching, and for illustrating several branches of study, have been greatly increased; and the collections of models, specimens, and tangible appliances of various kinds, although not yet complete, have been enriched by many new additions. The most valuable of these is one of Auzoux's best and largest manikins, the purchase of which was followed by an order sent to Dresden, Germany, for a full set of Dr. Schaufuss's anatomical models. The manikin is a fine specimen, five feet six inches high, and is composed of ninety separate pieces, which can be taken apart so as to show the human structure in all its details. The Schaufuss models, forty-three in number, and representing the different parts of the body singly, are well made of papier-maché, and have been found of great service in the educational institutions of Germany. The apparatus illustrative of the metric system, and a collection of minerals, fossils, crystals, seeds and dried plants, kindergarten materials, and stuffed birds and animals, have also been procured, and advantageously used by our pupils.

These additions, although increasing our educational facilities, are far from completing them, and making them such as they ought to be. We need more specimens, both of sensible objects from the animal and

vegetable kingdoms, and tangible models of various
kinds; so that in every case where it is possible the real
thing may be presented to the touch when it is studied
or taught.   This mode of instruction is of inestimable
value.   It bridges over the chasm from the known to
the unknown, from the concrete to the abstract, and lays
a solid foundation for the mind to work upon.   It rouses
the attention of the pupils, and excites their interest.
It appeals to experience, and stimulates their powers of
observation to intense activity.   It feeds the mind with
real food, and raises it out of the slough of inattention
and listless inactivity.

The first step in mental growth is to obtain knowledge which comes in the form of the perception of
the qualities of objects, or of facts in regard to their
relations; the next is a comparison of two or more
perceptions and the recognition of their points of likeness and unlikeness, then classification, then generalization, then law and principle, then definition.   Thus
ideas are formed in the mind by abstraction and generalization from facts revealed to it through the senses;
and the more numerous, varied, intense, and harmonious are the latter, the more complete and clear will
be the former, and the more profound the enjoyment
derived from them.   What the pupils themselves perceive of the tangible properties of things serves as the
basis of thought; and upon the vividness and fulness
of the impressions made upon them by external objects
depend the correctness of their inferences and the
soundness of their judgment.   In early childhood the
perceptive faculties are relatively stronger than at a
later period; and, while the understanding and reason

still sleep, the sensitive mind is receiving those sharp
impressions of external things, which, held fast by the
memory, transformed by the imagination, and finally
classified and organized through reflection, result in
the determination of thought and in the formation of
character.

Descartes, in his philosophy, attempts to show that
the only reality of which we are absolutely certain is,
that *we think,* — " *cogito, ergo sum,*" — and that the
materials and order of thought are furnished by the
outer world.   It is true, that the more we study natural
phenomena, and rise to a comprehension of the laws
that control them, the more thoroughly is the reasoning
faculty developed, and the better are we prepared to
perform the duties of life.   But we must not lose sight
of the fact that the final result of mental discipline is
the attainment, not of subsensuous, but of supersensuous
knowledge, and the ability to deal with abstract relations
and principles.   This consummation of education should
not be hindered, either by neglect of object-lessons, or
by an exclusive and too long continuation of them.
Either extreme is dangerous ; for culture in the one case
rests upon a narrow and insufficient basis of fact, and, in
the other, the mind is kept under the dominion of the
senses, and independent thought is rendered nearly impossible.

TEXT-BOOKS, THEIR USE AND ABUSE.

The evil tendency of obliging pupils to commit to
memory the words of the text-book has been constantly
disapproved and persistently avoided.

This practice is a pernicious one, and has been

severely criticised and emphatically condemned by great
philosophers and distinguished educators.   Hallam says,
that " Locke did not think that to pour the wordy book-
learning of pedants into the memory is the true discipline of childhood ; " and Montaigne observes, that " a
mere bookish learning is a poor stock to go upon.
Though it may serve for some kind of ornament, yet
there is no foundation for any superstructure to be raised
upon." It seems to have its origin in indolence or
ignorance, and lack of training, and is calculated directly
to narrow, rather than to expand, the mind.   It fixes the
attention on words, rather than on thoughts, and makes
more of forms and symbols than of the thing symbolized.
It is not merely because Moses, Socrates, Confucius,
Plato, and Aristotle were great men themselves, but
that they happily lived before text-books were manufactured, and had to invent their methods as they went' on
teaching, that their vast original force has so gone out
upon the world of thought.

Text-books are used in our school as aids, rather than
as fetters ; as helps to elucidate the study which they
present, rather than as all-sufficient treasures of information.   The keynote with us is an extension of the
sphere and uses of oral instruction, which furnishes the
best facilities for the acquisition of knowledge.   This
kind of teaching leads the mind to exert such activity
as will result in a thorough training of the intellectual
faculties and in the attainment of a good method of
thinking and acting.

But oral teaching, in order to be valuable, must be
systematic, connected, and harmonious, and not mere
random talk,   Its form must be dialectic, and not dog-

matic.   Socrates, and, after him, Arkesilaos, first made
their pupils speak, and then spoke to them ; and every
true teacher ought to follow their example.

MUSIC DEPARTMENT.

" By music, minds an equal temper know,
Nor swell too high, nor sink too low :
If in the breast tumultuous joys arise,
Music her soft, persuasive voice applies ;
Or, when the soul is pressed with cares,
Exalts her in enlivening airs." — *Pope.*

This department has fully sustained its high standing
in our system of education, and its work has been performed in a manner which is very creditable to those
who are engaged in it.

Eighty-seven scholars have received instruction in
music during the past year, and the branches taught
may be summarized as follows : piano-forte, the parlor
and church organ, class and solo singing, flute, clarinet, cornet, and other band instruments, harmony, counterpoint, and the art of teaching.

The progress of the pupils has been very satisfactory,
and those among them who are gifted with special
talent, and possess such general mental ability as is
essential for the attainment of excellence in any art,
advance rapidly.   But there are some who prove, after
a patient and fair trial, utterly destitute of natural aptitude for music.   These are required to discontinue
their music-lessons, and to devote their time out of
school-hours to the acquisition of some useful trade, or
to some other manual occupation.   In order to meet
the usual remonstrances of disappointed relatives and

friends in such instances, a record of each scholar's progress is kept, showing the number of lessons given to him, the exact amount of music learned at each of them, and the number of hours practised per week. From these data the actual standing of every pupil can be accurately obtained, and his ability or inaptitude for further musical instruction exactly ascertained. There are individuals who are afflicted with what Mr. Grant Allen has called note-deafness, — an imperfection in the nervous apparatus in the ear, analogous to color-blindness, which is supposed to be due to the loss of sensibility of one of the three sets of retinal nerve-fibres. To such persons, as well as to those who are wanting in mental capacity and calibre, instruction in music is of no avail whatever, and the sooner they turn their attention to some of the mechanical arts, the better it is for them.

Due attention is given to concerted music, such as class-singing, band-playing, and the like; but the fullest measure of attention and endeavor is directed towards those forms of instruction and training which aim at individual excellence both in vocal and instrumental music. In the arena of practical life, the success of a graduate who has been merely a member of a singing-class, or of a band or orchestra, is rather doubtful ; but if the culture of his voice has been such as to enable him to sing artistically, accompanying himself, if need be, on the piano-forte, or if he can play solos well on any string, reed, or brass instrument which shall be fit for the concert-room or for a select parlor-entertainment, he will find almost anywhere an open field of usefulness, and may derive substantial advantages from the practice of his profession.

Nearly all the individual lessons on instruments used in the band, and most of the instruction in vocal music, are given by three non-resident professors, — Messrs. H. C. Brown, C. Higgins, and Madame Rametti. These, with five resident teachers, one assistant, three music-readers, and some of the advanced pupils, constitute an able and efficient corps of instructors.

The Objectionable in Music.

Music, like literature, has its low and sensational forms, which tend to degrade both taste and feeling. Dime novels and vile fiction have their counterpart in musical compositions. This kind of music, which is either meaningless, or ends in mere sentiment, without exciting to generous and noble action, vulgarizing that which is lofty and pure, or appealing directly to the basest passions, is shunned in our curriculum, and that alone chosen which has a tendency to arouse the higher nature, to repress selfishness, to refine the taste, and to restrain the lower propensities. Music of this kind, while directly aiding in æsthetic culture, becomes an important element in moral education.

The possession of the æsthetic faculty, that is, of a well developed sense of the general fitness of beautiful things, is one of the most important requisites of a musician ; and this, together with the ability for sound analytical criticism of musical compositions, can be attained in the concert-room, where the compositions of the greater and lesser masters are interpreted by eminent artists. Thanks to the authorities and members of the best musical societies of Boston, to the proprietors of theatres, the managers of public entertainments, and

also to a brilliant array of distinguished musicians in
our city, — the names of all of whom will be hereafter
gratefully mentioned in the list of acknowledgments,
— our pupils continue to be generously permitted to
attend the finest concerts, rehearsals, operas, oratorios,
and the like, and are favored with many most exquisite
artistic performances given in our own hall.   They
actually live and move in a musical atmosphere, which
has, of course, a most powerful influence in the formation of the taste ; so that pure classical music is enjoyed
by them with the greatest zest and enthusiasm, and
concerts of a high order become favorite entertainments.

The True, the Beautiful, and the Useful in Music.

Herbert Spencer, in describing the importance of
the social and moral influence of music, says, —

" The tendency of civilization is more and more to repress the
antagonistic elements of our characters, and to develop the social
ones, to curb our purely selfish desires, and exercise our unselfish
ones, to replace private gratification by gratification resulting
from or involving the happiness of others ; and while, by this
adaptation to the social state, the sympathetic side of our nature
is being unfolded, there is simultaneously growing up a language
of sympathetic intercourse, — a language through which we communicate to others the happiness we feel, and are made to share
their happiness."

These words of the eminent scientist are in accordance with the views of the most distinguished writers
and celebrated thinkers on the subject.   Music is undoubtedly one of the spontaneous manifestations of that
intellectual activity which is the special characteristic
of man, and its value as a promoter of the beautiful,
and through it of the good, is universally admitted.   It

constitutes a very essential factor in the education of the
blind; and its study and practice are earnestly pursued
in our school for the æsthetic culture which it affords, —
for its beneficial results in mental and moral discipline, —
and for the substantial advantages, as well as the pleasure, which its devotees derive from its profession.   But,
on the other hand, the idea that music should or can
constitute the sole aim of the efforts of the blind is a
mistaken and very pernicious one.   It proceeds from
ignorance of the nature of the art itself, and rests upon
a mere illusion with regard to its effects upon man's
normal development.   While no one will agree in these
days with the stern-minded Romans of old in their con-
demnation of music as effeminating, it is obvious, that,
if pursued with a narrow and exclusive devotion, it may
become so.   The truest musician is he who is loyal to
his whole nature, who does not dwarf his mind, and
stunt his body, thereby in reality thwarting his art.
This fact, although apparently so self-evident, it is
always necessary to impress upon the minds of young
people, and especially upon those of the blind, in whom
neither pallid cheeks, sunken chests, sedentary habits,
lameness of the wrists, circumscribed mental horizon,
nor the limited circle of sympathies, can be improved or
remedied by exclusive devotion to one branch of education, which must produce an inharmonious development of all the faculties and powers.   The success of
our graduates as music-teachers and performers depends
in no small measure upon the breadth of their general
knowledge and the degree of mental discipline which
they have attained in school.   As in intellectual training the aim is to ascertain the true in facts and in the

relations of both the physical and mental worlds, so in music the end sought is the beautiful, which is the true in the relations of sound, and in their combinations and qualities as they affect the sense of hearing. The true includes all phenomena, and the beautiful refers to those objective relations and combinations which afford pleasure. Hence the two are so related to each other, that each is essential in an educational course for the ultimate success of the other, and that substantial attainment in the former is necessary to the highest proficiency in the latter. Without the assertion of the intellect in music, its sweetness would cloy, and become positively tiresome. Berlioz's remarks on this subject carry with them more than ordinary weight. They seem to be the embodiment of keen observation, mature experience, and sound judgment. " Music," says he, " is at once an art and a science ; to have a thorough knowledge of it, one must go through complex and quite long studies ; to feel the emotions it arouses, one must have a cultured intelligence and a practical ear ; to judge of the value of musical works, one must have a well-furnished memory in order to be able to make comparisons, and, in fine, to know many things, of which one is necessarily ignorant when one has not learned them."

The ancient Greeks, who, by the harmonious development and proper exercise of all the mental faculties and bodily powers, reached the *beau ideal* of physical, intellectual, and æsthetic perfection, embraced in the term *music* (μουσικὴ) the whole course of culture, from the gymnasium to the academia. This definition may seem over-wide at first, yet I venture to plead for its applica-

tion in the case of the blind.   Then, and then only, will
education light for them the path to a noble social
equalization and the domain of a rational individual
happiness, when, like Phœbus in Guido's famous picture, the luminous herald is permitted to ride in a car
of faultless workmanship, in which symbol I would
embody the idea of a perfect physical development
bearing along as in a beautiful chariot the glory of the
illuminated mind.

TUNING DEPARTMENT.

In order that our pupils may obtain the necessary
training for the productive employments of life, our
system of instruction is not confined to the ordinary
branches of an English education alone, or to the cultivation of music, the broadening of the intellect, or the
refinement of the æsthetic nature.   Addressing the
mind, it does not ignore the hands, or the whole range
of those faculties of which they are the special instruments, but aims to develop the mechanical aptitudes
and tastes of our pupils, and send them out sufficiently
prepared to earn their living by their own exertions.

The tuning department, infusing as it does a new
motive into the activities of the blind, is a valuable auxiliary to this end, and an important adjunct to our system of education.   It opens a new and lucrative field of
usefulness to our graduates ; and a considerable number
of young men who despaired of success in other callings are doing exceedingly well as tuners of piano-
fortes.

This department has received during the past year all
the attention which its practical ends and general pur-

poses deserve, and a great amount of work has been accomplished in it. Its present condition is excellent, and its future prospects very promising.

The number of pupils who have received instruction in tuning is seventeen ; and the time devoted by them to taking lessons and practising varies, according to their attainments and necessities, from five to twenty-four hours a week.

Two of the pupils graduated from this department at the close of the last term ; and one of the former graduates has been employed during the year on a regular salary to assist in tuning the piano-fortes used in the schools of the city of Boston.

Another piano-forte has been added to those already in use in this department, and our collection of appliances for the practical study of the internal mechanism of instruments of various kinds has been increased by the generous gift of Messrs. Steinway and Sons of two models of the actions of their upright and grand piano-fortes. For finished workmanship,· beauty, and completeness of construction, these models can hardly be surpassed, and they are great ornaments to the apparatus of our tuning department.

Manufacturers of piano-fortes in this and other cities will promote their own interests, as well as those of the blind, by placing models of their actions in this institution. Tuners who are thus assisted in mastering thoroughly the details and peculiarities of various instruments are able to recommend them among the *clientèle* which they almost invariably acquire on leaving school. Thus the sale of the instruments is increased, and a knowledge of their special characteristics diffused in different parts of the country. This is particularly desirable where any new principles are involved in their construction.

The contract for tuning and keeping in repair the piano-fortes used in the public schools of Boston has been renewed for another year on the same terms as before, and without the least opposition from any direction. This unanimous and prompt action of the committee is highly complimentary to our tuners, and speaks more eloquently for their skill and efficiency than words can do. It is a source of encouragement to the blind of New England and a noble example of justice and foresight which does honor to the members of the school board of Boston, and ought to be followed by the authorities of every city in America.

The popular prejudice against the ability of the blind as tuners, teachers, or adepts in any art or profession, which has for a long time blocked up their way to usefulness and independence, thus gratuitously increasing the grievous burden of their misfortune, is gradually yielding to a better understanding of their skill and capacity; and many of the best and most intelligent families of Boston and the neighboring towns unhesitatingly place their costly instruments under the care of our tuning department, and, so far as we know, not only has no fault been found with the work done upon them, but general satisfaction seems to echo from all directions. For this feeling of confidence in the proficiency of our tuners, and for the generous patronage which is constantly extended to them, we are greatly indebted to some of our most distinguished musicians and to many teachers and eminent citizens, who, by employing our men to keep their own piano-fortes in order, have manifested their reliance upon the work of the blind in the most practical and convincing manner.

It has been repeatedly stated in my previous reports, that the blind develop, in consequence of their infirmity, a remarkable power of distinguishing the pitch and quality of sounds; that, as a result of this ability, they acquire great proficiency in the art of tuning piano-fortes; that in this calling they labor under no disadvantage whatsoever, and therefore are exceedingly successful; and that their work is in many respects more thoroughly and satisfactorily done than that of most of their seeing brethren in the craft. I desire to repeat the assertion here with all the emphasis which proceeds from full conviction; for it does not rest upon mere *a priori* reasoning, but is warranted by experience gathered in the field of observation and study, and confirmed by facts obtained by scientific investigation. So far as the calling of a tuner is concerned, it is beyond doubt, that, other things being equal, the blind, living as they do in this institution in an atmosphere eminently musical, and enjoying uncommon advantages for theoretical study and thorough practical training in the art of tuning, are qualified to do their work more satisfactorily than their seeing competitors in the art. Hence it is earnestly hoped that the community in general, and piano-forte manufacturers in particular, will take more notice of this fact, and will favor our tuners in their efforts for self-maintenance with more encouragement in the future than they have done heretofore. As sight is a condition *sine qua non* in the pursuit of the mechanical arts, the sphere of employments for our graduates is a contracted one, and it is simply a matter of justice, that, in those branches of industry in which they compete successfully with other workmen, and even excel them, they should receive all the patronage, nay, the preference, which is due to them as an inherent part, and as active members, of the organic body of society.

TECHNICAL DEPARTMENT.

This department continues to perform its important part in the work of training our pupils for useful independence and happiness.

While we are deeply impressed with the magnitude of the benefits which intellectual and moral culture confer upon the blind, yet their education would be decidedly deficient, if not supplemented by instruction in some kind of handicraft, and the acquisition of a fair amount of skill for its pursuance. The system which makes the training of the hands keep pace with the mental development is of immense importance to the blind, and the good effects produced by it may be summed up as follows : —

First, it arouses the senses to activity, and provides the mental faculties with a gentle stimulus, while it-- prevents the morbid action of the brain which too much study is apt to produce in young persons.

Secondly, it trains the muscles to respond immediately to the will, and gives dexterity in the use of tools and in the handling of materials.

Thirdly, it furnishes pleasant, and, in most cases, profitable occupation, without which the time might be passed in idleness, despondency, and dissipation.

Fourthly, its influence may be likened to that of a

utilitarian gymnasium, and it exercises an important hygienic agency.

Finally, it aims to impart a healthy tonic against the sentimentalism and dilettanteism which are the bane of our age, and to inculcate the wholesome lesson that young people must work in order to enjoy; that they cannot accomplish any thing creditable without application and diligence; that they must not be daunted by difficulties, but conquer them by patience and perseverance; and that, above all, they should seek elevation of character, without which capacity is worthless, and worldly success is naught.

For these reasons manual labor has always been made one of the most prominent means of improvement in this institution; and its dignity and usefulness have been constantly asserted by precept and example. All our pupils, whether children of the rich or of the poor, are required to spend a part of their time daily in the industrial department, and to learn to work with their hands, so that, when they leave the school, they may not only be instructed in the various branches of study, but possessed of knowledge of some profession, or of one or more trades, and, above all, with bodily vigor, and with muscles trained to the performance of the tasks which await them in the wide field of industry.

As has been repeatedly stated in former reports, the technical department of the institution is divided into two branches, one for the boys, and the other for the girls. The business of both of these branches has been conducted with rare assiduity and fidelity by those in charge, and with very gratifying results.

I. — *Workshop for the Boys.*

Regular and systematic instruction in various trades, such as seating cane-bottomed chairs, manufacturing brooms, making mattresses, and upholstering parlor furniture, is given in this shop; and the pupils are occupied as much as possible with work of a solid and serviceable character, either for the use of the institution, or for sale.

The mode of instruction employed is simple and practical, and the advancement of its recipients very satisfactory.

The workshop for the boys, as well as that for the girls, was never designed as a source of pecuniary profit to the institution. We endeavor to make it pay its own expenses; but, if it did not quite do that, — as in reality it does not, — the benefit to the pupils in training them to mechanical skill, and habits of industry and regularity, would still make it our duty to maintain it, and keep it under the management and supervision of teachers employed directly for the purpose by the institution.

In some parts of the country an arrangement is made by which the pupils of educational establishments are placed for certain specified hours of the day under the charge of a contractor, who, in addition to the use of the shop free of rent, receives the avails of their labor in return for the instruction he may impart to them. Such a plan is very convenient indeed where it does not matter whether the training in handicraft is nominal or not. It saves to an institution a certain amount of money, and, what is more important than this, it lessens the work of those managers who have a natural con-

tempt for too much exertion; but it cannot be too
severely deprecated, if the workshops are intended to
play in all its completeness the rôle which is assigned to
them in the education of the blind. The advancement
of the objects of an institution is proportioned to the
degree of disinterestedness, zeal, efficiency, and aptitude,
displayed by those employed to carry on its work, and
the amount of influence and control which they exercise
over its beneficiaries. Now, a contractor who aspires
to reap as much pecuniary benefit from his undertakings
as possible, however tightly he may be bound to conform with the terms of his agreement, cannot perform
the duties of an experienced teacher in the different
branches of handicraft satisfactorily and acceptably.
He will be inclined to look out for his own interests
rather than for those of the pupils committed to his
charge; and instead of giving systematic and progressive instruction to all of them, and especially to those
who need it the most, he will pay particular attention
to those whose labor is profitable to himself, keeping
them at work on what they can do best at the expense
of breadth of training and the versatility which it imparts. He will not be disposed to be strict with them
by noticing whether they stand erect, are tidy, and free
from objectionable habits, and use proper language,
provided they work assiduously, and turn out as many
salable brooms or other articles as possible. He will
devote all his time and energy to the increasing of his
own business by urging on the older and more advanced, and will have none left to spend in guiding step
by step the young and unskilful, who are of feeble
temperament, and cannot use their hands to advantage.

Thus, while the latter are sure to be neglected, the former will be employed in the work which is most lucrative, without any reference to their improvement in the knowledge of their trades. The acquisition of the habits of prudence and economy in the use of stock is the only redeeming feature of the contract-system; but this is more than counterbalanced by the great disadvantages resulting from such an arrangement.

II. — Workrooms for the Girls.

The condition of the girls' branch of the technical department is flourishing, and its work progresses most satisfactorily. No pains have been spared in rendering the lessons here given interesting and attractive, and the responsive spirit shown by the pupils is very gratifying to their instructors.

A few of our girls learn seating cane-bottomed chairs, which is always a resource for a blind person, particularly in small towns and villages; but a livelier interest is shown by the greater number in the various branches of needlework which are taught in the sewing-room, where the majority of the older girls spend a part of the afternoon Fancy-work of different materials, and more especially of the kind known among blind people as bead-work, develops infinite ramifications in their hands. New forms are invented from time to time, and the ingenious work-mistress, Miss Dillingham, is constantly on the alert to obtain, and introduce into the school, the most recent and graceful patterns of various articles which are esteemed desirable for gifts, &c. The girls derive pecuniary profit from the disposal of the fruits of their industry, and a great deal of zeal is natu-rally displayed in their contrivance and manufacture.

Besides these lighter forms of work, the sewing-machines are kept constantly going; and linen for the household, as well as various other articles of use, are prepared by the pupils. The generosity of Messrs. Wheeler & Wilson has furnished this department with two of their new "improved machines," the number now amounting to nine in all. These machines continue to be held in the highest esteem among us, and are regarded as the most valuable adjunct to our sewing-rooms.

It has also been deemed necessary to add to our stock one of Franz & Pope's knitting-machines, which gives better satisfaction than those formerly purchased of Mr. Bickford of New York.

A variety of domestic occupations is moreover taught to our girls. Our cottage system affords an excellent opportunity for learning by daily practice and routine the economy of a frugal and orderly household. The pupils manifest interest, application, perseverance, a willingness to work, and a certain degree of pride in what they accomplish. A woman's sphere of knowledge is incomplete, unless it embrace some acquaintance with work of this sort; and it is especially necessary for blind girls to be trained in matters, which, if they had sight, would be to them almost a second nature. Milton says, —

> " To know
> That which before us lies in daily life
> Is the prime wisdom ; "

and every well-organized system of education should afford to its recipients ample facilities for instruction and practice in the ordinary callings of daily life.

Department of Physical Training.

That the perfection of the operations of the mind is dependent upon the soundness of the machinery by means of which it manifests itself, and that a healthy and vigorous body is indispensable to success in any active form of intellectual life, is too evident to need demonstration.

Emerson says that the first thing in every efficient man is a fine animal. Experience shows, that, without this, nothing that is truly remarkable can be achieved. Genius is very seldom, if ever, nurtured in a weak and diseased frame. No man is at his best without physical vigor. It is the strength of the body that nourishes the power of the mind. In endeavoring to bring out the beauty and brilliancy of the gem, we must not neglect the casket which enshrines it. There can be no healthful or wholesome action of the mind or the moral perceptions, if the physique is enervated. The age of an animal life preceded the unparalleled intellectual and æsthetic development of ancient Greece. The works of Ictinus and Phidias, of Zeuxis and Praxiteles, of Plato and Thucydides, of Æschylus and Demosthenes, were produced when the first care in that country was to make a man a magnificent creature, when corporeal weakness was considered a positive disgrace, and physical deformity was not allowed to exist, and when beauty and bodily vigor were classed among the noblest virtues.

Wiry muscles and firm flesh, good digestion, the power of endurance of all kinds of labor, and a fresh active brain, are highly essential for accurate perception, retentive memory, clear judgment, and a pleasant frame of mind; and these, as well as a blooming complexion, graceful mien, and erect carriage, can be secured and preserved only by regular and systematic exercise.

Physical training performs an important part in promoting bodily vigor and intellectual growth, as well as in combating the causes which tend to the deterioration of the material frame, and lead to disease. It prevents excessive stimulation and tension of the mind, which causes a greater or less congestion of the brain, manifesting itself by chronic headaches, and bleedings at the nose, and disorders of the digestive and nutritive functions and the circulation. It lays the foundation of permanent strength, and brings the powers of the material frame under the immediate control of the will. Its claims are urged by distinguished physiologists, and recognized by eminent educators; and the preaching of the gospel of good health and bodily vigor is no longer regarded as a sectarian hobby. On the contrary, it is universally admitted, that unless the wonderful mechanism, which is at once the domicile and the feeder of the mind, be kept in the highest state of efficiency, no success is attainable in any of the learned professions, and I may safely say in any calling.

Such, in brief, are the beneficial effects, and such the general considerations, which call for the physical culture of all children. But, besides these, the loss of sight is a positive hinderance to the free and almost ceaseless exercise of the muscular system which is necessary in youth for the full development of the bodily powers; and its unfavorable effects upon the material organization of the blind are so obvious, that a thorough course of gymnastic training is demanded with tenfold

force in all schools established for their benefit.   High
shoulders, drooping heads, a cadaverous complexion, contracted chests, lax muscles, a shuffling gait, a hacking
cough, and an embarrassing uncertainty regarding the
proper place to locate the arms and legs, are some
of the undesirable physical characteristics of our pupils;
and they must be remedied as far as may be, and the
proper means must be assiduously employed in order
to put their material mechanism in as good order as
possible.   The modes of exercise which brought forth
strength and beauty in ancient days, if adhered to persistently, will undoubtedly eradicate special weaknesses
and defects, promote symmetry, increase vigor to maturity, and sustain it unfailingly.   It is a self-evident
fact, that in order to make good scholars, efficient musicians, skilful mechanics, nay, men and women fit for life,
and able to perform its ordinary duties, we must first,
and above all, build securely the pedestal upon which
the statue of their education and professional training is
to be raised.   Without this, all attempts to reach the
highest intellectual and moral development will prove
abortive.   A school that makes no provision to prevent
its beneficiaries from becoming sickly, crooked, mal-
formed, and feeble, both in mind and body, is doing its
work in the wrong way, and its usefulness is of a very
doubtful character.

The erection of a new and spacious gymnasium upon
the premises of the institution is justly regarded as an
important step, from which the most beneficent results
may be anticipated.

During the past year the interior of the new structure has been finished with hard wood, and made ready

for use. Owing to the pressure of work, however, for completing the repairs and improvements undertaken in the main building before the commencement of the school session, there was hardly any time left for selecting and arranging the necessary apparatus. This will soon be accomplished, and there will be inaugurated a system of physical culture which is calculated to make the pupils well-proportioned, strong, and healthy, supple-jointed, and graceful in repose or in motion, and so erect, too, as to insure, whether on foot, sitting, or lying down, ample room for the proper working of all the organs of the human frame.

The female pupils have received regular and thorough physical training during the past year. Both the gallery and new gymnasium have afforded ample opportunities for this. They have been drilled with special care in calisthenic exercises, and the results are very satisfactory. Grace in attitude, and comeliness in appearance, have been developed, and a greater amount of intellectual work has been accomplished. Nervous restlessness is gradually allayed, and headaches and other ailments are not of as frequent occurrence as they used to be. The tendency to distortion incident to the effects of the loss of sight is overcome to a considerable extent, and, what is especially noticeable, a strong, free, and vigorous movement is substituted for the listless shambling or the nervous jerking, which are common characteristics among the pupils of those institutions where the claims of physical culture are utterly ignored. With the progress of time, and the improvements in our methods which experience will suggest, it is hoped that our system of bodily training will become still more complete,

and bear even more abundant fruit in the future than it
has done in the past.

LAURA BRIDGMAN.

This most interesting woman, the silent guest, now,
with one exception, the eldest inhabitant, of the institution, continues to reside with us, and to awaken. never-
failing interest in the minds of all who visit the establishment.   Her pathetic history encircles her with a
halo which no worldly success or brilliancy could give;—
and she appeals mutely to the tenderest feelings of the
human heart.   The story of her life is indissolubly bound
up with that of him who was more to her than a father,
the friend and teacher who struck the rock of silence that
the fountain of knowedge might gush forth, infusing with
Promethean fire the mind which must otherwise have
remained dormant forever.   Round him her earliest
memories entwine.   His loving care and watchfulness
were the gate through which she entered into intelligent
and conscious life.   It is not my purpose here to trace
the details of her rescue from the hopeless barriers
which hemmed her in on every side to an existence of
intelligence, activity, and happiness.   Enough is known
to you of the wonderful way in which that isolated
mind was liberated from its dark tomb.   The story of
Laura Bridgman is engraved in the memory of all who
were then living, and has been handed down as one of
the greatest monuments of human benevolence and
wisdom.   I would merely give a brief account of her
present condition, in which I am certain that all who
have known her will feel interested.

Laura's health is more delicate than of old; but her

mental activity and sprightliness continue to distinguish her as vividly to-day as they did in her earliest youth. She is decidedly a living and feeling person ; and there prevails more liveliness and animation in the room where she is than in a group of five or six people of phlegmatic temperament. If I may be permitted to use a simile, Laura, with her warm, excitable feelings, keen and quick perception, rapid intellectual processes, and vivid emotional nature, surrounded as she is by an impenetrable wall of silence, is like the snow-covered Hecla, whose icy barriers enshroud the burning fire within.

Her life is necessarily a quiet one ; but she welcomes every little variety with the enthusiasm of a child. One must be with Laura in order to learn how great may be the value of little pleasures. She is extremely fond of the institution, preferring it as a residence to any other place. Every new book which she reads with her delicate fingers is an era in her life, every piece of work accomplished a little triumph to rejoice over. The loss of her best earthly friend has cast a shadow over her life, and she treasures his memory with an orphan's fidelity. Her religious nature is very active ; and her remarks on such subjects are often original and striking. She also puts a great deal of warmth and vivacity into all her friendships and ac-quaintanceships. It is usually a fancy of hers to bestow the title of " brother " or " sister " upon a dear friend. Last spring she said to a young clergyman who re-newed his acquaintance with her, " I love to meet the saints." She is never so happy as when making herself useful, and is much interested in the sewing-room for the girls, where she assists.

A new work on Laura is in course of preparation by Professor G. Stanley Hall, now resident in Berlin. Professor Hall writes from that city, that the scientific men of Germany are very much interested in her case. Two articles from his pen have already been published, — one in " The Mind," an English psychological quarterly, and the other in " The Nation." Professor Hall spent some time in the institution, devoting every moment of his visit to a close scientific observation of Laura's case in all its bearings ; and his book is looked forward to as one of the highest value.

A kind and noble friend of Laura's in Edinburgh, Dr. David Brodie, conceived some time ago the idea of making up a present in money for her among people who were interested in her case in England and Scotland. His efforts met with a prompt and generous response. It was most touching to find, that, after the lapse of so many years since her misfortune first occupied the public mind, there were so many yet living who entertained the same warm and friendly interest that was called forth so long ago. Indeed, it may most truly be said, that, although afflicted, Laura has always been very rich in friends. Though born to the greatest of all calamities, that of being cut off from all communication with her kind, she was deeply blest in her redemption from that grievous misfortune. The noble act which rescued her from a doom too terrible for the mind to dwell upon drew the hearts of all men to her, and crowned her young life with joy and affections which must blossom and bear fruit to all eternity. Even the hardest heart must be softened in contemplating her afflictions. She has never awakened any but

the tenderest feelings in all who have come in contact
with her; and the path where so many thorns were
strewn has been spread with the fairest flowers that love
and friendship and unselfish benevolence could scatter;
and thus may it be to the end!

CLOSING REMARKS.

In submitting this report, gentlemen, to your forbear-
ing consideration, I beg leave to repeat in a few words
that no efforts have been spared to increase our educational facilities, and to secure to our pupils the highest
degree of usefulness, comfort, and happiness. Our
sphere of action is, of course, circumscribed by the
limited means at our disposal, and many desirable
things and helpful appliances are beyond our reach;
but nothing that seems to be essential for carrying out
the work of the institution in an efficient and thorough
manner is omitted. We endeavor to improve our system of instruction and training from year to year by
every possible means, to expand its scope, and to render
it a powerful agent for the amelioration of the condition
of the blind in general, and for their elevation in the
social and moral scale to the same level with their more
fortunate fellow-men. In spite of the many obstacles
and difficulties encountered in the application of this
system, its workings have thus far proved successful.
An aspiration after self-support and independence is the
primary manifestation of its effects; and dignity, self-
respect, and refinement are its ripe fruit. This is so
true, that we may as well expect to see the organized
beggary of southern Italy transplanted and thriving in
the uncongenial soil of Massachusetts, as to imagine the

educated and industrious blind of New England marching under the same banner with those of the old world,
asserting the rights of pauperism by the lamp-posts, or
clamoring for alms in the churchyards.

It is always a great satisfaction to me to acknowledge
my obligations to all who are associated with me, for
the valuable assistance which they have given in the
promotion of the comfort, happiness, and welfare of the
household, the efficiency of the school, and the general
prosperity of the institution.   By their genuine sympathy and kindness of heart, their rare combination of
perfect gentleness with a rational degree of firmness,
their tact, and their untiring devotion to their charge,
they have rendered most valuable services in the education and training of our pupils, and have won alike their
respect and gratitude.

In conclusion, gentlemen, I desire to express to the
members of your board my heartfelt thanks for your
courtesy, kindness, confidence, and cordial coöperation.
Whatever has been done during the last four years to
increase the efficiency, and advance the working power,
of the institution, is largely due to your broad views,
wise resolutions, and liberal policy.   If any thing has
been neglected which might have been accomplished,
the fault lies neither with your board, nor with my
assistants, but with myself.

Respectfully submitted by

M. ANAGNOS.

ACKNOWLEDGMENTS.

Among the pleasant duties incident to the close of the year is that of expressing our heartfelt thanks and grateful acknowledgments to the following artists, *littérateurs*, societies, proprietors, managers, editors and publishers, for concerts and various musical entertainments, for operas, oratorios, lectures, readings, and for an excellent supply of periodicals and weekly papers.

As I have said in previous reports, these favors are not only a source of pleasure and happiness to our pupils, but also a valuable means of æsthetic culture, of social intercourse, and of mental stimulus and improvement. As far as we know, there is no community in the world which does half so much for the gratification and improvement of its unfortunate members as that of Boston does for our pupils.

I. — Acknowledgments for Concerts, &c., in the City.

To the Harvard Musical Association, through its president, Mr. John S. Dwight, for fifty season-tickets to eight symphony concerts.

To Messrs. Tompkins and Hill, proprietors of the Boston Theatre, for admitting parties in unlimited numbers to ten operas, and also to H. M. S. Pinafore. To this latter, the invitation was given in the most cordial form of *carte blanche* for one week and a half; and all the members of our household, old and young, had an opportunity to attend the popular opera more than once, thanks to the great generosity of the proprietors, who, however crowded their theatre may be, always make room for " their friends," the blind.

To the Händel and Haydn Society, through its president, Mr. C. C. Perkins, for tickets to five of their grand concerts.

To Boylston Club, through its conductor, Mr. George L. Osgood, and its secretary, Mr. F. H. Ratcliffe, for admission to three concerts.

To Mr. R. M. Field, manager of the Boston Museum, for an invitation to children's Pinafore.

To Messrs. Hathaway and Pond, for fifty tickets to their Wilhelmj concerts.

To Mr. H. C. Brown, for admission to a series of concerts by his band.

To Miss Edith Abell, for admission to her concert, in which the "Stabat Mater" was given.

To Madame Cappiani and the Alpine quartette we are similarly indebted.

In the line of purely classical music we are under great obligations to the Euterpe Society, for admission to their series of four chamber concerts; to Mr. W. H. Sherwood, for permission to attend his series of ten piano-forte recitals; to Mr. B. J. Lang, for admissions to his series of two concerts; to Mr. J. A. Preston, for a similar favor; and to Miss Charlotte Hawes, for an invitation to attend one of her lectures on music.

Our pupils have also occasionally attended some of the concerts which are free to the public.

We are also under great obligations to Mr. J. T. Zimmerman for an invitation to the Siege of Paris, the particulars of which were clearly explained to our pupils by his agent.

II. — *Acknowledgment for Concerts given in our Hall.*

For a series of fine concerts and miscellaneous entertainments given in the hall of the Institution we are under great obligations to the following eminent artists : —

Miss Fanny Kellogg. Mr. John Orth, and Mr. Wulf Fries.

Madame Rametti and several of her pupils.

Mr. Hanchette and Miss Claybor.

Miss Ware, pianist, and Mr. Akeroid, violinist.

Mr. Preston, organist of St. Peter's Church, Cambridge.

Miss Dow, vocalist, and Miss Bennett, reader.

III. — *Acknowledgments for Lectures and Readings.*

For a series of lectures and readings we are greatly indebted to the following kind friends who have generously volunteered to interest and entertain our pupils: To Dr. F. W. Holland of Cambridge, Professor James Rosedale of Jerusalem, Mr. R. W. Jamieson of South Boston, Miss S. E. Oglevee of Springfield, O., Miss Ellen Reed of Nova Scotia, and Miss Mason of Boston.

IV. — *Acknowledgments for Periodicals and Newspapers.*

The editors and publishers of the following reviews, magazines, and semi-monthly and weekly papers, continue to be very kind and liberal in sending us their publications gratuitously, which are always cordially welcomed, and perused with interest: —

The N. E. Journal of Education	*Boston, Mass.*
The Atlantic	" "
The Christian	.. ..
The Christian Register	.. ..
The Folio	.. ..
The Sunday Herald	.. ..
Unitarian Review	..
The Watchman	.. ..
Wide Awake	" "
The Salem Register	*Salem, Mass.*
Illustrated Scientific News	*New York, N.Y.,*
Scribner's Monthly	" "
St. Nicholas	..
The Christian Union	..
The International Review	.. "
National Quarterly Review	.. "..
Musical Review	"
The N. Y. Weekly Post	" "
Journal of Health	*Dansville, N.Y.*
The Journal of Speculative Philosophy	*St. Louis, Mo.*
Lippincotts' Magazine	*Philadelphia, Penn.*
The Penn Monthly	" "..
Robinson's Epitome of Literature	..

The Normal Monthly Review .   *Shippensburg, Penn.*
Indiana School Journal   .   .   . *Indianapolis, Ind.*
Canada School Journal   .   .   .   *Toronto, Can.*
Goodson's Gazette, *Va. Inst. for Deaf-Mutes and Blind.*
Tablet   .   .   *West Va.* "   "   "   "
Mirror   .   .   *Michigan* "   "
Companion   .   *Minnesota* "   "   "   "
Philomathean Argus   .   . *Ohio Inst. for the Blind.*
Mistletoe .   .   .   .   . *Iowa* " " "   "
Il Mentore dei Ciechi   .   .   .   *Florence, Italy.*

I desire again to render the most hearty thanks, in behalf of all
our pupils, to the kind friends who have thus nobly remembered
them. The seeds which their friendly and generous attentions
have sown have fallen on no barren ground, but will continue to
bear fruit in after-years; and the memory of many of these
delightful and instructive occasions and valuable gifts will be
retained through life.

M. ANAGNOS.

Dr.   PERKINS INSTITUTION AND MASSACHUSETTS SCHOOL FOR THE BLIND, *in account with* H. ENDICOTT, *Treasurer.*   Cr.

Dr.			Cr.		
To cash paid on Auditor's drafts		$66,348 66	By balance from last account, Sept. 30, 1878		$2,049 67
city of Boston, taxes		156 40	cash from State of Massachusetts		30,000 00
		$66,515 06	New Hampshire		2,875 00
Re-investments.			Vermont		1,000 00
To loans secured by mortgages on real estate	$10,000 00		Rhode Island		3,000 00
10,000 Eastern Railroad bond,	7,579 91		Connecticut		3,300 00
10,000 Lowell Railroad bond,	10,219 44		Interest on mortgages		7,002 50
5,000 United States bond	5,115 62		Rents		259 56
		32,914 97	Boston and Providence Railroad dividends		180 00
balance to new account		579 21	Fitchburg Railroad dividends		270 00
			Interest on Eastern Railroad bonds		175 00
			Interest on deposits		238 86
			M. Anagnos, Director,—	$12,371 24	
			Work Department	3,507 41	
			Sundries		15,678 65
			By cash legacy account William Taylor, Tewksbury		700 00
			Payment of mortgage notes		32,000 00
		$100,009 24			$100,009 24
			1878.		
			Sept. 30, By balance to new account		579 21

BOSTON, Sept. 30, 1879.

The undersigned, a committee appointed to examine the accounts of the Perkins Institution and Massachusetts School for the Blind, have attended to that duty, and hereby certify that they find the accounts properly vouched and correctly cast, and that there is a balance in the hands of the Treasurer of five hundred and seventy-nine 21-100 dollars.

The Treasurer also exhibited to us evidence of the following property belonging to the Institution:—

Real Estate No. 11 Oxford Street, city valuation	$96,000 00	5,000 United States 6 per cent bond	5,000 00
No. 144 Prince Street, city valuation	5,500 00	20 shares Boston and Providence Railroad Company, market value $122	3,660 00
No. 197 Endicott Street, city valuation	3,900 00	45 shares Fitchburg Railroad, market value $118	5,310 00
Notes secured by mortgage on real estate	2,300 00		
10,000 Boston and Lowell Railroad 6 per cent bond	10,000 00		
10,000 Eastern Railroad bond	8,000 00		$139,670 00

E. E.   HENRY ENDICOTT, *Treasurer.*

G. HIGGINSON,
A. T. FROTHINGHAM, } *Auditing Committee.*

DETAILED STATEMENT OF TREASURER'S ACCOUNT.

DR.

1878-1879.

To cash paid on Auditor's drafts . . .		.$66,348 66
city of Boston for taxes . .		166 40
for re-investments . . .		. 32,914 97
on hand Sept. 30, 1879 . . .		. 579 21
		$100.009 24

CR.

1878.

Sept. 30. By balance of former account		. $2,649 67
Oct. 1. cash from State of Massachusetts . .		. 7,500 00
15. From six months' interest on note, $5,000, at 6 per cent		150 00
28. six months' interest on note, $3,500, at 6 per cent		105 00
30. interest on note, $12,000		390 00
dividend on Boston and Providence Railroad .		90 00
Nov. 29. six months' interest on note, $8,000, at 6 per cent		240 00
Dec. 11. six months' interest on note, $3,500, at 7 per cent		122 50

1879.

Jan. 1. six months' interest on note, $8,000, at 6 per cent		240 00
2. State of Massachusetts		7,500 00
4. interest on note of $18,000, at 6 per cent .		540 00
$20,000, at 6 per cent .		646 67
20. rents		239 56
25. M. Anagnos, Director, as per following:—		

J. B. Winsor, for board and tuition of son	$300 00	
income of legacy to Laura Bridgman .	85 00	
State of Rhode Island, for clothing for H. Lanergan . . .	20 00	
town of Dedham, account of Mary O'Hare	22 19	
Dr. A. W. Burnham, account of daughter	50 00	
city of Boston, for tuning . .	600 00	
sale of books in raised print . .	84 15	
receipts of work department:—		

for October .	.$1,315 28		
November .	. 1,037 56		
December .	. 871 50		
		3,224 34	
			4,385 68

Amount carried forward		.$24,799 08

	Amount brought forward		.$24,799 08

1879.

Jan. 25.	From six months' interest on note, $15,000, at 6 per cent		450 00
Feb. 1.	interest on deposit		155 11
21.	William Hunt, executor of will of William Taylor of Tewksbury, account legacy . .		700 00
24.	dividend on Fitchburg Railroad . .		135 00
Mar. 1.	six months' interest on note, $25,000, at 6 per cent		750 00
Apr. 1.	State of Massachusetts		7,500 00
15.	six months' interest on note, $5,000, at 6 per cent		150 00
25.	six months' interest on note, $3,500, at 6 per cent		105 00

28.	M. Anagnos, Director, as per following : —	
	sale of books in raised print . .	$229 36
	tuning	531 00
	J. B. Winsor, donation . . .	100 00
	Nebraska Institution, for map . .	37 00
	sale of brooms	38 63
	writing-tablets	8 43
	admission-tickets	27 44
	old barrels, junk, &c. . . .	66 78
	Mrs. Knowlton, account of daughter,	36 00
	salesroom, for storing coal . .	6 85
	town of Brimfield, account of George Needham	5 45
	Redmond Geary, for travelling expenses	1 38
	Mrs. Quimby, account of daughter,	5 00
	receipts of work department : —	
	for January . . $744 07	
	February . . 457 53	
	March . . 763 15	
	———— 1,964 75	

			3,058 07
May 20.	payment of note	.	12,000 00
	interest on note	.	379 17
27.	dividend from Boston and Providence R.R .		90 00
29.	six months' interest on note of $8,000, at 6 per cent	.	240 00
June 12.	six months' interest on note of $3,500, at 7 per cent	.	122 50
24.	interest ten days, $5,000		8 33
July 1.	State of Massachusetts	.	7,500 00
5.	six months' interest on note, $18,000, at 6 per cent	.	540 00

	Amount carried forward		.$58,682 26

Amount brought forward				.$58,682 26

1879.

July	9.	From payment of mortgage note			20,000 00
		interest on mortgage note			623 33
	28.	M. Anagnos, Director, as per following :—			
		city of Boston, for tuning . .	$300 00		
		sale of books in raised print . .	115 55		
		Henry T. Bray, for board and tuition			
		of self	200 00		
		receipts of work department :—			
		for April . . . $815 04			
		May . . . 1,366 15			
		June . . . 1,241 54			
				3,422 73	
					4,038 28
		six months' interest on note, $15,000, at 6			
		per cent			450 00
Aug.	1.	interest on deposit			83 75
	20.	State of Vermont			1,500 00
		Rhode Island			3,000 00
		Connecticut			3,300 00
Sept.	1.	six months' interest on Eastern R.R. bonds .			175 00
		Fitchburg Railroad dividend			135 00
	3.	six months' interest on note of $25,000, at 6			
		per cent			750 00
	17.	State of New Hampshire			2,875 00
	30.	M. Anagnos, Director, as per following :—			
		A. W. Burnham, account of daughter,	$50 00		
		income of legacy to Laura Bridgman,	40 00		
		C. A. Fairbanks, account of son .	25 00		
		tuning	103 00		
		J. J. Mundo, account of daughter .	25 00		
		sale of old junk, &c. . . .	54 80		
		books in raised print . .	38 36		
		writing-tablets . . .	19 46		
		brooms	37 26		
		receipts of concert	7 00		
		admission-tickets	37 57		
		Miss Morton, account of Ida House .	7 75		
		Mrs. Knowlton, account of daughter,	12 00		
		salesroom, for use of horse and wagon			
		one year	180 00		
		receipts of work department :—			
		for July . . . $1,100 76			
		August . . 788 18			
		September . . 1,870 48			
				3,759 42	
					4,396 62
					$100,009 24

ANALYSIS OF TREASURER'S ACCOUNTS.

The Treasurer's account shows that the total receipts during
    the year were $100.009 24
Less cash on hand at the beginning of the year . .   2,649 67

                                  $97,359 57

Ordinary Receipts.

From the State of Massachusetts . . . $30,000 00
    beneficiaries of other States and individuals . 11,559 77
    interest, coupons, and rent 8,105 92
                                  $49,665 69

Extraordinary Receipts.

From work department, for sale of articles made by
    the blind, &c. $12,371 24
    payment of mortgage notes 32,000 00
    sale of books and maps 504 42
    tuning 1,534 00
    legacy and donation 800 00
    sale of writing-tablets 27 89
        brooms, account boys' shop . . 75 89
        old junk, barrels, &c. . . . 121 58
        admission-tickets 65 01
    receipts of concert 7 00
    salesroom, for storing coal 6 85
    use of horse and wagon one year . . . 180 00
                              47,693 88

                                  $97,359 57

GENERAL ANALYSIS OF THE STEWARD'S ACCOUNT.

DR.

Receipts from Auditor's drafts . . . $66,348 66
Less amount due Steward Oct. 1, 1878 . $546 63
    balance in Steward's hands Oct. 1,
    1879 . . . . . . 773 16
                      1,319 79
                                $65,028 87

CR.

Ordinary expenses as per schedule annexed . $38,363 10
Extraordinary expenses as per schedule annexed . 26,665 77
                                $65,028 87

ANALYSIS OF EXPENDITURES FOR THE YEAR ENDING SEPT. 30, 1879,
AS PER STEWARD'S ACCOUNT.

Meat, 24,302 lbs.	$2,177 01
Fish, 3,997 lbs.	220 55
Butter, 4,755 lbs.	1,153 50
Rice, sago, &c.	99 30
Bread, flour, meal, &c.[1]	160 64
Potatoes and other vegetables	729 13
Fruit	325 50
Milk, 21,400 qts.	958 47
Sugar, 2,919 lbs.	245 98
Tea and coffee, 622 lbs.	83 54
Groceries	393 41
Gas and oil	371 92
Coal and wood	2,199 42
Sundry articles of consumption	214 60
Salaries, superintendence, and instruction	14,827 85
Domestic wages	3,964 94
Outside aid	181 14
Medicine and medical aid	32 57
Furniture and bedding	1,146 30
Clothing and mending	13 94
Musical instruments	83 31
Expenses of tuning department	807 90
" " boys' shop	74 36
" " printing-office	2,197 60
" " stable	344 42
Books, stationery, and school apparatus	1,663 89
Ordinary construction and repairs	1,322 48
Taxes and insurance	1,617 26
Travelling expenses	130 34
Rent of office in town	250 00
Board of blind men	252 13
" " man and clerk during vacation	85 72
Sundries	33 89
	$38,363 10

Extraordinary Expenses.		
Extraordinary construction and repairs	$11,621 34	
Bills to be refunded	65 57	
Beneficiaries of Harris Fund	600 00	
Expenses of work department	14,378 86	
		26,665 77
		$65,028 87

[1] There was a large stock of flour and meal on hand Oct. 1, 1878, which accounts for the smallness of this item.

GENERAL ABSTRACT OF ACCOUNT OF WORK DEPARTMENT,
OCT. 1, 1879.

Liabilities.

Due institution for investments at sundry times since the first date	$38,889 83	
Excess of expenditures over receipts . . .	2,007 62	
		$40,897 45

Assets.

Stock on hand Oct. 1, 1879	$4,467 83	
Debts due	1,400 66	
		5,868 49
		$35,028 96

Balance against work department Oct. 1, 1879 . . .	$35,028 96
" " " " " 1878 . . .	33,138 49
	$1,890 47

DR.

Cash received for sales, &c., during the year	$12,371 24	
Excess of expenditures over receipts . . .	2,007 62	
		$14,378 86

CR.

Salaries and wages paid blind persons . . .	$3,136 31	
" " " " seeing " . .	2,504 14	
Sundries for stock, &c.	8,738 41	
		$14,378 86

LIST OF APPLIANCES AND TANGIBLE APPARATUS,

Made at the Perkins Institution and Massachusetts School for the Blind.

GEOGRAPHY.

I. — *Wall Maps.*

1. The Hemispheres	size 42 by 52 inches.
2. United States, Mexico, and Canada . . .	" " "
8. South America	" " "
4. Europe	" " "
5. Asia	" " "
6. Africa	" " "
7. The World on Mercator's Projection . .	" " "

Each $35, or the set, $245.

II. — *Dissected Maps.*

1. Eastern Hemisphere	size 30 by 36 inches.
2. Western Hemisphere	" " "
8 North America	" " "
4. United States	" " "
5. South America	" " "
6. Europe	" " "
7. Asia	" " "
8. Africa	" " "

Each $23, or the set, $184.

These maps are considered, in point of workmanship, accuracy and distinctness of outline, durability, and beauty, far superior to all thus far made in Europe or in this country.

The "New-England Journal of Education" says, "They are very strong, present a fine, bright surface, and are an ornament to any school-room."

III. — *Pin-Maps.*

Cushions for pin-maps and diagrams . . . . . each, $0 75

ARITHMETIC.

Ciphering-boards made of brass strips, nickel-plated .	each, $4 25
Ciphering-types, nickel-plated, per hundred . . .	1 00

WRITING.

Grooved writing-cards	each, $0 10
Braille's tablets, with metallic bed	" 1 50
Braille's French tablets, with cloth bed . . .	" 1 00
Braille's new tablets, with cloth bed . . .	" 1 00
Braille's Daisy tablets	" 8 75

LIST OF EMBOSSED BOOKS,

Printed at the Perkins Institution and Massachusetts School for the Blind.

TITLE OF BOOK.	No. of Volumes.	Price per Volume.
Howe's Geography	1	2 50
Howe's Atlas of the Islands [1]	1	3 00
Howe's Blind Child's First Book [1]	1	1 25
Howe's Blind Child's Second Book [1]	1	1 25
Howe's Blind Child's Third Book [1]	1	1 25
Howe's Blind Child's Fourth Book [1]	1	1 25
Second Table of Logarithms	1	3 00
Astronomical Dictionary	1	2 00
Rudiments of Natural Philosophy [1]	1	4 00
Philosophy of Natural History	1	3 00
Guyot's Geography	1	4 00
Howe's Cyclopædia	8	4 00
Natural Theology	1	4 00
Combe's Constitution of Man	1	4 00
Pope's Essay on Man [1]	1	2 00
Baxter's Call	1	2 50
Book of Proverbs	1	2 00
Book of Psalms	1	3 00
New Testament (small)	4	2 50
Book of Common Prayer	1	4 00
Hymns for the Blind [1]	1	3 00
Pilgrim's Progress	1	4 00
Life of Melanchthon	1	2 00
Dickens's Old Curiosity Shop	3	4 00
Shakspeare's Hamlet and Julius Cæsar	1	4 00
Byron's Hebrew Melodies and Childe Harold	1	3 00
Anderson's History of United States	1	2 50
Dickens's Child's History of England	2	3 50
Selections from the Works of Swedenborg	1	–
Memoir of Dr. Samuel G. Howe	1	3 00
Cutter's Anatomy, Physiology, and Hygiene	1	4 00
Viri Romæ, new edition with additions	1	2 00
The Reader; or, Extracts from British and American Literature [1]	2	3 00
Musical Characters used by the seeing, with explanations	1	35
Milton's Paradise Lost	2	3 00
Higginson's Young Folks' History of the United States	1	3 50
Histories of Greece and Rome (in press)	–	–

[1] Stereotyped.

LIST OF APPLIANCES AND TANGIBLE APPARATUS,

Made at the Perkins Institution and Massachusetts School for the Blind.

GEOGRAPHY.

I. — *Wall Maps.*

1. The Hemispheres . . . . . . size 42 by 52 inches.
2. United States, Mexico, and Canada . . . " " "
3. South America . . . . . . " " "
4. Europe . . . . " " "
5. Asia . . . . " " "
6. Africa . . . . " " "
7. The World on Mercator's Projection . . " " "

Each $35, or the set, $245.

II. — *Dissected Maps.*

1. Eastern Hemisphere . . . . . . size 30 by 36 inches.
2. Western Hemisphere . . . . " " "
3 North America . . . . . . " " "
4. United States . . . . . . " " "
5. South America . . . . . . " " "
6. Europe . . . . " " "
7. Asia . . . . " " "
8. Africa . . . . " " "

Each $23, or the set, $184.

These maps are considered, in point of workmanship, accuracy and distinctness of outline, durability, and beauty, far superior to all thus far made in Europe or in this country.

The "New-England Journal of Education" says, "They are very strong, present a fine, bright surface, and are an ornament to any schoolroom."

III. — *Pin-Maps.*

Cushions for pin-maps and diagrams . . . . . each, $0 75

ARITHMETIC.

Ciphering-boards made of brass strips, nickel-plated . . each, $4 25
Ciphering-types, nickel-plated, per hundred . . . 1 00

WRITING.

Grooved writing-cards . . . . each, $0 10
Braille's tablets, with metallic bed . . . . " 1 50
Braille's French tablets, with cloth bed . . . " 1 00
Braille's new tablets, with cloth bed 1 00
Braille's Daisy tablets 8 75

TERMS OF ADMISSION.

Young blind persons between the ages of ten and nineteen, and of good moral character, can be admitted to the
school by paying $300 per annum. This sum covers all
expenses, except for clothing; namely, board, washing, the
use of books, musical instruments, &c. The pupils must
furnish their own clothing, and pay their own fares to and
from the Institution. The friends of the pupils can visit
them whenever they choose.

Indigent blind persons of suitable age and character, belonging to Massachusetts, can be admitted gratuitously, by
application to the Governor for a warrant.

The following is a good form, though any other will do : —

" *To his Excellency the Governor.*

"SIR, — My son (or daughter, or nephew, or niece, as the case may
be) named ——, and aged ——, cannot be instructed in the common
schools, for want of sight. I am unable to pay for the tuition at the
Perkins Institution and Massachusetts School for the Blind, and I request that your Excellency will give a warrant for free admission.

"Very respectfully,   —— ——."

The application may be made by any relation or friend, if
the parents are dead or absent.

It should be accompanied by a certificate from one or
more of the selectmen of the town, or aldermen of the city,
in this form : —

" I hereby certify, that, in my opinion, Mr. —— —— is not a wealthy
person, and that he cannot afford to pay $300 per annum for his child's
instruction.   (Signed)   —— ——."

There should be a certificate, signed by some regular physician, in this form : —

"I certify, that, in my opinion, —— —— has not sufficient vision to
be taught in common schools ; and that he is free from epilepsy, and
from any contagious disease.   (Signed)   —— ——."

These papers should be done up together, and forwarded to the DIRECTOR OF THE INSTITUTION FOR THE BLIND, *South Boston, Mass.*

An obligation will be required from some responsible persons, that the pupil shall be kept properly supplied with decent clothing, shall be provided for during vacations, and shall be removed, without expense to the Institution, whenever it may be desirable to discharge him.

The usual period of tuition is from five to seven years. Indigent blind persons residing in Maine, New Hampshire, Vermont, Connecticut, and Rhode Island, by applying as above to the Governor, or the "Secretary of State," in their respective States, can obtain warrants for free admission.

The relatives or friends of the blind who may be sent to the Institution are requested to furnish information in answer to the following questions : —

1. What is the name and age of the applicant?
2. Where born?
3. Was he born blind ?   If not, at what age was his sight impaired?
4. Is the blindness total, or partial?
5. What is the supposed cause of the blindness?
6. Has he ever been subject to fits?
7. Is he now in good health, and free from eruptions and contagious diseases of the skin?
8. Has he ever been to school ?   If yes, where ?
9. What is the general moral character of the applicant?
10. Of what country was the father of the applicant a native ?
11. What was the general bodily condition and health of the father, — was he vigorous and healthy, or the contrary?
12. Was the father of the applicant ever subject to fits or to scrofula?
13. Were all his senses perfect?
14. Was he always a temperate man?
15. About how old was he when the applicant was born?
16. Was there any known peculiarity in the family of the father of the applicant ; that is, were any of the grandparents, parents, uncles, aunts, brothers, sisters, or cousins, blind, deaf, or insane, or afflicted with any infirmity of body or mind?
17. If dead, at what age did the father die, and of what disorder?
18. Where was the mother of the applicant born?
19. What was the general bodily condition of the mother of the applicant, — strong and healthy, or the contrary?
20. Was she ever subject to scrofula, or to fits?
21. Were all her senses perfect?
22. Was she always a temperate woman?
23. About how old was she when the applicant was born?

24. How many children had she before the applicant was born?

25. Was she related by blood to her husband? If so, in what degree. — first, second, or third cousins?

26. If dead, at what age did she die, and of what disorder?

27. Was there any known peculiarity in her family ; that is, were any of her grandparents, parents, uncles, aunts, sisters, brothers, children, or cousins, either blind, or deaf, or insane, or afflicted with any infirmity of body or mind?

28. What are the pecuniary means of the parents or immediate relatives of the applicant?

29. How much can they afford to pay towards the support and education of the applicant?

For further particulars address M. ANAGNOS, DIRECTOR OF THE INSTITUTION FOR THE BLIND, *South Boston, Mass.*

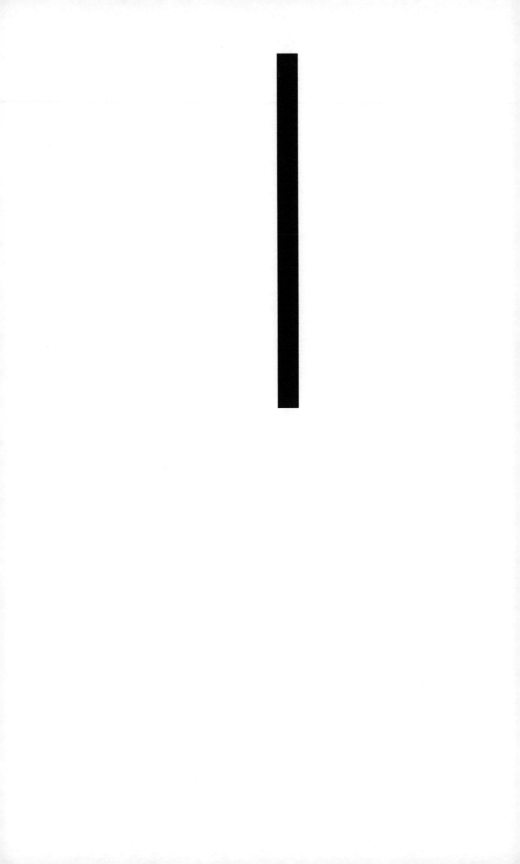

PUBLIC DOCUMENT. No. 27.

FORTY-NINTH ANNUAL REPORT

OF

THE TRUSTEES

OF THE

PERKINS INSTITUTION

AND

𝕸assachusetts 𝕾chool for the 𝕭lind,

FOR THE YEAR ENDING

SEPTEMBER 30, 1880.

BOSTON:
Rand, Avery, & Co., Printers to the Commonwealth,
117 Franklin Street.
1881.

TABLE OF CONTENTS.

Commonwealth of Massachusetts.

Perkins Institution and Mass. School for the Blind,
So. Boston, Oct. 19, 1880.

To the Hon. HENRY B. PEIRCE, *Secretary of State.*

DEAR SIR, — I have the honor to transmit to you for the use of the Legislature, a copy of the Forty-ninth Annual Report of the Trustees of this Institution to the Corporation thereof, together with the usual accompanying documents.

Respectfully,

M. ANAGNOS,

Secretary.

OFFICERS OF THE CORPORATION.
1880–81.

SAMUEL ELIOT, *President.*

JOHN CUMMINGS, *Vice-President.*

P. T. JACKSON, *Treasurer.*

M. ANAGNOS, *Secretary.*

BOARD OF TRUSTEES.

ROBERT E. APTHORP.	ANDREW P. PEABODY, D.D.
JOHN S. DWIGHT.	EDWARD N. PERKINS.
JOSEPH B GLOVER.	SAMUEL M. QUINCY.
J. THEODORE HEARD, M.D.	SAMUEL G. SNELLING.
HENRY LEE HIGGINSON.	JAMES STURGIS.
JAMES H. MEANS, D.D.	GEORGE W. WALES.

STANDING COMMITTEES.
Monthly Visiting Committee,

Whose duty it is to visit and inspect the Institution at least once in each month.

1881. January	. R. E. APTHORP.	1881. July	. . . A. P. PEABODY.
February	. J. S. DWIGHT.	August	. . E. N. PERKINS.
March	. . J. B. GLOVER.	September	. S. M. QUINCY.
April	. J. T. HEARD.	October	. S. G. SNELLING.
May	. . H. L. HIGGINSON.	November	. JAMES STURGIS.
June	. . J. H. MEANS.	December	. GEO. W. WALES.

Committee on Education.	House Committee.
J. S. DWIGHT.	E. N. PERKINS.
A. P. PEABODY.	G. W. WALES.
S. M. QUINCY.	J. H. MEANS.

Committee of Finance.	Committee on Health.
R. E. APTHORP.	J. THEODORE HEARD.
J. B. GLOVER.	E. N. PERKINS.
JAMES STURGIS.	H. L. HIGGINSON.

Auditors of Accounts.

ROBERT E. APTHORP.

SAMUEL G. SNELLING.

OFFICERS OF THE INSTITUTION.

DIRECTOR.
M. ANAGNOS.

MEDICAL INSPECTOR.
JOHN HOMANS, M.D.

LITERARY DEPARTMENT.

Miss M. L. P. Shattuck.
Miss J. R. Gilman.
Miss Julia Boylan.
Miss E. S. Adams.

Miss Della Bennett.
Miss S. L. Bennett.
Miss Mary C. Moore.
Miss S. E. Lane, *Librarian.*

MUSICAL DEPARTMENT.

Resident Teachers.

Thomas Reeves.
Frank H. Kilbourne.
Miss Freda Black.
Miss Lizzie Riley.
Miss Lucy Hammond.
Miss M. L. Drowne.
Henry W. Stratton, *Assistant.*

Non-Resident Teachers.

Mrs. Kate Rametti.
Henry C. Brown.
C. H. Higgins.

Music Readers.

Miss Allie S. Knapp.
Miss Mary A. Proctor.

TUNING DEPARTMENT.
J. W. Smith, *Instructor and Manager.*

INDUSTRIAL DEPARTMENT.

Workshops for Juveniles.

J. H. Wright, *Work Master.*
Miss A. J. Dillingham, *Work Mistress.*
Thomas Carroll, *Assistant.*
Miss H. Kellier, *Assistant.*

Workshop for Adults.

A. W. Bowden, *Manager.*
P. Morrill, *Foreman.*
Miss M. A. Dwelly, *Forewoman.*
Miss M. M. Stone, *Clerk.*

DOMESTIC DEPARTMENT.

Steward.

A. W. Bowden.

Matron.

Miss M. C. Moulton.
Miss E. Ware, *Assistant.*

Housekeepers in the Cottages.

Mrs. M. A. Knowlton.
Miss A. J. Dillingham.
Miss Bessie Wood.
Miss Lizzie N. Smith.

PRINTING DEPARTMENT.
Dennis A. Reardon, *Manager.*

Miss E. B. Webster, *Book-keeper.*

MEMBERS OF THE CORPORATION.

ALL persons who have contributed twenty-five dollars to the funds of the institution, all who have served as trustees or treasurer, and all who have been elected by special vote, are members.

Aldrich, Mrs. Aaron, Boston.
Alger, Rev. William R., Boston.
Amory, James S., Boston.
Amory, William, Boston.
Anagnos, M., Boston.
Appleton, T. G., Boston.
Apthorp, Robert E., Boston.
Apthorp, William F., Boston.
Atkinson, Edward, Boston.
Atkinson, William, Boston.
Austin, Edward, Boston.
Baldwin, William H., Boston.
Barrows, Rev. S. J., Dorchester.
Beard, Hon. Alanson W., Boston.
Bigelow, E. B., Boston.
Blake, G. Baty, Boston.
Bouvé, Thomas T., Boston.
Bowditch, J. I., Boston.
Bradlee, F. H., Boston.
Brewster, Osmyn, Boston.
Brimmer, Hon. Martin, Boston.
Brooks, Francis, Boston.
Brooks, Rev. Phillips, Boston.
Browne, A. Parker, Boston.
Bullard, W. S., Boston.
Chandler, P. W., Boston.
Chandler, Theophilus P., Brookline.
Childs, Alfred A., Boston.
Claflin, Hon. William, Boston.
Clapp, William W., Boston.
Coolidge, Dr. A., Boston.
Crosby, Joseph B., Boston.
Cummings, Charles A., Boston.

Cummings, Hon. John, Woburn.
Dalton, C. H., Boston.
Davis, James, Boston.
Dix, J. H., M.D., Boston.
Downer, Samuel, Dorchester.
Dwight, John S., Boston.
Eliot, Dr. Samuel, Boston.
Emerson, George B., Boston.
Emery, Francis F., Boston.
Emery, Isaac, Boston.
Emmons, Mrs. Nath'l H., Boston.
Endicott, Henry, Boston.
Endicott, William, jun., Boston.
Fisk, Rev. Photius, Boston.
Folsom, Charles F., M.D., Boston.
Forbes, J. M., Milton.
Freeman, Miss Hattie E., Boston.
Galloupe, C. W., Boston.
Gardiner, Charles P., Boston.
Gardner, George A., Boston.
Glover, J. B., Boston.
Goddard, Benjamin, Brookline.
Goddard, Delano A., Boston.
Gray, Mrs. Horace, Boston.
Gray, John C., Boston.
Greenleaf, R. C., Boston.
Hale, Rev. Edward E., Boston.
Hale, George S., Boston.
Hardy, Alpheus, Brookline.
Haskell, Edwin B., Auburndale.
Heard, J. T., M.D., Boston.
Higginson, George, Boston.
Higginson, Henry Lee, Boston.

Hill, Hon. Hamilton A., Boston.
Hilton, William, Boston.
Hogg, John, Boston.
Hooper, E. W., Boston.
Hooper, R. W., M.D., Boston.
Hovey, William A., Brookline.
Howe, Mrs. Julia Ward, Boston.
Houghton, Hon. H. O., Cambridge.
Hunnewell, H. H., Boston.
Hyatt, Alpheus, Cambridge.
Jackson, Edward, Boston.
Jackson, Patrick T., Boston.
Jackson, Mrs. Sarah, Boston.
Jarvis, Edward, M.D., Dorchester.
Jones, J. M., Boston.
Kendall, C. S., Boston.
Kennard, Martin P., Brookline.
Kidder, H. P., Boston.
Kinsley, E. W., Boston.
Lang, B. J., Boston.
Lawrence, Amos A., Longwood.
Lincoln, L. J. B., Hingham.
Lodge, Mrs. J. E., Boston.
Lord, Melvin, Boston.
Lothrop, John, Auburndale.
Lovett, George L., Boston.
Lowell, Augustus, Boston.
Lowell, John A., Boston.
Lyman, George W., Boston.
Mack, Thomas, Boston.
May, Miss Abby, Boston.
May, F. W. G., Dorchester.
Means, Rev. J. H., D.D., Dorchester.
Merriam, Mrs. Caroline, Boston.
Minot, William, Boston.
Montgomery, Hugh, Boston.
Morton, Edwin, Boston.
Motley, Edward, Boston.
Mudge, Hon. E. R., Boston.
Nickerson, George, Jamaica Plain.
Nickerson, S. D., Boston.
Noyes, Hon. Charles J., Boston.
Osborn, John T., Boston.
Paine, Mrs. Julia B., Boston.
Parker, H. D., Boston.
Parkman, Francis, Boston.
Parkman, George F., Boston.
Parkman, Rev. John, Boston.
Parsons, Thomas, Chelsea.

Payson, S. R., Boston.
Peabody, Rev. A. P., D.D., Camb'ge.
Peabody, F. H., Boston.
Perkins, Charles C., Boston.
Perkins, Edward N., Jamaica Plain.
Perkins, William, Boston.
Peters, Edward D., Boston.
Pickman, W. D., Boston.
Pierce, Hon. H. L., Boston.
Phillips, John C., Boston.
Pratt, Elliott W., Boston.
Preston, Jonathan, Boston.
Quincy, Hon. Josiah, Wollaston.
Quincy, Samuel M., Wollaston.
Rice, Hon. A. H., Boston.
Robeson, W. R., Boston.
Robinson, Henry, Reading.
Rogers, Henry B., Boston.
Rogers, Jacob C., Boston.
Ropes, J. S., Jamaica Plain.
Rotch, Benjamin S., Boston.
Russell, Mrs. S. S., Boston.
Saltonstall, H., Boston.
Saltonstall, Leverett, Newton.
Sanborn, Frank B., Concord.
Schlesinger, Sebastian, Boston.
Sears, David, Boston.
Sears, W. T., Boston.
Sherwood, W. H., Boston.
Shimmin, C. F., Boston.
Shippen, Rev. Rush R., Jamaica Pl.
Slack, C. W., Boston.
Snelling, Samuel G., Boston.
Stone, Joseph L., Boston.
Sturgis, Francis S., Jamaica Plain.
Sturgis, James, Jamaica Plain.
Taggard, B. W., Boston.
Taggard, Mrs. B. W., Boston.
Thaxter, Joseph B., Hingham.
Thayer, Rev. George A., Boston.
Thayer, Nathaniel, Boston.
Thorndike, S. Lothrop, Cambridge.
Tucker, Alanson, Boston.
Tucker, W. W., Boston.
Upton, George B., Boston.
Wales, George W., Boston.
Wales, Miss Mary Ann, Boston.
Wales, Thomas B., Boston.
Ware, Charles E., M.D., Boston.

Washburn, Hon. J. D., Worcester.
Weld, W. G., Boston.
Wheelwright, John W., Boston.
Wigglesworth, Edw., M.D., Boston.
Wigglesworth, Miss Mary, Boston.
Wigglesworth, Thomas, Boston.
Wilder, Hon. Marshall P., Dorch.
Winslow, Mrs. George, Roxbury.

Winsor, J. B., Providence, R. I.
Winthrop, Hon. Robert C., Boston.
Wolcott, J. H., Boston.
Wolcott, Mrs. J. H., Boston.
Woods, Henry, Paris, France.
Worthington, Roland, Roxbury.
Young, Charles L., Boston.

2

Commonwealth of Massachusetts.

REPORT OF THE TRUSTEES.

PERKINS INSTITUTION AND MASS. SCHOOL FOR THE BLIND,
SOUTH BOSTON, Sept. 30, 1880.

TO THE MEMBERS OF THE CORPORATION.

Gentlemen, — In accordance with the requirements of the by-laws of the institution, we, the undersigned trustees, present to you, and through you to the executive of the commonwealth and to the legislature, the following report for the year ending Sept. 30, 1880 : —

We are very desirous that the general state of the establishment should be known, and that every suitable means should be employed to keep the mind of the public enlightened and the sympathies of our fellow-citizens awake with regard to the blind wherever they may be found.

The publication of our annual report is one of the means for promoting this end, and the fact that those whom we thus address represent to a very great extent the enlightment and the benevolence of the community at large emboldens us to come forward year after year and ask attention for our affairs.

In reviewing the history of the past twelve months, we may say at the outset that the general condition of the institution has been entirely satisfactory to the board, and that nothing has occurred to mar its advancement.

The kind interest which the wise, the intelligent, and the benevolent of the community have continued to take in the welfare of the blind, has been a source of great encouragement to us.

The quarterly reports of the director made to our board have set forth in detail the statistics of entrances and discharges. The substance of these communications is, that there have been 179 blind persons immédiately connected with the institution, in all its departments, as pupils, instructors, employés, and work men or women. Present number, 156.

The health of the household has been remarkably good. No death and no case of serious illness has occurred during the year.

The sanitary arrangements of the establishment are in excellent condition, and the medical supervision of our physician, Dr. Homans, has been regular and thorough.

The trustees can speak in terms of approbation of the uniform cleanliness of the buildings, of the personal neatness of the pupils, and the quiet and order which have pervaded the school.

The teachers and officers have performed their part zealously, and have worked faithfully to further the welfare of those committed to their care.

The pupils in general merit commendation for their good behavior and obedience to the rules and regulations established for their government.

We have endeavored to adminster the affairs of the institution in such a manner as to attain the best results which the means at our disposal could effect; and, although we claim no infallibility, we cannot but be thankful for the degree of prosperity which has attended our efforts.

The institution is well appointed in all its departments, and its work is carried on with good results. We have aimed to improve those systematic arrangements which have heretofore proved satisfactory, to carry forward the original plan of the institution, to enlarge the sphere of its usefulness, to incorporate in its workings the fruits of enlightened experience and the results of the best thought given to this branch of education, and to perpetuate the spirit of beneficence towards those for whose good the school was founded. But, although we have continued to press on in the way of progress, we do not allow ourselves to think that our system of instruction and training is complete in its details and perfect in its appointments. On the contrary, we are aware of its shortcomings, and are ever ready to welcome all rational improvements, and make such changes as shall promise after thorough examination better results than we have yet attained.

Such is in brief the record of the year now closed. While we look back upon what has been accomplished during the past twelve months with gratitude, we regard the present with proper satisfaction, and the future with encouragement and hope.

The Present State of the School.

The main object of the institution — which is to give
to blind youth of both sexes the same kind and degree
of instruction as is afforded to other children in the best
common schools of New England, and to train them up
to industry and professional attainments — has been
steadily and successfully pursued, and has been followed
by good results. The means and methods employed to
promote this end have been improved and perfected
from year to year, and our course of education embraces
all branches which are necessary to fit pupils for a life
of enlightened activity and usefulness.

The modes of instruction followed in the various
departments of the institution are of the most approved
character, and its graduates will bear comparison in
point of intellectual attainments with those of any well-
organized academy. Those who attended the graduating exercises of our school, or who have become otherwise familiar with its workings and with the present
condition of its departments, will bear testimony to this
fact.

These exercises were held at the close of the term in
the music hall of the institution, and were witnessed by
a large number of distinguished citizens. The State of
Rhode Island was represented by Gov. Littlefield and
Secretary Addeman, and the Massachusetts Board of
Education by its secretary, Mr. Dickinson, and one of
its members, Mr. Hussey. Many clergymen and several prominent musicians were also present.

Diplomas were for the first time awarded to the
members of the graduating class, six in number, and

their award could not fail to be a very gratifying
ceremony to all witnesses who had even the faintest
feeling of interest in the welfare and prosperity of
the recipients. The giving of these simple rolls told
of a past of diligent application and meritorious endeavor, and prophesied a future of happy usefulness
and well-earned reward. No pupil could receive one
of these testimonials who had not gone through the
regular school course and attained a certain degree
of excellence by faithful and thorough work at his
lessons and in his calling. Besides being valuable
as a record of past exertions and distinction in the
school, the diploma is also of importance to the deserving and active graduate as a promise of a prosperous future. The diplomas were given out by the
Rev. Dr. Peabody of our board, accompanied by a
few well-chosen remarks, and were received by the
young people with very evident emotion, in which
the audience keenly sympathized.

FINANCES.

The report of the treasurer, Mr. P. T. Jackson,
accompanied by a detailed statement of his cash account, is herewith submitted, and shows the finances
of the institution to have been wisely and judiciously
administered.

The amount of money received from all sources
during the past year, as well as that of the disbursements made for all purposes, may be briefly set forth
as follows : —

Cash on hand Oct. 1, 1879 .	.	$579 21
Total receipts during the year	.	94,139 58
		———— $94,718 79
Total expenditures . . .	. .	. 92,491 36
Cash balance in the treasury .	. .	. $2,227 43

This result has been obtained only by the exercise in every department of the most rigid economy consistent with the proper administration of the affairs of the institution, and with the efficient training of the pupils, and the comfort and welfare of the household.

To aid in a more complete and minute examination of the financial concerns of the establishment, the report of the treasurer is accompanied by an analysis of the steward's accounts, which gives specific information in regard to the principal articles consumed, their quantity, and the aggregate price paid for each.

The director makes provision for all the wants of the institution, and is responsible for the prudent and judicious expenditure of its funds; but his accounts are scrutinized and audited monthly by a committee especially appointed by our board for this purpose, and the treasurer pays no money except upon their order.

It is our pleasant duty to allude in this connection to the continued zeal, care, and fidelity, with which the auditors, Messrs. R. E. Apthorp and S. G. Snelling, have discharged their duty. They have certified that the accounts have been properly and correctly kept, and that all items of expense have been authenticated by vouchers.

The books are open to your scrutiny, and we earnestly invite you to satisfy yourselves, by actual examination, that the funds of the institution have been applied with sound judgment and unwavering integrity.

Mr. Endicott's Resignation.

The trustees cannot close this part of their report without expressing their deep regret at the necessity which has compelled Mr. Henry Endicott to resign the office of treasurer. For twelve years his name and that of his elder brother, Mr. William Endicott, jun., have stood forth prominently among the kindest and most disinterested friends of the blind. Their efforts for the prosperity of the establishment were unremitting, and their generosity unceasing. An intimate knowledge of their benevolence and their devotion to the welfare of the school enables us to concur heartily in the well-chosen expressions of the following vote, which was unanimously passed by you at a special meeting held for the purpose of acting upon the treasurer's resignation:—

"*Voted*, that the warm thanks of the corporation be hereby tendered to Mr. Henry Endicott for the ability, disinterestedness, and courtesy, with which he has discharged his duties, and for his efficient and faithful services, which merit the highest praise and the expression of the deepest obligation from all friends of the institution."

To the present treasurer, Mr. P. T. Jackson, and to his brother, Mr. Edward Jackson, who succeeded Mr. Endicott, but who was obliged, after a brief period of service, to tender his resignation in order to go abroad,

we are greatly indebted for the diligence and promptness with which they have performed their duties.

REPAIRS AND IMPROVEMENTS.

The work of repairs and improvements inaugurated
several years since, and carried on with more or less
rapidity, is still far from complete. Yet an important
step towards this end has been made during the summer
vacation, in addition to the renovations effected in several parts of the establishment.

The erection of a new building in the girls' department
is the most prominent improvement made during the
year. This edifice is forty-nine feet long and twenty-
five feet wide, and consists of four stories with a good
basement, the windows of which are above ground.
The first and second flights, together with the basement,
when entirely finished, will furnish ample space for
school, music, sewing, and knitting rooms, while the
whole of the third story will be occupied by a library,
which will be provided with cases for books, minerals,
specimens of natural history, models, and educational
appliances of various kinds. This building is connected
with the girls' schoolhouse by a covered but well-
lighted bridge, and with the cottages by an underground
passage. It has been carefully planned in all its details
by the skilful manager of our printing-office, Mr. Dennis A. Reardon, — of whose ingenuity we had occasion
to speak in our last annual report, — and it is admirably
adapted for our purpose.

An underground arch has been built between the cottages, through which the steam-pipes are carried from
one block of houses to the other under such protection

as to prevent even the smallest waste of heat in the future. This tunnel is high enough to form a convenient underground passage.

In the main building the work of renovation, to which an impetus was given some time ago, has been carried some steps forward during the past year. One of the dining-rooms, the small boys' sitting-room, and three of the schoolrooms have been thoroughly repaired and put in good order. The walls and ceilings have been painted, the old pine sheathing has been replaced in hard-wood, the heating apparatus improved, the ventilation increased, and various conveniences for keeping things in their proper places have been provided wherever needed.

Several other alterations and improvements of a minor character, supplying urgent wants and calculated to preserve the buildings and to promote the welfare of the household, have been made during the past year; but the limited means placed at our disposition have compelled us to restrict our operations in this direction to a small area. The necessity for continuing the process of renovation in the interior of the main building as rapidly as may be is evidently pressing; for the effects of time and rough usage are very obvious, not only in the corridors and the most frequented rooms, but everywhere. Both safety and economy demand that the loose plastering, the rotten wood-work, the worn floors, the decayed window-frames, the soiled wall-paper, the shaky sashes, and the impaired painting should be replaced, or repaired and made sound, and the sooner this is done, the better. It is our intention to push on the work of reconstruction as fast as we can; but, as our means are not sufficient to meet the ever increasing wants of the establishment, we must depend upon the friends of the blind for assistance.

PRINTING DEPARTMENT.

The great book of nature, with its myriad pages of beauty, its endless variety of scenery, and its ever-changing aspects of sea and sky, is constantly open to the seeing. The achievements of art can be enjoyed by them at all times and seasons, and literature gives them daily something new and fair to feast upon. How different is the lot of the blind, and how few are the privileges of this sort which they enjoy! Yet even for these children of misfortune a brighter day is dawning, and literature, which is, next to music, their greatest solace, holds out to them its consolations and its joys. Music has indeed usually been considered to be the great delight and specialty of the blind; but it is the belief of those who are familiar with their tastes, that, besides their world-wide acknowledged devotion to and appreciation of this art, they are likewise among the most ardent worshippers at the shrine of literature. Enter a room where some seeing person is reading aloud to the blind, and note the intense interest with which the older members of the group hang on the lips of the reader, how they drink in his every word! This is their compensation for all the beautiful things which others enjoy and from which they are cut off. A seeing person may well imbibe the love of study, if he have it not by nature, from intercourse with the blind. It often happens that the seeing youth glances about the room while an important work is being read. He

grows restless, thinks he can peruse it as well himself
at another time (which often never comes), jerks his
chair, looks out of the window, and finally asks to be
excused.   His blind friend sits in an attitude of intense
enjoyment and appreciation, draws a long breath when
the reading is over, as if it had been almost too good,
treasures up all the historic facts or philosophic truths
in the storehouse of his memory, and leaves the room
enlightened and enriched.   Those golden hours are
treasures which he never forgets to count over with
pride and pleasure.   The mention of the title of each
well-prized book brings a smile to his face.   He has
"*lived through*" literature, not dreamed over it.

How more than happy, then, is he, when it offers
itself to the tips of his own fingers, when he need
look to no seeing person to step in as an interpreter
between his author and himself!   This is the work to
which the most earnest energies of the friends of the
blind should now be directed; namely, the foundation of
a choice library of embossed books for their personal
use.   The noble thoughts of great minds were never
meant to be shut off from those who are bereft of sight.
Nay, how gratifying must it be to an author to see that
his works have been laid open for their use!   It is as if
they had been translated into another language, so
difficult is the process which has to be gone through
before the "open sesame" can be pronounced.   But
the results thus far attained amply counterbalance the
obstacles which have been encountered, and bid us to
carry forward the enterprise of embossing books and
constructing tangible apparatus, which was commenced
in Boston forty-nine years ago.

This beneficent undertaking was the offspring of pure benevolence. It was adopted and improved by the fertile mind of Dr. Howe, cherished in its infancy by his warm enthusiasm and indomitable energy, and brought to maturity by the liberal contributions of some of the most distinguished members of our community. Works of various kinds have been published either by subscription or at the expense of generous and noble individuals; but these, compared with the riches of the realm of literature enjoyed by those who are blessed with sight, are but as a few crumbs, insufficient to satisfy the intellectual hunger of the blind. More are absolutely needed.

New Books and Donations.

During the past year the work of our printing-office has been carried on vigorously, and several new volumes have been added to the list of our publications.

We have reprinted from our own fund those admirable books for children, which the superintendent of the public schools and our own president, Dr. Eliot, and Mr. Henry Cabot Lodge, have given to the juvenile world; namely, "Six Stories from the Arabian Nights" and "Twelve Popular Tales." The munificence of one of the kindest friends and noblest benefactors of the blind, at whose expense Higginson's "Young Folks' History of the United States" was embossed and electrotyped last year, and whose modesty withholds his name from the public ken, has enabled us to prosecute the publication of the manuals of ancient and mediæval history without interruption. The Rev. Photius Fisk of the United-States Navy, a native of Greece and well known for various philanthropic deeds, has made a generous donation for embossing the history of his — fatherland, which was accompanied by the following correspondence : —

BOSTON, Feb. 24, 1880.

Friend Anagnos, — I send you herewith the sum of five hundred dollars in gold to be used by the Perkins Institution and Massachusetts School for the Blind in the publication of an edition of the history of Greece, which I understand is much needed. Hoping that such publication will be of great service to all who are so unfortunate as to be deprived of the inestimable gift of sight, I am, very truly, &c.,

PHOTIUS FISK,

U. S. Navy.

SOUTH BOSTON, Feb. 25, 1880.

My dear Mr. Fisk, — I know not how to thank you for this renewed proof of your goodness toward our school. Your munificent present was duly received, and, I assure you, it moved me deeply. Of all the monuments which you have been erecting, and the generous acts which you are incessantly performing, this is undoubtedly the most enduring and most beneficent ; for it adds oil to the lamp which lightens the intellectual horizon of a large class of our fellow-men, and serves as a beacon to lead them to the shore of knowledge, independence, and happiness. There is no calculating the good which it will do to our sightless children. May you, my dear friend, be rewarded for your noble kindness and generosity, and may your example be followed by those who have the stewardship of riches.

I shall have the greatest pleasure in carrying out your most benevolent plan. Your name will stand with those of Peter C. Brooks, John C. Gray, Samuel May, John Preston, Amos A. Lawrence, Charles Dickens, Thomas Roche, and others of our most prized benefactors, whose generosity has aided Dr. Howe in opening the realm of literature to the blind.

Believe me, my dear Mr. Fisk, with the kindest regards and heartfelt thanks, faithfully yours,

M. ANAGNOS.

Another kind friend of the blind, Mrs. Julia B. Paine, has contributed one hundred dollars towards the expense of the juvenile series; and Mr. Henry B. Rogers, whose beneficent acts are numerous in our community, has added one thousand dollars to the permanent fund of our printing-office.

Through these and many other generous gifts previously made, new paths of knowledge and happiness have been opened to the blind. Hundreds of them have felt in their solitude and darkness how cheering and useful is intellectual light. But what they have already received is not enough. They ask for more. Shall their call be heeded? May we not hope that the voice of the same benevolence which has inspired the hearts of so many noble men and women with a desire to ameliorate the lot of those whose night endures from the cradle to the grave will whisper to others of high aim and purpose, "Go ye and do likewise"?

Improvements in the Printing Department.

Our printing-office has recently undergone thorough renovation in every direction, and its working capacities have been greatly increased. It has been supplied with new machinery, types, cases, appliances, fixtures, and conveniencies of the most approved kind, and put in an excellent condition to do good and steady service. Of the improvements introduced since the reconstruction of this department, the two most important deserve a brief mention here : —

First, the completion of the " Howe Memorial Press" and its work.

Second, the contrivance of a mode of electrotyping specially adapted for our purpose.

I. Howe Memorial Press. — It has been found necessary to make some alterations and improvements in this press since its completion. It is now perfect in every particular, and the following cut gives a correct idea of its form and style : —

The above illustration shows clearly that the press is compact in form, and very simple in construction. It is of the type known as the platen press, as distinguished from the cylinder one. Solidity and strength are its main characteristics. Although it resembles ordinary machines of a similar pattern in some respects, it differs from them very essentially in others. The bed is raised and lowered vertically by a toggle joint, which is impelled directly by a connecting-rod two and one half inches in diameter, and not

4

by the action of a cam and gooseneck, as in the Adams Printing-Press. The complication of parts in the old-style platen presses has been entirely avoided in ours, and, by some very ingenious mechanical devices planned by the manager of our printing-office, Mr. Dennis A. Reardon, and designed and executed by the manufacturer, Mr. Francis Meisel, valuable improvements have been introduced. The masterly arrangement for automatic feed and delivery is not the least among these improvements. The press is sound in mechanism, and complete in all its appointments. It embosses eight hundred leaves per hour, and its work is so superior in point of legibility, height of relief, and evenness of impression, to any thus far produced, that it receives the cordial approbation and unreserved commendation of all who are familiar with the subject. The venerable and esteemed principal of the Pennsylvania institution for the blind, Mr. William Chapin, — than whom there is no better judge in the matter of embossing books, — having examined a few pages of our new print, writes as follows: "The specimen sent me of the work of the Howe Memorial Press is certainly as near perfection as any relief work can be. It is beautiful." The accomplished principal of the Ontario institution for the blind, Mr. J. Howard Hunter, a thorough scholar and an unbiassed critic, states the results of his observations in the following words: "The authors selected are exceedingly well chosen, the selections manifestly showing a thorough consideration of the requirements of the blind; and as to the paper, typography, and mechanical execution, it is difficult to see how they can possibly be surpassed.

The typography is extraordinarily fine, the relief being brought up to a very unusual fulness and height: the words fairly *leap off* the book." Mr. Morrison Heady, the deaf and blind author and inventor, and a constant reader of embossed books of various kinds, speaks thus: "Your print is indeed beautiful, the relief being wonderfully clear-cut, uniform, and sustained; and I believe that the letters are as distinctly legible to the touch as the Roman alphabet, so closely imitated, is capable of being made." The superintendent of the Louisiana institution for the blind, Mr. P. Lane, who is also an expert in raised print, writes as follows: "The typography of the history of the celebrated diamonds is excellent. The distinctness of relief and firmness of surface present all the conditions of easy legibility. . . . The print is as nearly perfect as relief print can be." Mrs. A. D. Lord of the New-York State institution, who has for many years been especially successful in teaching blind persons of all ages to read, says that one of her pupils, on taking up one of our recent publications, remarked, " It rests me to read this print after my fingers have grown tired with other books." The principal of the Minnesota institution for the blind, Professor J. J. Dow, — under whose able management the young school is doing excellent work, and is rapidly advancing to the front ranks among establishments of this kind, — writes as follows : " I am highly pleased with the appearance of the books ordered of you, and feel constrained to say that we have never received a more valuable addition to our raised-print library, both as regards the intrinsic worth of the matter selected for publication, and the manner in which the work is done."

These, and several other testimonials of a similar nature, given by competent judges, show how perfect is the work of the Howe Memorial Press, and how superior in more points than one are the books issued by it.

II. Electrotype Plates. — An important step has been made during the past year toward the solution of one of the most difficult problems in the work of embossing books for the blind. We refer to the process of stereotyping.

The ordinary modes of casting metal plates either by the clay or by the *papier-maché* process have been tried in succession, and proved very unsatisfactory. Several of our early publications have been stereotyped by the former method at considerable expense. The plates produced by either of these two processes, as well as those procured by means of thin brass foil embossed from them by strong pressure, and filled in on the back with cement, have been, and in the nature of things must always be, defective. They can never give an absolutely uniform and perfect impression. The lines of the letters embossed from plates made by these processes are either thinner or thicker than those of the types from which they are taken, and are generally uneven.

During the past few years the common method of electrotyping has been employed in our printing-office to great advantage, and the permanence of some of our recent publications has been secured by these means; but even the electrotype plates, although far superior to those produced by any other method, were far from being perfect in every particular. In most of them there was a want of evenness and exactness of outline, and a lack of uniformity in relief, which was especially noticeable in the embossed work of such a powerful press as ours. Through the ingenuity and persistent endeavors of the manager of our printing department, an improvement on the process of electrotyping has been devised, by means of which an exact copy of the faces and shoulders of the types can be transferred to a copper shell, while the cost is reduced to the lowest possible point. This process is very simple. A wax matrix is procured from the type form by means of a very powerful press. The mould thus obtained is coated with plumbago in order to form a metallic continuity for the passage of the electric current, and is placed in a tank. A battery is then applied which causes the uniform deposit of copper on the surface of the wax matrix. Thus a shell is made, which, when it has attained the required thickness, is removed from the mould. The lines of this shell are filled on the reverse side with melted tin, which is rubbed down to a true surface, and which renders them perfectly solid. Plates of absolute uniformity, and of a thickness of about one thirty-second of an inch, are thus finished, and made ready for the press. These plates have been used in our printing-office with entire satisfaction. The impression obtained from them is well nigh perfect. A number of pages of the histories of Greece and Rome and of the Popular Tales were embossed from them; and no one could perceive any difference between these pages and those printed from the type forms themselves.

In addition to the above-named improvements, a num-

ber of others of a minor character have been made in the
printing department of this institution during the past
year. Two smaller presses, one for taking proof and
embossing writing-cards, and the other for ink print,
have been procured. All possible measures have been
taken to improve the quality of embossed publications,
and great efforts have been made to increase their number while reducing their cost. The paper which we use
is made expressly for us from selected materials and
with an uncommonly strong fibre, and no pains have
been spared to have our books not only neatly but substantially bound.

Thus our printing-office is complete in all its appointments, and well equipped with the necessary appliances
for carrying on its work on a broad scale steadily and
vigorously. All that is now needed to promote its usefulness and make it what it ought to be — a perennial
source of blessing to the blind — is a permanent fund,
the income of which should be sufficient to defray its
expenses. Doubtless there are many benevolent persons in our community who, if they understood the
workings of this grand enterprise, would be willing to
contribute to its success from their abundance. To
them, and to all generous people whose hearts can be
touched by the magnitude of the calamity of blindness
and the needs of its victims, we appeal, and beg them
to consider the claims of those members of the human
family who cannot feast, as they do, at the broad table
of universal literature, but to whose touch a few of its
choicest morsels may be adapted if the means are given
to us. A select library for their use is truly a great
monument to benevolence and humanity ; and we can-

not but hope that some one will undertake to erect it in the near future.

Work Department for Adults.

This department continues to be conducted on the system adopted many years ago, and the general principles of its administration do not differ in any essential point from those which govern ordinary business establishments.

During the past twelve months, the receipts of the workshop from all sources have amounted to $13,943.07, being more by $1,571.83 than those of the previous year.

The expenses for all purposes have been $15,163.21.

Thus the balance against the department is $990.03, whereas the sum of $1,890.47 was paid out of the treasury of the institution the previous year.

The number of blind persons employed in this department was nineteen, and the amount paid in cash to them as wages for their work was $3,186.72, or $50.41 more than in 1879.

This *résumé* of the accounts of the workshop tells its story plainly. It shows clearly that there is nothing in the present condition and prospects of the institution which calls more emphatically for immediate consideration and definite action than the financial state of this department. Nor can temporary relief afford by any means adequate remedy. It is a necessity of the highest importance that something should be done without delay to protect the treasury of the establishment from this constant and almost chronic drain.

As we have repeatedly stated in our annual reports,

the workshop for adults has been a blessing to blind persons, and its preservation is a great boon to many of them.   It has supplied them with remunerative occupation, and thus rescued them from the grasp of poverty and the degradation of the almshouse.   It has smoothed the pathway of life to those on whom the hand of affliction pressed heavily, and has enabled them to secure for themselves, by industry and diligence, the comforts of home and the inestimable enjoyments of domestic happiness.   When, therefore, we reflect upon facts so vital and so pregnant with the whole future of a large number of blind persons, we must patiently but persistently present the case to our fellow-citizens, upon whose generosity and liberal patronage the very existence of this department rests, before having recourse to the extreme measure of discontinuing it.

We need hardly say that there will be no want of effort on our part to continue to uphold the industrial department for adults and cultivate this special field of beneficence in the future as we have done in the past. But we beg to report that, in order to be able to do so, our hands must be strengthened by an endowment, — the income of which shall be sufficient to pay the rent and all the necessary expenses of the salesrooms, — as well as by an increase of patronage.   Our rules, arrangements, and supplies of stock are such as to facilitate the prompt and faithful execution of all orders left at the office, No. 37 Avon street, for new mattresses, pillows, bolsters, comforters, and feather beds; for dressing, cleansing, and making over old ones; for repairing and re-upholstering all kinds of parlor furniture; for re-seating cane-bottomed chairs; for tuning and repairing piano-fortes; for supplying churches and vessels with cushions ; for brooms, brushes, door-mats, and the like. We solicit orders for all these on a strictly business footing. The articles manufactured are warranted to be of the best materials and faithfully made up.

Pains are taken by fidelity in the work and by all other means to render our industrial department one of the best and most reliable concerns of its kind in the city. We invoke for it the patronage and the serious consideration of all men and women who are truly interested in benevolent and philanthropic objects.

RETROSPECTIVE VIEW OF THE WORK OF THE SCHOOL.

Before bringing this, the forty-ninth in our series of public reports, to a close, we cannot forbear indulging in a few remarks of a retrospective character.

It is now almost half a century since the attention of a small band of benevolent citizens of Boston, given for the first time on this continent to the consideration of the condition of the blind, resulted in the foundation of this institution. It is just fifty years since Dr. Howe, at the suggestion of Dr. John D. Fisher, entered upon this enterprise, and sailed for Europe for the purpose of visiting establishments of a similar kind already in operation there, examining the methods of instruction therein employed, engaging the services of competent teachers, and procuring specimens of embossed books and tangible apparatus. Two generations have nearly passed away since the school entered upon its career of usefulness, and not one of its original projectors and benefactors, who reared the foundations carefully in its infancy and worked so assiduously for its maturity and success, is now living.

5

In looking back at that period, and comparing the present social and moral status and the prospects of the blind with what they then were, we cannot but see that a great work has been accomplished.

Since the foundation of our school the mind of the country has become so convinced of the justice and benevolence of the cause, that at least twenty-nine institutions have been established in different states, devoted to this special field of human culture. About two thousand children are at this moment pupils of these schools, and about six thousand have already gone forth from them, having received instruction in various branches, intellectual, artistic, and mechanical. It is very encouraging to note how large a number of these graduates have been able to fight the battle of life successfully, and have been not only useful but happy men. It is gratifying to know that in most cases education has so formed their principles and regulated their conduct, that, as they have mingled in society and engaged in business occupations, they have established a character for honor and integrity, and have obtained positions of trust and profit, from which they must otherwise have been excluded.

These facts are indeed remarkable, and ought to bear with them much satisfaction and hopefulness. But the advancement hitherto effected should be regarded as merely a prelude to that which is to come. Half a century is not a long period in the history of such a movement as this, and the art of educating the blind and awakening in them individual force and creative ability is still to be considered as comparatively recent. The torch of science is now, moreover, sending forth such a clear and constant flame, and throwing such abundance of light into every department of human thought, that what seemed to be excellent ten or twenty years ago may prove very incomplete and deficient if seen by its rays. Thus it is necessary for us to advance our standard continually in order to keep pace with the times, and carry the enterprise forward with ever-new vigor and energy, stimulated, by the success of the past, to greater achievements in the future.

GENERAL REMARKS.

In taking leave of the members of the corporation, we are happy to state that the affairs and interests of the institution have been so managed as to receive our approbation, and that its usefulness and importance are growing from year to year. From comparatively small beginnings the establishment has become an educational agency of great power and influence, constituting as it does an important link in the chain of our public schools, and co-operating with them in the fair distribution of knowledge among all classes of children.

It is to the credit of our community and to the honor of the state, that the institution stands to-day in the front rank of establishments of its kind as far as regards the completeness of its appointments, the breadth of its purpose, the comprehensiveness of its objects, the liberality of its policy, and the efficiency of its methods of instruction and training.

It is very gratifying to our board to be able to bear witness to the ability, zeal, and fidelity of the teachers and officers upon whom devolve the labor and responsibility of carrying on the work of the institution in its various departments.

The trustees again extend a cordial invitation to the members of the corporation and to those of the executive of the commonwealth and of the legislature, as well as to the chief magistrates and other officials of all the New-England States, to visit the school as often as they can, and to see for themselves the condition of the household, the progress of the pupils, and the benefits which they are deriving from the public aid afforded to them.

Commending the institution and all the interests of the blind to the representatives of the people, upon whose fairness and sense of justice the majority of our pupils depend for their education, to the benevolent, the intelligent, the wise and good everywhere, from many of whom we continually receive indications of sympathy and friendly approbation in our work, we close this report.

All which is respectfully submitted by

ROBERT E. APTHORP,
JOHN S. DWIGHT,
JOSEPH B. GLOVER,
J. THEODORE HEARD,
HENRY LEE HIGGINSON,
JAMES H. MEANS,
ANDREW P. PEABODY,
EDWARD N. PERKINS,
JOSIAH QUINCY,
SAMUEL G. SNELLING,
JAMES STURGIS,
GEORGE W. WALES,
Trustees.

South Boston, Oct. 13, 1880.

At the annual meeting of the corporation, summoned according to the by-laws, and held this day at the institution, the foregoing was accepted, and ordered to be printed, together with the reports of the director and treasurer and the usual accompanying documents; and the officers for the ensuing year were elected.

M. ANAGNOS, *Secretary.*

and responsibility of carrying on the work of the institution in its various departments.

The trustees again extend a cordial invitation to the members of the corporation and to those of the executive of the commonwealth and of the legislature, as well as to the chief magistrates and other officials of all the New-England States, to visit the school as often as they can, and to see for themselves the condition of the household, the progress of the pupils, and the benefits which they are deriving from the public aid afforded to them.

Commending the institution and all the interests of the blind to the representatives of the people, upon whose fairness and sense of justice the majority of our pupils depend for their education, to the benevolent, the intelligent, the wise and good everywhere, from many of whom we continually receive indications of sympathy and friendly approbation in our work, we close this report.

All which is respectfully submitted by

ROBERT E. APTHORP,
JOHN S. DWIGHT,
JOSEPH B. GLOVER,
J. THEODORE HEARD,
HENRY LEE HIGGINSON,
JAMES H. MEANS,
ANDREW P. PEABODY,
EDWARD N. PERKINS,
JOSIAH QUINCY,
SAMUEL G. SNELLING,
JAMES STURGIS,
GEORGE W. WALES,
Trustees.

South Boston, Oct. 13, 1880.

At the annual meeting of the corporation, summoned according to the by-laws, and held this day at the institution, the foregoing was accepted, and ordered to be printed, together with the reports of the director and treasurer and the usual accompanying documents; and the officers for the ensuing year were elected.

M. ANAGNOS, *Secretary.*

THE REPORT OF THE DIRECTOR.

To the Board of Trustees.

Gentlemen, — I have the honor to submit to your consideration the customary annual report on the workings of the institution and the management of its internal affairs.

It is a pleasure to review the history of such an auspicious year as the last has been, and to place its work on record ; to note the progress that has been effected ; to commend to your attention certain measures, the adoption of which would, in my judgment, tend to advance the interests and promote the welfare of the school ; and to present such thoughts and suggestions on the education of the blind in general as come within the scope of a document of this kind.

No interruption or disturbance has occurred to interfere with the usual quiet course of things, and the year has not been marked by any uncommon events.

The various departments of the institution have been conducted with ability and discretion, and the labors of the year have been productive of very satisfactory results.

The teachers and officers have been faithful in the performance of their duties, and have done all in their power to improve the minds and elevate the character of those placed under thei charge.

Good order has prevailed at all times; and the pupils have, as a general rule, responded with cheerfulness, and in a manly spirit, to the requirements of those in authority, and have shown a real interest in their work.

I may safely state here that the institution never stood higher in these respects than at present.

The ordinary means and methods of . intellectual, moral, musical, and technical instruction and training, have been steadily pursued with such improvements, modifications, and additions, as experience has suggested and progress has seemed to require.

A judicious division of the time into the hours of study, practice on musical instruments, handicraft, exercise, and rest, has been made as heretofore; and its legitimate results may be easily seen in the happiness and contentment of the scholars, as well as in their healthy appearance, and their advancement in their studies.

The aims and purposes of the school have been constantly kept in .view; and pains have been taken to enlarge our collections of specimens and appliances adapted to the sense of touch, and to procure such facilities as would contribute to the thorough training of the pupils.

All the systematic arrangements pertaining to the internal economy of the establishment which have heretofore proved satisfactory have not only been preserved, but improved more or less, so as to secure thorough efficiency in the management of the various details of the household, and regularity in the movements of the domestic machinery.

The general interest which the community has always

shown in all questions relating to the education and welfare of the blind has been fully sustained during the past year, and the principles and policy which were inculcated at the commencement of the institution by its great founder are bearing abundant fruit.

NUMBER OF INMATES.

The total number of blind persons connected with the various departments of the institution at the beginning of the past year, as teachers, pupils, employés, and work men and women, was 162. There have since been admitted 17; 23 have been discharged, making the present total number 156. Of these, 137 are in the school proper, and 19 in the workshop for adults.

The first class includes 125 boys and girls enrolled as pupils, 8 teachers, and 4 domestics. Of the pupils there are now 57 boys and 47 girls in attendance, 13 of the former and 8 of the latter being absent on account of physical disability, or from other causes.

The second class comprises 16 men and 3 women, employed in the industrial department for adults.

Of the 156 blind persons connected with the institution 151 belong to New England, and 5 have come to us from the West and South, — one from each of the states of Minnesota, Michigan, New York, Ohio, and Tennessee. A sixth, belonging to Indiana, is about to be admitted. Some of these young men have already passed through the course of study pursued at the several institutions of their respective states, and have graduated from them. They have come to Boston for the purpose of pursuing their musical education further, and of acquiring the art of tuning piano-fortes, both theoretically and practically.

GRADUATES AND THEIR GENERAL SUCCESS.

Six of those whose connection with the institution terminated at the end of the last school session were regular graduates, having gone through the entire course of study and training given here, and receiving diplomas at the close of the term. They have all labored faithfully and assiduously to qualify themselves for a career of activity and usefulness, and are all well fitted to enter the arena of practical life, and to become self-supporting.

I may add, in this connection, that we continue to receive interesting and favorable accounts from a large number of our graduates, who are succeeding remarkably well in obtaining a comfortable living, and are respected as useful citizens. Many of these have had great obstacles to overcome at the outset, and all of them have had to fight their way, more or less, through the clouds of incredulity and common prejudice as to their ability and skill to pursue any of the liberal professions, or to work at any of the mechanic arts. But, by diligent application and exemplary conduct, they have conquered all difficulties, and have not only taken their places in the ranks of society, but have, in some instances, even gained a certain degree of distinction.

SANITARY CONDITION.

The general health of the household throughout the year has been excellent. No epidemic of any kind has prevailed, and no case of death or of serious illness has occurred. This is the more extraordinary when we recollect the natural physical debility of the pupils, and their low stamina.

In a large number of cases blindness is caused by some severe illness in early life, which often leaves an indelible impression on the constitution, and renders it more liable to the attacks of disease ever after. In another class of those who come under our care, the extinction of sight is simply a visible symptom of some latent organic disorder; and in still another, which is quite numerous, dimness of vision is produced by what is called, in general terms, scrofula. This disease is usually hereditary, or, when not so, results from want of proper regard to diet, exercise, and habits of personal cleanliness during the early years of childhood. If left unchecked, it undermines the constitution, wastes its vitality, and leads to consumption and other fatal disorders. The fact is, that either from the same causes which bring about the loss of sight, or in consequence of the effects of this misfortune, and the habits which it superinduces upon its victims, there are but very few among the blind who may be considered as typical specimens of perfect health. I am aware that this is a very serious statement, but it is as true as it is grave.

The healthfulness of the mental life and activity of our pupils depends solely upon the soundness of their material organism; that is, the physical condition which secures the uniform and regular performance of all the functions of the body arising from the harmonious action of every one of its parts. Hence all possible means are taken in our institution for the improvement and conservation of the health of the household, and no object is considered of greater importance than that of carefully and wisely guarding against any and all influences that would impair or endanger it. Our sanitary arrangements and hygienic regulations are most cautiously made; cleanliness and regular habits of life are strictly enforced upon all, and special attention is paid to the preparation, quality, quantity, and variety of food, which is one of the fundamental agencies in the promotion of physical well-being, since from it is obtained the material necessary for the growth of the body, and for the supply of the waste occasioned by muscular and mental action. It should be remarked, however, that in all changes of diet the real, and not the imaginary, wants of the pupils are consulted. For it is often the case that a false demand is created by injudicious supplies, which becomes imperious in after life.

OBJECTS AND SCOPE OF THE EDUCATION OF THE BLIND.

The subject of education is one which has occupied many of the greatest minds from the remotest times down to the present day. Philosophers and writers have earnestly discussed and variously defined it. " I call that education," says Fellenberg, " which embraces the culture of the whole man with all his faculties, subjecting his senses, his understanding, and his passions, to reason and to conscience." According to Dugald Stewart, " To educate is to cultivate the principles of man's nature, both speculative and active, in such a manner as to bring them to the greatest perfection of which they are susceptible." Richter observes that " education should bring to light the ideal of the individual." Horace Mann remarks that, " it is to inspire truth as the supreme good, and to clarify the vision of the intellect to discern it ; " and Herbert Spencer sums up its functions as teaching us " in what way to treat the body, in what way to treat the mind, in what way to behave as a citizen, in what way to utilize all those sources of happiness which nature supplies, how to use our faculties to the greatest advantage of ourselves and others, how to live completely."

But, be the definitions of writers what they may, and let their opinions on the subject differ as widely as they can, the end and aim of education is now clearly understood as being to promote and guide the harmonious and normal growth of children, to unfold all their faculties and powers systematically and symmetrically, to impart to them the greatest possible capacity of thought and action, and to make of them complete human beings, endowed with a healthy and beautiful physical formation, with broad and enlightened minds, and with dignified and firm sentiments. In other words, its object is to give humanity its fullest expansion, its most perfect development.

Education begins almost spontaneously in the earliest stages of childhood with a mother's glance; with a father's nod of approbation or sign of reproof; a sister's gentle pressure of the hand; an elder brother's generous attention; a handful of flowers gathered in the green meadows; the thoughts directed in sweet and kindly tones and words to nature and beauty, to goodness and truth. This is all well and good as far as it goes, but it is not all sufficient. Something more is required; and this is a system of training so well organized and so completely arranged as to nurture and bring to the highest maturity the intelligence and the moral nature in children; to foster budding capacities for good, and even for what is great and noble in charac-

ter; to endow them with free and full use of all their
powers, and make them natural, modest, frank, and
real; and, finally, to give a sufficient scope for the
development of those activities which, in their combination, constitute life.

Such are, in brief, the ends and aims of education,
and such the requirements for their accomplishment.
But, while its general principles and essential laws are
equally applicable to both seeing and blind youth, the
means and methods, as well as the mechanical appliances and apparatus employed in the training of the
latter, compared with those used in the ordinary educational systems, must be as much more varied and
comprehensive as the peculiarities and obstacles are
greater in the one case than in the other.

In the case of ordinary children all the natural channels of communication between the mind and the external world are open. Sensation is a law of their being;
perception is the next direct step from it; and then
recognition, conception, memory, comparison, ratiocination, judgment, and imagination, as naturally follow.
Educated by these simple intellectual operations, their
attention naturally turns inward, and, with the exercise
of consciousness, children become capable of compre-
hending the laws and principles of their own minds.
The will undergoes a simultaneous development through
the reciprocating influences of intelligence and volition.

In the case of the blind, one of the broadest and
most important avenues of sense, through which at
least one-third of the nervous impressions necessary
for sensation and consciousness pass to the sensorium,
is entirely closed. This obstruction between the mind

and the outer world, aside from undermining the vitality of the physical organization, acts as a disturbing force in the order of the development of the various intellectual and moral faculties which go to form character, and renders its victims as weak and irresolute in thought and purpose as they are feeble and flabby in fibre. Its effects, as seen in a large number of individuals, are somewhat like those of light coming upon a plant from one side only, and causing it to grow crooked. They constitute a novel phasis of human development, which is surely worth the careful study of scientific men. Owing to their infirmity, the sensations of the blind are, in the natural order of things, imperfect. They awaken indistinct and limited perceptions, and consequently the intellectual processes that follow will be feeble. For the operation of the higher functions of the mind in solving the problems of thought and in arriving at just conclusions depends upon the faithfulness with which the powers of perception have been cultivated, and upon the variety and quality of the materials which these powers have gathered. From insufficient data and incorrect premises no right conclusions can be reached. Such are some of the most striking effects of the obstruction of the visual sense.

In arranging a system for the instruction and training of the blind, special cognizance should be taken of the physical peculiarities and psychological phenomena arising from their infirmity ; and efficient means should be employed for reducing its consequences to the minimum, for counteracting its undesirable effects as far as may be, for building up the whole character

of its victims, and for raising them as near as possible
to the social and moral standard of the community.
Careful attention to the thorough cultivation of the
remaining senses is not the least of these means,
since it is an undisputed fact, that, by proper training and efficient exercise, they acquire a power which
is quite remarkable, and which, although it cannot
substitute the specific functions of sight, yet goes far
enough to serve as a compensation in the pursuit of
knowledge.

The education of the blind, as well as that of all
classes of children, is purely an inductive science; and
its principles and rules must be based upon a long
and careful observation of the manifestations of the
mind, presented in its several stages of growth, and
must aim at the full development of the powers of
its recipients. It was upon this groundwork that the
great benefactor of the blind, Dr. Howe, aided by the
light of his day, labored through life with marvellous
success to rear the structure. But unhappily this interesting science does not seem to keep pace with the
march of progress, and, as it now exists in many
places, is even little less than empirical. It is founded
on no rigid laws gathered from the systematic observation of the physical difficulties and the consideration
of the various effects arising from the loss of sight.
Nor is its practice sufficiently consistent to deserve the
title of an art. This result is owing, not so much to
the uncertainties surrounding the subject, as to the
lack of scientific training and scholarly attainments in
its expounders. I am aware that in making this
assertion, even with the kindest intention, I am touch-

ing upon a very sensitive point; but loyalty to truth
and justice to the cause itself compel me to forego
my personal feelings, and to state candidly that no
educational enterprise for the blind can succeed, and
no system for their instruction and training can attain
perfection and bear ripe fruit, unless those who control
it be men of superior talents and learning, able to
branch off from the beaten tracks of mere routine
work, and follow progress in its higher flights, and
unless its importance be so fully recognized by the
community at large that the gates of the temples in
which the enterprise is enshrined are hermetically
closed against the whirlwinds of partisan strife and
capricious favoritism, which too often bring with them
confusion and desolation.

The success and happiness of the blind lie in the
thoroughness of their education, and in the just proportion in which their faculties are developed, their
powers increased, and their sentiments refined. The
provisions made for their instruction and training, both
intellectual and professional, must be so skilfully and
wisely administered as to enable them to reap the
greatest possible amount of good, to enter the domain
of social and industrial activities, to assume the responsibilities and enjoy the privileges of citizenship,
and fully to realize the grandeur of the continuity of
intellectual tradition, thus taking an active part in all
movements concerning human affairs, and toiling cheerfully in the ranks of their fellow-men. As Geoffroy
Saint-Hilaire's mental vision was brought to such a
point of clearness that the loss of the sense of sight
did not prevent him from beholding the future of

zoölogy, so his brethren in misfortune may be raised
by earnest and incessant effort to such an intellectual
and moral height as to be able to look with the eye
of faith and hope beyond the trials which now shroud
their lot, and "the struggle for the survival of the
fittest," and gaze on the blaze of the great destinies
of humanity.

When education is so well organized as to tend to
transfer the allegiance of all races and classes of people
to the wider interests of culture, freedom, and civilization, and rises to be the handmaid of ethical purpose,
then and then only may it worthily take its place beside
the grandest products of human development, having
as its objects to enrich and beautify the lives of men by
tuning them unconsciously into harmony with whatever
is noblest in nature and in humanity.

THE VARIOUS DEPARTMENTS OF THE INSTITUTION.

It is obvious from the above remarks that the first
and most fundamental principle in the work of the
institution is to unfold the mental faculties and
strengthen the bodily powers of its beneficiaries in
definite order by regular and constant exercises adapted
to the requirements of their case; to train them up in
virtuous and industrious habits; to increase, by thorough
cultivation, the quickness and accuracy of their remaining senses; and to develop to the utmost extent all their
capacities and aptitudes, so that the absence of sight
may not be for them a bar to social relationship upon
terms of entire equality.

Our system of education is, no doubt, far from being
perfect in every detail, or complete in all its appoint-

ments ; but it is on the whole sound in principle, practical in its purposes, broad in its views, liberal in its policy, and well adapted to the wants and peculiarities of the class of children for whose special benefit it is intended.

The principal instrumentalities employed for carrying out this system, although they have been repeatedly set forth in former reports, may be again briefly stated as follows : —

First, instruction in such branches of study as constitute the curriculum of our best common schools and academies.

Secondly, lessons and practice in music, both vocal and instrumental.

Thirdly, systematic instruction in the theory and practice of the art of tuning piano-fortes.

Fourthly, training in one or more simple trades, and work at some mechanical or domestic occupation.

Fifthly, regular gymnastic drill under the care of competent teachers, and plenty of exercise in the open air.

Of the working and effects of these instrumentalities during the past year, a full account will be found in the following pages, where each department of the institution is separately reviewed.

Literary Department.

Man is a hunter of truth ; this is the definition which Plato gives of him. But the greatest and most luminous star in the firmament of ideal philosophy omits to point out the place where human beings can be thoroughly qualified to follow this pursuit successfully.

In our own days, in addition to a good and sunny home, it would evidently be a well-organized and properly conducted school or academy. Here light breaks out of darkness, revealing the wonders of nature and the accumulated experience of mankind. Here the intellect is awakened from its winter torpor, and rejoices in a new and active life. Here the soil of the mind is carefully cultivated, and enriched with germs which have in them the virtue of perennial growth. Here confidence in the native powers and resources is fostered, and aptitude for invention is stimulated. Finally, here are provided the necessary means for laying the foundations of a refined and correct taste and of a noble character.

How great, then, is the responsibility of planning and organizing a school dedicated to the instruction of youth, and how delicate and difficult the task of carrying out the workings of its mechanism when once established! Even as the best and most perfectly constructed clock needs to be wound up at certain intervals, so would an institution for the training and teaching of children and youth run down, its machinery grow rusty, and its hands point stupidly and obstinately to the wrong time of day, if it were not wound up from time to time.

From the danger of becoming stationary or even retrograde, it has been our constant care to guard the literary department of this institution as thoroughly and conscientiously as might be; and it may safely be said that these efforts have not proved futile.

The progress of the school during the past year has been exceedingly satisfactory, and the amount and value of the work accomplished by both teachers and pupils may be weighed by the mental growth of the one and the increase in power and ability of the other.

The course of study has been arranged in exact accordance with the needs of each stage of mental development; and, as it now stands, it gives the pupils a fair quota of work without being burdensome or injurious. The branches embraced have been taught in a simple and thorough manner, and knowledge has been imparted in the way which science points out and experience approves.

At the close of the term a public examination was held, which was witnessed by the friends of the scholars and several members of your board, and which, according to the general testimony, would have been very creditable to any educational establishment.

Some of the pupils have needed occasional correction as regards their outward behavior; but more have required to be stimulated to greater energy, and to be cured of listless and inactive habits. Their progress, however, has been on the whole of the solid and lasting kind; in many cases rapid as well as thorough. They have been taught to observe carefully, to understand readily, to reflect accurately and rationally, to express their ideas concisely, and to use their hands skilfully; and have been trained to grow up to be vigorous thinkers, strong reasoners, and independent workers. Consistency and clearness of views, distinctness of statement, coherence of argument, and absence of repetition and tautology, have been persistently required in most of their recitations. In the mean time care has been taken that acquisition should not go beyond the pale of mental discipline, and that the taxation of the intellect should be kept entirely within the limits of the constitutional capacity and physical endurance of the children.

Whatever has been the success of the school, is mainly due to the zeal and fidelity with which the teachers have discharged their duties, and to their adaptability for their work. They have endeavored to raise the intellectual standard as well as the moral tone of the school, and have met with good success. They study its best interests, and are diligent and conscientious in their labors to advance them. They strive to acquaint themselves with the mental condition, habits, temperament, and capacity of each individual, so as to be able to make the necessary allowances and discriminations. They enforce habits of regularity, punctuality, industry, self-control, and politeness; but they do all this with genuine sympathy, and with a patience that no irritability of temper or dulness of intellect can exhaust. I can truly say that, in, the dealings of all our teachers and pupils, Shakspeare's counsel is often well carried out : —

> " What thou wilt,
> Thou rather shalt enforce it with a smile,
> Than hew to't with thy sword."

Most of our instructors, moreover, manifest a sincere fondness for their work ; and this is an invaluable qualification. Where this love of one's work is found, the course of things is like the smooth flowing of a stream sparkling and dancing in the sunlight. But where such love is wanting, many an effort, like a wave driven on the beach by a gale, returns baffled and wasted upon itself,

The same system of instruction which has been
described in preceding reports has been pursued during
the past year, with such modifications and improvements as the circumstances of particular classes have
seemed to demand, or the light of progress to indicate.

Linguistic formulæ, mechanical spelling, dry dates
and tables, vague geographical notions, obscure mathematical abstractions, and all that mass of antiquated
rubbish which has been palmed off on all schools as
educational wealth, has been gradually discarded, and
replaced by more rational methods. Instead of rattling
off definitions of grammar and parsing like automata,
the pupils have been taught to frame sentences and
learn practically the structure of language. Instead of
repeating glibly the contents of a text-book on history,
they have been required to state connectedly and in a
simple manner the most prominent events of the past
and their causes, and, if possible, to point out the effects
which they exercised on human affairs. Instead of
shouting out in concert the names of countries, states,
capitals, cities, rivers, and mountains, they have been
instructed first to examine tangible representations of
all parts of the globe, starting from the nearest and
most familiar ones, and then to name them, and state
briefly what they know about them. Instead of gab-
bling the rules of arithmetic like parrots, they have
been trained to solve new and unexpected problems.
Instead of prating forth confused ideas on the external
world enveloped in misty verbalism, they have been led
to study the rudiments of the natural sciences objectively, and to give a plain account of what they had
learned about them. That system of instruction which

combines naturalness with scientific efficacy, grace with
vigor, and simplicity with solidity, calls into exercise
the most useful faculties of the mind, opens to the
pupils vistas of research in the direction of general culture, and exerts a purifying and elevating influence
upon their character. In the training of children we
must keep constantly in view the creative and productive divinity of nature, which prefigures and determines
the future plant in the tenderest germ, shields and pro-
tects it carefully, and out of the smallest and simplest
develops gradually, step by step, the highest and noblest.

All available means conducing to the cultivation of
the habit of analytical observation have been eagerly
employed in our school. This faculty is a very important factor in education, and should receive all the
attention which can be bestowed upon it. As the young
Apollo is represented by one antique sculptor as watching the quick and alert movements of the saurus, and
divining from its motions things relating to humanity,
so children should be taught to notice or examine every
thing in the outer life of the glad and active earth.
Much of the force which discovers and originates is due
to this faculty. The incident of Archimedes and his
bath illustrates strikingly the effects of habitual observation.

In the pursuit of knowledge the pupils are generally
inspired with a determination to accomplish whatever
they undertake, rather than with a desire to attempt
great things. By the time that they reach such a degree of self-confidence as to think it within their power
to perform a certain kind of work, they are fully able
to do it. They *have learned to* believe in their own

capacity, to trust themselves, and to rely upon their own resources. As an eminent writer puts it, —

" Possunt quia posse videntur."

Most of the exercises of the school are calculated to train the senses of the pupils, and to enable them to perceive accurately, to form exact ideas, and to express them clearly in simple language. This practice opposes any tendency to exaggeration or to habitual mistakes, gives them access to correct and vital knowledge, and, above all, strengthens the sense and love of truth in every part of life. The latter quality contains in itself a potent charm which bears a man safely through the entanglements of the world. It not only makes him more simple and natural, and less liable to error, but it conduces to his highest' intellectual . development. Goethe says that the love of truth shows itself in discovering and appreciating what is good wherever it may exist.

The communication of knowledge is generally followed by an awakening of the active powers of the mind; so that the pupils seem as if they were discovering truth rather than learning it. The scholar becomes the potent creator of the study he apprehends. Sir William Hamilton says that " self-activity is the indispensable condition of improvement ; " and too much care can never be given to the development of this power. Children often become sick through the evils following upon the constant reception of knowledge in a passive manner, and can only be made healthy by working for its acquisition.

But, while incessant endeavors have been made to

give systematic instruction to the pupils, developing their faculties in definite order, and rendering them obedient to the commands of the central will, pains have also been taken not to compress the cerebral structure, which is the seat of their growth, but to cultivate it, and strengthen it by proper exercise. For upon the soundness and expansion of this marvellous organ much of the success of mental training depends. The broad, large, roomy brain, well balanced and counterpoised, is capable of taking in many ideas, and in weighing, comparing, and inwardly digesting them. The result in the pupil is the ability to form wise conclusions, solid arguments, and generous convictions. A strong intellect, nourished in the convolutions of a healthful brain, and favored with good powers of acquisition, and liberty to grow in free luxuriance, sends its roots into the various soils, and draws from them the constituents of wholesome saps.

On the re-assembling of the school in September, both pupils and teachers entered on their duties with renewed zeal, and the opening of the year seems to be very auspicious.

OBJECT TEACHING.

" Novus rerum nascitur ordo."

A marked change has taken place in our day in all the methods, not only of thought, but of instruction. The philosopher turns from the study to the laboratory. The natural sciences are raised to a post of dignity which they have never before held in the learned world. In the schoolroom the perfect cast or statue takes the place of the only half-suggestive wood-cut.

8

The flat-faced wall-map swells into the highly embossed chart or globe. There is a strong re-action against mere hearsay knowledge, a wish to touch and handle objects of interest, instead of merely reading about and describing them. With this change in the study and the schoolroom, many of the elements of mere routine and red tape have been cast aside. The duties of a teacher are now almost professional, when their present is compared with their past extent. It no longer suffices for the instructor to read his explanations from a book alone. He must give them from his own thoughts, and must therefore be thoroughly prepared for the lesson beforehand. He must also be more or less of a scientist, if he wishes to keep pace with the spirit of the day.

The re-action in favor of objective teaching, which has come in with the tendency towards greater thoroughness in all branches, may no doubt be pushed too far; yet there can be no question that the present movement is one which can be utilized to a very great extent in the instruction and training of the blind.

Many of the appliances and a great part of the apparatus manufactured for ordinary school uses at the present day are of a nature equally well adapted for the instruction and training of our pupils; and the education of the seeing, as it advances, carries that of the blind in its train. The conceptions of the mind on material subjects, unaided by any outward sense, are as vague in those who can see as in the sightless; and the little blind girl who said that a hen had three legs is hardly more an object of pity than the child at the Isle of Shoals who "had never seen a horse, but had once beheld a picture of one."

So prone is the mind to create images, whether true or false, that we often find ourselves surprised or almost shocked, on seeing a new scene or person for the first time, to discover that the reality has dared to differ from the image preconceived in our fancy. The mind of blind persons is equally quick in forming images of this sort, even as we ourselves see quite as lively shapes when our eyes are closed in sleep as at noonday. Even Laura Bridgman exercises this universal human privilege. Her description, given to Professor Hall, of the dream in which she thought she saw God, was very touching and beautiful.

Now comes the wonderful plastic skill of the present era of objective development, and furnishes to the eyes of the seeing and the fingers of the blind the shapes for which they have so long groped in darkness and doubt.

Perfect imitations of the human frame, whole and in parts, life-size and diminished, manikins and dissected models, are made with exquisite fidelity to nature, and can be purchased at comparatively moderate rates considering their really inestimable value. Animals and plants are also brought within the pupils' ken in all their beauty and completeness. The old saying, "Seeing is believing," is powerfully exemplified in the objective teaching of the present day. The taxidermist's art, too, can be called to the teacher's aid; and this has made great strides since what are familiarly called "old times," or that vaguely defined period when every one who is now grown up was a little child. Besides these most interesting guides to the studies of physiology, zoölogy, and botany, the gate of the mineral kingdom has been thrown much wider open than of old, and imitations of all forms of crystals and precious stones are now given to the market in the greatest possible beauty and perfection.

Armed with these instrumentalities, the teacher of to-day leads his young charges on board a full-rigged ship fairly equipped at all points for the voyage in pursuit of learning, where once he had only a small raft on which to embark with them on the wide ocean of knowledge. If he does not reach far-distant ports, and bring home a rich freight of fact and acquisition, the fault is with him, and not with the material which he has to work with. Indeed, art so vies with nature at the present day, that it might almost seem necessary for the latter to invent new forms, lest her subtle sister exhaust all her treasures, and find nothing more to imitate.

Collection of Tangible Objects.

During the past year the work of increasing our collections of models, specimens, and tangible objects of various kinds, has been carried on persistently, and our shelves have been enriched by many new additions. The most valuable of these consist in a complete set of the Schaufuss anatomical preparations (including birds, fishes, and silkworms), and in a large collection of minerals, rocks, fossils, specimens of woods, dried plants, seeds, stuffed animals, birds, fishes, reptiles, eggs, nests, shells, crustaceans, sponges, corals, star-fishes, crystal imitations of the most celebrated diamonds and of other precious stones, maps in relief of some of the volcanoes, and many other articles of great usefulness. The total number of tangible objects procured during the past

year is not far from seven hundred and fifty, and almost
every branch of natural history is represented in them. —
But, with all these additions, our collections are far from
being complete. They are mere nuclei. More are
absolutely needed. The changes which have been
gradually introduced into our methods of instruction
render their increase both in numbers and varieties
imperative; and it is earnestly hoped that the friends
of the blind will interest themselves in this matter, and
give their active co-operation in carrying it out.

A great part of the above-named articles were purchased from Dr. W. L. Schaufuss of Germany; and I
heartily avail myself of this opportunity to testify to the
reasonableness of his charges, and to the fairness and
honesty with which the business of his extensive establishment near Dresden, the Museum of Ludwig Salvator,
is conducted.

Library.

A good collection of well-chosen books is an important
adjunct to any school. It supplements the course of
instruction, and renders valuable assistance in carrying
on the work of education successfully. It is a sort of
intellectual gymnasium which helps to build up the
mental structure. It tends to create a literary atmosphere, and to encourage both teachers and pupils to
carry their researches and pursuits for information
beyond the limits of the text-books. In short, it really
is what the Greeks call it, "a sanatory of the soul," —
ψυχῆς ἰατρεῖον.

Although the necessity for obtaining various kinds of
apparatus was so great as to require immediate attention, the claims of the library have not been overlooked.

On the contrary, they have been promptly attended to, and the facilities for the widest possible diffusion of knowledge among the members of our school have been greatly increased.   The total number of volumes in our library is 4,590.   Of these, 294 in raised characters and 453 in ordinary print have been procured during the past year.   The latter are mostly either books of reference or standard works on history, philosophy, travel, and literature, both English and foreign.   All are substantially, and, to a very great extent, uniformly, bound.

As soon as the room appropriated for a library in the new building in the girls' department is finished, the books, as well as the rest of our collections, will be properly arranged, classified, numbered, and catalogued by the librarian, under whose charge they have been placed, and who is held responsible for their careful use and preservation.

KINDERGARTEN.

The system of Froebel, which has worked such widespread benefit in Germany, and is beginning to make its good influence felt in this country also, is in many of its departments admirably suited for the instruction of little blind children.   This system may be said to offer the A B C of objective teaching.   The industrial features of the plan, the weaving, block-building, and even the embroidery upon cardboard, have been taught to our younger pupils with excellent effect.   In fact, the whole system, with the exception of the part relating to colors, has been introduced into our school, and has proved exceedingly beneficial.   Of course the work accomplished has no intrinsic value ; but the manual

skill acquired is very considerable, and can be turned to
good account in more serious pursuits later. Every
thing which tends to strengthen in the minds of blind
children the conception of outward forms is of the
highest importance to them, and the kindergarten plan
contains elements which minister very largely to this
necessity. The simple modelling in clay, the rounding
of little balls, apples, dumb-bells, and the like, is extremely useful in developing the sense and perception of
shape, both in seeing and blind children. The mathematical faculty is quickened by the use and handling of
the cubes and other blocks, and the games and exercises
afford excellent physical training, besides promoting
pleasure and good spirits. In brief, the kindergarten
system is a most useful and beneficent factor in the education of children, since it trains the body at the same
time that it unfolds the mind, teaching them the use of
hand as well as brain, — a feature, the salutary effects
of which in after life are universally acknowledged.
This system is a great advance, in point of the genuine-
ness of the training which it imparts, even upon object-
teaching; since, while the latter strengthens the perceptive faculties, the former fosters also the growth of the
creative ones, to which the perceptive are but as servants or harbingers ploughing the mental soil for a
future harvest of activity. The introduction of the
kindergarten in our primary classes proves to be as
important an era in the development and progress of
education for the blind as it has in schools for the
seeing. It might only be wished that the means could
be provided for the establishment of a special department for sightless little children between the ages of

five and nine, who are now either suffering under the
rust of neglect in the corner of ill-ventilated kitchens or
other comfortless apartments, or living in such isolation
from the rest of the world as to not have any opportunity of becoming acquainted with any of their more
fortunate little fellow-creatures who can see and move
about and play.

Our kindergarten department is indirectly indebted
to the generosity of Mrs. Shaw, whose munificence in
providing means for spreading the system and making
happy hundreds of indigent children has been so widely
felt in this community, since the principal teacher, Mrs.
E. Bethmann, employed in the South-Boston district by
that beneficent lady, has kindly volunteered to assist us
in setting the little classes into working order, and to
give the necessary directions for their proper training.

Music Department.

"Music, soft charm of heaven and earth!
· Whence didst thou borrow thy auspicious birth?
Or art thou of eternal date,
Siro to thyself, thyself as old as fate?" — *Edmund Smith.*

The importance and necessary prominence of music
as a prime factor of the education of the blind has
too often been dwelt upon in these reports, and is too
widely known to need special amplification here.   It
is to them what Luther called it, "a shield in combat
and adversity, a friend and companion in moments of
joy, a comforter and refuge in the hours of despondency and solitude."   It is their guide to higher regions
of thought and activity long after they have ceased to
need the kind hand of friendship to lead them along

life's narrow paths.   By it they earn not only their
bread, but that mental nourishment, the need of which
is so much higher than that of mere material sustenance.   It is their passport into the realms of art,
and the key to noble and beautiful achievements.   Nor
is this all.   Higher than the mere sense of improvement
in ourselves, of accomplishment and achievement, is the
consciousness of usefulness to others, of being a helping
force in this busy world.   This gives the widest scope
to all the faculties, enabling them to grow and blossom
to the fullest and fairest extent, and from this blessing
the blind are far from being excluded.   Their usefulness as teachers in spreading a thorough knowledge
and a love of the study of music is generally acknowledged.

But, in order that they may be able to continue to
occupy an area of fertile soil in this field of usefulness,
and reap a rich harvest on it, they require something
more than mere mechanical attainments, or even
acknowledged proficiency in the art of music *per se.*
They need an enlightened intellect, a broad purpose,
and a strong will.   In other words, their professional
skill must be accompanied and sustained by a liberal
general culture.

The mental discipline which real education insures
is of inestimable advantage to those who intend following music as a profession.   It gives to them that
mental grasp, that grip, that firm hold of a subject,
that power of concentration, and that energy of purpose,
which are indispensable for success in the domain of
art.   The man of culture is accustomed to hard thinking, close reasoning, clear definition, and the tracing

out of subtle distinctions. He carries his habits of
mind into his work. His music will bear the unmistakable impress of his intellectual training. Unaided
genius is powerless, and sinks baffled if it cannot fall
back upon those mental qualities which only a thorough
education can bring to perfection. The great masters
of music were undoubtedly all men of genius; but
they were more than this. They were cultured men,
trained thinkers, logical reasoners, systematic workers.
Their works prove this beyond controversy.

In consideration of these facts, our system of education is so arranged that instruction in music, which is
one of its prime constituents, is blended in just proportion with the graces of a thorough mental culture,
and with the substantial advantages of a systematic
physical training. It is from the harmony of this broad
union, and not from the narrowness of any isolated and
one-sided attainments, that the blind may confidently
expect to derive the means and strength necessary to
their career.

The music department of the institution has received,
during the past year, all the attention which its importance requires, and its present condition is very creditable to those by whom its work is carried on.

The number of pupils who have enjoyed the advantages of this department during the last twelve months
was eighty-two. Of these, seventy received instruction
on the piano-forte, thirty-two in harmony, two in counterpoint and composition, five on the organ, four on the
flute, five on the clarinet, five on the cornet, thirteen
on other brass instruments, fifty-seven belonged to the
singing-classes, and thirty-four took lessons in vocal
music separately.

An exact record of the standing of each individual
case, carefully kept by the teachers, shows the progress
of the pupils to have been very satisfactory. Those
among them who are endowed with special talent, and
who possess such general mental ability as is essential
for the attainment of excellence in any art, advance
rapidly.   But there are some who prove, after a patient
and fair trial, utterly devoid of natural aptitude for
music.   These are required to discontinue their music
lessons, and to devote their time out of school-hours to
the acquisition of some useful trade, or to some other
manual occupation.

Two of the scholars who graduated from the music
department at the close of the last term — Joseph R.
Lucier of Worcester, and William H. Wade of Lawrence — were specially gifted, and manifested great perseverance and application in the pursuit of their studies.
The former, while possessing a fair knowledge of
several branches of music, such as the piano-forte,
harmony, and singing, takes rank among the best
cornet soloists, and will, no doubt, earn a good living by
playing and teaching this instrument. The latter has
devoted his time principally to the organ and piano-
forte. His part in the music of the graduating exercises was the great fugue in G minor by Bach, and
number two of Liszt's rhapsodies, both of which were
executed with brilliancy and good taste.   Ordinarily
young men of Wade's attainments would enter upon
their professional career, and commence teaching; but
he is preparing to go to Germany for the purpose of
continuing his studies for several years.

During the past year three new piano-fortes have

been added to our collection of musical instruments, and all the old ones have been kept in good working order.

The pupils are generally provided with sufficient means for regular practice, as well as with ample opportunities for a thorough drill in the principles upon which the science of music rests. This is a very essential part of their professional training. The grammar of music affords an invaluable aid in the acquisition of the power of interpreting the master-pieces of art correctly and intelligibly. Mechanical skill kept up by incessant labor is good as far as it goes, but a clear comprehension of the science of music enhances its value incalculably.

Music makes large claims upon its devotees, and no one can succeed in it without patient submission to a discipline which is far from being attractive or enter-taining. Most of our pupils show a keen appreciation of the uncommon facilities afforded by the institution for a thorough study of this art, and many among them endeavor by steady application and unflagging industry to turn them to the greatest possible advantage. Praise and honor belong to all who succeed in surmounting the obstacles which they find in the way, and reaching the regions of independence and usefulness; but those who have to scale the height of Helicon with hard labor and measured step deserve more admiration than those who fly to its lofty summits on the wings of natural talent. As Pope expresses it, —

> " Though the same sun, with all-diffusive rays,
> Blush in the rose and in the diamond blaze,
> We prize the stronger effort of his power,
> And justly set the gem above the flower."

But however extensive may be the internal advantages afforded by the institution for the purpose of making thorough musicians and good teachers of those of its beneficiaries who possess the requisite talent and ability, they cannot be entirely complete by themselves. External opportunities for the cultivation and refinement of the musical taste are indispensable. To enable the pupils to become suitably familiar with the larger works of the classical school, and to learn to appreciate and enjoy such noble compositions as Bach's fugues, Händel's oratorios, Haydn's symphonies, Beethoven's sonatas, Chopin's Polonaises, and Liszt's rhapsodies, is not a simple matter, nor is it so easy a task as to be accomplished in the teaching or practising room. Aside from a full development of the musical sensibility and of the intellectual powers, is required that æsthetic culture, which can be derived solely from constant attendance upon concerts and other musical performances, in which the works of the greater and lesser masters are interpreted by eminent artists. Thanks to the officers and members of the best musical societies of Boston, to the proprietors of theatres, the managers of public entertainments, and also to a long chain of eminent musicians in our city, — the names of all of whom will be hereafter mentioned in the list of acknowledgments, — our scholars have continued to be generously permitted to attend the finest concerts, rehearsals, operas, oratorios, and the like, and have also been favored with many brilliant, artistic performances given in our hall. There is often a great deal of latent musical ability in young people, and opportunities like these serve as the touchstone which occasionally brings a hidden talent to the surface.

Tuning Department.

This department continues to perform its important part in the work of training our pupils for their share in the remunerative employments of life; and the uncommon advantages offered here for a thorough study of the art of tuning, both in theory and practice, have not suffered the least relaxation during the past year. On the contrary, pains have been taken to improve them still further, and to render them as efficient as possible, and productive of the highest good to the blind of New England.

Eight pupils have graduated from the tuning department during the past year, and four have been added to the ranks of those who are receiving instruction in it. Most of those whose connection with the school ceased at the close of the last term were well qualified to enter the practical walks of life with hope and courage; for in the thoroughness and efficiency of their training they have the elements, as well as the promise, of good success.

It is very pleasant to be able to report that the work of our tuners has continued to give entire satisfaction to our customers; and the steady increase of patronage which has been extended to them by some of the most intelligent families of Boston and the neighboring towns indicates that the popular prejudice against the ability and skill of the blind to take good care of musical instruments and keep them in excellent working condition is slowly but surely dying away.

That our pupils, receiving such thorough training as they do in this institution, become efficient tuners of piano-fortes, and that their infirmity is no obstacle whatever to them in the exercise of their profession, has been repeatedly stated in these reports, and can be easily shown by a brief explanation of the nature of their art.

A tuner of piano-fortes has nothing to do with the form, the color, or the carvings of the legs of an instrument. His work is principally and mainly confined to the regulation of the musical tones produced by it. These sounds belong exclusively to the domain of hearing, and not to that of sight, or of any other sense. Tones are the concomitants in the stimulation of those fibres which have their terminals in the cochlea of the ear. They are excited by the regular and periodic vibrations of certain definite frequencies. Some of the fibres vibrate in sympathy with the undulations of slow periods, and others with those of rapid ones. The former produce low, and the latter high, tones. The pitch, therefore, depends upon the particular fibre of the cochlea which has been affected.

It is evident from this brief explanation that it is not mechanics which have full sway, or even play an important part in the art of tuning, but the cultivation of the sense of hearing, coupled with the science of acoustics, — that branch of physics which treats of the nature of sound and the laws of its production and propagation.

Now the blind, in consequence of their infirmity, begin early to concentrate their attention upon the impressions received through the auditory nerves. They constantly employ the ear for various purposes for which seeing persons use the eyes, and they let it rest only when they are asleep. While in the institution they live and move in an atmosphere which resounds with musical tones. By this incessant exercise their sense of hearing becomes so improved, and acquires such an acuteness and nicety, that the relations of sounds, imperceptible to ordinary listeners, are apparent to them. In addition to this, a thorough study of physics constitutes an integral part of our system of instruction. Hence, all other things being equal, a sightless person, whose power and accuracy in distinguishing the pitch and quality of sounds is truly astonishing, makes a better tuner of piano-fortes than a seeing one.

This assertion does not rest upon mere *a priori* reasoning. It has been clearly demonstrated by an array of facts gathered from the field of experience and practice, and it is firmly sustained by the verdict of distinguished artists and prominent music-teachers, who have had an opportunity of obtaining a personal knowledge of the work of our tuners, and by the readiness with which the wise and intelligent of the community employ them. In addition to the many previously published testimonials bearing upon this matter, there are three of a recent date, — one from the committee on supplies of the school board of the city of Boston, one from the world-renowned firm of Messrs. Steinway & Sons of New York, and a third from Messrs. William Bourne & Son, manufacturers of piano-fortes in this city.

The work of our tuners in taking care of the piano-fortes used in the public schools of Boston, and keeping them in good repair, has been so well and conscientiously done that the contract was again renewed for another year; and the committee on supplies have touched upon the subject in their last annual report, in the following words : —

" The tuning of pianos in the public schools has been performed in a very satisfactory manner during the last three years by the Perkins Institution for the Blind ; and a new contract for one year, from May 1, 1880, has been made with that institution, on the same terms as for preceding years."

This statement, together with the fact that the renewal of the contract was made with uncommon unanimity and promptness, does great honor to the sense of justice and fairness of the members of the school board, and is very gratifying to our tuners.

Messrs. Steinway & Sons have for a long time employed a blind man as head-tuner of their great establishment in New York ; and, in reply to a letter which I addressed to them, asking for information with regard to his success, they speak as follows : —

NEW YORK, Jan. 9, 1880.

M. ANAGNOS, Esq.

Dear Sir, — In answer to your letter of the 29th ult., we desire to inform you that one of our principal tuners is a blind man named Armin Schotte.

This gentleman tunes the concert grand pianos for the concerts at Steinway Hall, &c., which work is considered the highest achievement in the art of tuning. Mr. Schotte's tuning is simply perfect, not only for its purity, but in his skill of so setting the tuning-pins that the piano can endure the largest amount of heavy playing without being put out of tune.

Very respectfully yours,

STEINWAY & SONS.

Messrs. William Bourne & Son of Boston have also employed one of the graduates of this institution, Mr. Joseph H. Wood, as principal tuner for seventeen years; and their views on his work and on the fitness of the blind in general to deal with musical instruments are embodied in the following letter: —

Boston, Sept. 27, 1880.

Dear Sir, — We would say in reply to your letter of the 25th inst., that Mr. Joseph H. Wood has been in our employ as principal tuner since the year 1863. It gives us the greatest pleasure to take this opportunity of testifying to the efficient and excellent service rendered by him to our establishment, and to say that his able and skilful workmanship has always been much prized by us. We see no reason why blindness should be a drawback in the tuner's profession. On the contrary, we have been convinced by long observation that persons deprived of sight succeed remarkably well in this calling. Their ear is much more delicate than that of ordinary tuners, and the objection made by some people that they corrode the strings by handling them is wholly unfounded. We never knew Mr. Wood to touch the strings while he was tuning a piano. Many years of experience in the business of manufacturing piano-fortes has shown us that the judgment of the blind in selecting these instruments for the trade is of the first order.

This is our candid opinion on Mr. Wood's work, and on the efficiency and ability of the blind as tuners. If it can be of any service in the promotion of their cause, you are at liberty to use it in any way that you may see fit.

Yours truly,

WILLIAM BOURNE & SON.

Mr. M. Anagnos,
  Director Perkins Institution for the Blind, South Boston, Mass.

These testimonials speak sufficiently for themselves. They need no comments; but they compel the utterance of an earnest hope that the noble example of the above two firms may soon be followed by other piano-makers of high standing and 'influence, and that the reasonable claims of our tuners to a fair share of work may be favored with more justice and less prejudice in the future than they have received heretofore.

' One of the essays which were included in the programme of our closing exercises treated in a simple and clear manner of sound, of the construction of the piano-forte, and of the carefulness of instruction necessary to qualify a tuner of this instrument. This paper was written by a member of the graduating class, George G. Goldthwait of Lynn, who has devoted a large part of his time to the tuning department; and, as it gives a fairer illustration of the thoroughness and comprehensiveness of the training of our scholars than any words of mine can convey, I copy it herewith *in toto:* —

"THE PIANO-FORTE AND PIANO-FORTE TUNING.

" The five senses possessed by man enable him to perceive whatever passes around him, and not the least in value is that knowledge received through the sense of hearing.

" According to the theory now universally accepted, sound is produced by vibrations. If these vibrations exceed 38,000 per second, consciousness of sound ceases because the ear is not capable of receiving impressions beyond that limit.

" Musical sounds are produced by vibrations succeeding each other at regular intervals. The lowest tone is produced by sixteen vibrations in a second. The highest tone which the ear is capable of receiving is the result of six thousand vibrations in the same time. This range embraces about eight octaves.

" By the aid of music man expresses his thoughts and emotions more clearly, sometimes, than by language. Music comforts the oppressed, strengthens the weary, cheers the sorrowing, nerves the soldier on to battle and to victory, and gives expression to the loftiest aspirations of the soul. Should it not then be cherished and cultivated to its fullest extent?

"Instruments for the production of music may be classed under two general heads, wind and stringed instruments. Your attention is called to a representative of the latter class.

"Instrumental music was attempted at an early date. We read of David's harp and the shepherd's flute; but long before that time, back in geologic ages, we find rude bone flutes among the relics left behind the tertiary man. The harp is formed of a sounding-board, lengthwise of which are passed stretched strings. These strings differ in length according to the degree of pitch to be attained by each note. The strings are attached at either end, and the tension is changed at pleasure. In other words, it is tuned by means of screws or pegs. Upon the principle involved in the construction of the harp is built our modern piano-forte. The immediate forerunners of the piano were the clarichord and the harpsichord, founded upon the principle of the harp, with this difference, — the strings, instead of being picked by the fingers, were plucked by metallic quills, which were forced against them by jacks that were raised by pressing down keys. The sounds thus produced were metallic, and not altogether agreeable as musical tones. To obviate this difficulty, the hammers were made of wood, and covered with some soft material. The tones produced when the wires were struck by such hammers were more agreeable. Since that time innumerable improvements have been made, resulting in the modern piano.

"The invention of the piano-forte is claimed by Italy, France, Germany, and England. There is good reason to believe that Bartolommeo Christophori, a native of Padua, was the inventor of an instrument which he called piano-forte, because he could play both *piano* (or softly) and *forte* (or loud) upon it. At the present day these instruments are made in three distinct forms, — square, grand, and upright. In the first two the strings lie in a horizontal position; in the latter they run either in an oblique or perpendicular direction.

"In England the favorite instrument is the upright, in Germany the grand takes the lead, while on this side of the water the square has, until lately, been the most popular.

"In 1822 Jonas Chickering, the founder of the present house of Chickering & Sons, manufactured, in Boston, his first piano. Soon after this time two very important improvements, which gave a great impulse to the manufacture of these instruments in America, were introduced. These improvements were the invention of the iron frame and the introduction of the over-strung scale. Alpheus Babcock, in 1825, received the first patent on the iron frame, and in 1837 Chickering used the first frame with cross-bars cast entire.

"In 1856 the house of Steinway & Sons commenced the manufacture of grand pianos on the European plan, with this improvement however, — they introduced the iron plate. Subsequently they made many improvements, and to-day their instruments are celebrated for superior quality and volume of tone, and capacity of standing in tune.

"The materials for the construction of the piano should be of the best quality. Porous wood, having a strong fibre and resonant qualities, is best adapted for the sound-board. The strings should be of the best steel to withstand the tension brought upon them. It requires a tension of two hundred pounds to raise the highest note on a seven-octave piano to the required pitch, and the combined strain upon a full concert grand is about twelve tons. The pitch of a note depends upon the length of the string. The lowest notes upon a piano would require a string sixteen feet long. To prevent this inconvenient length in the instrument the strings producing the lower notes are shortened, and wound with soft wire to retard the vibrations.

"The lowest notes upon a piano vibrate about twenty-seven times, and the highest notes four thousand times, in a second, giving a range of seven and one-third octaves. The rate of vibration of a musical tone is ascertained from a knowledge of the number of vibrations of any note of the scale; for example, the middle C on the piano vibrates two hundred and fifty-six times per second, which number, divided by $\frac{8}{9}$, the fraction of D in the inverse ratio, will give the number of vibrations for D; or, in

other words, taking C as a standard, and dividing it by the
inverse ratio of the fraction of the vibrations, which we know,
we obtain the number of vibrations for any note.

"Difficulty arises in tuning from the fact that the whole tones
in the scale differ in size. The larger intervals are called major
whole tones; the smaller, minor whole tones. This difference
in the size of intervals renders it impossible to tune perfect intervals in all the scales; for, if this were done, a part of them
would be so imperfect, that the chords would be offensive to the
ear. Therefore, to make the scales equally agreeable, it is necessary to temper them, or divide these inequalities in different
intervals equally between all the twelve keys. To secure this
result it is necessary to flatten all the fifths and sharpen the
fourths. The only perfect interval on the piano is the octave.

"We have tried to give a brief sketch of the fundamental
principles embodied in the production of music from stringed
instruments as it has been developed and perfected in the piano-
forte, the natural outgrowth of all other stringed instruments,
and, at present, the favorite.

"Its construction, care, and use afford occupation to a large
number of manufacturers, tuners, and musicians. Very important
among these is the tuner, although, perhaps, he receives the smallest share of credit.

"He necessarily precedes the pianist, not before an appreciative
audience, for the necessities of the case are such that he demands
a private interview with the instrument.

"If the piano-forte is the most popular instrument, and the demand for it is steadily increasing, then the work of the tuner grows
in importance. The yearly increasing number of musicians and
critics render it necessary that the tuner be educated and skilled in
his profession; and the required degree of skill can only be acquired by careful study and constant practice, for, to become a
tuner of any note, years are required to cultivate the ear to distinguish readily and accurately imperfect unisons and intervals: nor
is this all; the hand and wrist must be trained to control the hammer in such a manner as to secure the solidity and permanency of
the work, this being of the first importance, as upon it rests the
value of piano-forte tuning."

Among the legions of seeing tuners who are scattered all over the country there are no doubt some who may have as good a knowledge of the philosophy of their art as the writer of the above essay seems to possess; but I venture to say that their number is not very large.

TECHNICAL DEPARTMENT.

A well-organized and properly conducted workshop, where the pupils of an institution can repair daily at fixed hours and be employed in acquiring skill and facility in the practice of the mechanic arts, is an important branch of a complete system of education. It is of great benefit to young persons in more ways than one. It furnishes them with occupation out of school-hours, and provides the mental faculties with a gentle stimulus, while it prevents the morbid action of the brain, which too much study is apt to produce in children. It rouses the senses to activity, and trains the hands to dexterity and the muscles to agility, so that they may respond immediately to the commands of the will. It induces confidence in the use of the bodily powers, and independence of character. Finally, it offers to a large number opportunities for the profitable employment of their time, and for self-support.

It has been the policy of this institution since the date of its foundation to pay particular attention to the industrial training of the blind. One of the two instructors whom Dr. Howe engaged in Europe in 1831 was a master of handicraft. The so-called "developing school," which has been of late years claimed as a new discovery, has been in operation here for nearly half a century, and its main features form a very essen-

tial part of our system of education. Thus, while our
pupils are acquiring such knowledge as will fit them to
be enlightened members of the community, it is deemed
absolutely necessary that they should also learn a trade
or become familiar with some branch of manual labor
which shall prepare them for usefulness and self-reliance in after life.

To compass this end, a commodious shop for the boys
and suitable workrooms for the girls are provided, the
services of skilful and efficient teachers are secured,
and all the requisite machines, tools, appliances, and
materials are furnished.

I. — Workshop for the Boys.

The affairs of this department have been managed
with discretion and sound judgment, and its present
state is very satisfactory.

The usual trades of manufacturing brooms, seating
cane-bottomed chairs, upholstering parlor furniture, and
making mattresses, have been regularly and systematically taught, and the pupils have been diligently trained
to work steadily, and to acquire an ease and skill in the
use of their hands which will be a practical help to
them at every step of their lives.

During the past year, as in previous ones, this workshop has been carried on at a comparatively moderate
expense. It was never designed as a source of income
to the institution, and never will be. All that can be
reasonably expected is, that the avails of the labor of
the learners should pay the cost of materials. The
advantages are looked for in the acquisition of manual
dexterity and mechanical aptitude, and still more in the

feeling of independence and habits of industry, regularity, and economy, on which depend in so large a measure the usefulness and happiness of man in society. It is a great pleasure to be able to state that in many cases these expectations are more than fully realized.

II. — *Workrooms for the Girls.*

The girls' branch of the technical department has been conducted with great ability and efficiency, and is making excellent progress in the direction both of useful and ornamental work.

New and graceful patterns are constantly introduced and skilfully executed, and the articles made by the girls are no less serviceable than beautiful.

There is ample room in the devising of various shapes and designs for the exercise of the inventive faculty by the scholars ; and they generally have something new in hand, which is a source of interest and delight to them, and often of profit as well.

The table, which is spread with the handiwork of the pupils at the weekly exhibitions, is always an attraction to visitors, and the little manufacturers are much pleased when their wares bring them in a small profit. This encourages them to fresh exertions in the same line ; and the result is that many of the girls leave us quite accomplished in sewing and knitting, both by hand and machine, in crocheting, and in making a great variety of articles of fancy, worsted, and bead work.

The exhibit sent from this department to the Melbourne International Exposition last summer was the finest and most tasteful which has yet been gotten up here, and did great credit to the pupils and to their teacher.

11

The quarters appropriated for workrooms in the new building are extensive and commodious, and the girls are rejoicing in the prospect of more scope and greater conveniences than they have heretofore enjoyed.

The art of making fancy baskets was taught during a portion of the past year by an Indian woman, who resided in the establishment for that purpose, with great success, and it will again be resumed during the present year.

Manual Occupations of the Blind in Ontario.

The circle of industrial employments for the blind is already very much contracted by the invention of machinery; and the problem of "how to enable the great mass of our pupils to earn their living by the work of their hands," instead of approaching solution, becomes more and more complicated year by year. There are but few articles made by hand without the guidance of sight which can be profitably disposed of, and we must seek for new fields of industry for our graduates.

In compliance with a vote of your board, I have visited the Ontario Institution for the Blind at Brantford for the purpose of examining its industrial department and obtaining a clear idea of its workings. I was cordially received by Mr. Hunter, the principal, and his teachers, and promptly assisted in all my investigations. I found, on careful inspection of the workrooms, that the rule of the thumb was truly in the ascendency there, but not to the detriment of the literary and musical departments. The pupils of both sexes are well trained in handicraft, and some of them are experts in

their trades.   Willow-work, and knitting and sewing by
hand and machine, are the principal manual occupations.
During the past year the boys have manufactured a
large number of baskets of various kinds, shapes, colors,
and sizes; and the girls have knit four thousand one
hundred pairs of socks by machine, and one thousand
and fifty of mittens by hand, for sale, besides *cutting* and
making about fifty-three underwaists and dresses for
their own use.   There is no other institution for the
blind on this continent with which I am acquainted that
can show equal results with regard to the handicraft of
its female apprentices.   All the wares made by the
pupils are readily disposed of to advantage.   The baskets are sold in open market, without sharp competition,
at good prices; and the stockings and mittens are purchased by order of the government of Ontario for the
use of the inmates of the eleëmosynary and penal institutions of the province.   Thus the industrial activity of
the scholars is stimulated by the wise policy of the government and by other circumstances peculiar to the location of the school at Brantford, and is promoted by such
prudent and systematic arrangements that it does not
interfere in the least with the work of the other departments of the establishment, which are in a thriving
condition.   The management of the institution is not
only efficient, but decidedly progressive.   It is successful
in every respect; for it is intrusted to the hands of a gentleman who combines in himself two excellent qualities
which are rarely found together, — that of broad and
thorough scholarship with uncommon executive ability
enhanced by truthfulness and strict honesty.   Mr. Hunter is, moreover, gifted with considerable mechanical

ingenuity; and the invention of a new tablet for point-writing, far superior to those previously in existence, is not the least important among his contrivances.

DEPARTMENT OF PHYSICAL TRAINING.

The necessity of physical culture as the basis for the higher departments of education has been so fully demonstrated in previous reports, and is so generally acknowledged by thoughtful men everywhere, that I hardly need devote to it more than a few passing remarks here.

The body and mind are twin sisters, co-ordinate companions. Their functions are interwoven in such a manner that they may be considered as the two well-fitting halves of a perfect whole, designed in true accord to sustain and support each other mutually. So close and intimate is their relation that the mind can no more reach the height of intellectual and moral excellence when enshrined in an enervated and weak frame than a bird can soar through the mid-heavens without the full strength of its wings. There is no error more profound or more prolific of evil consequences than that which views the mental and bodily powers as antithetic and opposed to each other. The truth is precisely the reverse of this. The welfare and efficiency of the one are greatly promoted by the soundness of the other. Their union constitutes one of the laws of nature which never can be broken with impunity. Hence, intellectual and physical culture must advance hand in hand; for, if permitted to go apart, either will stray from its appropriate sphere, and the result will be feebleness, decline, and premature decay.

In the education of children the fact must always be
kept in view that it is not a mind or a body that we
are training up, — it is a man, and that we ought not to
divide him; or, as Plato says, we are not to fashion one
without the other, but make them draw together like
two horses harnessed to a coach. Every attempt to
cultivate the intellect without its co-ordinate power,
the body, will end in an ignoble failure or a miserable
defeat. But, when the two parts are made to act in
unison and harmony, any thing within the limits of
possibility may be accomplished.

It is therefore obvious that every well-organized system of education should provide its participants with
adequate and efficient means for regular and uniform
physical training, which shall call forth and cultivate
the latent powers and capacities of the body, and aid
the full development and expansion of its various parts
and organs.

But, if physical culture is so great a factor in the
education of ordinary children, in that of the blind,
whose infirmity is unquestionably a positive hinderance
to the free and uninterrupted exercise of the muscular
system, and very seriously affects the development of the
bodily powers, it is demanded with tenfold force. No
school established for their benefit can be complete or
do its work properly without making ample provision
for training of this nature. Force of character, strength
of will, mental vigor, clearness of views and ideas,
activity, energy, dexterity, tenacity, and endurance constitute the secret of success in every undertaking, and
are indispensable qualities for all youth who are about
to enter on the career of practical life. It is a well-

established fact that not a few among the blind are more or less wanting in these requirements, and they must attain them by proper training before they can reasonably aspire to great achievements in their intellectual and professional pursuits.

Physical culture has been followed systematically and persistently in our school during the past year, and has assumed a position commensurate with its importance.

The gymnasium has been supplied with the necessary apparatus ; and the pupils, divided into five classes, have repaired there regularly at fixed hours, and have gone through such a series of systematic and progressive exercises as were calculated to strengthen every part of the physical frame, and to cause the blood, which, owing. to close application to study, is apt to crowd towards the brain and produce languor and stupor, to leap through the veins. Muscular development is thus promoted, the respiration and circulation are quickened, and the whole system is toned up. Grace and beauty are imparted to the person, and ease to the manner ; and at the same time a pleasing recreative occupation is afforded to the mind.

The exercises have been carefully selected and wisely conducted by competent teachers ; and their effect upon the appearance, health, and strength of the pupils, has been quite remarkable. The pale countenances, nerveless looks, puny forms, drooping heads, want of elasticity and facility in the movements, tendency to spinal curvature, flat and narrow chests, slouching shoulders, haggard cheeks, — these and all other imperfections which are generally noticed in almost every school for the blind, and which are indications of stunted growth and muscular flabbiness, have slowly but steadily diminished, if not altogether disappeared, from among our pupils, giving place to comely figures, fresh complexions, a resolute bearing, buoyant spirits, and a fair share of nerve-power and agility. In fact, life itself seems to spread before them like a fair field, of which every acre is their own.

Military drill, which has been introduced into our gymnasium during the past year, and carried on in accordance with the rules of tactics, has proved an invaluable adjunct to our course of exercises, and has already conferred a great and lasting benefit upon our young men. It has helped to promote an erect carriage and neatness of appearance, and to foster habits of promptness, exactness, and unanimity in action. It has enabled them to acquire a manly gait and a better command of their muscles. Lastly, it has taught them self-control, and has given them correct ideas of order, discipline, and subordination.

Thanks to the cordial co-operation of the officers of the institution, and most especially to the endeavors of those of the teachers who have entered into the work of the gymnasium with genuine enthusiasm and unabating faith in its beneficent effects, this important department of our system of education has been made a success, and a great amount of good has already been and is being accomplished in it. The current which has so auspiciously begun to flow in this direction will run stronger and deeper until every child in the institution shall reach the highest point of physical amelioration which lies within the possibilities of his constitution and organization.

Concluding Remarks.

In bringing this report to a close, I beg leave, gentlemen, to bespeak your forbearance for its numerous short-comings, and most especially for the crudeness which is apparent in the treatment of some of its topics. The time allotted for writing it has been so crowded with business and cares, that it has been impossible for me to bestow upon its preparation the attention requisite for putting it into a better form.

It is with no small degree of satisfaction that I avail myself again of this opportunity to express my unqualified approbation of the valuable services of the matron and of all the officers and teachers with whom I am associated in the management of the institution. Each and all of them have performed their duties faithfully and efficiently, have spared no efforts in promoting the best interests of the pupils, and have labored with zeal, perseverance, and cheerfulness, for the attainment of the highest results.

To you, gentlemen of the board, I would offer my warmest thanks for the readiness and promptness with which you have responded to every claim upon your time and attention, for the great interest you have invariably manifested in all movements concerning the welfare of the blind, and for the uniform kindness and courtesy with which you have received and considered my suggestions.

Respectfully submitted by

M. ANAGNOS.

ACKNOWLEDGMENTS.

AMONG the pleasant duties incident to the close of the year is that of expressing our heartfelt thanks and grateful acknowledgments to the following artists, *littérateurs*, societies, proprietors, managers, editors, and publishers, for concerts and various musical entertainments, for operas, oratorios, lectures, readings, and for an excellent supply of periodicals and weekly papers, minerals, and specimens of various kinds.

As I have said in previous reports, these favors are not only a source of pleasure and happiness to our pupils, but also a valuable means of æsthetic culture, of social intercourse, and of mental stimulus and improvement. As far as we know, there is no community in the world which does half so much for the gratification and improvement of its unfortunate members as that of Boston does for our pupils.

I. — Acknowledgments for Concerts and Operas in the City.

To the Harvard Musical Association, through its president, Mr. ·John S. Dwight, for fifty season-tickets to eight symphony concerts. The blind of New England are under great and lasting obligations to this association for the uncommon musical advantages which it has always extended to them in the most liberal and friendly manner since the inauguration of its concerts.

To Messrs. Tompkins & Hill, proprietors of the Boston Theatre, for admitting parties in unlimited numbers to six operas.

To Mr. John Stetson of the Globe Theatre, for admission to one opera ; and to Mr. Thomas, to one children's operetta in Horticultural Hall.

To the Händel and Haydn Society, through its president, Mr. C. C. Perkins, and its secretary, Mr. A. Parker Browne, for tickets to one oratorio and five rehearsals.

12

To Mr. C. C. Perkins, for tickets to five of the Euterpe concerts.

To the Boylston Club, through its secretary, Mr. F. H. Ratcliffe, for admission to four of its concerts.

To the Apollo Club, through the kindness of its secretary, Mr. Arthur Reed, for tickets to six concerts ; and to the Cecilia Club, through the same gentleman, for an invitation to four concerts.

To the following distinguished artists we are under great obligations for admitting our pupils to their classical chamber-concerts : Mr. B. J. Lang, Mr. Ernst Perabo, Mr. H. G. Tucker, Mr. Henry Hanchett, Mr. Arthur Foote, Mr. John A. Preston, Madame Frohock, and Madame Cappiani. Mrs. S. W. Farwell of Boston generously sent to the pupils twenty-five tickets to one of Mr. Perabo's concerts.

For popular concerts we are indebted to Mrs. Manley Howe, Dr. L. B. Fenderson, Mr. Charles Poole, Mr. B. W. Williams, and Mr. H. C. Brown.

II. — Acknowledgments for Concerts given in our Hall.

For a series of fine concerts given from time to time in the hall of the institution we are greatly indebted to the following artists : —

To the Polish violinist, Mr. Timothée Adamowski, assisted by Mr. C. L. Capen, Mrs. H. T. Spooner, Miss Sarah Winslow, Miss Teresa Carreno Campbell, and Miss Mary M. Campbell.

To Mr. and Mrs. Ole Bull.

To Mr. W. H. Sherwood, assisted by Mrs. Sherwood and Mr. Alfred Wilkie.

To Mr. W. H. Sherwood a second time, assisted by Mr. Whiting and Miss Emma Howe.

To Mr. John Orth, assisted by Mr. Dunnreuter, Mrs. Knowles, and Madame Dietrich Strong.

To Miss Teresa Carreno Campbell, violinist, and Miss Mary M. Campbell, pianist.

To Miss Mary Underwood, assisted by Miss Ella Abbott, Miss Laura Underwood, Miss Josephine Ware, and Miss Alice Vars.

To Mrs. Kate Remetti, assisted by her friends, for two concerts.

To Mr. Eugene Thayer, for a series of classical organ recitals, assisted by his chorus, Miss Marion Osgood, violinist, and some of his best organ pupils.

III. — Acknowledgments for Lectures and Readings.

For a series of lectures and readings our thanks are due to the following kind friends: Mrs. Julia Ward Howe, Miss Lutie M. Marsh, Miss Helen Harding, Professor J. H. Dickson, Miss Florence Bachelder, Miss F. S. Sayles, Miss Emily Esterbrook, Mrs. Fred Flanders, Miss Mary Washburn, Miss Alice Barnicoat, and Mr. Frank Pope.

IV. — Acknowledgments for Minerals, Specimens, Tangible Objects, &c.

For a collection of minerals, specimens, and tangible objects of various kinds, we are greatly indebted to the following persons: Gen. John Eaton, Commissioner of Education, Gen. William G. LeDuc, Commissioner of Agriculture, Mr. William Reed, Mr. James E. Mills, Miss M. C. Moulton, Mrs. V. B. Turner, Miss Sophia Ann Wolfe, and Miss Mamie Mayer.

We are also under great obligation to Mr. G. W. Eddy, manager of the Twombly Knitting Machine Co., for the gift of one of their machines; and to our good friend, Rev. Photius Fisk, for a great abundance of various kinds of fruit.

V. — Acknowledgments for Periodicals and Newspapers.

The editors and publishers of the following reviews, magazines, and semi-monthly and weekly papers, continue to be very kind and liberal in sending us their publications gratuitously, which are always cordially welcomed, and perused with interest: —

The N. E. Journal of Education	Boston, Mass.
The Atlantic	" "
Boston Home Journal	.. ..
N. E. Medical Gazette	
The Christian	
The Christian Register	.. ..
The Musical Record	.. ..
The Musical Herald	.. ..
The Folio	..

The Sunday Herald . . . . *Boston, Mass.*
Littell's Living Age . . . . " "
Unitarian Review . . . . .
The Watchman . . . . .
The Congregationalist . . . .
The Golden Rule . . . . .
Wide Awake . . . . . "
The Salem Register . . . . *Salem,* "
Scribner's Monthly . . . . *New York, N. Y.*
St. Nicholas . . . . . " "
The Christian Union . . .
National Quarterly Review . .
The Journal of Speculative Philosophy "
Journal of Health . . . . *Dansville,* "
Lippincott's Magazine . . *Philadelphia, Penn.*
The Penn Monthly . . . . " "
Weekly Notes . . . . " "
Church's Musical Journal . . *Cincinnati, Ohio.*
Our Reporter . . . . . *Concord, Mich.*
The Bystander . . . . *Toronto, Canada.*
Hours of Recreation . . . *Chicago, Ill.*
Goodson's Gazette, *Va. Inst. for Deaf-Mutes and Blind.*
Tablet . . *West Va.* " " " "
Mirror . . *Michigan* " "
Companion . *Minnesota* " " " "
Mute Ranger . *Texas Inst. for the Deaf and Dumb.*
Mistletoe . . . . *Iowa Inst. for the Blind.*
Il Mentore dei Ciechi . . . *Florence, Italy.*

I desire again to render the most hearty thanks, in behalf of all our pupils, to the kind friends who have thus nobly remembered them. The seeds which their friendly and generous attentions have sown have fallen on no barren ground, but will continue to bear fruit in after years; and the memory of many of these delightful and instructive occasions and valuable gifts will be retained through life.

M. ANAGNOS.

Dr.   PERKINS INSTITUTION AND MASSACHUSETTS SCHOOL FOR THE BLIND in *Account with* P. T. JACKSON, *Treasurer.*   Cr.

Dr.			Cr.		
To cash paid, Auditors' drafts, Nos. 153 to 172,	$72,787 86		By balance from last year's account, Sept. 30, 1879		$579 21
city of Boston, taxes	146 25		cash from State of Massachusetts		30,000 00
repairs on houses	531 50		Maine		7,125 00
rent of box at Safe Deposit Vaults	20 00		Connecticut		3,300 00
check-book	5 75		Rhode Island		3,150 00
		$73,491 36	Vermont		1,925 00
			Interest on mortgages		6,385 57
			rents collected		648 57
			Boston and Providence Railroad dividends		225 00
Re-investments in			Fitchburg Railroad dividends		135 00
Loans secured by mortgages on real estate	$19,000 00		Eastern Railroad bonds interest		90 00
Balance to new account	2,227 43		interest on deposits		230 08
			interest United States bonds		50 00
			interest Boston and Lowell Railroad bonds		150 00
			M. Anagnos, Director, —		
			Work Department	$13,943 07	
			Sundries	5,722 51	
					19,665 58
			By cash legacy from William Taylor		891 30
			William Munroe		100 00
			gift from Henry B. Rogers for permanent printing fund,		1,000 00
			United States bonds sold,	$5,090 62	
			Boston and Lowell Railroad bonds sold,	9,061 34	
			Eastern Railroad bonds sold	4,966 50	
				$19,118 46	
			Less commission and interest	49 41	
					19,069 05
		$94,718 79			$94,718 79
1880. Sept. 30,			Balance to new account .		2,227 43

BOSTON, Sept. 30, 1880.   E. & O. E.   P. T. JACKSON, *Treasurer.*

The undersigned, a committee appointed to examine the accounts of the Treasurer of the Perkins Institution and Massachusetts School for the Blind, for the year ending Sept. 30, 1880, have attended to that duty, and hereby testify that they find the payments properly vouched, and the accounts correctly cast, resulting in a balance of twenty-two hundred and twenty-seven dollars and forty-three cents on hand, deposited at the New England Trust Company to the credit of the Institution.
The Treasurer also exhibited to us evidence of the following property belonging to the Institution : —

Notes secured by mortgages on real estate	$115,000 00	Bond of Eastern Railroad, par value $4,000 at 4½ per cent	$4,000 00
Estate No. 11 Oxford street, city valuation	5,500 00	30 shares Boston and Providence Railroad, par value at $140	4,200 00
No. 144 Prince street, city valuation	3,500 00	45 shares Fitchburg Railroad Company, par value at $120	5,360 00
No. 197 Endicott street, city valuation	2,300 00		$141,760 00
Bond of Boston and Lowell Railroad, par value $1,000 at 5 per cent	1,000 00		

G. HIGGINSON,
A. T. FROTHINGHAM, } *Auditing Committee.*

DETAILED STATEMENT OF TREASURER'S ACCOUNT.

DR.

1879-1880.

To cash paid on Auditors' drafts . . .	$72,787	86
city of Boston for taxes . . .	146	25
repairs on houses . . .	531	50
rent of box at Safe Deposit Vaults .	20	00
check-book	5	75
re-investments	19,000	00
on hand Sept. 30, 1880 . . .	2,227	43
	$94,718	79

CR.

1879.

Sept. 30.	By balance of former account. . . .	$579	21
Oct. 10.	From State of Massachusetts	7,500	00
13.	Maine, 1878-79	3,500	00
15.	6 months' interest on note for $5,000 at 6 per cent	150	00
16.	interest on $5,000 United-States bonds, 3 months, at 4 per cent	50	00
21.	$5,000 United-States 4 per cent bonds, sold at 101$\frac{13}{16}$	5,090	62
	$4,000 Boston and Lowell 5 per cent bonds, sold at par value, $4,000, and interest, $55.78	4,055	78
25.	6 months' interest on note, $3,500, at 6 per cent	105	00
29.	R. E. Apthorp, agent, rents collected . .	227	75
Nov. 29.	6 months' interest on note, $8,000, at 6 per cent	240	00
Dec. 9.	6 months' interest on note, $3,500, at 7 per cent	122	50
1880.			
Jan. 2.	6 months' interest on note, $5,000, at 5 per cent	125	00
3.	State of Massachusetts	7,500	00
5.	6 months' interest on note of $18,000 at 6 per cent	540	00
10.	12 months' interest on note of $8,000 at 5 per cent	400	00
	dividend on 45 shares Fitchburg Railroad .	135	00
	6 months' interest on Boston and Lowell Railroad bonds	150	00
15.	$6,000 Eastern Railroad bonds, sold at .81$\frac{1}{2}$, $4,890; and interest to Dec. 12, $76 50 . . . . . $4,966 50		

Amounts carried forward . . .	$4,966 50	$30,470	86

Amounts brought forward $4,966 50 $30,470 86

1880.

Jan. 15. From $5,000 Boston and Lowell bonds,
sold 5,000 00
interest on same to 9th inst.. . 5 56
<hr>
$9,972 06

Less interest on loan. $21 91
commission on
$11,000 . . 27 50
<hr>
49 41
<hr>
9,922 65

17. executors of will of William Taylor, final payment 891 30

23. 6 months' interest on note, $2,500, at 6 per
cent 75 00

29. 6 months' interest on note, $2,500, at 6 per
cent 75 00
6 months' interest on note, $10,000, at 6 per
cent 300 00

M. Anagnos, Director, as per following:—
City of Boston for tuning . . $500 00
J. H. M'Cafferty, account of
daughter. . . . 45 00
State of Rhode Island, account
of Henry Lanergan . . 20 00
Sale of embossed books . . 268 76
J. B. Winsor, account of son . 300 00
Town of Dedham, account of
Mary O'Hare. . . . 27 22
Town of Brimfield, account of
George Needham . . . 14 00
Income of legacy to Laura Bridg-
man 131 20
Hubert Baker, on account. . 20 00
F. Meisel, for old iron . . 86 11
receipts of work department :—
For October . . $1,291 05
November . . 1,095 38
December . . 938 77
<hr>
3,325 20
<hr>
4,737 49

March 1. 6 months' interest on note, $25,000, at 6 per
cent 750 00
6 months' interest on $4,000, Eastern Rail-
road bonds 90 00

20. 6 months' interest on note, $5,000, at 5 per
cent 125 00

24. interest on deposits 176 17

April 5. State of Massachusetts 7,500 00
<hr>
Amount carried forward $55,113 47

Amount brought forward $55,113 47

1880.

April 5. From M. Anagnos, Director, as per following:—

Sale of books in embossed print, tablets, &c.	$351 32	
From tuning	520 00	
Nebraska Institution, for map .	87 00	
A. D. Cadwell, account of son .	85 00	
Rev. Photius Fisk, to print "History of Greece" . , .	500 00	
A friend, donation to print Higginson's "History of United States"	1,186 00	
Mrs. Charles C. Paine, donation to printing fund . . .	100 00	
J. J. Mundo, acc't of daughter,	25 00	
Mrs. Knowlton, account of daughter	24 00	
Sale of admission-tickets . .	50 61	
brooms, account of boys' shop	24 30	
old barrels, junk, &c. .	60 69	
Hubert Baker, on account . .	30 00	

receipts of work department:—

For January . . $839 91		
February . . 1,005 79		
March . . . 859 07		
	——— 2,704 77	
		——— 5,698 69

12.	6 months' interest on note, $9,000, at 6 per cent	270 00

1879.

Oct. 29.	dividend, 30 shares Boston and Providence Railroad	105 00

1880.

April 15.	6 months' interest on note, $5,000, at 6 per cent	150 00
17.	6 months' interest on note, $3,500, at 6 per cent	105 00
May 5.	Boston and Providence Railroad dividends .	120 00
28.	6 months' interest on note, $8,000, at 6 per cent	240 00
June 13.	6 months' interest on note, $10,000, at 6 per cent	300 00
3.	6 months' interest on note, $3,500, at 7 per cent	122 50
July 1	interest on deposit	53 91
	6 months' interest on note of $8,000 at 5 per cent	200 00

Amount carried forward $62,478 57

Amount brought forward		.$62,478 57

1880.

July	1.	From 6 months' interest on note of $5,000 at 5 per cent	125 00
	3.	6 months' interest on note of $18,000 at 6 per cent	540 00
	8.	State of Massachusetts. . . .	7,500 00
	16.	rents collected by R. E. Apthorp, agent .	420 82
		H. B. Rogers, for permanent printing .	1,000 00
	23.	fund 6 months' interest on note, $2,500, at 6 per cent.	75 00
	26.	6 months' interest on note, $2,500, at 6 per cent	75 00
Aug.	2.	estate of William Munroe . . .	100 00
	10.	State of Connecticut	8,800 00
	11.	Maine	3,625 00
		Rhode Island	3,150 00
	13.	Vermont.	1,925 00

M. Anagnos, Director, as per following: —

Tuning	$400 00	
Sale of books in raised print .	126 35	
maps	74 00	
J. H. M'Cafferty, account of daughter	· 55 00	
A. D. Cadwell, account of son .	90 00	
Income of legacy to Laura Bridgman	40 00	

receipts of work department : —

For April . .	$894 02		
May . .	1,378 86		
June . .	1,446 24		
July . .	1,692 10		
		5,411 22	
			6,196 57

	10.	6 months' interest on note, $10,000, at 6 per cent	300 00
Sept.	1.	6 months' interest on note, $5,000, at 5 per cent	125 00
	2.	6 months' interest on note, $25,000, at 6 per cent	750 00
	30.	M. Anagnos, as per following: —	

Sale of books and writing-tablets,	$154 64	
Tuning	250 00	
Mrs. Knowlton, account of daughter	24 00	
Sale of brooms, account of boys' shop	14 13	

Amounts carried forward . . · .	. $442 77	$91,685 96

13

Amounts brought forward	$442 77	$91,685 96

1880.

Sept. 30.   From sale of old junk, &c. . . . 48 10

admission-tickets . . 40 08

receipts of work department: —

| For August . . $957 30 |
| September . . 1,544 58 |

——— 2,501 88

——— 3,032 83

$94,718 79

ANALYSIS OF TREASURER'S ACCOUNTS.

The Treasurer's account shows that the total receipts during
    the year were $94,718 79
Less cash on hand at the beginning of the year . . . 579 21

$94,139 58

Ordinary Receipts.

From the State of Massachusetts . . . $30,000 00
    beneficiaries of other states and individuals, 16,430 42
    interest, coupons, and rent . . . 7,913 65

——— $54,344 07

Extraordinary Receipts.

From work department, for sale of articles made
    by the blind, &c. $13,943 07
    sale of bonds 19,069 05
       embossed books and maps . 1,012 07
    tuning 1,670 00
    legacies and donations . . . 3,777 30
    sale of brooms, account of boys' shop . 38 43
       old junk, barrels, &c. . . . 194 90
       admission-tickets . . . 90 69

——— 39,795 51

$94,139 58

GENERAL ANALYSIS OF THE STEWARD'S ACCOUNT.

DR.

Amount in Steward's hands Oct. 1, 1879 . . $773 16
Receipts from Auditors' drafts . . . 72,787 86

$73,561 02
Less amount in Steward's hands Oct. 1, 1880 . 2,054 82
——— $71,506 20

CR.

Ordinary expenses as per schedule annexed . $42,476 53
Extraordinary expenses as per schedule annexed . 29,029 67
——— 71,506 20

ANALYSIS OF EXPENDITURES FOR THE YEAR ENDING SEPT. 30, 1880,
AS PER STEWARD'S ACCOUNT.

Meat, 25,893 lbs.	$2,153 42
Fish, 3,528 lbs.	191 90
Butter, 4,017 lbs.	1,538 37
Rice, sago, &c.	73 61
Bread, flour, and meal	1,437 84
Potatoes and other vegetables	616 16
Fruit	242 09
Milk, 16,447 quarts	1,008 25
Sugar, 8,411 lbs.	822 09
Tea and coffee, 686 lbs.	173 75
Groceries	622 38
Gas and oil	372 19
Coal and wood	2,464 69
Sundry articles of consumption	226 29
Salaries, superintendence, and instruction	15,009 41
Domestic wages	4,084 73
Outside aid	163 55
Medicines and medical aid	36 45
Furniture and bedding	1,468 17
Clothing and mending	32 86
Musical instruments	902 47
Expenses of tuning department	822 19
boys' shop	39 44
printing-office	3,011 82
stable	232 59
Books, stationery, and school apparatus	2,146 06
Ordinary construction and repairs	1,480 42
Taxes and insurance	609 76
Travelling expenses	73 33
Rent of office in town	250 00
Board of men and clerk during vacation	118 86
Sundries	51 89
	$42,476 53

Extraordinary Expenses.

Extraordinary construction and repairs	$13,073 36	
Bills to be refunded	90 10	
Beneficiaries of the Harris Fund	703 00	
Expenses of work department	15,163 21	
		29,029 67
		$71,506 20

GENERAL ABSTRACT OF ACCOUNT OF WORK DEPARTMENT,
OCT. 1, 1880.

Liabilities.

Due institution for investments at sundry times since the first date	$40,897 45	
Excess of expenditures over receipts . . .	1,220 14	
		$42,117 59

Assets.

Stock on hand Oct. 1, 1880	$4,698 78	
Debts due	1,399 82	
		6,098 60
		$36,018 99

Balance against work department Oct. 1, 1880 . . .	$36,018 99
Balance against work department Oct. 1, 1879 . . .	35,028 96
Cost of carrying on workshop	$990 03

DR.

Cash received for sales, &c., during the year .	$13,943 07	
Excess of expenditures over receipts . .	1,220 14	
		$15,163 21

CR.

Salaries and wages paid blind persons . . .	$3,186 72	
Salaries and wages paid seeing persons . .	2,608 75	
Sundries for stock, &c.	9,367 74	
		$15,163 21

ACCOUNT OF STOCK OCT. 1, 1880.

Real estate		$247,800 00
Railroad stock		15,050 00
Notes secured by mortgage		115,000 00
Cash		4,282 25
Stock in work department		4,698 78
Household furniture		16,581 41
Provisions and supplies		1,101 26
Wood and coal		2,877 90
Musical department, viz., —		
One large organ	$5,500 00	
Three small organs	730 00	
Forty-four pianos	11,000 00	
Violins	100 00	
Brass and reed instruments . . .	1,500 00	
		18,830 00
Books in printing-office		4,700 00
Stereotype plates		2,100 00
School furniture and apparatus . . .		5,700 00
Musical library		625 00
Library of books in common type . .		1,950 00
Library of books in raised type . . .		5,500 00
Boys' shop		108 75
Stable and tools		625 75
Boat		15 00
		$447,546 10

LIST OF EMBOSSED BOOKS

Printed at the Perkins Institution and Massachusetts School for the Blind.

TITLE OF BOOK.	No. of Volumes.	Price per Volume.
Howe's Geography	1	$2 50
Howe's Atlas of the Islands	1	3 00
Howe's Blind Child's First Book	1	1 25
Howe's Blind Child's Second Book	1	1 25
Howe's Blind Child's Third Book	1	1 25
Howe's Blind Child's Fourth Book	1	1 25
Second Table of Logarithms	1	3 00
Astronomical Dictionary	1	2 00
Rudiments of Natural Philosophy	1	4 00
Philosophy of Natural History	1	3 00
Guyot's Geography	1	4 00
Howe's Cyclopædia	8	4 00
Natural Theology	1	4 00
Combe's Constitution of Man	1	4 00
Pope's Essay on Man, and other Poems	1	2 50
Baxter's Call	1	2 50
Book of Proverbs	1	2 00
Book of Psalms	1	3 00
New Testament (small)	4	2 50
Book of Common Prayer	1	4 00
Hymns for the Blind	1	3 00
Pilgrim's Progress	1	4 00
Life of Melanchthon	1	2 00
Dickens's Old Curiosity Shop	3	4 00
Shakspeare's Hamlet and Julius Cæsar	1	4 00
Byron's Hebrew Melodies and Childe Harold	1	3 00
Anderson's History of the United States	1	2 50
Dickens's Child's History of England	2	3 50
Selections from the Works of Swedenborg	1	–
Memoir of Dr. Samuel G. Howe	1	3 00
Cutter's Anatomy, Physiology, and Hygiene	1	4 00
Viri Romæ, new edition with additions	1	2 00
The Reader; or, Extracts from British and American Literature	2	3 00
Musical Characters used by the seeing, with explanations	1	35
Milton's Paradise Lost	2	3 00
Higginson's Young Folks' History of the United States	1	3 50
Schmitz's History of Greece	1	3 00
Schmitz's History of Rome	1	2 50
Freeman's History of Europe	1	2 50
Eliot's Six Arabian Nights	1	3 00
Lodge's Twelve Popular Tales	1	2 00
An Account of the Most Celebrated Diamonds	1	50
Huxley's Science Primers, Introductory	1	2 00
American Prose	2	3 00

LIST OF APPLIANCES AND TANGIBLE APPARATUS

Made at the Perkins Institution and Massachusetts School for the Blind.

GEOGRAPHY.

I. — *Wall-Maps.*

1. The Hemispheres . . . . . . size 42 by 52 inches.
2. United States, Mexico, and Canada . . . " " "
3. South America . . . . " " "
4. Europe . . . . " " "
5. Asia . . . . " " "
6. Africa . . . . " " "
7. The World on Mercator's Projection . . . " " "

Each $35, or the set, $245.

II. — *Dissected Maps.*

1. Eastern Hemisphere . . . . . . size 30 by 36 inches.
2. Western Hemisphere . . . . . . " " "
3. North America . . . . " " "
4. United States . . . . " " "
5. South America . . . . " " "
6. Europe . . . . " " "
7. Asia . . . . " " "
8. Africa . . . . " " "

Each $23, or the set, $184.

These maps are considered, in point of workmanship, accuracy, and distinctness of outline, durability, and beauty, far superior to all thus far made in Europe or in this country.

"The New-England Journal of Education" says, "They are very strong, present a fine, bright surface, and are an ornament to any school-room."

III. — *Pin-Maps.*

Cushions for pin-maps and diagrams . . . . . each, $0 75

ARITHMETIC.

Ciphering-boards made of brass strips, nickel-plated . . each, $4 25
Ciphering-types, nickel-plated, per hundred . . . " 1 00

WRITING.

Grooved writing-cards . . . . each, $0 10
Braille's tablets, with metallic bed . . . . " 1 50
Braille's French tablets, with cloth bed . . . . " 1 00
Braille's new tablets, with cloth bed . . . . " 1 00
Braille's Daisy tablets . . . . " 5 00

TERMS OF ADMISSION.

YOUNG blind persons between the ages of ten and nineteen, and of good moral character, can be admitted to the school by paying $300 per annum. This sum covers all expenses, except for clothing; namely, board, washing, the use of books, musical instruments, &c. The pupils must furnish their own clothing, and pay their own fares to and from the institution. The friends of the pupils can visit them whenever they choose.

Indigent blind persons of suitable age and character, belonging to Massachusetts, can be admitted gratuitously by application to the Governor for a warrant.

The following is a good form, though any other will do : —

" *To his Excellency the Governor.*

"SIR, — My son (or daughter, or nephew, or niece, as the case may be), named ——, and aged ——, cannot be instructed in the common schools, for want of sight. I am unable to pay for the tuition at the Perkins Institution and Massachusetts School for the Blind, and I request that your Excellency will give a warrant for free admission.

"Very respectfully,   —— ——."

The application may be made by any relation or friend, if the parents are dead or absent.

It should be accompanied by a certificate from one or more of the selectmen of the town, or aldermen of the city, in this form : —

"I hereby certify, that, in my opinion, Mr. —— —— is not a wealthy person, and that he cannot afford to pay $300 per annum for his child's instruction.   (Signed)   —— ——."

There should be a certificate, signed by some regular physician, in this form : —

"I certify, that, in my opinion, —— —— has not sufficient vision to be taught in common schools; and that he is free from epilepsy, and from any contagious disease.   (Signed)   —— ——."

These papers should be done up together, and forwarded to the DIRECTOR OF THE INSTITUTION FOR THE BLIND, *South Boston, Mass.*

An obligation will be required from some responsible persons, that the pupil shall be kept properly supplied with decent clothing, shall be provided for during vacations, and shall be removed, without expense to the institution, whenever it may be desirable to discharge him.

The usual period of tuition is from five to seven years. Indigent blind persons residing in Maine, New Hampshire, Vermont, Connecticut, and Rhode Island, by applying as above to the Governor, or the "Secretary of State," in their respective states, can obtain warrants for free admission.

The relatives or friends of the blind who may be sent to the institution are requested to furnish information in answer to the following questions: —

1. What is the name and age of the applicant?
2. Where born?
3. Was he born blind? If not, at what age was his sight impaired?
4. Is the blindness total or partial?
5. What is the supposed cause of the blindness?
6. Has he ever been subject to fits?
7. Is he now in good health, and free from eruptions and contagious diseases of the skin?
8. Has he ever been to school? If yes, where?
9. What is the general moral character of the applicant?
10. Of what country was the father of the applicant a native?
11. What was the general bodily condition and health of the father, — was he vigorous and healthy, or the contrary?
12. Was the father of the applicant ever subject to fits or to scrofula?
13. Were all his senses perfect?
14. Was he always a temperate man?
15. About how old was he when the applicant was born?
16. Was there any known peculiarity in the family of the father of the applicant; that is, were any of the grandparents, parents, uncles, aunts, brothers, sisters, or cousins, blind, deaf, or insane, or afflicted with any infirmity of body or mind?
17. If dead, at what age did the father die, and of what disorder?
18. Where was the mother of the applicant born?
19. What was the general bodily condition of the mother of the applicant, — strong and healthy, or the contrary?
20. Was she ever subject to scrofula or to fits?
21. Were all her senses perfect?
22. Was she always a temperate woman?
23. About how old was she when the applicant was born?

14

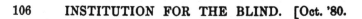

24. How many children had she before the applicant was born?

25. Was she related by blood to her husband? If so, in what degree, — first, second, or third cousins?

26. If dead, at what age did she die, and of what disorder?

27. Was there any known peculiarity in her family; that is, were any of her grandparents, parents, uncles, aunts, sisters, brothers, children, or cousins, either blind, or deaf, or insane, or afflicted with any infirmity of body or mind?

28. What are the pecuniary means of the parents or immediate relatives of the applicant?

29. How much can they afford to pay towards the support and eduction of the applicants?

For further particulars, address M. ANAGNOS, DIRECTOR OF THE INSTITUTION FOR THE BLIND, *South Boston, Mass.*

PUBLIC DOCUMENT. No. 27.

FIFTIETH ANNUAL REPORT

OF

THE TRUSTEES

OF THE

PERKINS INSTITUTION

AND

Massachusetts School for the Blind,

FOR THE YEAR ENDING

SEPTEMBER 30, 1881.

BOSTON:

Rand, Avery, & Co., Printers to the Commonwealth,

117 FRANKLIN STREET.

1882.

TABLE OF CONTENTS.

Commonwealth of Massachusetts.

PERKINS INSTITUTION AND MASS. SCHOOL FOR THE BLIND,
SOUTH BOSTON, Oct. 18, 1881.

To the Hon. HENRY B. PEIRCE, *Secretary of State*, Boston.

DEAR SIR, — I have the honor to transmit to you, for the use of the legislature, a copy of the fiftieth annual report of the trustees of this institution to the corporation thereof, together with the usual accompanying documents.

Respectfully,

M. ANAGNOS,

Secretary.

OFFICERS OF THE CORPORATION.
1881–82.

SAMUEL ELIOT, *President.*
JOHN CUMMINGS, *Vice-President.*
EDWARD JACKSON, *Treasurer.*
M. ANAGNOS, *Secretary.*

BOARD OF TRUSTEES.

ROBERT E. APTHORP.
JOHN S. DWIGHT.
JOSEPH B. GLOVER.
J. THEODORE HEARD, M.D.
HENRY LEE HIGGINSON.
JAMES H. MEANS, D.D.

ROBERT TREAT PAINE, Jun.
EDWARD N. PERKINS.
SAMUEL M. QUINCY.
SAMUEL G. SNELLING.
JAMES STURGIS.
GEORGE W. WALES.

STANDING COMMITTEES.
Monthly Visiting Committee,
whose duty it is to visit and inspect the Institution at least once in each month.

1882. January . . R. E. APTHORP.
February . . J. S. DWIGHT.
March . . . J. B. GLOVER.
April . . . J. T. HEARD.
May . . . . H. L. HIGGINSON.
June . . . J. H. MEANS.

1882. July . . . R. T. PAINE, Jun.
August . . E. N. PERKINS.
September . S. M. QUINCY.
October . . S. G. SNELLING.
November . JAMES STURGIS.
December . GEO. W. WALES.

Committee on Education.
J. S. DWIGHT.
R. T. PAINE, Jun.
S. M. QUINCY.

House Committee.
E. N. PERKINS.
G. W. WALES.
J. H. MEANS.

Committee of Finance.
R. E. APTHORP.
J. B. GLOVER.
JAMES STURGIS.

Committee on Health.
J. THEODORE HEARD.
E. N. PERKINS.
H. L. HIGGINSON.

Auditors of Accounts.
ROBERT E. APTHORP.
SAMUEL G. SNELLING.

OFFICERS OF THE INSTITUTION.

DIRECTOR.
M. ANAGNOS.

MEDICAL INSPECTOR.
JOHN HOMANS, M.D.

LITERARY DEPARTMENT.
Miss J. R. Gilman.
Miss E. S. Adams.
Miss Annie E. Carnes.
Miss Julia Boylan.

Miss Della Bennett.
Miss Mary C. Moore.
Miss Cora A. Newton.
Miss S. E. Lane, *Librarian.*

MUSICAL DEPARTMENT.
Thomas Reeves.
Frank H. Kilbourne.
Miss Freda Black.
Miss Lizzie Riley.
Miss Lucy Hammond.
Miss M. L. Drowne.
Orville Cadwell, *Assistant.*

Mrs. Kate Rametti.
C. H. Higgins.
Joseph R. Lucier.

Music Readers.
Miss Allie S. Knapp.
Miss Mary A. Proctor.

TUNING DEPARTMENT.
J. W. Smith, *Instructor and Manager.*

INDUSTRIAL DEPARTMENT.
Workshops for Juveniles.
J. H. Wright, *Work Master.*
Miss A. J Dillingham, *Work Mistress.*
Thomas Carroll, *Assistant.*
Miss H. Kellier, *Assistant.*

Workshop for Adults.
A. W. Bowden, *Manager.*
P Morrill, *Foreman.*
Miss M. A. Dwelly, *Forewoman.*
Miss M. M. Stone, *Clerk.*

DOMESTIC DEPARTMENT.
Steward.
A. W. Bowden.

Matron.
Miss M. C. Moulton.
Miss E. Ware, *Assistant.*

Housekeepers in the Cottages.
Mrs. M. A. Knowlton.
Mrs. L S. Smith.
Miss Bessie Wood.
Miss Lizzie N. Smith.

PRINTING DEPARTMENT.
Dennis A. Reardon, *Manager.*

Miss E. B. Webster, *Book-keeper.*

MEMBERS OF THE CORPORATION.

ALL persons who have contributed twenty-five dollars to the funds of the institution, all who have served as trustees or treasurer, and all who have been elected by special vote, are members.

Aldrich, Mrs. Sarah, Boston.
Alger, Rev. William R., Boston.
Ames, Mrs. II. A , Boston.
Amory, C. W., Boston.
Amory, James S., Boston.
Amory, William, Boston.
Anagnos, M., Boston.
Appleton, Miss Emily G., Boston.
Appleton, T. G., Boston.
Appleton, Mrs. William, Boston.
Apthorp, Robert E., Boston.
Apthorp, William F., Boston.
Atkinson, Edward, Boston.
Atkinson, William, Boston.
Austin, Edward, Boston.
Baldwin, William H., Boston.
Baker, Mrs. E. M., Boston.
Baker, Miss M. K., Boston.
Barbour, E. D., Boston.
Barrows, Rev. S. J., Dorchester.
Beal, J. H., Boston.
Beard, Hon. Alanson W., Boston.
Bennett, Mrs. Eleanor, Billerica.
Bigelow, E. B., Boston.
Blake, G. Baty, Boston.
Blanchard, G. D. B., Malden.
Bouvé, Thomas T., Boston.
Bowditch, Mrs. E. B., Boston.
Bowditch, J. I , Boston.
Bradlee, F. H., Boston.
Brewster, Osmyn, Boston.
Brimmer, Hon. Martin, Boston.
Brooks, Francis, Boston.

Brooks, Rev. Phillips, Boston.
Brooks, Shepherd, Boston.
Brooks, Susan O., Boston.
Browne. A. Parker, Boston.
Bullard, W. S., Boston.
Burnham, J. A , Boston.
Chandler, P. W., Boston.
Chandler, Theophilus P., Brookline.
Chase, Mrs. Theodore, Boston.
Cheney, Benjamin P., Boston.
Chickering, George II., Boston.
Childs, Alfred A., Boston.
Claflin, Hon. William, Boston.
Clapp, William W., Boston.
Clement, Edward II., Boston.
Cobb, Samuel T , Boston.
Conant, Mrs. Rebecca, Amherst, N.H.
Coolidge, Dr. A , Boston.
Coolidge, J. R., Boston.
Coolidge, Mrs. J. R , Boston.
Coolidge, J. T., Boston.
Coolidge, Mrs J. T., Boston.
Crane, Zenas M., Dalton.
Crosby, Joseph B , Boston.
Cummings, Charles A., Boston.
Cummings, Hon. John, Woburn.
Curtis, Mrs Charles P., Boston.
Dana, Mrs. Samuel T., Boston.
Dalton, C. II., Boston.
Dalton, Mis. C. H., Boston.
Davis, James, Boston.
Deblois, Stephen G., Boston.

Devens, Rev. Samuel A., Boston.
Ditson, Oliver, Boston.
Dix, J. H., M.D., Boston.
Dwight, John S., Boston.
Eliot, Dr. Samuel, Boston.
Emery, Francis F., Boston.
Emery, Isaac, Boston.
Emmons, Mrs. Nath'l H., Boston.
English, James E., New Haven, Conn.
Endicott, Henry, Boston.
Endicott, William, jun , Boston.
Farnam, Mrs. A. G., New Haven, Conn.
Farnam, Henry, New Haven, Conn.
Fay, Miss Sarah B., Boston.
Fay, Mrs. S. S , Boston.
Fellows, R. J., New Haven, Conn.
Fisk, Rev. Photius, Boston.
Folsom, Charles F., M.D., Danvers.
Forbes, J. M., Milton.
Freeman, Miss Hattie E , Boston.
Frothingham, A. T., Boston.
Galloupe, C. W., Boston.
Gardiner, Charles P., Boston.
Gardiner, William II., Boston.
Gardner, George, Boston.
Gardner, George A., Boston.
Glover, J. B., Boston.
Goddard, Benjamin, Brookline.
Goddard, Delano A., Boston.
Gray, Mrs. Horace, Boston.
Greenleaf, Mrs. James, Charlestown.
Greenleaf, R. C., Boston.
Grover, W. A., Boston.
Guild, Mrs. S. E., Boston.
Hale, Rev. Edward E , Boston.
Hale, George S., Boston.
Hall, J. R., Boston.
Hall, Miss L. E., Charlestown.
Hardy, Alpheus, Boston.
Heard, J. T., M D., Boston.
Higginson, George, Boston.
Higginson, Henry Lee, Boston.
Hill, Hon. Hamilton A., Boston.
Hilton, William, Boston.
Hogg, John, Boston.
Hooper, E. W., Boston.

Hooper, R. W., M.D., Boston.
Hovey, George O., Boston.
Hovey, William A., Brookline.
Howe, Mrs. Julia Ward, Boston.
Howes, Miss E., Boston.
Houghton, Hon. H. O., Cambridge.
Hunnewell, H. H., Boston.
Hunt, Moses, Charlestown.
Hyatt, Alpheus, Cambridge.
Inches, H. B , Boston.
Jackson, Charles C., Boston.
Jackson, Edward, Boston.
Jackson, Patrick T., Boston.
Jackson, Mrs. Sarah, Boston.
Jarvis, Edward, M.D., Dorchester.
Jones, J. M., Boston.
Kendall, C. S , Boston.
Kennard, Martin P., Brookline.
Kidder, H. P., Boston.
Kinsley, E. W., Boston.
Lang, B. J., Boston.
Lawrence, Abbott, Boston.
Lawrence, Amos A., Longwood.
Lawrence, Edward, Charlestown.
Lawrence, William, Boston.
Lincoln, L. J. B., Hingham.
Littell, Miss S. G., Brookline.
Lockwood, Mrs. Alice, Providence, R I.
Lodge, Mrs. A. C., Boston.
Lord, Melvin, Boston.
Lothrop, John, Auburndale.
Lovett, George L., Boston.
Lowell, Augustus, Boston.
Lowell, Miss A. C , Boston.
Lyman, Arthur T., Boston.
Lyman, George H., M.D., Boston.
Lyman, George W., Boston.
Lyman, J. P., Boston.
Mack, Thomas, Boston.
May, Miss Abby, Boston.
May, F. W. G., Dorchester.
May, Mrs. Samuel, Boston.
Means, Rev. J. H., D D., Dorchester.
Merriam, Mrs. Caroline, Boston.
Merriam, Charles, Boston.
Minot, William, Boston.
Montgomery, Hugh, Boston.
Morrill, Charles J., Boston.

Morton, Edwin, Boston.
Motley, Edward, Boston.
Nichols, J. Howard, Boston.
Nichols, R. P., Boston.
Nickerson, Mrs. A. T., Boston.
Nickerson, George, Jamaica Plain.
Nickerson, S. D , Boston.
Noyes, Hon. Charles J., Boston.
Osborn, John T., Boston.
Paine, Mrs. Julia B., Boston.
Paine, Robert Treat, jun., Boston.
Parker, Mrs. E. P., Boston.
Parker, E. F., Boston.
Parker, H. D., Boston.
Parker, Richard T., Boston.
Parkman, Francis, Boston.
Parkman, George F. Boston.
Parkman, Rev. John, Boston..
Parsons, Thomas, Chelsea.
Payson, S R., Boston.
Peabody, Rev. A. P., D.D., Camb'ge.
Peabody, F. H., Boston.
Peabody, O. W., Milton.
Perkins, Charles C , Boston.
Perkins, Edward N., Jamaica Plain.
Perkins, William, Boston.
Peters, Edward D., Boston.
Phillips, John C , Boston.
Pickman, W. D , Boston.
Pickman Mrs. W. D., Boston.
Pierce, Hon. H. L., Boston.
Pratt, Elliott W., Boston.
Pratt, Miss Mary, Boston.
Prendergast, J M. Boston.
Preston, Jonathan, Boston.
Quincy, Hon. Josiah, Wollaston.
Quincy, Samuel M., Wollaston.
Rice, Hon. A. H., Boston.
Robeson, W. R., Boston.
Robinson, Henry, Reading.
Rogers, Henry B., Boston.
Rogers, Jacob C., Boston.
Ropes, J. S., Jamaica Plain.
Rotch, Benjamin S., Boston.
Rotch, Mrs. Benjamin S., Boston.
Russell, Miss Marian, Boston.
Russell, Mrs. S. S., Boston.
Salisbury, Stephen, Worcester.

Saltonstall, H., Boston.
Saltonstall, Leverett, Newton.
Sanborn, Frank B., Concord.
Sargent, I., Brookline.
Schlesinger, Sebastian, Boston.
Sears, David, Boston.
Sears, Mrs. K W., Boston.
Sears, Mrs. S. P., Boston.
Sears, W. T., Boston.
Shaw, Mrs. G. H., Boston.
Shaw, Quincy A. Boston.
Sherwood, W. H., Boston.
Shimmin, C. F., Boston.
Shippen, Rev. Rush R., Jamaio
  Plain.
Slack, C. W., Boston.
Snelling, Samuel G , Boston.
Stone, Joseph L , Boston.
Sturgis, Francis S., Jamaica Plain.
Sturgis, James, Jamaica Plain.
Sullivan, Richard, Boston.
Sweetser, Mrs. Anne M., Boston.
Taggard, B. W., Boston.
Taggard, Mrs. B. W., Boston.
Thaxter, Joseph B , Hingham.
Thayer, Miss A. G., Andover.
Thayer, Rev. George A., Boston.
Thayer, Nathaniel, Boston.
Thorndike, S. Lothrop, Cambridge.
Tucker, Alanson, Boston.
Tucker, W. W., Boston.
Turner, Miss Abby W., Boston.
Upton, George B., Boston.
Wales, George W., Boston.
Wales, Miss Mary Ann, Boston.
Wales, Thomas B., Boston.
Ward, Samuel, New York.
Ware, Charles E., M.D., Boston.
Warren, S D , Boston.
Washburn, Hon. J. D., Worcester.
Weld, W. G., Boston.
Wheelwright, A. C., Boston.
Wheelwright, John W., Boston.
Whitman, Sarah W., Boston.
White, B. C , Boston.
Whiting, Ebenezer, Boston.
Whitney, Edward, Belmont.
Whitney, E., Boston.

Whitney, Mrs., Boston.

Whitney, Miss, Boston.

Wigglesworth, Miss Ann, Boston.

Wigglesworth, Edw., M.D., Boston.

Wigglesworth, Miss Mary, Boston.

Wigglesworth, Thomas, Boston.

Wilder, Hon. Marshall P., Dorch.

Winslow, Mrs. George, Roxbury.

Winsor, J. B., Providence, R.I.

Winthrop, Hon. Robert C., Boston.

Winthrop, Mrs. Robert C., Boston.

Wolcott, J. H., Boston.

Wolcott, Mrs. J. H., Boston.

Woods, Henry, Paris, France.

Worthington, Roland, Roxbury.

Young, Charles L., Boston.

PROCEEDINGS

OF THE

ANNUAL MEETING OF THE CORPORATION.

Boston, October 12, 1881.

THE meeting was called to order by the president, Dr. Samuel Eliot, at 3 P.M.

The minutes of the last annual meeting were read by the secretary, and declared approved.

The report of the trustees and that of the director were presented, accepted, and ordered to be printed with the usual accompanying documents.

The following preamble and resolutions, presented by Mr. John S. Dwight, were unanimously passed : —

"In view of the fact that this institution has now entered upon the fiftieth year of its existence, and in accordance with the suggestions contained in the annual report of the trustees, as well as in the very interesting and instructive history of all that Europe and America have done toward the education of the blind, to which we have just listened from the director, it is hereby

"*Resolved*, 1, that the semi-centennial anniversary of the Perkins Institution and Massachusetts School for the Blind shall be publicly celebrated at the close of the current school year, in June, 1882, by appropriate exercises, in which pupils, teachers, graduates, and friends of the school shall take part in one of the largest halls or theatres of the city.

"*Resolved*, 2, that the chair do here and now appoint three members of the corporation, who shall mature the plan, and have charge of all the arrangements of the festival."

Messrs. Dwight, William F. Apthorp, and Samuel M. Quincy, were appointed by the president to arrange for the festival.

Mr. Dwight presented also the following resolution, which was unanimously accepted: —

"*Resolved*, that the corporation feels it a pleasant duty, in the name of the school, past and present, and of all friends of the blind, to acknowledge a long-standing debt of gratitude to the musical societies of Boston, which have year after year freely extended to the pupils of this institution such abundant opportunities of hearing the best performances of what is best in music; and equally to the many individual artists who have sent them invitations to their concerts, or have even sought them here in their school home, and sung and played to them through many a delightful evening in their own music-hall." [For the names of societies and artists, see list of acknowledgments, pp. 121, 122 and 123.]

On motion of Mr. Samuel G. Snelling, the following votes were unanimously passed: —

" *Voted*, that the thanks of the corporation be hereby tendered to the contributors to the printing fund, to whose kindness and generosity the blind will be forever indebted; and to the editors of the leading newspapers for the efficient and disinterested aid which they have so promptly and gratuitously rendered.

" *Voted*, that further subscriptions be solicited to the amount of thirty-eight thousand dollars, which will complete the sum of the printing endowment asked for by the board of trustees."

All the officers of the past year were then re-elected, with the exception of the treasurer, Mr. P. T. Jackson, who expressed a wish to retire, and in whose place Mr. Edward Jackson, his brother, was chosen.

" *Voted*, that the thanks of the corporation be presented to the retiring treasurer, Mr. P. T. Jackson, for the faithful discharge of his duties, and for the interest which he has manifested in the prosperity of the institution."

The following persons were afterwards added to the list of the corporators by a unanimous vote: A. C. Wheelwright, Benjamin P. Cheney, Edward H. Clement, Samuel T. Cobb, Miss L. E. Hall, and Miss Eveline A. Everett.

The meeting was then dissolved, and the members of the corporation proceeded, with the invited guests, to visit the school and inspect the premises.

M. ANAGNOS,

Secretary.

Commonwealth of Massachusetts.

REPORT OF THE TRUSTEES.

PERKINS INSTITUTION AND MASS. SCHOOL FOR THE BLIND,
SOUTH BOSTON, Sept. 30, 1881.

To THE MEMBERS OF THE CORPORATION:

Gentlemen, — The undersigned trustees respectfully submit to your consideration their FIFTIETH annual report for the financial year ending September 30, 1881.

This communication embraces a brief account of their transactions and of the progress and present condition of the school, and is accompanied by such documents as are required by law and custom.

It is with a feeling of sincere pleasure that we proceed to place on record the events of the past year. On no former occasion have circumstances so auspicious attended the performance of this duty.

A high degree of prosperity has been enjoyed by the institution. Its objects have been pursued with diligence and success, and the state of its affairs is generally satisfactory.

The present total number of blind persons immediately connected with the institution, in all its departments, as pupils, instructors, employés and work men and women, is 162.

The health of the household has again been remarkably good, and it is a cause of much thankfulness that neither any of the epidemic diseases which have been prevalent in the community, nor death, have entered the school.

Order and discipline have been admirably preserved without resort to severe or harsh measures, and the march of progress is observable in all the departments of the institution.

In the management of the affairs of the school there is a fixed and definite policy, which consists in adhering to what is good, in improving what is imperfect, in strengthening what is weak but useful, and in adopting what is pointed out by the light of experience and science as best adapted to the wants of the blind.

The trustees express themselves with entire approbation with regard to the state of the school, the fidelity and efficiency with which instruction has been imparted, and the disposition and capacity of the greater portion of the pupils to profit by it. They feel that a great amount of good work has been accomplished, and that the establishment has continued to dispense among the blind of New England intelligence and culture, making them diffusive as sunshine, causing them to penetrate into every hamlet and dwelling, and, like the vernal sun, quickening into life the seeds of usefulness and worth, wherever the prodigal hand of nature may have scattered them.

The institution continues to be in a flourishing condition, and its influence and importance as the most effective agency for developing the capacities of the blind, and enabling them to become independent workers with hand and brain, increase from year to year.

The establishment is provided with appliances and apparatus of the most approved kind, and is well appointed in all its departments, which are so arranged as to form a cluster of fruitful branches to crown the solid trunk of the parent tree.

The business of the school has been carried on in a very satisfactory manner, and the results of its workings, which have been witnessed from time to time during the year by members of our board, have been thorough and solid. This was manifestly shown in the searching examinations, and at the graduating exercises, which were held at the close of the term in the music-hall of the institution.

Few occasions could be more interesting and gratifying than these exercises. They were attended by a select and cultivated audience, and proved enjoyable in every particular. The pupils showed careful training, and proficiency in their literary studies and music; and, as one of the leading newspapers said, seemed to stand quite on a par with seeing youth of the same age; the compositions and essays which they read displayed excellent taste and good culture; and their bearing and appearance were everything that could be desired.

The interest of the occasion was enhanced by the eloquent and appropriate remarks of the president of the corporation, Dr. Samuel Eliot (who presented the diplomas to the graduates), Mrs. Julia Ward Howe, Hon. A. W. Beard (collector of the port), Rev. Phillips Brooks, D.D., Col. T. W. Higginson, and Mr. William H. Baldwin.

Owing to the smallness of our hall, the invitations to the exercises were limited to the benefactors and immediate friends of the institution, and a large number of eager applications for admission were necessarily refused. This circumstance was certainly very disadvantageous, and no one could regret it more deeply and more sincerely than the authorities of the institution.

FINANCES.

The report of the treasurer, Mr. P. T. Jackson, which is herewith submitted, shows the financial condition of the institution to be very satisfactory.

It appears therefrom that the amount of cash on hand Oct. 1, 1880, was,

On general fund	. $1,227 43	
Total receipts during the year. .	. 77,324 20	
		$78,551 63
Total expenditures	.	79,839 79
Balance due to the treasurer		$1,288 16

To aid in a thorough examination of the financial concerns of the establishment, the report of the treasurer is accompanied by an analysis of the steward's accounts, which gives specific information in regard to the principal articles consumed, their quality, and the aggregate price paid for each.

The general work of the establishment has been directed with discretion, and efficiency has been secured

at a moderate cost. Wise foresight and system in all
things; the utmost economy consistent with the health
and comfort of the household; care to avoid losses, and
judicious expenditure of money, are items of paramount
importance in the management of the finances of the
institution, and have received constant and undivided
attention.

The accounts have been regularly audited at the end
of each month by a special committee appointed by our
board for the purpose, and have been found properly
cast and correctly kept.

The trustees take this opportunity of acknowledging
their great obligation to the treasurer of the corporation,
Mr. P. T. Jackson, for the diligence, courtesy and
promptness with which he has discharged his onerous
duties, and for the personal interest which he has shown
in the welfare and prosperity of the school.

REPAIRS AND IMPROVEMENTS.

The work of renovating the interior of the main
building, which was begun several years since, has been
carried a few steps forward during the summer vacation.

In the rotunda, the ceiling and walls have been
replastered, painted and decorated; the old and dilapidated doors and frames have been replaced by new ones
of hard wood; new marble tiles have been laid, and
the whole appearance of this part of the building has
been refreshed and greatly improved.

The large and small reception-rooms and the office
have been wainscotted with hard wood, replastered and
frescoed, and all the doors, frames and blinds in the
same rooms renewed.

One of the boys' sitting-rooms has undergone a similar process of renovation, and has been made as attractive as might be.

A tunnel has been constructed from the southern to the northern end of the west wing of the building for the purpose of running all the steam and water pipes through it, and thus rendering them accessible for examination and repairs.

Several other alterations and improvements of a minor character have been made during the past year; but the high price of labor and materials, and the want of funds at our disposal, have compelled us to restrict our operations in this direction to a very small area, and to undertake a great deal less than ought to have been done.

A desirable piece of land of about forty-one thousand square feet, adjacent to the lot on which our stable and the workshop for adults stand, and facing Fifth street, has been purchased at a reasonable price.

This land is a valuable addition to our grounds, and will afford great facilities for the future development of the institution. There is space enough upon it for the reconstruction and re-arrangement of the workshop and the printing-office, and for the erection of a kindergarten, or primary department, for such poor little children as are too young to be received in a mixed school like ours, and are wasting away under the rust of neglect and the want of sufficient food and proper care and training.

Embossing Books for the Blind.

We take great pleasure in reporting that the work of our printing department has been carried on during the past year with unusual vigor and on a larger scale than heretofore, and that ten new books have been issued by our press. At no previous period in the history of this enterprise has such activity been exhibited, and so much matter embossed in so short a time, as in the course of the last eleven months.

Our publications have been mostly confined to two series of selections from the works of British and American authors: one of prose and the other of poetry.

The first of these series comprises Freeman's "Elementary History of Europe;" Huxley's "Introductory Science Primer;" Goldsmith's "Vicar of Wakefield;" Dickens's "Christmas Carol," with copious extracts from the "Pickwick Papers;" and two volumes of brief stories, sketches, and essays selected from the writings of Hawthorne, Washington Irving, Longfellow, Whittier, Holmes, Lowell, Thoreau and Emerson.

In the second series one volume is devoted to Pope's works, two to Longfellow's, one to Tennyson's, and one to Whittier's. In each of these four volumes, in addition to a large number of the smaller favorite poems, are included such masterpieces as the "Essay on Man" and the "Rape of the Lock;" "Evangeline" and the "Courtship of Miles Standish;" "In Memoriam," "Enoch Arden" and the "Lady of Shalott;" "Snow-bound," "Among the Hills" and the "Hero." A comprehensive biographical and critical sketch of each author is prefixed to the selections from his works.

Both of these series will be continued, and a number of other books adapted to the wants of juvenile readers, as well as to those of advanced pupils, are either in preparation or in contemplation.

The first edition of Higginson's "History of the United States," which was printed and electrotyped at the expense of a generous friend and benefactor of the blind, was received with such eagerness and appreciation, that it was entirely exhausted, and a second one has just been issued.

Through the generosity of Mr. Robert Treat Paine, jun., we have in press a volume of Lowell's poems. This is to be followed by selections from the works of Holmes, Bryant, Emerson, Scott, Macaulay, Moore, Byron, and others.

A collection of appliances and tools, which was intended to be used in an establishment for embossing books and manufacturing tangible apparatus for the blind, was recently to be sold, and we took the opportunity of purchasing such of them as could be made serviceable by alterations and improvements, effected at a moderate additional expense.

Our printing department is now complete in all its equipments, and supplied with ample facilities to do good and steady work for many years to come.

The Printing Fund.

The necessity of a library, in the more positive and permanent sense of the word, for the use of the blind has been acknowledged since the organization of the institution ; and the earnest efforts of Dr. Howe for the multiplication of select books in embossed print were unwearied and incessant. Great as was his success, however, and generous as had been the response which his enthusiastic exertions met with, the public mind was hardly yet ripe for the idea of raising an adequate endowment, the income of which should be sufficient to render our printing department a perennial source of happiness and improvement to the blind all over the country.

For the attainment of this grand object, a movement was inaugurated last winter, which, fostered by the distribution of a large number of copies of a circular issued by our press in raised print, and sustained by the active sympathy and the disinterested aid of the leading newspapers, resulted in the voluntary contribution of about seven thousand dollars. The conjuncture seemed an opportune one for the promotion of the cause, and measures were taken to improve it.

On the 18th of March, a committee was appointed to solicit subscriptions to the amount of seventy-five thousand dollars in addition to that which had already been contributed, and on the first day of April an. appeal was made at a public meeting, which was held for the purpose in Tremont Temple. This occasion was in the highest sense characteristic of Boston, and proved exceedingly interesting. His Excellency Governor Long presided, and made the opening address, and Rev. Phillips Brooks, Rev. E. E. Hale, Mrs. Julia Ward Howe, Rev. A. A. Miner, Rev. F. M. Ellis, and Rev. James Freeman Clarke presented in the most eloquent and impressive manner the wants and claims of the blind, supported by an array of undisputed facts which it may not be out of place to rehearse and sum up in this connection.

The cost of printing in relief very much exceeds that of producing a book in the ordinary way. The fact that the blind cannot obtain a copy of the Bible which they can read for less than twenty dollars, while seeing people pay from twenty-five to fifty cents for one, is a striking illustration of this point. But, even if the price of embossed books were not so high, there are but very few sightless persons who are so favored with the goods of this world as to be able to purchase them, for blindness is usually begotten of poverty, and in some instances it begets it. On the other hand, a little reflection will convince us that they need books more than we do.

The blind possess all the human attributes, and are endowed with native capacities for improvement and for enjoying the delights of nature. Their sentiments, feelings, affections, desires, ambitions, and aspirations are identical with ours; but a part of the objective knowledge which ministers to all these, and which is specially the legitimate product of the power of vision, is not so easily attainable in their case. The majestic forms of the clouds, the colors of the rainbow, the plumage of the birds, the tints of the flowers, all the glad outward world, the varieties of trees and plants, the products of art, the wonders of nature, and the marvellous creations of man's genius, so far as the physical perceptions are concerned, are a blank to the blind. The dark veil which covers their eyes renders all the vast wealth of information and the means of daily comfort and enjoyment which are derived from the mere sight of natural objects inaccessible to them. Wherever they go they carry with them their chamber of

darkness and isolation.   Their night is in many cases a
continuous one from the cradle to the grave.   They
long, therefore, for intellectual light, for the means of
cheering their lonely hours, of lightening the burden
of their calamity, and of brightening their existence.
They pine and parch within a very short distance of the
fountain.   Dr. Brooks has aptly likened the embossed
page to the "window through which the blind can look
upon the great world of wit and wisdom, poetry and
science."   But the supply of such publications as are
calculated to introduce into the mind of the blind,
through the tips of their fingers, a flood of light is
exceedingly inadequate to the evident need.   When
the strong and striking contrast between the library of
the sightless and that of the seeing is remembered, the
scantiness of the one is pathetic as compared with the
overflowing abundance of the other.   One hundred
books stand on the shelves of our institution, some of
which are nearly worn out by constant use: three hundred and ninety thousand on those of the public library of the city of Boston.   In order to remedy this
inequality, and to provide the inestimable blessing for
the blind of an adequate library, we have brought their
case before the public, and have appealed for a fund of
seventy-five thousand dollars, which, added to previous
contributions and donations, would make the total
amount one hundred thousand dollars.   The income of
this endowment will enable us to issue from ten to
twelve new books every year, and to place sets of them
in the leading libraries of New England and of all the
large cities of the union for free use, thus rendering
embossed publications as accessible to the sightless as
works in common print are to those who can see.

Perhaps no feature in the whole history of the development of the educational system for the blind is of greater interest or more full of encouragement than the generous spirit with which the plan of raising a permanent printing-fund was received by the community. The energy, nay the enthusiasm, which this project has awakened is only comparable to that benevolent activity which marked the beginnings of the first movement in behalf of the blind, of which the present is the legitimate outcome and continuation. Its spirit is indeed precisely identical with that which prompted the early efforts in this field of beneficence. The original instructors said: "Give us light to clear these darkened paths." To-day we say: "Give us more oil to keep that light burning." Like the perpetual lamp of the sanctuary, it must not be suffered to go out for an instant; and it is our constant aim and desire to preserve its bright flame. But no man can work alone and unaided, however sacred and important his task; and the helping hands which have been stretched forth to us have brought the attainment of our object as near as could be reasonably expected within so short a space of time.

Words fail to express the deep gratitude of the blind towards these their generous benefactors; but their brightened minds, like polished mirrors, will reflect, through the far years, the goodness and beauty which radiate towards them from the noble hearts of their friends and well-wishers. To the beneficent kindness of these munificent donors the projected library for the blind will stand as a monument in perpetuity. We may liken it to a grand column of light and wisdom; but the capital is still missing. Thirty-eight thousand dollars are wanting to complete it. Let us appeal once more for this amount, hoping that the generous and the benevolent of the community will respond readily to the need of the blind, and will not deny to them the whole loaf of that bread of intellectual life for which they ask.

Work Department for Adults.

A fair amount of work has been done in this department during the past year, but its financial condition is still far from satisfactory.

The receipts from all sources, from the first day of October, 1880, to the 30th of September, 1881, have amounted to $14,118.41, being more by $175.34 than those of the previous year.

The expenses for materials, labor, and all other items have been $15,658.69.

Thus the balance on the wrong side of the sheet is $1,186.33, whereas the sum of $990.03 was paid out of the treasury of the institution the previous year.

The number of blind persons employed in this department was 19 ; and the amount paid in cash to them, as wages for their work, was $3,435.03, or $248.31 more than in 1880.

This department was never designed as a source of income to the institution. Its main object is to assist adult blind persons in deriving support from their own industry, by providing them with more regular work than they would be able to obtain by their own individual efforts. This laudable end has been persistently pursued amidst great and discouraging difficulties, and a number of respectable men and women have been rescued from the grasp of poverty and the degradation of dependence upon alms.

But this department is far from being self-sustaining: on the contrary, it has for many years entailed a heavy loss upon the institution; and we feel again constrained to request our fellow-citizens to come to our relief by increasing their patronage, and extending orders for goods made in our workshops, which we warrant to be such as they are represented in every respect.

EXHIBITS OF THE WORK OF THE INSTITUTION.

The fine exhibit of articles of fancy-work, books in raised print, and educational appliances, sent last year to the world's fair at Melbourne, Australia, has received due notice, and we are informed that a medal has been awarded to the institution. This new mark of approbation is quite gratifying, and bears witness to the spirit of progress and improvement which permeates the various departments of the establishment.

We have also another exhibit at the Mechanics' Fair this year, which is presided over by one of the graduates of the school. It represents the work of the institution in several of its branches; and comprises mattresses, pillows, door-mats, cushions, specimens of embossed books issued by our press, maps in relief, and fancy-work from the girls' department, ranging all the way from fine lace to hammocks and Indian baskets. The whole makes an attractive display.

SEMI-CENTENNIAL ANNIVERSARY.

The institution entered upon the fiftieth year of its organization in August last, and with the close of the present school session will occur the first semi-centennial anniversary of its existence.

The time which has elapsed since then has seen wondrous changes ; and in no instance more remarkable than in the matter of the education of the blind. The little band of six pupils first gathered together by Dr. Howe, in his father's house on Pleasant street, has expanded into whole ranks and files of pupils, graduates and candidates. Useful blind citizens have finished their honored career and gone to their graves. Young children are constantly coming to us for the first rudiments of education. Music teachers, tuners of pianofortes, mechanics, men of business, trained and fitted for the efficient practice of their respective professions and arts under the fostering care of the school, ply their avocations actively in all the towns and villages of New England. The timid blind child, hardly trusting his feet to move alone, or his hands to trace the first letters of the alphabet, to-day walks among us as the self-poised, self-dependent man, managing his own affairs, assisting in those of others, scorning the idea of being a recipient of alms, helpful, respected, intelligent and industrious.

In looking over the annals of the institution, and recounting the changes through which it has passed and the work it has accomplished, we cannot but see that it has been to the blind of New England what the heart is to the human body, — the centre and source of their mental vitality and power, the spot from which the young, fresh, and bright stream of intellectual and moral light is distributed in every direction to strengthen their character, awaken their dormant powers, and illumine their darkened path in life.

The report of the director, which is herewith submitted, instead of being confined to a review of the work of the past year, with suggestions for changes and improvements, is mostly devoted to a brief historical sketch of the origin, rise and progress of the science of the education of the blind, from the earliest times to this day. As the present is the fiftieth report of the institution, — the first one having been issued in the form of an address a few months after its organization, — the occasion seems eminently suitable for such an account.

We trust that the corporation will also take the necessary measures to celebrate the semi-centennial anniversary of the establishment at the close of the school year in a fitting manner.

Closing Remarks.

Before taking leave of the corporation, we would fain express our conviction that the institution is successfully performing the work assigned to it, as one of the agencies which have for their object the weal of humanity, and that it deserves the confidence, sympathy and support of the community. As regards the number of those who are benefited by it, and the degree of relief which their affliction receives from its ministrations, there is, in our opinion, no manifestation of benevolence more striking, and no enterprise of philanthropy more important, than that which raises the blind to a participation in the enjoyments and responsibilities of life.

It is gratifying to remark that the spirit which seems to prevail everywhere in the establishment is that of a well-ordered and harmonious home, and that the end kept in view by its management is to supply to the pupils those kindly domestic influences which are so important in the education of youth. The school is particularly fortunate in having its work carried on by a band of teachers and officers highly qualified for the performance of the duties of their respective places. The general improvement made under their care and exertions is not a mere sign of spasmodic activity, but a solid manifestation of the steady application of a well-conceived and matured plan.

Conscious that the duties devolving upon our board have been faithfully discharged, we gladly invite examination and criticism of our administration of the affairs of the institution.

In conclusion, we would tender our thanks and grateful acknowledgments to the legislative bodies of Massachusetts and the other states of New England, and to all who have afforded their assistance and coöperation in the promotion of the great cause of the education of the blind.

All which is respectfully submitted by

ROBERT E. APTHORP,
JOHN S. DWIGHT,
JOSEPH B. GLOVER,
J. THEODORE HEARD,
HENRY LEE HIGGINSON,
JAMES H. MEANS,
ROBERT TREAT PAINE, Jun.,
EDWARD N. PERKINS,
SAMUEL M. QUINCY,
SAMUEL G. SNELLING,
JAMES STURGIS,
GEORGE W. WALES,

Trustees.

THE REPORT OF THE DIRECTOR.

To the Trustees.

Gentlemen, — With the revolution of another year, it has again become my duty to submit to your board a report of the progress and present condition of the institution, touching incidentally upon such topics as may be germane to the education of the blind.

It is a pleasant and encouraging task to review the work of the past year, for it shows a steady progress in its character and a preponderance of good in its results.

The method of conducting the affairs of the institution, the daily routine of its internal life, the system of instruction, and the general principles upon which the physical, intellectual and moral training of the pupils is based, although modified and improved in some of their details, have, in the main, been preserved the same as heretofore.

The house has been kept in good condition; the pupils have been properly cared for; and additional facilities, of more or less importance, for the efficient prosecution of our work, have been introduced in nearly every department of the establishment.

Progress in knowledge, good order, happiness and contentment, resulting from a judicious division of their time into hours of study and practice, labor and amusement, exercise and rest, is noticeable among the scholars, and may be considered as the legitimate fruit of the well-matured plans and earnest endeavors of the teachers and officers of the institution.

Increased experience in our work stimulates our energies and quickens our zeal for its more thorough and satisfactory performance. Full well we know that we are far from having reached the highest attainable point; and yet we cannot but hope that the amount of positive good gained, and of evil removed, through the agency of the school from year to year, is steadily increasing. A mere repetition, however, in a perfunctory fashion, of what has hitherto been done, or the performance of approximately the same work in a somewhat better manner, is not sufficient. In order to advance the cause of the education of the blind, and bring it within the limits indicated by science and prescribed by the nature of their case, we must strive to overcome more difficulties, and to surmount every obstacle that can be reached by human perseverance.

NUMBER OF INMATES.

The total number of blind persons connected with the various departments of the institution at the beginning of the past year, as teachers, pupils, employés, and work men and women, was 156. There have since been admitted 27; 21 have been discharged, making the present total number 162. Of these, 144 are in the school proper, and 18 in the workshop for adults.

The first class includes 128 boys and girls, enrolled as pupils, 13 teachers, and 3 domestics. Of the pupils there are now 109 in attendance; 19 being temporarily absent on account of illness, or from various other causes.

The second class comprises 14 men and 4 women, employed in the industrial department for adults.

The number of pupils is rapidly increasing. There never were so many young children, and particularly little girls, received at the beginning of any previous school session as this year. Most of them seem to be quite intelligent and promising, while in a few cases the disease which has caused the loss of sight has undermined the constitution and weakened the mental faculties.

SANITARY CONDITION.

It is a source of great pleasure to be able to report again that during the past year the school has not been visited by death, and that the members of the household have been entirely free from epidemic or other diseases.

We are, no doubt, greatly indebted to the salubrity of the location of the institution for the general prevalence of health, which is the more remarkable from the fact that many of our inmates are victims of scrofula, or have a predisposition to some form of disease, often, perhaps, that which originally caused their blindness. But regularity of living, wholesomeness of diet, a proper regard to personal habits, and prompt attention to ordinary ailments, together with exercise in the open air and under shelter, serve in many cases to mitigate or remove these tendencies, and conduce to the good measure of health which our pupils enjoy, as well as to their success in their various pursuits.

SCOPE OF THE EDUCATION OF THE BLIND.

" Sightless to see and judge through judgment's eyes,
  To make four senses do the work of five,
To arm the mind for hopeful enterprise,
  Are lights to him who doth in darkness live."

These words of an old poet concisely express and
strikingly set forth the object of the education of the
blind. They show the nature of its work and the extent of its scope. They indicate that it should be
broad in its aims, comprehensive in its purposes, and
thorough in its character.

A system for the efficient and proper training of the
blind, in order to be successful and productive of good
results, should be adapted to the special requirements
of their case, and calculated to meet the exigencies
resulting from their affliction, and to promote the full
development of their remaining faculties and the harmonious growth of their powers. It should constitute
a sort of physical, intellectual and moral gymnasium,
preparatory for the great struggle in the arena of life,
and should include that finishing instruction as members
of society which Schiller designated as the " education
of the human race," consisting of action, conduct, self-
culture, self-control, — all that tends to discipline a man
truly, and fit him for the proper performance of his
duties and for the business of life. A mere literary
drill, or any exclusive and one-sided accomplishment,
cannot do this for the blind. It will prove insufficient
and incomplete at its best. Bacon observes, with his
usual weight of words, that " studies teach not their
use; but there is a wisdom without them and above

them, won by observation;" and all experience serves
to illustrate and enforce the lesson, that a man perfects
himself by work blended with reading ; and that it is
life elevated by literature, action quickened by study,
and character strengthened by the illustrious examples
of biography, which tend perpetually to purify and
renovate mankind.

A brief review of the work of the various departments of the institution will show that neither efforts
nor any means within our reach have been spared to
" arm the mind of the blind for hopeful enterprise," to
equip them well to make a successful struggle with the
odds that are against them, and to enable them to grapple resolutely with the difficulties opposing their advancement to usefulness and independence.

LITERARY DEPARTMENT.

The work of this department has been carried on
with earnestness and success ; and its present condition
is highly satisfactory.

The course of instruction marked out some time
since has been followed, during the past year, steadily
and with satisfactory results.

The progress made by the pupils in their respective
studies is generally commendable, and attests their diligence and application, as well as the skill and fidelity of
their teachers.

No means have been spared during the past year to
render the school efficient in its workings, progressive
in its methods, well supplied with apparatus for tangible
illustration, and complete in its curriculum.

The instruction of our teachers has been mostly given

in the form of direction, rather than in that of
didactics. They have taken câre that the natural activity of the scholars should have an opportunity for
free exercise.

Mechanical teaching has been persistently avoided;
and the system of requiring the pupils to commit stol-
idly to memory the contents of text-books, to recite
meaningless rules glibly, and to learn crude and obscure
statements of abstract theories and wordy definitions by
heart, has no place whatever in our school. On the
contrary, the time is devoted to the nurture of the intellectual faculties, to the development of the mental
powers from which ideas are born, and to the acquisition of those great truths which relate to the happiness
of the human race and to the general welfare of mankind.

In the primary departments of the school the educational processes have been preëminently objective, syn-
thetic, inductive, and experimental; while in the advanced divisions they have been subjective and analytic
as well, — deductive as well as inductive, and philosophical as well as experimental. In the high classes, a
broad and deep foundation has been laid for future
achievement. Here the pupils have attained a good
degree of scholarship and culture, which increases the
strength and fertilizes the resources of their mind.
Here they have been taught how to command their
powers and direct their energies. Here they have been
furnished with all available facilities to prepare themselves for a useful career in life.

I•am exceedingly sorry to be obliged to report that
the corps of teachers has not preserved its integrity;

On
lar p
tivc

A
the
the
thr
exa

mi
bu
of
o
a

ıd
.nd
due

these
, in all
impetus
acquiring
from mere

ıf the Misses
scholars, Miss ..
ouraged to go ..
xcellent normal ·
ıluated, and has
ıcting the system,
:nnett in the girls'

ıur school have been
scemed entirely help-
ıtever of their hands,
ıl activity by the agency
, the simple but interest-
.ı of block-building, weav-
ıı clay, and the like, they
ı of muscular elasticity and
-ists them in tracing on the
.iphering the embossed print
.ʒs of their shoes neatly, in
. in using their needle adeptly,
ı of things readily which they
to undertake without this train-

but that two changes have occurred in it during the past year. Miss S. L. Bennett, having found, after a few weeks' rest, that her strength was not sufficiently restored to enable her to discharge her duties efficiently and conscientiously, felt obliged to decline a re-appointment, and Miss Cora A. Newton, of Fayville, a graduate of the State Normal School at South Framingham, was elected to fill her place. Miss M. L. P. Shattuck resigned a few weeks before the commencement of the term to accept the principalship of the training-school for girls at Haverhill, and Miss Julia R. Gilman, a lady of long experience and devotion to our work, was promoted as first teacher in the boys' department. Miss Annie E. Carnes, of Attleborough, a graduate of the State Normal School at Bridgewater, was appointed to fill the vacancy created by this promotion.

Kindergarten and Object-teaching.

The blind usually experience great difficulty, not only in getting a clear idea of things from mere descriptions, but in obtaining, by feeling, correct notions of the forms of objects to which they have not been accustomed; and this is a serious drawback to their acquiring much valuable and practical information. This difficulty arises not from any general defect in their powers of sensation, — for these are in the majority of cases not in the least affected by the causes which produce blindness, — but rather from the want of a special and thorough training of the sense of touch.

To remedy this important evil as far as we may, and at the same time to awaken and exercise the powers of observation, comparison, combination, invention, memory, reflection and action, the kindergarten system and object-teaching have been found among the best and most efficient auxiliaries; and both have received due and earnest attention in our school.

The means and appliances for carrying out these methods of instruction and training successfully in all their details have not been wanting, and an impetus has been given in most branches of study for acquiring knowledge from tangible objects rather than from mere abstract descriptions.

Thanks to the kindness and generosity of the Misses Garland and Weston, one of our advanced scholars, Miss Annie E. Poulson, was permitted and encouraged to go through the regular course in their excellent normal training kindergarten, where she graduated, and has since aided very materially in perfecting the system already introduced by Miss Della Bennett in the girls' department.

The workings of the system in our school have been most beneficent. Children who seemed entirely help-less, and had no command whatever of their hands, have been roused to energy and activity by the agency of the kindergarten. Through the simple but interesting and attractive occupations of block-building, weaving, embroidery, moulding in clay, and the like, they have acquired a great degree of muscular elasticity and manual dexterity, which assists them in tracing on the maps with alacrity, in deciphering the embossed print easily, in tying the strings of their shoes neatly, in stringing beads promptly, in using their needle adeptly, and in doing a number of things readily which they would have felt unable to undertake without this training. Modelling is particularly beneficial to the blind: it helps them to acquire a more or less correct idea of forms of various kinds, which it is almost impossible for them to obtain by the mere handling of objects.

Kindergarten work may thus be likened to the exercises given to beginners in music, which prepare the student for rendering difficult pieces more brilliantly; and no training of primary classes of blind children can attain a high degree of efficiency without its assistance.

Music Department.

Steady advancement has marked this important branch of our school, and a great amount of practical work has been accomplished in it during the past year.

Music has been taught in all its branches both theoretically and practically; and its refining and elevating influence has been seen in the taste and inclinations of those of our pupils who have entered into its study with an earnest desire to overcome difficulties and be benefited by it.

The usual course of instruction has been continued during the past year, with such alterations and improvements as have seemed necessary; and the piano, harmony, counterpoint and composition, class and solo singing, the church and reed organ, flute, clarinet, cornet, and various other wind instruments, have all been taught by competent and patient teachers, and with satisfactory results.

Two new reed organs have been recently purchased, and all the instruments in our collection have keen kept in good repair and sound condition.

There has been no want of appreciation of the inter-

nal means and facilities afforded by the institution for
making good musicians and efficient teachers of our
pupils; and those among them who are gifted with
special talent, and possess such general mental ability
as is essential for the attainment of excellence in any
profession, advance rapidly and give promise of success
in their career.   But it cannot be too strongly stated
or too often repeated that an exclusive and absorbing
devotion to music, to the neglect of other branches
of education, does an incalculable amount of mischief
among the blind.   It dwarfs their mind, disturbs the
harmony of their development, contracts their intellectual horizon, undermines their nervous system, stunts
their physical growth, narrows their sympathies, and
renders them unfit for the duties and amenities of life.
Illiteracy among musicians is becoming so palpable and
crying an evil everywhere, thwarting and degrading
their art, that a number of distinguished men in England have recently organized themselves into an association for the purpose of promoting intellectual education
among those who follow the study of the "accord of
sweet sounds;" and there is no class of people whose
success as music teachers and performers depends in so
great a measure upon the degree of mental discipline
which they have attained at school, and the breadth of
their general knowledge, as that of the blind.   With
them professional skill, however perfect it may be in
itself, will not find full scope for display unless it be
accompanied by those accomplishments with which every
musician ought to adorn his intellect, and enhanced by
those moral beauties and graces which embellish the
character.

6

Besides the means for thorough instruction and practice afforded at the institution, external opportunities
for the cultivation and refinement of the musical taste
of the pupils, and the development of their artistic
sense, have been eagerly sought and amply enjoyed.
Owing to the kindness of the officers and members of
the leading musical societies of Boston, to the proprietors of theatres, the managers of public entertainments,
and also to a long chain of eminent musicians in the
city, — the names of all of whom will be printed in the
list of acknowledgments, — our scholars have continued
to be generously permitted to attend the finest concerts,
rehearsals, operas, oratorios, recitals, and the like, and
have also been favored with many exquisite performances given in our own hall.   The week beginning with
the thirtieth of January and ending with the fifth of
February was in this respect remarkable.   Our pupils
had the daily opportunity of enjoying one or two concerts of a high order.   On Sunday evening they heard
Mozart's " Requiem," and Beethoven's " Mount of
Olives," by the Händel and Haydn society.   On Monday evening they attended a concert by Mr. Georg
Henschel, in Tremont Temple.   On Tuesday afternoon
they were invited to an organ recital in the same place ;
and in the evening they had a musical entertainment in
our own hall, given by M. A. De Sève, the violinist,
and M. Otto Bendix, pianist, with the assistance of Miss
Sarah Winslow, Mrs. H. T. Spooner, and Miss Daisy
Terry, of Rome.   On Wednesday evening they attended
the Euterpe concert.   On Thursday afternoon they
heard the Harvard symphony concert, and in the evening had another interesting entertainment in our hall,

given by Mr. George Parker, of King's chapel, and
Dr. and Mrs. Fenderson, of South Boston. On Friday
afternoon they were invited to a concert of the New
England conservatory, and in the evening to one of the
Apollo club. On Saturday evening they attended Mr.
Arthur Foote's piano recital. This was, of course, an
avalanche of opportunities of uncommon occurrence;
but I am sure that there is no city in the whole civilized world in which the blind enjoy one-half of the
advantages which are so liberally bestowed upon our
scholars by the musical organizations of Boston.

TUNING DEPARTMENT.

The art of tuning pianofortes was introduced into this
institution a few years after its organization as a lucrative employment for the blind; and as early as 1837 the
trustees were able to announce, in their fifth annual
report, that the pupils were prepared to keep instruments in order, by the year, at a reasonable rate, and
that their "work was warranted to give satisfaction to
competent judges."

Experience has since confirmed the value of the
tuning department as one of the most important
branches in our system of training; and it has received all the attention which its practical aim and
useful purposes merit.

The instruction given in this department during the
past year has been as thorough and systematic as heretofore, and the results have been quite satisfactory.

The pupils have had excellent opportunities for a
careful study and steady practice of the art of tuning;
and those of the graduates who have mastered it in all

its details meet with favor and encouragement from the public, and are, as a whole, successful.

It is a matter of congratulation that the care of the pianofortes in the public schools — one hundred and thirty in number — has again for the fifth time been entrusted to the tuning department of this institution. The confidence which this charge implies aids to strengthen our tuners in the good opinion of the public, and by so doing ensures to them an increased and extended patronage throughout the community. Their work is in all cases most carefully and satisfactorily executed, and draws forth encomiums from their employers, as well as from some of the best musicians in the city, which show that they are worthy of the trust reposed in their ability and skill.

Orders for tuning are coming in continually from some of the best and most intelligent families in Boston and the neighboring towns, and are invariably attended to with promptitude and despatch.

TECHNICAL DEPARTMENT.

" Other creatures all day long
Rove idle, unemployed, and less need rest;
Man hath his daily work of body or mind
Appointed, which declares his dignity
And the regard of Heaven on all his ways."

Milton.

This department continues to perform its important part in our system of education, both as an essential element in enlarging the sphere of the activities of the blind and as an agent in training them in habits of industry and in the practice of useful handicraft.

As has been often stated in these reports, the influence of manual labor is of inestimable value to all men, but most especially to the blind. It promotes physical strength and soundness of health. It induces confidence in the use of their bodily powers, and independence of character. It prevents them, in the midst of the mental exercises required of them, from underestimating the practical needs of life. While their studies add to their intelligence, increase their social accomplishments, and dignify their calling, patient and daily labor will prove the real source of their material prosperity. Moreover, experience has proved that pupils who are occupied a part of the day with books in the schoolroom, and the remainder with tools in the workshop, or with practice on the piano or in singing, make about as rapid intellectual progress as those of equal ability who spend the whole time in study and recitation.

For these reasons the work has been carried on during the past year in both branches of the technical department with the same earnestness as heretofore, and with equally satisfactory results.

I. — Workshop for the Boys.

The pupils in this branch of the industrial department have been carefully trained during the past year in the elements of handicraft, and have worked at the usual trades with more or less success, which is attainable in proportion to the natural activity and aptitude of the learner.

Instruction has been given in a simple and practical way, and the boys have been made to feel that, from

the moment that they are able to use their hands skilfully and manufacture a few plain articles, they enter
into the sphere of real business.   Moreover, they are
constantly taught, by precept and example, that practical
industry, wisely and vigorously applied, always produces
its due effects, and that it carries a man onward, brings
out his individual character, and stimulates others to a
like activity.

Several of the advanced pupils, — in whose case some
handicraft seemed to be the chief reliance for self-maintenance, — after having learned the rudiments of upholstery in the juvenile department, have devoted most of
their time to the practice of making mattresses in the
workshop for adults, under the immediate care of one
of the experienced journeymen.

II. — Workrooms for the Girls.

It affords me great pleasure to report that a higher
degree of efficiency has been attained in this branch of
industry during the past year than ever before, and
that particular pains have been taken to render the
workrooms attractive and useful.

The girls have been taught to sew and knit, both by
hand and machine, and have given much attention to
various kinds of fancy-work.   The articles manufactured
by them indicate a degree of skill, taste and thoroughness which does honor to their teacher and credit to
themselves.   Perhaps the specimens which represent
the work of our pupils in the Mechanics' Fair this year
are among the finest ever produced.

The art of making Indian baskets of different sizes
and forms has again received as much attention as the

private affairs of an experienced instructress permitted
her to devote to it.   It is hoped that some of our advanced scholars will soon have a fair opportunity to
master this trade.

Our girls have continued to take turns in the lighter
household work, and a few of them have received such
special training in the domestic circle as to be able to -
become useful to themselves and helpful to others in --
this direction in after-life.

DEPARTMENT OF PHYSICAL TRAINING.

During the past year our system of physical training
has been improved and perfected in many of its details,
and has been carried on with unusual efficiency and
precision.

In addition to the out-door exercise at the end of
every hour in the day, the pupils, divided into six
classes, have repaired regularly to the gymnasium at
fixed times, and, under the direction of discreet and
competent teachers, have gone through a systematic and
progressive course of gymnastics.

These exercises, although mild in character and
rather limited in some respects, are of sufficient force
and variety to ensure the energetic movement of the
muscles, and facilitate the vital process of the destruction and renovation of the tissues of the body, which it
is the object of physical training to accomplish.   They
consist of calisthenics, swinging, jumping, marching,
military drill, and the like, and are calculated to give
strength to the muscles, elasticity to the limbs, suppleness to the joints, erectness of carriage, and above all,
and with infinitely greater force than all, to promote

the expansion of those parts of the body, and stimulate the activity of those of its organs, upon the health and fair conformation of which happiness and success are in a great measure dependent.

Experience and daily observation enable me to state confidently that, as the result and legitimate reward of a strict adherence to our system of physical training, a class of children will leave us loftier in stature, firmer in structure, fairer in form, and better able to perform the duties and bear the burdens of life.

Collections of Tangible Objects, Library, etc.

The efforts to increase our collections of tangible objects and apparatus of various kinds, and to multiply the books both in raised and ordinary print, have continued during the past year without relaxation, and our shelves have been enriched by many new additions.

The most important of these consist in a complete set of Auzoux's botanical models, several of his other anatomical preparations, and in a large supply of stuffed animals, birds, fishes, shells, specimens of woods and plants, fossils, and many curiosities which are calculated to interest our children, and stimulate their minds to inquiry and the examination of external things.

The total number of tangible objects of various kinds in our collection is about 1,261. Of these, 501 have been procured during the past year. I avail myself of this opportunity to express my high appreciation of the kindness of many friends of the blind who have volunteered to assist them in this direction. I am especially indebted to one of our graduates, Mr. Clement Ryder, of Chelsea, whose valuable contributions to our little museum include, among numerous other things, three fine albatrosses.

The present total number of volumes in our library is 5,383. Of these, 793 — 450 in common and 343 in — raised print — have been obtained during the past year. Most of these books have been selected with care, and are not only tastefully but substantially bound.

EDUCATION OF THE BLIND.

Historical Sketch of its Origin, Rise and Progress.

The institution has now entered upon the last year of its first semi-centennial ; and it seems 'fitting to give in the present, its fiftieth report, an outline of the history of its origin, rise and progress.

But, in order to take a comprehensive view of the work of the education of the blind, it will be necessary to glance at the springs of its original inception in France, to go back to the early stages of its development, and to trace the course of the marvellous stream of beneficence, which has transformed a desolate wilderness into a fair and blooming garden.

The present sketch will therefore treat concisely of the following topics : —

First, of the general condition of the blind in the past, and the neglect formerly endured.

Second, of the early attempts at their education made in different countries.

Third, of the organization of the Paris school by Valentin Haüy.

Fourth, of the establishment of similar institutions in Great Britain and on the continent of Europe.

Fifth, of the foundation and development of the New England institution.

Sixth, of the education and training of Laura Bridgman; and,

Seventh, of the establishment of schools for the blind throughout the United States of America.

A brief comparison of the distinctive features of the systems of instruction and training for the blind in this country and in Europe will bring this sketch to a close.

I. — *Condition of the Blind in the Past.*

History has preserved sundry particulars regarding blind persons who have of themselves acquired great knowledge in various branches of learning, and won distinction in science, literature and art; but these were phenomenal cases, — mere shooting stars on the horizon of deep darkness, ignorance and neglect. The great mass of this afflicted class were everywhere mere objects of charity, which, however wisely it may be administered, wounds the spirit while it soothes the flesh. From Bartimeus to Lesueur — the first pupil of Haüy — the blind were left to procure a precarious subsistence by begging at the entrance of the temples, in the churchyards, or by the wayside. Their infirmity was considered a sufficient cause to prevent them from participating in the activities of life, and from enjoying the blessings of instruction or the benefits of industry. Discouraged by the apparent incapacity of the blind, men shrank from the task of endeavoring to combat the ills which their affliction had entailed upon them, and to rescue them from the evils of idleness and the horrors of intellectual darkness. They were even allowed,

at times, to become the objects of harsh and inhuman
pastimes in the hands of ignorant and vicious people.
The following instance may give some idea of the condition and treatment of the blind during the fifteenth
century: —

In the month of August, 1425, under the reign of
Charles VII., four blind men, cased in full armor and
provided with clubs, were placed in a fenced square of
the Hôtel d'Armagnac with a large hog, which was to
be the prize of whoever should kill it. The struggle
having begun, the poor sightless creatures, in endeavoring to hit the animal, struck each other with such
violence that, but for their armor, they would certainly
have killed each other. With this cruel sport the
savage and unfeeling spectators were much diverted.

It is curious that a pagan and uncivilized nation
should have set a good example to enlightened chris-
tians in this respect. It is stated, in Charlevoix's history, that in Japan the blind were long ago made to
fill a comparatively useful sphere. The government
kept a large number of them in an establishment, and
their business was to learn the history of the empire
through all the remote ages, to arrange it systematically by chapter and verse in their memories, and to
transmit it from generation to generation, thus forming
a sort of perennial walking and talking library of useful historical knowledge.

II. — *Early Attempts at the Education of the Blind.*

During the sixteenth century, thoughtful and benevolent men sought to devise processes for the instruction
of the blind, but with no great success. Several un-

fruitful attempts were also made in the early part of
the seventeenth century to prepare some sort of books
for them, both in engraved and raised letters. Among
others, Jérôme Cardan had conceived that it would be
possible to teach the blind to read and write by means
of feeling, and cited, in support of this view, several
facts reported by Erasmus.

The first book which called attention to the condition
and miseries of the blind was published in Italy, in
1646. It was written by one of the learned sons of
that favored country, in the form of a letter addressed
from S. D. C. to Vincent Armanni, and was printed in
Italian and French under the title *Il cieco afflitto e con-
solato ;* or, *L'aveugle affligé et consolé.*

In 1670, padre Lana Terzi, a Jesuit of Brescia, who
had previously devoted a few pages to the education of
the deaf, published a treatise on the instruction of the
blind.

Jacques Bernouilli, being at Geneva in 1676, taught
Mademoiselle Elizabeth Waldkirch, who had lost her
sight two months after birth, to read; but he did not
make known the means which he employed.

Dr. Burnet, bishop of Salisbury, gives, in his "Journey in Switzerland," a detailed account of Mademoiselle
Walkier, of Schaffhousen, whose eyes had been burned
when she was a year old. She spoke five languages,
and was a theologian, a philosopher, and a good musician. This young person had learned to write by
means of hollow characters cut in wood, which she at
first passed over with a pointed iron. She had afterwards made use of a pencil, and finally, when Bishop
Burnet was at Schaffhousen, in October, 1685, he saw
her write very rapidly and very correctly.

Two years later appeared Locke's famous "Essay on the Human Understanding," in which was discussed the problem proposed to him by Molyneux, — a scholarly writer and member of the Irish parliament, — whether a person blind from his birth would, upon being suddenly restored to sight, be able to distinguish, by his eyes alone, a globe from a cube, the difference between which he had previously recognized by feeling? The question was answered in the negative, both by the author of the essay and by his "learned and worthy friend."

In 1703, Leibnitz took up the subject, and his conclusions were at variance with those of Locke and Molyneux.

A few years later, that sightless mathematical wonder, Nicholas Saunderson, appeared on the literary horizon of England, and made such advances in the higher departments of science, that he was appointed, "though not matriculated at the university," on the recommendation of Sir Isaac Newton, to fill the chair which a short time previous had been occupied by himself at Cambridge. Expounding from the depths of the eternal night in which he lived the most abstruse points of the Newtonian philosophy, and especially the laws of optics, or the theory of solar refraction, and communicating his ideas with unequalled perspicuity and precision, he filled his audience with surprise, and became the object of general admiration.

In 1729, while Saunderson was still at the zenith of his fame at Cambridge (having just been created doctor of laws by a mandate of George II.), Locke's answer to Molyneux's problem was receiving confirma-

tion from the experience of a boy blind from birth,
whom Cheselden, the celebrated anatomist, had successfully couched for cataracts and restored to perfect sight
at the age of thirteen.   This youth was not able at
first to recognize by vision the objects which were most
familiar to his touch.   It was long before he could
discriminate by his eye between his old companions, the
family cat and dog, dissimilar as such animals appear
to us in color and conformation.   Being ashamed to
ask the oft-repeated question, he was observed one
day to pass his hand carefully over the cat, and then,
looking at her steadfastly, to exclaim, " So, puss, I shall
know you another time."   This case, the most remarkable of the kind, faithfully detailed by the surgeon himself in No. 402 of the " Philosophical Transactions," led
to similar experiments afterwards, the conclusions of
which did not differ essentially from those of Locke.

The spirit of free inquiry, which had been unchained
in the preceding century, having passed by a natural
transition from expatiation in the regions of taste and
abstract philosophy into those of social science and
human life, became bold and restless, longing for
greater triumphs than those achieved heretofore.   The
French *savans*, who were endeavoring to dissipate the
clouds of authority and the foggy mists of error, were
on the alert for events touching upon important psychological questions, and calculated to help the cause of
humanity.

In 1746, Condillac took up Locke's problem and the
experiments of Cheselden, and discussed with much
clearness and dialectic skill the mental processes of the
blind.

Simultaneously with his *Essai sur l'origine des connaissances humaines* was first published a volume of the poems of Dr. Blacklock, of Scotland, who, although deprived of sight in early infancy, went through the usual course of studies at the university of Edinburgh, and distinguished himself by his proficiency in classical literature, in *belles-lettres*, in metaphysics, and in all other branches of knowledge. The productions of his muse are marked by elegance of diction, ardor of sentiment, and accurate descriptions of visible objects. His writings will be searched in vain, however, for poetry of a very high order. He says of himself, what doubtless is true of all persons similarly situated, that he always associated some moral quality with visible objects.

The following year appeared in Dublin a biography of Saunderson from the pen of his disciple and successor in the professorship at Cambridge, William Inchlif or Hinchliffe. This work contained a minute description, with illustrative drawings, of the appliances used by the sightless mathematician, and was most eagerly read in France.

The abbé Deschamps, treating of the education of the deaf-mutes, also sketched the outlines of the art of teaching the blind to read and write.

Meanwhile Lenôtre, the famous blind man of Puiseaux, appeared on the stage, and, by the originality which stamped everything that he did, attracted universal attention. He was the son of a professor of philosophy in the university of Paris, and had attended with advantage courses of chemistry and botany at the *Jardin du Roi*. After having dissipated a part of his

fortune, he retired to Puiseaux, a little town in Gatinais,
where he established a distillery, the products of which
he came regularly once a year to Paris to dispose of.
It was his custom to sleep during the day and rise in
the evening. He worked all night, "because," as he
himself said, "he was not then disturbed by anybody."
His wife used to find everything perfectly arranged in
the morning. Having found in the resources of his
mind and in his own activity a shelter from poverty, he
lived happily in the midst of his family. His retired
and extraordinary mode of life earned for him a sort of
reputation. Diderot, then looking out for philosophical
sensations, visited him at his home, and found him occupied in teaching his seeing son to read with raised
characters. The blind man put to him some very singular questions on the transparency of glass, colors, and
such matters. He asked if naturalists were the only
persons who saw with the microscope; if the machine
which magnified objects was greater than that which
diminished them; if that which brought them near was
shorter than that which removed them to a distance.
He conceived the eye to be "an organ upon which the
air produces the same effect as the staff on the hand,"
and defined a mirror as "a machine by which objects
are placed in relief. out of themselves." On being in-
terrogated as to whether he felt a great desire to have
eyes, he answered, "Were it not for the mere gratification of curiosity, I think I should do as well to wish for
long arms. It seems to me that my hands would inform me better of what is going on in the moon than
your eyes and telescopes; and then the eyes lose the
power of vision more readily than the hands that of

feeling. It would be better to perfect the organ which
I have than to bestow on me that which I have not."
This interview, together with the knowledge of Saunderson's appliances obtained from a perusal of his biography, called out, in 1749, Diderot's ingenious *Lettres
sur les aveugles à l'usage de ceux qui voint*, which set
Paris ablaze with enthusiasm and inquiry, and which
procured for him at once an acquaintance with Voltaire
and three months' imprisonment at Vincennes. Of the
many stupid blunders and imbecile acts which emanated
from the government of Louis XV., this incarceration
was the most unaccountable. Like any other unpro-
voked outrage, it created great surprise. It added one
more stigma of violence to the crown of that rapacious
monarch, — whose tyranny and debauchery had already
stripped him of the early appellation of " well-beloved,"
— wrought up public feeling in favor of the persecuted
author to a state of fervor, and converted the current of
astonishment into a cataract of popular indignation.
Diderot was released ; but the resistance shown to his
liberal opinions had set the minds of men afloat, and
restlessness was followed by high excitation. He became at one stroke the lion of the day and the champion of the blind, and, his speculations about them being
widely spread, enlisted general interest in their cause.
Captivated by the novelty of the ideas which he developed in the famous letters, dazzled by the eloquence
which he employed, and moved by his recital of the
woes and disadvantages which beset the void of sight,
people naturally began to think about the amelioration
of the condition of the blind.

In 1763, Dr. Thomas Reid endeavored to show in his

essay, entitled " An Inquiry into the Human Mind,"
that the blind, if properly instructed, are capable of
forming almost every idea and attaining almost every
truth which can be impressed on the mind through the
medium of light and color, except the sensations of
light and color themselves. The object of this work
was to refute the opinions of Locke and Hartley respecting the connection which they supposed to exist
between the phenomena, powers and operations of the
mind, and to found human knowledge on a system of
instinctive principles. Dr. Reid's views concerning
those pleasures of which the sense of sight is commonly
understood to be the only channel were similar to the
observations made by Burke in 1756, in his treatise on
the "Sublime and Beautiful." This author appeals not
only to the scientific acquirements of Saunderson, but
also to the poetry of Dr. Blacklock, as a confirmation of
his doctrine. "Here," says he, "is a poet, doubtless as
much affected with his own descriptions as any that
reads them can be; and yet he is affected with this
strong enthusiasm by things of which he neither has,
nor possibly can have, any idea further than that of bare
sound."

While in prison, Diderot was often visited by the
celebrated philosopher of the age, Jean Jacques Rousseau, whose warm interest in all sufferers, and particularly in the blind, was manifest. This master spirit of
progress, who was soon to become not merely the fore-
runner but the creator of a new era in the history of
mankind, was already the champion of humanity, and
the apostle of nature in all things. As Villemain expresses it, " his words, descending like a flame of fire,

moved the souls of his contemporaries." While, on the one hand, Rousseau was teaching, in a calm, logical manner, that "true philosophy is to commune with one's self," and that reason is the source, the assurance and the criterion of truth, he was, on the other, thrilling two continents with his memorable declaration, that "man is born free, but is everywhere in chains," — which later became the gospel of the Jacobins. His passionate feeling, deep thought, stupendous learning, refined taste, profound pathos and resolute bearing had such effect not only upon the minds of the lower classes of society, but even upon those of the nobility and the courtiers themselves, that thunders of applause shook the theatre of Versailles at the celebrated lines of Voltaire, —

" Je suis fils de Brutus, et je porte en mon cœur
La liberté gravée et les rois en horreur.''

By the touch of the magic wand of Rousseau's eloquence the tree of tyranny was to be uprooted and the whole framework of despotism torn down. No sooner had he opened his lips than he restored earnestness to the world, replaced selfishness by benevolence, engrafted the shoots of tenderness on the stock of hardness of heart and exclusiveness, wrought up France into a mood of sympathy with afflicted humanity, and rendered the eighteenth century an earnest and sincere one, full of beneficence, replete with faith in man's capacity for improvement, productive of grand ideas, and adorned by many virtues. Charity never was more active than at this period, when philanthropy had become a sort of fashion, and the movements for the suppression of men-

dicancy and the elevation of individual independence,
self-respect and dignity, common enterprises. The
great designs and inventions for the removal or palliation
of physical or mental disabilities which stand as significant indices on the road of modern civilization were
all of them fostered on the fertile soil of France.
Prominent among these was unquestionably the one
which aimed at the deliverance of the blind; and there
is no doubt that the conception of its importance is
due rather to the genius of the celebrated author of
"Émile" than to the mental resources of any one else.
True, Diderot was the first writer who called special
and direct attention to the condition and wants of this
afflicted class, and made them popularly known; but
neither he, nor Locke, nor Leibnitz, nor Reid, nor Condillac, nor any of the encyclopædists, went beyond the
boundaries of abstract psychological speculation. They
proposed no measures of practical utility or relief, nor
did they devise any plans for the instruction and training of sightless persons. It was Rousseau who first
asked the momentous question, "What can we do to
alleviate the lot of this class of sufferers, and how shall
we apply to their education the results of metaphysics?"
It was he who suggested the embossed books which
were afterwards printed by Haüy in a crude form. It
was under the genial warmth of his marvellous pen that
the plant of the education of both the blind and the
deaf-mutes grew, blossomed and throve.

But, although Rousseau's keen observations and
practical suggestions gave form and wise direction to
the fugitive glimpses of abstract speculation and isolated individual effort, yet the blind had still to await

the coming of their deliverer. An accidental circumstance sent him to them.

III. — Valentiñ Haüy and the School at Paris.

In the summer of 1783, the proprietor of a place of
refreshment in one of the principal thoroughfares of
Paris, desirous of increasing his custom, procured the
services of eight or ten blind persons, whom he arranged before a long desk, with goggles on nose and
instruments in their hands. Upon the stand were
placed open music-books, and the sightless men, feign-
ing to read their notes from these, executed, at short
intervals, the most " discordant symphonies." The object of the proprietor of the place, — which was afterwards known by the name of *Café des Aveugles*, — was
gained. The music drew a large crowd, who received
the ridiculous performances with boisterous and heartless
mirth, while consuming refreshments. Among the most
interested by-standers was Valentin Haüy, the brother
of the eminent crystallologist, and a man of large heart
and head, with deep feeling for the woes of humanity
and the power of thought to invent means for their
alleviation. He began at once to ponder upon the condition of the blind, and to question whether a method
of reading might be devised which should in some measure counterbalance their privation and give them some
comfort and consolation for the affliction under which
they labored. In his famous " Essay on the Education of
the Blind," Haüy describes with charming simplicity and
impressive modesty the bitter feelings and serious re-
flections which the performances at the *Café des Aveugles* had given him. " A very different sentiment from

that of delight," he says, " possessed our soul, and we
conceived, at that very instant, the possibility of turning
to the advantage of those unfortunate people the means
of which they had only an apparent and ridiculous enjoyment. Do not the blind, said we to ourselves, distinguish objects by the diversity of their form? Are
they mistaken in the value of a piece of money? Why
can they not distinguish a C from a G in music, or an *a*
from an *f* in orthography, if these characters should be
rendered palpable to the touch? While we were
reflecting on the usefulness of such an undertaking,
another observation struck us. A young child, full of
intelligence but deprived of sight, listened with profit
to the correction of his brother's classical exercises.
He often even besought him to read his elementary
books to him. He, however, more occupied with his
amusements, turned a deaf ear to the solicitations of
his unfortunate brother, who was soon carried off by a
cruel disease.

" These different examples soon convinced us how
precious it would be for the blind to possess the means
of extending their knowledge, without being obliged to
wait for, or sometimes even in vain to demand, the
assistance of those who see."

Having got so far, Haüy gathered together all the
information which could be drawn from the history of
celebrated congenital blind persons with regard to the
special processes which they had employed.

In England, Saunderson had devised a ciphering-
tablet. In France, the blind man of Puiseaux and
Mademoiselle de Salignac had used raised letters, and
Lamouroux had invented tangible musical characters.

In Germany, Weissemburg, blind from the age of seven, had accustomed himself to trace signs in relief. He had made maps of ordinary cards divided by threads, on which beads varying in size were strung, to indicate the different orders of towns, and covered with glazed sands in various ways to distinguish the seas, countries, provinces, etc. By means of these processes he had instructed a young blind girl, named Maria Theresa von Paradis.

This gifted child was born in Vienna, in 1759, and lost her sight at three years of age. Her parents were persons of rank and fortune, — her father being aulic councillor of the empire, — and they spared no expense in cultivating her extraordinary talents, and procuring for her the various ingenious contrivances then known for facilitating the education of the blind. Under the instruction of Weissemburg and the baron von Kempelen, the deviser of the *mechanical chess-player* and the speaking automaton, she had learned to spell with letters cut out of pasteboard, and to read words pricked upon cards with pins. Herr von Kempelen built for her a little press, by means of which she printed with ink the sentences which she composed, and in this way maintained a correspondence with her teachers and friends. She made use of a large cushion, into which she stuck pins to form notes or letters.

Having devoted much of her time to the study and practice of the pianoforte and organ, under the care of Herr Hozeluch and other masters, Mademoiselle von Paradis suddenly appeared before the musical world as an accomplished *pianiste*. She was the godchild of the empress Maria Theresa, — who allowed her an annual pension of two hundred florins, — and her performances at the palace and in the aristocratic circles of Vienna were received with *éclat*. Accompanied by her mother, she made a grand professional tour through the capitals and principal towns of central Europe and England, and charmed the rulers, the high functionaries, and the cultivated classes of society everywhere. In 1784, she ventured to Paris, and there she took part in the brilliant concerts of the winter, and achieved her grandest triumphs. No one was more enthusiastic at her magnificent success than Haüy, who immediately sought and made her acquaintance, and to whom she exhibited her appliances and apparatus and explained their use. Profiting by these observations, he began at once to lay the foundations of a complete system of education for those who had hitherto been left entirely untaught and uncared for. The abbé de l'Épée had at about the same period, in a certain sense, restored the deaf-mutes to intelligence and communion with the world around them.

Haüy, having determined to test his plans and methods by the instruction of one or more sightless persons, found, after some time, a congenital blind lad of seventeen years, named Lesueur, who was in the habit of soliciting alms at the door of the chapel *Bonne Nouvelle*. In order to dissuade him from his degrading profession, the eager philanthropist promised to pay him from his own pocket an amount of money equal to that which he gained as a mendicant. Lesueur accepted the offer, and proved a very tractable pupil. On him Haüy tried his inventions almost as rapidly as they proceeded from his own brain, and with such remarkable success that, as a proof of the positions which he had taken in an essay on the education of the blind, read by him before the Royal Academy of Sciences, at their invitation, he exhibited his pupil's attainments. The members of the assembly were carried as if by storm, and a commission was appointed to examine the matter more fully, and report. Meanwhile the Philanthropic Society, which had undertaken, as soon as it was organized, to assist twelve indigent sightless children by giving them twelve livres per month, entrusted them to the care of Haüy. Thus the first school for the blind was established in a small house in the *rue Coquillière.*

Nothing further was wanting to the founder of the institution but the public support of the *savans.* This was soon to be given. During the interval, however, the establishment was rapidly progressing, and the art of embossing books for the blind was an undisputed triumph of Haüy's ingenuity. This discovery had been long, though dimly, foreshadowed. According to Francesco Lucas, letters engraved on wood had been used in Spain as early as the sixteenth century, which were reproduced in Italy, with some modifications, by Rampazzetto, in 1573; but these were in intaglio instead of being in relief, and all attempts to ascertain their configuration by feeling proved fruitless. In 1640, a writing-master of Paris, named Pierre Moreau, caused movable raised characters to be cast in lead for the use of the blind; but he relinquished the scheme for reasons unknown to us. Movable letters on small tablets were also tried; but these were well adapted only for instructing seeing children to read. In fact, it was by means of similar characters that Usher, afterwards arch-

9

bishop of Armagh, was taught to read by his two aunts, who were both blind. Various other methods were employed, but none of them received general approbation until Haüy's great invention, which seems to have been partly the result of accident. Mr. Gailliod, who at a later date became one of his most celebrated pupils, thus relates the circumstance:

" Lesueur was sent one day to his master's desk for some article, and passing his fingers over the papers, they came in contact with the back of a printed note, which, having received an unusually strong impression, exhibited the letters in relief on the reverse. He distinguished an o, and brought the paper to his teacher to show him that he could do so. Haüy at once perceived the importance of the discovery, and testing it further by writing upon paper with a sharp point, and reversing it, found that Lesueur read it with great facility."

The ingenious inventor proceeded to produce letters in relief by pressing the type strongly on sized paper, and his success was complete. Thus the art of embossing books for the blind was discovered. The first characters adopted by Haüy were those of the Illyrian or Sclavonic alphabet, which were doubtless preferred on account of their square form; but these were afterwards altered and improved.

In February, 1785, the commission of the Royal Academy made its report, and while pointing out the features which the system of Haüy had in common with the agencies previously employed by individual blind persons, declared that to him alone were due their perfection, extension, and arrangement into a veritable

method. They concluded by saying that " if the success which we have witnessed does honor to the intelligence of the pupils, it is no less satisfactory and
creditable to their instructor, whose beneficent labors
merit the public gratitude."

This report had a marvellous effect upon the community. The school for the blind became one of the
lions of Paris, and was for some time absolutely the
rage. All classes of society were interested in the establishment, and each one strove to put-do the other.
Eminent musicians and actors gave performances for its
benefit. The Lyceum, the Museum, the *Salon de Correspondence* soon vied with one another for the privilege of
having the young sightless pupils stammer (to borrow
the expression of their instructor) the first elements of
reading, arithmetic, history, geography, and music at
their sessions ; and these exercises were always concluded
by collections for their benefit. Donations poured in
from all sides, and the funds were placed in the treasury
of the Philanthropic Society (still charged, at that time,
with providing the expenses of the establishment), which
had been removed to the *rue Nôtre Dame des Victoires*,
No. 18.

Finally, on the 26th December, 1786, the blind children of Haüy's school, to the number of twenty-four, and
a seeing lad taught by them, were admitted at Versailles
to the presence of the royal family. They were lodged
and cared for at the palace for eight days, and their
exercises made a deep impression upon the hearts of the
king, the queen, and princes. Haüy became a favorite
of Louis XVI., and was made interpreter to his majesty,
the navy department, and the *Hôtel de Ville*, for the Eng-

lish, German, and Dutch languages; royal interpreter
and professor of ancient inscriptions; and lastly, secretary to the king.   These honors were no doubt as gratifying to the recipient as they were creditable to the royal
giver; but they were ephemeral. Haüy's fame rests
upon a higher plane and more solid ground than this.
He proved himself worthy of the name of the "father
and apostle of the blind;" a reward richer than a
crown; a title more truly glorious than that of con-
queror.

At about this time Haüy published his "Essay on the
Education of the Blind," which,was printed under the
superintendence of M. Clousier, printer to the king,
partly in relief and partly with ink, by his pupils. It is
hardly possible to ascertain precisely the proportion of
the work performed by the latter. A literal translation
of this treatise into English was made by Blacklock, the
blind poet. It was first published in 1793, two years
after his death, and was chiefly remarkable for its inaccuracies.

The prosperity of the institution continued for about
four years longer, at the end of which period its days of
adversity and gloom commenced.   In 1791, the revolution was fairly inaugurated, and the Philanthropic Society,
which had taken charge of this noble enterprise from its
inception, was broken up, its members imprisoned, ex-
iled, and many of them subsequently guillotined.   On
the 21st of July of that year the school for the blind was
placed under the care of the state, and on the 28th of
September the national assembly passed an act providing
for its support. On the 10th Thermidor, anno III., it
was reorganized by a decree of the convention, and joined

with the school for the deaf-mutes, the two classes occupying the convent of the Celestins. All yet looked fair
for the institution; but the reign of terror soon followed,
and philanthropy, which had so lately been the fashion
in Paris, gave place to a demoniac and blood-thirsty cruelty which has no parallel in the history of nations. The
best blood of France flowed like water, and all thought
of humanity seemed banished from the minds of the
frantic barbarians who ruled her. Amid all the confusion and discord, Haüy quietly continued his course of
instruction, though sorely straitened for the means to
sustain the children confided to his care. The government nominally provided for them; but the orders on a
bankrupt treasury were nearly worthless. Haüy freely
gave up his own little fortune; and when this was gone,
with the aid of his pupils, he worked faithfully at the
printing-press, procured in their better days, and eked
out the means for their existence by issuing the numberless bulletins, hand-bills, *affiches*, and tracts, which so
abounded in that period of anarchy. It is said that
Haüy for more than a year confined himself to a single
meal a day, that his scholars might not starve. In addition to all other misfortunes the union of the blind and
the deaf-mutes proved unwise and unblest. The managers quarrelled and conducted matters so badly, that the
existence of both schools was in danger. At last this
discreditable state of things was terminated by a decree of the national convention, July 27, 1794, which
separated the disputants, and placed the deaf-mutes in
the seminary of *Saint Magloire* and the blind in the
maison Sainte Catherine, rue des Lombards. But the suffering, resulting mainly from the want of pecuniary

means, was not ended. It lasted more or less until
1800. During this period of darkness and misery,
Haüy had been able, amidst the gigantic difficulties by
which he was surrounded, to educate some pupils, whose
subsequent renown reflected its splendor upon his patient
labors. Among these were Gailliod, the musical com-
poser; Penjon, who afterwards filled the chair of professor of mathematics at the college of Angers for thirty
years, with high distinction; and Avisse, whose early
death deprived France of one of her sweetest poets.

At length brighter days began to dawn and prosperity
seemed about to revisit the sufferers of a whole decade.
But in 1801 a terrible blow fell suddenly upon the
institution, in comparison with which all its privations
and misery seemed light. The consular government
decided to incorporate the school for the young blind
with the *hospice des Quinze-Vingts*. This establishment,
which was founded by Louis IX. in 1260, was a retreat
or home for adults; and was occupied at this time by a
large number of blind paupers with their families, who
were indolent, degraded, depraved and vicious. To
place the children, for whom Haüy had sacrificed so
much, in constant association with these idle, dissolute
and profligate men and women was more than he could
bear. Calmly had he endured hunger and privation for
their sake, and as cheerfully would he do it again; but
to see their minds and morals contaminated and cor-
rupted, their habits of industry and study abandoned,
was too much. The government of Bonaparte, however,
was inexorable, and Haüy resigned his position. In
acknowledgment of his past services, a pension of four
hundred dollars was decreed to him.

Unwilling to abandon a class for whom he felt so deep and intense an interest, Haüy opened a private school for the blind, under the title of *Musée des Aveugles*. He maintained it for three years; and in that time educated, among others, two pupils, whose names and reputation are still remembered throughout Europe: Rodenbach, the eloquent writer and eminent statesman of Belgium, who took an active part in the revolution of 1830, and played an important *rôle* in the political arena of his country; and Fournier, hardly less distinguished in France. The undertaking, however, proved pecuniarily unsuccessful; and in 1806, Haüy accepted a pressing invitation from the Czar to establish a school for the blind in his empire. Accompanied by his faithful pupil and constant friend, Fournier, he started for Russia, and on his way thither visited Berlin. Here he was presented to the king of Prussia, who extended to him a cordial and flattering reception, and to whom he exhibited his methods of instruction. On his arrival at St. Petersburg, Haüy organized an institution over which he presided for nine years with great ability.

For thirteen years the place of the "father of the blind" in the school at Paris was supplied by an ignorant instructor named Bertrand, under whom the establishment lost nearly all its early reputation. He died suddenly on the 4th of March, 1814; and in the following month, Dr. Guillié, a man of learning, tact and energy, but harsh, unscrupulous, untruthful and excessively vain, was appointed to his place. As the Bourbons had just returned to France, the new director availed himself of every possible opportunity to bring his pupils under their notice and make known to them their

condition and wants. The government soon became
satisfied that a grave error had been committed in the
union of the two institutions ; and they hastened to
rectify it.   During the year 1815 ample funds and
separate quarters, in the seminary of St. Firmin, *rue St.
Victor*, were assigned to the school, which again assumed
the title of the *Royal Institution for Blind Youth*.   The
removal of the establishment to the new building was,
however, delayed by the political events of the time
until 1816, when Dr. Guillié reörganized it with pomp
and parade.   He at once expelled forty-three of the
pupils, whose morals had been contaminated by their
associations at the *maison des Quinze-Vingts*.   M. Dufau
was appointed second instructor of the boys ; and Mlle.
Cardeilhac, a young lady distinguished by her youth,
proverbial beauty, and accomplishments, as teacher of
the girls.   Under Dr. Guillié's administration the study
of music was in a flourishing condition.   He knew how
to interest the first artists of the day in his pupils ; and
procured lessons and counsel gratis from such eminent
professors as Jadin, Habeneck, Dacosta, Duport, Perne,
Dauprat, Benazet and Vogt.   Under these great masters,
Marjolin, Charraux, Lamaury, Dupuis, and the *pianiste*
Sophie Osmond became veritable artists.   But, with this
exception, everything else was done for effect and show.
Manufactured articles were purchased at the bazaars
and were exhibited as the work of the blind children.
Greek, Latin, English, German, Italian, and Spanish
were professedly taught, and the scholars made glib
public recitations in them by the aid of interlinear
translations ; while at the same time they were not
versed even in the elements of arithmetic and history.

The necessary was sacrificed to the superfluous. Add
to this flagrant charlatanism Dr. Guillié's malignity and
narrowness, and you will have a complete picture of the
character of the man. He seemed to regard any reference to Haüy as a personal insult; and forbade the
teachers, many of whom had been instructed and trained
by him, even to mention the name of their early
benefactor. In 1817, Dr. Guillié published the first
edition of his *Essai sur l'Instruction des Aveugles*, in
the two hundred and forty pages of which he labored
studiously wholly to ignore the great services and sacrifices of the noble founder of the institution (alluding to
his name only twice *en passant*), and to attribute its
origin to Louis XVI.

In the very same year Haüy, feeling the pressure of
disease as well as the effects of old age, determined to
return to his native land to die. His parting with the
Czar Alexander was very affecting. The emperor embraced him repeatedly, and conferred upon him the
order of St. Vladimir. On his arrival in Paris, Haüy
was domiciled with his brother, the abbé. His heart
was, however, overflowing with affection for the school
which he had organized, and he hastened, feeble as he
was, to pay it a visit. But Dr. Guillié refused him admission, under the sham excuse that, as he had taken
an active part in the revolution, it would be displeasing
to the royal family to have him recognized. It is difficult to believe that even a Bourbon, imbecile as Louis
XVIII. was, could have authorized so contemptible an
act. This cruelty, added to numerous other misdeeds of
the director, led to such a clamor against Dr. Guillié,
that the government was compelled to order an investi-

gation of his management of the institution. After
careful and thorough inquiry, the commission appointed
for this purpose reported that in every department they
had found ample evidence of fraud, humbug, trickery,
and deception. This statement was so abundantly illustrated by a detailed array of facts, that the miserable
man, finding the poisoned chalice which he had drugged
for others commended to his own lips, was fain to resign amid a storm of popular indignation, followed in
his retirement by the fair Mademoiselle Cardeilhac, who
had often tempered the harshness of the proceedings of
her chief, and willingly served as a channel through
which his graces descended upon the heads of offenders.

Dr. Guillié was succeeded in February, 1821, by Dr.
Pignier, who was a man of truth and honor, but whose
education, which had been received entirely in the
monkish seminaries, rendered him illiberal, suspicious,
and utterly unfit for the post. After reörganizing the
school, and adopting regulations which should prevent
the repetition of the disgraceful practices of the preceding administration, the new director felt that it was due
to Haüy that his eminent services should be recognized
by a suitable ovation. Accordingly, on the 22d of
August, 1821, a public concert, in his honor, was given
at the institution, and the pupils and teachers vied with
each other in their expressions of gratitude to the
"father of the blind." Songs and choruses, composed
for the occasion, commemorated his trials, his hardships
and his successes; and, as the good old man, with
streaming eyes, witnessed the triumphant results of his
early labors, and listened to the expressions of thankfulness, he exclaimed, "Give not the praise to me, my

children; it is God who has done all." It was his last
visit to the institution. His health, long feeble, gave
way during the succeeding autumn ; and, after months
of suffering, he died on the 18th of March, 1822, in the
seventy-seventh year of his age. Thus ended the career
of Valentin Haüy, one of the noblest men and the
greatest benefactors of humanity, whose name will always be pronounced with profound veneration among
the blind of the civilized world.

Dr. Pignier's administration lasted nineteen years.
During this period there were but few innovations
made either in the matter or the manner of the instruction in the literary department; but a new era was inaugurated in several other respects. The character of
music was entirely changed. The art of tuning as a
lucrative employment for the blind was developed and
introduced by Montal, one of the pupils, to whom the
director, disregarding the clamor and bitter opposition
of the seeing tuner hired by the institution, gave first
opportunities of studying the construction of the piano-
forte, and afterwards the place of teacher; and whose
subsequent career as one of the great piano-manufac-
turers of Paris, and the author of the best manual on
tuning, is well known. The system of writing and
printing in raised points likewise came into use at this
time. It was really invented, in principle, by a seeing
man, named Charles Barbier, in 1825; but was improved, perfected and arranged in its present form by
a sightless musician, Louis Braille, whose name has
been attached to it ever since.

Dr. Guillié, whose principal object was to dazzle the
public, considered a fine orchestra and a few brilliant

soloists as the best means for this purpose, and devoted
all his energies to its accomplishment. His successor
had altogether different views on the subject. Fashioned in religious habits, Dr. Pignier attributed very
little importance to secular music, and sought to direct
the efforts of his instructors and pupils to that of the
church, and most especially to the organ. Thus a great
impetus was given in this direction, the result of which
was the production of a large number of eminent organists, who found their way into the parochial churches of
Paris, and the cathedrals of Blois, Évreux, Limoges,
Orléans, Tours, Meaux and Vannes. Among these were
Gauthier, who subsequently became principal teacher of
music at the institution, and author of a treatise on the
" Mechanism of Musical Composition," and of several
other works; Marius Gueit, Poissant, Braille, and Mon-
couteau, who afterwards published a manual on " Musical Composition," and a treatise on " Harmony," which
was most favorably commended by several competent
musicians, and particularly by Berlioz, the severest critic
of the time. Thorough and careful study of the organ,
both in theory and practice, has ever since been one of
the prominent features of this pioneer institution for the
blind ; and there are to-day no less than two hundred blind
organists and choristers employed in the churches of the
capital and the provinces of France. · The names of a
large number of these are given in full in a pamphlet
recently published in Paris by Maurice de la Sizeranne,
under the title *Les aveugles utiles.*

The institution was thriving in 1825, when Dr. Pignier spoke with much satisfaction in his report of the
effects of the direction which he had given to its affairs,

and earnestly recommended, among other projects, the removal of the establishment to a healthier location and the provision of better accommodations than those which they had in the *rue St. Victor.* But the tide of prosperity and progress seemed to have reached its highest mark at this time; for soon after signs of decadence and retrogression began to appear on all sides, and their sinister work was so rapidly and effectually accomplished, that in 1832 one of the ministers proclaimed from the national tribune that "the condition of the establishment was deplorable in every respect." This state of things continued, only going from bad to worse, for several years. At length the vices and weaknesses of the administration, the want of union among the instructors, and internal quarrels, dissensions, strife, and heart-burnings, brought about such confusion and anarchy that a new organization became inevitable.

On the 20th of May, 1840, M. Dufau, the second instructor, succeeded Dr. Pignier as director. Soon afterwards, the administrative commission, which had managed the establishment since 1814, gave place to an advisory board, consisting of four members. The new director regenerated the institution completely. He modified the somewhat cloistral manners into a life more in harmony with the present state of society; freed the discipline from all elements of arbitrariness and absolutism, and rendered it more liberal; laid anew the foundations of instruction, and restored to the school its old prestige. In 1843, the institution was transferred to its present beautiful building, the cornerstone of which was laid in 1838. The want of harmony existing between the older administration and the organization which followed it, required new regulations. These were issued in 1845, and have remained in full force ever since.

I have given the history of the pioneer school for the blind at considerably greater length than is admissible in the limits of a brief sketch like this, for three reasons: firstly, on account of the importance of the causes and events which brought it into existence; secondly, on account of the pleasant memories and the noble examples of enthusiasm, self-denial, and disinterestedness which cluster around its infancy; and thirdly, because it served more or less as a model in the formation of similar establishments all over the civilized world. This last fact renders a thorough knowledge of the details of its rise and development indispensable to all who labor in the same field; but particularly to those who are earnestly endeavoring to clear that field from chronic errors, weed out abuses, and rid it of all parasitical evils and noxious plants.

IV. — Schools for the Blind in Great Britain and Europe.

The seeds of Haüy's marvellous creation were sown everywhere, and schools for the blind sprang up first in England, and afterwards in all the principal countries of Europe.

The second institution for sightless children, in point of time, was founded in Liverpool, in 1791, by Mr. Pudsey Dawson, who died in 1816. It was supported by subscriptions, donations, and legacies, and its object was to teach poor blind children to work at trades, to sing in church, and to play the organ. Literary education was not included within its scope.

Dr. Blacklock, of Edinburgh, had often wished to erect a school for children similarly afflicted with himself, and communicated his views on the subject to Mr. David Miller, who was also blind from birth, and a competent instructor. It was for this purpose that Dr. Blacklock made a careful study of Haüy's methods, and even translated his famous essay; but he took no steps toward carrying out his intention. After Dr. Blacklock's death, which occurred in 1791, Mr. Miller enlisted the interest of Dr. David Johnston in the enterprise, and through their combined efforts the project was placed before the public, and the necessary means were raised for the foundation of a school, which was opened in 1793 with nine pupils. Mr. Robert Johnston, the secretary of the establishment, devoted his energies to its welfare and prosperity, and Dr. Henry Moyes, the celebrated blind professor of philosophy and natural history in Edinburgh, announced a public *séance* in behalf of his fellow-sufferers, which was attended by a large number of the best citizens, and proved remarkably successful in a pecuniary point of view.

At about the same time the Bristol asylum and industrial school for the blind was established, the object of which was to teach sightless children such handicraft as would enable them to earn their own living.

In 1799, Messrs. Ware, Bosanquet, Boddington, and Houlston founded a similar institution in London, which, in 1800, had only fifteen inmates, and attracted very little attention. Subsequently generous subscriptions poured into its treasury, and the school at St. George's in the Fields increased both in numbers and usefulness.

The next institution for the blind in Great Britain

was organized at Norwich, in 1805. It was a blind man named Tawell, who not only inaugurated a public movement, but ceded a house with the surrounding grounds for this purpose.

Similar establishments were afterwards founded in Glasgow, York, Manchester, and elsewhere; but most of the British schools for the blind have never taken a high stand in their literary or musical training.

At the beginning of the present century institutions for the blind were established in various parts of Europe in the following order: that of Vienna in 1804, by Dr. Klein, who was its director for about fifty years; that of Berlin, — the soil for which was thoroughly prepared by Haüy himself while on his way to Russia, — in 1806, under the superintendence of Herr Zeune, and that of Amsterdam in 1808, by an association of free-masons. In the same year, two more institutions were founded: that of Prague, by a charitable society, and that of Dresden. In 1809, Haüy put the school in St. Petersburg in operation, and Dr. Hirzel organized that of Zürich. Two years later an institution for the blind was established at Copenhagen by the *society of the chain*, an organization similar to that of the free-masons; and many others soon after followed.

The schools for the blind on the continent were mainly fashioned after the model set by Haüy in Paris. Dr. Klein, the blind founder of the Vienna institution, claimed that the idea of arranging a system of education for his companions in misfortune, and the processes for carrying it out, originated with him without any previous knowledge of what had been done elsewhere in this direction. A writer in the *Encyclopédie Théologique* remarks, that "pretensions of this kind are not new," and asks, "How could Dr. Klein be ignorant in 1804 of a creation so original as that of Haüy, which was demonstrated in 1784?" Other French authors do not dispute the truthfulness of the statement. It is hardly necessary for us to enter into a further discussion on this point. We cannot refrain from saying, however, that it is a common practice in our days with unscrupulous men of small mental calibre and doubtful veracity to lay claim to inventions and processes for the blind which were conceived and publicly tried by others within a stone's throw of their abode several years before they ever dreamed of them.

Some of the European institutions were founded in a moment of passing enthusiasm; but, like seed thrown upon the rock, they found no genial earth whence to draw the necessary vital elements for their development, and have sadly dwindled. Others, though planted in a propitious soil, and watered by copious showers of patronage, have not attained that lofty and luxuriant growth which their nature seemed to promise at first.

V. — Foundation of the New England Institution.

The first attempts to educate the blind on this side of the Atlantic were made in Boston, and the merit of proposing the establishment of an institution for their instruction and training belongs to Dr. John D. Fisher of this city. While pursuing his medical studies in Paris, he paid frequent visits to the royal institution for the young blind, and conceived the design of transplanting to his own country the advantages there enjoyed. After his return to Boston, in 1826, he kept the matter

11

constantly in view, and opened a correspondence with
Mr. Robert Johnston, secretary of the asylum for the
blind in Edinburgh, Scotland. Many other Americans
had, it is true, visited these beneficent establishments
of the old world, and on their return had delighted
their friends with the details of the curious methods of
instruction and training therein pursued; but none
of them had ever before this time attempted, by appeals
to the public or otherwise, to bring these means within
the reach of the blind of the new world.

Having consulted with his friends on the subject, Dr.
Fisher was advised to call a meeting of such persons as
it was supposed would favor the plan and take an interest in promoting it. This meeting was held on the
10th of February, 1829, at the Exchange Coffee-house.
The legislature being in session, many representatives
from various parts of the commonwealth were in
attendance. The Hon. Robert Rantoul of Beverly, a
member of the house, was appointed chairman, and
Charles H. Locke, of Boston, secretary. At this meeting Dr. Fisher gave a detailed and minute account of
the several processes employed to communicate knowledge to the blind; described the various manufactures
by which they were enabled to obtain a livelihood, and
exhibited specimens of embossed books printed for their
use. His statements excited a deep interest in all present, and remarks were made by Mr. Edward Brooks of
Boston, Mr. Stephen Phillips of Salem, Mr. Caleb
Cushing of Newburyport, and Hon. William B. Calhoun of Springfield, speaker of the house, expressive
of their warm approbation of the design and of the
usefulness of such an institution. On motion of Dr.

Fisher, it was then voted, "that a committee be appointed to consider what measures should be adopted to promote the establishment of an institution for the blind of New England;" and the following gentlemen were accordingly appointed : — Hon. Jonathan Phillips, Mr. Theodore Sedgwick, Mr. Richard D. Tucker, Mr. Edward Brooks, and Dr. John D. Fisher.

At an adjourned meeting held on the 19th of February, at the representatives' hall in the state-house, the above-named committee made a report, which closed with the following resolution : —

"*Resolved*, that we are impressed with a deep sense of the utility of institutions for the education of the blind, and that a committee be appointed to take all measures necessary for the establishment of such an institution for the blind of New England."

After the reading of the report, Dr. Fisher repeated the statements which he had made at the previous meeting. The nature and object of the proposed institution were explained and recommended by Mr. Edward Brooks and Mr. Theodore Sedgwick of Stockbridge. The above resolution was then unanimously adopted, and the following gentlemen were put on the committee : — Hon. Jonathan Phillips, Mr. Richard D. Tucker, Mr. Edward Brooks, Mr. Theodore Sedgwick, Dr. John D. Fisher, Hon. William B. Calhoun, Mr. Stephen C. Phillips, Mr. George Bond, Mr. Samuel M. M'Kay, Hon. Josiah J. Fiske, Mr. Isaac L. Hedge, Dr. John Homans, and Hon. William Thorndike.

This committee applied immediately to the legislature for an act of incorporation, which was granted unanimously in both houses without debate. The act is dated March 2, 1829. The name of the corporation was " *The New England Asylum for the Blind*," and the purpose of its formation was to educate sightless persons. Hon. Jonathan Phillips, of Boston, was authorized by the act to call the first meeting of the corporation, by giving three weeks' notice in three of the Boston newspapers. The legislature passed, moreover, a resolve directing the secretary of state to send circulars to the several towns, to ascertain the number of blind persons in the commonwealth, and their condition.

The corporation thus formed proceeded somewhat slowly in organizing and starting this new enterprise, and for more than two years little progress was apparently made. Its first meeting, which was held at the Marlborough House, April 17, 1829, resulted in the acceptance of the act of incorporation granted by the legislature, and the appointment of a committee to prepare by-laws and an address to be circulated in its behalf. Two subsequent meetings were held during the same year, at the Exchange Coffee-house, at which a set of by-laws was adopted, and measures were taken for obtaining reliable information as to the number and condition of the blind in the city of Boston and throughout the state of Massachusetts. In the following year, the corporation elected its first board of officers, consisting of the following gentlemen : — Hon. Jonathan Phillips, *president ;* Hon. William B. Calhoun, *vice-president ;* Mr. Richard D. Tucker, *treasurer ;* Mr. Charles H. Locke, *secretary ;* Dr. John D. Fisher, Dr. John Homans, and Messrs. Joseph Coolidge, Pliny Cutler, William H. Prescott, Samuel T. Armstrong,

Edward Brooks, and Stephen C. Phillips, *trustees*. In
accordance with the act of incorporation, four other
trustees were chosen by the state board of visitors, consisting of the governor, the lieutenant-governor, the
president of the senate, the speaker of the house of
representatives, and the chaplains of the legislature.
A motion was made to change the name of the corporation from that of the *New England Asylum for the
Blind*, to the *American Asylum for the Blind;* but after
discussion it was withdrawn.   Meanwhile Dr. Fisher,
who had been foremost in promoting this noble enterprise, being unable to engage in it personally, had
enlisted the sympathy and coöperation of Dr. Samuel
G. Howe, who had just returned from the scenes of his
philanthropic mission and military exploits in Greece.
A small fund for commencing the work had been provided by the legislature, which, by a resolve of March
9, 1830, allowed to the institution for the blind the un-
expended balance of the appropriation for the deaf-
mutes at the Hartford asylum ; and on the 18th of
August, 1831, the trustees entered into an agreement
with Dr. Howe, by which he was engaged as " principal " or " superintendent " of the asylum for the education of blind persons.   In article III. of this contract
he was intrusted as follows : — " The first duty of Dr.
Howe will be to embark for Europe, in order to make
himself fully acquainted with the mode of conducting
such institutions; to procure one, or at most two, instructed blind as assistant teachers; also, the necessary
apparatus."

In accordance with these instructions, Dr. Howe immediately sailed for Europe, where he visited and care-

fully studied all the principal institutions for the blind; and in his report to the trustees he says that he " found in all much to admire and copy, but also much to avoid." On the whole, however, he " considered them as beacons to warn rather than as lights to guide." In an article on the education of the blind, published by him two years later in the " North American Review," he criticized their work at some length, and said that " the school of Edinburgh was decidedly of a higher order than any other in Great Britain." Of that of Paris his impressions were very unfavorable, and were expressed as follows: " There pervades that establishment a spirit of illiberality, of mysticism, amounting almost to charlatanism, that ill accords with the well-known liberality of most French institutions. There is a ridiculous attempt at mystery, — an effort at show and parade, which injure the establishment in the minds of men of sense. Instead of throwing wide open the door of knowledge, and inviting the scrutiny and the suggestions of every friend of humanity, the process of education is not explained, and the method of constructing some of the apparatus is absolutely kept a secret. We say this from personal knowledge."

Dr. Howe returned to Boston in July of 1832, bringing with him, as assistants, Mr. Émile Trencheri, a graduate of the Paris school, as literary teacher, and Mr. John Pringle, of the Edinburgh institution, as master of handicrafts. In August of the same year he opened a school at his father's residence, No. 144 Pleasant street, having as pupils six " blind persons from different parts of the state, varying in age from six to twenty years." These scholars had been under instruc-

tion five months, and had already learned to read embossed print; had made considerable progress in the
study of geography from maps in relief, in arithmetic,
and in music, when a memorial was presented to the
legislature, in January, 1833, setting forth the condition and wants of the institution and praying for aid.
At the annual meeting of the corporation in that year,
Dr. Howe was elected secretary, and this office, together
with that of superintendent, or " director," of the institution, he held from that time until his death in 1876,
a period of forty-three years.

Early in the year 1833, the half-dozen pupils with
whom Dr. Howe had commenced the experiment of
teaching sightless children exhibited the results of their
six months' tuition before the legislature of Massachusetts, and the practicability of educating the blind
was so satisfactorily proved by their performances, that
the general court at once made an appropriation of six
thousand dollars per annum to the institution, on condition that it should receive and educate, free of cost,
twenty poor blind persons belonging to the state. A
number of public exhibitions were given in Boston,
Salem, and elsewhere, and an address, containing much
valuable information collected by Dr. Howe while in
Europe, was widely circulated. The result of these
efforts was far more favorable than had been expected,
and the interest and sympathy of the community were
so thoroughly roused and excited, that subscriptions and
donations were freely given. The ladies of Salem first
suggested the idea of a fair; and, assisted by those of
Marblehead and Newburyport, they got up a splendid
fête, which, besides calling forth a display of all the

energy of female character and all the kindlier feelings of the human heart, resulted in a net profit of $2,980. Resolving not to be outdone, the ladies of Boston entered the field with great ardor, and, persevering for several weeks, they opened a bazaar on the first of May, in Faneuil Hall, which exceeded in splendor and taste anything of the kind ever got up in this, or perhaps in any other, country. A vivid description of the fair, from the pen of Dr. Howe, was published in the " New England Magazine," and its net profits amounted to $11,400.

The institution had now taken firm hold upon the sympathies of a generous public, and it needed something to call forth and direct its expression; this was the donation of Col. Thomas H. Perkins of his mansion-house and grounds on Pearl street, valued at twenty-five thousand dollars, for a permanent location for the school, provided that a fund of fifty thousand dollars could be raised. The following imperfect cut of the mansion is copied from the " Penny Magazine for Useful Knowledge."

The liberal spirit of Col. Perkins was so warmly seconded by the community, that within one month the sum of fifty thousand dollars was contributed. Exhibitions were also given in other states, and the legislature of Connecticut voted an appropriation of one thousand dollars per annum, for twelve years, for as many blind children as could be educated for that sum ; Vermont made an appropriation of twelve hundred dollars, for ten years ; and New Hampshire a temporary appropriation of five hundred dollars. The states of Maine and Rhode Island afterwards adopted a similar course, and thus the institution at Boston became the educational establishment for the blind of all the New England states, as the asylum at Hartford already was for the deaf-mutes.

MANSION-HOUSE AND GROUNDS OF COL. THOMAS H. PERKINS.

Sufficient means to insure the permanent establishment of the school having been thus provided, such alterations as were necessary to accommodate a large number of pupils were made upon the premises in Pearl street, and an adjoining estate was purchased, which was much needed for a play-ground.   By this addition the corporation became owners of the whole

square between Pearl and Atkinson streets. The institution was advertised as open to pupils from all parts of
the country, and the little school already opened at Dr.
Howe's residence was removed to its new home in
September, 1833. At the close of the year the number of pupils had increased to thirty-four.

The school being now well established, and in a condition of vigorous growth, Dr. Howe began to devote
himself to the study and improvement of the means and
appliances for teaching the blind. By his own exertions
he raised subscriptions for a printing-fund; and, after
many and costly experiments with the ordinary printing-
press, a new one, especially adapted to the work of embossing books for the blind, was obtained at considerable
expense. A series of experiments made by the doctor
in arranging an alphabet legible to the touch, resulted
in the adoption of a slight modification of the ordinary
Roman letter of the lower-case; and this has been
known as the Boston type. This was the first printing-
office for the blind opened in any American institution;
and its work was so actively carried on that very flattering testimonials of its worth were soon received in the
shape of orders from England, Ireland and Holland.
The British and Foreign Bible society ordered a complete edition of the book of psalms, for which they paid
seven hundred and fifty dollars. The exertions of Dr.
Howe to establish a printing-fund for the blind on a
solid and permanent basis were incessant and unwearied,
in season and out of season. For this end he visited
Washington with three of his pupils, whose attainments
he exhibited to the members of congress, hoping to
induce them to found a national printing-establishment

for the blind. Failing in his first effort, he organized a second visit to Washington in 1846, accompanied by the superintendents and select scholars of the institutions of New York and Philadelphia, as well as pupils from this school, and proposed to congress either to give a portion of the fund of the Smithsonian Institute for this purpose, or to make an endowment similar to that received by the asylum for deaf-mutes at Hartford. The prospects looked hopeful for the accomplishment of so great and noble an end, when the darkening of the political horizon by the breaking out of the Mexican war precluded the furtherance of the enterprise by the entire engrossment of congress in that momentous subject.

Instruction in the literary department of the institution included not only the simple branches of a common-school education, but some of the higher mathematics, a knowledge of history, astronomy and natural philosophy; and the study of languages was early introduced. In addition to vocal music and instruction upon the piano and organ, the foundation for an orchestra was immediately commenced. The tuning of pianofortes was taught as a practical employment, and a mechanical department was opened for male pupils, in which they learned to manufacture mattresses, cushions, mats and baskets; while the girls were taught sewing, knitting, braiding, and some household duties.

The institution grew so rapidly that within a short time increased accommodations were necessary; and a new wing, as extensive as the original building, was erected in 1835.

The state continued its annual appropriation for its

beneficiaries; and upon this the institution was mainly
dependent for the means of meeting its current expenses.
This income was, however, supplemented by the smaller
appropriations made by the other New England states,
by fees received from private pupils (some of whom
came from distant parts of the country), by donations,
and an occasional legacy.

In 1839, an opportunity occurred for advantageously
changing the location of the establishment. The Mount
Washington House, on Dorchester Heights, at South
Boston, was thrown into the market; and Col. Perkins
having very generously and promptly withdrawn all the
conditions and restrictions attached to the gift of his
mansion for a permanent residence for the blind, an
even exchange of the Pearl street estate for the Mount
Washington House was effected. In grateful appreciation of the liberality of Col. Perkins, not only in his
first gift, but also in the alacrity with which he withdrew
all its restrictions when they became a hindrance to the
growth of the institution, the trustees desired to connect
his name permanently with the establishment, and accordingly, at their recommendation, the corporation
passed, at a meeting held March 15, 1839, a resolve,
" *That from and after the first day of April next, this
institution shall be called and known by the name of the
Perkins Institution and Massachusetts Asylum for
the Blind.*"

The establishment was removed to the new premises
in South Boston in May, 1839. The elevated situation,
the abundance of open ground in the neighborhood, the
unobstructed streets, and the facilities for sea-bathing,
made this change of location highly desirable on account

of its superior healthfulness; and the spacious building, which afforded large and airy rooms for the various needs of the school, and gave ample space, not only for a large increase in the number of pupils, but also for entirely separate arrangements for each sex, combined to render it such an acquisition as the best friends of the institution would desire, but such as the most sanguine would scarcely have dared to hope for.

PERKINS INSTITUTION AND MASSACHUSETTS ASYLUM FOR THE BLIND.

In 1840, an additional department was opened "for the purpose of providing employment for those pupils who have acquired their education and learned to work, but who could not find employment or carry on business alone." The making, cleansing and renovating of beds, mattresses and cushions; the manufacture of mats and brooms and cane-seating chairs, were the occupations chosen as those in which the blind could best compete with seeing workmen. In reference to the need of such a department, the trustees in their annual report wrote as follows: —

"Many a blind person has acquired a knowledge of some handicraft, but he cannot work at it as seeing workmen do, or be employed in a common workshop. He has no capital, perhaps. and cannot buy materials, or wait uncertain times for the sales, and he is idle. It is for the sake of such persons, and we are happy to say, that a separate work department has been opened during the past year ; and a beginning made of an establishment which, if successful, will become of great value to the blind."

The test of years proved this department to be a valuable auxiliary in assisting the blind to self-maintenance, not only by furnishing the necessary aid by which many of the adult pupils could carry on their trades in fair competition with ordinary workmen, but also in providing for another class, who had hitherto been left uncared for, viz., those who, dependent upon manual labor for self-support, had by accident or sickness been deprived of sight at too advanced an age to enter the school as ordinary pupils. To many such persons the opportunity thus afforded for learning a trade was their only salvation from pauperism.

At about this period the several departments of the school were arrayed in admirable working order, and promised good harvest. That of music — in which the seeds of excellence were planted and fostered by such eminent professors as Lowell Mason, Joseph A. Keller, and later by H. Theodore Hach — had entered upon that career of beneficence which it has so long and so fully sustained; while a number of young men and women were remarkably successful in the field of literature, and some of the former were preparing to enter one or two of the leading colleges of New England.

The evils attendant upon congregating together so
many persons laboring under a common infirmity were
perceived at an early date in the history of this institution, and the unfavorable effects were especially felt in
connection with the industrial department.   The result
was that the first steps towards correcting this evil were
taken in 1850; when, a new workshop having been ·
erected (partly by a special appropriation of the state
and partly at the expense of the institution), the adult
blind were entirely removed from the building and scattered about the neighborhood, boarding in different families where they could find accommodation, and going
daily to the shop like ordinary workmen.   They were
paid regularly every month, and their wages were usually sufficient, by prudent management, for their support.
Some who could work successfully in their own neigh-
borhoods were aided by the purchase of stock for their
use, and by the privilege of leaving their goods for sale
at the store opened in the city mainly for the benefit of
this department.   Those who, from loss of sight in later
life, entered the workshop to learn some kind of handicraft were expected to pay the cost of their board until
the trade was acquired; after which, if they remained,
they received wages in proportion to the character of
their work.   The workshop for the pupils, however, continued to be carried on within the walls of the institution.

The industrial department for adults furnished employment mainly to men, and having proved so successful after a trial of many years, it was thought advisable,
in order to meet the great need of more occupations for
blind women, to try the experiment of a laundry conducted on the same plan.   Accordingly, in 1863, a build-

ing was hired for the purpose and a laundry opened, which, in addition to the washing and ironing for the institution, and for the school for feeble-minded youth, also sought the patronage of private families. The experiment was continued for nearly five years ; but much seeing help was needed to secure the satisfactory performance of the finer parts of the work furnished by customers, and the cost of their services left so small a sum for the wages of the blind women, that the scheme was abandoned as impracticable, save for doing the work of the institution.

The evils of the congregate system were more and more felt as years went on and the growth of the establishment increased. The subject of reörganizing the institution by building several dwelling-houses and dividing the blind into families had been repeatedly discussed in the annual reports for several years, and a claim for an appropriation for buildings was urged upon the attention of the legislature. With the exception of five thousand dollars toward the erection of the new workshop, in 1850, the state had furnished no means for building purposes until, by a resolve of 1868, the sum of fifteen thousand dollars " was allowed for buildings, — workshop, laundry, etc., — to be paid when a similar sum had actually been raised by the friends of the institution." But as the experiment of a public laundry was abandoned, and the building would soon demand such extensive repairs and alterations as would far exceed the appropriation, it was decided to let this remain until a sufficient sum could be raised for such new buildings, alterations, and improvements as the proper reörganization of the school demanded. Accordingly the trustees applied to the legislature, and their petition was referred to the committee on charitable institutions, who reported unanimously in its favor, urging the claim as follows : —

"It would be a waste of words to urge the claim which blind children have for a full share of the means of instruction which the state accords to all the young. They have even stronger claims than common children; they carry a burden in their infirmity, because they come mostly of poor and humble parents; and because, without special instruction and training, they are almost certain, sooner or later, to become a public charge. All children have a right to instruction. The children of the rich are sure to get it; and the state is bound, alike by duty and interest, to see that none lacks the means of obtaining it.   .   .   .

"The trustees ask that the commonwealth will furnish them with the means of educating her blind children in some slight degree proportionate to the means she has so liberally furnished for educating her seeing children. They do not ask it as a charity, but they expect it as a part of the obligation early assumed to educate every son and daughter of the commonwealth. For her seeing children Massachusetts opens primary, grammar and high schools. Every town is required by law to provide adequate instruction, free, for all seeing children of suitable age.   .   .   .

"We believe that blind children have the same claim upon the state for education as seeing children, and that their needs are greater; that the commonwealth owes to her blind children the opportunities for better education than those hitherto enjoyed, which have been confined almost entirely to merely elementary studies; that she is abundantly able to furnish them means, and cannot afford to withhold them; that she has an institution where these children can be educated more cheaply and more successfully than in any other institution in the world, and that every consideration of economy and of humanity appeals to the legislature to place at the disposal of the trustees of this institution the means of increasing its usefulness, and of enlarging and perfecting the efforts which have made the Massachusetts institution for the blind an honor to the commonwealth and a blessing to mankind."

13

This report closed with the following resolve, which, as here amended, passed both branches of the legislature unanimously: —

"*Resolved*, That there be allowed and paid to the trustees of the Perkins Institution and Massachusetts Asylum for the Blind the sum of eighty thousand dollars, and the same is hereby appropriated, for the purpose of erecting suitable buildings for the use of the institution, the same to be paid from time to time in instalments, as may be certified to be necessary by the trustees: *provided*, that no portion of the said sum shall be paid until the said trustees shall have conveyed to the commonwealth, by a good and sufficient deed, and free from all incumbrances, the land on which the buildings to be erected shall stand, and so much adjacent thereto as the governor and council shall require; and until the plans for said buildings shall have been approved by the governor and council."

This resolve was passed in 1869, and in accordance with its terms the corporation deeded the required portion of land to the commonwealth. But the sum granted was insufficient to accomplish all the necessary changes, and in order to meet the conditions of the appropriation of fifteen thousand dollars made in the preceding year, contributions to a similar amount were raised among the friends of the blind. The plans for buildings were prepared, submitted to the governor and council, and approved by them, and the work was soon commenced. Four dwelling-houses were erected on Fourth street, and a schoolhouse, with recitation and music-rooms, was built at a convenient distance. The premises occupied by the new buildings were divided from those on which the old structure stood by a fence. This arrangement afforded easy and pleasant means for entire separation of the sexes. The cottages, with the

new schoolhouse, were occupied by the girls, who were
gradually arranged into four distinct families, while the
main building was entirely devoted to the use of the
boys.   An attempt was made to classify the latter, as
far as the internal conveniences of the house permitted,
by dividing them into small families, each group having
a particular flat for sleeping chambers and the like, and
separate tables in the dining-rooms.   Though this
arrangement could not be as satisfactorily carried out
as in the girls' department, it was a great improvement
upon the preceding one.

The buildings having been entirely completed, the
institution was reörganized upon the new system in
October, 1870 ; and the experience of the past eleven
years has proved the sagacity, foresight and broad-
mindedness of its great founder and benefactor, who
strove persistently to the very last day of his noble
career to reform traditional evils and bring about a new
order of things more in harmony with advanced civilization and the long-cherished idea of a home.

By the death of Dr. Howe, which took place on the
9th of January, 1876, the institution lost not merely its
director, but its lifelong friend and champion.   He had
devoted himself to the cause of the blind in the zeal
and enthusiasm of early manhood; he had given to it
the wisdom and experience of his mature years, and it
continued to be the object of his tenderest care until the
end of his life.   He had organized the first attempts in
this country to educate the blind, and had not only arranged for them a system of instruction and training
imbued with the spirit of manliness and progress, and
calculated to raise their social and moral status, but had

pleaded their cause in fifteen states with the eloquence of earnestness and with remarkable success. He appeared before the legislatures and other notable assemblies in

DR. HOWE.

Ohio, Virginia, South Carolina, and Kentucky, and his addresses, with the performances of three of his first pupils, — Sophia and Abby Carter and Joseph B. Smith, — were so effective, that provision for the education of the blind was made in those states before the representatives of the people had time to wipe the tears from their eyes. In order to promote the interests of the class to whose welfare he devoted his best energies, he addressed large audiences, and exhibited before them the attainments of his pupils, not only in most of the cities of New England, but in New York, Washington, Baltimore, Augusta (Georgia), Louisville, and later in several places in the provinces of Ontario and Quebec, in Canada. Words with Dr. Howe were as sparingly used as the few tools around the mason — his trowel, hammer, and mortar — when he raises the substantial fabric of wall or house ; but those which he employed seemed as if they were forged in the fire of his enthusiasm and made resistless. He was tireless in his endeavors for the amelioration of the condition of the blind, and his achievements in their behalf will always stand out like the majestic purple of the clouds against the azure sky of philanthropy. When the experience of years and the growth of the school under his immediate care demanded improved methods, Dr. Howe was among the first to "read the signs of the times," and reörganized his work upon a better system. During the later years of his life he labored especially to remove – the school from the class of charitable institutions, and · to put it on the same footing with other educational establishments. His work was taken up and carried on in the same spirit, and the final act necessary to remove from it entirely the idea of an asylum was accomplished when, at a meeting of the corporation held Oct. 3, 1877, – it was " *Voted*, that the institution shall hereafter be called and known by the name of PERKINS INSTITUTION AND MASSACHUSETTS SCHOOL FOR THE BLIND."

The means for the support of the establishment are supplied by the same sources as when first established. The state of Massachusetts gradually increased its annual appropriation from six thousand dollars in 1833 to thirty thousand dollars in 1869. The other New England states continue to pay in proportion to the number of their pupils ; and friends of the blind have aided from time to time by donations and bequests.

The character of the institution has always been that

of a school for blind youth of both sexes. Its main object has been from the beginning to furnish them with the means and facilities for a thorough practical education, and thus to enable them to depend upon their own exertions for their support, and to become useful and happy members of society. To compass this end a system of instruction was gradually arranged which, although not differing in its principal features from those employed in educational establishments for seeing youth, was, in some of its details, better adapted to the requirements of the class of children for whose special benefit it was intended. This system was sound in principle, practical in its methods, broad in its purposes, and liberal in its policy. It aimed at the full development of the energies and capacities of the blind, and embraced the following instrumentalities: —

First, instruction in such branches of study as constitute the curriculum of our best common schools and academies.

Secondly, lessons and practice in music, both vocal and instrumental.

Thirdly, systematic instruction in the theory and practice of the art of tuning pianofortes.

Fourthly, training in one or more simple trades, and work at some mechanical or domestic occupation.

Fifthly, regular gymnastic drill under the care of competent teachers, and plenty of exercise in the open air.

The main object of this comprehensive system was to unfold the mental faculties and strengthen the bodily powers of the blind in definite order; to cultivate in them the æsthetic element and prepare them for liberal professions; to train them up in industrious and virtuous habits; to develop to the utmost extent all their faculties and aptitudes; and lastly, to make them hardy and self-reliant, so that they might go out into the world, not to eat the bread of charity, but to earn a livelihood by honest work. A comparison of the present condition of the blind of New England with that of fifty years ago will show that this system has proved a complete success and produced abundant fruit, and that the institution, conceived in the benevolence of the citizens of Boston, and nurtured by the tender and fostering care of such distinguished men as Jonathan Phillips, Peter C. Brooks, Thomas H. Perkins, Samuel Appleton, Samuel May, Edward Brooks, William Oliver, and a host of others, has kindled in America the Promethean fire of enlightenment for the sightless, and wrought a wonderful revolution in the realm of humanity.

VI. — Instruction and Training of Laura Bridgman.

An account of this institution would be incomplete if it failed to mention the remarkable success achieved in the education of Laura Bridgman. Cases of combined loss (or lack) of sight, hearing and speech are so extremely rare, that able writers and philosophers had discussed the possibility of teaching beings so deprived of the senses necessary for communion with their fellows any systematic language for such intercourse. But no such person seems to have come to the knowledge of these teachers and philosophers, and it was considered an open question whether such education were possible, when Dr. Howe, having found " in a little village in the mountains a pretty and lively girl about six years old,

who was totally blind and deaf, and who had only a
very indistinct sense of smell," resolved to try the experiment of establishing a means of communication between
the human soul thus buried in darkness and silence and
the world outside.

Laura Bridgman was born at Hanover, N.H., Dec.
21, 1829. She was a bright, pretty infant, but very
delicate, and subject to fits until she was eighteen
months old, when her health began to improve, and at
two years of age she was an active, intelligent and
healthy child. She was then suddenly prostrated by a
fever, which raged violently for seven weeks, and deprived her entirely of the senses of sight and hearing,
and blunted those of taste and smell. For five months
she lay in a darkened room ; and two years had passed
before her health was fully restored. Though thus deprived of most of the usual means of communication
with others, she was interested in things about her, and
showed a desire to learn. She soon began to make a
language of her own ; and had a sign to indicate her
recognition of each member of the family. Her power
of imitation led her to repeat what others did, and by
means of this faculty she had learned to sew a little,
and to knit. When Dr. Howe first saw her, he described her as having " a well-formed figure ; a strongly-
marked, nervous-sanguine temperament ; a large and
beautifully-shaped head ; and the whole system in healthy
action." Her parents were willing to allow the trial of
Dr. Howe's plan of teaching their unfortunate child, and
on the 4th of October, 1837, she was brought to the
institution.

The first lessons were given by taking small articles

of common use, such as a *key*, a *pen*, etc., having labels
pasted upon them with their names in raised letters,
and allowing her to feel of these very carefully, over
and over again, until she came to associate the word
thus printed with the article itself; and when shown
the name apart from the object, would at once bring the
object which the name called for. In order to teach
her the value of the individual letters of which these
names were composed, short monosyllabic words were
first selected, such as *pin* and *pen*; and by repeatedly
examining these, she came to perceive that they consisted of three separate signs or characters, and that
the middle sign of one differed from the middle sign of
the other. The task of teaching these early lessons was
a very slow one; but Laura began by being a willing
and patient imitator, even before she had any conception of the meaning or object of these lessons; and
when, by degrees, some idea of their signification
dawned upon her, her delight was so unmistakably
manifested, and her zeal and interest became so great,
that the slow process became a pleasant work. After
learning to associate the printed names upon the labels
with the articles, the letters were given her on detached
pieces of paper, and she was taught to arrange them so
as to spell the words which she had already learned
upon the labels. She was next supplied with a set of
metal types with the letters of the alphabet cast upon
their ends, and a board containing square holes, into
which the types could be set, so that only the letters
upon the ends could be felt above the surface; and with
these she soon learned to spell the words which she
knew, as she had with the paper slips. After several

weeks of this practice she was taught to make the different letters by the position of her fingers, and thus dispense with the more cumbrous aid of board and types. About three months were spent in thus teaching her the names of some common objects, and the means of expressing them by setting up type, or by the manual alphabet. She was so eager to learn the name of every object with which she came in contact that much time was spent in teaching her these. Next came words expressing positive qualities; then the use of prepositions; and she easily acquired the use of some active verbs, such as to *walk*, to *run*, to *sew*, etc., although the distinctions of mood and tense came later. The process of teaching was necessarily so slow, that, notwithstanding the unusual quickness of apprehension and eagerness to learn, she had attained only about the same command of language as that possessed by ordinary children at three years of age when she had been under instruction twenty-six months, and was ten years old. But as she now possessed the means for the acquirement of all knowledge, and she became capable of expressing her own thoughts, feelings and impressions, the process of teaching her and watching the development of her moral and intellectual nature became more and more interesting. Her sense of touch became more acute, and there was some improvement in the senses of taste and smell. Laura seems to have possessed an innate love of neatness and modesty which, even in early childhood, prevented her from ever transgressing the rules of propriety. She had a bright and sunny disposition, which delighted in fun and merriment; an affectionate and sympathetic nature, and a ready confi-

dence in others; and her conscientiousness and love of
truth were early developed. When she had acquired a
sufficient command of language to converse freely by
means of the manual alphabet, her circle of friends and
acquaintances began to enlarge, and the development of
her character was greatly aided by coming into contact
with a variety of persons. A few years later she took

LAURA BRIDGMAN TEACHING OLIVER CASWELL TO READ
EMBOSSED PRINT.

great interest in assisting in the education of Oliver
Caswell, who was similarly afflicted with herself. By
the special teaching adapted to her condition, Laura has
acquired a good education, and is very skilful in many
of the employments of women: such as sewing (both by
hand and by machine), knitting, crocheting, and some
fancy work; and she is also capable of performing many
household duties. She is very intelligent, and fond of

reading and of social intercourse; and, notwithstanding the isolation which her lack of sight, hearing and speech necessarily involves, her life is an industrious and a happy one.

Dr. Howe watched and guided the development of this little shut-in human treasure with a father's care from the beginning. She was never absent from his thoughts; and to her training he devoted the best and freshest powers of his mind and life. Laura, as the first-fruits of his genius, commanded his time, his energies and his attention; but, like other great architects, he also employed the assistance of skilled workmen, and Laura had, on the whole, good and efficient teachers, of whom the one distinguished by breadth of mind and capacity for carrying out the work so wonderfully begun by his creative mind was Miss Wight, afterward the wife of Mr. George Bond.

VII.—Establishment of other Institutions in America.

Even as the Paris school served as a model and stimulus for the establishment of similar institutions all over Europe, so did that of Boston in America. The initiatory steps taken in this city gave an impulse to the active philanthropy of Dr. Samuel Akerly and Mr. Samuel Wood, and through their influence and exertions the New York institution for the blind was incorporated on the 22d of April, 1831. On the 15th of March, 1832, three blind boys were taken from the almshouse of the city and placed under the direction of Dr. John D. Russ, who was invited to coöperate with the managers of the institution from the beginning, and who kindly volunteered his services to give instruction to the pupils. On the 19th of May of the same year, three other children were added to their number, and with the six a school was opened at No. 47 Mercer street. The experiment proved a success, as was anticipated; and at the end of the year 1833 the institution was removed to its present location on Ninth avenue. During his connection with the school, Dr. Russ devised, among other educational facilities, a phonetic alphabet which showed some ingenuity, but did not come into use. He resigned his place in 1836, and was succeeded by Mr. Silas Jones in August of that year; but he continued to manifest, from time to time, great interest in the improvement of educational appliances for the blind. He was the first projector and advocate of the horizontal system of point writing, and the alphabet in that system which he arranged in the year 1862 and 1863 is identical in its main principles with that which is used in many American institutions to-day, and differs from it only in some of the minor details. A little sheet which was periodically published by Dr. Russ, under the title of the " Experiment," for the purpose of explaining and illustrating his contrivances, bears ample testimony to this statement. Among other things, the doctor devised a method of printing between the lines on both sides of the paper, which was readily adopted at the Paris school for the blind in 1867, and from that institution was carried to England by Dr. T. R. Armitage, who, although always eager to profit by inventions in this direction, does not seem inclined to disclose any of his own. Fortunately, however, there is no danger of great loss to the blind in general from secrecy of this kind, for the real value of the contrivances made in such a spirit seldom exceeds the cost of the ink and paper required for their description.

With regard to the early administrations of the New York institution, it may be said that no one was thoroughly successful, and the progress of the school was retarded by the want of an efficient head to direct its affairs. In 1845, Mr. James F. Chamberlain was elected superintendent, and under his management an era of prosperity and advancement dawned for the establishment.

The third American institution was founded in Philadelphia, by the society of friends, on the 5th of March, 1833. A house was soon provided, and the services of Mr. Julius R. Friedlander, as principal, were secured by the managers. Mr. Friedlander was of German origin, and began to occupy himself with the blind in the year 1828, when he resided for a little while at the school in Paris. He continued this study in London, and finally entered the institution for the blind at Bruchsal, in the grand duchy of Baden, as sub-master. The description which the duke of Saxe Weimer had given of the city of Philadelphia, and of the hospitality of its inhabitants, produced in the mind of Friedlander an earnest desire to expatriate himself in order to establish in that city an institution for the education of sightless children. He organized the school with great care and deliberation; gave exhibitions of the attainments of his pupils before the legislatures of Pennsylvania, Delaware and New Jersey, and obtained appropriations for the support of beneficiaries from each of these states, and later from that of Maryland. The institution occupied its present location on Race street in October, 1836.

Mr. Friedlander was obliged to spend the winter of that
year in the West Indies, for the restoration of his impaired health; and his place was temporarily supplied
by Mr. Sprout, assistant instructor, and Mr. A. W. Penniman, a graduate from the New England school.   Mr.
Friedlander returned from the South on the 4th of
March, 1839, and died at the institution on the 17th of
the same month, lamented by managers, teachers and
pupils, and was succeeded by Dr. Joshua Roades, who
subsequently became superintendent of the Illinois institution for the blind, where he remained until near the
end of his life.

Ohio comes next in order in the good work of the
education of the blind.   The idea of establishing a
school in Columbus for that purpose was first conceived by Dr. William M. Awl, as early as 1835.
Through his efforts, on the 11th of March, 1836, the
legislature passed a resolution, by which he, with two
others, Dr. James Hodge and Col. N. H. Swayne, were
appointed trustees to collect information in relation to
the instruction of the blind, and submit a report to the
next general assembly.   Circulars were at once sent to
the justices of the peace in all the townships in the
state; and in order to create a public interest in the
subject, Dr. S. G. Howe was invited to lend his assistance.   He promptly offered his services, and in the
latter part of December, 1836, he appeared before the
legislature and a large number of influential persons
who were gathered at the state-house, and made a
stirring address which, supplemented by an exhibition
of the attainments of three of his pupils whom he had
brought with him, made so deep an impression upon

the community in general, and upon the minds of the representatives of the people in particular, that in April, 1837, an act incorporating the institution was triumphantly passed, and an appropriation for commencing the building made. The school was organized by Mr. A. W. Penniman, who was recommended to the trustees by Dr. Howe, and on the 4th of July, 1837, was publicly opened in the First Presbyterian church in Columbus. Maps, globes, books and all other educational appliances and apparatus for the young institution were prepared in this establishment, and there exists in our records a copy of a long and exceedingly interesting letter, addressed by Dr. Howe to Dr. Awl, in which a complete plan of buildings adapted to the wants of the blind is sketched. I need hardly add in this connection that long experience, keen observation, and mature reflection had so essentially modified Dr. Howe's early views on this point, that he became the irreconcilable foe to expensive piles of bricks and mortar and vast congregations of human beings under one roof, and the enthusiastic and irresistible advocate of the family or cottage system.

The fifth American institution was founded in the state of Virginia; and the following letter of Dr. Howe, dated Boston, March 14, 1837, and addressed to Rev. W. S. Plummer, of Richmond, clearly shows its origin: —

" Dear Sir, — With this letter you will receive a copy of our annual report for the past year. Has anything been done yet towards establishing an institution for the education of the blind in your section of the country? If not, the work should be commenced, and that soon; for since Providence has pointed out the

way by which so much knowledge and happiness and benefit, both
to soul and body, may be conferred upon this hitherto neglected
class, it seems to me imperative upon us to be acting in it.

"I would gladly have visited Virginia with my pupils on my
return from Ohio; but strong necessity bade me return here at
once.

"I feel confident that if the subject could be brought before the
public and your legislature, the foundation of a noble establishment which would confer benefit through future ages might be laid
broad and deep. I believe, too, that a more vivid impression
could be made now, while the subject is comparatively new, than
hereafter.

"Can I in any way be useful in such an undertaking? I shall
have a vacation and short release from my duties here in May. I
would gladly devote the time to any effort for the benefit of the
blind in any other section of the country, provided there was a
reasonable hope of success, and prospect of coöperation from
others. Will you give me your views on the subject?

"With much respect, truly yours,

"S. G. Howe."

The words of this letter found a peculiarly congenial
soil for fruition in the tender heart of Mr. Plummer,
and a correspondence ensued between the two philanthropists which resulted in an arrangement for a visit
of Dr. Howe, with three of his pupils, to Virginia.
Meanwhile the proposition of Mr. F. A. P. Barnard, of
New York, to unite the deaf-mutes with the blind, was
accepted, and a combined exhibition was given before
the legislature in Richmond, in January, 1838, which
produced the desired effect. On the 31st of March of
the same year the bill to incorporate a dual institution
for the deaf-mutes and the blind was passed, and the
sum of twenty thousand dollars was appropriated for
the purpose of procuring a suitable site and erecting

15

thereon the necessary buildings, together with ten thousand dollars for the support of the establishment. A board of visitors was appointed during Governor Campbell's administration, and, after some delay for preliminary arrangements, the two schools of the institution at Staunton got into full operation, with the Rev. Joseph D. Tyler as principal of the department for deaf-mutes and Dr. J. C. M. Merrillat of that for the blind. Virginia's example of bringing the two classes together under one organization and government was unfortunately followed by eight other states, three of which — those of Louisiana, Minnesota and Michigan — have dissolved the unnatural and vexatious union, and formed separate institutions for each class.

Next to Virginia, Kentucky fell into the line of the good cause. The first attempt to induce the legislature of that state to establish a school for the blind was prompted by a former pupil of Dr. Howe, Mr. Otis Patten, in 1840; but, so far as I can judge from the correspondence which I have before me, it was not crowned with success. Mr. Patten wrote to his teacher and friend of the failure; and from Dr. Howe's reply, dated July 7th, 1841, I make the following extract : — " Do not attempt anything unless you are sure that every possible provision has been made for every possible contingency. I have it very much to heart to see institutions for the instruction of the blind built up in every part of the country, and I would willingly make any personal sacrifice or effort to effect it. If it is thought I can be of any use, I will come to Louisville and take the matter in hand. I will devote myself entirely to it, and ask no compensation for my time or expenses." On the 15th

of November of the same year, Dr. Howe addressed a
letter to Dr. J. B. Flint, of Louisville, on the subject, in
which, after referring to Mr. Patten's earnest efforts, he
speaks as follows: — " I am very desirous of making the
attempt this winter myself, with the aid of two of my
pupils, to persuade your legislature to some immediate
action on the subject, and if I can obtain a hearing I am
sure I shall succeed."   Arrangements were at once made,
and Dr. Howe, with his two favorite pupils, Abby and
Sophia Carter, proceeded to Kentucky, where — joined
by Mr. William Chapin, then superintendent of the Ohio
institution, with some of his best pupils — they gave
together an exhibition before the legislature.   On the
5th of February, 1842, an institution was incorporated
by an act of the general assembly, and visitors or managers were soon appointed.   A suitable house was rented
in Louisville, which was furnished by the liberality of the
inhabitants of that city, who also generously contributed
funds sufficient to sustain the institution during the first
six months of its infancy ; and the school was opened
on the 9th of May, with Mr. Bryce Patten as director,
Mr. Otis Patten as teacher, and five pupils, whose number increased to ten before the end of the year.

On his way to Kentucky, Dr. Howe stopped at Columbia, South Carolina, and made a strong plea in behalf
of the blind before the legislature of that state.   From
a long correspondence relating to the preliminary arrangements of this visit I make a few extracts, which
are characteristic of the great champion of humanity.
In a letter dated July 4th, 1841, and addressed to Dr.
H. S. Dickenson, of Charleston, Dr. Howe speaks as
follows : — " I am inclined to the opinion that no pre-

paration will be necessary; because I have not the
slightest doubt about being able to carry the feelings of
your legislators entirely away with the subject. I do
not mean that I have any peculiar power of enlisting
the feelings, so far from it, the very absence of eloquence
gives additional effect to the irresistible appeal which
the blind children themselves make." To governor T.
P. Richardson, Dr. Howe wrote as follows on the subject: — " I desire most ardently, before taking my hand
from the plough, to see schools for the blind established in every part of the country, or at least provision
made for their support. With this view I intend to address the legislature of South Carolina this winter, and
so endeavor to induce them to do for the blind of the
state what they do for the deaf and dumb, viz., make
an appropriation for their education." To his friend,
Dr. Francis Lieber, who was then professor of history
and political economy in the South Carolina college, at
Columbia, Dr. Howe wrote as follows on the 30th of
November, 1841: — " It has occurred to me that you
might be of essential service to the cause of the blind, if
you would exert your influence to create an interest in
this subject. From Columbia I shall go to Kentucky,
where I think an institution will be founded immediately.
I am very desirous of seeing ample provision made in
every part of my country for the education of the blind,
and I doubt not I shall be gratified."

Yes, Dr. Howe's most ardent wishes in this direction
were fulfilled; for, in addition to the above-named states,
twenty-four others established institutions in the following chronological order: — Tennessee, 1844; Indiana,
1847; Illinois, 1849; North Carolina, 1849; Wiscon-

sin, 1850; Missouri, 1851; Georgia, 1852; Maryland, 1853; Michigan, 1854; South Carolina, 1855; Texas, 1856; Alabama, 1858; Arkansas, 1859; California, 1860; Minnesota, 1862; Kansas, 1867; New York State, 1867; West Virginia, 1870; Oregon, 1872; Colorado, 1874; Nebraska, 1875. Thus twenty-nine States support their own institutions for the education of the blind, while the rest make provision for the instruction of their sightless children in the nearest schools.

European and American Institutions Compared.

In order to measure and compare the value and importance of the schools of Europe and of this country correctly and fairly, it is necessary to look at the principles which underlie them and the purpose with which they are administered.

In most of the European institutions the prevailing idea is, that what is done for the blind is in the spirit of favor and charity, rather than of right and obligation. The liberal and elevating influences of a free and thorough education, which alone can assist this afflicted class to rise above the clouds of ignorance and common prejudice, and breath the free air of independence, are wanting, and a depressing atmosphere of social inferiority and dependence surrounds them. A large number of the so-called schools, especially those in Great Britain, are mere asylums, chiefly supported by annual contributions, which are made and received in the nature of alms. This helps to strengthen and perpetuate what it is most desirable to destroy, namely, the old, unhappy and disadvantageous association in the public mind of blindness with beggary. But even in those establishments which

are endowed and supported by the governments, the
pupils are brought up under such influences as favor the
⁚ segregation of the blind into a class by themselves, and
are neither inspired with those higher views of man's
dignity and self-respect, nor fired up with that uncon-
querable desire for usefulness and self-maintenance
which are so indispensable for their success in life.
Hence the greatest number of their graduates relapse
into their original state of inanition, and the glimmering
of happiness which they have caught while under instruction is followed by a doubly dark and wretched
future.   The fact that even so eminent a man as Penjon,
who held a professorship of mathematics at the college
of Angers for thirty years with success and distinction,
spent the latter part of his life, either willingly or from
force of circumstances, amidst the misery of the *hospice
des Quinze-Vingts*, illustrates strikingly the unfavorable
effects of early education and training at so famous a
school as that of Paris.

The most valuable distinctive feature of the American institutions is that they constitute an integral part
of the educational system of the country.   Their existence is planted in the letter and nourished by the liberal
spirit of its fundamental laws.   They are the creations
of justice and equity, and not the offspring of charity
and favor.   Thus the right of the blind to participate
in all the educational benefits provided for every child
in the commonwealth is acknowledged by the state in
its sovereign capacity; and since they cannot be taught
in the common schools, an express provision is made
for their instruction.   This policy has acted very favorably upon the blind.   It has strengthened their good im-

pulses, and fostered in them an upward tendency and noble determination to become useful and independent. It has inspired them with self-respect, and made them aim at a higher place in the social scale than they would otherwise have sought. The fruits of this policy began to appear soon after the organization of the American institutions. As early as 1837, Madame Eugénie Niboyet made the following remarks on the schools of this country in her valuable work entitled *Des aveugles et de leur éducation :* — " The American institutions, recently founded, are in many respects much superior to that of Paris." Again she says elsewhere : — " The Americans have left us behind. The pupil has become stronger (*plus fort*) than the master."

Another distinctive feature in the American schools is the spirit of individual independence and self-reliance which Dr. Howe breathed into the system of education and training which he arranged for the sightless children of New England, and which was afterwards more or less copied everywhere. He taught the blind that the maxim, " Heaven helps those who help themselves," is a well-tried one, embodying in a small compass the results of vast human experience. He inculcated among them the healthy doctrine of self-help as the most potent lever to raise them in the social scale ; and as soon as it was understood and carried into action, ignorance and dependence upon alms and charity were reduced to their minimum : for the two principles are directly antagonistic ; and what Victor Hugo says of the pen and the sword applies alike to them : " This kills that." I can give no better estimate of the powers of the great philanthropist in this respect than the one made by Mr. George Combe in his "Tour in the United States," vol. I. p. 228, which runs as follows : — "It appears to us that Dr. Howe has a bold, active, enterprising mind, and to a certain extent he impresses his own character on the minds of his pupils. He enlarges the practical boundaries of their capacities by encouraging them to believe in the greatness of their natural extent."

In bringing this sketch to a close, I must add that the blind have availed themselves of the advantages offered by the schools, and have proved that in the stream of life they are not mere straws thrown upon the water to mark the direction of the current, but that they have within themselves the power of strong swimmers, and are capable of striking out for themselves ; of buffeting with the waves, and directing their own independent course to some extent. Thus they have furnished a remarkable illustration of what may be effected by the energetic development and exercise of faculties, the germs of which at least are in every human heart.

All which is respectfully submitted.

M. ANAGNOS.

ACKNOWLEDGMENTS.

AMONG the pleasant duties incident to the close of the year is that of expressing our heartfelt thanks and grateful acknowledgments to the following artists, *littérateurs*, societies, proprietors, managers, editors and publishers, for concerts and various musical entertainments; for operas, oratorios, lectures, readings, and for an excellent supply of periodicals and weekly papers, minerals and specimens of various kinds.

As I have said in previous reports, these favors are not only a source of pleasure and happiness to our pupils, but also a valuable means of æsthetic culture, of social intercourse, and of mental stimulus and improvement. As far as we know, there is no community in the world which does half so much for the gratification and improvement of its unfortunate members as that of Boston does for our pupils.

I. — *Acknowledgments for Concerts and Operas in the City.*

To the Harvard Musical Association, through its president, Mr. John S. Dwight, for fifty season-tickets to eight symphony concerts. The blind of New England are under great and lasting obligations to this association for the uncommon musical advantages which it has always extended to them in the most liberal and friendly manner since the inauguration of its concerts.

To Messrs. Tompkins & Hill, proprietors of the Boston Theatre, for admitting parties in unlimited numbers to ten operas.

To the Händel and Haydn Society, through its president, Mr. C. C. Perkins, and its secretary, Mr. A. Parker Browne, for tickets to the oratorio of " St. Paul," Mozart's " Requiem," Beethoven's " Mount of Olives," and the public rehearsal of Bach's Passion music.

16

To the Boston Philharmonic Society, for admission to five public rehearsals.

To Mr. C. C. Perkins, for tickets to the Dwight testimonial concert, to the Wulf Fries testimonial concert, and to five of the Euterpe concerts.

To Dr. Louis Maas, for admission to his orchestral concert, given for the benefit of the printing-fund of this institution.

To Mr. Benjamin Bates, for admission to one opera at the Gaiety Theatre; and to Miss Jessy Cochrane, to one operetta at the Boston Museum.

To the managers of the Tremont Temple, through the kindness of deacon Charles A. Roundy, for an invitation to attend the performance of the oratorio "Elijah" by the Händel and Haydn Society, two Morgan organ and harp matinées, and four Swan organ recitals.

To Mr. Joseph Winch, for admission to the oratorio of "Samuel" in Phillips church.

To the Apollo and Cecilia clubs, through the kindness of their secretary, Mr. Arthur Reed, for tickets to six concerts each.

To Boylston club, through Mr. G. L. Osgood, director, and Mr. F. H. Ratcliffe, secretary, for tickets to three concerts.

To the following distinguished artists we are under great obligations for admitting our pupils to their concerts: Mr. B. J. Lang, to two concerts and three rehearsals of the "Damnation of Faust," by Berlioz; to Mr. W. H. Sherwood, to four concerts; to Mr. Ernst Perabo, to two; to Mr. Arthur Foote, to eight; to M. Otto Bendix, to two; to Madame Dietrich Strong, to one; to Mr. J. A. Conant, to one; to Mr. Georg Henschel, to one recital; and to Mr. J. W. Brackett, to one of the Satter concerts.

We are also indebted to the managers of Dudley Hall for admission to four historical concerts; to Dr. E. Tourjée, director of the New England conservatory, to four concerts, three organ recitals, and to all the performances of the festival week; to Mr. Henry M. Dunham, to four organ recitals, and to Mr. John A. Preston to three; to Rev. J. J. Lewis, and Mr. A. G. Ham, to several concerts in the Universalist church, South Boston; to the Broadway Methodist Society, through Dr. L. D. Packard, to a course of lectures and concerts; and to Mr. B. W. Williams, to three jubilee concerts.

II. — *Acknowledgments for Concerts given in our Hall.*

For a series of fine concerts given from time to time in the music-hall of the institution we are greatly indebted to the following artists : —

To Mr. Ernst Perabo, assisted by one of his pupils, Miss Amy Marcy Cheney.

To Madame Marie Fries Bishop, assisted by Mrs. Georgie Pray, Miss Louisa Fries, Mr. John Little, and Mrs. Alice Lee McLaughlin, reader.

To Mr. Wulf Fries and daughter.

To Madame Rametti, assisted by Miss Jessy Rametti, Mrs. G. Gibbs, Mrs. Freeman Cobb, Miss Ella Chamberlain, Mr. John F. Winch, and Mr. Henry Pray.

To Madame Dietrich Strong, Mr. Gustav Dannreuther, and Mrs. H. M. Knowles.

To Mrs. Dr. Fenderson, Mrs. Freeman Cobb, and Mr. George Parker.

To M. Alfred de Sève, M. Otto Bendix, Miss Annie Lawrence, Miss Sarah Winslow, Miss Daisy Terry, Mrs. H. T. Spooner, Mr. and Mrs. J. C. Miller, and Mr. Arthur T. Burns.

To Dr. Louis Maas, for a pianoforte recital.

To St. Augustine's sanctuary choir, directed by Mr. Albert Meyers, and assisted by Miss Nellie McLaughlin, Miss Nellie Moore, Miss Cecilia Mooney, Mr. J. G. Lennon, and Mr. J. P. Leahy, elocutionist.

To Mr. Eugene Thayer, for a series of organ concerts, assisted by Miss Osgood (violinist), Mrs. Geraldine Morris (vocalist), Miss Black, and Mr. Harris.

III. — *Acknowledgments for Lectures and Readings.*

For a series of lectures and readings our thanks are due to the following kind friends : Rev. E. E. Hale, D.D., Dr. L. B. Fenderson, Mrs. Annie D. C. Hardy, Mrs. Alice McLaughlin, Miss

Jenny Morrison, Miss Selma Borg, Miss E. V. Adams, Miss Emma Clifford, and Miss Stratton.

IV. — Acknowledgments for Tangible Objects, Specimens, etc.

For a collection of specimens, curiosities and tangible objects of various kinds, we are greatly indebted to the following persons : Mr. Clement Ryder, Mr. David Denio, Mr. James R. Cocke, Mr. Charles H. Dillaway, Miss M. C. Moulton, Mr. William C. Howes, Miss Sophia Ann Wolfe, Mr. William P. Garrison, and Mr. John N. Marble.

We are also under great obligations to Mrs. S. N. Russell of Pittsfield, Mass., and Mrs. Henry Farnam of New Haven, Conn., for generous and useful gifts to our girls; to Automatic Organ Company, for one of their instruments ; and to Rev. Photius Fiske, for several acts of kindness and thoughtfulness performed at various times and in various ways.

V. — Acknowledgments for Periodicals and Newspapers.

The editors and publishers of the following reviews, magazines and semi-monthly and weekly papers, continue to be very kind and liberal in sending us their publications gratuitously, which are always cordially welcomed, and perused with interest : —

The N. E. Journal of Education . .	Boston, Mass.
The Atlantic	" "
Boston Home Journal	-- --
The Christian	-- --
The Christian Register	-- --
The Musical Record	-- --
The Musical Herald	
The Folio	-- --
Littell's Living Age	-- --
Unitarian Review	-- --
The Watchman	
The Congregationalist	-- --
The Golden Rule	-- --
The Missionary Herald . . .	"
The Salem Register . . .	Salem, --

Scribner's Monthly   .   .   .   *New York, N.Y.*
St. Nicholas.   .   .   .   .   "   "
The Christian Union   .   .   .
The Journal of Speculative Philosophy   "   "
Journal of Health   .   .   .   *Dansville, N.Y.*
The Penn Monthly   .   .   .   *Philadelphia, Penn.*
Church's Musical Journal   .   .   .   *Cincinnati, O.*
Our Reporter   .   .   .   .   *Little Rock, Ark.*
Goodson Gazette, *Va. Inst. for Deaf-Mutes and Blind.*
Tablet .   .   .   *West Va.* "   "   "   "
Companion .   .   *Minnesota Institute for Deaf-Mutes.*
Mistletoe   .   .   .   *Iowa Institute for the Blind.*
Il Mentore dei Ciechi   .   .   .   .   *Florence, Italy.*

I desire again to render the most hearty thanks, in behalf of all our pupils, to the kind friends who have thus nobly remembered them. The seeds which their friendly and generous attentions have sown have fallen on no barren ground, but will continue to bear fruit in after years; and the memory of many of these delightful and instructive occasions and valuable gifts will be retained through life.

M. ANAGNOS.

PERKINS INSTITUTION AND MASSACHUSETTS SCHOOL FOR THE BLIND *in account with* P. T. JACKSON, *Treasurer.*

General Fund.

Dr.			Cr.
To cash paid, Auditor's drafts, Nos. 174 to 101	$63,698 20	By balance from last years account, Sept. 30, 1881,	$1,227 43
taxes	177 84	By cash from State of Massachusetts	30,000 00
insurance on house 11 Oxford st.	30 00	Maine	3,450 00
rent of box, Union Safe Deposit Vaults	20 00	New Hampshire	6,725 00
five rights on new stock in Fitchburg Railroad	24 00	Connecticut	3,775 00
assessments on same	500 00	Rhode Island	3,100 00
land on Fifth street, by order of Trustees	10,380 75	Vermont	2,300 00
		interest on mortgages	6,008 10
		rents collected	563 51
		Boston and Providence Railroad dividends,	240 00
		Fitchburg Railroad dividends	202 50
		interest on Chicago and Milwaukee Railroad bonds	150 00
		interest on Eastern Railroad bonds	90 00
		interest on Lowell Railroad bonds	75 00
		interest on deposit	250 05
		M. Anagnos, Work Department, $14,118 41	
		M. Anagnos, sundries 5,582 57	10,700 98
	$79,830 70	Debit to new account	1,288 10
			$79,830 70

1881. Oct. 1,	Debit to new account	$1,288 16

E. & O. E. P. T. JACKSON, *Treasurer.*

BOSTON, Oct. 1, 1881.

PERKINS INSTITUTION AND MASSACHUSETTS SCHOOL FOR THE BLIND *in account with* P. T. JACKSON, *Treasurer.*

Printing Fund.

Dr.			Cr.		
To cash paid for two bonds, $10,000 each, of the Chicago, Milwaukee, and St. Paul Railroad Company .	$2,150 17		1880. Oct. 1, By balance, cash on hand .	$1,000 00	
loan, secured by mortgage note .	10,000 00		cash received from contributors as per schedule .	44,365 20	
paid for five bonds of Ottawa and Burlington Railroad Company .	5,550 00		cash interest on note of $10,000, 8 months, at 8¾ per cent .	236 25	
accrued interest on the same .	91 07				
paid for five bonds Kansas City and St. Joseph and Council Bluffs Railroad .	6,226 07				
paid to Mr. Anagnos for Laura Bridgman .	50 00				
Balance to new account .	21,523 04			$45,601 45	
	$45,601 45		1881. Sept. 30, Balance to new account .	$21,523 04	

PERKINS INSTITUTION AND MASSACHUSETTS SCHOOL FOR THE BLIND *in account with* P. T. JACKSON, *Treasurer.*

Harris Fund.

Dr.			Cr.
1881. July 21,	To cash paid for three bonds of Milwaukee and St. Paul Railroad Company . . .	$3,238 75	**1880.** Oct. 18, Cash received from note collected . . $3,500 00
	Balance uninvested . . .	3,761 25	**1881.** July 15, Cash received from note collected . . 3,500 00
		$7,000 00	$7,000 00
			Sept. 30, Balance to new account . . . $3,761 25

Balance of Printing Fund uninvested . . . $21,523 94
Balance of Harris Fund uninvested . . . 3,761 25
$25,285 19

General Fund, excess of expenditure over income . . $1,298 16
Balance in New-England Trust Company . . 23,987 03
$25,285 19

Boston, Oct. 1, 1881. E. & O. E.

P. T. JACKSON, *Treasurer.*

CERTIFICATE OF THE AUDITING COMMITTEE.

BOSTON, Oct. 11, 1881.

The undersigned, a committee appointed to examine the account of the treasurer of the Perkins Institution and Massachusetts School for the Blind, for the year ending Sept. 30, 1881, have attended to that duty, and hereby certify that they find the payments properly vouched, and the accounts correctly cast, resulting in a balance of twenty-three thousand, nine hundred and ninety-seven dollars, and three cents on hand, deposited in the New England Trust Company to the credit of the institution.

The treasurer also exhibited to us evidence of the following property belonging to the institution, viz.: —

HARRIS FUND.

Notes secured by mortgage on real estate . .	$70,000	
1 bond Boston & Lowell Railroad Company . .	1,000	
3 bonds Eastern Railroad Company . . .	3,000	
3 bonds Chicago, Milwaukee, & St. Paul Railroad Company	3,000	
		$77,000

GENERAL FUND.

Notes secured by mortgage on real estate . .	$38,000	
2 bonds of Eastern Railroad, $500 each . .	1,000	
30 shares Boston & Providence Railroad . . .	4,200	
50 shares Fitchburg Railroad	6,874	
Estate No. 11 Oxford street, Boston . . .	5,500	
Estate No. 44 Prince street, Boston . . .	3,900	
Estate No. 197 Endicott street, Boston . . .	2,300	
		61,274

PRINTING FUND.

Note	$10,000	
5 bonds of the Ottawa & Burlington Railroad .	5,550	
5 bonds of the Kansas City, St. Joseph, & Council Bluffs Railroad	6,200	
2 bonds of the Chicago, Milwaukee, and St. Paul Railroad	2,000	
		23,750
		$162,024

A. T. FROTHINGHAM, } *Auditing Committee.*
GEO. L. LOVETT, }

DETAILED STATEMENT OF TREASURER'S ACCOUNT.

GENERAL FUND.

DR.

1880–1881.

To cash paid on auditor's drafts	.$68,698	20
city of Boston for taxes . . .	177	84
insurance	30	00
rent of box in Safe Deposit Vaults .	20	00
five rights on new stock in Fitchburg Railroad	24	00
assessments on new stock in Fitchburg Railroad	500	00
land in Fifth street . . .	. 10,389	75
	$79,839	79

CR.

1880.

Oct.	1. By balance from former account . . .	. $1,227	43
	6. Interest on note of $9,000, 6 months . .	270	00
	10. 5,000, 6 months . .	150	00
	•18. 3,500, 6 months . .	105	00
	23. From State of New Hampshire . .	. 3,575	00
Nov.	2. dividend on Fitchburg Railroad shares .	135	00
	interest on Eastern Railroad bonds .	90	00
	Lowell Railroad bonds .	25	00
	20. State of Massachusetts . . .	. 7,500	00
	27. interest on note of $8,000, 6 months .	240	00
Dec.	9. 3,500, 6 months .	122	50
	13. 10,000, 6 months .	300	00
	29. rents collected, R E. Apthorp, agent .	234	82
	31. interest on deposit in New England Trust Co.	126	45
	31. note of $5,000, 6 months .	125	00
1881.			
Jan.	1. interest on note of $8,000, 6 months .	200	00
	15. 18,000, 6 months .	540	00

M. Anagnos, director, as per following:—		
sale of books in raised print .	. $507	07
tuning	. 500	00
W. D. Garrison, account of son .	150	00
A. D. Cadwell, account of son .	100	00

Amounts carried forward $1,257 07 $14,966 20

Amounts brought forward $1,257 07		$14,966 20

1881.

Jan.	15.	From J. R. Cocke, account of self. .	150 00	
		J. H. M'Cafferty, acct. of daughter,	50 00	
		Mrs. Heine, account of daughter .	25 00	
		town of Dedham, account of Mary O'Hare	28 10	
		Mrs. Müller, acct. of Henry Boesch,	125 00	
		State of New Hampshire, account of B. F. Parker . . .	22 00	
		J. J. Mundo, account of daughter .	25 00	
		receipts of work department : —		
		for month of October, $1,333 66		
		November, 1,165 27		
		December, 983 52		
			3,482 45	
				5,164 62
Jan.	28.	dividend from Fitchburg Railroad Company .		157 50
		interest on Boston and Lowell Railroad bonds,		25 00
	29.	dividend from Boston and Providence Railroad,		120 00
Mar.	23.	State of Massachusetts		7,500 00
April	6.	interest on note of $15,000, 6 months . .		450 00
		5,000, 6 months . .		125 00
		25,000, 6 months . .		750 00
	8.	State of Massachusetts		7,500 00
		interest on note of $9,000, 6 months . .		270 00
	16.	5,000, 6 months . .		150 00
	29.	M. Anagnos, director, as per following: —		
		Mrs. Heine, account of daughter .	$25 00	
		income legacy to Laura Bridgman,	40 00	
		W. D. Garrison, account of son .	150 00	
		C. G. Dennison, acct. of daughter .	65 00	
		A. D. Cadwell, account of son .	100 00	
		J. H. M'Cafferty, account of daughter	50 00	
		W. Easley, account of J. R. Cocke,	150 00	
		Mrs. Knowlton, acct. of daughter .	36 00	
		sale of old junk, etc. . . .	56 34	
		tablets	41 09	
		admission tickets . .	36 90	
		brooms, acct. of boys' shop,	29 48	
		books in raised print .	726 58	
		tuning	590 00	
		receipts of work department: —		
		for month of January, $845 70		
		February, 654 81		
		March, 1,023 05		
			2,523 56	
				4,619 95
		Amount carried forward		$41,798 27

Amount brought forward			$41,798 27
1881.			
May 28. From interest on note of $8.000, 6 months . .		240 00	
June 9.	3.500, 6 months . .	122 50	
11.	10.000, 6 months . .	300 00	
	8,000, 6 months . .	200 00	
July 1.	5,000, 6 months . .	125 00	
	on balance at New England Trust Co.	129 60	
5.	interest on note of $15,000, 6 months . .	450 00	
	18,000, 6 months . .	540 00	
15.	collected . . .	18 66	
Aug. 3.	State of Massachusetts	7,500 00	
6.	interest on Boston and Lowell Railroad bonds,	25 00	
	State of New Hampshire	3,150 00	
	interest on Milwaukee and St. Paul Railroad bonds	150 00	

M. Anagnos, director, as per following:—

C. G. Dennison, acct. of daughter,	$60 00	
George E. Fairbanks, acct. of son,	100 00	
Mrs. Müller, acct. of Henry Boesch,	125 00	
A. D. Cadwell, account of son .	50 00	
tuning	200 00	
sale of old junk, etc, . .	30 52	
books in raised print .	524 46	

receipts of work department:—

for month of April .	$1,333 19		
May .	1,093 74		
June .	1,509 52		
		3,936 45	
			5,026 43

10.	State of Vermont		2,300 00
	Rhode Island		3,100 00
22.	Maine		3,450 00
	Connecticut		3,775 00
	dividend on Boston and Providence Railroad bonds		120 00
30.	rents collected by R. E. Apthorp, agent .		328 69
	interest on note		125 00
	" "		687 50

M. Anagnos, director, as per following: —

tuning	$335 59	
sale of books in embossed print .	220 95	
Mrs. Heine, account of daughter .	50 00	
Mrs. Knowlton, acct. of daughter .	12 00	
State Almshouse, account of A. Sullivan	21 09	
sale of old junk, etc. . .	5 26	
tablets . . .	24 17	

Amounts carried forward	$669 06	$73,661 65

Amounts brought forward	$669 06	$73,661 65

1881.
Aug. 30. From sale of brooms, acct. of boys' shop, ... 24 75
admission tickets . . 20 22
receipts of work department: —
for month of July . $1,140 01
August. 1,073 84
Sept. . 1,962 10
————— 4,175 95
——————— 4,889 98
——————
$78,551 63

ANALYSIS OF TREASURER'S ACCOUNT.

The treasurer's account shows that the total receipts for
the year were $78,551 63
Less cash on hand at the beginning of the year . . 1,227 43
——————
$77,324 20

Ordinary Receipts.

From the State of Massachusetts . . . $30,000 00
beneficiaries of other states and individuals 21,050 19
interest, coupons, and rents . . . 8,273 22
—————— $59,332 41

Extraordinary Receipts.

From work department for sale of articles
made by the blind, etc. . . . $14,118 41
sale of embossed books and maps . . 1,979 06
writing tablets 65 26
tuning 1,625 59
sale of brooms, account of boys' shop . 54 23
sale of old junk, etc. 92 12
admission tickets . . . 57 12
—————— 17,991 79
——————
$77,324 20

GENERAL ANALYSIS OF THE STEWARD'S ACCOUNT.

DR.

Amount in steward's hands Oct. 1, 1880 . $2,054 82
Receipts from auditors' drafts . . . 68,698 20
Due steward for supplies, etc., Oct. 1, 1881 . 1,185 01
——————— $71,938 03

CR.

Ordinary expenses, as per schedule annexed . $47,290 82
Extraordinary expenses, as per schedule annexed 24,647 21
——————— $71,938 03

ANALYSIS OF EXPENDITURES FOR THE YEAR ENDING SEPT. 30, 1881, AS PER STEWARD'S ACCOUNT.

Meat, 26,131 lbs.	$2,548 57	
Fish, 3,373 lbs.	190 10	
Butter, 5,250 lbs.	1,601 08	
Rice, sago, etc.	47 22	
Bread, flour, and meal	1,743 54	
Potatoes and other vegetables	611 96	
Fruit	305 12	
Milk, 21,182 quarts	1,098 44	
Sugar, 5,938 lbs.	576 27	
Tea and coffee, 423 lbs.	140 58	
Groceries	681 23	
Gas and oil	414 30	
Coal and wood	2,950 87	
Sundry articles of consumption	417 92	
Salaries, superintendence, and instruction	15,513 85	
Domestic wages	3,882 21	
Outside aid	274 53	
Medicines and medical aid	51 09	
Furniture and bedding	1,936 57	
Clothing and mending	25 22	
Musical instruments	290 00	
Expenses of tuning department	827 47	
Expenses of boys' shop	84 53	
Expenses of printing-office	5,922 82	
Expenses of stable	215 21	
Books stationery and apparatus	2,507 75	
Ordinary construction and repairs	1,498 29	
Taxes and insurance	356 50	
Travelling expenses	204 02	
Rent of office in town	250 00	
Board of man and clerk during vacation	51 00	
Sundries	72 56	
		$47,290 82

EXTRAORDINARY EXPENSES.

Extraordinary construction and repairs	$7,783 78	
Bills to be refunded	36 19	
Beneficiaries of the Harris Fund	880 00	
Printing proceedings of meeting at Tremont Temple	288 55	
Expenses of work department	15,658 69	
		24,647 21
		$71,938 03

GENERAL ABSTRACT OF ACCOUNT OF WORK DEPARTMENT,
Oct. 1, 1881.

Liabilities.

Due institution for investments since the first date	$42,117 59	
Excess of expenditures over receipts . .	1,540 28	
		$43,657 87

Assets.

Stock on hand Oct. 1, 1881 . . .	$4,656 77	
Debts due Oct. 1, 1881	1,795 78	
		6,452 55
		$37,205 32

Balance against work department, Oct. 1, 1881 . . .		$37,205 32
Balance against work department, Oct. 1, 1880 . . .		36,018 99
		$1,186 33

DR.

Cash received for sales, etc., during the year,	$14,118 41	
Excess of expenditures over receipts during the year	1,540 28	
		$15,658 69

CR.

Salaries and wages paid blind persons .	$3,435 03	
Salaries paid seeing persons . . .	2,352 16	
Sundries for stock, etc.	9,871 50	
		$15,658 69

ACCOUNT OF STOCK, OCT. 1, 1881.

Real estate		$258,189 00
Railroad stock		11,574 00
Notes		38,000 00
Harris fund		80,761 25
Printing fund		45,273 94
Household furniture		16,700 00
Provisions and supplies		1,304 60
Wood and coal		3,302 49
Stock in work department		4,656 77
Musical department, viz., —		
One large organ	$5,500 00	
Four small organs	750 00	
Forty-four pianos	10,800 00	
Brass and reed instruments	900 00	
		17,950 00
Books in printing-office		5,700 00
Stereotype plates		2,800 00
School furniture and apparatus		6,700 00
Musical library		625 00
Library of books in common type		2,400 00
Library of books in raised type		6,000 00
Boys' shop		108 10
Stable and tools		1,154 35
		$503,199 50

LIST OF EMBOSSED BOOKS

Printed at the Perkins Institution and Massachusetts School for the Blind.

TITLE OF BOOK.	No. of Volumes.	Price per Volume.
Howe's Blind Child's First Book	1	$1 25
Howe's Blind Child's Second Book	1	1 25
Howe's Blind Child's Third Book	1	1 25
Howe's Blind Child's Fourth Book	1	1 25
Howe's Cyclopædia	8	4 00
Baxter's Call	1	2 50
Book of Proverbs	1	2 00
Book of Psalms	1	3 00
New Testament (small)	4	2 50
Book of Common Prayer	1	4 00
Hymns for the Blind	1	2 00
Pilgrim's Progress	1	4 00
Life of Melanchthon	1	2 00
Natural Theology	1	4 00
Combe's Constitution of Man	1	4 00
Selections from the Works of Swedenborg	1	–
Second Table of Logarithms	1	8 00
Philosophy of Natural History	1	8 00
Huxley's Science Primers, Introductory	1	2 00
Memoir of Dr. Samuel G. Howe	1	3 00
Cutter's Anatomy, Physiology and Hygiene	1	4 00
Viri Romæ, new edition with additions	1	2 00
Musical Characters used by the seeing, with explanations	1	35
Guyot's Geography	1	4 00
Dickens's Child's History of England	2	3 50
Anderson's History of the United States	1	2 50
Higginson's Young Folks' History of the United States	1	3 50
Schmitz's History of Greece	1	3 00
Schmitz's History of Rome	1	2 50
Freeman's History of Europe	1	2 50
Eliot's Six Arabian Nights	1	3 00
Lodge's Twelve Popular Tales	1	2 00
An Account of the Most Celebrated Diamonds	1	50
Extracts from British and American Literature	2	3 00
American Prose	2	3 00
Hawthorne's Tanglewood Tales	2	2 00
Dickens's Old Curiosity Shop	3	4 00
Dickens's Christmas Carol, with extracts from Pickwick	1	3 00
Goldsmith's Vicar of Wakefield	1	3 00
Milton's Paradise Lost	2	3 00
Pope's Essay on Man and other Poems	1	2 50
Shakspeare's Hamlet and Julius Cæsar	1	4 00
Byron's Hebrew Melodies and Childe Harold	1	3 00
Tennyson's In Memoriam and other Poems	1	3 00
Longfellow's Evangeline	1	2 00
Longfellow's Evangeline and other Poems	1	3 00
Whittier's Poems	1	3 00
Lowell's Poems	1	3 00
Bryant's Poems	1	3 00

Amount brought forward		**$7,143 20**
1881.		
Mar. 15. Received from Mrs. A. C. Lodge		100 00
Miss A. C Lowell		50 00
Stephen G. Deblois		25 00
Mrs. S. P Sears		25 00
Henry Saltonstall		200 00
Mrs. Rebecca Conant . . .		125 00
23. A Friend		15 00
E. A. G.		8 00
Mrs. B. S. Rotch . . .		50 00
Mrs. Samuel May . . .		100 00
Miss A. W. May . . .		100 00
26. J. P. Lyman		50 00
R. J. Fellows		25 00
James E. English		25 00
Mrs. Hoppin		5 00
H. Farnam		100 00
Mrs. A. G. Farnam . . .		45 00
H. W. Farnam		20 00
Dr. Dix		100 00
Friend to Printing . . .		20 00
31. A Friend		100 00
Sito		100 00
B. C. White		50 00
April 6. W. E. Fette		5 00
George H. Lyman . . .		100 00
Mrs. Tinkham		5 00
Mrs. Sarah Aldrich . . .		100 00
Miss Marian Russell . . .		100 00
A Friend		20 00
William Minot		50 00
8. A Friend		500 00
11. Oliver Ditson		500 00
Arthur T Lyman . . .		200 00
14. Miss M. V. Iasigi . . .		10 00
Mrs. M. E. Lowell . . .		10 00
Mrs. J. T. Coolidge . . .		100 00
Mrs. S. T. Dana . . .		100 00
20. A Friend		200 00
A. B.		100 00
A Bostonian		1,000 00
29. Miss Palfrey		10 00
Anonymous		25 00
John A. Lowell		100 00
Augustus Lowell		100 00
May 6. George Gardner		100 00
Amount carried forward		**$12,016 20**

Amount brought forward $12,016 20

1881.

May 6. Received from Rev. Samuel A. Devens . . .	50 00
	S. S. of South Congregational Church,	25 00
	G. D. B. Blanchard	25 00
	Mr., Mrs., and Miss Whitney . .	50 00
16.	Mrs. Theodore Chase . . .	30 00
	Mrs. M. Davis	10 00
	Miss M. J. Davis	5 00
	" F."	10 00
	Mrs. Susan O. Brooks . . .	1,000 00
19.	J. M. Prendergast	25 00
	Mrs. E. B. Bowditch . . .	450 00
	Miss H. P. Rogers	5 00
	" From a Friend " (through M. K. Baker)	500 00
	Mrs. E. M. Baker . . .	100 00
	" G. R."	5 00
	Miss M. J. Garland . . .	5 00
	Miss R. J. Weston . . .	5 00
	Friends of Katie Grant . .	15 00
June 14.	Miss M. A. Wales . . .	50 00
	Mrs. S. S. Fay	1,000 00
	A Friend	100 00
	Mrs. Robert Swan . . .	15 00
20.	Samuel Ward	500 00
	George L. Lovett . . .	25 00
	Miss Mary Pratt , . .	500 00
30.	Arthur Reed	10 00
	Miss Mary Russell . . .	5 00
	A. D. Cadwell, Fairmont, Minn. .	5 00
	" Friend D."	5,000 00
	Moses Hunt, on subscription of $1,000,	100 00
	Nathaniel Thayer . . .	5,000 00
July 7.	W. A. Grover	1,000 00
15.	Mrs. William Appleton . .	500 00
	William Amory . . .	1,000 00
	E. D. Barbour	200 00
	Samuel Eliot	100 00
	William Lawrence . . .	50 00
	Mrs. Sarah W. Whitman . .	50 00
	" F."	20 00
	A Friend	5 00
20.	S. D. Warren	1,000 00
	Miss E. Howes	100 00
	H. P. Kidder	1,000 00
	Mrs. K. W. Sears . . .	46 00

Amount carried forward $31,712 20

Amount brought forward $31,712 20

1881.

July 20. Received from Moses Hunt (on $1,000) . . . 200 00
     Mrs. H. A. Ames 500 00
     Mrs. R. C. Winthrop . . . 100 00
 25.   John A. Burnham 1,000 00
     Henry Saltonstall ($1,000 in all) . 800 00
     F. H. Peabody 250 00
     O. W. Peabody 100 00
     Ignatius Sargent 100 00
     J. R. Coolidge 50 00
     Miss A. G. Thayer 100 00
     J. R. Hall 100 00
     C. J. Morrill 300 00
     H H. Hunnewell 2,000 00
     C. H. Dalton 100 00
 28.   " W." 50 00
     " C. S. C." 5 00
     Thomas G. Appleton . . . 1,000 00
     J. H. Beal 100 00
Aug. 3.   George H. Chickering . . . 100 00
     Amos A. Lawrence 200 00
     Samuel Downer 20 00
     Miss Ann Wigglesworth . . . 100 00
     Edward Lawrence 50 00
 6.   Ladies' Domestic Missionary Society,
      Portsmouth, N.H. . . . 25 00
     Moses Hunt (on $1,000) . . . 200 00
     R. P. Nichols 25 00
 15.   Abbott Lawrence 500 00
     Richard T. Parker 200 00
     Thomas Wigglesworth . . . 200 00
 25.   Q. A. Shaw 3,000 00
 30.   H. B. Inches 100 00
     Phillips Brooks 100 00
Sept. 3.   Mrs. James Greenleaf . . . 200 00
 22.   Martin Brimmer 200 00
     E. F. Parker 100 00
     Mrs. Gibson 5 00
     William H. Gardiner . . . 200 00
     Moses Hunt (on $1,000) . . . 200 00
 30.   A Friend 50 00
     Mrs. Phenister, Chelsea . . . 10 00
     Mrs. L. D. James, Williamsburg . 5 00
     Mrs. H. A. Spelman . . . 3 00
     Charles Davis, jun. . . . 5 00

            $44,365 20

LIST OF EMBOSSED BOOKS

Printed at the Perkins Institution and Massachusetts School for the Blind.

TITLE OF BOOK.	No. of Volumes.	Price per Volume.
Howe's Blind Child's First Book	1	$1 25
Howe's Blind Child's Second Book	1	1 25
Howe's Blind Child's Third Book	1	1 25
Howe's Blind Child's Fourth Book	1	1 25
Howe's Cyclopædia	8	4 00
Baxter's Call	1	2 50
Book of Proverbs	1	2 00
Book of Psalms	1	3 00
New Testament (small)	4	2 50
Book of Common Prayer	1	4 00
Hymns for the Blind	1	2 00
Pilgrim's Progress	1	4 00
Life of Melanchthon	1	2 00
Natural Theology	1	4 00
Combe's Constitution of Man	1	4 00
Selections from the Works of Swedenborg	1	–
Second Table of Logarithms	1	3 00
Philosophy of Natural History	1	3 00
Huxley's Science Primers, Introductory	1	2 00
Memoir of Dr. Samuel G. Howe	1	3 00
Cutter's Anatomy, Physiology and Hygiene	1	4 00
Viri Romæ, new edition with additions	1	2 00
Musical Characters used by the seeing, with explanations	1	35
Guyot's Geography	1	4 00
Dickens's Child's History of England	2	3 50
Anderson's History of the United States	1	2 50
Higginson's Young Folks' History of the United States	1	3 50
Schmitz's History of Greece	1	3 00
Schmitz's History of Rome	1	2 50
Freeman's History of Europe	1	2 50
Eliot's Six Arabian Nights	1	3 00
Lodge's Twelve Popular Tales	1	2 00
An Account of the Most Celebrated Diamonds	1	50
Extracts from British and American Literature	2	3 00
American Prose	2	3 00
Hawthorne's Tanglewood Tales	2	2 00
Dickens's Old Curiosity Shop	3	4 00
Dickens's Christmas Carol, with extracts from Pickwick	1	3 00
Goldsmith's Vicar of Wakefield	1	3 00
Milton's Paradise Lost	2	3 00
Pope's Essay on Man and other Poems	1	2 50
Shakspeare's Hamlet and Julius Cæsar	1	4 00
Byron's Hebrew Melodies and Childe Harold	1	3 00
Tennyson's In Memoriam and other Poems	1	3 00
Longfellow's Evangeline	1	2 00
Longfellow's Evangeline and other Poems	1	3 00
Whittier's Poems	1	3 00
Lowell's Poems	1	3 00
Bryant's Poems	1	3 00

LIST OF APPLIANCES AND TANGIBLE APPARATUS
made at the Perkins Institution and Massachusetts School for the Blind.

GEOGRAPHY.

I. — *Wall-Maps.*

1. The Hemispheres . . . . . . size 42 by 52 inches.
2. United States, Mexico, and Canada . . . " " "
3. North America . . . . " " "
4. South America . . . . -- --
5. Europe . . . . -- --
6. Asia . . . . -- --
7. Africa . . . . -- --
8. The World on Mercator's Projection . . . -- --

Each $35, or the set, $280.

II. — *Dissected Maps.*

1. Eastern Hemisphere . . . . . . size 30 by 36 inches.
2. Western Hemisphere . . . . . " " "
3. North America . . . . " " "
4. United States . . . . -- ..
5. South America . . . . -- --
6. Europe . . . . -- --
7. Asia . . . . -- --
8. Africa . . . . -- --

Each $23, or the set, $184.

These maps are considered, in point of workmanship, accuracy and distinctness of outline, durability and beauty, far superior to all thus far made in Europe or in this country.

"The New-England Journal of Education" says, "They are very strong, present a fine, bright surface, and are an ornament to any schoolroom."

III. — *Pin-Maps.*

Cushions for pin-maps and diagrams . . . . . each, $0 75

ARITHMETIC.

Ciphering-boards made of brass strips, nickel-plated . . each, $4 25
Ciphering-types, nickel-plated, per hundred . . . . " 1 00

WRITING.

Grooved writing-cards . . . . each, $0 10
Braille tablets, with metallic bed . . . . . " 1 50
Braille French tablets, with cloth bed . . . . " 1 00
Braille new tablets, with cloth bed . . . . . -- 1 00
Braille Daisy tablets . . . . -- 5 00

PUBLIC DOCUMENT.   No. 27.

FIFTY-FIRST ANNUAL REPORT

OF

THE TRUSTEES

OF THE

PERKINS INSTITUTION

AND

Massachusetts School for the Blind,

FOR THE YEAR ENDING

SEPTEMBER 30, 1882.

BOSTON:
WRIGHT & POTTER PRINTING CO., STATE PRINTERS,
18 Post Office Square.
1883.

PUBLIC DOCUMENT.   No. 27.

FIFTY-FIRST ANNUAL REPORT

OF

THE TRUSTEES

OF THE

PERKINS INSTITUTION

AND

Massachusetts School for the Blind,

FOR THE YEAR ENDING

SEPTEMBER 30, 1882.

BOSTON:
WRIGHT & POTTER PRINTING CO., STATE PRINTERS,
18 POST OFFICE SQUARE.
1883.

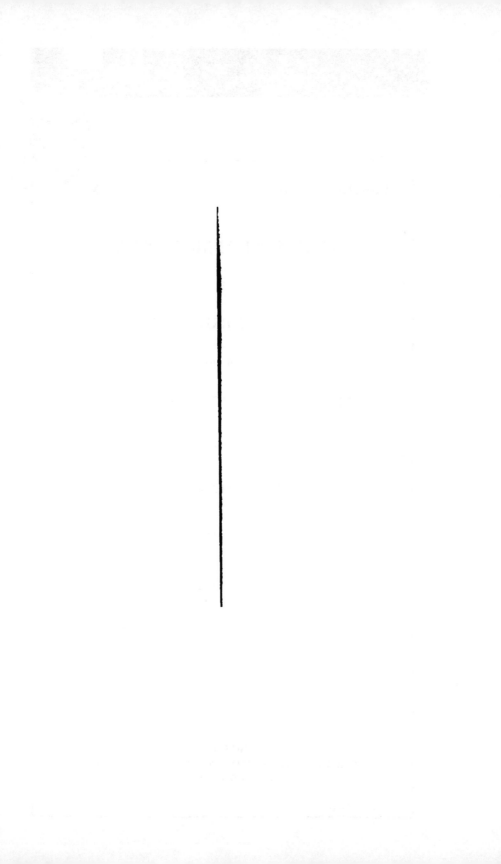

FIFTY-FIRST ANNUAL REPORT

OF

THE TRUSTEES

OF THE

PERKINS INSTITUTION

AND

𝔐assachusetts 𝔖chool 𝔣or the 𝔅lind,

FOR THE YEAR ENDING

SEPTEMBER 30, 1882.

BOSTON:
WRIGHT & POTTER PRINTING CO., STATE PRINTERS,
18 POST OFFICE SQUARE.
1883.

TABLE OF CONTENTS.

Commonwealth of Massachusetts.

PERKINS INSTITUTION AND MASS. SCHOOL FOR THE BLIND,
SOUTH BOSTON, Oct. 23, 1882.

To the Hon. HENRY B. PEIRCE, *Secretary of State*, Boston.

DEAR SIR : — I have the honor to transmit to you, for the use of the legislature, a copy of the fifty-first annual report of the trustees of this institution to the corporation thereof, together with the usual accompanying documents.

Respectfully,

M. ANAGNOS,
Secretary.

OFFICERS OF THE CORPORATION.

1882-83.

SAMUEL ELIOT, *President.*
JOHN CUMMINGS, *Vice-President.*
EDWARD JACKSON, *Treasurer.*
M. ANAGNOS, *Secretary.*

BOARD OF TRUSTEES.

JOHN S. DWIGHT.	EDWARD N. PERKINS.
JOSEPH B. GLOVER.	JOHN C. PHILLIPS.
J. THEODORE HEARD, M.D.	SAMUEL M. QUINCY.
HENRY LEE HIGGINSON.	SAMUEL G. SNELLING.
JAMES H. MEANS, D.D.	JAMES STURGIS.
ROBERT TREAT PAINE, Jun.	GEORGE W. WALES.

STANDING COMMITTEES.

Monthly Visiting Committee,

Whose duty it is to visit and inspect the Institution at least once in each month.

1883. January, .	J. S. DWIGHT.	1883. July, . . .	E. N. PERKINS.
February, .	J. B. GLOVER.	August, . .	JOHN C. PHILLIPS.
March, . .	J. T. HEARD.	September,	S. M. QUINCY.
April, . .	H. L. HIGGINSON.	October, .	S. G. SNELLING.
May, . .	J. H. MEANS.	November,	JAMES STURGIS.
June, . .	R. T. PAINE, Jun.	December, .	GEO. W. WALES.

Committee on Education.	House Committee.
J. S. DWIGHT.	E. N. PERKINS.
R. T. PAINE, Jun.	G. W. WALES.
S. M. QUINCY.	J. H. MEANS.

Committee of Finance.	Committee on Health.
J. B. GLOVER.	J. THEODORE HEARD.
JAMES STURGIS.	JOHN C. PHILLIPS.
SAMUEL G. SNELLING.	H. L. HIGGINSON.

Auditors of Accounts.

SAMUEL G. SNELLING.
JAMES STURGIS.

OFFICERS OF THE INSTITUTION.

DIRECTOR.
M. ANAGNOS.

MEDICAL INSPECTOR.
JOHN HOMANS, M.D.

LITERARY DEPARTMENT.

Miss JULIA R. GILMAN.
Miss ETTA S. ADAMS.
Miss ANNIE E. CARNES.
Miss JULIA A. BOYLAN.

Miss DELLA BENNETT.
Miss MARY C. MOORE.
Miss CORA A. NEWTON.
Miss EMMA A. COOLIDGE.

Miss SARAH E. LANE, *Librarian.*

MUSICAL DEPARTMENT.

THOMAS REEVES.
FRANK H. KILBOURNE.
Miss FREDA BLACK.
Miss MARY L. RILEY.
Miss LUCY A. HAMMOND.
Miss CONSTANCE A. HEINE.
Miss MARY A. PROCTOR.

Mrs. KATE RAMETTI.
C. H. HIGGINS.
EZRA M. BAGLEY.

Music Readers.

Miss ALLIE S. KNAPP.
Miss CAROLINE L. BATES.

TUNING DEPARTMENT.
JOEL W. SMITH, *Instructor and Manager.*
GEORGE E. HART, *Tuner.*

INDUSTRIAL DEPARTMENT.

Workshops for Juveniles.
JOHN H. WRIGHT, *Work Master.*
Miss A. J. DILLINGHAM, *Work Mistress.*
Miss CORA L. DAVIS, *Assistant.*
THOMAS CARROLL, *Assistant.*

Workshop for Adults.
A. W. BOWDEN, *Manager.*
P. MORRILL, *Foreman.*
Miss M. A. DWELLY, *Forewoman.*
Miss M. M. STONE, *Clerk.*

DOMESTIC DEPARTMENT.

Steward.
A. W. BOWDEN.
Matron.
Miss M. C. MOULTON.
Miss VIRTILINE HASKELL, *Assistant.*

Housekeepers in the Cottages.
Mrs. M. A. KNOWLTON.
Mrs. L. S. SMITH.
Miss BESSIE WOOD.
Miss LIZZIE N. SMITH.

PRINTING DEPARTMENT.
DENNIS A. REARDON, ... *Manager.*
Miss ELIZABETH HOWE, *Printer.*
Miss MARTHA F. ROWELL, "

Miss E. B. WEBSTER, *Book-keeper.*

MEMBERS OF THE CORPORATION.

All persons who have contributed twenty-five dollars to the funds of the institution, all who have served as trustees or treasurer, and all who have been elected by special vote, are members.

Adams, John A., Providence.
Aldrich, Mrs. Sarah, Boston.
Alger, Rev. William R., Boston.
Ames, F. L., Boston.
Ames, Mrs. H. A., Boston.
Ames, Oliver, Boston.
Amory, C. W., Boston.
Amory, James S., Boston.
Amory, William, Boston.
Amory, Mrs. William, Boston.
Anagnos, M., Boston.
Andrews, Francis, Boston.
Anthony, Hon. Henry, Providence·
Appleton, Miss Emily G., Boston.
Appleton, T. G., Boston.
Appleton, Mrs. William, Boston·
Apthorp, William F., Boston.
Arnold, A. B., Providence.
Atkins, Mrs. Elisha, Boston.
Atkinson, Edward, Boston.
Atkinson, William, Boston.
Austin, Edward, Boston.
Aylesworth, H. B., Providence.
Baldwin, William H., Boston.
Baker, Mrs. F. M., Boston.
Baker, Mrs. E. W., Dorchester.
Baker, Ezra H., Boston.
Baker, Miss M. K., Boston.
Barbour, E. D., Boston.
Barker, Joseph A., Providence.
Barstow, Amos C., Providence.

Barrows, Rev. S. J., Dorchester.
Beal, J. H., Boston.
Beard, Hon. Alanson W., Boston.
Beckwith, Miss A. G., Providence
Beckwith, Mrs. T., Providence.
Beebe, J. A., Boston.
Bennett, Mrs. Eleanor, Billerica.
Bigelow, E. B., Boston.
Binney, William, Providence.
Black, G. N., Boston.
Blake, G. Baty, Boston.
Blake, James H., Boston.
Blanchard, G. D. B., Malden.
Bourn, A. O., Providence.
Bouvé, Thomas T., Boston.
Bowditch, Mrs. E. B., Boston.
Bowditch, J. I., Boston.
Bowditch, Mrs. J. I., Boston.
Bradlee, F. H., Boston,
Bradlee, Mrs. F. H., Boston.
Bradlee, J. P., Boston.
Brewer, Miss C. A., Boston.
Brewer, Mrs. Mary, Boston.
Brewster, Osmyn, Boston.
Brimmer, Hon. Martin, Boston.
Brooks, Francis, Boston.
Brooks, Mrs. F. A., Boston.
Brooks, Peter C., Boston.
Brooks, Rev. Phillips, Boston.
Brooks, Shepherd, Boston.
Brooks, Mrs. Susan O., Boston.

Brown, John A., Providence.
Brown, Mrs. John C., Providence.
Browne, A. Parker, Boston.
Bullard, W. S., Boston.
Bullock, Miss Julia, Providence.
Bundy, James J., Providence.
Burnett, Joseph, Boston.
Burnham, J. A., Boston.
Cabot, Mrs. Samuel, Sen , Boston.
Cabot, W. C., Boston.
Callender, Walter, Providence.
Carpenter, Chas. E., Providence.
Cary, Mrs. W. F., Boston.
Chandler, P. W., Boston.
Chandler,Theophilus P., Brookline.
Chace, J. H., Providence.
Chace, J., Providence.
Chapin, E. P., Providence.
Chase, Mrs. Theodore, Boston.
Cheever, Dr. David W., Boston.
Cheney, Benjamin P., Boston.
Chickering, George H., Boston.
Childs, Alfred A., Boston.
Claflin, Hon. William, Boston.
Clapp, William W., Boston.
Clarke, Mrs. Jas. Freeman, Boston.
Clement, Edward H., Boston.
Coats, James, Providence.
Cobb, Samuel C., Boston.
Cobb, Samuel T., Boston.
Cochrane, Alexander, Boston.
Coffin, Mrs. W. E., Boston.
Colt, Samuel P., Providence.
Conant, Mrs. Rebecca, Amherst, N. H.
Coolidge, Dr. A., Boston.
Coolidge, J. R., Boston.
Coolidge, Mrs. J. R., Boston.
Coolidge, J. T., Boston.
Coolidge, Mrs. J. T., Boston.
Corliss, George H., Providence.
Cotting, C. U., Boston.
Crane, Zenas M., Dalton.
Crosby, Joseph B., Boston.
Crosby, William S., Boston.
Cruft, Miss Annah P., Boston.

Cruft, Miss Harriet O., Boston.
Cummings, Charles A., Boston.
Cummings, Hon. John, Woburn.
Curtis, George S., Boston.
Curtis, Mrs. Margarette S., Boston.
Dana, Mrs. Samuel T., Boston.
Dalton, C. H., Boston.
Dalton, Mrs. C. H., Boston.
Danielson, G. W., Providence.
Darling, L. B., Providence.
Davis, Miss A. W., Boston.
Day, Daniel E., Providence.
Deblois, Stephen G., Boston.
Denny, George P., Boston.
Devens, Rev. Samuel A., Boston
Ditson, Oliver, Boston.
Dix, J. H., M.D., Boston.
Dunnell, Jacob, Providence.
Dwight, John S., Boston.
Eaton, W. S., Boston.
Eliot, Dr. Samuel, Boston.
Emery, Francis F., Boston.
Emery, Isaac, Boston.
Emmons, Mrs. Nath'l H., Boston.
English, Jas. E., New Haven, Conn.
Endicott, Henry, Boston.
Endicott, William, Jr., Boston.
Farnam, Mrs. A. G., New Haven.
Farnam, Henry, New Haven, Conn.
Fay, H. H., Boston.
Fay, Mrs. H. H., Boston.
Fay, Miss Sarah B., Boston.
Fay, Mrs. S. S., Boston.
Fellows, R. J., New Haven, Conn.
Ferris, M. C., Boston.
Fisk, Rev. Photius, Boston.
Fiske, J. N., Boston.
Folsom, Charles F., M.D., Boston
Forbes, J. M., Milton.
Foster, F. C., Boston.
Freeman, Miss Hattie E., Boston.
French, Jonathan, Boston.
Frothingham, A. T., Boston.
Frothingham, Rev. Fred'k, Milton
Galloupe, C. W., Boston.
Gammell, Prof. Wm., Providence.

Gammell, Mrs. Wm., Providence.
Gardiner, Charles P., Boston.
Gardiner, William H., Boston.
Gardner, George, Boston.
Gardner, George A., Boston.
Gardner, Henry W., Providence.
Gardner, John L., Boston.
George, Charles H., Providence.
Glidden, W. T., Boston.
Glover, A., Boston.
Glover, J. B., Boston.
Goddard, Benjamin, Brookline.
Goddard, T. P. I., Providence.
Goddard, William, Providence.
Goff, Darius L., Pawtucket, R. I.
Goff, L. B., Pawtucket.
Gray, Mrs. Horace, Boston.
Greene, Benj. F., Providence.
Greene, S. H., Providence.
Greenleaf, Mrs. Jas., Charlestown.
Greenleaf, R. C., Boston.
Grosvenor, William, Providence.
Grover, W. A., Boston.
Guild, Mrs. S. E., Boston.
Hale, Rev. Edward E., Boston.
Hale, George S., Boston.
Hall, J. R., Boston.
Hall, Miss L. E., Charlestown.
Hardy, Alpheus, Boston.
Haskell, Edwin B., Auburndale.
Hayward, Hon.Wm. S.,Providence.
Hazard, Rowland, Providence.
Heard, J. T., M.D., Boston.
Hemenway, Mrs. A., Jr., Boston.
Hendricken, Rt. Rev. T. F., Providence.
Higginson, George, Boston.
Higginson, Henry Lee, Boston.
Hill, Hon. Hamilton A., Boston.
Hill, Mrs. T. J., Providence.
Hilton, William, Boston.
Hogg, John, Boston.
Hooper, E. W., Boston.
Hooper, R. W., M.D., Boston.
Hoppin, Hon. W. W., Providence.
Hovey, George O., Boston.

Hovey, William A., Boston.
Howard, Hon. A. C., Providence.
Howard, Mrs. Chas. W., California.
Howard, Hon. Henry, Providence.
Howe, Mrs. Julia Ward, Boston.
Howes, Miss E., Boston.
Houghton, Hon. H. O., Cambridge.
Hunnewell, F. W., Boston.
Hunnewell, H. H., Boston.
Hunt, Moses, Charlestown.
Hyatt, Alpheus, Cambridge.
Inches, H. B., Boston.
Ives, Mrs. Anna A., Providence.
Jackson, Charles C., Boston.
Jackson, Edward, Boston.
Jackson, Patrick T., Boston.
Jackson, Mrs. Sarah, Boston.
Jarvis, Edward, M.D., Dorchester.
Johnson, Samuel, Boston.
Jones, J. M., Boston.
Joy, Mrs. Charles H., Boston.
Kendall, C. S., Boston.
Kendall, Henry L., Providence.
Kennard, Martin P., Brookline.
Kent, Mrs. Helena M., Boston.
Kidder, H. P., Boston.
Kinsley, E. W., Boston.
Lang, B. J., Boston.
Lawrence, Abbott, Boston.
Lawrence, Amos A., Longwood.
Lawrence, Edward, Charlestown.
Lawrence, Mrs. James, Boston.
Lawrence, William, Boston.
Lee, Henry, Boston.
Lincoln, L. J. B., Hingham.
Linzee, J. W., Boston.
Linzee, Miss Susan I., Boston.
Lippitt, Hon. Henry, Providence.
Littell, Miss S. G., Brookline.
Little, J. L., Boston.
Littlefield, A. H., Pawtucket.
Littlefield, D. G., Pawtucket.
Lockwood, A. D., Providence.
Lodge, Mrs. A. C., Boston.
Lodge, Henry C., Boston.
Lord, Melvin, Boston.

Lothrop, John, Auburndale.
Lovett, George L., Boston.
Lowell, Augustus, Boston.
Lowell, Miss A. C., Boston.
Lowell, Francis C., Boston.
Lowell, George G., Boston.
Lowell, Miss Lucy, Boston.
Lyman, Arthur T., Boston.
Lyman, George H., M.D., Boston.
Lyman, J. P., Boston.
Lyman, Theodore, Boston.
McAuslan, John, Providence.
Mack, Thomas, Boston.
Macullar, Addison, Boston.
Marcy, Fred I., Providence.
Marston, S. W., Boston.
Mason, Miss E. F., Boston.
Mason, Miss Ida M., Boston.
Mason, L. B., Providence.
May, Miss Abby, Boston.
May, F. W. G., Dorchester.
May, Mrs. Samuel, Boston.
McCloy, J. A., Providence.
Means, Rev. J. H., D.D.,Dorchester.
Merriam, Mrs. Caroline, Boston.
Merriam, Charles, Boston.
Metcalf, Jesse, Providence.
Minot, Mrs. G. R., Boston.
Minot, William, Boston.
Mixter, Miss Helen K., Boston.
Mixter, Miss Madelaine C., Boston.
Montgomery, Hugh, Boston.
Morrill, Charles J., Boston.
Morse, S. T., Boston.
Morton, Edwin, Boston.
Motley, Edward, Boston.
Nevins, David, Boston.
Nichols, J. Howard, Boston.
Nichols, R. P., Boston.
Nickerson, A., Boston.
Nickerson, Mrs. A. T., Boston.
Nickerson, George, Jamaica Plain.
Nickerson, Miss Priscilla, Boston.
Nickerson, S. D., Boston.
Noyes, Hon. Charles J., Boston.
Osgood, J. F., Boston.

Osborn, John T., Boston.
Owen, George, Providence.
Paine, Mrs. Julia B., Boston.
Paine, Robert Treat, Jun., Boston.
Palfrey, J. C., Boston.
Palmer, John S., Providence.
Parker, Mrs. E. P., Boston.
Parker, E. F., Boston.
Parker, H. D., Boston.
Parker, Richard T., Boston.
Parkman, Francis, Boston.
Parkman, George F., Boston.
Parsons, Thomas, Chelsea.
Payson, S. R., Boston.
Peabody, Rev. A. P., D.D., Cam-
    bridge.
Peabody, F. H., Boston.
Peabody, O. W., Milton.
Peabody, S. E., Boston.
Perkins, A. T., Boston.
Perkins, Charles C., Boston.
Perkins, Edward N., Jamaica Plain.
Perkins, William, Boston.
Peters, Edward D., Boston.
Phillips, John C., Boston.
Pickett, John, Beverly.
Pickman, W. D., Boston.
Pickman, Mrs. W. D., Boston.
Pierce, Hon. H. L., Boston.
Potter, Mrs. Sarah, Providence.
Pratt, Elliott W., Boston.
Prendergast, J. M., Boston.
Preston, Jonathan, Boston.
Quincy, Samuel M., Wollaston.
Rice, Hon. A. H., Boston.
Rice, Fitz James, Providence.
Richardson, George C., Boston.
Richardson, John, Boston.
Robbins, R. E., Boston.
Robeson, W. R., Boston.
Robinson, Henry, Reading.
Rodman, S. W., Boston.
Rodocanachi, J. M., Boston.
Rogers, Henry B., Boston.
Rogers, Jacob C., Boston.
Ropes, J. C., Boston.

Ropes, J. S., Jamaica Plain.
Rotch, Mrs. Benjamin S., Boston.
Russell, Henry G., Providence.
Russell, Mrs. Henry G., Providence.
Russell, Miss Marian, Boston.
Russell, Mrs. S. S., Boston.
Salisbury, Stephen, Worcester.
Saltonstall, H., Boston.
Saltonstall, Leverett, Newton.
Sanborn, Frank B., Concord.
Sargent, I., Brookline.
Sayles, F. C., Providence.
Sayles, W. F., Providence.
Schlesinger, Barthold, Boston.
Schlesinger, Sebastian B., Boston.
Sears, David, Boston.
Sears, Mrs. David, Boston.
Sears, Mrs. Fred, Jr., Boston.
Sears, F. R., Boston.
Sears, Mrs. K. W., Boston.
Sears, Mrs. S. P., Boston.
Sears, W. T., Boston.
Sharpe, L., Providence.
Shaw, Mrs. G. H., Boston.
Shaw, Henry S., Boston.
Shaw, Quincy A., Boston.
Shepard, Mrs. E. A., Providence.
Sherwood, W. H., Boston.
Shimmin, C. F., Boston.
Shippen, Rev. R. R., Washington.
Sigourney, Mrs. M. B., Boston.
Slack, C. W., Boston.
Slater, H. N., Jr., Providence.
Snelling, Samuel G., Boston.
Spaulding, J. P., Boston.
Spaulding, M. D., Boston.
Sprague, S. S., Providence.
Steere, Henry J., Providence.
Stone, Joseph L., Boston.
Sturgis, Francis S., Boston.
Sturgis, J. H., Boston.
Sturgis, James, Boston.
Sullivan, Richard, Boston.
Sweetser, Mrs. Anne M., Boston.
Taggard, B. W., Boston.
Taggard, Mrs. B. W., Boston.

Thacher, Isaac, Boston.
Thaxter, Joseph B., Hingham.
Thayer, Miss Adele G., Boston.
Thayer, Miss A. G., Andover.
Thayer, Rev. George A., Cincinnati.
Thayer, Nathaniel, Boston.
Thomas, H. H., Providence.
Thorndike, Delia D., Boston.
Thorndike, S. Lothrop, Cambridge.
Thurston, Benj. F., Providence.
Tingley, S. H., Providence.
Torrey, Miss A. D., Boston.
Troup, John E, Providence.
Tucker, W. W., Boston.
Turner, Miss Abby W., Boston.
Turner, Mrs. M. A., Providence.
Upton, George B., Boston.
Wales, George W., Boston.
Wales, Miss Mary Ann, Boston.
Wales, Thomas B., Boston.
Ward, Samuel, New York.
Ware, Charles E., M.D., Boston.
Warren, S. D., Boston.
Warren, Mrs. Wm. W., Boston.
Washburn, Hon. J. D., Worcester
Weeks, A. G., Boston.
Weeks, J. H., Boston.
Weld, R. H., Boston.
Weld, Mrs. W. F., Philadelphia.
Weld, W. G., Boston.
Wesson, J. L., Boston.
Wheelwright, A. C., Boston.
Wheelwright, John W., Boston.
White, B. C., Boston.
White, C. J., Cambridge.
Whiting, Ebenezer, Boston.
Whitman, Sarah W., Boston.
Whitney, Edward, Belmont.
Whitney, E., Boston.
Whitney, H. A., Boston.
Whitney, H. M., Boston.
Whitney, Mrs., Boston.
Whitney, Miss, Boston.
Wigglesworth, Miss Ann, Boston.
Wigglesworth, Edw., M.D., Boston.
Wigglesworth, Thomas, Boston.

Wightman, W. B., Providence.	Winthrop, Mrs. Robert C., Boston.
Wilder, Hon Marshall P., Dorch.	Wolcott, J. H., Boston.
Willard, Mrs. Harry, New York.	Wolcott, Mrs. J. H., Boston.
Williams, Geo. W. A., Boston.	Woods, Henry, Paris, France.
Winslow, Mrs. George, Roxbury.	Worthington, Roland, Roxbury.
Winsor, J. B., Providence.	Young, Mrs. B. L., Boston.
Winthrop, Hon. Robert C., Boston.	Young, Charles L., Boston.

SYNOPSIS OF THE PROCEEDINGS

OF THE

ANNUAL MEETING OF THE CORPORATION.

BOSTON, October 11, 1882.

The annual meeting of the corporation, duly summoned, was held today at the institution, and was called to order by the president, Samuel Eliot, LL. D., at 3 P. M.

The proceedings of the last annual meeting were read by the secretary, and declared approved.

The report of the trustees was presented, accepted, and ordered to be printed with that of the director and the usual accompanying documents.

The treasurer, Mr. Edward Jackson, read his report, which was accepted, and ordered to be printed.

All the officers of the past year were reëlected, Mr. John C. Phillips having been chosen to fill the vacancy caused by the death of the late Robert E. Apthorp.

The meeting was then dissolved, and all in attendance proceeded, with the invited guests, to visit the various departments of the school and inspect the premises.

M. ANAGNOS,
Secretary.

Commonwealth of Massachusetts.

REPORT OF THE TRUSTEES.

PERKINS INSTITUTION AND MASS. SCHOOL FOR THE BLIND,
SOUTH BOSTON, Sept. 30, 1882.

TO THE MEMBERS OF THE CORPORATION.

Gentlemen, — The undersigned, trustees, respectfully submit their annual report upon the affairs of the institution, together with an account of the celebration of the semi-centennial anniversary, prepared by the committee in charge of the arrangements of the festival, and other documents relating to the progress and conduct of the establishment.

We take great pleasure in reporting, at the outset, that the school has maintained its usual high standard of usefulness during the year, and that its prosperity is undiminished.

The completion of the printing fund is a theme for especial congratulation; but of this the story will be fully told in the report of the director.

The present total number of blind persons connected with the establishment, in all its departments, is 165.

The household has been entirely exempt from disease or severe illness, and blessed with the usual degree of health.

The general results of the year's experience have been very satisfactory, both in an educational and material aspect, and call for grateful acknowledgment.

The teachers and officers have performed their respective duties with commendable zeal and indefatigable energy, and have proved themselves worthy of the fullest confidence and praise.

The pupils have been diligent in their studies, attentive to their occupations, orderly in their manners and obedient in their conduct.

The favors bestowed upon the institution during the past year have been numerous and substantial. Their recollection is a source of great happiness to the friends of the blind, and urges us on to still greater efforts to deserve their continuance.

Members of our board have made frequent visits to the school and close examination of its operations, and are satisfied that kindness is the law and spirit of its administration, that great care is taken to regulate the diet, exercise and discipline of the pupils, and that the domestic department is conducted with systematic neatness and reasonable frugality.

In closing these preliminary remarks, we may

be permitted to add that, mindful of the trust
committed to our keeping, of the powers which it
delegates, and of the responsibility which it imposes, we have endeavored to direct our action in
such a manner as to improve the efficiency of the
institution, promote the welfare of its beneficiaries,
subserve the interests of the community, and advance the cause of humanity.

Semi-Centennial Anniversary.

In accordance with a vote passed at the last
annual meeting of the corporation, the semi-centennial anniversary of the institution, together
with the commencement exercises of the school,
was held at Tremont Temple, on Tuesday, June
13th, at 3 p. m. A very large and cultivated audience, representing the intelligence, benevolence
and wealth of our community, filled the large hall.
The occasion was one of exceeding interest, and
roused feelings of the deepest gratitude in the
hearts of all lovers of the cause of humanity. It
showed, in a striking manner, the workings of the
school in its various departments, and the marvellous
changes effected through its agency in the mental,
physical, moral and social status of the blind.

Half a century ago this afflicted class were mere
objects of pity and charity. They were entirely
dependent upon the mercy and sympathy of their
fellow men. No day of hopefulness returned to
them with the seasons of the year. They were

surrounded by "cloud and enduring dark." The doors of usefulness were closed to them, and the field of industry was an unexplored region for them. Their calamity was so appalling to the eyes of the casual beholders, that no one thought it feasible to turn into their minds the stream of education, and fertilize the soil of their activity by means of enlightenment. Thus the circle of their lives may be likened to a mere pool of stagnant waters, pregnant with the ills of idleness and sorrow, poverty and gloom, unhappiness and neglect.

Such was the condition of the blind on this continent, when Fisher and Howe and Prescott proclaimed the gospel of their deliverance from the dungeon of intellectual and moral darkness, and pointed out the means which could be used as a powerful lever to raise them in the scale of independence and dignity. These glad tidings touched a responsive chord in the noble hearts of such generous men as Colonel Perkins, Jonathan Phillips, Peter C. Brooks and a host of others among the public-spirited sons of Massachusetts, and the infant school was auspiciously planted and tenderly nurtured by the munificence of their philanthropy. Thus a new departure was inaugurated in the fortunes of the blind, and fifty years of labor and struggle, of anxiety and encouragement, of toil and hope under gigantic difficulties, ended in triumph and success, and wrought a remarkable revolution in the realm of humanity. The little

timid band that gathered around Dr. Howe has
grown to the ranks of hundreds and thousands of
active and self-supporting men and women, whose
usefulness is one of the fairest flowers of the age,
and·is now so well established that it can never
be uprooted or impaired.

As we look back upon this half century of interesting and important events in the history of the
education of the blind, it seems like a great avenue
leading upward to that goal, which Dr. Eliot so
nobly pointed out in his address to the graduating class, and which they have at length so
nearly reached. Weary has been the journey for
themselves and for their helpers; but they are
there, and Heaven be praised for their having thus
attained the object for which fifty years have been
so worthily spent. Many have died ere that half
cycle was completed. Others of· the old pupils
have lived on to see with their mind's eye the victory which has crowned their cause, and to bear
testimony to the fact that the blind man of today
needs no longer to be pleaded for. He takes his
place among his peers. He shares with them all
the privileges and duties of citizenship. He constitutes an integral part of society. True, while
his fellow men are sailing towards the harbor of
success, provided with every possible facility and
convenience, he is steering his imperfect and scant-
ily supplied craft under immense difficulties and
enormous privations; but the hardships and an-

noyances of the voyage, discomforting and trying
as they are to him, are not profitless and without
good effects either to himself or the community in
which he lives.

Miss Sophia Carter, one of the first six pupils
of Dr. Howe, after witnessing the exercises at
Tremont Temple, wrote to her friends at the
institution that, if during the coming fifty years
as much shall be done as has been accomplished
since the foundation of our school, blindness will
almost cease to be a calamity. Let the noble
work, so auspiciously begun, go on steadily to
such a glorious consummation as to render these
words a verity. Let Massachusetts which, for half
a century, has led the way in the cause of the education of the blind, suffer none to go before her
now. Let her still bear aloft the torch. Her
bright example is already emulated through the
length and breadth of the whole land.

Embossing Books for the Blind.

The work in the printing department of the institution has been carried on during the past year
with unusual vigor and exceedingly satisfactory
results, and numerous valuable books have been
issued by the "Howe Memorial Press."

"Silas Marner," which is considered one of the
most finished of George Eliot's novels, and two
volumes of poems, one consisting of selections
from the works of Lowell and the other from

those of Bryant, have been added to our series of standard books. The whole of the expense for printing and electrotyping Lowell's poems, amounting to five hundred dollars, was defrayed by our colleague, Mr. Robert Treat Paine, Jr.

In the line of juvenile publications the following books have been issued during the past year: Selections from the tales of Hans Christian Andersen; "Children's Fairy Book," a collection of stories in prose and verse; "Scribner's Geographical Reader;" a series of seven small readers, with a primer, and three volumes of the "Youth's Library." Of the character and usefulness of this last work, the following explanations, copied from its preface, will give a sufficient idea:

"'The Youth's Library,' consisting of seven volumes of full size, is a continuation of the small-sized readers, which have just been published in seven parts, with a primer, under the title of 'The Child's Book.' The two series of books form together a complete set of systematically arranged and carefully graded readers. The character and classification of the lessons and exercises contained in them have been determined by special study of the wants of the blind. Almost all the pieces present a freshness and attractiveness not less welcome than novel. They have been selected from a great variety of books of child-lore, natural history and philosophy, mythology, astronomy and general literature, with a view of interesting the pupils in learning to read, and at the same time of giving them a large fund of useful information regarding the world around them. The lessons of some of the readers relate mainly to zoölogy, while in others botany or mineralogy, physics or history, biography or literature, predominate. The principal idea

in each of the volumes is, however, to teach children and youth
to read, to awaken in them the greatest possible interest in
everything that is beautiful, good, or useful, and to sustain it
by such guidance as tends to a gradual and systematic educational development."

For the publication of Andersen's stories and
tales, and the seven small readers, with the primer,
we are indebted to the great and ceaseless generosity of Mrs. Peter C. Brooks, who has befriended
the blind in various ways, and whose munificent
liberality will always shine forth like a bright gem
in the annals of beneficent actions.

The arrangements of our printing office are now
complete in all their details. The appliances and
facilities for doing steady and thorough work have
been improved and increased, while the cost of
embossed books has been greatly reduced. The
impression obtained from our electrotyped plates
is even, sharp, firm and durable. The quality of
the paper and all other materials used, continues
to be excellent. According to the uniform testimony, volunteered by intelligent and experienced
readers from various parts of the country, the productions of our press are in every respect finer
and superior to those of any other. Moreover, a
careful examination of the prices marked on our
catalogue will show that they are at least seventeen per cent. lower than those charged elsewhere.

Wishing to extend the benefits flowing from our
printing establishment to all blind persons who

may be in need of them, the following preamble
and resolutions were unanimously passed at the
last quarterly meeting of our board:

"*Whereas*, The object of the friends of the blind in raising
an endowment of one hundred thousand dollars for the 'Howe
Memorial Press,' is not only to provide the pupils of our institution with an adequate supply of embossed books and tangible apparatus, but also to render our publications accessible
to all sightless readers in New England, and to aid, so far as
it lies in our power, all other schools similar to our own in
their efforts to increase and improve their educational facilities :

"*Resolved*, That copies of the books issued by our press be
placed in the public libraries of Providence, Rhode Island ;
Worcester, Massachusetts ; Hartford, Connecticut, and Lew-
iston, Maine, to be loaned free of charge to all blind persons
who may desire to read them.

"*Resolved*, That all our publications be sold to regular institutions at fifteen per cent. below the actual cost marked on
our catalogue."

We earnestly trust and hope that we shall soon
be so favored by circumstances as to increase this
discount to forty per cent. at least, and reduce the
cost of embossed books to the lowest possible
figure.

KINDERGARTEN AND PRIMARY SCHOOL.

It was stated in the course of the exercises of
the semi-centennial anniversary at Tremont Temple, that the most urgent need in the cause of the
education of the blind is the establishment and
endowment of a kindergarten or primary school.

A careful investigation of the matter will prove, beyond doubt, that the organization of an institution of this kind is not a mere desideratum; it is an imperative necessity.

There is in New England a large number of blind children between the ages of five and nine, who are too young to be received in a mixed school like ours. They live and move in a very unhealthy atmosphere. Their minds are contaminated by low influences, and their growth stinted by their confinement in ill-ventilated and comfortless quarters. They waste away under the rust of neglect, and the want of sufficient food and proper care. They parch and pine within a short distance of the refreshing waters of a benevolence known all over the civilized world.

For such children the kindergarten system, with the genial warmth of kindness radiating from its principles, with its methodically arranged gifts and games, its block building, weaving, sewing and modelling, affords the best and most efficient means of training. It is calculated to awaken, strengthen and regulate their faculties of imagination, volition and action, which are weakened by their infirmity, depressed by the wretchedness of their surroundings, and benumbed by the frost of their privations. It promises to raise them up from a state of misery, sloth and torpor, to that of comfort, activity and diligence. It will create a new era in the history of the education of the blind, by laying the foundations and increasing the possibilities of a higher standard of attainments than has hitherto been reached.

The necessity for immediate action in this matter is thoroughly discussed and plainly shown in the report of the director, and an appeal is made in behalf of these unfortunate children for the foundation and endowment of such a school as would be the means of their deliverance from their present condition. The call for aid to this end is clear, broad, pathetic and to the point. We heartily commend it to the favorable consideration of a generous public.

FINANCES.

The report of the treasurer, Mr. Edward Jackson, is hereto annexed.

It is as usual clear, concise and accurate in every particular, and shows the financial affairs of the institution to be in as favorable a state as ever before.

It may be summarized as follows:

Total receipts during the year, .	$79,306 42	
Total expenditures, . . .	69,667 83	
		$9,638 59
Deducting amount due at the beginning of the year,		1,288 16
Cash balance in the treasury, ...		$8,350 43

For an easier and more minute examination of the financial concerns of the establishment, the report of the treasurer is accompanied by an analysis of the steward's accounts, by which both the ordinary and extraordinary receipts and expenses may be seen and understood at a glance.

Owing to the advanced prices of provisions and all other articles of household consumption, it has been necessary for us to spend, during the past year, a larger sum of money than during the previous one; but we have endeavored to be strictly prudent in all disbursements. We have lavished nothing on show or ornamentation. Our rule has been, however, that the best and most approved system is the cheapest in the end; and when a question has occurred as to the adoption of one of two methods of procedure, we have asked which is the best and most promotive of the interests of the school, and not which costs the least.

The auditors have kept a constant supervision over the expenditures of the establishment. They have examined the accounts regularly at the end of each month, and have certified that they have found them correctly kept, and all entries properly authenticated by vouchers, which are approved, numbered and placed on file.

It is with a feeling of much gratitude, that we desire to express our obligations to these gentlemen, as well as to the treasurer of the corporation, for the fidelity, wisdom and promptness which they have shown in the discharge of their respective duties.

DEATH OF MR. APTHORP.

Since the last meeting of the corporation our board has met with a great loss in the death of Mr. Robert East Apthorp, which took place at his home on the 10th of February last, at the age of seventy. Mr. Apthorp has been associated with us for fifteen years, and has at all times and on all occasions been a wise, faithful and useful counsellor and coöperator. He was deeply interested in the institution. He made frequent informal visits to the school, and ever gave his affectionate and cheering sympathy and encouragement to the teachers, the officers and the children. He never declined any labor, or shrank from any responsibility. He took an active part in the movement for raising the printing fund, and several of his pathetic appeals which appeared in the "Daily Advertiser," the "Evening Transcript," the "Christian Register," and other newspapers, touched many a tender heart and rendered the task of soliciting subscriptions somewhat easier for Mr. Snelling. The trustees embodied their sense of his character and services in the following resolutions, which were communicated to his family and entered on the records: —

" *Resolved*, 1. That in the death of Robert East Apthorp, we mourn the loss of a dear and honored associate and friend, whose long and faithful service in the many difficult and delicate trusts and functions which have fallen to him among the duties of this board ; whose hearty and untiring devotion, even in his days of suffering, to the best good of the Perkins Institution ; whose warm personal interest and friendship for the blind pupils and the officers and teachers of the school ; and whose uniform, consistent courtesy and dignity, and charm of manner, — a courtesy that sprang from a sincere regard and sympathy for others, high or low, — a dignity in which self-respect meant true respect for human nature ; in short, whose whole influence and example as a member of this board have endeared him to every inmate, manager and friend of the institution, and made our intercourse with him a sweet memory for all our lives.

" 2. That we heartily indorse the touching resolutions passed in honor of his memory at a recent meeting of the officers, teachers and pupils of the school.

" 3. That we are thankful for his long and effectual coöperation with us, and for the example he has set us ; and we trust that the spirit and the influence of that example may still live in us and those who shall succeed us in the responsible charge which we have undertaken.

" 4. That the respectful sympathies of this board are hereby tendered to the family and nearest friends of the deceased in this their deep affliction ; and that a copy of these resolutions be transmitted to the family by the secretary and entered on the records."

The resolutions of the officers, teachers and pupils, to which reference is made in the above, were as follows : —

" *Resolved*, That the members of the household of the institution are deeply affected by the sudden death of Mr. Robert E. Apthorp, late a member of the board of trustees, and that we are called upon to mourn in his decease the loss of one of the

most constant and efficient friends of the cause of the education
of the blind, one whose intelligent interest, active labors and
wise counsels have contributed largely to the career of usefulness and beneficence of our school.

" *Resolved*, That we desire to express our profound gratitude
for his warm sympathy, his genial courtesy and his noble
friendliness toward each and all the members of our household.

" *Resolved*, That the secretary be directed to transmit a copy
of these resolutions to the family of the deceased."

We mourn also the death of three other esti-
mable friends of the institution, — that of Mr.
Benjamin S. Rotch, who served for many years as
a trustee; that of Miss Mary Wigglesworth, who
has shown her good-will toward its beneficiaries
by generous voluntary contributions to its funds,
and that of Mr. Delano A. Goddard, late editor-in-
chief of the " Boston Daily Advertiser," who took a
deep interest in the school, visited it repeatedly,
and rendered valuable aid to the advancement of
the cause of the education of the blind through the
influential columns of his journal.

WORK DEPARTMENT FOR ADULTS.

The operations of this department have been
carried on steadily during the last year, but its
financial condition, although improved somewhat,
is still far from satisfactory.

The receipts from all sources have amounted to
$15,680.86, being an increase of $1,562.45 over
those of the previous year.

The expenses for stock, labor, rent of store and all other items have been $16,748.06.

Thus the actual loss of this department during the last twelve months is $1,117.29, while that of the preceding year amounted to $1,186.33.

The number of blind persons employed in the workshop is 20; and the sum paid in cash to them, as wages for their labor, is $3,600.81, or $165.78 more than in 1881.

This exhibit shows that, although the sales of our industrial department have slightly increased, they are not yet sufficient to pay the expenses and to give employment to all meritorious blind men and women who need it.

The patronage of our fellow citizens to this beneficent enterprise is again earnestly solicited, and with the fullest confidence that the mattresses, feather-beds, pew and boat cushions, door-mats, and the rest of the articles manufactured in our workshop, are as good in material and as strong in fabric as the best in the market. They are put at the lowest possible price, and the public are requested to call and examine them without being expected to pay any more than their real value, with no increase of charges for the benefit of the blind who make them. The current of a liberal patronage must float an enterprise which affords to a number of afflicted men and women the means for self-support and comfort.

FINAL REMARKS.

In summing up the review of last year's work, we rejoice to think that you will find ample evidence in it that the trust committed to our charge has been faithfully and successfully administered, and has furnished renewed cause for the most grateful remembrance of the illustrious founders of the institution.

We cannot take leave of the benefactors and friends of the school without thanking them heartily for the continuance of the favors which they have bestowed upon it, and their kind appreciation of our endeavors to render it a rich blessing to its beneficiaries. We assure them that no pains shall be spared on our part to make it even more efficient and useful in the future than it has been in the past.

Finally, we would commend the institution and the interests of the blind to the fostering care of the executives and the legislative bodies of New England; to the special attention of the corporation, and to the generous aid of the public. They still have, each and all, important duties to perform. The establishment still requires their kind countenance, encouragement and assistance, for it has not yet reached its highest point of usefulness; nor can it ever do so without the earnest efforts and hearty coöperation of all with whom rests the responsibility of its success.

All which is respectfully submitted by

JOHN S. DWIGHT,
JOSEPH B. GLOVER,
J. THEODORE HEARD,
HENRY LEE HIGGINSON,
JAMES H. MEANS,
ROBERT TREAT PAINE, Jun.,
EDWARD N. PERKINS,
JOHN C. PHILLIPS,
SAMUEL M. QUINCY,
SAMUEL G. SNELLING,
JAMES STURGIS,
GEORGE W. WALES,

Trustees.

REPORT ON THE FIFTIETH ANNIVERSARY.

To the Members of the Corporation.

Gentlemen,—The committee on the celebration of the fiftieth anniversary feel that there is little left for them to report after the signally fine report made by the festival itself and by the school. They entered at once upon the work of preparation, which for them was limited mainly to the outward aspects of the affair, the engaging of eminent speakers, the issuing of invitations to governors, mayors, distinguished men and women, and the friends of the blind in general, being relieved of all anxiety or labor about the exercises in themselves, and the whole plan and arrangement of the programme (beyond some general consultation), by the admirable judgment, the fruitful invention and the enthusiastic, timely, thorough and well-ordered work of the whole hive of pupils, teachers and director.

The festival came off as announced on the afternoon of June 13, 1882, at the Tremont Temple, which was filled at an early hour with an audience of culture and of character, attracted by no idle curiosity, but full of tender human interest in the education and the welfare of the blind.

Several of the most eloquent philanthropists of our country had expressed the deepest interest in the occasion, and a desire to take part in it personally and *viva voce*, and were detained only by imperative engagements. His Excellency Governor Long had heartily consented to preside and speak, but was prevented by an absolute necessity of rest and change of scene. Col. Higginson with joy consented to make the principal address, but illness interfered; yet the disappointment was soon forgotten in the admirably pertinent, impressive, eloquent remarks made by the honored president of our corporation, who took the chair, and who also spoke words of wisdom and good cheer to those pupils who received at his hands their diplomas on the completion of their studies.

The exercises of the pupils were of the most interesting description, covering a wide and varied field of reading from raised type, declamation, original essays, well conceived and well expressed both in the writing and delivery, strikingly beautiful exercises in geography, in military drill and calisthenics, and touchingly so those of the kindergarten class in modelling from clay, etc. And the whole was sweetened and enlivened by excellent music from the school band, and airs, part-songs, and instrumental solos of really artistic character. To these were added a beautiful poem, written and recited by Mrs. Anagnos, and an off-hand address by the indefatigable director, Mr. Anagnos, presenting a very earnest, cogent plea for the means of founding the next most needed auxiliary and complement to the school : to wit, a preparatory or kindergarten school for the youngest children who are blind.

The audience listened with delighted interest, many with moist eyes, to all this, in spite of the unexpected great length of the exercises. A new life, too, was given to the occasion by the announcement of the completion of the printing fund of $100,000.

Respectfully submitted.

J. S. DWIGHT,
SAMUEL M. QUINCY,
WM. F. APTHORP,
Committee.

THE REPORT OF THE DIRECTOR.

To the Trustees.

Gentlemen,—Another year in the life of our institution has passed, and it affords me very great pleasure to say that so even has been the tenor of its way, that in turning back the record of its days, weeks and months, little is found which calls for special notice.

The general state of the school has been both pleasant and prosperous, and no adverse event has occurred to retard the progress or impair the usefulness of the institution.

The total number of blind persons connected with the various departments of the establishment at the beginning of the past year, as pupils, teachers, employés, and work men and women, was 162. There have since been admitted 29; 26 have been discharged; making the present total number 165. Of these, 145 are in the school proper, and 20 in the workshop for adults.

The first class includes 129 boys and girls, enrolled as pupils, 12 teachers and 4 domestics. Of the pupils there are now 108 in attendance, 21 being temporarily absent on account of illness or from various other causes.

The second class comprises 16 men and 4 women, employed in the industrial department for adults.

The doors of the school have thus far been wide open to all applicants of proper age and mental qualifications. This will undoubtedly continue to be the policy of the institution so long as the space at our command enables us to receive the yearly increasing numbers of sightless children who are sent to us for education and training.

The health of the household has continued to be remarkably good. No death has invaded our circle, nor has any case of severe disease occurred at the institution. This exemption from mortality and illness during a season which has been noted for its unhealthiness, demands special recognition and grateful mention.

The usual course of study, music, physical training and handicraft work, has been pursued during the past year with uninterrupted regularity and excellent results. The fruits of every year's work bring renewed confirmation to the earnest hopes of those who are deeply interested in the welfare and progress of the institution, and although all the recipients of its.benefits are not able at once to provide for themselves, they are, as a class, elevated intellectually, morally and socially, and become more active and independent, and less of a burden to themselves and to their relations and friends.

REVIEW OF THE VARIOUS DEPARTMENTS.

A brief review of what has been accomplished during the past year in each of the departments of the institution will show that our general course of instruction and training has been so improved as to give definiteness to the work of the school and to secure regular and permanent results.

LITERARY DEPARTMENT.

The degree of success which has attended the operations of this department is exceedingly gratifying, and augurs still better results and greater usefulness in the future.

The course of study has been regularly and assiduously pursued, and the progress made by the pupils in their respective studies is generally commendable.

All suggestions of improvements in the processes of mental development and discipline have been carefully considered, and expedients have often been devised for the more sure and rapid attainment of the desired results.

Several changes in the administration of this important department, pointed out by mature experience, have been made, and no efforts have been spared to promote its efficiency, invigorate its organic forces, increase its educational facilities, multiply its mechanical appliances, and keep its light burning steadily and brightly.

Instruction in most of the common branches has been freed from all typical oppressiveness, and given in a simple and natural way. Various contrivances have at times been resorted to as a relief from monotony, and the fog of dulness has been shut out from the atmosphere of the school-room by the charm of novelty and the warmth of ever fresh and unfailing interest. Whenever the objective method was admissible or possible, it has been unhesitatingly adopted and put into practice in preference to any and all others.

Reading by the touch has been taught with the greatest care, and the utmost pains have been taken with the intonation of the voice and the articulation of the throat. The fresh and valuable books recently embossed in our printing office have served as a powerful impetus in this direction, and created an ardent desire among the blind for choice literature adapted to their wants. This craving, fostered and strengthened by every new addition made to our library, has already exercised a salutary influence upon many a sightless child and youth, inciting them to a more frequent use of their fingers, and a desire to drill and train them more perseveringly than heretofore. As a consequence, of the whole number of pupils in attendance at our school during the past year, there were only four who could not read with more or less facility the products of our press. Two of these, owing either to mental weakness or physical incapacity,

were unable to decipher the letters of the alphabet
in any of the line or point systems of printing.
Of the remaining two, one could read both Moon's
and Braille's characters, while the other was only
able to make out with great difficulty a few sentences in Moon's publications.

Thoroughness has continued to be the leading
principle in whatever the pupils have undertaken
to do. Every particular of their work has received
due attention, and nothing has been slighted or
neglected on account of its being insignificant
from a material point of view. The reason for this
insistance is very obvious. In the light of education details or objects which may at first sight
appear comparatively valueless, are really of the
greatest practical importance, not so much for the
amount of information which they yield, as because
of the development which they compel. The
mastery of certain subjects in all their minutiæ
evokes effort and cultivates powers of application,
which otherwise might have lain dormant. Thus
one thing leads to another, and so the work
goes on through life. But indulging in discouragement has never helped any one over a difficulty,
and never will. D'Alembert's advice to the student
who complained to him of his want of success in
mastering the elements of mathematics was the
right one. " Go on, sir, and faith and strength
will come to you."

At the reopening of the school, after the summer vacation, both teachers and pupils have promptly returned to their work, and resumed their respective duties with fresh zest and new sense of power. There is a feeling of activity and vigor in the air, and they all seem to be animated by an earnest desire to profit by the boundless possibilities of a promising year which stretch before them.

MUSIC DEPARTMENT.

This department has been conducted upon the same general plan as in previous years. No changes either in organization or in management have been attempted, and no new theories have been adopted. Improvements, however, in the processes of instruction and the details of administration have been made from time to time, and warrant a feeling of great satisfaction.

The number of pupils in the music department during the past year was 73. Of these, 68 received instruction in the piano, 47 in class singing, 17 in private vocal training, 21 in harmony, 10 in the cabinet and church organ, and 21 in reed and brass instruments.

There were four normal classes with an average membership of five each for instruction in the art of teaching.

The Braille system of musical notation has been used by the pupils, as heretofore during the last eight or nine years, in copying portions of text-books for the piano, harmony and counterpoint, for permanent use. It has also been used for band music.

The practical utility and thoroughness of the course of instruction pursued in our music department may be illustrated by the experience of a young man, who was a graduate from another school and came here at the close of his course for a single year only. After leaving his *alma mater*, he obtained some pupils on the pianoforte, and, although he was a good player, he neither knew how or what to teach them, not having committed any instruction book or books of *études* for this instrument to memory. His collection of pieces was small and not sufficiently varied. After spending nine months here, these defects were remedied, and he returned to his home in Buffalo, N. Y., and again obtained pupils, but this time he knew how to teach them. It is just a year since he left us, and during all this time he has had plenty to do. He is the organist of a Roman catholic church, has twenty-three scholars on the pianoforte, and one on the violin. His success is complete in every respect.

Violin playing is the only important branch of music absent from our course. This instrument is unquestionably the most favorite one at the present time. Judged by its wide popularity, it reigns supreme over all others. It charms and delights alike the young and the old, the wise and the unlearned, the student and the man of affairs,

the sedate and the gay. The brilliancy and intrinsic
sweetness of its sound infuse a sense of liveliness
and create a feeling of joy and happiness which
are unequalled.   While the range of its organic
resources and the compass of its harmonic combinations and rhythmic successions are neither as
extensive nor as comprehensive as those of the
organ and the pianoforte, its melodious effects, its
power and nobleness of expression, its suppleness
of tone are, on the other hand, superior to those
of any other instrument.   No school of music can,
in our days, be considered as complete without the
study of the violin.   The seriousness of the objec-
tions which were cogent in the early part of the
history of the institution and caused its discontin-
uance is invalidated, or at least greatly modified,
by the present intellectual, moral and social status
of the blind; and I earnestly recommend that provision should be made for its speedy introduction
into both branches of the music department.

Extensive as are the facilities afforded at the
institution itself for thorough instruction and practice, and great as are the actual benefits accruing
from them, their value is vastly enhanced by the
rare external opportunities for the cultivation and
refinement of the artistic taste, which are freely
offered to those of our scholars who are gifted with
natural ability for the study of music.

Through the great kindness and generosity of
the leading musical societies of Boston, of the

proprietors of theatres, the managers of public
entertainments, and also of the most eminent musicians in the city,— the names of all of whom will
be given elsewhere,— our pupils have continued to
be permitted to attend the finest concerts, rehearsals, operas, oratorios and recitals, and to hear the
compositions of the greater and lesser masters
interpreted by distinguished individual artists or
well drilled orchestras. I avail myself of this
opportunity to express in the name of the school,
to each and all of them, our warm thanks and
grateful acknowledgments, and to join the public
at large in the hearty wish for their future success
and prosperity.

But the discharge of this pleasant duty is, I am
grieved to say, blended with a feeling of sincere
regret and disappointment, caused by the announcement that the concerts of one of the most prominent of these organizations, the Harvard musical
association, will be heard no longer. This society
has been a constant friend, an efficient educator
and a great benefactor to the blind of New England. For sixteen years it has opened its doors to
them with unparalleled liberality, and freely extended to them abundant opportunities for hearing the best performances of the *chefs d'œuvre* of
classic music, thereby contributing largely to the
full development of their artistic sensibilities, critical acumen and general musical culture. These
uncommon advantages were so highly valued and

fully appreciated by our pupils, that their loss is keenly felt and deeply regretted by all of them.

Let us hope and trust that the noble example of the Harvard musical association will be followed by others, and that the cause of the education of the blind will not cease to be remembered by those who have it in their power to befriend and advance it.

TUNING DEPARTMENT.

This department has received its wonted share of attention and shows results quite as encouraging as those of former years.

As the circle of possible pursuits and remunerative employments for the blind becomes more and more restricted by the invention and use of machinery in all manufacturing processes, by the division of labor and by the enormous development of absorbing monopolies, it is more urgent that the most perfect provision should be made for those in which they can excel. Experience has proved that the art of tuning pianofortes is the most prominent among them, and no institution for the blind can afford to neglect or slight it. In our system of training the pupils for useful occupations it holds a very important position.

During the past year several improvements have been made in the appliances employed in the tuning department, and new facilities have been added for carrying on its operations successfully, and rendering the instruction and practice of the recipients of its benefits thorough and efficient.

The contract for tuning and keeping in repair the pianofortes of the public schools of Boston has again, for the sixth time, been awarded to the tuning department of this institution, on the same terms as heretofore, and without the least opposition from any direction. This unanimous and prompt action of the committee, together with the steady increase of patronage which has been extended to our tuners by some of the very best families of Boston and the neighboring towns, is very gratifying to them, and speaks more eloquently for their skill and efficiency than words can do. Moreover, it constitutes in itself a complete answer and consummate refutation to the base aspersions, sneering insinuations and unfriendly remarks, which are now and then, either thoughtlessly or designedly, directed against the abilities of the blind.

The most contemptible criticism of this kind appeared last July in the editorial columns of the "Musical Critic and Trade Review" of New York. The writer of this curious paragraph asserts that, having watched the method of a blind tuner, he saw that "he had no conception of the principles of proper tuning." He says: "His musical ear was true, but he did not understand the mechanical construction of the piano, and *there is no doubt* that he succeeded in ruining the instrument.

Some persons may be actuated by a spirit of charity in engaging a blind man for the purpose of
tuning their pianos, but they could better afford
to pay the unfortunate man a few dollars to keep
him from touching the piano, and at the same time
make money by the operation, as the damage
usually done is equal to twenty times the cost of
tuning."

This statement is as reckless and untrue as it is
cruel and unjust to a large class of our fellow men,
who are striving determinedly to reach the goal of
independence and grapple resolutely with the for-
midable difficulties opposing their advancement to
the dignity of self-maintenance.   It misrepresents
the nature of their work, gives false impressions
of the thoroughness of their training, undervalues
their capacities, and adds a vast amount of
anguish to their sore calamity.   Conceived in supreme selfishness and mean jealousy, if not in des-
picable malice, and couched in terms of hypocrisy
and pretence, it is calculated to strengthen the
common prejudices against sightless tuners, create
mistrust in their endeavors, deprive them of their
share in the public patronage, and thus condemn
them to the evils of idleness and the mercy of
charity.

Now the facts of the case are simply these.   In
consequence of their infirmity the blind begin
early to concentrate their attention upon the impressions received through the auditory organs.

They constantly employ the ear for various purposes for which seeing persons use their eyes,
and they let it rest only when they are asleep.
While in school, they live and move in an atmosphere which resounds with musical tones. By
this incessant exercise their sense of hearing is so
improved, and acquires such an acuteness and
nicety, that the relations of sounds, and the imperfections of unisons and intervals, imperceptible to
ordinary listeners, are apparent to them. This
power and accuracy of the musical ear of our
pupils is coupled and sustained by a practical and
systematic knowledge of the construction of the
pianoforte and its internal mechanism which they
acquire in the tuning department of this institution. Here, aided by the use of models and the
dissection of old instruments, they study with
great care and under efficient guidance the differences in the structure of the various kinds of
actions, learn the details of their workings, and
become familiar with the form, size and relations
of every part, the materials of which it is composed, and the office it performs. In addition to
this, special attention is paid to that branch of
physics which treats of the nature of sound and
the laws of its production and propagation. Thus,
all things being considered, our tuners are far
better prepared in theory as well as in practice for
the successful pursuit of their art than the great
majority of their seeing competitors, and have

positive advantages over them, both in their natural aptitudes and in their acquired qualifications.

This assertion does not rest upon mere speculation or *a priori* reasoning.   It is based upon
undisputed facts which, warranted by history and
confirmed by daily experience, ought to dispel all
reasonable doubts as to the competency and success
of the blind as tuners of pianofortes.   Some of
these are herewith given in the briefest possible
manner.

1. Claud Montal, a graduate of the school for
the young blind in Paris, has been one of the most
distinguished tuners in that city, and be not only
made improvements in his art but contributed
more than any other individual to its present perfection.   His treatise on the subject is still a work
of unsurpassed merit.   His knowledge of the
mechanism and construction of pianofortes was so
thorough and extensive that he became the head
of one of the leading and most prosperous factories of these instruments.   His talents were generally recognized and fully appreciated by eminent
artists everywhere.   He was the author of several
inventions; but the most valuable of these was
that concerning the pedals.   He exhibited in London in 1862 a "*pédale d'expression*," diminishing
the range of the hammers instead of shifting them,
an expedient now employed by American and
German makers, and a "*pédale de prolongement*,"
by using which a note or notes may be prolonged

after the fingers have quitted the keys. Montal's genius has planted the art of tuning pianofortes so firmly in the curriculum of his *alma mater*, that about one-third of the graduates of that school continue to become skilled in it and to earn their living by its practice in the capital and provinces of France.

2. Messrs. Steinway & Sons of New York have for a long time employed a blind man, named Arnim Shotte, as head tuner of their celebrated establishment, and in reply to a letter which I addressed to them, asking for information with regard to his success, they speak as follows: " Mr. Shotte's tuning is simply perfect, not only for its purity, but for his skill of so setting the tuning pins that the piano can endure the largest amount of heavy playing without being put out of tune." With this opinion coincides that of Messrs. Wm. Bourne & Son of Boston, who have employed one of the graduates of this institution, Mr. Joseph H. Wood, as principal tuner for nineteen years, and write: " It gives us the greatest pleasure to testify to the efficient and excellent service rendered by him to our establishment, and to say that his able and skilful workmanship has always been much prized by us." Other factories and dealers of pianofortes in Boston, Providence, Cleveland, Ohio, and elsewhere have availed themselves of the services of sightless tuners, and they all bear testimony to the uniform success of their work.

3. The tuners of this institution have for six years taken charge of the pianofortes used in the public schools of Boston — one hundred and thirty-one in number. Their tuning, and the lesser repairs which they themselves do, have received unqualified commendation and cordial approbation from both the music teachers and the proper authorities, and never to my knowledge has a word of dissatisfaction been breathed, or any complaint made of the slightest injury to any of the instruments.

4. A number of prominent musicians, teachers and critics in this city, such as Messrs. Carl Zerrahn, B. J. Lang, W. H. Sherwood, Julius Eichberg, John S. Dwight, J. B. Sharland, H. E. Holt, J. W. Mason, the late Robert E. Apthorp, and many others, after a patient and conscientious trial of our tuners, have declared themselves "perfectly satisfied with their work," have characterized it as "equal to the best," and some of them have earnestly recommended the services of the blind to their pupils and friends, and have obtained orders for them. The most emphatic of the testimonials cheerfully given to them was that of Mr. Sherwood, in which he says: "My grand piano was recently tuned and regulated by tuners from the institution for the blind. They put it in better repair and condition (in both action, hammer-felts and perfect tune) than it has been for a long time past. I cordially endorse their abilities in this line as apparently unsurpassed."

The chain of these testimonials and historic facts
could be greatly lengthened by the addition of
many others of a similar nature; but the above-
mentioned will suffice to prove the correctness of
my assertions, and to show that the blind are
remarkably successful as tuners of pianofortes, and
that the slurs cast upon their work by unprincipled
critics and heartless traducers are unmerited and
unjustifiable. That now and then there may be
found one of their number who is not an expert in the
art which he professes to pursue, and who may do
harm to an instrument entrusted to his care, no one
can reasonably deny. But is it fair, is it honorable,
is it humane to condemn a whole class of industrious and meritorious people by the misconduct of
a few, to exclude them on that ground from the
active occupations of life and assign them arbitrarily to the unmitigated miseries of the almshouse, from which they have been delivered through
the indefatigable toil and sagacious efforts of
eminent reformers and distinguished philanthropists? Are the instigators of the paragraph published in the " Musical Critic and Trade Review "
prepared to stamp as perfect or " well done " the
work of the legions of seeing persons who swarm
the country heralded by flaming advertisements and
circulars as first-class tuners, but who are both by
taste and training more competent to split wood or
till the soil than to handle and regulate musical
instruments? Yet it would be simply absurd to

use their failings and misdeeds as a weapon against a whole class of artisans, amongst whom there are many of acknowledged skill and dexterity.

In closing these remarks, which duty and the sense of justice compel me to write in defence of the assailed rights and misjudged abilities of the blind, I beg leave to state that the work of all the graduates from the tuning department of this institution who are supplied with certificates is warranted to be thorough in every respect; and I herewith appeal to the public to continue to favor them with employment on the solid basis of business and not on that of charity.

TECHNICAL DEPARTMENT.

A brief review of the work accomplished in the two branches of the technical department will show that its affairs have been managed with commendable diligence and with satisfactory results.

I. *Workshop for the Boys.*

Under the faithful care and general supervision of Mr. John H. Wright, our boys have been regularly employed in this shop in working at the usual trades, and have acquired more or less skill in their pursuance.

The mode of instruction has been very simple and eminently practical, and its chief object has been to enable the pupils to use their hands with dexterity, to exercise their faculties upon things

tangible and actual, to manipulate materials, and
to learn how to construct various articles. The
valuable effects of this training are manifest not
only in the exactness or fitness with which mattresses, or brooms, or cane seats, or other special
articles are prepared for the market, but in the
development of the powers and increase of the
capacities of the apprentices for the transaction of
business and for general usefulness.

II. *Work-rooms for the Girls.*

Of the condition and prospects of this branch
of our technical department I am able to give a
most favorable account.

Under the efficient management of Miss Abby J.
Dillingham, the work-rooms for the girls have continued to be bee-hives of industry, and the articles
there manufactured have been most creditable both
to teachers and learners, and found so ready a sale
that only a few specimens could be seen in our
cases at any one time.

The training which the girls receive in the workrooms, added to the experience which they obtain in
domestic employments, is of incalculable benefit to
them. It enables them to engage in various occupations adapted to their sex, and to become helpful
members of their families.

DEPARTMENT OF PHYSICAL TRAINING.

The pupils, divided as usual into six classes of
moderate size, have repaired to the gymnasium at

stated hours, and have been regularly instructed and trained in those graduated trials of strength, activity and adroitness by which the size and power of the muscles are fully developed, the vital processes of respiration, digestion and circulation are promoted, the general health and agility in motion improved, and the whole frame is invigorated and prepared for sustaining prolonged and sudden efforts.

The exercises comprised in our course of physical training have been selected with a view to their suitableness to the capacity of learners of different ages and of every grade of bodily strength, and . have been arranged in a progressive and systematic manner, each step leading to that directly in advance of it. They have been invariably conducted by experienced and prudent teachers, who allow no attempts of extraordinary or exaggerated feats that might cause accidents, and their effect upon the appearance, health, and strength of the pupils has been quite remarkable.

THE PRINTING FUND.

It was a source of no small gratification to have been able to announce at the celebration of the semi-centennial anniversary of the institution, that the total amount of one hundred thousand dollars for the permanent endowment of the "Howe Memorial Press" had been contributed. The generosity and benevolence of our citizens were

never more signally manifested than in the completion of this enterprise, which will stand in perpetuity, like a beautiful fountain, breathing forth
comfort and life-giving power.

About a year ago, while rendering a brief account
of the progress made in raising the printing fund,
we stated that the sum requisite was still incomplete, and urgently asked for further subscriptions.
Our appeal met with a prompt and hearty response.
The names of new contributors were almost daily
added to our list, and some of the noblest families
and constant benefactors of the blind, whose
modesty screens them from the public ken, sent us
the glad and refreshing order to double their original donations of one thousand dollars, and in
several instances to multiply them by five. Such
a grand use of the rules of arithmetic for the
benefit of suffering humanity is not a common
occurrence. It is, indeed, a rare phenomenon.
Nor is it the practice of men of ordinary mental
and moral calibre, who come into the possession of
riches by a mere stroke of luck or accident, and
whose charitable gifts are either exceedingly
slender in size or capricious and showy in character.
It is the privilege of great souls and hearts full of
sympathy and good-will. It is the ripe fruit of
pure unselfishness and benign philanthropy.

The completion of the printing fund is an act of
public-spirited beneficence which, we believe, has
no parallel in history, and reflects the greatest

honor on the munificent liberality of the donors
and the organic fabric of the community in which
such enterprises are accomplished. The books
which will be annually issued will prove not only
valuable treasures of enlightenment and wisdom,
but a perennial source of consolation under an
affliction which closes upon its victims the delights
and charms of the visible world. They will gladden
many a saddened heart, raise many a drooping
spirit, and comfort many a joyless dwelling. Like
balm and anodyne, they will assuage the pangs of
calamity and misfortune. For good literature is
one of the best remedies to a sorrowing soul.
Pliny says :

> " At unicum doloris levamentum studia confugio ; "

and Montesquieu declared that no grief is so deep
as not to be dissipated by reading for an hour :

> " Je n'ai jamais eu de chagrin si profond qu'une heure de
> lecture ne l'ait dissipé."

In the case of the blind this remedy acts with
tenfold force. The shadowed outward vision
causes the light within to burn more brightly, as
the window-curtains drawn at dark increase the
glow of the fire and intensify the cheerfulness
inside the room.

To a generous and enlightened public, and to
the editors and proprietors of the leading newspapers we are under great and lasting obligations
for the active aid and coöperation readily given

to our earnest efforts to bring the enterprise of
embossing books to its consummation. Encouraged
by the success thus attained, we are determined to
prosecute this grand object with all our energies,
until every sightless person who can read with the
tips of his fingers is provided with a sufficient
supply of choice and healthy literature.

ABSOLUTE NEED OF A KINDERGARTEN.

Eloquent the children's faces —
  Poverty's lean look, which saith,
Save us! save us! woe surrounds us;
Little knowledge sore confounds us;
  Life is but a lingering death.

Give us light amid our darkness;
  Let us know the good from ill:
Hate us not for all our blindness;
Love us, lead us, show us kindness,
  You can make us what you will.

We are willing; we are ready;
  We would learn if you would teach;
We have hearts that yearn towards duty;
We have minds alive to beauty;
  Souls that any heights can reach.
                          MARY HOWITT.

These lines give a striking picture of the condition of a large number of little blind children who
are scattered in all parts of New England, living
in total physical darkness and indescribable destitution.   They set forth clearly and concisely their
wants and capabilities, and present in plain and

simple words a pathetic and resistless appeal in
their behalf.

Like other human beings, these afflicted children
of night are endowed with faculties and capacities
susceptible of development, growth and improvement, but, unlike most of them, they are considered
as hopelessly disabled by their infirmity, and are
thoughtlessly doomed to sloth and inertia. Pale,
nerveless, haggard, and evidently reduced in
vitality, they are confined to wretched lodgings,
and are permitted to lead a distressing existence.
All the natural pleasures of childhood are unknown
to them. Not a ray of joy enters the dark chamber of their isolation; not a breath of happiness
lightens the heavy pressure of the clouds of their
calamity. They are usually born in poverty, and
often in moral depravity. They are nursed by
sorrow, surrounded by vice, accompanied by misfortune, brought up in neglect, and tortured by
inexpressible misery. They live in a world of
seclusion and suffering, with the woes of which
very few of our citizens are acquainted. Hunger,
filth, fou lair, stifling heat, or severe cold — these
and their like are the daily attendants and constant
companions of these unfortunate human beings.

But it is beyond doubt that the souls of these
children have in them something of that cloud of
glory of which the poet sings. No matter how
hideous and squalid their lives may be, they have
susceptibilities that can be touched by kindness,

beauty and goodness. They have hearts which can
be reached by love and sympathy. They have the
germs of natural aptitudes and mental abilities
which can be fostered by care and brought to fruition by training.

Now the salvation and future welfare of these
children of misfortune depend wholly upon their
being removed from the poisonous effects of their
environment, and placed in neat and healthy quarters, where the means for physical well-being and
systematic training are sufficiently provided, and
the spirit of good-will and benevolence all pervad-
ing and guiding, and where faith in man's capacity
for improvement and elevation is firmly adhered to,
and parental care and affection freely bestowed.
This salutary change should be effected before corrupt tendencies and vicious propensities are hardened and crystallized into permanent habits; and
the tender age between five and nine years seems
most appropriate for it. Being brought so early in
life under favorable influences and a regular course
of bodily, mental and moral culture, the children
will prove better subjects for reformation than if
taken in charge later on. Good principles and
aspirations will sink more deeply into their minds
while these are still in a plastic state and comparatively free from low impressions and mean encum-
brances; and when sound seed is sown before the
tares have time to take root, the probability is that

the harvest will be more abundant and of a purer
and better quality.

For the accomplishment of this noble purpose,
the foundation of a primary school for little blind
children is imperatively needed. As there is
neither room nor conveniences for such an establishment on the premises of this institution, and as
it is, moreover, neither advisable nor desirable to
have its tender inmates associated and brought up
together with youth between the ages of fifteen
and nineteen years, it should be placed elsewhere
within the limits of the city. It should have a
pleasant and healthy location, and occupy a lot of
land comprising five acres at least. It should be
organized on sound principles, and conducted on a
broad and liberal policy. There should be nothing
about either its title or arrangements which would
in any way compromise its educational character.
Its existence should be secured by an endowment
fund of about two hundred and fifty thousand dollars, and its doors should be freely opened not only
to such indigent blind children as are above
described, but to all others who are deprived of
the visual sense and may be desirous of entering
the school. They should be retained until the age
of twelve, and taught and trained objectively according to the simple and rational methods developed in Froebel's kindergarten.

This system is admirably suited for the instruction of little blind children, containing, as it does,

within itself, that principle of organic life manifested in gradual development, and the power of
counteracting the undesirable effects produced by
the loss of sight and by weakening and degrading
influences.   It turns innocent play to useful
account, and cultivates happiness on the fertile soil
of industry.   By the felicitous combination of
"doing with knowing," the intellectual activity is
unconsciously promoted while the physical strength
is steadily increased.   In the simple and delicate
crafts of folding, weaving, block-building, sewing,
embroidering upon cardboard, modelling in clay,
and the like, a grand purpose is subserved, that of
unfolding the various powers of the body and
mind just at the time when they are particularly
capable of harmonious growth, eager for improvement and most pliable in every respect.

Of the numerous beneficent results obtained
from the above-named occupations and from similar interesting and attractive exercises, the following are the most noticeable: Good physical
development; muscular strength and elasticity;
habits of attention and order; clearness and precision in thinking; freedom and grace of movement;
quickness of invention and fertility of imagination;
a keen sense of symmetry and harmony, together
with love of construction and appreciation of utility;
great mechanical skill in the use of the hands, and
initiation into the conventionalities of polite society,
in their demeanor toward each other, and in mat-

ters of eating, drinking and personal cleanliness.

The average intelligence of pupils taught in the kindergarten is decidedly superior to that of children who enter the primary schools without such training. The former are more or less accustomed to exert themselves in the search for information, and prepared to derive greater benefit from instruction and mental discipline than the latter. They generally observe accurately, seize ideas rapidly and definitely, illustrate readily, work independently and express their thoughts with correctness and fluency. To persons bereft of sight, Froebel's system promises even higher results than these. It affords them unequalled facilities for gaining an adequate conception of forms of various kinds, and rare opportunities for the practice and refinement of their remaining senses, especially of that of touch, which is their chief reliance for the acquisition of all concrete knowledge, and consequently the most important factor of their education. Above all, the drill obtained through its exercises so early in life and under such genial influences, will prove a valuable auxiliary for future achievements and the most effective agent for raising the standard of attainments in this school. For a great part of the time which is now necessarily spent in mere primary routine work and elementary training, can then be devoted to the pursuit of advanced studies both in the literary and musical departments, and to a thorough preparation for a professional or other calling. Thus there will be a positive and most significant gain at both ends, which will in some measure pave the way for the solution of the great problem of the higher education for the blind and their thorough equipment for the struggle of existence.

It is obvious from these facts and from a careful consideration of the matter, that a well-fitted and sufficiently provided kindergarten will be to little sightless children what the light of the sun and the dew of heaven are to tender plants, — a source of life and growth and strength, a flame dispelling the clouds of darkness, a fountain of happiness and strength, aiding them to outsoar the shadows of their night. It will be a psalm of their deliverance from the clutches of misery, a hymn to the dawn of an era of freedom and independence, a benediction to the benevolence of our age.

In behalf of these afflicted children, who from the midst of the wretchedness and neglect in which they are plunged, stretch their helpless hands towards the shore and call for a life-boat, we make an earnest appeal to the generous and wealthy members of our community, and hope that it will touch a responsive chord in their hearts. When they determine to pronounce the grand verdict and say, " let there be a permanent source of light and happiness for little blind children," there

will be no intellectual and moral darkness for them
any longer.

Cicero says, that men resemble the gods in nothing so much as in doing good to their fellow
creatures. "*Homines ad deos nulla se propius
accedunt, quam salutem hominibus dando*." There
may possibly be some, however, who are disposed to bestow their gifts upon works of an
artistic nature, upon the cause of higher or professional education, upon the furtherance of culture
and refinement, but not inclined to aid an enterprise which is calculated to seek its beneficiaries
in the humblest social ranks and lighten one of the
greatest human calamities of half its weight. If
there be such among our generous citizens, let me
remind them of the words of Richter: "Very beautiful is the eagle when he floats with outstretched
wings aloft in the clear blue; but sublime when he
plunges down through the tempests to his eyrie on
the cliff, where his unfledged young ones dwell
and are starving."

Occasions of Interest during the Year.

Though a little shut in from the world, our
young people are not behindhand in echoing the
movements which characterize the day, and the
celebration of anniversaries and other occasions
during the past year has marked this tendency to
a very special and interesting degree.

The first of these festivals was held in honor of

the seventy-fourth birthday of New England's favored poet, John Greenleaf Whittier, on the 17th of December, 1881.

Inspired by the new and welcome delight of being enabled to read his works for themselves unaided by any one save their own printer, the pupils of the advanced class in the girls' department conceived the idea of celebrating both the poet's birthday and their own gratitude by appropriate festal exercises; and a very charming and much enjoyed evening was the result of this happy thought. Some of the most beautiful of Whittier's poems were read with much spirit and feeling, their tender purity and pathetic grace being brought out in high relief. Music and appropriate remarks ensued and added considerably to the liveliness of the occasion. The following exquisite letter from the veteran poet, written in the touching vernacular of the interesting sect of Friends, was received by one of our teachers who had written to Mr. Whittier, informing him of the great pleasure and delight which her pupils experienced in reading his works:

DANVERS, MASS., Dec. 12th, 1881.

To MARY C. MOORE :—

Dear Friend,—It gives me great pleasure to know that the pupils in thy class at the institution for the blind have the opportunity afforded them to read some of my writings, and thus hold what I hope will prove a pleasant communion with me. Very glad I shall be if the pen-pictures of nature and homely country firesides, which I have tried to make, are understood and appreciated by those who cannot discern them by natural vision. I shall count it a great privilege to see for them, or rather to let them see through my eyes. It is the mind after all that really sees, shapes and colors all things. What visions of beauty and sublimity passed before the inward and spiritual light of blind Milton and deaf Beethoven!

I have an esteemed friend, Morrison Heady of Kentucky, who is deaf and blind; yet under these circumstances he has cultivated his mind to a high degree, and has written poems of great beauty and vivid descriptions of scenes which have been witnessed only by the " light within."

I thank thee for thy letter, and beg of thee to assure thy students that I am deeply interested in their welfare and progress, and that my prayer is that their inward and spiritual eyes may become so clear that they can well dispense with the outward and material ones.

I am very truly thy friend,

JOHN G. WHITTIER.

The celebration of the birthday of Longfellow, preceding, as it did, his death by so few weeks, seemed in particular a very beautiful and, as it were, almost prophetic feature of the intellectual life of the school.

The garlands, the flowers, the pictures of the great poet and of his home, were probably seen in many celebrations of the occasion, which was wonderfully and, as we have said, prophetically kept all over the country. But perhaps there was something peculiarly touching in this outburst of gratitude towards Longfellow from the hearts of the blind, to whom the difficulty of reading his works, as compared with the ordinary methods of publication, rendered them infinitely more precious, and who welcomed his birthday with an enthusiasm which only the afflicted can know.

Again, the singing of several of Longfellow's pieces in their musical and well-tuned voices, was a tribute *sui generis* to the genius of the day, and the pupils entered into their dialogue on his birthday with an ardor which showed their worship of the hero.

Mr. Longfellow himself was interested in hearing of the histrionic attempt, which had been made earlier in the winter, and in which the play of "Maurice, the Woodcutter," was given in a very lively and untrammelled manner. No blind person unexpectedly entering the audience on that occasion would have supposed that the actors before him were sightless. Indeed, he would have imagined from the animation of their speech and the promptness of their actions, that he himself was the only person in the room who could not see. The pupils had been well drilled in the entrances, exits, and other practical points of the little drama, and their interest in the story carried them wholly out of themselves, so that awkwardness, self-consciousness and stage-fright were really left far behind.

Passing over the amusing costume party got up by our girls in the gymnasium of the institution, which was highly enjoyed and a great success, the memory dwells with delight and with lingering glance upon the day chosen to acknowledge in a suitable manner the ceaseless and devoted efforts of Mr. Samuel G. Snelling in behalf of the blind. Mr. Snelling was himself totally unaware of the festivity intended in his honor, coming out on the afternoon appointed with a party of friends to go over the institution.   As was natural in the case of distinguished visitors, the pupils were assembled *en masse* in the hall, ready with their beautiful music, with recitations and with reading.   Gradually it appeared that all the transactions centered toward one object; and the demonstration becoming more pointed, a climax was reached when a crayon portrait of Mr. Snelling was unveiled, to which the following inscription was attached: "This portrait of Mr. Samuel G. Snelling was made at the expense of the pupils and teachers of the Perkins Institution and Massachusetts School for the Blind, as a slight token of their great and deep gratitude for his persistent exertions and laborious efforts in raising the printing fund for the blind of New England."   Mrs. Julia Ward Howe made one of her happiest speeches on the occasion, closing with the following appropriate verse:

> " These friends who in the shadows sit,
>   Your kindly face cannot behold,
>   But your soul features in their hearts
>   They 'll keep enshrined in memory's gold."

Two crowns of roses were presented to Mr. Snelling by a little boy and girl, on behalf of both departments of the school, and were gracefully acknowledged by him in a few well-chosen words.

Remarks by Mr. John S. Dwight, and music by the celebrated pianist, Mr. Baerman, added greatly to the delightfulness of the occasion. The guests then visited the schools, and those who were able to stay later had the pleasure of listening to a recital by the eminent vocalist, Mrs. Clara Doria Rogers, and in the evening to a concert of much merit, given by Mr. S. B. Whitney, with the assistance of Mrs. Topliffe and other well-known musicians.

Thus the day was made thrice happy and trebly noteworthy, and as such it will be remembered by all who had the great pleasure of being present.

Closing with the celebration of the semi-centennial anniversary, the past school year has certainly been a memorable one. Yet, after all, it has only exemplified, on a larger scale, the enjoyments and advantages always open to the blind of New England.

MOVEMENT FOR THE BLIND IN PROVIDENCE.

Among the many interesting and gratifying demonstrations in behalf of the blind, none was more so than the action of the people of Providence, Rhode Island, in furtherance of the printing fund.

A public meeting was held in the music hall of that city on the 12th of April last, which was

attended by a large, intelligent and enthusiastic audience.   Governor Littlefield presided, and opened
the exercises with a brief address.   About thirty
members of our school gave an exhibition in reading and in various branches of study and vocal and
instrumental music, and illustrated, in a striking
and touching manner, the results of the beneficent
work begun by Dr. Howe fifty years ago.   Pertinent speeches were made by the Rev. Dr. Robinson, president of Brown university, ex-governor
Van Zandt, Bishop Clark, the Rev. A. Woodbury,
the Rev. Dr. Behrends and the Rev. George Harris, and a committee was appointed to take charge
of the matter, composed of Governor Littlefield,
Mayor Hayward, and ten other members representing the business interests, the social status and the
benevolence of the community.

Thus the work of soliciting subscriptions to the
printing fund was auspiciously inaugurated, and a
regular system of canvassing was pursued, by
means of which the amount of about seven thousand dollars was raised.

For so satisfactory a consummation of this
movement the blind of New England are greatly
indebted to the prominent citizens and clergymen
of Providence who encouraged and promoted it,
to the editors of the two leading newspapers,
the "Journal" and the "Press," who cheerfully
espoused the cause and lent their influence to its
advancement, and especially to our good friend,

Mr. James B. Winsor, who devoted himself to it from its very inception and labored persistently and with marked disinterestedness until success was fully attained.

EFFECTS OF POLITICAL INTERFERENCE.

The public institutions of Great Britain and America have their origin in the same causes, are carried on for similar purposes, and are alike in many respects; but they differ essentially in three important points: in the fundamental principles of their organization, in the sources from which they derive their means of existence, and in the scope of their administration.

In Great Britain no provision is made by the state in its sovereign character in favor of its crippled and defective children. The budget annually presented by the government and adopted by the parliament contains no items of expense either for their education or for their care and maintenance. It is true that humane enterprises are not neglected in England, and that the field of philanthropy receives due attention and is rendered productive of good harvest in some of its parts: but the means of its cultivation are not furnished from the public treasury; they are raised by the donations and contributions of benevolent individuals. Society, as such, in its organic capacity, recognizes no obligation towards its unfortunate members. It is entirely left to private charity to perform this duty. History and experience suggest, however, that whatever is done under this form is often so hampered by conditions calculated to minister to the whims and vanity of the donors, is so ludicrously encumbered by a complicated machinery of parade and show, of empty titles and long subscription lists, of arrogant distinctions and humiliating ceremonies, of annual dinners and begging sermons, that although it may be very gratifying to the feelings and ambition of the givers, its blessedness is rather questionable so far as the recipients are concerned.

In this country the case is entirely different. The state adheres to broader considerations and higher principles, and its fixed policy is to take care of every disabled or incapacitated citizen, and to provide the means of education for every child within its borders, in view not only of his assumed rights, but also for the protection of the community itself against ignorance as a source of pauperism, and as unfitting men for the duties of citizenship. Thus public institutions for the poor and the perverse, the halt and the lawless, the idiots and the insane, the deaf and the blind, are established everywhere by legislative enactments and are supported by funds to which each taxpayer contributes his share.

This policy is unquestionably the right one. Viewed in the light of social economy, it is just to the sufferers, creditable to the community at large,

and admirable in every respect; but, considered
in its practical workings, it is not entirely free
from grave disadvantages and certain perils. The
most serious of these arise from political or partisan interference in the administration of the
affairs of public establishments and the control of
their interests.

The disastrous effects of this contemptible practice are so enormous that it would be very difficult
to exaggerate them. The lamentable condition of
many state institutions in various parts of the
country, especially in the West and South, shows
conclusively, that it is the most threatening as it is
the most insidious danger that besets them. In its
concrete application it eats "as doth a canker"
into the very heart of their existence. It is a crying evil, affixing a stigma upon the communities
which encourage or tolerate it. Born of no other
incentives than the lust of spoils and the thirst
for lucrative positions, it has already done an
incalculable amount of mischief. However it may
be disguised under this pretence or that excuse,
it is obviously pernicious in its character, demor-
alizing in its influences, unscrupulous in its
attempts, plunderous in its aims, vindictive in its
purposes, destructive in its tendencies, and reckless in its action. Through the viciousness of this
system the usefulness of state institutions is greatly
impaired, the essential powers on which their efficiency rests are consumed, and the foundations of

the moral dikes that shut out the waters of a sea of ills are sapped. Honesty, fitness, capacity and fidelity cannot possibly thrive or find adequate protection under it. As a consequence, accomplished superintendents, trained and intelligent teachers, experienced officers and faithful employés are summarily dismissed from their places for no other cause but simply in order to make room for corrupt politicians and to gratify the hunger for office of their henchmen and satellites who were howling on the confines of party strife. Under such circumstances the vital forces of public service are undermined, the springs of enthusiasm and earnest devotion to duty are dried, activity and hopefulness are succeeded by apathy and despondency, and men of talent, acknowledged ability, scholarly attainments and independence of character are driven out of their professions in disgust. They seem to prefer retirement to the yoke of unreasonable and exacting despotism.

This evil has already assumed such immense dimensions in several sections of the country that it cannot be cured by the ordinary means of grace. It has become a terrible incubus which must be torn up by the roots, a nightmare which must be shaken off without delay. It has grown to a monstrous wrong, which deserves universal and unrelenting opprobrium, and which imposes upon the good people of all political parties and religious sects the solemn obligation to unite in a strenuous and determined effort to close the gates of public institutions against the whirlwinds of political antagonisms, partisan influences, and capricious favoritism, bringing with them confusion, anarchy and desolation. Unless this be effectually done, the provision made by the state for the maintenance and support of educational or charitable establishments will prove in many instances a source of trouble and annoyance, instead of a means of convenience, prosperity, and permanent peace.

It is with sincere pleasure that we are able to say that such practices are almost unknown in New England, and can hardly be tolerated by its people. May their absence be perpetual!

Misapprehensions to be Avoided.

It is well known that some public institutions have their origin in the idea of the supreme reign of law and order and the protection of society, others in pity and sympathy for the disabled and suffering members of the human family, and still others in the right to a thorough education which the state accords to all its children, irrespective of creed, color, social condition, or physical defects. In other words, these establishments are either penal, reformatory, eleemosynary, or educational in their character. A thorough understanding of these distinctions, as well as of the specific aims and purposes of the different institutions, will help those

in authority not only to minister properly to the
wants and training of their beneficiaries, but likewise to do perfect justice to all of them individually, and to infuse into those among them who
hope to depend upon their own efforts for self-
maintenance that spirit of manliness, dignity and
independence which is indispensable to general success in life. A misapprehension of these points
will lead, on the other hand, either to mistaken
views of imaginary economy, or to mere illusions
as to the magnificent results of centralization in
the administration of public charities; or, again, to
the adoption of unwise rules and measures proving
in time positively detrimental to the welfare of the
wards of the state, and to the interests of the
community itself.

It is with sincere regret that I am constrained to
say in this connection that the unaccountable
attachment of the schools for the blind to the
national conference of charities and corrections as
one of its departments, coupled with a call to their
managers to join in the deliberations of this body
last August, is a striking illustration of such misunderstanding. It shows clearly that the nature
and scope of the education of sightless children
and their legal right to it are not as widely and as
thoroughly known as they ought to have been. In
consequence of this want of knowledge, they are
arbitrarily separated from the deaf-mutes by the

brief dictum of a convention, and indiscriminately classed with paupers, criminals and lunatics.

I earnestly hope that the representatives of the various schools for the instruction of the blind in the country did not assent tacitly to this unfortunate misunderstanding. It would have been very unwise, to say the least, on their part to do so. Duty, as well as the fundamental principles of their work and the vital interests of their charge, alike demanded that they should endeavor to rectify this error promptly and in the most emphatic manner. For myself, I felt compelled to remonstrate against it as uncalled for. It is a well established fact, known to all who are familiar with the affairs of this commonwealth, that our school is founded upon the solid rock of equity, and not upon the piers of pity and favor. It has therefore no official relation whatever with the state board of charities. It has been placed by law where it properly belongs, namely, under the supervision of the state board of education. It is classed with the normal schools, the state art school, the Massachusetts agricultural college, and the institutions for deaf-mutes; and I could not allow myself to do the slightest thing which might have even the appearance of dragging it back among the eleëmosynary and reformatory establishments. In my judgment, the meetings in which the cause of the blind ought to be regularly and officially represented by their instructors are not those of the national conference

of charities and corrections, but those of the
American institute of instruction, and the national
educational association.   No doubt much practical
benefit can be derived from the deliberations of
the former body, or from personal acquaintance and
comparison of notes with men and women who
labor in the field of benevolence, and are more or
less familiar with the management of public institutions; but the experience and knowledge obtained
from active coöperation with the leading educators
of the country, and from participation in such dis-
cussions as pertain to the improvement of the
methods of teaching, mental development, moral
culture, physical and technical training, school
discipline, and the like, are of far greater importance.

For these reasons I felt constrained not only to
request that my name should be dropped from the
list of members of a standing committee of the
national conference of charities, but to raise my
feeble voice against the injustice of classifying the
schools for the blind with eleëmosynary, penal, or
reformatory institutions.

CONCLUSION.

In bringing this report to a close, I beg leave to
say that the institution, which hardly dared to call
itself a nucleus fifty years ago, to-day stands on
the firmest foundations of public confidence and
beneficent activity.   As we cast a glance over the

history of the past, and trace the wandering course of the river of memory, its earlier rills lead us up among the hills of high endeavor, the thinner atmosphere, where the first pioneers of the blind labored for them in the midst of immense and often disheartening difficulties, struggled for them with the mightiest odds, and drove from their path the demons of doubt, incredulity, discouragement and despair. Oh! if but a breath of the intrepid spirit of these earliest days still animates us, we can never fail, even in the most arduous and perplexing undertakings! If there still remains within us a spark of the old zeal which led our Cadmus onward, until nothing, not even the walls of darkness and silence shutting in the most secluded of human beings, could resist his magic touch, the smallest child will feel the contagion of the divine enthusiasm for wisdom, usefulness, and the bringing about of a more perfect good on earth.

May the grand motives and noble purposes of the originators and fathers of our enterprise, who nursed it in its infancy, and carried it forward to the fair goal of a brilliant and permanent success, abide by their successors now and for ever.

Respectfully submitted by

M. ANAGNOS.

ACKNOWLEDGMENTS.

Among the pleasant duties incident to the close of the year is that of expressing our heartfelt thanks and grateful acknowledgments to the following artists, *littérateurs*, societies, proprietors, managers, editors, and publishers, for concerts and various musical entertainments ; for operas, oratorios, lectures, readings, and for an excellent supply of periodicals and weekly papers, minerals and specimens of various kinds.

As I have said in previous reports, these favors are not only a source of pleasure and happiness to our pupils, but also a valuable means of æsthetic culture, of social intercourse and of mental stimulus and improvement. As far as we know, there is no community in the world which does half so much for the gratification and improvement of its unfortunate members as that of Boston does for our pupils.

I. — Acknowledgments for Concerts and Operas in the City.

To the music committee of the Harvard Musical Association, we are indebted for twelve tickets to each of their five symphony concerts.

To Mr. Henry Lee Higginson, for thirty tickets to each of the public rehearsals of his series of twenty symphony concerts.

To the Philharmonic Society, for twelve tickets to each of their eight public rehearsals.

To the Händel and Haydn Society, through Mr. C. C. Perkins, president, and Mr. A. Parker Browne, secretary, for admission to two oratorios and two public rehearsals.

To Messrs. Tompkins and Hill, proprietors of the Boston theatre, for admission of unlimited numbers to five operas.

To Mr. Frye, for eighty-five tickets to the opera of Lucia in the Mechanic Charitable Association building.

To Mr. George H. Wilson, for seven tickets to the opera of Fidelio, given as a concert.

To the Cecilia society, through its secretary, Mr. Arthur Reed, for four tickets to each of five concerts.   To Mr. C. C. Perkins, for five tickets to two of these concerts.

To Mr. B. J. Lang, for admission to the rehearsal of Berlioz's Requiem.

To the Apollo Club, through its secretary, Mr. Arthur Reed, for six tickets to each of six concerts.

To the Boylston Club, through its secretary, Mr. F. H. Ratcliffe, for eight tickets to each of five concerts.

To the president of the Euterpe society, Mr. C. C. Perkins, for nine tickets to each of four concerts.

To Mr. Wm. Winch, conductor of the Arlington Club, for four tickets.

To Mr. Georg Henschel, for thirty tickets to each of his three concerts.

To Dr. Louis Maas, for ten tickets to each of his two piano recitals.

To Mr. A. P. Peck, for forty tickets to one of Joseffy's piano recitals.

To Mr. E. W. Tyler for ten tickets to each of Mr. Otto Bendix's piano recitals.

To Mr. Loring B. Barnes, for forty tickets to Miss Fannie Barnes's concert.

To Mr. Ernst Perabo, for twenty-five tickets to each of his two piano recitals.

To Mr. Arthur Foote, for six tickets to one piano recital, and the same number to five trio concerts.

To Mr. Wm. H. Sherwood, for six tickets to one piano recital.

To Dr. Tourjée, for admission to two classical and three quarterly conservatory concerts.

To Madame Terese Liebe, for twenty tickets to her concert.

To Mr. Arthur Whiting, for admission to one piano recital.

To Mr. Albert Conant, for twelve tickets to one of the Petersilea conservatory concerts.

To Mrs. Leavitt, of the W. C. T. U. committee, for twenty tickets to the children's temperance festival.

To Miss Anna Dunlap, for six tickets to each of her two concerts.

To Mr. J. F. Winch, for ten tickets to one concert.

II. — Acknowledgments for Concerts given in our Hall.

For a series of recitals and concerts given from time to time in the music hall of the institution, we are greatly indebted to the following artists :—

To Prof. Carl Baerman and Mrs. Clara Doria Rogers.

To Mr. S. B. Whitney, organist, Mrs. G. F. Topliffe, pianist, Mr. G. B. Van Sanvoord, flutist, Mr. E. B. Marble, violinist, and Mr. Arthur Stockbridge, cellist.

To Mr. Albert Meyers, assisted by Miss Annie C. Westervelt, Miss Nellie M. Moore, Mr. B. F. Hammond of Worcester, Mr. Frank Donahoe, organist and pianist, and Mr. J. P. Leahy, elocutionist.

To Mrs. Freeman Cobb, assisted by Miss Fannie Barnes, Miss Hunneman, Mrs. Ella Cleveland Fenderson, Mr. Smith, and Dr. Fenderson.

To Mr. Stark, assisted by Mrs. Starkweather, Mrs. Scott James, Mr. E. R. Eaton, Mr. George Buckmore, and Miss Nason, reader.

To Mr. Clayton Johns, for a piano recital.

To Miss Woodward, for a lecture on Norwegian music, with illustrations.

III. — Acknowledgments for Lectures and Readings.

For various lectures, addresses and readings, our thanks are due to the following friends: Miss Helen McGill, Ph.D., Mrs.

Julia Ward Howe, Mr. F. H. Underwood, Samuel Eliot, LL.D., G. Stanley Hall, Ph.D., W. D. Howells, Mr. R. W. Jamieson, and others.

IV. — *Acknowledgments for Shells, Specimens, etc.*

For a valuable collection of shells and specimens of various kinds we are under lasting obligations to the Boston Natural History Society, through its custodian, Prof. Alpheus Hyatt, who has taken a kind interest in our little museum and has shown his good will and friendliness towards the institution and its beneficiaries in many ways.

V.—*Acknowledgments for Periodicals and Newspapers.*

The editors and publishers of the following reviews, magazines and semi-monthly and weekly papers, continue to be very kind and liberal in sending us their publications gratuitously, which are always cordially welcomed, and perused with interest :—

The N. E. Journal of Education, .	*Boston, Mass.*
The Atlantic, ...	" "
Wide Awake, ...	.. ..
Boston Home Journal, . . .	.. ..
Youth's Companion, ...	.. ..
The Christian, ...	.. ..
The Christian Register, ...	.. ..
The Musical Record, . . .	
The Musical Herald, ...	.. ..
The Folio, ...	.. ..
Littell's Living Age, ...	.. ..
Unitarian Review, ...	
The Watchman, ...	.. ..
The Golden Rule, ...	.. ..
Zion's Herald, ...	.. ..
The Missionary Herald, . . .	

The Salem Register, ... *Salem, Mass.*
The Century, ... *New York, N. Y.*
St. Nicholas, ...   "   "
The Christian Union,   .   .
The Journal of Speculative Philosophy,   "   "
Journal of Health,   .   .   . *Dansville, N. Y.*
Church's Musical Journal,   .   . *Cincinnati, O.*
Goodson Gazette, *Va. Inst. for Deaf-Mutes and Blind.*
Tablet,   .   . *West Va.* "   "   "   "
Companion,   . *Minnesota Institute for Deaf-Mutes.*
Il Mentore dei Ciechi,   .   . *Florence, Italy.*

I desire again to render the most hearty thanks, in behalf of all our pupils, to the kind friends who have thus nobly remembered them. The seeds which their friendly and generous attentions have sown have fallen on no barren ground, but will continue to bear fruit in after years; and the memory of many of these delightful and instructive occasions and valuable gifts will be retained through life.

M. ANAGNOS.

PERKINS INSTITUTION AND MASSACHUSETTS SCHOOL FOR THE BLIND *in account with* EDWARD JACKSON, *Treasurer.*

General Fund.

Dr.		Cr.	
To balance from last year,	$1,288 16	By cash from State of Massachusetts,	$30,000 00
cash paid, Auditors' drafts,	65,281 61	Maine,	3,600 00
taxes,	221 01	New Hampshire,	3,620 00
surveying 197 Endicott st.,	15 00	Connecticut,	4,300 00
Hatch's bill for selling,	96 15	Rhode Island,	3,544 00
stationery,	1 25	Vermont,	2,550 00
estate of R. E. Apthorp, commissions,	66 53	Interest on mortgages,	6,985 00
loaned on mortgage 197 Endicott st.,	2,000 00	rents,	450 00
Chicago, Burlington, and Quincy 4 per cent. bonds,	1,696 28	Boston and Providence R.R. dividends,	240 00
balance on hand,	8,650 43	Fitchburg R.R.,	457 50
		interest on Eastern R.R. bonds,	360 00
		Chicago, Milwaukee and St. Paul,	180 00
		Boston and Lowell,	50 00
		deposits with N.E. Trust Co.,	189 22
		sale of 197 Endicott st.,	3,650 00
		M. Anagnos, director Work Department, $15,680 98	
		sundries, 3,449 84	19,130 70
	$79,306 42		$79,306 42

| | | 1882. | |
| | | Oct. 1, Credit to new account, | 8,650 43 |

EDWARD JACKSON, *Treasurer.*

BOSTON, Oct. 1, 1882.

PERKINS INSTITUTION AND MASSACHUSETTS SCHOOL FOR THE BLIND *in account with* EDWARD JACKSON, *Treasurer.*

Harris Fund.

Dr.			Cr.	
1882.			**1881.**	
Aug. 24, $15,000 C. B. & Q. R. R. 4 per cent. bonds,	$12,732 08		Oct. 1, Balance on hand, ...	$3,761 25
			1882.	
Oct. 1, Balance uninvested, ...	29 17		July 2, Collected on mortgage note, . .	9 000 00
	$12,761 25			$12,761 25
			Oct. 1, Credit to new account, . . .	29 17

EDWARD JACKSON, *Treasurer,*

BOSTON, Oct. 1, 1882.

PERKINS INSTITUTION AND MASSACHUSETTS SCHOOL FOR THE BLIND *in account with* EDWARD JACKSON, *Treasurer.*

Printing Fund.

DR.   CR.

To cash paid, Auditors' drafts,	$5,298 41	
loaned on notes,	92,500 00	
10 C. B. & Q. R. R. 4 per cent. bonds,	8,360 00	
loaned on mortgage,	2,500 00	
	$108,658 41	
1882. Oct. 1, Debit to new account,	39 40	

1881. Oct. 1, Balance,	$21,523 94	
Subscriptions to date,	61,295 50	
1882. Oct. 1, Interest on Ottawa and Burlington R. R. bonds,	300 00	
Interest on Kansas City, St. Joseph and Council Bluffs,	350 00	
Interest on Chicago, Milwaukee and St. Paul,	120 00	
Interest on notes,	2,538 93	
" " Chicago, Burlington and Quincy R. R. bonds,	171 33	
Interest on Deposits at N. B. Trust Co.	150 00	
Amounts received from M. Anagnos,	1,502 89	
" Am. Printing House, Louisville, Ky.	666 42	
" Notes collected,	20,000 00	
Debit to new account,	39 40	
	$108,658 41	

Balance of Harris Fund uninvested,	$29 17	
Balance of General Fund,	8,650 43	
	$8,679 60	
Printing Fund, excess of expenditures over income,	$39 40	
Balance in N. B. Trust Co.,	8,640 20	
	$8,679 60	

BOSTON, Oct. 1, 1882.

EDWARD JACKSON, *Treasurer.*

CERTIFICATE OF THE AUDITING COMMITTEE.

BOSTON, Oct. 9, 1882.

The undersigned, a committee appointed to examine the accounts of the treasurer of the Perkins Institution and Massachusetts School for the Blind, for the year ending Sept. 30, 1882, have attended to that duty, and hereby certify that they find the payments properly vouched and the accounts correctly cast, resulting in a balance of eight thousand six hundred and forty dollars and twenty cents on hand, deposited in the New England Trust Co. to the credit of the institution.

The treasurer also exhibited to us evidence of the following property belonging to the institution.

A. T. FROTHINGHAM,
GEO. L. LOVETT,
Auditing Committee.

General Fund.

Notes secured by mortgage, . .	$40,000 00
30 shares Boston & Providence R. R.,	4,200 00
50 shares Fitchburg R. R , ...	6,374 00
Estate No. 11 Oxford street, Boston, . .	5,500 00
2 Eastern R. R. bonds, ...	1,000 00
2 Chicago, Burlington & Quincy bonds, .	1,686 28
	——— $58,760 28

Harris Fund.

Notes secured by mortgage, . . .	$61,000 00
1 Boston & Lowell R. R. bond, . . .	1,000 00
3 Eastern R. R. bonds, ...	3,000 00
3 Chicago, Milwaukee & St. Paul R. R. bonds, ...	3,000 00
15 Chicago, Burlington & Quincy R. R. bonds, ...	12,732 08
	——— 80,732 08

Printing Fund.

Notes secured by mortgage, . . .	$2,500 00
Temporary notes, ...	82,500 00
2 Chicago, Milwaukee & St. Paul R. R. bonds, ...	2,159 00
5 Ottawa & Burlington R. R. bonds, . .	5,550 00
5 Kansas City, St. Joseph & Council Bluffs bonds, ...	6,200 00
10 Chicago, Burlington & Quincy R. R., .	8,360 00
	——— 107,269 00
	$246,761 36

DETAILED STATEMENT OF TREASURER'S RECEIPTS.

1881.

Oct.	1. Balance on hand, ...	$23,997 03
	7. Interest on note, ...	270 00
	15. Interest on note, ...	150 00
	31. State of Massachusetts, ...	7,500 00
Nov.	17. Discount on note, ...	362 18
	25. Interest on Ottawa & Burlington R. R. bonds,	150 00
	25. Sale of estate No. 11 Endicott street, . .	3,650 00
	29. Interest on note, ...	240 00
Dec.	20. Boston & Providence R. R. dividend, . .	120 00
	24. Interest on note, ...	300 00
	Interest on New England Trust Co., . .	239 82

1882.

Jan.   14 State of Massachusetts, ...   7,500 00

25. Receipts from M. Anagnos, director, as per
   following :—

Income of legacy to Laura Bridgman, ...	$167 90	
State of N. H., acc't B. F. Parker,	45 02	
J. J. Mundo, account of daughter,	50 00	
W. D. Garrison, account of son, .	300 00	
J. R. Cocke, account of self, . .	40 00	
Sale of admission tickets, . .	12 00	
Tuning, ...	500 00	
P. Thatcher, acc't of Henry Boesch,	100 00	
J J. M'Cafferty, acc't of daughter,	50 00	
Gift of Sir Moses Montefiore, . .	21 97	
Receipts of work department:—		
For month of October, $1,591 50		
November, 1,164 44		
December, 1,350 11		
	4,106 05	
Sale of books acc't printing dep't, .	747 10	
		6,140 04

27. Interest on note, ...	303 75
30. " " "	75 00
" " "	75 00
" " "	300 00
Amount carried forward, ...	$51,372 82

Amount brought forward,	.	.	.	$51,372 82

1882.

Jan. 30. Interest on note,	. . . . .	200 00
" " "	. . . . .	125 00
" " "	. . . . .	540 00
Feb. 6. Note collected, .	. . . . .	5,000 00
Interest,	. . . . .	31 25
14. Interest on Kansas City, St Joseph & Council Bluffs R. R. bonds,	. . . .	175 00
Feb. 14. Interest on Milwaukee & St. Paul R. R. bonds,	. . . . .	150 00
Interest on Boston & Lowell R. R. bonds,	.	25 00
28. Interest on note,	. . . .	125 00
March 1. Eastern R. R. coupons,	. . . .	270 00
Sale of note,	. . . . .	10,000 00
Interest on note,	. . . .	687 50
Interest on note,	. . . .	156 57
April 1. Discount on note,	. . . .	155 56
3. State of Massachusetts,	. . . .	7,500 00
5. Interest on Ottawa & Burlington R. R. bonds,	. . . .	150 00
20. Interest on note,	. . . .	305 00
Estate of R. E. Apthorp, for rents collected,	. . . .	200 00

25. M. Anagnos, director, as per following :—

Tuning, ...	$590 00	
Mrs. Knowlton, account of daughter,	. 24 00	
Sale of brooms, account of boys' shop,	. 37 18	
Admission fees, . . .	. 55 47	
Printing department, for boxes, etc.,	. 74 34	
Income of legacy to Laura Bridgman,	. 40 00	
Sale of old junk etc., . . .	. 48 83	
Receipts of work department :—		
For month of January, $1,119 99		
February, 696 53		
March, 890 50		
	2,707 02	
Sale of books, acc't of printing department, ...	487 55	
		4,064 39

29. Interest on note,	. . . .	270 00
Interest on note,	. . . .	150 00
May 1. Boston & Providence R. R. dividend,	. .	120 00
8. American printing house, for the blind, Louisville, Ky., .	. . .	581 25

Amount carried forward,	. . . .	$82,354 34

Amount brought forward, ...				$82,354 34

1882.

May	27. Interest on note, ...			240 00
	" " "			99 40
	" " "			300 00
	30. " " "			200 00
July	1. " " "			125 00
	6. " " "			540 00
July	7. State of Massachusetts, ...			7,500 00
	13. Interest on Kansas City, St. Joseph & Council Bluffs R. R. bonds, . . .			175 00
	15. " " Chicago, Burlington & Quincy R. R. bonds, ...			150 00
	" " Boston & Lowell R. R. bonds, .			25 00
July	25. Interest on note, ...			300 00
	" " "			75 00
	" " "			75 00
	28 Payment of one-half mortgage note, . .			9,000 00
	Interest on mortgage note, ...			810 00
Aug.	4. Interest on Chicago, Burlington & Quincy R. R. bonds, ...			200 00
	Note collected, ...			10,000 00

M. Anagnos, director, as per following:—

J. J. M'Cafferty, acc't of daughter,	$50 00			
F. A. Hosmer, account of son, .	300 00			
J. R Cocke, account of self, . .	60 00			
Tuning, ...	300 00			
Sale of soap-grease, . .	31 24			

Receipts of work department:—

For month of April,	$1,234 29			
May,	1,322 53			
June,	1,687 43			
	———— 4,244 25			
Sale of books, acc't of printing dep't, ...	71 00			
				5,056 49
12. American printing house for the blind, Louisville, Ky., ...				85 75
J. V. Apthorp, rents collected, . . .				250 00
State of Connecticut for board and tuition of beneficiaries, ...				4,300 00
Discount on note, ...				228 75
15. Interest on notes, ...				303 13

Amount carried forward, ...				$122,392 86

Amount brought forward, ... $122,392 86

1882.
Aug.   15. State of Vermont for board and tuition of
               beneficiaries, ...   2,550 00
           State of Rhode Island, board and tuition of
               beneficiaries, ...   3,544 00
           State of Maine for board and tuition of bene-
               ficiaries, ...   3,600 00
           Notes collected, ...   15,000 00
Sept   12. Interest on Eastern R. R. bonds, . . .   90 00
       18. Interest on note, ...   125 00
           Discount on note, ...   300 00
       26. Fitchburg R. R. dividends, ...   457 50
           Notes collected, ...   10,000 00
           Interest   " 30 55
       29. Note   " 10,000 00
           Discount on note, ...   362 19
       30. State of New Hampshire for board and tui-
               tion of beneficiaries, ...   3,620 00
           Interest on note, ...   687 50
           M. Anagnos, director, as per following :—
           Mrs. Knowlton account of daughter, $24 00
           Tuning, ...   314 24
           Sale of brooms, ...   23 36
           Admission tickets, ...   27 96
           Seating bench and tools, . .   23 55
           Sale of old junk etc., . . .   45 98
           Printing department, for maps, etc.,   92 80
           Receipts of work department :—
           For month of July, $1,697 26
                      August,   934 06
                      September, 1,992 22   4,623 54
           Sale of books, acc't of printing de-
               partment, ...   197 24
                                                  ──────
                                                  5,372 67
           Subscriptions to printing fund, . .   61,296 00
                                                  ──────────
                                                  $239,428 27

───────────────

ANALYSIS OF TREASURER'S RECEIPTS.

The treasurer's account shows that the total receipts
    for the year were $239,428 27
Less cash on hand at the beginning of the year, . .   23,997 03
                                                  ──────────
                                                  $215,431 24

Ordinary Receipts.

From State of Massachusetts, . . .	$30,000 00	
beneficiaries of other states and individuals, ...	18,864 92	
interest, coupons and rents, . .	12,570 65	
		$61,435 57

Extraordinary Receipts.

From work department for sale of articles made by the blind, etc., . . .	$15,680 86	
sale of embossed books, maps, etc., .	2,169 89	
sale of real estate, ...	3,650 00	
tuning, ...	1,704 24	
sale of brooms at boys' shop, . .	60 54	
sale of admission tickets, . . .	95 43	
donation, ...	21 97	
sale of bench and tools, . . .	23 55	
printing department, maps, boxes, etc.,	167 14	
sale of old junk, soap-grease, etc., .	126 05	
notes, ...	69,000 00	
subscriptions to printing fund, . .	61,296 00	
		153,995 67
		$215,431 24

GENERAL ANALYSIS OF STEWARD'S ACCOUNT.

DR.

Receipts from auditors' drafts, General Acct.,	$65,281 61	
Receipts from auditors' drafts, Printing, .	5,298 41	$70,580 02
Less amount due steward Oct. 1, 1881, . . .		1,185 01
		$69,395 01

CR.

Ordinary expenses as per schedule annexed,	$44,748 28	
Extraordinary expenses as per schedule annexed, ...	18,389 76	
Expenses of printing department, . .	5,276 16	
	$68,414 20	
Cash on hand, General Acct., . $958 56		
Cash on hand, Printing Acct , . 22 25	980 81	
		$69,395 01

ANALYSIS OF EXPENDITURES FOR THE YEAR ENDING SEPT. 30, 1882,
AS PER STEWARD'S ACCOUNT.

Meat, 28,318 lbs.,	$3,057 33	
Fish, 4,285 lbs.,	242 87	
Butter, 5,458 lbs ,	1,918 62	
Rice, sago, etc.,	53 42	
Bread, flour and meal,	1,273 82	
Potatoes and other vegetables,	929 49	
Fruit,	512 40	
Milk, 21,516 qts ,	1,371 13	
Sugar, 7,343 lbs.,	710 17	
Tea and coffee, 610 lbs.,	201 25	
Groceries,	907 33	
Gas and oil,	487 13	
Coal and wood,	2,192 12	
Sundry articles of consumption,	111 61	
Salaries, superintendence, and instruction,	15,685 12	
Domestic wages,	4,137 00	
Outside aid,	253 49	
Medicines and medical aid,	45 42	
Furniture and bedding,	3,751 00	
Clothing and mending,	20 30	
Musical instruments,	443 38	
Expenses of tuning department,	756 38	
Expenses of boys' shop,	87 60	
Expenses of stable,	180 33	
Books, stationery and apparatus,	1,493 62	
Ordinary construction and repairs,	2,873 62	
Taxes and insurance,	570 10	
Travelling expenses,	51 32	
Rent of office in town,	250 00	
Board of men and clerk during vacation,	79 00	
Sundries,	101 91	
		$44,748 28
Extraordinary Expenses.		
Extraordinary construction and repairs,	335 97	
Bills to be refunded,	137 00	
Beneficiaries of Harris Fund,	880 00	
Lawyer's fees,	213 73	
Expenses at Mechanics' Fair	75 00	
Expenses of work department	16,748 06	
		18,389 76
		$63,138 04

ANALYSIS OF ACCOUNTS OF PRINTING DEPARTMENT.

Type, ...	$313 98
Machinery, ...	418 10
Labor, ...	1,331 67
Stock, ...	920 52
Electrotyping, ...	1,172 90
Binding, ...	922 70
Circulars, stationery, etc., ...	86 38
Travelling expenses, ... •	109 91
	$5,276 16

GENERAL ABSTRACT OF ACCOUNT OF THE WORK DEPARTMENT,
October 1st, 1882.

Liabilities.

Due to the institution for investments since the first date, ...	$43,657 87	
Excess of expenditures over receipts, .	1,067 20	
		$44,725 07

Assets.

Stock on hand Oct. 1, 1882, . . .	$4,803 89	
Debts due Oct. 1, 1882, ...	1,543 12	
		6,347 01
		$38,378 06

Balance against the work department, Oct. 1, 1882, .	$38,378 06	
Balance against the work department, Oct. 1, 1881, .	37,205 32	
		$1,172 74
Less uncollectable bills from Dec. 6, 1878 to April 2, 1880, charged off, ...		55 45
Cost of carrying on the work department for the year ending Sept. 30, 1882, ...		$1,117 29

Cash received for sales during the year, .	$15,680 86	
Excess of expenditures over receipts, .	1,067 20	
		$16,748 06

Salaries and wages paid to blind people,	$3,600 81	
Salaries paid to seeing people, . .	2,445 79	
Sundries for stock, etc., ...	10,701 46	
		$16,748 06

ACCOUNT OF STOCK, OCT. 1, 1882.

Real estate, ...		$254,539 00
Railroad stock, ...		13,260 28
Notes, ...		40,000 00
Harris fund, ...		80,732 08
Printing fund, ...		107,269 00
Household furniture, ...		17,200 00
Provisions and supplies, ...		604 53
Wood and coal, ...		2,739 12
Stock in work department, ...		4,803 89
Musical department, viz.,—		
One large organ, ...	$5,500 00	
Four small organs, ...	750 00	
Forty-five pianos, ...	11,000 00	
Brass and reed instruments, . .	950 00	
		18,200 00
Books in printing office, ...		8,100 00
Stereotype plates, ...		3,900 00
School furniture and apparatus, . . .		7,700 00
Musical library, ...		600 00
Library of books in common type, . .		2,900 00
Library of books in raised type, . .		6,000 00
Boys' shop, ...		105 00
Stable and tools, ...		755 00
		$569,407 90

LIST OF SUBSCRIBERS TO PRINTING FUND.

Amount acknowledged in the last Report,	$44,365 20
Moses Hunt,	200 00
A Bostonian, through C. P. Curtis,	4,000 00
P. C. Brooks,	100 00
F., through S. G. Snelling,	40 00
B. S. Rotch,	500 00
F. R. Sears,	200 00
S. T. Morse,	25 00
Mrs. B. L. Young,	200 00
Moses Hunt (final),	100 00
R. T. Paine, Jr. (to be used as income),	500 00
A Friend, through S. G. S.,	500 00
Children's Mission Society, North Adams,	25 00
A Lady, through R. E. Apthorp,	1,000 00
A. Nickerson,	25 00
J. L. Gardner,	300 00
James Sturgis,	50 00
R. H. Weld,	25 00
Mrs. E. F. Lang, sales of her blind daughter's poems,	10 50
J. R. Coolidge,	50 00
F. W. Hunnewell,	100 00
Mrs. James Lawrence,	25 00
George W. A. Williams,	250 00
Henry Lee,	5,000 00
G. S. Curtis,	100 00
Mrs. S. E. Guild (second donation),	50 00
Dr. David W. Cheever,	25 00
Henry S. Shaw,	100 00
W. Endicott, Jr.,	1,000 00
R. C. Greenleaf,	1,000 00
A Friend, through S. G. Snelling,	500 00
Theodore Lyman,	50 00
Mrs. P. C. Brooks (to be used as income),	500 00
C. W Amory,	100 00
Mrs. Gardner Brewer,	100 00
H. B. Rogers,	1,000 00

Amount carried forward,	$62,115 70

Amount brought forward,	$62,115 70
Mrs. William Amory,	500 00
L. M. Standish,	20 00
Woburn Unitarian Sunday School,	18 87
F. W. Palfrey,	10 00
C. J. White,	30 00
Two Friends,	2 00
Seven Friends, in Randolph,	520 00
A Friend,	5 00
J. B. Glover,	200 00
Mrs. J. T. Coolidge,	100 00
F. C. Foster,	100 00
Two Friends,	11 00
G. M. W.,	5 00
A Friend, through S. G. S.,	200 00
G. A. Gardner,	200 00
Willard G Gross,	5 00
A sincere Friend,	5 00
Mrs. B. W. Taggard,	25 00
Miss M. A. Wales,	50 00
Miss Susan Weld,	5 00
F. C. Lowell,	25 00
Mrs. C. P. Curtis, Senior,	35 00
A. Parker Browne,	10 00
C. C. J.,	100 00
Mrs. W. Appleton,	500 00
Mrs. P. C. Brooks (second donation to be used as income),	500 00
Mrs. M. R. Peabody,	5 00
John Richardson,	35 00
Friends, through Miss Cruft,	100 00
Mrs. and Miss ——,	115 00
Charles L. Young,	100 00
Mrs. J. F. Clarke,	25 00
Miss Cora H. Clarke,	5 00
Mrs. William W. Warren,	100 00
Miss E. F. Mason,	500 00
Miss Ida M. Mason,	500 00
Mrs. Sarah S. Fay (second subscription),	1,000 00
A Friend,	200 00
Mrs. Caroline Merriam,	100 00
W.,	50 00
George C. Richardson,	500 00
Mrs. A. W. Davis,	50 00
Mrs. M. B. Sigourney,	100 00
Amount carried forward,	$68,782 57

Amount brought forward, ...	$68,782 57
W. D. Pickman, ...	500 00
Jona. French, ...	100 00
J. C. Palfrey, ...	50 00
R. A. & M. G., ...	• 50 00
A Friend, through S. G. S., ...	250 00
Samuel C Cobb, ...	50 00
Three Friends, ...	3 00
Mrs. J. H. Wolcott (second donation), . . .	300 00
J. H. Weeks, ...	25 00
S. W. Rodman, ...	50 00
A Friend, ...	50 00
S. E. and A., ...	10 00
Miss Madelaine C. Mixter, ...	250 00
Miss Helen K. Mixter, ...	250 00
Macullar Parker & Co., ...	250 00
A. T Lyman, ...	50 00
Mrs. Fred Sears, Jr., ...	25 00
E. D. Peters, ...	25 00
Delia D. Thorndike, ...	50 00
J. P. Bradlee, ...	100 00
Miss Black, ...	100 00
G. N. Black, ...	500 00
Nevins & Co., ...	1,000 00
W. S. Eaton, ...	100 00
J. C. Ropes, ...	50 00
T. Lyman, ...	50 00
Mrs. Isaac Sweetser, ...	300 00
E. Whitney, ...	500 00
Mrs. W. E. Coffin, ...	50 00
Francis Andrews, ...	25 00
Mrs. G. R. Minot, ...	25 00
Mrs. David Sears, ...	50 00
M. D. and J. P. Spaulding, ...	1,000 00
J. N. B., ...	5 00
Oliver Ames, ...	250 00
Mrs. Elisha Atkins, ...	300 00
C. E. Ware, ...	100 00
A Friend, through S. G. S., ...	50 00
Miss A. D. Torrey, ...	50 00
Mrs. Charles Webb Howard, California, . . .	250 00
James H. Blake, ...	100 00
Mrs. J. I. Bowditch, ...	200 00
George P. Denny, ...	100 00
Amount carried forward, . . .	$76,375 57

Amount brought forward,	$76,375 57
J. W. Wheelwright,	50 00
S. Johnson,	200 00
M. C. Ferris,	50 00
H. C. Grant,	10 00
Mrs. Caroline Merriam,	50 00
Charles Merriam,	100 00
John Pickett, Beverly	200 00
Rev. Frederick Frothingham,	1,000 00
George G. Lowell,	50 00
Mrs. C. H. Joy,	500 00
Mrs. Theodore Chase,	20 00
R. E. Robbins,	500 00
Miss A. G. Thayer,	500 00
Rev. J. H. Means,	25 00
S. G. Deblois,	25 00
A. T. Perkins,	50 00
Mrs. A. Hemenway, Jr.,	200 00
Mrs. S. Piper,	5 00
W. T. Piper,	5 00
Anonymous,	10 00
R.,	1 00
Mrs. W. F. Cary,	200 00
Mrs. F. A. Brooks,	50 00
Miss Susan I. Linzee,	100 00
W. T. Glidden,	100 00
S. R Payson,	500 00
Mrs. S. Cabot, Sen.,	200 00
J. M. Prendergast,	50 00
Mrs. Walter Baker,	300 00
Miss S. F. King,	10 00
Mrs. King, Attleboro',	5 00
A. J. Templin,	1 00
H. B. Cross,	1 00
A. B. T. Myers,	5 00
Mrs. E. Pickering,	5 00
Thomas Mack,	100 00
J H Sturgis,	50 00
Stephen Salisbury, Worcester,	3,000 00
B. P. Cheney,	1,000 00
B. Schlesinger,	200 00
J. L. Little,	500 00
Miss C. A. Brewer,	100 00
Sebastian B. Schlesinger,	25 00
Amount carried forward,	$86,428 57

Amount brought forward, ...	$86,428 57
Mrs. F. G. Willard, ...	25 00
Hon. W. W. Hoppin, Providence, ...	35 38
A. B. Aruold, "	25 00
D. R. Brown, "	5 00
Two Friends in Boston, ...	100 00
Mrs. Helena M. Kent, ...	100 00
A. G. Weeks, ...	200 00
S E. Peabody, ...	200 00
H. M. Whitney, ...	200 00
Easter collection in Trinity church, . . .	20 00
Mrs. H. H. Fay, ...	50 00
Alexander Cochrane, ...	250 00
H. A. Whitney, ...	100 00
H. C. Lodge, ...	100 00
F. L. Ames, ...	1,000 00
E. H. Baker, ...	100 00
C. U. Cotting, ...	*200 00
J. F. Osgood, ...	200 00
Mrs. Wm. F. Weld (last thousand to make up $100,000),	1,000 00
A Friend, ...	50 00
G. Higginson, ...	500 00
Isaac Thacher, ...	100 00
Mrs. F. H. Bradlee, ...	100 00
K. W. Sears, ...	100 00
S. W. Marston, ...	250 00
F. H. Bradlee, ...	100 00
Joseph Burnett, ...	100 00
Mrs C. H. Joy, ...	500 00
J. A Beebe, ...	50 00
J. W. Linzee, ...	50 00
Cash, ...	50 00
W. S. C., ...	250 00
C. F. Shimmin, ...	25 00
H. B. Rogers ($5,000 in all), ...	2,000 00
W. Endicott, Jr. ($5,000 in all), ...	4,000 00
C. W. Galloupe, ...	100 00
A. Glover, ...	100 00
J. N. Fiske, ...	100 00
Through W. F. Apthorp, ...	100 00
Mrs. G. W. Hammond, ...	10 00
Mrs. S. A. Miller, ...	5 00
S. Weaver, ...	5 00
L. A. Tillinghast, ...	5 00
Amount carried forward, ...	$98,988 95

Amount brought forward, ...	$98,988 95
T. Little, ...	1 25
Joshua Gray, ...	2 00
B. F. Gilman, ...	2 00
W. C. Cabot, ...	100 00
Mrs. Robert Swan, ...	20 00

Providence, R. I.

Cash, through Mr. Howard, ...	10 00
J. H. and J. Chace, ...	100 00
Henry W. Gardner, ...	50 00
Rt. Rev. Thomas M. Clark, ...	20 00
Jacob Dunnell, ...	100 00
A. D. Lockwood, ...	100 00
James Boyce, ...	20 00
T. P. I. Goddard, ...	200 00
Mr. and Mrs. William Gammell, ...	1,000 00
A Friend, ...	50 00
A. H. Okie, ...	10 00
A. O. Bourn, ...	25 00
Miss A. G. Beckwith, ...	50 00
Cash, ...	102 00
Hon. Wm. S. Hayward, ...	100 00
Fitz James Rice, ...	100 00
William Goddard, ...	250 00
S. S. Sprague, ...	100 00
Mrs. E. A. Shepard, ...	200 00
James Coats, ...	300 00
Rowland Hazard, ...	200 00
D. Goff & Sons, ...	200 00
Miss Caroline Richmond, ...	20 00
Joseph A. Barker, ...	50 00
Callender, McAuslan & Troup, ...	100 00
Hon. Henry Howard, ...	25 00
Edwin Barrows, ...	5 00
Mr. and Mrs. Henry G. Russell, ...	300 00
Mrs. Anna A. Ives, ...	200 00
S. H. Greene & Sons, ...	100 00
Daniel E. Day, ...	100 00
Henry L. Kendall, ...	50 00
Fred I. Marcy, ...	50 00
W. F. Sayles, ...	100 00
R. Sherman, ...	10 00
Geo. W. Dart, ...	10 00

Amount carried forward, ...	$103,521 20

Amount brought forward, ...	. $103,521 20
Mrs. J. C. Brown, ...	50 00
A Friend, ...	50 00
Hon. A. C. Howard, ...	100 00
Miss Julia Bullock, ...	100 00
Whitford, Aldrich & Co., ...	25 00
L. Sharpe, ...	50 00
Hiram B. Aylesworth, ...	25 00
Fannie Kimball (collected from friends), . . .	15 00
Free Religious School, ...	5 00
Mrs. Col. William Earle, ...	10 00
William Grosvenor, ...	50 00
Mrs. T. Beckwith, ...	25 00
Benjamin F. Greene, ...	100 00
D. G. Littlefield, ...	50 00
L. B. Darling, ...	25 00
John A. Adams, ...	25 00
H. H. Thomas, ...	25 00
H. N. Slater, Jr., ...	25 00
L. B. Mason, ...	50 00
Augustus Woodbury, ...	10 00
Rev. C. A. L. Richards, ...	20 00
William Binney, ...	25 00
Edward Jollie, ...	10 00
Emily Waterman, ...	20 00
D. C. Jenckes, ...	10 00
George H. Corliss, ...	300 00
James J. Bundy	25 00
J. A. McCloy, ...	. 25 00
Mrs. Sarah Potter, ...	25
Willard Manchester, ...	5
Walter H. Manchester, ...	5
C. D. Wiggin, ...	5
C. A. Darling, ...	5
S. N. Smith, ...	5
J. S. Hudson, ...	5
J. E. Sturdy, ...	5
W. H. Fenner, ...	5
Knowles, Anthony & Danielson, ...	100 00
Cash, ...	98 00
A Friend, ...	2
George L. Claflin & Co., ...	25
F. C. Sayles, ...	100 00
Benj. F. Thurston, ...	25 00
Amount carried forward, ...	. $105,186 20

Amount brought forward,	$105,186 20
George Owen,	25 00
Potter & Buffington,	25 00
Rt. Rev. Thomas F. Hendricken,	25 00
Charles H. George,	25 00
E. P. Chapin,	25 00
Charles E. Carpenter,	50 00
Hon Henry Lippitt,	200 00
Henry J Steere,	100 00
J. T. Snow,	10 00
A. L. Calder,	10 00
A. B. Gardiner,	5 00
W. B. Wightman,	25 00
Mrs. M. A. Turner,	25 00
A. B. McCrillis,	10 00
G. W. Ladd,	15 00
John A. Brown,	25 00
Jesse Metcalf,	25 00
E. H. Brown,	10 00
F. M. Ballou,	10 00
L. K. J.,	10 00
H. B. M.,	10 00
John S. Palmer,	25 00
Mrs. T. J. Hill,	50 00
George M. Turner,	10 00
A. B. Hawes,	10 00
Amos R. Turner,	5 00
Mrs. W. H. H. Brayman,	5 00
Mrs. N. B. Horton,	5 00
C. Wiggin,	5 00
J. C. Nichols,	5 00
James T. Bower,	1 00
Sadie E. Bower,	1 00
Russell Vaughn,	2 00
J. C. Ellis,	1 00
S. B. Wickes,	1 00
H. Phinney,	2 00
J. H. Eldredge,	1 00
Mrs. W. H. Cornell,	1 00
Samuel P. Colt,	25 00
Isaac Lindsley,	2 00
B. B. Edmands,	5 00
L. D. C.,	5 00
S. H. Tingley,	25 00
Mrs. Fielden and Miss Chace's school,	26 00
	$106,069 20

LIST OF EMBOSSED BOOKS,

Printed at the Perkins Institution and Massachusetts School for the Blind.

TITLE OF BOOK.	No. of Volumes.	Price per Volume.
Howe's Cyclopædia,	8	$4 00
Baxter's Call,	1	2 50
Book of Proverbs,	1	2 00
Book of Psalms,	1	3 00
New Testament,	3	2 50
Book of Common Prayer,	1	4 00
Hymns for the Blind,	1	2 00
Pilgrim's Progress,	1	4 00
Life of Melanchthon,	1	1 00
Natural Theology,	1	4 00
Combe's Constitution of Man,	1	4 00
Selections from the Works of Swedenborg,	1	–
Second Table of Logarithms,	1	3 00
Philosophy of Natural History,	1	3 00
Huxley's Science Primers, Introductory,	1	2 00
Memoir of Dr. Samuel G. Howe,	1	3 00
Cutter's Anatomy, Physiology and Hygiene,	1	3 00
Viri Romæ, new edition with additions,	1	2 00
Musical Characters used by the seeing,	1	,35
Guyot's Geography,	1	4 00
Scribner's Geographical Reader,	1	2 50
Dickens's Child's History of England,	2	3 00
Anderson's History of the United States,	1	2 50
Higginson's Young Folks' History of the United States,	1	3 50
Schmitz's History of Greece,	1	3 00
Schmitz's History of Rome,	1	2 50
Freeman's History of Europe,	1	2 50
An Account of the Most Celebrated Diamonds,	1	50
Extracts from British and American Literature,	2	3 00
American Prose,	2	3 00
Hawthorne's Tanglewood Tales,	2	2 00
Dickens's Old Curiosity Shop,	3	4 00
Dickens's Christmas Carol, with extracts from Pickwick,	1	3 00
Goldsmith's Vicar of Wakefield,	1	3 00
George Eliot's Silas Marner,	1	3 50
Biographical Sketch of George Eliot,	1	25
Milton's Paradise Lost,	2	3 00
Pope's Essay on Man and other Poems,	1	2 50
Shakspeare's Hamlet and Julius Cæsar,	1	4 00
Byron's Hebrew Melodies and Childe Harold,	1	3 00
Tennyson's In Memoriam and other Poems,	1	3 00
Longfellow's Evangeline,	1	2 00
Longfellow's Evangeline and other Poems,	1	3 00
Whittier's Poems,	1	3 00
Lowell's Poems,	1	3 00
Bryant's Poems,	1	3 00
Longfellow's Birthday, by J. R. Anagnos,	1	25
Commemoration Ode, by H. W. Stratton,	1	10

LIST OF EMBOSSED BOOKS,

Printed at the Perkins Institution and Massachusetts School for the Blind.

TITLE OF BOOK.	No. of Volumes.	Price per Volume.
JUVENILE BOOKS.		
An Eclectic Primer,	1	$0 40
Child's First Book, .	1	40
Child's Second Book,	1	40
Child's Third Book,	1	40
Child's Fourth Book,	1	40
Child's Fifth Book, .	1	40
Child's Sixth Book,	1	40
Child's Seventh Book, .	1	40
Youth's Library, vol. 1st,	1	1 25
Youth's Library, " 2d, .	1	1 25
Youth's Library, " 3d, .	1	1 25
Youth's Library, " 4th,	1	1 25
Youth's Library, " 5th,	1	1 25
Youth's Library, " 6th,	1	1 25
Youth's Library, " 7th,	1	1 25
Children's Fairy Book, by M. Anagnos, .	1	2 50
Andersen's Stories and Tales, .	1	3 00
Eliot's Six Arabian Nights, .	1	3 00
Lodge's Twelve Popular Tales,	1	2 00

N.B.   The prices in the above list are set down per volume, not per set.

LIST OF APPLIANCES AND TANGIBLE APPARATUS

Made at the Perkins Institution and Massachusetts School for the Blind.

GEOGRAPHY.

I. — *Wall-Maps.*

1. The Hemispheres, ... size, 42 by 52 inches.
2. United States, Mexico and Canada, . . " " "
3. North America, ... " " "
4. South America, ... " " "
5. Europe, ... " " "
6. Asia, ... " " "
7. Africa, ... " " "
8. The World on Mercator's Projection, . . " " "

Each $35, or the set, $280.

II. — *Dissected Maps.*

1. Eastern Hemisphere, ... size, 30 by 36 inches.
2. Western Hemisphere, ... " " "
3. North America, ... " " "
4. United States, ... " " "
5. South America, ... " " "
6. Europe, ... " " "
7. Asia, ... " " "
8. Africa, ... " " "

Each $23, or the set, $184.

These maps are considered, in point of workmanship, accuracy and distinctness of outline, durability and beauty, far superior to all thus far made in Europe or in this country.

"The New England Journal of Education" says, "They are very strong, present a fine, bright surface, and are an ornament to any school-room."

III. — *Pin-Maps..*

Cushions for pin-maps and diagrams, ... each, $0 75

ARITHMETIC.

Ciphering-boards made of brass strips, nickel-plated, . each, $4 25
Ciphering-types, nickel-plated, per hundred, . . . " 1 00

WRITING.

Grooved writing-cards, ... each, $0 10
Braille tablets, with metallic bed, ... " 1 50
Braille French tablets, with cloth bed, ... " 1 00
Braille new tablets, with cloth bed, ... 1 00
Braille Daisy tablets, ... 5 00

TERMS OF ADMISSION.

"Candidates for admission must be over nine and under nineteen years of age, and none others shall be admitted." — *Extract from the by-laws.*

Blind children and youth between the ages above prescribed and of sound mind and good moral character, can be admitted to the school by paying $300 per annum. Those among them who belong to the State of Massachusetts and whose parents or guardians are not able to pay the whole or a portion of this sum, can be admitted gratuitously by application to the governor for a warrant.

The following is a good form, though any other will do : —

To His Excellency the Governor.

"SIR, — My son (or daughter, or nephew, or niece, as the case may be), named ——, and aged ——, cannot be instructed in the common schools, for want of sight. I am unable to pay for the tuition at the Perkins Institution and Massachusetts School for the Blind, and I request that your Excellency will give a warrant for free admission.
                    Very respectfully,   —— ——."

The application may be made by any relation or friend, if the parents are dead or absent.

It should be accompanied by a certificate, signed by some regular physician, in this form : —

"I certify, that, in my opinion, —— —— has not sufficient vision to be taught in common schools; and that he is free from epilepsy, and from any contagious disease.
                    (Signed)   —— ——."

These papers should be done up together, and forwarded to the DIRECTOR OF THE INSTITUTION FOR THE BLIND, *South Boston, Mass.*

Blind children and youth residing in Maine, New Hampshire, Vermont, Connecticut and Rhode Island, by applying as above to the Governor, or the "Secretary of State," in their respective States can obtain warrants for free admission.

The sum of $300 above specified covers all expenses (except for clothing), namely, board, lodging, washing, tuition, and the use of books and musical instruments. The pupils must furnish their own clothing, and pay their own fares to and from the institution.

An obligation will be required from some responsible persons, that the pupils shall be kept properly supplied with decent clothing, shall be provided for during vacations, and shall be removed, without expense to the institution, whenever it may be desirable to discharge him.

The usual period of tuition is from five to seven years.

The friends of the pupils can visit them whenever they choose.

The use of tobacco, either in smoking or otherwise, is strictly prohibited in the institution.

Persons applying for admission of children must fill out certain blanks, copies of which will be forwarded to any address on application.

For further information address M. ANAGNOS, DIRECTOR PERKINS INSTITUTION FOR THE BLIND, *South Boston, Mass.*

APPENDIX.

PROCEEDINGS

OF THE

SEMI-CENTENNIAL ANNIVERSARY

AND

COMMENCEMENT EXERCISES

OF THE

PERKINS INSTITUTION AND MASSACHUSETTS SCHOOL FOR THE BLIND.

CELEBRATION

OF THE

FIFTIETH ANNIVERSARY

OF THE

𝔓erkins 𝔦nstitution and 𝔐assachusetts 𝔖chool for the 𝔅lind.

It was in the summer of 1832 that Dr. Howe first gathered, in his father's house, on Pleasant street, the little group of six children with which he commenced the enterprise which, under his paternal care, developed into the Perkins Institution and Massachusetts School for the Blind. It was thought fitting, therefore, that this fiftieth anniversary should be especially and publicly celebrated, and that this celebration should be held in connection with the commencement exercises of the school. The following circular was therefore issued :—

PERKINS INSTITUTION AND MASS. SCHOOL FOR THE BLIND,
BOSTON, May 25, 1882.

In accordance with a vote passed at the last annual meeting of the corporation of this institution, the semi-centennial anniversary of the establishment, together with the commencement exercises of the school, will be held at Tremont Temple, on Tuesday, June 13, at 3 P. M. His Excellency Governor Long has kindly consented to preside, and most of the chief magistrates and some of the mayors and eminent citizens of New England have expressed the intention of attending the exercises. Col. T. W. Higginson will give an address.

You are most cordially invited to honor the occasion with your presence, and witness the performances, which will be to some extent indicative of the character of the work accomplished during the last fifty years for the amelioration of the condition of the blind, and their elevation in the scale of humanity.

JOHN S. DWIGHT,
SAMUEL M. QUINCY,
WILLIAM F. APTHORP,
Committee of Arrangements.

Similar notices and paragraphs calling attention to it were published in most of the Boston journals and in some others. Tickets of admission were printed in raised type in the printing office of the institution, and, accompanied by the following programme of exercises, were sent by order of the committee to former pupils, to members of the corporation, and to benefactors and friends of the institution. Others wishing to attend could obtain tickets by application to the director.

SEMI-CENTENNIAL ANNIVERSARY

AND COMMENCEMENT EXERCISES OF THE

Perkins Institution and Massachusetts School for the Blind,

TREMONT TEMPLE,

TUESDAY, JUNE 13, AT 3 O'CLOCK, P. M.

Doors open at 2.30 o'clock,

HIS EXCELLENCY GOV. LONG PRESIDING.

ADDRESS BY COL. T. W. HIGGINSON.

PROGRAMME.

PART I.

1. Operatic Selections by the   .   .   .   . Band.
2. Introductory Remarks by.   .   His Excellency Gov. Long.
3. Address, ... Col. T. W. Higginson,
4. Aria, — "The trumpet shall sound" (with trumpet obligato),
   from the Messiah (*Handel*),   .   . Wm. B. Hammond.
5. Essay, — "History,"   .   .   .   . Miss Jennie M. Colby.
6. Commemoration Ode, ... Henry W. Stratton.
7. Piano Solo, — Polonaise, opus 53 (*Chopin*), Miss C. A. Heine.
8. Essay, — "Telegraphy" (illust'd by apparatus), Wm. C. Bolles.
9. Declamation, — "The Present Age" (*Channing*),
   Henry B. Thomas.
10. Solo for Alto Horn, Swiss Air and Variations, *Arr. by B. F. Bent*,
    Christopher A. Howland.
11. Essay, — "Literature,"   .   .   .   . Henry E. Boesch.
12. Reading by touch, ... Second Class of Girls.
13. Chorus for Female Voices, — "The Psalm of Life," (*Pinsuti.*)

PART II.

1. Poem, — "An Old Enterprise," by .   .   . Mrs. Anagnos.
2. Exercise in Geography, ... Little Boys.
3. Military Drill and Gymnastics.
4. Fantasie for Cornet (*Gustave Rosarie*),   .   . J. R. Lucier.
5. Essay, — "Energy,"   .   .   . Miss Lenna D. Swinerton.
6. Kindergarten Exercise, ... Little Girls.
7. Valedictory, ... Wm. B. Hammond.
8. Chorus, — a, "Ave Verum," (*Mozart.*)
   b, "Receive the May with Blossoms," (*Franz.*)
9. Award of Diplomas by .   .   .   . Dr. Samuel Eliot.
10. Band, — March, (*J. R. Lucier.*)

There was a very great demand for tickets. The day was beautiful, cool and clear, and an eager crowd awaited the opening of the doors. Quite a number of persons endeavored to enter without tickets, and were greatly disappointed to find that even the offer of payment would not secure them admission. The auditorium and balconies contained a very large assembly, — large not only in numbers, but in its representation of the best culture, refinement and wealth of the city and its suburbs. The platform was occupied by the pupils of the school, the teachers, trustees and a few invited guests. The tasteful grouping of the pupils and the bright dresses of the little girls made it a very attractive scene, and the presence of Laura Bridgman, who was seated among the teachers, greatly enhanced its interest.

Mr. John S. Dwight, chairman of the committee of arrangements, opened the meeting, expressing his regret at having to announce a double disappointment, Governor Long, who had expected to preside, being unavoidably absent in Maine, whither he had gone to take a much-needed rest; and Col. T. W. Higginson, who was to have delivered the address, being prevented from attending by a relapse of his recent severe illness. As a substitute for both, Mr. Dwight said that he knew he should name a most acceptable gentleman in the person of Dr. Samuel Eliot. This announcement was very cordially received, for the warm personal interest of Dr. Eliot in the school renders him its best representative to the public. On taking the chair, Dr. Eliot said, " No words are needed from my lips to tell you what the work is that is accomplished by the school. What the pupils do will be the best comment on the institution."

A medley of operatic selections was then performed
very creditably by the band, after which Dr. Eliot
addressed the audïence as follows :—

ADDRESS OF SAMUEL ELIOT, LL.D.

Members and Friends of the Institution:

We celebrate our semi-centennial at this time because the
first pupils of the school were gathered, half a century ago, in
1832. We might have celebrated it last year, for it was then
fifty years from the appointment of Dr. Howe as director. If it
is true that the teacher makes the school, Dr. Howe made this
school. He brought to it in 1831, and he gave it in every succeeding year until his death, all the energy, all the aspiration
which belonged to him; he formed its character from the first,
and trained not only its pupils, but its teachers ; nor these alone,
but its trustees, its benefactors, the very community, in a wise
understanding of the blind — their powers, their desires, their
destinies. He did not lay the actual foundations, but he built
upon them almost immediately after they were laid, and it is
his design, the idea which he conceived and gradually executed,
which we see and for which we are grateful today. Not to legis-
lation or incorporation, not to any conventional organization
does an institution like this owe its life, but to the heads and
hearts of living men and women. They breathe into it, and it
breathes ; they live for it, and it lives. Our organization dates
from 1829, when the founders of the school obtained an act of
incorporation from the Massachusetts legislature. But that was
not the year when the school was really born, and its fiftieth
anniversary passed without commemoration. Then the work of
the institution was proposed. In 1832 it was begun.

The first to conceive this work, now reaching its half century,
was John D. Fisher. While pursuing his medical studies in
Paris, he had been much interested in the education of the blind in
that city, and what was done there he believed might be done here.
It seems simple enough to us, but it must have seemed difficult
to him, to induce Boston, then a place of comparatively limited
resources, to follow the example of the great capital, and he but
a young man just entering on a profession which claimed his
time and strength as its own. He was brave, however, as well
as benevolent, and went on from one man to another until he had

persuaded a sufficient number of his fellow-citizens to hold a formal meeting, and to take the steps which resulted in the incorporation of the institution. He did more, far more than this. He found Dr. Howe, engaged him in the service which he could not undertake himself and made it certain as anything earthly can be, that the institution would be a reality. Dr. Fisher will always be remembered as our founder. He was one of the first trustees, and continued to promote the work which he had started. But in promoting it he was one of many; in starting it he was alone. Let some, at least, of the recollections which this day stirs centre in him and renew our sense of his high-minded devotion.

The first president of the corporation was Jonathan Phillips, a name for many years before and after synonymous with public spirit. He gave of his wealth, and better still, of his wisdom, to the cause of the blind, as he was wont to give to every good cause of his time. He was a very close friend of Channing, who not only loved him, but leaned upon him. " That noble intellect," wrote the great preacher, " was made for a world of light, that noble heart, for a society of truth and honor." It was fortunate, indeed, for this institution to find such a man to preside over its infancy, and we can believe without any effort that our history would have been a different one but for Jonathan Phillips. Let him, too, be reverently remembered at this hour.

Among the first trustees was a man now of world-wide fame, but then known to few beyond his own circle here, — William H. Prescott. He had a personal interest in the blind, being half blind himself, sometimes unable to use his eyes at all, and always subject to painful restrictions with regard to them. His most important service to this institution appears to have been an article of his writing in the " North American Review " for July, 1830. He wrote not merely to show the need of a school for the blind and the imperative duty of the community to supply it, but yet more to make that duty a hopeful one. The prevailing sentiment concerning the blind, even among their well-wishers, was compassion rather than confidence: they were a sorely afflicted class who could do little or nothing for themselves, and must depend upon the charitable care of those around them. Our trustee spoke in a very different tone. He pointed out the compensations of the blind, showed how their mental grasp might be strengthened by their infirmity, how memory and

reflection might be developed in a life of thought unbroken by
the sights which often distract the minds of the seeing. This
was an inspiring view. It opened new hopes to the blind and to
their friends. It led those about them to trust in their capacity
for independence, in their ability to support themselves, nay, in-
their ability to support others; and from that day to this there
has been no brighter thought in all the thinking about them.
No one can undervalue Prescott's histories. They have glorified
the name of his country as well as his own name. But were he
here to choose between them and the article which gave fresh
spirit to the blind and their friends, he would have reason to be
prouder of the article.

Not long after the earliest pupils were taken under instruction,
the women of Essex county were moved to assist them, and a
fair held in Salem in the early part of 1833 secured nearly three
thousand dollars. Their example was followed by the women of
Boston and the neighborhood, whose fair in Faneuil Hall brought
eleven thousand dollars and upwards to the treasury. The result
in sympathy was worth far more. Thomas Handasyd Perkins
took the lead in expressing what was in many hearts, and gave his
mansion, valued at twenty-five thousand dollars, on condition
that an equal amount in money should be contributed by others.
The subscription proved not only equal to, but double the sum
proposed. Thus in a few months about a hundred thousand dollars was bestowed upon the school, and more than a hundred
thousand friends were led to interest themselves in its welfare.
The poet says, " 'Tis always morning somewhere in the world,"
and it was evidently morning in our institution in the year 1833.
The day which began so brightly has never been overcast. Its
light has gone on increasing towards the noon, and as it has
spread over earth and sky, and filled new spaces with its lustre,
it has been reflected by hundreds of sightless eyes. Of the inner
life into which this illumination has penetrated, of the minds that
have been expanded, of the souls that have been uplifted under
its deep-reaching influence, the story has been written in heaven.

In face of such a record as this, without attempting to make
it fuller, we may well be thankful to keep our anniversary. We
do not keep it for the sake of the past alone, but for that of the
future. This semi-centennial year has witnessed the completion
of the noblest subscription yet made in behalf of the institution
and its constituency. One hundred thousand dollars have been

given to the Howe Memorial Printing Fund, and from this, as from a living fountain, a rich stream of literature for the blind will flow on to the generations yet to be. Books which the blind read with little less facility than we with eyes can show in our reading, will now be multiplied. Libraries will grow up here and everywhere to minister to the intellectual and moral growth of those who have long been waiting for them; and not the blind only, but their seeing neighbors, will rejoice in the abundant harvest.

Nothing done here but bears fruit elsewhere. The opening of this institution was a blessing felt far beyond its borders. Its example was followed in other states, and even in other countries; and many a blind man and woman besides those educated in our school owe their education indirectly to it, and have cause to count its existence a benefit to them. So it will be with our printing fund, so with every good thing that can be grafted on our stock; it will all tell, and wide as the world of the blind will be the effect of each new movement in their behalf originating here. Let us never doubt that our school is capable of doing more for the blind than even the generous name of Massachusetts can fully cover. Let us never cease to hope, and, as far as in us lies, to exert ourselves, that the promise of the last fifty years may be fulfilled in the next fifty, so that when the full centennial anniversary shall come, it may be greeted with heartfelt joy by the children and the children's children who rise up to call this institution doubly blessed.

At the close of the address, Händel's aria, "The trumpet shall sound," was sung by Wm. B. Hammond, with trumpet obligato, and was greeted with hearty applause. It was followed by an essay on "History," which was commended for terseness of phrase, and for the clear and forcible manner in which it was read by the authoress, Jennie M. Colby. Mr. H. W. Stratton then read from his embossed manuscript the following —

COMMEMORATION ODE.

For him to whose large heart each noble cause
  A potent magnet proved,
Whose deeds to yet re-echoing applause,
  The soul of nations moved, —

For him today strong beats our pulse of love.
    A path he slowly oped
That led from depths of gloom to light above;
    With trials well he coped.
They ne'er his hope or might of will could foil,
    Nor patience could consume.
What joy he felt when burst his bud of toil
    Full into triumph's bloom!

What mines of bliss on us hath he bestowed!
    His key of sympathy
The garden gates of knowledge oped, and showed
    The realm within, where we
Now roam and pluck the choicest flowers and fruits,
    Or quench from founts of lore
Our thirst, or analyze thought's deepest roots,
    Drawn forth from learning's store.
And while amid these fragrant walks of truth,
    Another boon is ours, —
The teaching of that golden-sandalled youth,
    Which to us yieldeth powers
To run existence's race and gain a goal
    That equalleth in worth
The highest aim of any artist soul.
    Not all, howe'er, is mirth,
Although we joyful dwell 'mid Pleasure's bowers
    And gardens of delight,
Though compensation's law doth make the hours
    Wing quickly on their flight.

Care's lash on us inflicts as fierce a sting
    As on all other lives;
In us the knife of mental suffering
    Its blade regardless drives;
Affliction and true happiness do not
    Necessity obey,
And ride in friendship's golden chariot
    Along life's rugged way.
Not few are they who foolishly suppose
    Felicity is chief
Companion of our days. We say to those,

Though known to us is grief,
Whate'er the storms that faith doth bring upon
   Life's billowy expanse,
Contentment's ever ready galleon
   A voyage of safety grants.

Our sips from labor's cup, indeed, are few,
   But nourishment they yield ;
From countless scenes are we deprived, 'tis true ;
   But hope doth ever wield
Within our breasts her sceptre.   Time's fast wheel
   With new work e'er is fraught,
Which we shall find.   Our precious books reveal
   The soaring wing of thought.
Ah ! when, upon our fingers, shall we cease
   To number their amount?
Oh, may the years to come, their sum increase
   Beyond the power to count !

From seeds our patron sowed so long ago,
   That climbed progression's path,
Whose steep, full well all enterprises know,
   A goodly harvest hath
By us been reaped of golden knowledge-sheaves,
   Which we have gathered fast
In Memory's bands.   His work today receives
   An impulse ne'er surpassed,
Upon whose chord of influence may deeds
   Of future years be strung.

Our name depends on how each nature heeds
   Its acts and careless tongue ;
All words and deeds form fabrics which the loom
   Of time relentless weaves ;
From these the world of thought within its womb
   Opinions soon conceives,
And reputation thereupon is based.
   It thus behooveth each
To be 'neath caution's willing wing well placed,
   For she doth wisdom teach.

Let us present Minerva with the key
  That opes the treasure-room,—
The thought-filled chambers of the mind; for she,
  As weaver to the loom,
Will feed it with our wisest words and ways;
  And thus the light of fame
Won by our peerless school shall brighter blaze.
  The fabric of a name
Unsullied, pure, may all who in it move
  Bequeath, and, year by year,
More worthy of its founder shall it prove,
  And grow to us more dear.
And when our barks the future's tide shall sweep
  Afar from this loved home,
The cable of remembrance then will keep
  It near, where'er we roam.

For all whose generous gifts afford us aid,
  Within our hearts and lives
The green of gratitude can never fade,
  And ne'er oblivion's gyves
Their names, when tombed in ages, shall surround;
  But shining in the scroll
Of love for fellow-men shall they be found, —
  All time shall them extol.
To those who wisely guide the helm of this
  The flagship of our fleet,
We who have known their care and sympathies,
  Our thanks can ne'er complete.

To ye whose work completion doth await
  Within, our honored walls,
To all our class in every land and state,
  The smiling future calls
To add fresh fuel to the glowing flame
  Of our desire to press
Upon the paths of knowledge, art and fame,
  And capture proud success!
That flame doth generate the steam of will,
  Which turns progression's wheels
Upon the track of life. The eye of skill
  Each danger-sign reveals.

Then let us on, and destinations reach
  Of moral excellence,
As well as other aims of worth : may each
  Heed well experience.
Our efforts let coöperation guide ;
  They who would wed Success
Must woo her well with energies allied
  E'er she will answer — yes.
From out the zenith of the firmament
  Of our advancing cause,
Hope's sun a disk refulgent doth present,
Whose shining ne'er will pause ;
  Nor 'neath the horizon of doubt shall sink
  That orb which lights our way.
Relying in the Guide divine, we link
  Our hearts and lives for aye.

The piano solo (Chopin's Polonaise, Opus 53) which followed, was so finely executed by Miss Constance A. Heine that it won a most enthusiastic encore, to which the young lady responded. Commenting upon this performance, the musical critic of one of our journals remarks that it was played " with a really artistic comprehension of its meaning," adding, " The shading of this pianist is excellent, and she has a brilliancy of execution which is, under the circumstances, marvellous."

The essay on " Telegraphy," by Wm. C. Bolles, which he illustrated by the use of apparatus, giving as a specimen the first despatch ever transmitted, " What hath God wrought?" was listened to with marked attention. It was followed by a declamation, " The Present Age," delivered in a very creditable manner by Henry B. Thomas ; after which Christopher Howland played an alto horn solo, " Swiss Air and variations," which was critically described as being " in every respect a fine performance."

Henry E. Boesch then gave a thoughtful essay on

"Literature," which was favorably received; and four girls of the second class read fluently and gracefully, from embossed volumes, some well-chosen selections from Longfellow, Whittier, Lowell, and Dr. Howe, after which the singing of the "Psalm of Life" by a chorus of female voices finished the first part of the programme.

The second part began with the following poem by Mrs. Anagnos, which was cordially appreciated : —

AN OLD ENTERPRISE.

Fair and bright are trifles new,
But the great is ever true ;
When those trifles fade in dust,
Shines the gold that cannot rust.

Shines through springtide's budding fair,
Shines through summer's ardent air ;
Autumn's frosts cannot impair,
Winter finds it glowing there.

Be our emblem, fairest Gold !
Strong as thou the cause we hold,
Bright as thou our hope and trust,
Firm the faith that cannot rust.

Then from thee a crown we 'll build,
Which no artist needs to gild ;
Circling form gives emblem free
Of thy course, Eternity.

Not the serpent, but the dove,
Heralds forth the cause we love ;
Cause which all conspire to aid,
Which the great their own have made,
And the gentle for it prayed,
And the strong worked undismayed.

Cause we love and love the giver,
Who loves right and helps it ever ;
Who forsakes its banners never,
When the stoutest quail and quiver.

Yes! that cause and thee, its king,
Let the friends of freedom sing!
Freedom from the bands of fate,
Which she weaves with cruel hate;
Freedom for the groping blind,
Freedom for the deathless mind,
Freedom for the healing light,
All its lovers to requite.

The exercise in geography for little boys proved very interesting to the audience. A basket of blocks, each. representing some state or country of a dissected map, was produced, and as fast as they were handed to the boys, they gave the name and locality of each, and answered sundry questions as to form of government, present ruler, etc.; nor did they allow themselves to be entrapped by misleading questions occasionally asked by the teacher.

Perhaps the most striking feature of the occasion, and one which was especially pleasing as showing the attention given to physical development, was the military drill for boys, and the dumb-bell exercise for girls. The former was conducted by Capt. J. H. Wright, and was highly commended for precision of movement both in marching and in the manual of arms. The girls were dressed in a pretty uniform of white with red sashes and trimmings; and their prompt and easy movements in harmony with the music made their performance especially pleasing to the eye.

The cornet solo played by Mr. J. R. Lucier, although very difficult, was rendered clearly even in the most trying passages, and was encored by the audience, and highly praised by musical critics.

The lateness of the hour made it necessary to shorten

the programme, and the essay on " Energy " was accordingly omitted.

A class of little girls then came forward so that the audience could see their work, and began modelling figures from clay ; and while they were thus occupied Wm. B. Hammond delivered the

VALEDICTORY ADDRESS.

If we stand upon a lofty mountain and behold the scenery which stretches before us, we experience feelings of wonder and grandeur ; and it is so to-day. As we stand upon an eminence of fifty years and look down upon the past history of Perkins Institution, we are thrilled with similar emotions. Let us linger for a few moments upon these heights, and briefly picture the scenes which dot the landscape of its history.

Dr. Fisher of Boston first conceived the idea of establishing a school for the blind in this country. While pursuing his studies in Paris, he often visited the institution of the young blind in that city ; and he was so deeply impressed by the advantages which this school afforded its pupils, that he resolved to give the sightless of America similar opportunities. On his return to Boston in 1826 he communicated his intentions to several prominent persons in this city. As a result several meetings were held in behalf of the blind, and in 1829 it was voted that a committee be appointed to ask the legislature for a charter of incorporation. This petition was unanimously granted by both houses.

Dr. Fisher being unable to undertake the enterprise himself, enlisted the sympathies and coöperation of Dr. Samuel G. Howe, who opened a school at his father's residence in Pleasant street, in August, 1832, with a little band of six pupils ; but soon the number of applicants for admission became so numerous that to accommodate them it was necessary that a larger building should be provided. Col. Perkins, realizing this fact, offered his mansion in Pearl street, on condition that the amount of $50,000 be raised by subscriptions. The citizens of Boston responded to the appeal with that generosity and liberality which has always characterized them; and so great was the interest manifested, that in one month this large sum was raised, and in less than one year the legislatures of the several New England states made appropriations, so that their blind children might be educated at the Boston school.

In 1839 the facilities of the institution were greatly increased by the exchange of the Pearl street mansion for the large and commodious building which we now occupy on Dorchester Heights. Year after year witnessed improvements in the building itself, while its utility as an educational establishment was increased with the constant addition of school apparatus, musical instruments, and modes of instruction in handicraft.

The course of study pursued is essentially the same as in the high schools and academies of the United States. The aim of its instructors has been to give the pupils such practical information as will enable them to take their places as intelligent men and women in society.

On the 9th of January, 1876, the institution sustained an irreparable loss in the death of its noble and great founder, Dr. Howe, who had been our beloved and revered director for forty-four years. Mr. Anagnos was then elected by the trustees to fill the vacancy. During his administration the school has made rapid progress in the various branches; but the crowning effort of his labors in our behalf is the recent work of completing the fund for printing embossed books. To him and our dear friend, Mr. Samuel G. Snelling, the blind of New England will owe a lasting debt of gratitude; and we are glad to have this opportunity of returning our heartfelt thanks to them, and to all who by their generosity have afforded us, and those who will come after us, the means of reading for ourselves the best books of the best authors of every age.

That our institution has done a great work, no one can doubt; for she has not only elevated the blind of New England, but her influence has fallen upon the world like the beneficent rays of the sun, to bring forth germs which should spring up into institutions like herself. How well she has done her work may be shown by the statement that at the present time twenty-nine states have their own educational establishments for the blind, the others making provisions for the instruction of their sightless children at the nearest school. The Royal Normal College, which is the pride and boast of England, may be rightly considered as an outgrowth of our institution. Thus far across the Atlantic have the beacon lights of the Boston institution been seen.

In considering the achievements of this school our minds naturally turn to those who by their benevolence have enabled it to accomplish so much. Yet, while we admire these noble men and women, we can only linger upon the name of its founder, Dr. Samuel G. Howe. And though his deeds have inspired the poet, singer and orator to breathe immortal words, we, the children of his labor and love, would bring our offering, though it may be only a simple flower, among the floral tributes to his memory. There are certain phenomena in nature,—the roar of the cataract, thunder, lightning, and the deep bass of the ocean, which fill the mind with awe. Still, I think, as one contemplates a human character which reveals a holy ambition and philanthropic efforts for suffering humanity, that a feeling of sublimity is produced which even the grandeur of nature cannot surpass. Such emotions as these I experience in treating of the character of Dr. Howe,— a character so grand and so vast in its proportions that an abler pen than mine might well hesitate to attempt to portray it. Genius is the shrine at which humanity has always worshipped, and those men upon whom it has been bestowed have too often been honored and immortalized, regardless of true character. Thus it is that we admire the military achievements of Alexander, Cæsar and Napoleon. Yet they were men whose histories were written in blood and in desolated kingdoms, and who sacrificed humanity to an extent which has never been equalled by the greatest pestilence that has scourged the earth. If such men as these claim admiration, how much more must Dr.

Howe, whose genius was not only great, but whose character was above reproach.

There have lived few men to whom humanity owes more than to him whose name we honor today, and it is not too much to affirm that, had he never lived, many men and women who are today enlightened and happy, might be groping in darkness and despair. His philanthropy cannot be better expressed than it has been by our poet Whittier :—

> " Wherever outraged nature
> Asks word or action brave,
> Wherever struggles labor,
> Wherever groans a slave,
> The throbbing heart of freedom finds
> An answer in his own."

It is needless for me to recount the history of this great man, for the whole world knows it. It is written in the annals of Greece, it is proclaimed through the happy countenances of the blind, it is revealed through the intelligence of Laura Bridgman, and it is stamped upon the face of the poor idiot. And what was it that led him to accomplish these deeds which have made his name so famous? Was it to establish an immortal fame? Was it to have his name emblazoned upon the banners of civilization, that all might see his glory? No! for at the time when he was doing these great works, the skeptical public laughed in derision. It was simply the outpouring of his love and pity, which was so great that as we contemplate it we become lost in its vastness ; and as we review its history, we can only exclaim, " Greater works than these can no man do." There have lived great men who have written their glories upon granite and marble ; yet these monuments, like the bodies of their founders, have crumbled into dust. But far different is the fate which the fame of our hero will experience ; for it is not inscribed upon perishable granite or marble, but upon human character itself. As we lay our garland of praise upon his memory, let us not bedeck his tomb with mourning, but rather let us rejoice, for our benefactor is not dead. The truly great never die. Humanity has given him the title of philanthropist, which is the noblest gift it can bestow; and he has won for himself a name which will endure as long as a Greek shall take pride in the glory of his nation, as long as the world shall rejoice in philanthropy, virtue, and the love of God. Until these shall vanish will the name of Dr. Howe stand as one of the brightest stars which adorn the pages of history,—a star which shall never fade, but will always be in the zenith of its glory, shedding its lustre on coming generations, and revealing to the ages the splendor of the nineteenth century.

Today brings us to the close of another year; and as we look back there is much that is pleasant to remember, though it is with sadness that we speak of our friend, the late Mr. Apthorp, who was so long one of our trustees, and who endeared himself to us by his friendly visits and personal interests in our welfare. We shall always treasure in our hearts his kindness, and that of the many friends who have contributed to our happiness.

To His Excellency the Governor of Massachusetts, and to the executives and the legislatures of the several New England states, we are greatly indebted for their liberal appropriations that have enabled the school to carry on its work.

Director, teachers and officers, we who graduate today would pour out our gratitude to you for your kindness and self-sacrifice, for your timely reproofs and watchful care; and though our thanks be but poorly expressed, our gratitude is none the less sincere.

Fellow-classmates, the hour of parting is at hand. We who have journeyed together for so many years, who have been sheltered under the same roof, and have formed ties of brotherhood which death only can sever, are soon to separate; each to go to his own field of labor; and let us seek to live so that we shall be a credit to ourselves, and an honor to our *alma mater*. It has often been said that school days are the happiest in life, and perhaps when our circuit of existence is nearly completed we shall realize this statement; for I am sure that we can never

look back upon the past with other than feelings of gratitude for
the dear friends who have done so much for us, and with joy to
the hours when we played and sang together; yes, and the dear
old building itself, each room of which could tell a story that
would fill our countenances with smiles, and our eyes with tears.

>   " This fond attachment to the well-known place,
>   Where first we started into life's long race,
>   Will maintain its hold with unfailing sway,
>   And we'll feel it in age and our latest day."

At the close of the address the little girls had finished
their modelling, the products of which represented geometrical shapes, articles of common use, fruits and animals.   Each exhibited to the audience the models she had
made, and gave a brief account of their nature and uses.

Mr. Anagnos then spoke, briefly explaining that these
exercises were a specimen of the regular instruction of the
school, and calling attention to the need of a primary or
kindergarten school for those who are too young for admission to this institution, and are, in consequence, suffering
deeply from the lack of early training.   He announced a
determination to effect the establishment of such a school,
and made a brief but earnest appeal for assistance and co-
operation in the work, pointing out that no better monument could be reared to the memory of any philanthropic
lady or gentleman who should feel disposed to endow it.

After the singing of the choruses by the pupils, the
diplomas were presented to the graduates, Wm. B. Hammond, Henry B. Thomas, Wm. C. Bolles and Henry E.
Boesch, by Dr. Eliot, who addressed them as follows :—

I have the privilege of presenting the diplomas which have
been awarded to you by the director and faculty of the school.
You are well aware that they have made the award, and that I
am merely their instrument in transferring these rolls to your
hands.

I congratulate you on receiving them today. We have been keeping an anniversary full of precious memories and precious hopes, and the diplomas associated with such an event have an exceptional value. They will call up these exercises in after years, and give you new courage as you remember the high and solemn day on which you received them.

I congratulate you also on having enjoyed the great advantages of your training at a time when they have been constantly on the increase, and especially on receiving your education in a period when the blind have proved themselves as fit to be highly educated and highly trusted as any class among us. May you add your own proofs to those already given to this effect, and may your lives be crowned with independence and success.

You will not, I am sure, consider yourselves separated from the school by your graduation. On the contrary, you become, by virtue of having reached the end of your undergraduate course, fuller members of the institution than you have hitherto been. You will be followed with watchful interest by those you leave behind, and you will turn back to them with ever-growing affection and gratitude. Farewell.

A march composed by J. R. Lucier, and played by the band, closed the exercises, which, though lasting nearly three hours and a half, held the close attention of the audience to the end.

The exercises, both individually and collectively, received very high commendation by the press. Of the literary exercises one writer says, " There was manifest throughout a thorough knowledge and appreciation of the subject, and it even required a mental effort on the part of the spectators to realize that the performers were not in full possession of all faculties of body as well as of mind ; " and a musical critic says, " The outcome of such a concert must inspire the public with confidence in the practical musicianship of the blind."

The following lines, a voluntary contribution from a former graduate, were to have been read, but were crowded out by lack of time.

LINES FOR THE FIFTIETH ANNIVERSARY.

By P. Reeves.

The day was dawning o'er us
Just fifty years ago,
And now we sing in chorus,
Though the master is laid low.
To him we pay a tribute,
And for him we will pray ;
For he changed the clouded night
To a bright and sunny day.

A darker night in Egypt
The Egyptians never saw ;
He found us in the darkness,
He travelled near and far,
And the most afflicted ones
He gathered in a band,
Taught them how to read and write,
And led them by the hand.

He gave his time and talents
To educate the blind.
The star is still ascendant :
His work is well defined.
Dr. Howe, — the name we love
And ever shall revere !
Blest among the saints above,
His chair is vacant here.

They knew him in the East,
They knew him in the West :
In deeds of love and mercy
He ranks among the best.
And we should all be thankful,
And ever happy be,
And praise the man and master
Who made us proud and free.

CORRESPONDENCE.

The following letters were sent in response to invitations to take part in the celebration of the semi-centennial anniversary :

LETTER FROM GOVERNOR LITTLEFIELD.

STATE OF RHODE ISLAND, EXECUTIVE DEPARTMENT,
PROVIDENCE, June 7, 1882.

MY DEAR SIR : — I desire through you to thank the committee of arrangements for an invitation to be present at the semi-centennial anniversary of the " Perkins Institution for the Blind," to be held in connection with the commencement exercises of your school, on the 13th inst.

I regret to say I am obliged to deny myself the pleasure of being with you on that day, on account of public duties, which call me to Newport.

I feel the disappointment keenly, as I had made up my mind some weeks since to be with you on that occasion, which I supposed would occur a few days later in the month.

I am pleased to see our little commonwealth so well represented on your programme. I am sure the scholars from this and other states will perform the part assigned them to the full satisfaction of teachers and friends, and with credit to the institution over which you preside with such marked ability. May it be your pleasure on that day to report the *one hundred thousand dollars* printing fund complete, and may the good work of the institution be extended and strengthened with each successive year, until every child in New England, deprived of sight, may share its benefits.

Permit me to extend the cordial congratulations of the people of Rhode Island to your presiding officer. His Excellency the Governor of the Commonwealth of Massachusetts, your distinguished orator of the day, the committee of arrangements, and all engaged in the celebration of the semi-centennial anniversary of your noble institution.

Faithfully yours,
A. H. LITTLEFIELD.

Prof. M. ANAGNOS,
BOSTON, Mass.

LETTER FROM MR. WILLIAM CHAPIN OF PHILADELPHIA.

The revered and honored principal of the Pennsylvania
Institution for the Blind, Mr. William Chapin, whose noble
life has been devoted to the cause of the blind, not being
able to be present at the celebration, sent the following
letter : —

> PENN. INSTITUTION FOR THE INSTRUCTION OF THE BLIND,
> PHILADELPHIA, June 13, 1882.

MY DEAR MR. ANAGNOS : — I have failed to acknowledge
your kind invitation to be present at the *semi-centennial anniversary and commencement exercises* of your school, which are
really in full accomplishment at the time of this writing (Tuesday, 4 P. M.)   I regret the necessity of my absence, for I much
enjoy such commemorations.   Your programme presents a very
happy and appropriate variety of exercises ; and I shall hope to
have the pleasure of reading the address of the occasion, by
Col. Higginson.

Be so kind as to furnish me with any paper which may give
a report of the exercises.

Your institution stands pre-eminent in our country.   And its
present director ably sustains the prestige which it gained by its
eminent founder, Dr. S. G. Howe.   Believe me to be,

> Very truly your friend,
>
> WILLIAM CHAPIN.

M. ANAGNOS, Esq.

LETTER FROM MRS. JULIA WARD HOWE.

> BOSTON, June 13, 1882.

MY DEAR FRIENDS : — It is with a regretful heart that I turn
my steps westward today, in compliance with an engagement
which I made in ignorance of the precise date of your semi-
centennial celebration.   Though absent in person, my heart will
be with you at your festival ; and my most earnest good wishes
will always attend the progress of the institution whose past fifty
years make us hope for still nobler achievements in the future.

> Yours most affectionately,
>
> JULIA WARD HOWE.

DESPATCH FROM MR. B. B. HUNTOON.

LOUISVILLE, KY., June 14, 1882.

To M. ANAGNOS, *Supt. Inst. for the Blind:*

The Kentucky Institution for the Blind, as one of the children, sends congratulations upon the celebration of the golden wedding between the hearts of all New England and the Perkins Institution for the Blind.

B. B. HUNTOON, *Supt.*

LETTER FROM MR. OTIS PATTEN.

Mr. Otis Patten, superintendent of the Arkansas institution for the blind, and one of the early pupils of Dr. Howe, explained his absence from the festival in the following letter :—

ARKANSAS SCHOOL FOR THE BLIND,
LITTLE ROCK, ARK., June 10, 1882.

GENTLEMEN :— Your kind invitation to attend the semi-centennial celebration of the Perkins Institution for Blind I found waiting me this evening on my return home after nearly a week's absence. I regret that I shall not be able to be present on that interesting occasion, as my own school does not close till the 27th inst., and we are very busy preparing for the closing exercises. I had hoped that your celebration would be later in the season, and looked forward to it with many pleasant anticipations. I entered the Perkins Institution as a pupil nearly forty-seven years ago, and whatever of success I have had in life I owe in great measure to that school, and to its noble founder, Dr. S. G. Howe, whose kindness to me, an orphan boy, is among my most precious memories.

Yours respectfully,

OTIS PATTEN.

To MESSRS J. S. DWIGHT,
SAMUEL M. QUINCY,
WM. F. APTHORP,
Committee of Arrangements.

LETTER FROM J. HOWARD HUNTER, M. A., OF TORONTO.

Mr. J. Howard Hunter, formerly principal of the Ontario institution for the blind, and a gentleman of high scholarly attainments and rare ability, sent the following letter :—

OFFICE OF THE INSPECTOR OF INSURANCE, ONTARIO.
PARLIAMENT BUILDINGS,
TORONTO, CANADA, 12th June, 1882.

MY DEAR ANAGNOS : — I am very greatly obliged for your kind invitation to the semi-centennial of your noble institution for the blind ; but owing to the pressure of official engagements I must deny myself the sincere pleasure that it would have afforded to offer you, in person, my best congratulations.

Now — and formerly ! What a half century for the blind ! The transformation is surely the most marvellous that this wonderful half century can show. What Boston and Howe and Anagnos have contributed towards this transformation will, to the full extent, be admitted only when reflection ripens and when the disturbing influence of personal rivalry is removed. Competition, so valuable and necessary a spur in even works of philanthropy produces — like any other sharp spur — a temporary soreness of the sides.

I have often thought, will some grateful blind student in the better days that are to be become the historian of the education of the blind? The class for whom these long years of ceaseless, anxious, ingenious toil have been expended will doubtless yield a distinguished example of thankful recollection combined with brilliant literary expression. Assuredly, if ever that history comes to be written in the spirit of gratitude or simple truth, your name, my dear Anagnos, must constantly recur.

That you would succeed in your latest enterprise, — the establishment of a fund sufficiently large to keep your embossing presses constantly employed, — this was a foregone conclusion : for, though the undertaking seemed gigantic, it was a man of

Titanic energy that undertook it.   I most sincerely congratulate you and your distinguished board of trustees on this happy issue of your joint labors, which so auspiciously completes the half-century of your institution annals.

With kindest remembrances to Mrs. Anagnos and my Boston friends,

Yours, very faithfully,

J. HOWARD HUNTER.

FIFTY-SECOND ANNUAL REPORT

OF

THE TRUSTEES

OF THE

PERKINS INSTITUTION

AND

𝔐assachusetts 𝔖chool for the 𝔅lind,

FOR THE YEAR ENDING

SEPTEMBER 30, 1883.

BOSTON:
WRIGHT & POTTER PRINTING CO., STATE PRINTERS.
18 POST OFFICE SQUARE.
1884.

FIFTY-SECOND ANNUAL REPORT

OF

THE TRUSTEES

OF THE

PERKINS INSTITUTION

AND

𝕸assachusetts 𝕾chool for the 𝕭lind,

FOR THE YEAR ENDING

SEPTEMBER 30, 1883.

– ————

BOSTON:

WRIGHT & POTTER PRINTING CO., STATE PRINTERS,

18 POST OFFICE SQUARE.

1884.

TABLE OF CONTENTS.

Commonwealth of Massachusetts.

PERKINS INSTITUTION AND MASS. SCHOOL FOR THE BLIND,
SOUTH BOSTON, Oct. 23, 1883.

To the Hon. HENRY B. PEIRCE, *Secretary of State*, Boston.

DEAR SIR : — I have the honor to transmit to you, for the use of the legislature, a copy of the fifty-second annual report of the trustees of this institution to the corporation thereof, together with the usual accompanying documents.

Respectfully,

M. ANAGNOS,
Secretary.

OFFICERS OF THE CORPORATION.

1883-84.

SAMUEL ELIOT, *President.*
JOHN CUMMINGS, *Vice-President.*
EDWARD JACKSON, *Treasurer.*
M. ANAGNOS, *Secretary.*

BOARD OF TRUSTEES.

FRANCIS BROOKS.
JOHN S. DWIGHT.
M. ENGELHARDT.
JOSEPH B. GLOVER.
J. THEODORE HEARD, M.D.
EDWARD N. PERKINS.

JOHN C. PHILLIPS.
SAMUEL M. QUINCY,
SAMUEL G. SNELLING.
JAMES STURGIS.
GEORGE W. WALES.
JOHN H. WETHERBEE.

STANDING COMMITTEES.

Monthly Visiting Committee,

Whose duty it is to visit and inspect the Institution at least once in each month.

1884.		1884.	
January,	F. BROOKS.	July,	J. C. PHILLIPS.
February,	J. S. DWIGHT.	August,	S. M. QUINCY.
March,	M. ENGELHARDT.	September,	S. G. SNELLING.
April,	J. B. GLOVER.	October,	JAMES STURGIS.
May,	J. T. HEARD.	November,	G. W. WALES.
June,	E. N. PERKINS.	December,	J. H. WETHERBEE.

Committee on Education.

J. S. DWIGHT.
FRANCIS BROOKS.
S. M. QUINCY.

House Committee.

E. N. PERKINS.
G. W. WALES.
FRANCIS BROOKS.

Committee on Finance.

J. B. GLOVER.
JAMES STURGIS.
JOHN C. PHILLIPS.

Committee on Health.

J. THEODORE HEARD.
M. ENGELHARDT.
J. H. WETHERBEE.

Auditors of Accounts.

SAMUEL G. SNELLING.
JAMES STURGIS.

OFFICERS OF THE INSTITUTION.

DIRECTOR.
M. ANAGNOS.

MEDICAL INSPECTOR.
JOHN HOMANS, M.D.

LITERARY DEPARTMENT.

Miss Julia Roxana Gilman.
Miss Etta S. Adams.
Miss Frances B. Winslow.
Miss Julia A. Boylan.

Miss Della Bennett.
Miss Mary C. Moore.
Miss Cora A. Newton.
Miss Emma A. Coolidge.

Miss Sarah Elizabeth Lane, *Librarian.*

MUSICAL DEPARTMENT.

Thomas Reeves.
Frank H. Kilbourne.
Miss Freda Black.
Miss Mary L. Riley.
Miss Lucy A. Hammond.
Miss Annie Keith.
Miss Mary A. Proctor.

Mrs. Kate Rametti.
C. H. Higgins.
Ezra M. Bagley.
Julius Akeroyd.
Music Readers.
Miss Allie S. Knapp.
Miss Caroline L. Bates.

TUNING DEPARTMENT.

JOEL WEST SMITH, *Instructor and Manager.*
GEORGE E. HART, *Tuner.*

INDUSTRIAL DEPARTMENT.

Workrooms for Juveniles.

John H. Wright, *Work Master.*
Miss A. J. Dillingham, *Work Mistress.*
Miss Cora L. Davis, *Assistant.*
Thomas Carroll, *Assistant.*

Workshop for Adults.

Anthony W. Bowden, *Manager.*
P. Morrill, *Foreman.*
Miss M. A. Dwelly, *Forewoman.*
Miss Mattie M. Stone, *Clerk.*

DOMESTIC DEPARTMENT.

Steward.

Anthony W. Bowden.

Matron.

Miss Maria C. Moulton.
Miss Dora M. Morrell, *Assistant.*

Housekeepers in the Cottages.

Mrs. M. A. Knowlton.
Mrs. L. S. Smith.
Miss Bessie Wood.
Mrs. Sophia C. Hopkins.

PRINTING DEPARTMENT.

Dennis A. Reardon, ... *Manager.*
Miss Elizabeth S. Howe, *Printer.*
Miss Martha F. Rowell,   "

Miss Ellen B. Webster, *Book-keeper.*

MEMBERS OF THE CORPORATION.

All persons who have contributed twenty-five dollars to the funds of the institution, all who have served as trustees or treasurer, and all who have been elected by special vote, are members.

Adams, John A., Providence.
Adams, Waldo, Boston.
Aldrich, Mrs. Sarah, Boston.
Alger, Rev. William R., Boston.
Ames, F. L., Boston.
Ames, Mrs. H. A., Boston.
Ames, Oliver, Boston.
Amory, C. W., Boston.
Amory, James S., Boston.
Amory, William, Boston.
Amory, Mrs. William, Boston.
Anagnos, M., Boston.
Andrews, Francis, Boston.
Anthony, Hon. Henry, Providence.
Appleton, Miss Emily G., Boston.
Appleton, T. G., Boston.
Appleton, Mrs. William, Boston.
Apthorp, William F., Boston.
Arnold, A. B., Providence.
Atkins, Mrs. Elisha, Boston.
Atkinson, Edward, Boston.
Atkinson, William, Boston.
Austin, Edward, Boston.
Aylesworth, H. B., Providence.
Baldwin, William H., Boston.
Baker, Mrs. E. M., Boston.
Baker, Mrs. E. W., Dorchester.
Baker, Ezra H., Boston.
Baker, Miss M. K., Boston.
Barbour, E. D., Boston.
Barker, Joseph A., Providence.

Barstow, Amos C., Providence.
Barrows, Rev. S. J., Dorchester.
Beal, J. H., Boston.
Beard, Hon. Alanson W., Boston.
Beckwith, Miss A. G., Providence.
Beckwith, Mrs. T., Providence.
Beebe, J. A., Boston.
Bennett, Mrs. Eleanor, Billerica.
Bigelow, E. B., Boston.
Binney, William, Providence.
Black, G. N., Boston.
Blake, G. Baty, Boston.
Blake, James H., Boston.
Blanchard, G. D. B., Malden.
Bourn, A. O., Providence.
Bouvé, Thomas T., Boston.
Bowditch, Mrs. E. B., Boston.
Bowditch, J. I., Boston.
Bowditch, Mrs. J. I., Boston.
Bradlee, F. H., Boston.
Bradlee, Mrs. F. H., Boston.
Bradlee, J. P., Boston.
Brewer, Miss C. A., Boston.
Brewer, Mrs. Mary, Boston.
Brewster, Osmyn, Boston.
Brimmer, Hon. Martin, Boston
Brooks, Francis, Boston.
Brooks, Mrs. F. A., Boston.
Brooks, Peter C., Boston.
Brooks, Rev. Phillips, Boston.
Brooks, Shepherd, Boston.

Brooks, Mrs. Susan O., Boston.
Brown, John A., Providence.
Brown, Mrs. John C., Providence.
Browne, A. Parker, Boston.
Bullard, W. S., Boston.
Bullock, Miss Julia, Providence.
Bundy, James J., Providence.
Burnett, Joseph, Boston.
Cabot, Mrs. Samuel, Sen., Boston.
Cabot, W. C., Boston.
Callender, Walter, Providence.
Carpenter, Charles E., Providence.
Cary, Mrs. W. F., Boston.
Chandler, P. W., Boston.
Chandler, Theophilus P., Brookline.
Chace, J. H., Providence.
Chace, J., Providence.
Chapin, E. P., Providence.
Chase, Mrs. Theodore, Boston.
Cheever, Dr. David W., Boston.
Cheney, Benjamin P., Boston.
Chickering, George H., Boston.
Childs, Alfred A., Boston.
Claflin, Hon. William, Boston.
Clapp, William W., Boston.
Clarke, Mrs. Jas. Freeman, Boston.
Clement, Edward H., Boston.
Coats, James, Providence.
Cobb, Samuel C., Boston.
Cobb, Samuel T., Boston.
Cochrane, Alexander, Boston.
Coffin, Mrs. W. E., Boston.
Colt, Samuel P., Providence.
Conant, Mrs. Rebecca, Amherst, N. H.
Coolidge, Dr. A., Boston.
Coolidge, J. R., Boston.
Coolidge, Mrs. J. R., Boston
Coolidge, J. T., Boston.
Coolidge, Mrs. J. T., Boston.
Corliss, George H., Providence.
Cotting, C. U., Boston.
Crane, Zenas M., Dalton.
Crosby, Joseph B., Boston.
Crosby, William S., Boston.
Cruft, Miss Annah P., Boston.

Cruft, Miss Harriet O., Boston.
Cummings, Charles A., Boston.
Cummings, Hon. John, Woburn.
Curtis, George S., Boston.
Curtis, Mrs. Margarette S., Boston.
Dana, Mrs. Samuel T., Boston.
Dalton, C. H., Boston.
Dalton, Mrs. C. H., Boston.
Danielson, G. W., Providence.
Darling, L. B., Providence.
Davis, Miss A. W., Boston.
Day, Daniel E., Providence.
Deblois, Stephen G., Boston.
Denny, George P., Boston.
Devens, Rev. Samuel A., Boston.
Ditson, Oliver, Boston.
Dix, J. H., M.D., Boston.
Dunnell, Jacob, Providence.
Dwight, John S., Boston.
Eaton, W. S., Boston.
Eliot, Dr. Samuel, Boston.
Emery, Francis F., Boston.
Emery, Isaac, Boston.
Emmons, Mrs. Nath'l H., Boston.
English, Jas. E., New Haven, Conn.
Endicott, Henry, Boston.
Endicott, William, Jr., Boston.
Ernst, C. W., Boston.
Farnam, Mrs. A. G., New Haven.
Fay, H. H., Boston.
Fay, Mrs. H. H., Boston.
Fay, Miss Sarah B., Boston.
Fay, Mrs. Sarah S., Boston.
Fellows, R. J., New Haven, Conn.
Ferris, M. C., Boston.
Fisk, Rev. Photius, Boston.
Fiske, J. N., Boston.
Folsom, Charles F., M.D., Boston.
Forbes, J. M., Milton.
Foster, F. C., Boston.
Freeman, Miss Hattie E., Boston.
French, Jonathan, Boston.
Frothingham, A. T., Boston.
Frothingham, Rev. Fred'k, Milton.
Galloupe, C. W., Boston.
Gammell, Prof. Wm., Providence.

Gammell, Mrs. Wm., Providence.
Gardiner, Charles P., Boston.
Gardiner, William H., Boston.
Gardner, George, Boston.
Gardner, George A., Boston.
Gardner, Henry W., Providence.
Gardner, John L., Boston.
George, Charles H., Providence.
Glidden, W. T., Boston.
Glover, A., Boston.
Glover, J. B., Boston.
Goddard, Benjamin, Brookline.
Goddard, Miss Matilda, Boston.
Goddard, Miss Rebecca, Boston.
Goddard, T. P. I., Providence.
Goddard, William, Providence.
Goff, Darius L., Pawtucket, R. I.
Goff, L. B., Pawtucket.
Gray, Mrs. Horace, Boston.
Greene, Benj. F., Providence.
Greene, S. H., Providence.
Greenleaf, Mrs. Jas., Charlestown.
Greenleaf, R. C., Boston.
Grosvenor, William, Providence.
Grover, William O., Boston.
Guild, Mrs. S. E., Boston.
Hale, Rev. Edward E., Boston.
Hale, George S., Boston.
Hall, J. R., Boston.
Hall, Miss L. E., Charlestown.
Hardy, Alpheus, Boston.
Haskell, Edwin B., Auburndale.
Hayward, Hon. Wm.S.,Providence.
Hazard, Rowland, Providence.
Heard, J. T., M.D., Boston.
Hemenway, Mrs. A., Jr., Boston.
Hendricken, Rt. Rev. T. F., Providence.
Higginson, George, Boston.
Higginson, Henry Lee, Boston.
Hill, Hon. Hamilton A., Boston.
Hill, Mrs. T. J., Providence.
Hilton, William, Boston.
Hogg, John, Boston.
Hooper, E. W., Boston.
Hooper, R. W., M.D., Boston.

Hoppin, Hon. W. W., Providence.
Hovey, George O., Boston.
Hovey, William A., Boston.
Howard, Hon. A. C., Providence.
Howard, Mrs. Chas. W., California.
Howard, Hon. Henry, Providence.
Howe, Mrs. Julia Ward, Boston.
Howes, Miss E., Boston.
Houghton, Hon. H. O., Cambridge.
Hunnewell, F. W., Boston.
Hunnewell, H. H., Boston.
Hunt, Moses, Charlestown.
Hyatt, Alpheus, Cambridge.
Inches, H. B., Boston.
Ives, Mrs. Anna A., Providence.
Jackson, Charles C., Boston.
Jackson, Edward, Boston.
Jackson, Mrs. J. B. S., Boston.
Jackson, Patrick T., Boston.
Jackson, Mrs. Sarah, Boston.
Jarvis, Edward, M.D., Dorchester.
Johnson, Samuel, Boston
Jones, J. M., Boston.
Joy, Mrs. Charles H., Boston.
Kellogg, Mrs. Eva D., Boston.
Kendall, C. S., Boston.
Kennard, Martin P., Brookline.
Kent, Mrs Helena M., Boston.
Kidder, H. P., Boston.
Kinsley, E. W., Boston.
Lang, B. J., Boston.
Lawrence, Abbott, Boston.
Lawrence, Amos A., Longwood.
Lawrence, Edward, Charlestown.
Lawrence, Mrs. James, Boston.
Lawrence, William, Lawrence.
Lee, Henry, Boston.
Lincoln, L. J. B., Hingham.
Linzee, J. W., Boston.
Linzee, Miss Susan I., Boston.
Lippitt, Hon. Henry, Providence.
Littell, Miss S. G., Brookline
Little, J. L., Boston.
Littlefield, A. H., Pawtucket.
Littlefield, D. G., Pawtucket
Lockwood, A. D., Providence.

Lodge, Mrs. A. C., Boston.
Lodge, Henry C., Boston.
Lord, Melvin, Boston.
Lothrop, John, Auburndale.
Lovett, George L., Boston.
Lowell, Abbott Lawrence, Boston.
Lowell, Augustus, Boston.
Lowell, Miss A. C., Boston.
Lowell, Francis C., Boston.
Lowell, George G., Boston.
Lowell, Miss Lucy, Boston.
Lyman, Arthur T., Boston.
Lyman, George H., M.D., Boston
Lyman, J. P., Boston.
Lyman, Theodore, Boston.
McAuslan, John, Providence.
Mack, Thomas, Boston.
Macullar, Addison, Boston.
Marcy, Fred I., Providence.
Marston, S. W., Boston.
Mason, Miss E. F., Boston.
Mason, Miss Ida M., Boston.
Mason, L. B., Providence.
May, Miss Abby W., Boston.
May, F. W. G., Dorchester.
McCloy, J. A., Providence.
Means, Rev. J. H., D.D., Dorchester.
Merriam, Mrs. Caroline, Boston.
Merriam, Charles, Boston.
Metcalf, Jesse, Providence.
Minot, Francis, M.D., Boston.
Minot, Mrs. G. R., Boston.
Minot, William, Boston.
Mixter, Miss Helen K., Boston.
Mixter, Miss Madelaine C., Boston.
Morrill, Charles J., Boston.
Morse, S. T., Boston.
Morton, Edwin, Boston.
Motley, Edward, Boston.
Nevins, David, Boston.
Nichols, J. Howard, Boston.
Nichols, R. P., Boston.
Nickerson, Andrew, Boston.
Nickerson, Mrs. A. T., Boston.
Nickerson, George, Jamaica Plain
Nickerson, Miss Priscilla, Boston

Nickerson, S. D., Boston.
Noyes, Hon. Charles J., Boston.
O'Reilly, John Boyle, Boston.
Osgood, J. F., Boston.
Osborn, John T., Boston.
Owen, George, Providence.
Paine, Mrs. Julia B., Boston.
Paine, Robert Treat, Jun., Boston.
Palfrey, J. C., Boston.
Palmer, John S., Providence.
Parker, Mrs. E. P., Boston.
Parker, E. F., Boston.
Parker, H. D., Boston.
Parker, Henry G., Boston.
Parker, Richard T., Boston.
Parkman, Francis, Boston.
Parkman, George F., Boston.
Parsons, Thomas, Chelsea.
Payson, S. R., Boston.
Peabody, Rev. A. P., D.D., Cambridge.
Peabody, F. H., Boston.
Peabody, O. W., Milton.
Peabody, S. E., Boston.
Perkins, A. T., Boston.
Perkins, Charles C., Boston.
Perkins, Edward N., Jamaica Plain.
Perkins, William, Boston.
Peters, Edward D., Boston.
Phillips, John C., Boston.
Pickett, John, Beverly
Pickman, W. D., Boston.
Pickman, Mrs. W. D., Boston.
Pierce, Hon. H. L., Boston.
Potter, Mrs. Sarah, Providence.
Pratt, Elliott W., Boston.
Prendergast, J. M., Boston.
Preston, Jonathan, Boston.
Pulsifer, R. M., Boston.
Quincy, Samuel M., Wollaston.
Rice, Hon. A. H., Boston.
Rice, Fitz James, Providence.
Richardson, George C., Boston.
Richardson, John, Boston.
Robbins, R. E., Boston.
Robeson, W. R., Boston.

Robinson, Henry, Reading.
Rodman, S. W., Boston.
Rodocanachi, J. M., Boston.
Rogers, Henry B., Boston.
Rogers, Jacob C., Boston.
Ropes, J. C., Boston.
Ropes, J. S., Jamaica Plain,
Rotch, Mrs. Benjamin S., Boston.
Russell, Henry G., Providence.
Russell, Mrs. Henry G., Providence.
Russell, Miss Marian, Boston.
Russell, Mrs. S. S., Boston.
Salisbury, Stephen, Worcester.
Saltonstall, II., Boston.
Saltonstall, Leverett, Newton.
Sanborn, Frank B., Concord.
Sargent, I., Brookline.
Sayles, F. C., Pawtucket, R. I.
Sayles, W. F., Pawtucket, R. I.
Schlesinger, Barthold, Boston.
Schlesinger, Sebastian B., Boston.
Sears, David, Boston.
Sears, Mrs. David, Boston.
Sears, Mrs. Fred., Jr., Boston.
Sears, F. R., Boston.
Sears, Mrs. K. W., Boston.
Sears, Mrs. S. P., Boston.
Sears, W. T., Boston.
Sharpe, L., Providence.
Shaw, Mrs. G. H., Boston.
Shaw, Henry S., Boston.
Shaw, Quincy A., Boston.
Shepard, Mrs. E. A., Providence.
Sherwood, W. H., Boston.
Shimmin, C. F., Boston.
Shippen, Rev. R. R., Washington.
Sigourney, Mrs. M. B., Boston.
Slack, C. W., Boston.
Slater, H. N., Jr., Providence.
Snelling, Samuel G., Boston.
Spaulding, J. P., Boston.
Spaulding, M. D, Boston.
Sprague, S. S., Providence.
Stanwood, Edward, Boston.
Steere, Henry J., Providence.
Stone, Joseph L., Boston.

Sturgis, Francis S., Boston.
Sturgis, J. H., Boston.
Sturgis, James, Boston.
Sullivan, Richard, Boston.
Sweetser, Mrs. Anne M., Boston.
Taggard, B W., Boston.
Taggard, Mrs. B. W., Boston.
Thaxter, Joseph B., Hingham.
Thayer, Miss Adele G., Boston.
Thayer, Miss A. G., Andover.
Thayer, Rev. George A., Cincinnati.
Thomas, H. H., Providence.
Thorndike, Delia D., Boston.
Thorndike, Mrs. J. H., Boston.
Thorndike, S. Lothrop, Cambridge.
Thurston, Benj. F., Providence.
Tingley, S. H., Providence.
Tompkins, Orlando, Boston.
Torrey, Miss A. D., Boston.
Troup, John E., Providence.
Tucker, W. W., Boston.
Turner, Miss Abby W., Boston.
Turner, Mrs. M. A., Providence.
Underwood, F. II., Boston.
Upton, Geo. B., Boston.
Wales, George W., Boston.
Wales, Miss Mary Ann, Boston.
Wales, Thomas B., Boston.
Ward, Rev. Julius H., Boston.
Ward, Samuel, New York.
Ware, Charles E., M. D., Boston.
Warren, J. G., Providence.
Warren, S. D., Boston.
Warren, Mrs. Wm. W., Boston.
Washburn, Hon. J. D., Worcester.
Weeks, A. G., Boston.
Weeks, James H., Boston.
Weld, R. H., Boston.
Weld, Mrs. W. F., Philadelphia.
Weld, W. G., Boston.
Wesson, J. L., Boston.
Wheelwright, A. C., Boston.
Wheelwright, John W., Boston.
White, B. C., Boston.
White, C. J., Cambridge.
Whiting, Ebenezer, Boston.

Whitman, Sarah W., Boston.
Whitney, Edward, Belmont.
Whitney, E., Boston.
Whitney, H. A., Boston.
Whitney, H. M., Boston.
Whitney, Mrs., Boston.
Whitney, Miss, Boston.
Wigglesworth, Miss Ann, Boston.
Wigglesworth, Edw., M.D., Boston.
Wigglesworth, Thomas, Boston.
Wightman, W. B., Providence.
Wilder, Hon. Marshall P., Dorchester.

Willard, Mrs. Harry, New York.
Williams, Geo. W. A., Boston.
Winslow, Mrs. George, Roxbury.
Winsor, J. B., Providence.
Winthrop, Hon. Robert C., Boston.
Winthrop, Mrs. Robert C., Boston.
Wolcott, J. H., Boston.
Wolcott, Mrs. J. II., Boston.
Woods, Henry, Paris, France.
Worthington, Roland, Roxbury.
Young, Mrs. B. L., Boston.
Young, Charles L., Boston.

SYNOPSIS OF THE PROCEEDINGS

OF THE

ANNUAL MEETING OF THE CORPORATION.

BOSTON, Oct. 10, 1883.

The annual meeting of the corporation, duly summoned, was held to-day at the institution, and was called to order by the president, Samuel Eliot, LL. D., at 3 P. M.

The proceedings of the last annual meeting were read by the secretary, and declared approved.

The report of the trustees was presented, accepted, and ordered to be printed with that of the director and the usual accompanying documents.

The treasurer, Mr. Edward Jackson, read his report, which was accepted, and ordered to be printed.

All the officers of the past year were reëlected, J. Theodore Heard, M.D., having been chosen to fill the vacancy caused by the absence abroad of Mr. Henry Lee Higginson.

The following persons were afterwards added to the list of the members of the corporation by a

unanimous vote : Waldo Adams, Edward Stan-
wood, Henry G. Parker, Orlando Tompkins, John
Boyle O'Reilly, Francis H. Underwood, C. W.
Ernst, R. M. Pulsifer, Rev. Julius H. Ward and
Mrs. Eva D. Kellogg.

The meeting was then dissolved, and all in
attendance proceeded, with the invited guests, to
visit the various departments of the school and
inspect the premises.

M. ANAGNOS,
Secretary.

Commonwealth of Massachusetts.

REPORT OF THE TRUSTEES.

PERKINS INSTITUTION AND MASS. SCHOOL FOR THE BLIND,
SOUTH BOSTON, Oct. 1, 1883.

TO THE MEMBERS OF THE CORPORATION.

Gentlemen: — In compliance with the requirements of law and custom, we have the honor to
present to you, and, through you, to the legislature, a brief account of the history of the institution under our charge for the financial year
ending Sept 30, 1883.

There is no significant event to record, and no
important change to notice in the manner of conducting the affairs of the establishment.

The school has now been fifty-two years in
actual operation. Its successive annual reports
have contained such full and minute statements of
its internal concerns, the course and modes of
instruction, the management and government of
the pupils, the accommodations for the health and

comfort of the household, and the various arrangements for prosecuting its work successfully, that we do not deem it necessary to enter again upon the details of these topics. Suffice it to say that during the last twelve months the usual good order has prevailed, and the same satisfactory progress has been made throughout.

The present total number of blind persons immediately connected with the institution, in all its departments, is 160. The details of the admissions and discharges will be given in the report of the director.

The general health of the inmates has not been so good as heretofore. In fact, owing perhaps to the protracted severity of the cold weather and the prevalence of epidemic diseases in the city, the amount of sickness has been greater than usual. Besides the appearance of the measles and other ailments, the scarlet fever suddenly invaded the household, and we have to mourn the loss of the assistant matron, Miss Virtiline Haskell, who died of this disease on the 13th of June. She was a person of good abilities, tender heart and excellent character, and her memory will long be cherished by all who knew her.

The affairs of the institution have been administered acceptably to our board, and advantageously to the recipients of its benefits.

The report of the director will show that the school is well equipped in all its departments, and

that the officers and teachers have performed their respective duties with their accustomed fidelity and ability.

Members of our board who have made frequent visits to the institution, have observed that the best feelings exist between the members of the household, and that proper attention is paid to the comfort of the children, and due care is bestowed upon their mental development, physical training and moral improvement.

COMMENCEMENT EXERCISES.

These exercises were held at Tremont Temple on Tuesday, June 5, at 3 P. M. Tickets of admission, with a circular of invitation, were sent to all the members of the corporation, and to the benefactors and friends of the institution. Every seat was occupied, and a large number of applicants were refused admission for want of room.

Our president, Dr. Samuel Eliot, occupied the chair, and made a brief but exceedingly eloquent and admirably pertinent address, in which, among other things, he said that "the institution has existed deep and strong in the benevolence of its founders and the community for fifty years, and will exist deeper and stronger for many a half century to come. It makes no unusual claim, and asks for no exceptional sympathy. It only shows that, while all education is interesting, in that it overcomes difficulties, here it overcomes far more than ordinary difficulties." He also spoke earnest words of friendly encouragement and wise counsel to the six graduates who received their diplomas at his hands.

The exercises of the school were of unusual interest, and gave not only pleasure, but a real surprise to the immense audience. They were brief, appropriate, incisive, convincing and sparkling with taking points. They reflected credit of the very highest kind on the assiduity and industry of the pupils, on the talents and fidelity of their teachers, and on the completeness and efficiency of the educational advantages afforded by the institution.

It might have been feared that, after the novelty of the spectacle had begun to lose its freshness, the interest which the exercises of our pupils originally excited in the public mind would gradually subside. But, on the contrary, we are happy to report that each successive year shows an increase of interest.

THE APPEAL FOR A KINDERGARTEN.

The kindergarten exercises were made a special feature in the festival, and the greatest interest centered about them. Dr. W. T. Harris of Concord made an excellent address, in which he spoke earnestly of the peculiar significance and value of Froebel's system; and his remarks were heartily applauded.

A brief circular, printed in raised characters
and distributed extensively among the audience,
called attention to the need of money to establish
a primary school for the many little sightless children, who are now, at the tenderest and most
impressionable age, either neglected or being per-
verted in a vicious atmosphere. We quote as
follows: —

" With all the progress and advancement, our system of
education for the blind is not yet complete. A vital element is
still lacking for its perfection.

" There is in New England a large number of blind children
between the ages of five and nine, who are too young to be
received in a mixed school like ours. They live and move in
a very unhealthy atmosphere. Their minds are contaminated
by low influences, and their growth is stunted by confinement in
ill-ventilated and comfortless quarters. They waste away under
the rust of neglect and the want of sufficient food and proper
care.

" Humanity, justice, expediency and imperative duty, all
alike demand that immediate and vigorous measures should be
taken for the establishment and endowment of such a school as
will be not only an auxiliary, but a complement to our institution."

The force of this call was increased tenfold, by
the exquisite work of the little boys and girls of
the kindergarten classes. They demonstrated in a
most practical and convincing manner the great
promise and possibilities of this fruitful branch of
education, and pleaded eloquently and fervently by
the deftness of their fingers the cause of their

smaller brothers and sisters in misfortune, for whose early instruction and training there is no provision whatever.

The number of self-supporting and independent blind men and women will increase in proportion to the efficiency and thoroughness of this early training, and beggary and the sum of human suffering will diminish correspondingly.

Such is the scope and character of this new enterprise. The favor with which its announcement has been received by the leading newspapers of New England is already a powerful encouragement, and we trust that the community will be disposed to give it the support which it merits. It is hard to conceive of a more practical or less objectionable form of beneficence. It is based upon sound principles and aims at great results. May it commend itself to the reason as well as the hearts of those to whom much has been given, and who wish so to employ their trust as to make it produce the greatest good in the present and in the future.

FINANCES.

The report of the treasurer, examined and approved by the auditing committee of the corporation, is herewith presented.

It shows the finances of the institution to be in a satisfactory condition, and may be condensed as follows: —

Cash in hands of treasurer, general
fund, Oct 1, 1882, .   .   . $8,650 43
Total receipts of the treasurer from
all sources during the year,.   .   100,128 99
                       ———— $108,779 42
His total expenditures and investments,   .   .   106,055 11

   Cash balance in treasury, ... $2,724 31

To facilitate a thorough and minute examination of the expenses of the establishment, the treasurer's report is accompanied by an analysis of the director's account, which gives specific information in regard to the principal articles consumed, with prices paid. By this all items of expense may be seen at a glance.

Frugality and rigid economy have been practised in the administration of the institution, and no expense has been incurred which was not obviously required either for the efficiency of the school or for the health and comfort of the household.

In the management of the funds strict accountability has been invariably observed. All moneys are received by the treasurer, and paid out by him upon written requisitions of the auditors, who act in place of an executive committee. They scrutinize the accounts of current expenses at the end of each month, and not one dollar is allowed by them, except upon exhibition of a proper voucher.

We should do injustice to our feelings if we did not express our high appreciation of the valuable services readily and gratuitously rendered both by the treasurer of the corporation, Mr. Edward Jackson, and the members of the auditing committee, Messrs. Samuel G. Snelling and James Sturgis.

We feel the need of larger funds for every department of the institution. We must look to benevolent and high-minded citizens for an endowment fund, which will yield a sufficient annual income for the wants of the school, and secure its independence permanently, so that it may continue to be second to none in the educational facilities which it offers.

Repairs and Improvements.

Although there has been a great deal done in the way of repairs and improvements during the last eight or ten years, still, both the internal and external condition of most of our buildings, especially the former, is yet very far from what it ought to be. Walls, ceilings, floors, windows, doors, staircases, all seem more or less out of order, and require constant and steady attention. Hence the work of renovation was again taken up during the summer vacation, and carried forward as many steps as the means at our disposal would allow.

The four cottages for the girls have been thoroughly attended to, and put in excellent condition. The plastering has been repaired throughout, the walls and woodwork painted in various tints, the mantelpieces reset, and all defects carefully remedied, so far as they could be discovered.

In the main building about one thousand yards of plastering have been renewed, and the walls of ten chambers and three of the lower entries have been painted; while in one of the latter, the dilapidated doors and frames have been replaced by new ones of hard wood, and the entire hall has been wainscotted.

Moreover, the matron's sitting-room has been completely renovated, tastefully decorated, and made very comfortable and attractive.

Several other repairs and improvements of a minor character have been carried out with a view to increasing the conveniences, promoting the health, and securing the safety of the household.

The accomplishment of this work has cost the institution the sum of $3,461.76. This amount of money, like all others previously applied for the same purpose, was mainly spent for the mere preservation of the buildings from further decay and deterioration, without adding anything to the increase of the value of the real estate of the establishment.

EMBOSSING BOOKS FOR THE BLIND.

Thanks to the generosity of the friends and benefactors of the blind, the income of the printing fund has enabled us to carry on the work of this department with the usual vigor and steady regularity, and to issue several new books of great merit.

Of the "Youth's Library," five volumes have been printed during the past year, which, added to the three previously embossed, make eight in all. Two more will complete the series. This work is of great importance to juvenile pupils; for, besides interesting them by the freshness and attractiveness of its contents while learning to read with the fingers, it furnishes them with a vast fund of useful information regarding the world around them, which is a valuable auxiliary in object-teaching.

A good-sized volume of biographical sketches of noted blind persons and the eminent pioneers in the cause of their education, together with those of such distinguished leaders of human thought as Socrates, Plato, Kant, and others, has been compiled from various sources and published in June last.

New editions of several books on our list have also been published, and in order to keep our sets of the New Testament complete, we have been obliged to reprint and electrotype the whole of the first volume.

According to the voluntary testimony of experienced readers residing in different sections of the country, the works issued by the "Howe Memorial Press" continue to be superior both in subject-matter and in mechanical execution and durability to those printed elsewhere, while their cost has been greatly reduced.

The eagerness with which our pupils are waiting for new books to come out of the printing office, the zest with which they peruse them, and the vast amount of pleasure and knowledge which they derive from reading them, bear witness to the wisdom and benevolence of the patrons of the enterprise, who must be gratified by the thought, that they have contributed from their abundance to provide this inestimable boon for the blind of New England.

Work Department for Adults.

Owing to the depression which has generally prevailed in business circles, this department has suffered more or less in common with all industrial enterprises.

The receipts from all sources have amounted to $15,390.91, being a decrease of $289.95 from those of the previous year.

The expenses for stock, labor, rent of store, wages of employés, insurance and all other items have been $16,876.68.

The cost of carrying on the workshop, over and above the receipts, has been $556.27. Hence the loss to the treasury of the institution, compared with that of the previous year, has been decreased by $561.02.

There have been twenty blind persons employed to do the work, and the sum paid in cash to them, as wages for their labor, has been $3,579.34, or $21.47 less than in 1882.

This *résumé* of the accounts of the workshop shows that its operations have not been so extensive as heretofore, and that there is but little improvement in its financial status, which has been quite unsatisfactory for a long time.

It is highly desirable that the business of this department should be increased, in order that it may pay its expenses, and that its benefits may be extended to a larger number of meritorious and industrious persons, who are striving to keep away from the almshouse, and to whom the bread of charity is not palatable. It ought to have an income of its own. The scanty funds of the institution are too limited to supply the wants of the workshop. Indeed, they do not suffice to carry out other plans relating to the development of the school, which have been so often commended to the attention of the corporation and approved by it.

We earnestly recommend this beneficent branch of our institution to the patronage of the public. It is scarcely necessary to renew the assurance that the work is done faithfully and thoroughly, and that our charges are very reasonable.

Closing Remarks.

In summing up the record of the events of another year, we beg leave to say, that the school is moving steadily forward on the road of progress, that its work has been crowned with a reasonable measure of success, and that all the just expectations of its noble founder, and its generous and benevolent friends, have been realized to a very great degree.

We again extend a cordial invitation to the executive and council of the commonwealth of Massachusetts, to the legislature and members of the corporation, as well as to the chief magistrates and other officials of the New England states, and to all citizens interested in the education and welfare of the blind, to visit the institution as often as they can, and to see for themselves the condition of its internal affairs, the improvement of the pupils, and the benefits which they derive from the public aid afforded to them.

For further information relating to the details of the instruction of the blind and the modes of their training, we refer you to the report of the director, which is hereto appended, and which gives an account of the present state of the various departments of the institution, of the work that has been accomplished or inaugurated during the year, and of the harvest which is being reaped in this most interesting field of beneficence and human culture.

All which is respectfully submitted by

FRANCIS BROOKS,
JOHN S. DWIGHT,
M. ENGELHARDT,
JOSEPH B. GLOVER,
HENRY LEE HIGGINSON,
EDWARD N. PERKINS,
JOHN C. PHILLIPS,
SAMUEL M. QUINCY,
SAMUEL G. SNELLING,
JAMES STURGIS,
GEORGE W. WALES,
JOHN H. WETHERBEE,
Trustees.

THE REPORT OF THE DIRECTOR.

To the Trustees.

Gentlemen:—A brief retrospect of the work and progress of the school during the past year, and an attempt to set forth its present wants and future prospects, and to touch upon such subjects as relate to the education of the blind, will constitute the materials of the report of the director, which I have the honor to present to your board.

Whoever seeks information regarding the nature, objects and condition of the institution, naturally looks for it in its annual reports. He cannot find it elsewhere. To meet this want, these documents must of necessity contain statements which are more or less repetitions of similar ones formerly made.

It is a great privilege to be able again to speak of the continued prosperity of the institution and refer to most of the events of the year with satisfaction.

The ordinary courses of study, music and industrial and physical training have been pursued with undeviating regularity, and gratifying improvement has been made in all the departments of the establishment.

The pupils have prosecuted their several occupations with assiduity, cheerfulness and success. Their time has been divided as usual between the school-rooms, the music-rooms, the workshops, the gymnasium and the play-ground.

The teachers and officers of the institution have performed their respective duties in a way not only to elicit my approbation, but to merit and secure my gratitude. It is but simple justice and ungarnished truth to say that the prosperity and progress of the establishment are in a great measure due to their hearty coöperation, uncommon tact and discretion, and to their faithful labors.

The customary vacations during the year have given variety and rest to the scholars, relaxation and strength to the teachers, and the pleasure of change and home to all.

The advancement made by the pupils, the order which has reigned in the school, and the harmony and good-will which have pervaded the household, are highly commendable, while diligence in study, industry in work and practice, and readiness in attention to duty, have given an assurance of positive progress in knowledge, virtue and happiness.

The organization of the institution and all its internal arrangements and regulations are in perfect harmony with the requirements of the present time, and are calculated to promote the best interests of the blind. No clannish spirit, or a disposition to monkish seclusion is fostered by them. On the contrary, everything is done to arm the pupils efficiently for the battle of common, social life, and to inspire them with courage to contend resolutely, but generously, for their share of its duties, its responsibilities, and its blessings.

On the whole, the record of the year may be filed away among the annals of the past with the inscription, "Read, examined and approved." Nothing therein contained should be considered, however, as assuming that all has been done that might have been accomplished, or as lessening the obligation to attain better and higher results in the future. Such a notion would weaken the springs of activity, and render powerless the wings of progress.

Fifty-two years ago the field of the education of the blind in this country was of little promise. It was a mere wilderness. Shrubs and thistles grew on its borders, and literal barrenness was in the midst. But through the sagacity and tireless toil of Dr. Howe, who undertook its cultivation with the resolution of a pioneer and the enthusiasm of a devotee, it was transformed into a fresh and verdant garden, and its appearance now delights the hearts of the friends of humanity. While we rejoice with them at the close of another year in the hope of its continued fertility, let us follow the steps of our noble Cadmus and strive to enrich its soil, and not only increase the quantity but improve the quality of its fruits.

NUMBER OF INMATES.

The total number of blind persons connected with the various departments of the institution at the beginning of the past year as pupils, teachers, employés and work men and women, was 165. There have since been admitted 23; 28 have been discharged; making the present total number 160. Of these, 140 are in the school proper, and 20 in the workshop for adults.

The first class includes 125 boys and girls enrolled as pupils, 11 teachers and 4 domestics. Of the pupils, there are now 108 in attendance, 17 being temporarily absent on account of bodily weakness or from various other causes.

The second class comprises 16 men and 4 women, employed in the industrial department for adults.

No applicant of proper age, of good moral character, and of average intelligence is ever refused admission. On the contrary, all who appear to be fit subjects for the school are promptly received on probation, and retained on the list of pupils or discharged after a fair and patient trial.

For many years past the number of male pupils has been considerably larger than that of the

females, and the preponderance of the sterner sex
among the new comers was always noticeable.
This order has of late been reversed, and the proportion of the girls to that of the boys admitted at
the beginning of the present session is more than
double; it is nearly three to one.

HEALTH OF THE HOUSEHOLD.

By attention to the immutable natural laws
which govern life, by considering them as divine
commands, and by obeying them as strictly as
possible, we have endeavored to secure the blessing of health for our household. But with all
these efforts, there has been, during the past year,
an unusual amount of illness, first in the girls'
department and afterwards in that of the boys,
attributable, probably, to so protracted a season of
steady cold weather as we had last winter, and to
the prevalence of epidemic diseases in the city and
the neighboring towns.

Among other minor ailments, there occurred in
the cottages during the months of December,
January and February two cases of pneumonia,
three of erysipelas, and one of scarlet fever. On
the appearance of the latter disease the most
vigorous measures were taken to prevent its
spreading among the pupils, and it was stamped
out effectually.

For about a month afterwards the usual degree
of good health prevailed in both departments ; but

in the middle of April, the measles broke out among the boys, in a light form, and all those who had not had the disease before, seven in number, were attacked by it. Soon the sanitary horizon of the school was clear again, and the preparations for the commencement exercises were completed without further interruptions.

In the midst of the pleasure and gratification which followed the striking success of the performances at our exhibition at Tremont Temple, a cloud rose to shadow our household. The assistant matron, Miss Virtiline Haskell, was taken ill on Sunday, the 10th of June. On Tuesday, her disease was found to be scarlet fever, of a malignant nature, and she was removed at once to the city hospital, where she received the most skilful medical aid and watchful care and nursing; but all was of no avail. She died on Wednesday night, June 13th, lamented by all who knew her amiable disposition, her devotion to the duties of her office and the welfare of the children, and her sterling qualities of character and heart. One of the scholars, who had gone to a friend's house to spend Sunday, was attacked, simultaneously with Miss Haskell, by the same disease. He soon recovered, however, as did also two others, who were taken ill immediately after the close of the school term and their arrival home for the summer vacation.

On the whole, in point of health, the past year

has been the most trying and unsatisfactory one since my connection with the institution.

I take this opportunity to express my deepest obligations and grateful acknowledgments to the superintendents of both the City and the Massachusetts General hospitals, Dr. George H. M. Rowe and Dr. James H. Whittemore, for the readiness with which they received such pupils as our medical inspector, Dr. Homans, deemed it necessary to send to them, and for the kind attention and considerate care which they bestowed upon them.

Before the beginning of the present school term, the drainage of our buildings was thoroughly examined by a sanitary expert for the second time during the past year, and was pronounced to be flawless.

GOVERNMENT AND DISCIPLINE.

The government of the institution is parental in its character, and moral suasion is the leading principle in our system of discipline. No corporal punishment or harsh measures of treatment of any kind are permitted. The rules are as simple and reasonable as the necessities and exigencies of a family like ours allow them to be. They aim at the maintenance of strict decorum, which means proper conduct, good manners and becoming behavior, and are carefully observed. Further than this, nothing is required of the pupils, who are left to that wholesome liberty of action, which is the leaven for the development of individual independence.

The members of the higher classes of the school are granted the privilege of self-government. They are neither marked, nor reprimanded or reproved, but are expected to comply with the rules and regulations of the establishment. and to conduct themselves like young ladies and gentlemen. If they fail to do so. they are classed with the younger children, and treated as such, until they redeem their character and regain their rank.

This system of self-discipline by the pupils is rather a gradual evolution than a new and sudden departure from existing methods. Its chief object is to raise the standard of self-control and reliance, and build up an atmosphere of manhood. womanhood and truth. So far it has worked wonderfully well, and my faith in its beneficent effects is so unbounded that I earnestly trust that we shall soon be able to extend it to some of the lower divisions of the school.

PLAN OF OPERATIONS.

Our general system of education and training has been pursued with such alterations and improvements as experience seemed to suggest and progress to require. But, as in the fundamental principles of our plan, so in all the changes and modifications of its methods, the main aim and end is to secure for the blind better physical, intellect-

ual and social advantages than they have hitherto
enjoyed. The prime object constantly kept in
view is to lessen their sense of dependence and
strengthen their feeling of self-respect ; to call
into play those faculties which are necessary for
self-guidance, and to develop such powers as are
indispensable for self-support ; and, lastly, to give
to all individuals that freedom of action which
generates and fosters self-reliance, and the largest
possible liberty, conditioned only on the observance
of the rules of the establishment and consistent
with the order of the household and the rights of
others.

This system is carried on in the various departments of the institution, which are to its organic
force what the brooks and upland springs are to a
great river. We shall notice each one of these
more in detail hereafter.

These departments have been conducted in a
quiet and unostentatious manner; and, although
there is undoubtedly much room for improvement
in the quality of their work, as well as in the
means and methods of performing it, yet what has
been accomplished is on the whole satisfactory
and very creditable to those who are employed in
them. As a rule, whatever degree of excellence
is attained in any of the branches of the establishment is not considered as a final triumph, but only
serves as a vantage-ground, from which to survey

the whole field of operations and discover still further improvements to be made.

LITERARY DEPARTMENT.

During the past year the results of this important department, which constitutes the foundation of our system of education, have been exceedingly satisfactory.

There has been a marked improvement in the ethical and intellectual atmosphere of the school, and the continual adoption of rational and progressive methods of instruction has kept on a constant advance all along the line in the several branches of study.

The prominence given to teaching objectively, of which mention has been made in previous reports, has been fully sustained, and the merit resulting therefrom is of a higher order than ever before. In this connection the classes in botany, physiology, zoölogy, geography, and even arithmetic, deserve special praise.

The study of natural history by means of the use of specimens and models is of prime importance everywhere, but especially in a school like ours; and I am exceedingly glad to notice the enthusiasm manifested in this department by both teachers and pupils. The additions recently made to our collections of tangible objects and apparatus have perhaps aided to refresh and strengthen this tendency.

The matter and methods of instruction have, as a general rule, been adapted to the capacity of the learners. No fetters of any kind have been imposed on the minds of the children. Independent and glad effort has been invariably stimulated.

The pupils have been made to understand, that their improvement depends upon their application, and that labor is still, and ever will be, the inevitable price set upon everything which is valuable. They have been taught to work with a purpose, and wait the results with patience. The spirit of industry, embodied in the daily life of the scholars, will gradually lead them to exercise their powers on objects external to themselves of greater dignity and more extended usefulness.

All available measures have been taken to increase the vital sap and suppleness of fresh life in the school, and to prevent it from running the risk of becoming petrified. As a consequence, there has been an earnest desire for improvement in intellectual pursuits, a thirst for useful knowledge, a hunger for mental stimulus of a powerful kind.

Special efforts have been made to suppress the tendency to cram. This process, like a noxious weed, not only sterilizes the soil of the mind, but has a moral taint fostering ostentation and conceit. It is quite as likely to make pupils flippant as fluent, confounding gabble with smartness. It is multiplying Shakespeare's " knave very voluble," while better methods would, in Isaac Taylor's phrase, "put flippant scorn to blush."

The results of the progress made by the pupils during the past year are very apparent in the more general development among them of the power of observing carefully and thinking understandingly concerning that which has been studied. Among the most hopeful signs for the future is the fact, that the school has become a field, in which the teachers are themselves making various improvements and helpful discoveries in the true work of education, instead of contentedly following the traditionary and venerable customs of the past.

Much of the refinement of manner and nobleness of purpose with which visitors to the institution are impressed, is due to the rare qualities of head and heart of the instructors. They are loyal to right and duty, are moved by high moral considerations, and possess that indescribable charm which comes from native worth, gentle breeding and nice culture. The more quiet and peaceful the school appears to the observer, the greater the evidence that it is a constant and ceaseless care to the teachers. If he notices no friction, it is because they are such skilful engineers. If he sees no machinery, it is because they make it run so smoothly. If he finds pleasant light and genial warmth in the class-room, it is because they keep the lamps of cheerfulness and the fires of patient endeavor burning steadily.

To the careful planning and unwearied labors of the teachers we are chiefly indebted for the very unique and beautiful exhibition in connection with the commencement exercises held at Tremont Temple on the 5th of June last.

One of the young ladies, who, having completed their course of studies, received diplomas on this occasion, Miss Julia E. Burnham of Lowell, has since passed the requisite examination successfully and entered the State Normal School at Framingham, in order to qualify herself as a teacher for seeing children. Our graduates generally compare very favorably with those of the high schools and academies of New England. As a specimen of the thoroughness of their training and the character of their literary attainments, I venture to copy herewith *in toto* the brief but excellent valedictory address, prepared and delivered by Miss Lenna D. Swinerton of Danvers: —

" Before saying the reluctant yet hopeful farewell, those for whom we speak are reminded of the great debt due to our educational benefactors. Mere words cannot cancel it; and yet, on this occasion, we have nothing else to offer. So please accept words as gratitude's promissory notes, payable in that specie possessed by every individual — namely, the best that he or she may do and be; your aim in educating us having been to raise such specie to the standard value.

" To His Excellency the governor and the legislature of Massachusetts, and to the corresponding representatives of the other New England states, we tender our sincere thanks for their generous and unfailing support of this special public school.

"To our board of trustees we express our gratitude for their hearty sympathy and coöperation with each step of our school progress.

"To our director and teachers we owe more than we yet realize, but we are deeply grateful for their unceasing faithfulness and forbearance.

"Schoolmates, though henceforth our paths diverge, our interest in the coming kindergarten — childhood's Aurora — and in all that is noble and beautiful, will ever be one and the same.

> "On the hill where Washington
> Viewed the foe from Boston flying,
> By his vigilance outdone,
> Stands our school to-day dispelling
> Ignorance and want, its dower,
> Record of a great conception, —
> Giving us what made the nation,
> Freedom from a tyrant's power.
>
> "Leave we now our places here,
> Fare-thee-well and flourish ever,
> As from these whose constant care
> Makes thee what thou art, we sever,
> This our constant aim shall be,
> To live worthy of thy teaching,
> Virtue's fragrant flowers wearing,
> Growing in activity.
>
> "Farewell to thy household dear!
> Joy with grief combines at parting.
> For as children seek the cheer
> Of the mother's smile and blessing,
> Ere they launch where life's seas swell,
> So for thine we ask and linger,
> Comforted if thou canst answer,
> 'Go approved,' 'God speed you well.'"

A few days after our annual festival the principal teacher of the boys' department, Miss Julia Roxana Gilman, sailed for Europe for the purpose of travel and recreation. Our entire community joined in wishing her heartily a prosperous voyage and delightful stay abroad. But, great as was the interest manifested in her journey and its pleasures, her happy and safe return home was greeted with genuine joy and most cordial congratulations.

There has occurred but one change in the corps of teachers during the past year. Miss Annie E. Carnes, a young lady of great ability and uncommon industry, resigned at the close of the last term, and Miss Frances B. Winslow of Brewster, a graduate of the normal school at Bridgewater, was appointed to fill the vacancy.

The present session of the school has commenced under the most favorable auspices. After the rest and relaxation of the summer vacation, both pupils and teachers have returned promptly to their work, and have entered upon their respective duties with their accustomed earnestness and zeal.

MUSIC DEPARTMENT.

Plutarch says that " music is something so superior, so divine, so great, — something so beautiful and so sublime, — that our fathers were right in holding it in high estimation in education.' In the case of the blind these words of the Chæronean philosopher and historian may be applied with

additional force. For, besides being an exhaustless source of æsthetic culture and moral refinement, this queen of the fine arts opens to them
vistas of delightful enjoyment, and so wide a field
of practical advantages, that no curriculum of any
school specially intended for their benefit can be
complete without giving it a most prominent and
conspicuous place.

In this institution music has continued to receive
all the attention which its vast importance merits,
and the department devoted to its study and practice has been well conducted, and its aims and
purposes have been pursued with assiduity and
with satisfactory results.

The number of pupils who received instruction
in music during the past year was ninety-one. Of
these eighty-two studied the piano; ten, the cabinet and church organ; eighteen, harmony; four,
the violin; eighteen, reed and brass instruments;
sixty-eight practised singing in classes; twenty-
one received individual vocal training, and sixteen
participated in the practical exercises of the normal teaching classes.

There has been but one change in the corps of
teachers of this department. Miss Constance A.
Heine, a talented musician and brilliant performer,
resigned her position at the end of the first quarter
of the school session, and the vacancy was filled
by the appointment of Miss Annie Keith of
Middleborough.

In compliance with a vote passed by your board, the violin was introduced into this department — during the last term, and a competent teacher, Mr. Julius Akcroyd, was engaged to give instruction on that instrument. We augur much good from its reappearance·as a factor in our course of musical study. Special professors have been for many years employed to teach the cornet, the flute, the clarionet, and the higher classes in singing and vocal training, with great success; but the violin, the king of the stringed instruments, was absent from our school for a long period, and the importance of its readoption cannot be overestimated. It raises our pupils at one step to the highest round of the ladder of musical endeavor, and places them, still more emphatically than before, in the front ranks of the musical students and aspirants of the age.

This is a point which, in all the departments of the institution, I am most anxious to hold up before our eyes. Never to lose our date, never to fall behindhand, always to keep pace with the current of educational progress, never to post-date it. The familiar adage, that "the early bird gets the worm," is as true in artistic and intellectual matters as in the business sphere to which these accomplishments introduce our pupils, and which we must therefore keep in view.

No efforts or expense within the limits of our means have been spared to increase the facilities

and improve the advantages offered by our music
department, and the thoroughness of its work
and the efficiency of its training can be easily
judged by its fruits. Our graduates continue to
be very successful in their vocations as teachers
of vocal and instrumental music. Their instruction is sought after in the various communities
where they establish themselves after leaving the
school, and they are generally regarded as reliable
and faithful ministers of their art.

The numerous opportunities of hearing excellent music afforded in so friendly a spirit by those
who have the direction and management of our
best concerts, oratorios, operas and recitals, have
been as generously and munificently offered as
heretofore, and the visits of artists to our establishment have continued from time to time to delight its pupils. To those among them who have
more than ordinary taste and talent for music,
these external advantages are of as much importance as the thorough instruction which they
receive at the institution; for they introduce them
into the higher spheres of art, and enable them to
appreciate and enjoy the masterpieces of the great
composers, interpreted by eminent artists and by
well-drilled orchestras and choruses.

For these most valuable contributions to the
musical culture and artistic refinement of our
scholars, our warmest thanks and grateful acknowledgments are hereby tendered to their kind

friends and liberal benefactors, whose names will be given elsewhere. Perhaps it will be gratifying to them to know, that nowhere in the whole civilized world do the blind enjoy one-half the benefits which are so freely and cheerfully bestowed upon those of New England by the musical societies and organizations, and the distinguished artists of Boston.

While I was finishing this paragraph, a letter came to me from one of the ablest and most noted musicians of Boston, Mr. William H. Sherwood, who has for many years taken a deep interest in the welfare and progress of our scholars, and whose exquisite performances on the pianoforte have many a time delighted them. From this note I take the liberty of copying the following extract as an illustration of my statement: "Several of my most advanced pupils will be glad to play at the institute this winter. Mrs. Sherwood and I will also play, if you desire it. Will you please send me the choice of evenings?"

TUNING DEPARTMENT.

This department is eminently a practical and useful one, and constitutes a very important branch of our system of training the blind for the remunerative occupations of life. It infuses a new spur and stirring motive into their activities, and opens to them a field of congenial and lucrative employment.

The number of pupils who have received instruction in tuning pianofortes during the past year was thirteen. Two of these — Benjamin F. Parker of Nashua, New Hampshire, and William P. Garrison of Vernon, Michigan — graduated at the close of the last school session, and are exceedingly well qualified both in the theory and practice of their art, so as to turn it to advantage and render it profitable to themselves and serviceable to the communities in which they live.

Increased attention and care have been bestowed upon this department, and the modes of training therein pursued have been as thorough and systematic as heretofore, while the mechanical appliances and tangible apparatus have been kept in excellent condition.

The pianofortes in the public schools of the city of Boston, one hundred and thirty-two in number, have been entrusted to our charge for another year, on the same terms as the last. Our tuners have taken such great care and pains to do their work promptly and to the entire satisfaction of the music teachers employed by the city, and of all competent judges, that not a word of complaint or unfavorable criticism has been breathed from any direction. This contract is a strong endorsement of our graduates, and a high recommendation of their skill and ability, silencing effectually the base aspersions and sneering insinuations of unscrupulous rivalry, and for its seventh renewal we are under lasting obligations to the fair-mindedness and sense of justice of those members of the school board who have charge of the matter.

The services of our tuners continue to be steadily sought everywhere, and the patronage extended to them by some of the best and most intelligent families of Boston is constantly on the increase. During the past year the earnings of the tuning department amounted to $1,789. Of this sum, only a small fraction, — $65, — remains to be collected, the balance, $1,724, having already been paid to the treasurer. Besides the young men who are regularly employed to do the work on the pianofortes belonging to the public schools and on those of our customers, several of the present pupils are called on from time to time to assist them. These, in addition to the practice which they gain, receive pecuniary remuneration for their services, which in many instances is of great help to them.

. About a score and a half of our graduates, who have been trained in the tuning department, and have left the school during the last ten or twelve years, are scattered all over the country, from the Atlantic to the Pacific, and the majority of them are doing exceedingly well and are quite prosperous. Two, Orville C. Cadwell and William C. Bolles, are employed by a music firm in St. Paul, Minnesota, at a salary of $600 per annum apiece. Three, Henry E. Boesch, Edward E. Ware and

Eugene A. Bigelow, are working very advantageously and successfully in Cleveland, Ohio. One, James H. Stirling of Providence, Rhode Island, has been employed by a piano concern in his native city. Charles F. Spencer of San Francisco, California, Charles W. Lindsay of Montreal, Canada, Arthur Andrew of Willimantic, Connecticut, John Vars of Newport, Rhode Island, William A. Severance of Lewis, New York, John N. Marble of Fitchburg, Henry T. Bray of Boylston, and others, are either pursuing their calling as tuners, or dealing in various musical instruments in their respective places, with great profit and excellent prospects of improvement. The rest are settled in Boston, Worcester, Lowell, Lynn and elsewhere, supported by their own exertions, and seconded by the encouragement of their friends and the good-will of their neighbors.

This list, hastily made up from memory, without any reference to the records of the institution, is far from complete. It may be considered as a simple memorandum, or mere skeleton. But, imperfect as it is, it gives some idea of the nature of the work of our tuning department, and of the quality of the harvest which is being reaped on the fertile field of its practical usefulness.

TECHNICAL DEPARTMENT.

A part of each day has, as usual, been devoted by the pupils to handicraft. Both boys and girls

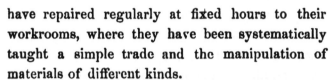

have repaired regularly at fixed hours to their workrooms, where they have been systematically taught a simple trade and the manipulation of materials of different kinds.

This practice is of immense importance to the blind in an educational, as well as in an industrial and sanitary point of view. It trains them to habits of regularity and activity, the value of which is readily seen in contrast with the feverish listlessness of idle hours and vacant thoughts. It gives them elasticity and dexterity in the use of their fingers, and thus it prepares them for a career of usefulness, and for doing something at least towards earning their own livelihood.

There have been no changes made either in the general principles or in the details of the management of the industrial department, and an examination of what has been accomplished in each of its two branches during the past year, will show that its affairs have been conducted with fidelity and with good results.

I. *Workshop for the Boys.*

Most of our male pupils have been regularly employed in this workshop, and have been taught the usual trades with more or less success, the degree of which is determined by the energy and natural aptitude of the learner.

The acquisition of a fair amount of skill and perseverance in the pursuance of handicrafts has been insisted upon as a helpful auxiliary in every undertaking. Moreover, attention, application, accuracy, method, punctuality and despatch have been invariably required of all the apprentices as the principal qualities, which are indispensable in the efficient conduct of business of any kind. These at first sight may appear to be small matters; and yet they are of essential importance to the happiness, well-being and usefulness of mankind. They are trivial things, it is true : but, as Smiles observes, life is made up of comparative trifles. It is the repetition of little acts which constitutes the sum of human character.

Some of our older pupils, who will have to depend wholly upon the labor of their hands for their support, are permitted to devote during the last year of their tuition a great portion of their time to mattress making and to the upholstering and repairing of parlor furniture. For a thorough practice in the first of these trades they are placed under the immediate care of one of the experienced journeymen in the workshop for adults.

II. *Workrooms for the Girls.*

A high degree of activity has prevailed in these rooms, — which have at all times the appearance of a hive of cheerful workers, — and much has been therein accomplished which is very creditable both to the ingenuity and taste of the principal teacher, Miss Abby J. Dillingham, and her assistants, and to the assiduous industry of the pupils.

Owing to the limited demand for bead work, less care has been bestowed upon it, and more upon sewing and knitting by hand and machine, upon crochetting, cane-seating, hammock-making, and manufacturing a great variety of articles of fancy work.

In addition to the instruction which our female pupils have received in the workrooms, they have also been regularly trained in such domestic occupations as seem to come within the special sphere of a housekeeper. On this point unrelaxed insistence has been laid, and whatever may be the attainments of our girls in literary and musical pursuits, a practical knowledge of household duties and of provident economy has been considered as one of their most prominent virtues and useful accomplishments. Darning and patching, washing dishes and polishing knives and forks, setting the table and dusting furniture, sweeping rooms and cleaning floors, peeling potatoes and doing all things of this sort, may be foreign to the regions of silly fashion, and excluded from the education of children born in the dominions of wealth; but they are essential elements and important factors in the welfare of every family of moderate means, and should under all circumstances receive due and undivided attention in a school like ours.

DEPARTMENT OF PHYSICAL TRAINING.

Of the children annually received at this institution many are of slender frame, enervated constitution and frail health, and none are so robust and hardy as the average of seeing youth, or can equal them in resolute, persevering, hard work. This is in most cases probably owing to the want of early rigid discipline, but it is still more due to lack of bodily vigor and activity.

Be the causes what they may, however, the fact remains undisputed, that the blind as a class have not only to struggle against the barriers imposed upon them by the loss of sight, but moreover to contend against consequent inferiority in physical health and stamina. Hence no system of education can be regarded as efficient or even suitable for them, unless it includes ample provision for securely preparing the groundwork upon which the temple of intellectual achievements and moral excellences is to be built.

In this institution a system of physical training, consisting of free gymnastics, calisthenics and military drill, has been carried on with the usual energy and regularity, and I venture to affirm, with the facts before me, that during the last four years there has been a marked improvement in the symmetrical growth, as well as in the appearance and disposition of our pupils. Their muscular system is stronger, their carriage more erect, their limbs are firmer, their lips fuller than heretofore, and even the bloom of their cheeks is in many instances flushed with faint vermilion. By means of the military drill especially, some of the most awkward peculiarities of blind youth, such as a heavy use of the feet, a stooping gait, arms stuck out from the side, and an uncertain and irregular movement, have been perceptibly corrected. In brief, the exercises in the gymnasium, added to the sports and frolic in which the pupils engage spontaneously in the open air during recesses, have in general given tone to the body and animation to the mind, vivified the circulation of the blood, promoted digestion and the process of assimilation and waked up the whole being.

But although the results so far attained in this vital department of our system of education are quite satisfactory, yet there is still room for greater improvement and richer harvest. There should be a decided increase in the variety and attractiveness of the exercises, both in the gymnasium and out of doors, and an eagerness and enthusiasm on the part of those who practise them. Our pupils must constantly bear in mind the fact, that, unless systematic physical culture is vigorously pursued and persistently carried out to such an extent as to lessen their organic weakness, raise the standard of their strength, improve the capital stock of their nervous force, and bring them out hale, sound, and well built, all efforts for intellectual development and professional acquirements will prove at the end futile and unavailing. No lasting monument was ever erected on a foundation of shifting sands and decaying timbers.

GIVE US A KINDERGARTEN!

Children are God's apostles, day by day
Sent forth to preach of love and hope and peace.

LOWELL.

It has been previously stated in these reports, that much as has already been done for the amelioration of the social and moral condition of the blind, the system of their education is not as yet complete. A vital element is still wanting for its perfection. The soil in which its first roots are planted still needs to be tilled and carefully prepared. There is no present provision for the instruction and training of little sightless children between the ages of four and nine. If they remain at home, they seem doomed to idleness and inertia, left to bask in the sun in summer and to hang over the fire in winter, passing through the tenderest period of their life without any discipline or direction. The early practice of Dr. Howe of receiving them under the roof of the institution and bringing them up with older youth, has been necessarily discontinued by the rapid growth of the school. There is scarcely room enough in it now for the development of its own legitimate plans and the full growth of its departments.

Hence the organization of a separate establishment devoted to the education of the smallest blind children is not a mere desideratum: it is a grand want and an imperative necessity.

To secure this, the most valuable, although the lowest round in the ladder of our system of instruction and training, an earnest and energetic appeal was made a year ago to the public for the foundation and endowment of a kindergarten, and the lapse of time only makes the project seem more important and indispensable.

Whenever we reflect, that whatever good or ill we see in the active world around us was cultivated in the nurseries of a generation ago, we can scarcely exaggerate the importance of a little child. In him is folded up, as it were, the hope of posterity, just as the future pride of the forest is enclosed in a tiny acorn. As Richter says, "The clew of our destiny, wander where we will, lies at the cradle-foot." But the little creature, the incipient man or woman, is in our power. The opening intellect, the budding feelings and capacities and the dawning conscience are committed to our care; and the child, in all his vast relations, will largely be just what we make him. We hold in our hand the seal with which the soft, ductile, impressive wax of infant character is to be moulded.

Educated our children must be, whether we will or not. Whether we think of it or not, we are forming them every day. By our speech and by our silence, by our looks and by the tones of our voice, by our habits and peculiarities, by our conversation with each other, by our companions, by every incident which our little ones witness, they are swiftly and surely trained to what they will be hereafter.

It is of vast importance therefore to adopt the right principles of education for all children as soon as they begin to notice things around them, and to protect them by watchful care and parental solicitude from all moral infections at the time when lasting impressions are made either for good or for evil, and when character is first taking form. But this necessity is immeasurably greater in the case of those among them upon whom the hand of affliction and misery is heavily laid, and to whom no day of hopefulness returns with the seasons of the year.

It is beyond doubt that the souls of these tiny human beings have in them something of that cloud of glory of which the poet sings. No matter how hideous and unclean their lives may be, they have susceptibilities that can be touched by the magic wand of kindness and beauty. They have hearts which can be reached by the radiance of love and sympathy. Like all other children, they are blessed with the germs of mental faculties, natural aptitudes and moral excellences, which can be fostered by culture and brought to

fruition by training. But, born for the most part,
in the folds of misery and vice and the by-ways of ·
ignorance and depravity, and cut off in so great a
degree from communion with the external world,
they are the prisoners of wretchedness and the
stricken lambs of the human flock. The enjoyments of childhood, the pleasures of life and the
comforts of home are utterly unknown to them.
Not a glimmer of gladness enters the dark chamber of their isolation, not a breath of happiness
lightens the heavy pressure of the iron veil of their
calamity. There is no affectionate sympathy
enveloping them in its ample mantle of charity,
until, with love's searching lens, some saving germs
can be found and nourished. Their environment,
is pregnant with pernicious influences, which stunt
their natural growth, and produce such physical
peculiarities, intellectual distortions and moral
deformities, as no amount of skilful training in
later years can eradicate. Thrust out of sight in
ill-ventilated and unhealthy quarters, or crowded
into the street, abandoned to negligence and rust,
or kicked and cuffed and driven about, these
unfortunate children tread with weary feet and
wasted strength their thorn-strewn path of early
life through the midst of indigence and distress,
want and privation, sorrow and suffering. The
bread they eat, the air they breathe and the talk
they hear, are all either injurious to their health or
poisonous to their character. The foxes in their

holes, the birds in their nests and the insects in
their habitations have far better care and guidance
than these little human forms. When I think of
the dens in which most of them are housed, and of
the squalid dwellings in which they are herded,
without furniture, without clothing save a few rags
for decency, and with a very limited quantity of
unwholesome food, sufficing only to maintain a
dwarfed existence, — and compare them with the
homes of the rich, with satin and velvet for their
soft seats, and costly, warm carpets and hangings
and wasteful profusion of luxuries, and fires and
bright lights, with books and pictures and per-
fumes, and pure air and spring water, and cleanliness, and all that the others lack, — oh! I cannot
but wonder at the magnitude of the inequality, and
I feel compelled to raise my feeble voice, and, in
the name of humanity and eternal justice, to ask a
fair and prompt cure for some of its most striking
features at least.

The remedy for this palpable injustice, and the
salvation and future welfare of these children, who,
in the words of Richter, unfortunate as they may
be, are "nearest to the throne of glory, as the
smallest planets are most approximate to the sun,"
are to be found exclusively in the immediate provision of means and measures for their early care
and systematic training. They should be speedily
removed from their surroundings and placed under
the most genial influences and thorough cultiva-

tion. It is by this means that the seeds of good qualities in them are to be vivified and germinate before the ground is given to weeds and tares. It is this that will prevent their humble talent from being buried in the depths of helplessness, or becoming rotten in the marshes of abuse or in the morasses of indulgence. It is this, more than anything else, that will kindle in them that sacred spark which illumines life with beauty and lights the flame on every altar where man sacrifices his baser instincts to lofty ideals. It is this alone that will develop and strengthen the wings or dignity and self-respect, so as to enable them to out-soar the enduring darkness of affliction and the distressing atmosphere of pauperism. Energetic husbandry in the spring brings good fruition in the autumn. We can hardly expect to see a perfect tree if we let the twig get warped and twisted at the outset. By raising these little waifs from a state of sloth and torpor to one of comfort and diligence, by teaching them by precept and example to love truth and uprightness of conduct and to hate falsehood and deception, and by instructing them in habits of industry and cleanliness, we shall engender in them a spirit of self-reliance and independence, and a feeling of respect for others, lay the foundations of sterling manhood and womanhood, and turn the whole current of their lives in the right direction. The blind persons whom we see occasionally in the streets of our large cities

with a placard on the breast heralding their misfortune, and with a forlorn little dog for a guide,
deeply touch the hearts of the passers-by, and the
pennies drop into the basket held in the poodle's
mouth at no slow and niggard rate: but at the
same time their presence reflects very unfavorably
upon the wisdom of our social economy, and
attaches a disgrace to our civilization; and I know
of no measure which will help more effectually to
erase these blots and create a new era of advancement and happiness than careful education and
thorough training during the first four or five years
of the lives of these infants, which are now either
wasted or, what is worse than this, given to the
devil and his ministers.

The difference between the neglected and the
educated sightless child is almost incredibly great.
While the former "wends his way" through life
like an unkempt creature, the latter, gladdened by
the genial warmth of knowledge and fitted for the
discharge of duty and general usefulness, takes
his station as a member of the human family, contributes his share to the common weal, and enjoys
the privileges and fulfils the obligations of citizenship, thus forming an integral part of society.
The crowning of all these inestimable advantages
is that the clouds of night folded round him no
longer render his existence unhappy. For a cultivated mind is not dark and gloomy because the
light of the sun and of the stars is shut out from it ;

but, like the fabled cavern, it glows with the gems which adorn it within.

For the accomplishment of this grand end, and the attainment of such valuable results in the largest possible number of cases, a primary school for little sightless children should be at once established. As there is not room for it on the premises of this institution, and, moreover, as it is not desirable on many accounts to locate it here, it should be placed in Dorchester, Roxbury, Jamaica Plain, or elsewhere within three or four miles of the state house. It should occupy a lot of high and well-drained land, in a healthy and pleasant situation, comprising five acres at least. It should be organized on sound progressive principles, and controlled by a board of trustees consisting of the most disinterested and public-spirited citizens of Boston. Its aims and purposes should be clearly defined, and there should be nothing eleëmosynary either in its title, charter, rules or regulations which might compromise its educational character. Its permanent existence and entire independence of political or sectarian influences should be secured and guaranteed by an endowment fund of $250,000, and its doors should be wide open to all little sightless children of whatever station and condition, and to a limited number of seeing ones, who would serve as their associates, playmates and companions. They should be kept until the age of twelve, and taught and trained objectively according to the rational and philosophic methods developed in Froebel's kindergarten.

This system is admirably suited for the instruction of blind infants, containing, as it does, within itself the power of awakening an inner force compelling them to manliness and righteousness, and of counteracting morbid feelings and peculiarities flowing from the loss of sight. It is founded on the broad principle that the highest type of humanity which education can produce is to be attained by the equal and simultaneous development of every faculty. It provides for the nourishment of each root of the character in its earliest stage, on the ground that all are indispensable to a noble and perfect growth. It seeks to create in the child whatever tends to unify him in every direction of his evolution. Unity is the fundamental thought which pervades the system. It is the main stay of the whole structure. Everything rests on it, proceeds from it, strives for it, leads and returns to it. The real difference between the kindergarten and the ordinary school-room is in the spirit, not in the methods. In the one, the order is made and the work mostly done by the pupils themselves ; in the other, by the teachers. Froebel does not treat children as parrots, who are to be made to perform certain tasks and to acquire such and such tricks, but views them as creatures of infinite capability for doing and learning, whose own instincts and desires must be turned towards the things that we deem desirable. The standard of this system is not one of attainment for a given age, but of the full and perfect development of humanity. Its games, while they doubtless are a source of amusement to the children in school, are also the tools, so to speak, to aid the teacher in her labors. Attention, accuracy, quickness of invention, a sense of harmony, fertility of imagination, the love of construction, and the first principles of reasoning, are taught by means of the gifts or simple toys, while nicety and dexterity of handling and pleasure in active exertion are promoted by every exercise. The peculiarity of the kindergarten is, that the play is invariably turned to a useful account. Through its instrumentality slumbering faculties are to be aroused, drowsy inclinations to be enlivened, and the power of reflection cultivated. In this system there is no end of learning, no acme of perfection. Moreover, Froebel is never weary of repeating that man must not only *know*, but *produce*, not only *think*, but *do;* and that the capacity for work must be fostered in early life, side by side with the faculty of observation and comprehension, before the memory is burdened with words and symbols.

These habits, valuable as they may be, are only a part of the choice fruits of the kindergarten. Nor is the training thereby obtained directed solely, or even principally, to the mind. It takes the child's whole nature, aiding its expansion physically and morally, as well as intellectually. The rhythmical movement, the marching and singing, the play and the merriment, all contribute to health. They improve the senses, increase the muscular strength, and make the limbs supple and the heart cheery.

Moral culture is also carried on through the habit of strict obedience under a gentle law. Froebel appeals to the higher nature of little human beings, to their generosity, their sense of right, their devotion to truth, their appreciation of goodness and self-sacrifice, in the most effective and practical manner. The ordinary dogmatic method pursued in the common schools is far inferior to his. The one orders conduct, the other cultivates motives. The one teaches catechisms to little children, the other sharpens their mental vision to see beauty and goodness, and leads the soul heavenward. The one uses habit, — the great power of education, — as an outward restraint, the other as an inward regulator. The one disapproves of a lie as much as the other; but the latter brings intellectual tendencies and associations to aid the moral precepts and makes clearness and precision so essential to the pupil's daily enjoyment of his occupations and diversions, that all the channels to untruth, such as exaggeration, confusedness of mind and incorrectness of speech, are cut off. So far as the child's horizon extends, he perceives distinctly and speaks plainly, and this atmosphere of intellectual veracity in which he lives is promotive of the growth of moral rectitude.

The average intelligence and mental activity of children taught in the kindergarten is infinitely superior to that of pupils who enter primary schools without such training. The former are more or less accustomed to exert themselves in the search for information, and prepared to advance more surely and steadily than the latter. They generally perceive things accurately, seize ideas rapidly and definitely, illustrate readily, work independently, and express their thoughts with correctness and fluency. To persons bereft of sight Froebel's system promises even higher and richer results than these. It affords them unequalled facilities for gaining an adequate conception of forms of various kinds and rare opportunities for the practice and refinement of their remaining senses, especially that of touch, which is their chief reliance for the acquisition of all concrete knowledge, and consequently the most important factor of their education. Above all, and with infinitely greater force than all, the drill obtained through its exercises so early in life, under such genial influences, will save many a blind child from dwindling and becoming dwarfed, and will prove a valuable auxiliary for future achievements. It will help to raise the standard of attainments in this school to a higher plane, to enlarge its curriculum so as to include the study of sciences and languages, and to increase and extend still more widely the sphere of its general usefulness. A great part of the time which is now necessarily spent in mere primary routine work and elementary training, can then be devoted to the pursuit of advanced studies, both in the literary and musical departments, and to a thorough preparation for a professional or other calling. Moreover, the path up the steep hill of knowledge will start from the lowest point and be a continuous one to its summit. There will be no chasms for the tender feet to leap, no precipices for them to scale. Thus there will be a positive and most significant gain at both ends, which will in some measure pave the way for the solution of the great problem of the higher education for the blind and their thorough equipment for the struggle of existence.

So far as our pupils are concerned, the great and lasting benefits of the kindergarten system are not imaginary. Nor do they rest upon mere speculation or *a priori* reasoning. They are real, substantial, tangible, gathered in the field of experience and confirmed by the test of time. Froebel's wonderful methods have been introduced and practised in our school for the last three years, and their results have been truly marvellous. Children whose faculties had been weakened and enervated by unwise indulgence or benumbed by the frost of privation, and who, sinking gradually into sluggishness and feeble-mindedness, were averse even to locomotion and unable to do anything elsewhere, have made remarkable advancement under its influence. Boys and girls who seemed entirely helpless and had no command whatever of their hands, have been roused to energy and activity by its agency. Through the simple but lively and attractive occupations of sewing, stick-laying, weaving, cube building, moulding in clay and the like, they have acquired a great degree of muscular elasticity and manual dexterity, which is of infinite assistance to them in deciphering the embossed print easily, in writing their letters skilfully, in tracing on the maps with alacrity, in examining objects intelligently, in stringing beads promptly, in using their needles deftly, in tying the strings of their shoes neatly, and, moreover, in doing readily a number of other things which they would have felt unable to undertake without this training.

These effects are succinctly but graphically described in the October number of the Wide Awake by Miss Emilie Poulsson, a graduate of our school and a teacher of broad culture and uncommon talent. Her excellent account of the " blind children's kindergarten," beautifully illustrated by the artistic hand of Miss L. B. Humphrey, and teeming with points in which the necessary faculty of judicious criticism is tempered by sympathetic feeling and keen insight blended with unfailing discrimination, is so interesting and so exhaustive, that I take great pleasure in reprinting it as an appendix to this report, by the kind and courteous permission of Messrs. D. Lothrop & Co., publishers of the magazine.

Those of our pupils who have tasted the fruits of the kindergarten and have learned to appreciate their value and importance, have become so infatuated with it, that they are most eager to secure its blessings permanently for their smaller brothers and sisters in misfortune. To this end they labor incessantly, unswervingly, enthusiastically. As the sudden termination of the last school session thwarted the plans and preparations of our girls for giving a concert in one of the neighboring towns at their own risk for the benefit of this enterprise, they have determined to make up the loss in various other ways. The members of the third class especially, who furnished most of the incidents related in Miss Poulsson's article, have shown an exemplary perseverance and touching devotion in this direction. One of them, Fanny E. Jackson of Bridgewater, twelve years of age, raised $5.30 for the " blind children's kindergarten," by taking care of a baby and washing dishes during the summer vacation. Another, Mary Callahan of Palmer, earned a smaller sum by scrubbing floors and making wool mats. A third, Mary Meleady of East Boston, sewed pieces for a bedquilt, thereby earning one dollar for the same purpose. Several others have endeavored to help the cause to

the best of their ability, and have raised money to
contribute to its furtherance either by taking care
of infants and cleaning kitchen and table utensils,
or by bringing the matter to the notice of their
neighbors and soliciting subscriptions from their
friends and acquaintances. The most striking
feature of this juvenile movement was its spon-
taneity and the enthusiasm of the little workers.
To be sure, the amount of money raised through
their exertions is small, very small indeed, —
only $11.55; —but the earnestness of their efforts
is full of pathos and significance. It tells the
whole story so eloquently and persuasively, that in
its light all mere arguments in favor of the project
seem pale and flat by comparison. Moreover, it
shows to those who roll in the abundance of riches,
that "sweet mercy is nobility's true badge."

> " Who does the best his circumstance allows,
> Does well, acts nobly ; angels could no more "

May the small sum raised in the spirit of true
love and self-denial be like leaven to the generous
contributions of the wealthy, and render them the
bread of life for hungering humanity!

In view of these facts and in consideration of
the beneficent and far-reaching aspects of the plan,
it will easily be seen, that a well-fitted and sufficiently endowed kindergarten will be to little sightless children what the light of the sun and the dew
of heaven are to tender plants, — a source of life and

growth and power, a flame dispelling the clouds of darkness, a fountain of happiness and strength, a radiant centre of illuminating force, helping them to out-soar the shadows of their night. It will prove an armory from which they will draw the most effective weapons to fight the battle of life successfully. It will be a psalm of their deliverance from the clutches of misery, a hymn to the dawn of an era of freedom and independence, a benediction on the benevolence of our age. To those who aid it to spring into being, such an institution will be a monument of enduring fame, reaching to the stars, yea, to the great white throne itself, studded on all sides with the gems of the lives of honorable men and women saved from the stagnant pools of vice by a kind hand reached out in season.

Scores of little children are now virtually waiting to partake of the benefits of such an establishment. They are famishing for the intellectual and moral food which it promises to supply to them. Plunged in a sea of ills, they stretch their helpless hands towards the shore, calling for a life-boat, and I almost seem to hear them speak in the language of the poet, and say, in mournful accents of supplication, —

"Save us! save us! woe surrounds us;
Little knowledge sore confounds us;
Life is but a lingering death.

> Give us light amid our darkness;
>   Let us know the good from ill;
> Hate us not for all our blindness;
> Love us, lead us, show us kindness,
>   You can make us what you will.
>
> We are willing; we are ready;
>   We would learn if you would teach;
> We have hearts that yearn towards duty;
> We have minds alive to beauty;
>   Souls that any heights can reach."

Who that hath a heart not palsied by selfishness can resist such an entreaty? Who can turn a deaf ear to so piteous and pathetic a call? Think of this imperative need, ye friends of humanity, and then say how much longer it shall be permitted to exist! Reflect upon the sufferings of these poor blind waifs, ye fathers and mothers, and then, gathering your darlings to your bosoms, rejoice that they do not go down darkling to the grave, and that they have the pure wheat and the sweet waters of life in plenitude. But at the same time remember, that the "faintest flaw in one of the links of circumstance, or an imperceptible turn or stoppage in the wheel of fortune," might leave your little ones homeless, sightless, speechless or mere lumps of clay, without care and protection! These helpless children are in no manner to blame that they are blind. The fault is that of others, perhaps is to be found in the very social fabric which pours gold into the coffers of the rich; — the misfortune alone, and the consequent privations, alas! are theirs.

But be the cause where it may, are these poor infants to be allowed to run the cycle of their life under the crushing weight of their infirmity? Is it fair that a great blight should be permitted to settle down on their character like a foul vapor, and prevent healthy growth? Is it just, is it human that the current of their existence should be left to flow in a tumultuous course from the sunny fountain-head to the dark ocean? Are there no men and women in the folds of benevolence generous enough and willing to help in this work of pure philanthropy and reformation, thus bending their heads to receive the crown, in which will shine like pearls and diamonds, the tears of joy and gratitude shed by those whom their munificence has saved and blessed?

This enterprise has already been considered in all quarters, and it seems to have gained friends everywhere. The preliminaries are now despatched, and the necessary preparations for active canvassing are nearly completed. The time for real work and for practical generosity and support has come. All the omens are favorable. But no great undertaking goes on its own feet. We have to furnish it with wings born of our earnestness, our fidelity and our devotion. The fact that so much has recently been done for the blind in the way of embossing books may deter some of their best friends from urging their claims vigorously on the attention of the public. For myself, deeply grate-

ful as I am for past favors, and much as I shrink
from calling again upon the benevolent for aid, I
deem it my solemn duty to do so promptly and without hesitation, notwithstanding the unpleasant
features of the task. I feel the sting of the neglect
endured by suffering humanity piercing my soul,
and I cannot be lukewarm any longer. I have cheerfully, gladly, deliberately and unequivocally accepted Froebel's grand call to " live for little children,"
and have determined to devote whatever powers I
may possess heartily and disinterestedly to the
amelioration of their condition. My own experience in early childhood brings their woes nearer to
my heart, and every cry for bread or raiment, for
shelter or education finds a responsive chord in it.
My desire to help them is so sincere and warm,
that I am prepared to put aside all personal considerations and convenience in order to carry it
out. Here or elsewhere, under the auspices of
your organization or those of a new one, with others
or alone, I am determined to labor for them with
the zeal of a true friend and the enthusiasm of a
believer in their cause. This is not a statement
made at random or on the spur of impulse. It is
a resolve formed from a profound sense of duty.
It is a conviction made strong and permanent by
the actual observation of so much misery and wick-
edness. It is a decision produced by the careful
study of the effects of blindness and of the means
for their alleviation. This project is uppermost in

all my thoughts, feelings, actions and aspirations.
" Bating not a jot of heart or hope," I must work
in season and out of season, until it is accomplished.
Perplexed as I often am by its difficulties,
now urged forward, now discouraged and held
back, always striving after success, wearied and
hampered by various obstacles, the only pleasure
that never fails me is the faith, that a kindergarten
for sightless children will ere long be founded and
endowed. The consummation of this noble enterprise will be the realization of the sweetest dream
that I may have beneath the skies.

Notable Anniversaries.

Two very interesting anniversaries were celebrated at the institution during the past year, the
thirtieth of Miss Moulton's matronship and the
fiftieth of Miss Caroline Augusta Sawyer's connection with the establishment.

The festival in honor of Miss Moulton was held
on the 3d of January, and was a very touching
occasion. The hall was very tastefully decorated,
and was crowded with friends and acquaintances,
as well as with the pupils and officers of the institution. Beautiful presents were brought as offerings, and a great deal of delightful music was furnished by the school. Pertinent addresses were
made by Mrs. Julia Ward Howe, — who also
wrote a song for the occasion, — Rev. James Reed,
Samuel G. Snelling and Prof. T. O. Paine, and

poems were prepared by Mrs. Anagnos, Henry W. Stratton and others. A life-size portrait of Miss Moulton had been placed under the folds of the flags which draped the organ, and was unveiled at a given signal. All in attendance were deeply moved by the pathos and the sweet spirit of the occasion, and our honored matron was hailed with all the enthusiasm which her lifelong devotion to the institution, to the blind and to the cause of humanity in general richly merit.

Another fête of a similar character was celebrated on the 19th of March, in commemoration of the semi-centennial anniversary of Miss Caroline Augusta Sawyer's connection with the institution. The occasion was as complete a surprise to the honored lady as that of Miss Moulton had been to her. The exercises were opened with a brief account of her arrival in Boston on the 18th of March, 1833, and joining the little group of nine sightless children, whom Dr. Howe had already gathered in his father's house on Pleasant street as the nucleus of the institution, and of the valuable services which she has rendered to the school most of the time since her graduation. At the conclusion of these remarks, an excellent programme was performed, consisting of music, both vocal and instrumental, original poems and a most appropriate address by the Rev. William P. Tilden, who gave in his inimitable and exquisite style some delightful reminiscences of Dr. Howe and of Miss

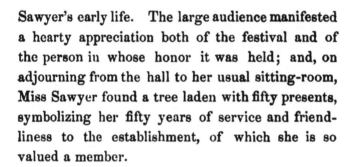

Sawyer's early life. The large audience manifested
a hearty appreciation both of the festival and of
the person in whose honor it was held; and, on
adjourning from the hall to her usual sitting-room,
Miss Sawyer found a tree laden with fifty presents,
symbolizing her fifty years of service and friendliness to the establishment, of which she is so
valued a member.

AID THOSE WHO STRIVE TO HELP THEMSELVES.

There is a large number of blind young men and
women all over the country, who are striving earnestly to overcome the difficulties of their infirmity
and become self-supporting; but who cannot possibly succeed unless they are thoroughly equipped
for the purpose.

These persons are as a general rule very industrious and exceedingly intelligent. They are
mostly graduates of institutions in their respective states, where they labor for many years faithfully and assiduously to get what they consider a
good education. But soon after graduation they
find that their training is incomplete and their
professional acquirements are too inadequate to enable them to earn their living. Consequently they
often seek admission here, in order that they may receive further instruction and qualify themselves for
the duties of practical life. From several applications of this kind addressed to me recently I select
the following, which was written by a graduate of

one of the largest schools for the blind in the West,
and which states the whole matter concisely and
vividly: —

"Dear Sir : — Although a graduate of the —— institution
for the blind, I do not feel competent to make my way in life.
I wish to study music and prepare myself for a teacher's post
and render my life useful, so that I may not be a burden to my
friends. My parents are poor, and it is impossible for me to
attend a conservatory or study privately. I ask of you therefore as a favor of kindness to admit me to your school. I am
not able to pay $300 tuition as stated in your catalogue. If it
is impossible for you to admit me free, please to send me the
very best terms which you can possibly give me. I know of no
other place, where I will receive proper instruction, and I do
beg of you to give me the best terms possible."

It was with sincere regret that I could not
grant this request, for two reasons: first, on account of the writer's being beyond the age prescribed by the by-laws of this institution; and
secondly, because we had no means at our disposal
to pay the whole or a portion of the actual cost for
his board and tuition. My grief was intensified by
the fact that I was perfectly aware that a little
help given to him at so critical a period in his life,
might have brightened his future prospects and
opened to him a career of usefulness and independence. This has been previously accomplished in
numerous cases. Many young men and women
who have come to us at different times from New
York, Ohio, Indiana, Michigan, Minnesota, Kentucky, Tennessee, Canada and elsewhere, for the

purpose of completing the course of their education and arming themselves efficiently for the battle of life have become self-reliant and prosperous in business, occupying a respectable place in the social scale, instead of sitting idly in their darkness and eating the bitter bread of charity.

There is a large number of others, who are thirsting for a systematic education and eager for a thorough professional training; and, if there were a " students' fund," the income of which could be annually applied to supplying a plank for those who are determined to learn to swim across the broad river of life, and strike out for themselves, many a meritorious young man or woman might be saved from sinking into the depths of want and dependence.

Enormous sums of money are constantly bequeathed for the higher education and æsthetic culture of those who are blessed with all their faculties. May we hope and trust that it may enter into the hearts of those who have the stewardship of wealth to dispose of a small portion of it for the benefit of the blind?

The Blessings of the Printing Fund.

As has been repeatedly said in these reports, the books issued by the "Howe Memorial Press" are becoming a perpetual source of intellectual light and happiness to the blind, gladdening many a saddened heart, raising many a drooping spirit, and brightening the life of many a suffering person. The following account of a touching scene at the "Colored Women's Home," written at the request of Dr. Samuel Eliot by one of the managers of that establishment, will be gratifying to the friends and promoters of the printing fund.

"It is very touching to see the pleasure and enjoyment which these books of raised letters give to the blind. A poor colored girl who is still sick and suffering at the "Colored Home," told one of the visitors, with a smile on her face, that the "Tanglewood Tales" and a book of fairy stories had helped her for a time to forget all her pains and trouble. These were among several books kindly lent her by the institution, and her expression was very sweet, as, unable to sit up, she moved her fingers slowly across the page, and gathered the meaning and point of the story. Afterward she described the characters and events as clearly and with as much exactness as if she had read with open eyes. She wished she were able to write and express the comfort the books had given her, especially during the long hot summer days while confined to her bed."

Most of the inmates of the Home are more or less illiterate, and we are told that they have derived much comfort and pleasure from being read to by their blind friend and companion from her books in raised letters.

CONCLUSION.

In bringing this report to a close, I beg leave to say, gentlemen, that each succeeding year that we render an account of our work deepens the conviction of the importance and value of the school as an efficient and powerful agent in raising the blind in the scale of humanity, and in opening to them avenues of usefulness, industry and social equality. That which ends to-day forms no exception in this respect; and it is a great pleasure to me to state, that all my assistants have faithfully endeavored, by steadily pursuing the principal objects of the institution, to soften the sting of affliction, and to enable as many of our graduates as possible to rely upon their own exertions and to lead independent, upright and happy lives. This is truly a grand undertaking, worthy of all the care, labor and means expended in carrying it out. How far our efforts have been successful, it is not for us to say. Be this as it may, however, our solemn and imperative duty is to press forward and onward, so long as sightless children call for our aid and sympathy.

That the success attained heretofore by the school may continue undiminished in the future, its usefulness increase and its educational light burn steadily and brightly for the guidance of those of our fellow-men who grope in unceasing physical darkness, is the humble and ardent prayer and will ever be the constant and unremitting endeavor of the undersigned.

Respectfully submitted by

M. ANAGNOS.

ACKNOWLEDGMENTS.

Among the pleasant duties incident to the close of the year is that of expressing our heartfelt thanks and grateful acknowledgments to the following artists, *littérateurs*, societies, proprietors, managers, editors and publishers, for concerts and various musical entertainments; for operas, oratorios, lectures, readings, and for an excellent supply of periodicals and weekly papers, minerals and specimens of various kinds.

As I have said in previous reports, these favors are not only a source of pleasure and happiness to our pupils, but also a valuable means of æsthetic culture, of social intercourse and of mental stimulus and improvement. So far as we know, there is no community in the world which does half so much for the gratification and improvement of its unfortunate members as that of Boston does for our pupils.

I. — *Acknowledgments for Concerts and Operas in the City.*

To Mr. Henry Lee Higginson we are under great and lasting obligations for thirty tickets to the public rehearsals of his twenty-six orchestral concerts.

To Messrs. Tompkins and Hill, proprietors of the Boston theatre, for a generous invitation of unlimited numbers to three operas and two operettas.

To Mr. E. H. Hastings, manager of the Bijou theatre, for thirty-five tickets to one operetta.

To the Händel and Haydn society, through its president and secretary, Mr. C. C. Perkins and Mr. A. Parker Browne, for thirty tickets to the oratorio of the Creation, thirty-five tickets to the Messiah, and admittance to the rehearsals of five other concerts.

To the Boylston club, through its secretary, Mr. F. H. Ratcliffe, for eight tickets to each of five concerts.

To the Cecilia society, through its secretary, Mr. Charles W. Stone, for four tickets to each of five concerts.

To the Apollo club, through its secretary, Mr. Arthur Reed, for six tickets to each of six concerts.

To the Euterpe society, through its president, Mr. C. C. Perkins, for an average of four tickets to each of four concerts.

To Mr. B. J. Lang, for nine season tickets to six piano recitals, devoted to Schumann music.

To Mr. Arthur Foote, for ten tickets to each of four trio concerts.

To Mr. H. G. Tucker, for ten tickets to one piano recital.

To Mr. John A. Preston, for a pass to one concert.

To Mr. Ernst Perabo, for a pass to two concerts.

To Mr. J. A. Hills, for twelve tickets to one concert.

To Mr. Frank F. Marshall, for ten tickets to one concert.

To Mr. E. W. Tyler, for admission to two piano recitals by Mr. Otto Bendix.

To Mr. Henry F. Miller, for admission to one piano recital by Mr. Edmund Neupert, to three piano recitals by Dr. Louis Maas, and for admission to Mr. William H. Sherwood's testimonial concert and to several of his pupils' concerts.

To Messrs. Harwood and Beardsley, for twenty-five tickets to each of two concerts.

To Dr. Tourjée, of the New England Conservatory, for an average of twenty tickets to each of three concerts.

To Miss Charlotte Hawes, for twenty-five tickets to her illustrated musical lecture.

To Miss Henrietta Maurer, for twelve tickets to one concert.

To Mrs. Manley Howe, for twelve tickets to one concert.

To Miss Anna Dunlap, for twenty-four tickets to one concert.

To Miss E. M. Stark, for twelve tickets to the Phillips church concert.

To Mr. W. J. Colville, for four tickets to a soirée musicale.

II. — *Acknowledgments for Concerts given in our Hall.*

For a series of recitals and concerts given from time to time in the music hall of the institution, we are greatly indebted to the following artists : —

To Mrs. William H. Sherwood, pianist, assisted by Mrs. Dr. Fenderson, vocalist, and Mr. J. Dudley Hall, accompanist.

To Dr. and Mrs. Fenderson, assisted by Miss Simonton, violinist, Miss Dunlap, pianist, and Mrs. Flanders, elocutionist.

Through the kindness of Mr. R. M. Chase, to Prof. Shortis for a delightful concert on the banjo.

To Mr. Louis K. Stark, assisted by Mrs. J. Arthur Jacobs, pianist, Mrs. J. D. Buckingham, vocalist, Miss Nellie B. Callender, vocalist, and Miss Abby Holbrook, elocutionist.

To Mr. Albert Meyers, assisted by Miss Annie C. Westervelt, soprano, Miss Theresa Flynn, alto, Mrs. Anna Mayhew Simonds, pianist, Mr. E. P. Murphy, elocutionist, and Mr. J. G. Lennon, organist and pianist.

III. — *Acknowledgments for Lectures and Readings.*

For various lectures, addresses and readings, our thanks are due to the following friends: Dr. Edward Everett Hale, Mrs. Julia Ward Howe, Rev. James Reed, Rev. William P. Tilden, Miss Adela Rankin and the late Mr. Charles L. Heywood.

IV. — *Acknowledgments for Birds, Musical Instruments, etc.*

To Mr. Andrew H. Newell, of Boston, for a fine collection of sixty birds from Australia, and the skin of a small kangaroo.

To Mr. P. C. Brooks, for a mechanical French pianoforte, and to Mr. Alfred A. Marcus, for several smaller musical instruments.

To Mr. Francis Brooks for a fine ebony and velvet case for the medals belonging to the institution.

For various specimens, curiosities, etc., we are indebted to the following friends: Mrs. W. C. Wendte, Capt. Perry, Mr. Richard Sullivan, Mr. C. H. Dillaway, Miss E. B. Webster and Miss Fannie E. Webster.

V. — Acknowledgments for Periodicals and Newspapers.

The editors and publishers of the following reviews, magazines and semi-monthly and weekly papers, continue to be very kind and liberal in sending us their publications gratuitously, which are always cordially welcomed, and perused with interest: —

The N. E. Journal of Education, . *Boston, Mass.*
The Atlantic, ... " "
Wide Awake, ...
Boston Home Journal, . . .
Youth's Companion, ...
The Christian, ...
The Christian Register, ...
The Musical Record, ...
The Musical Herald, ...
The Folio, ...
Littell's Living Age, ...
Unitarian Review, ...
The Watchman, ...
The Golden Rule, ...
Zion's Herald, ...
The Missionary Herald, . . . " "
The Salem Register, ... *Salem, Mass.*
The Century, · . . . *New York, N. Y.*
St. Nicholas, ... " "
The Christian Union, ...
The Journal of Speculative Philosophy, " "

Church's Musical Journal, . . . *Cincinnati, O.*
Goodson Gazette, *Va. Inst. for Deaf-Mutes and Blind.*
Tablet, . . *West Va.* " " " "
Deaf-Mute Index, *Colorado,* " " " "
Companion, . *Minnesota Institute for Deaf-Mutes.*
Il Mentore dei Ciechi, . . *Florence, Italy.*

I desire again to render the most hearty thanks, in behalf of all our pupils, to the kind friends who have thus nobly remembered them. The seeds which their friendly and generous attentions have sown have fallen on no barren ground, but will continue to bear fruit in after years; and the memory of many of these delightful and instructive occasions and valuable gifts will be retained through life.

M. ANAGNOS.

DR.   PERKINS INSTITUTION AND MASSACHUSETTS SCHOOL FOR THE BLIND, *in account with* EDWARD JACKSON, *Treasurer.*   CR.

GENERAL FUND.

1882. Oct. 1,			**1882.** Oct. 1,	
To cash paid, auditors' drafts,	$60,636 75		By balance from last year's account, Sept. 30, 1882,	$3,850 43
taxes, 11 Oxford street,	83 05		cash from state of Massachusetts, $30,000 00	
J. V. Apthorp, commissions,	185 06		Maine, 3,700 00	
rent of safe, Union Safe			New Hampshire, 3,660 00	
Deposits,	20 00		Connecticut, 4,075 00	
Interest,	30 25		Rhode Island, 3,618 40	
Investments,	44,600 00		Vermont, 1,800 00	46,853 40
Balance on hand,	2,724 31		interest on mortgages, $3,079 00	
			interest on notes, 381 25	
			rent of 11 Oxford street, 635 00	
			Boston & Providence Railroad dividends, 240 00	
			Fitchburg Railroad dividends, 300 00	
			Interest on Eastern Railroad bonds, 240 00	
			Chicago, Milwaukie & St. Paul, 179 70	
			Chicago, Burlington & Quincy, 680 00	
			Boston & Lowell, 50 00	
			deposits with N. E. Trust Co., 204 21	7,989 17
			M. Anagnos, director, receipts of —	
			work department, $15,390 91	
			tuning, 1,724 00	
			sale of brooms, boys' shop, 96 30	
			tuition, 530 00	
			admission tickets, 79 95	
			sundries, 521 35	
			balance of legacy from Mrs. De Witt,	18,341 43
			mortgages collected,	1,500 00
			donations,	28,000 00
				16 00
	$108,279 42			$108,279 42
			1882. Oct. 1,	
			Credit to new account,	$2,724 31

PRINTING FUND.

1883. Oct. 1,							
To balance from last year,			$39 40	By subscriptions,		$500 00	
cash paid, auditor's drafts,			4,124 08	interest on Ottawa & Burlington R.R. bonds,		350 00	$182 00
loaned on mortgage,			75,000 00	Kansas City & Council Bluffs R.R. bonds,			
loaned on notes,			1,500 00	Chicago, Milwaukie & St. Paul R.R. bonds,		120 00	
				Chicago, Burlington & Quincy R.R. bonds,		400 00	
				notes,		1,586 26	
				mortgages,		1,546 20	
							4,901 56
				amounts received from M. Anagnos, director, for sale of books,			1,014 57
				notes collected,			75,000 00
				amounts received from American Printing House, for books,			204 00
				Debit to new account,			11 23
			$80,663 46				$80,663 46
1883. Oct. 1,	Debit to new account,		$11 23				

KINDERGARTEN FUND.

1883. Oct. 1,							
To loan on note,		$2,900 00		By subscriptions to date,		$2,355 00	
balance on hand,		5 83		legacy from Miss Morton,		500 00	
			$2,905 83	interest on notes,		50 83	
							$2,905 83
				Credit to new account,			$5 83
			$2,905 83				
Balance of Kindergarten Fund,		$5 83		Printing Fund over-invested,		$11 23	
Harris Fund uninvested,		29 17		Balance in New England Trust Co.,		2,748 08	
General Fund,		2,724 31					
			$2,759 31				$2,759 31

BOSTON, Oct. 1, 1883.

EDWARD JACKSON, *Treasurer.*

DR. AUDITORS OF PERKINS INSTITUTION AND MASSACHUSETTS SCHOOL FOR THE BLIND *in account with* M. ANAGNOS, *Director.* CR.

Cash paid for maintenance, salaries, superintendence and instruction as per schedule annexed, .	$39,998 32			**1882.** Oct. 1,	Balance of draft on hand, General Fund, . . .	$958 56
					Printing Fund, .	22 25	$980 81
Extraordinary expenses, annexed, .	22,530 06	$62,528 37		**1883.** Oct. 1,	Drafts to date as per Treasurer's acct, General Fund, .		60,636 75
Expenses of printing department, .		4,333 86			Printing Fund, .		4,124 06
		$66,862 23			Cash due Director, General Fund, . .	$933 06	
					Printing Fund, .	187 55	1,120 61
1883. Oct 1, Balance to new account, . . .		$1,120 61				$66,862 23

M. ANAGNOS, *Director.*

ANALYSIS OF EXPENDITURES

For the Year ending Sept. 30, 1883.

Maintenance, Salaries, Superintendence, and Instruction.

Meat, 24,861 lbs.,	$2,833 25
Fish, 4,501 lbs.,	230 95
Butter, 5,208 lbs.,	1,645 65
Rice, sago, etc., 593 lbs.,	56 72
Bread, flour, and meal,	1,384 59
Potatoes and other vegetables,	797 34
Fruit,	352 48
Milk, 23,336 qts.,	1,414 10
Sugar, 6,971 lbs.,	624 38
Tea and coffee, 520 lbs.,	176 28
Groceries,	829 77
Gas and oil,	459 86
Coal and wood,	2,930 43
Sundry articles of consumption,	332 40
Salaries, superintendence, and instruction,	16,218 99
Wages,	4,255 27
Outside aid,	255 71
Medicines and medical aid,	20 09
Furniture and bedding,	1,221 78
Clothing and mending,	9 09
Musical instruments,	284 76
Expenses of stable,	173 56
Books, stationery, and apparatus,	1,534 67
Ordinary construction and repairs,	1,436 38
Water taxes and insurance,	336 00
Travelling expenses,	78 98
Sundries,	104 84
	$39,998 32

Amount brought forward, ... $39,998 32

Extraordinary Expenses.

Extraordinary construction and repairs,	.	$3,461 76
Rent of office in Avon Street,	. . .	250 00
Expenses of tuning department,	. . .	*775 94
" " boys' shop,	. . . .	84 85
Bills to be refunded,	. . . . .	138 69
Beneficiaries of the Harris Fund,	. . .	855 00
Board of beneficiary,	. . . . .	87 13
Bills of work department,	. . . .	†16,876 68

22,530 05

$62,528 37

* NOTE. — The receipts from tuning, amounting to $1,724.00, have been paid by the director to the treasurer. They show a balance in favor of this department of $948.06.

† The earnings of the shop, amounting to $15,390.91, were in like manner paid by the director to the treasurer. After deducting increased value of stock on hand, $929.50, there is a balance against the workshop amounting to $556.27.

EXPENSES OF PRINTING DEPARTMENT.

Labor, ...	$1,434 88
Stock, ...	1,289 60
Machinery, ...	276 76
Type, ...	39 76
Electrotyping, ...	570 82
Binding, ...	703 60
Sundries, ...	18 94

$4,333 86

GENERAL ABSTRACT

Of Account of the Work Department, Oct. 1, 1883.

Due to the institution for investments since
the first date, ... $44,725 07
Excess of expenditures over receipts, . . 1,485 77
————— $46,210 84

Assets.

Stock on hand Oct. 1, 1883, ... $5,192 54
Debts due Oct. 1, 1883, ... 2,083 97
————— 7,276 51

$38,934 33

Balance against the work department Oct. 1,
1883, ... $38,934 33
Balance against the work department Oct. 1,
1882, ... 38,378 06

Cost of carrying on the work department for
the year ending Sept. 30, 1883, ... $556 27

Cash received for sales during the year, . $15,390 91
Excess of expenditures over receipts, . . 1,485 77
————— $16,876 68

Salaries and wages paid blind people, . $3,579 34
" paid to seeing people, . . . 2,360 04
Sundries for stock, etc., ... 10,937 30
————— $16,876 68

INVENTORY OF STOCK

Oct. 1, 1883.

Real estate, South Boston, . . .	$250,000 00	
" " 11 Oxford street, . . .	5,500 00	
		$255,500 00
Railroad stock, ...		11,000 00
Notes, ...		59,600 00
Cash in treasury, ...	$2,748 08	
Less due Director, ...	1,120 61	
		1,627 47
Harris Fund, ...		83,000 00
Printing Fund, ...		108,500 00
Kindergarten Fund, ...		2,900 00
Household furniture, ...		16,320 00
Provisions and supplies, ...		895 06
Wood and coal, ...		3,288 80
Work department, stock, . . .	$5,192 54	
" " debts due, . . .	2,083 97	
		7,276 51
Musical department, viz., —		
One large organ, ...	$5,000 00	
Four small organs, ...	450 00	
Forty-five pianos, ...	10,450 00	
Brass and reed instruments, . . .	900 00	
Violins, ...	35 00	
Musical library, ...	600 00	
		17,435 00
Amount carried forward, ...		$567,342 84

Amount brought forward, ...			$567,342 84
Printing department, viz.,			
Stock and machinery, ...	$1,800 00		
Books and maps, ...	8,291 45		
Stereotype plates, ...	4,470 82		
			14,562 27
School furniture and apparatus, . . .			7,700 00
Library books in common type, . . .	$2,900 00		
" " in raised type, . . .	6,500 00		
			9,400 00
Boys' shop, ...			100 70
Stable and tools, ...			1,066 17
			$600,171 98

LIST OF EMBOSSED BOOKS,

Printed at the Perkins Institution and Massachusetts School for the Blind.

TITLE OF BOOK.	No. of Volumes.	Price per Volume.
Howe's Cyclópædia, ...	8	$4 00
Baxter's Call, ...	1	2 50
Book of Proverbs, ...	1	2 00
Book of Psalms, ...	1	3 00
New Testament, ...	3	2 50
Book of Common Prayer, ...	1	4 00
Hymns for the Blind, ...	1	2 00
Pilgrim's Progress, ...	1	4 00
Life of Melanchthon, ...	1	1 00
Natural Theology, ...	1	4 00
Combe's Constitution of Man, ...	1	4 00
Selections from the Works of Swedenborg, . .	1	–
Second Table of Logarithms, ...	1	3 00
Philosophy of Natural History, ...	1	3 00
Huxley's Science Primers, Introductory, . .	1	2 00
Memoir of Dr. Samuel G. Howe, . . .	1	3 00
Cutter's Anatomy, Physiology and Hygiene, . .	1	3 00
Viri Romæ, new edition with additions, . .	1	2 00
Musical Characters used by the seeing, . .	1	35
Key to Braille's Musical Notation, . . .	1	35
Guyot's Geography, ...	1	4 00
Scribner's Geographical Reader, . . .	1	2 50
Dickens's Child's History of England, . .	2	3 00
Anderson's History of the United States, . .	1	2 50
Higginson's Young Folks' History of the United States, .	1	3 50
Schmitz's History of Greece, ...	1	3 00
Schmitz's History of Rome, ...	1	2 50
Freeman's History of Europe, ...	1	2 50
An Account of the Most Celebrated Diamonds, . . .	1	50
Extracts from British and American Literature, . .	2	3 00
American Prose, ...	2	3 00
Hawthorne's Tanglewood Tales, . . .	2	2 00
Dickens's Old Curiosity Shop, ...	3	4 00
Dickens's Christmas Carol, with extracts from Pickwick, .	1	3 00
Goldsmith's Vicar of Wakefield, ...	1	3 00
George Eliot's Silas Marner, ...	1	3 50
Biographical Sketch of George Eliot, . . .	1	25
Milton's Paradise Lost, ...	2	3 00

LIST OF EMBOSSED BOOKS — *Continued.*

TITLE OF BOOK.	No. of Volumes.	Price per Volume.
Pope's Essay on Man and other Poems, ...	1	$2 50
Shakespeare's Hamlet and Julius Cæsar, ...	1	4 00
Scott's Lay of the Last Minstrel and 37 other Poems,	1	3 00
Byron's Hebrew Melodies and Childe Harold, . .	1	3 00
Tennyson's In Memoriam and other Poems,. . .	1	3 00
Longfellow's Evangeline, ...	1	2 00
Longfellow's Evangeline and other Poems, . .	1	3 00
Whittier's Poems, ...	1	3 00
Lowell's Poems, ...	1	3 00
Bryant's Poems, ...	1	3 00
Longfellow's Birthday, by J. R. Anagnos, . .	1	25
Constitution of the United States, . . .	1	40
Biographical Sketches of Distinguished Persons, .	1	3 00
Commemoration Ode, by H. W. Stratton, . .	1	10
JUVENILE BOOKS.		
Script and point alphabet sheets per hundred, .	—	5 00
An Eclectic Primer, ...	1	40
Child's First Book, ...	1	40
Child's Second Book, ...	1	40
Child's Third Book, ...	1	40
Child's Fourth Book, ...	1	40
Child's Fifth Book, ...	1	40
Child's Sixth Book, ...	1	40
Child's Seventh Book, ...	1	40
Youth's Library, vol. 1st, ...	1	1 25
Youth's Library, vol. 2d, ...	1	1 25
Youth's Library, vol. 3d, ...	1	1 25
Youth's Library, vol. 4th, ...	1	1 25
Youth's Library, vol. 5th, ...	1	1 25
Youth's Library, vol. 6th, ...	1	1 25
Youth's Library, vol. 7th, ...	1	1 25
Youth's Library, vol. 8th, ...	1	1 25
Children's Fairy Book, by M. Anagnos, . .	1	2 50
Andersen's Stories and Tales, ...	1	3 00
Eliot's Six Arabian Nights, ...	1	3 00
Lodge's Twelve Popular Tales, ...	1	2 00
Bible Stories in Bible language, by Emilie Poulsson, .	1	3 50

N. B. The prices in the above list are set down per volume, not per set.

LIST OF APPLIANCES AND TANGIBLE APPARATUS,

Made at the Perkins Institution and Massachusetts School for the Blind.

--- ---

GEOGRAPHY.

I. — *Wall-Maps.*

1. The Hemispheres, ... size, 42 by 52 inches.
2. United States, Mexico and Canada, . . . " " "
3. North America, ... " " "
4. South America, ... " " "
5. Europe, ... " " "
6. Asia, ... " " "
7. Africa, ... " " "
8. The World on Mercator's Projection, . . " " "

Each $35, or the set, $280.

II. — *Dissected Maps.*

1. Eastern Hemisphere, ... size, 30 by 36 inches.
2. Western Hemisphere, ... " " "
3. North America, ... a . " " "
4 United States, ... " " "
5. South America, ... " " "
6. Europe, ... " " "
7. Asia, ... " " "
8. Africa, ... " " "

Each $23, or the set, $184.

These maps are considered, in point of workmanship, accuracy and distinctness of outline, durability and beauty, far superior to all thus far made in Europe or in this country.

☞ "The New England Journal of Education" says, "They are very strong, present a fine, bright surface, and are an ornament to any school-room."

III. — *Pin-Maps.*

Cushions for pin-maps and diagrams, ... each, $0 75

ARITHMETIC.

Ciphering-boards made of brass strips, nickel-plated, . each, $1 25
Ciphering-types, nickel-plated, per hundred, . . . " 1 00

WRITING.

Grooved writing-cards, ... each, $0 10
Braille tablets, with metallic bed, . . " 1 50
Braille French tablets, with cloth bed, ... " 1 00
Braille new tablets, with cloth bed, . . 1 00
Braille Daisy tablets, . . . " 5 00

TERMS OF ADMISSION.

<hr>

"Candidates for admission must be over nine and under nineteen years of age, and none others shall be admitted." — *Extract from the by-laws.*

Blind children and youth between the ages above prescribed and of sound mind and good moral character, can be admitted to the school by paying $300 per annum. Those among them who belong to the state of Massachusetts and whose parents or guardians are not able to pay the whole or a portion of this sum, can be admitted gratuitously by application to the governor for a warrant.

The following is a good form, though any other will do : —

" *To His Excellency the Governor.*

" SIR, — My son (or daughter, or nephew, or niece, as the case may be), named ——, and aged——, cannot be instructed in the common schools, for want of sight. I am unable to pay for the tuition at the Perkins Institution and Massachusetts School for the Blind, and I request that your Excellency will give a warrant for free admission.
Very respectfully,   —— ——."

The application may be made by any relation or friend, if the parents are dead or absent.

It should be accompanied by a certificate, signed by some regular physician, in this form : —

" I certify, that, in my opinion, —— —— has not sufficient vision to be taught in common schools ; and that he is free from epilepsy, and from any contagious disease.
(Signed)   —— ——."

These papers should be done up together, and forwarded to the DIRECTOR OF THE INSTITUTION FOR THE BLIND, *South Boston, Mass.*

Blind children and youth residing in Maine, New Hampshire, Vermont, Connecticut and Rhode Island, by applying as above to the governor, or the "Secretary of State," in their respective states, can obtain warrants for free admission.

The sum of $300 above specified covers all expenses (except for clothing), namely, board, lodging, washing, tuition, and the use of books and musical instruments. The pupils must furnish their own clothing, and pay their own fares to and from the institution.

An obligation will be required from some responsible persons, that the pupil shall be kept properly supplied with decent clothing, shall be provided for during vacations, and shall be removed, without expense to the institution, whenever it may be desirable to discharge him.

The usual period of tuition is from five to seven years.

The friends of the pupils can visit them whenever they choose.

The use of tobacco, either in smoking or otherwise, is strictly prohibited in the institution.

Persons applying for admission of children must fill out certain blanks, copies of which will be forwarded to any address on application.

For further information address M. ANAGNOS, DIRECTOR, PERKINS INSTITUTION FOR THE BLIND, *South Boston, Mass.*

COMMENCEMENT EXERCISES

OF THE

PERKINS INSTITUTION AND MASSACHUSETTS SCHOOL FOR THE BLIND,

Held at Tremont Temple, on Tuesday, June 5, 1883, at 3 P.M.

SAMUEL ELIOT, LL.D., Presiding.

PROGRAMME. PART I.

1. ORGAN SELECTIONS.
   MISS FREDA BLACK and MR. WM. B. HAMMOND.

2. BAND, — Potpourri, ... *arr. by Heinicke.*

3. ESSAY, — "Our Library."
   MISS JULIA E. BURNHAM.

4. EXERCISE IN CHEMISTRY.
   BENJAMIN F. PARKER.

5. SOLO FOR ALTO HORN, — "Morceau
   de Salon," Variations, } . . *H. Painpare.*
   CHRISTOPHER A. HOWLAND.

6. ESSAY, — "The Steam-Engine," (illustrated).
   WILLIAM P. GARRISON.

7. QUARTETTE, — "Parting
   Ode," } *Music by Miss Mary McCaffrey.*
   MISSES MABEL BROWN, LENNA D. SWINERTON, MARY
   McCAFFREY, and EMMA PATTERSON.

8. ESSAY, — "The Practice of Massage, a Possibility for the Blind."
   MISS JENNY M. COLBY.

Part II.

1. MILITARY DRILL AND GYMNASTICS.

2. PIANO DUET, — Scherzo from 7th Symphony, . . *Beethoven.*
   MISS MARY McCAFFREY and MISS SARAH A. HAMSON.

3. READING WITH THE FINGERS, — Exercise in Geography.
   A CLASS OF BOYS.

4. KINDERGARTEN EXERCISES.

5. DUET, — "The Fisherman," . . . . *V. Gabussi.*
   MESSRS. WM. B. HAMMOND and L. TITUS.

6. VALEDICTORY.
   MISS LENNA D. SWINERTON.

7. CHORUS FOR FEMALE VOICES, — "Oh haste, } . *Donizetti.*
   Crimson Morning," }

8. AWARD OF DIPLOMAS,
   BY DR. SAMUEL ELIOT.

9. CHORUS, — "Where in Rocky Inlets," from } . *Rubenstein.*
   the Tower of Babel, }

NAMES OF GRADUATES.

JULIA E. BURNHAM.	MARY McCAFFREY.
JENNY M. COLBY.	BENJAMIN F. PARKER.
WILLIAM P. GARRISON.	LENNA D. SWINERTON.

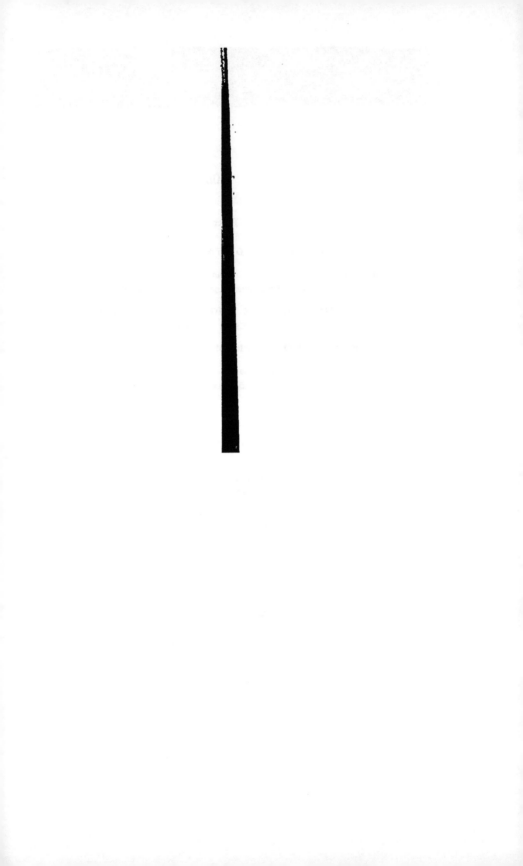

APPENDIX.

The Blind Children's Kindergarten.

BY

EMILIE POULSSON.

Reprinted from the October number of the WIDE AWAKE by kind permission of
Messrs. D. Lothrop & Co., publishers of the magazine.

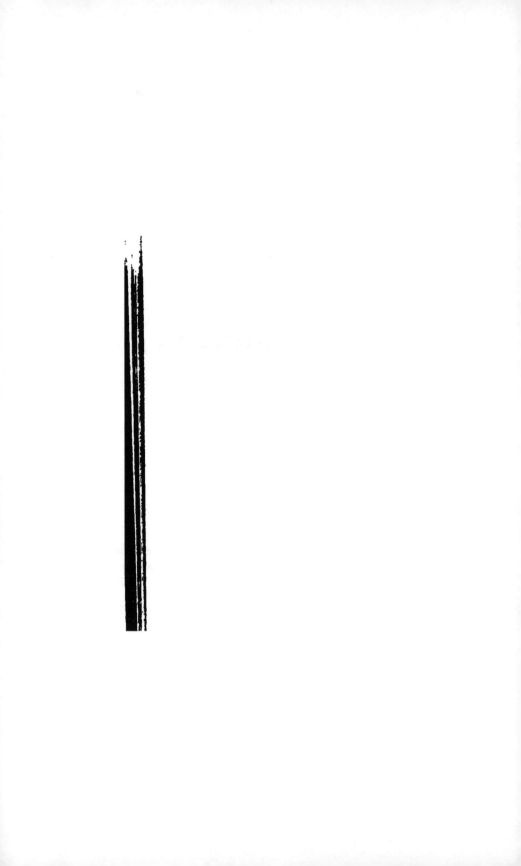

THE BLIND CHILDREN'S KINDERGARTEN.

BY EMILIE POULSSON.

Do you remember the article about the Perkins Institution for the Blind, in the " Wide Awake " for March,
1878, — that noble supplementary public school for those
brothers and sisters of yours over whose eyes a heavy
hand has been mysteriously laid? Since that account was
written, a kindergarten experiment has been tried, and
it promises to be the best " happy thought " yet for the
benefit of blind children. It really seems that knowledge
and usefulness and self-reliance were to be reached by a
blind person some years sooner by way of the kindergarten than by any of the slow, slow progresses over the
long, long roads of other years.

To be sure object-teaching had been used in the school.
The botany class had its vegetable garden; there had
been weighing and measuring, buying and selling, in the
arithmetic classes; the physiology class had fine anatomical models; and there were stuffed birds and other
animals for the student in natural history, to say nothing
of the orders given to the wondering Peter for lobsters,
clams, heart and lungs of an ox, the bones of fowls, and
many like objects.

Seeing that what was touched was comprehended far
more completely and quickly than what was described by

voice, Mr. Anagnos, after much careful study of the kindergarten, resolved to introduce it into the school; resolved to teach great boys and girls just as baby-folks are taught; resolved, if he succeeded as he expected, to give the world no peace until a great, noble kindergarten should be built and endowed that would take in all the blind baby-folks at the outset, just as soon as they came to true kindergarten age, so that they might begin to learn at the time of life when other children begin.

He started with two classes; one in the boys' school, and one in the girls'. Both classes are composed mostly of the pupils of the lowest grade. But he also brings in for a time those in the higher classes who are conspicuously lacking in dexterity, or whose conceptions of form are unusually vague and confused.

The idea that a blind person is ever without a marvelously delicate touch will be new to many people; but the truth is, that the sensitive touch, instead of being a compensatory gift, has been the result of harder work than you or I know anything about — the most patient, long-continued effort to see and think and imagine and remember with the fingers.

Mr. Anagnos finds kindergarten work to be his most valuable means in the cultivation of this sensitiveness of the fingers, and he would esteem it indispensable in the institution for this result alone. But beside this, there seems no way so effective of affording a systematic study of form — it is the true A B C in the education of the blind.

The geometrical training which any child gets in the kindergarten helps the blind wonderfully to definitely imagine objects which they cannot handle.

The little girls who have taken up geography after

their kindergarten training are far readier in their map-work than previous classes. They are very quick to notice peculiarities in the shape of the states and countries, and they listen to descriptions most understandingly.

" Reading by touch," too, is far easier to the fingers which have been trained in tracing the embroidered patterns on the sewing-cards, weaving the delicate papers and modelling in clay. The work of square handwriting is taken up with great delight and courage by pupils who already know lines and angles well through the stick-laying and sewing. The Braille point writing (a system of raised dots, and used because it can be read by touch) and the written arithmetic of the blind, which is done with type placed in different positions to represent the different figures, both require the clearness concerning " upper right," " lower right," " upper left" and " lower left," which is constantly cultivated by the kindergarten work with cubes, planes and sticks. The teacher of the girls' work school, under whom the girls learn hand-sewing, machine-sewing, knitting, crochetting, hammock-making, and cane-seating, speaks heartily in praise of kindergarten as a preparatory training. So it is in music; the awakened mind and flexile hand, with muscles already trained in the kindergarten to obey, tell at once in the progress of the pupil.

The youngest children in these two classes are ten years of age; the majority older. But they are found to need the same development and the same simple lesson as ordinary children from three to six years of age; not because of any natural mental lack, but because the aimless, neglected lives they have led before coming to the institution have kept them dull and unawake. The little blind child, following its natural instinct of play, gets hurt so often that it soon feels it safest to curl up in a corner and keep still. If it try to play games with active, seeing children, it finds itself in the way; and in the way still when there is work to do — it is naturally shoved to one side; play, work, conversation pass it by — growth stops or goes on slowly and weakly.

By and by, perhaps, some one takes the necessary steps and sends the big girl or boy to the school for the blind. And until the establishment of these classes, there has been no kindergarten into which to receive this big, clumsy infant. One girl said to me, piteously, "When I was at home, my stepmother used always to be a-scolding to me and my father, about my being blind and not being able to work in the factory like the others, and I not doing the housework either. But nobody showed me how to do anything till I came here. How could I do things?" The same girl has since written to an aunt who, she says, was always "feeling bad" because of her blindness: "I don't mind it now being blind, because I can go all around, and I can sew and wash dishes and have my lessons, and do just like other people."

But it is not always unkindness which leaves the poor things so untrained. Some suffer from the unwise tenderness which has led their friends to wait upon them always. A girl of twenty, who came to the institution, could scarcely pin her collars, and preferred to have some one put her gloves and shawl on for her. The kindergarten has done much for her already in giving her hands their normal *handiness*.

"What did you do at home, Sarah?" I asked another girl one day.

"Look at me," she replied; "do you see the way I am sitting?" She had her hands folded in her lap, her whole attitude as listless as possible. "That is what I used to do all day long."

Such are many of the girls in our kindergarten; grown-up, but as little children in their use of both muscle and mind: others have been more fortunate in home circumstances and training, and many are winsome, and dear, and interesting; but all need either the mental or manual drill, or both, of the kindergarten, before going into the usual classes.

Let me tell you how we train these great, piteous children:

Monday is sewing-day — they scarcely have any other names for days than "clay-day," "weaving-day," "cushion-day," etc.; — not for hemming, over-handing, basting and stitching; these come in the afternoon work school; but the embroidering of white cards with worsteds in patterns. The cards being pricked, the girls can feel the holes easily for working, and by tracing the worsted lines when completed they "see just how it looks." *They observe* with their fingers and their imaginations.

Among the outlines, that of a house is a favorite with both teacher and pupils. It brings up enough interesting information to keep them listening and questioning for a long time. Seeing people do not realize that a blind person may not know the shape of a house roof, the color of a chimney, and hundreds of other every-day things beyond the reach of investigating fingers; so the suggestiveness of the sewing cards is a valuable help in leading

these pupils to a correct knowledge of things about
them.

Tuesday is " cushion-day." The girls come to the
pleasant east room, where there are plants and sunshine
enough to satisfy any kinder-
gartener, and a knowing little
canary besides, and gather
around the horseshoe
table.

ON SEWING—DAY.

On it are red and grey cushions, each with a plentiful
supply of tiny doll-hairpins in the upper right-hand corner. When stick-laying is the work, the girls soon have
on their cushions a fine array of lines, squares, triangles,

ladders, chairs, and here and there a bird-house or other fancy figure. They fasten the sticks down carefully at each end with a hairpin, and thus have the same satisfaction as in card-sewing — that of examining their work themselves. Their imagination seems to awake. One worker sees four tall soldiers marching in a row, where you

ON CUSHION DAY.

notice only four vertical lines. After the soldiers were mentioned, some one suggested they ought to have tents. These they were sure they could make, as they had had a little descriptive talk about tents only a few days before; so they went to work.

Most of the class considered a triangle a satisfactory representation, and soon pronounced the tents ready.

Mary was busy longer with hers. She had made a square for the floor, and then put a pole up from each corner, letting the four meet, thus forming the framework of as cunning a little tent as you could imagine.

Belle had a flag on hers, the sticks that outlined it slant-
ing enough to give it a graceful droop. Abbie, too, had
a flag, but not having thought to make it droop, explained its extremely stiff appearance by saying that
there was a " strong wind blowing from the north-
west." Another put a sentry by the tent, and another
gave her soldiers guns, and so they kept on till the bell
struck.

The cushions are also used for the work with tablets.
These are inch squares of wood, red on one side, white
on the other; and for blind children's use they have holes
drilled in them, so that they may be fastened on the cushion with a pin, and also a tiny notch on the edge of the
red side so that they may know what color they have
uppermost. They delight to make red and white patch-
work in this way.

They also have triangular pieces drilled and notched
in the same way. Their first work with these is to combine them into squares. This was easy for most of
them, but one girl exclaimed, after painstaking efforts,
" Well, I seem to have made a very sad square somehow ! "

It was indeed a funny-looking irregular figure with
several sides and corners pointing in every direction. A
little talk about the sides and corners of a true square
showed Minnie what caused the " sadness," and she soon
showed us a very cheerful square indeed, with a correspondingly cheerful look on her face. This is valuable
training for the work schools in which they learn trades
for future support.

Weaving with colored papers is the Wednesday work,
and I think it ranks next the clay in their affections.

You can get a little idea of how bewildering it is to do this weaving if you should try it some time in the dark — trusting only to your finger tips. Under and over, under and over, patiently and carefully, the big blind pupils work. Wee Katie calls her papers men walking under and over the bridges; and another says, "They are men who do not know the way, and we have to lead them aright." This work, like the card sewing and the little tablets, brings out the girls' delight in colors. It seems strange that they should like so much what they can have no conception of.

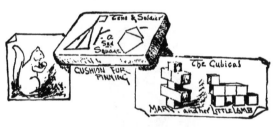

SOME OF THEIR HANDIWORK.

They have decided preferences in color, and the choosing of a new paper mat and the color of the strands to weave in it, is a work of just as much interest to them as to seeing children; and the guidance which their taste receives in this way, the lessons in combinations, and the little talks about the appropriateness of certain colors to certain articles and uses must help them to a somewhat clearer appreciation of the beauty and effectiveness of color.

Of all the occupations the paper weaving bears the most direct relation to future handiwork. For besides the sewing and ordinary " womanly work," many of the girls learn cane-seating and basket-making, and in both, the skill required in weaving will be of great service.

On Thursday they have cubes. The little boxes containing eight tiny cubes look rather insignificant; but wait till you have seen the fun that can be had with

" AS A LITTLE CHILD."

them, and the variety of things made with them. The class work together for a while, following the teacher's directions, and succeed fairly, though this is their hardest work. All is so easily demolished by a touch in the wrong place — and that cannot always be avoided, as they must "see" the forms with their fingers. In their first days with cubes, when they were constructing the sim-

plest forms, they made a line of the eight, and called it a
" procession," and I remember how one girl had displaced
hers quite badly, having a very loose, crooked line indeed,
and I was about to criticize it, when she said, " Mine is
a democratic procession, and the men are going to fall
out and go home." As it was the morning after the Gar-
field election, this was certainly not a clumsy turn.

When the girls work by themselves — without directions, that is — they invent forms just as other children
do, imitating things about them, or expressing their conceptions of something described to them. The whole furniture of the gymnasium was copied one day by little
Katie, each piece being announced with much enthusiasm.

We have great fun sometimes telling stories and making the forms suggested by them. One day the teacher
gave directions for a form which when completed was
hailed with delight by the class as a little girl. A form
followed this which they could not name at first — but
when I told them the little girl's name was Mary, they
recognized the " lamb," with great glee.

Left free to invent they went on and made the schoolhouse, the teacher's desk and chair, and the other furniture of Mary's school-room in great variety. One made
a horseshoe table like the one at which the class was
sitting, one made a square table and four desks for the
children, and one made an oblong table ; little May, who
went to a public school a year ago, before she lost her
sight, placed her children's desks far apart, with a broad
aisle between them, " so they shouldn't whisper." Mary's
home and her lamb's would probably have been made, but
there was no more time.

Another day they had the story of " The Three Bears."

I gave them that most delightful version of it, for which all the children of the land have to thank Mrs. Clara Doty Bates and the "Wide Awake."

> Silver Locks was a little girl,
> Lovely and good;
> She strayed out one day
> And got lost in the wood,
> And was lonely and sad
> Till she came where there stood
> The house that belonged to the bears.

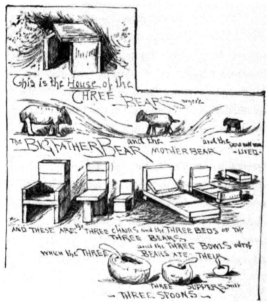

AN ILLUSTRATED STORY.

Of course we made the house with a door that would open wide; and the big chair and the middle-sized chair, and the wee baby bear's chair, which had to be broken

all into pieces; and the big bed and the middle-sized
bed, and the wee baby bear's bed.

And when clay-day came we made the three bowls for
the milk — the father bear's bowl with a big ladle in it, the
mother bear's bowl with a big spoon, and the baby bear's
with a wee little spoon.

This was as far as I had thought of making forms to
accompany the story; but several pairs of nimble hands
finished the bowls and made one or another of the bears,
so that we had the whole family complete as well as the
house and furniture. "Silver Locks" was attempted,
but was too far short of the darling ideal to be shown even
to me, though the intention and failure were confided.

Aside from what is gained in deftness, care and precision and development of the imagination, there are many
lessons given in connection with the cubes, so that there
is more than mere amusement in the towers, furniture,
steamboats, tents, candles, stairs, etc., that the pupils
make.

To copy these forms with their square tablets, is what
the girls call picture-making, and it is always done with
the liveliest interest. They were first shown that one
square was exactly like one face of the little cube, and then
letting their fingers trace down one side of the tower, they
saw how they could copy it on their cushions, and I think
no children enjoy drawing more than these children enjoy
making pictures in this way. They get puzzled sometimes, in trying to observe only one side of a figure, as
their fingers are apt to touch several sides, or even the
whole at once; but they are gradually learning the meaning of " front view," " side view," etc.

It is certainly incomprehensible to blind people that

things can be represented naturally and accurately on a surface which presents only smoothness to their touch. But the square tablets give tangible surface-representations of the solid forms made with the cubes, and through this it is hoped that the children may gain a notion of real pictures.

I suppose every kindergarten has clay on Friday. That delight finishes the week with the Perkins Institute kindergarten children too. There is a joyous bustle as they put on the oversleeves to protect their dresses, and then they listen with beaming faces to the soft thuds which tell that a lump of clay is being put on each board, and try to make the most fanciful things with as much faith as when they undertake every-day forms. Fortunately for the girls, their teacher has the ready tact and imagination needed often to detect the ideal in the rude clay forms. Once, however, even she was at a loss. Little Polly, dear child, full of quaint fancies, had made a puzzling figure, which looked as if she had meant it for a tallow candle which had melted and run down the sides. This guess was hazarded, but received with such surprise that it was hastily withdrawn, and the teacher begged for enlightenment, whereupon Polly explained with much enthusiasm that it was a "May-pole wreathed with flowers." *She* could even tell which were the full-blown roses in the garlands, where we could only see ragged lumps of clay. One of the other girls had attempted a cream pitcher, but finding it a clumsy one, she put a bail on instead of a handle, and a little curved piece near the bottom to lift by, and there it stood, an unmistakable coal hod !

Having only one hour a day for kindergarten, we cannot use all its varied occupations in each week, so we

choose those which seem most useful to our pupils; but
such have been the results from this " hour," that Mr.
Anagnos feels that all further pupils ought to be received
directly into thorough kindergarten modes of instruction.
Its importance seems a matter for universal consideration;
and we here commend the building and the endowment
of kindergartens for the blind children of the nation,
alike to the youth of the United States, and the wealthy
philanthropists of our time and country. Into such homes,
planned expressly for them, the little blind children now
living in comfortless quarters with but little or unwise care
could be gathered at the true kindergarten age; and there
with games and exercises prepared and adapted expressly
for them to suit their needs, they would be guarded from
hurt in their free frolickings; so that instead of dreading,
they would enjoy motion and be tempted into activity,
and thus gain physical development, which so many blind
people lack. Such children, by the time they reached the
age of those now in the kindergarten class, would have the
trained fingers, the active disciplined mind and the established character, which never belong to the blind youth
whose early years are spent in idleness and depression.

The Perkins Institution as it now stands cannot furnish
kindergarten for these little folks. It is already a village
in itself, with the main buildings, the cottages, school-
houses, gallery, printing-house and workshop. The land
is too crowded with buildings, and the buildings with the
older pupils, to afford room for any new department, for
any such kindergarten and primary school for little blind
children from five to ten years of age, as is now demanded;
and there is absolutely no national, state or private provision made for the instruction of the blind children under

ten years of age. Mr. Anagnos has issued an earnest appeal for the foundation and endowment of such a department in his last annual report. From it we gather that

In the Gymnasium

TEMPTED INTO ACTIVITY.

the first thing to be done is to secure about five acres of land in a pleasant, healthy location. Making allowance for the buildings which will be needed sooner or later, five acres would be none too much for the out-of-door life of the pupils, their gardens, playgrounds and walks.

Then they would need a house to live in; for, like the pupils at the institution, they would only go to their own homes in the vacations. Schoolrooms, too, or a school-house, would be demanded immediately, of course, and some big people to take care of the little people — a matron to do the "mothering" and the housekeeping, and others to help her, and two or three or four or more, kindergartnerin — the best, wisest, and most loving of them that could be found.

Mr. Anagnos estimates the sum needed in such a beginning to be twenty-five thousand dollars, for the land, the house, the schoolhouse, the salaries, for one year, of the people who would have the care and teaching of the children and the food and fuel for one year, with other plain necessities.

There is no doubt that this kindergarten must be a work of benevolence; for by far the greater number of blind children are among the very poor. Not more than eight per cent. among the pupils at the institution could possibly pay their own expenses.

But surely there are those among American parents and American children who have the sentiment of Jean Paul, "I love God and little children," and who will be touched by the pitiable condition of these dear sightless little ones, and who will give of their dollars and their pennies to found for them a true kindergarten home.

LIST OF CONTRIBUTORS

To THE KINDERGARTEN FUND.

Mrs. E. B. Bigelow, ...	$50 00
Mrs. J. H. Thorndike, . . . , . . .	100 00
Francis Minot, M.D., ...	100 00
Richard Sullivan, ...	50 00
Mrs. B. L. Young, ...	100 00
Mrs. Mary G. Burt, ...	5 00
Miss Matilda and Miss Rebecca Goddard, ...	50 00
Mrs. Sarah S. Fay, ...	1,000 00
"No Name Club," Brookline, Mass., ...	30 00
S. G. Deblois, ...	25 00
Mrs. P. C. Brooks (two donations), ...	600 00
Mrs. J. H. Wolcott, ...	200 00
Miss Morton (through Mr. Thompson Baxter), . . .	500 00
Abbott Lawrence Lowell, ...	25 00
Mrs. J. B. S. Jackson, ...	20 00

Further contributions and subscriptions are most earnestly solicited, and will be thankfully received by

EDWARD JACKSON, *Treasurer*,

No. 178 Devonshire Street,

BOSTON, MASS.

FIFTY-THIRD ANNUAL REPORT

OF

THE TRUSTEES

OF THE

PERKINS INSTITUTION

AND

𝔐assachusetts 𝔖chool for the 𝔅lind,

FOR THE YEAR ENDING

SEPTEMBER 30, 1884.

———

BOSTON:
WRIGHT & POTTER PRINTING CO., STATE PRINTERS,
18 POST OFFICE SQUARE.
1885.

TABLE OF CONTENTS.

Commonwealth of Massachusetts.

PERKINS INSTITUTION AND MASS. SCHOOL FOR THE BLIND,
SOUTH BOSTON, Oct. 23, 1884.

To the Hon. HENRY B. PEIRCE, *Secretary of State*, Boston.

DEAR SIR : — I have the honor to transmit to you, for the use of the legislature, a copy of the fifty-third annual report of the trustees of this institution to the corporation thereof, together with the usual accompanying documents.

Respectfully,

M. ANAGNOS,

Secretary.

OFFICERS OF THE CORPORATION.

1884-85.

SAMUEL ELIOT, *President.*
JOHN CUMMINGS, *Vice-President.*
EDWARD JACKSON, *Treasurer.*
M. ANAGNOS, *Secretary.*

BOARD OF TRUSTEES.

FRANCIS BROOKS.	SAMUEL M. QUINCY.
JOHN S. DWIGHT.	LEVERETT SALTONSTALL.
JOSEPH B. GLOVER.	SAMUEL G. SNELLING.
J THEODORE HEARD, M. D.	JAMES STURGIS.
EDWARD N. PERKINS.	GEORGE W. WALES.
JOHN C. PHILLIPS.	JOHN H. WETHERBEE.

STANDING COMMITTEES.

Monthly Visiting Committee,

Whose duty it is to visit and inspect the Institution at least once in each month.

1885.		1885.	
January,	. . . F. BROOKS.	July,	. . . S. M. QUINCY.
February,	. . . J. S. DWIGHT.	August,	. . LEVERETT SALTONSTALL.
March,	. . . . J. B. GLOVER.	September,	. S. G. SNELLING.
April,	. . . . J. T. HEARD.	October,	. . JAMES STURGIS.
May,	. . . . E. N. PERKINS.	November,	. G. W. WALES.
June,	. . . . J. C. PHILLIPS.	December,	. J. H. WETHERBEE.

Committee on Education.

J. S. DWIGHT.
FRANCIS BROOKS.
S. M. QUINCY.

House Committee.

E. N. PERKINS.
G. W. WALES.
FRANCIS BROOKS.

Committee on Finance.

J. B. GLOVER.
JAMES STURGIS.
JOHN C. PHILLIPS.

Committee on Health.

J. THEODORE HEARD, M.D.
L. SALTONSTALL.
J. H. WETHERBEE.

Auditors of Accounts.

SAMUEL G. SNELLING.
JAMES STURGIS.

OFFICERS OF THE INSTITUTION.

DIRECTOR.
M. ANAGNOS.

MEDICAL INSPECTOR.
JOHN HOMANS, M. D.

LITERARY DEPARTMENT.

Miss OLIVE A. PRESCOTT.
Miss ETTA S. ADAMS.
Miss FRANCES B. WINSLOW.
Miss JULIA A. BOYLAN.

Miss DELLA BENNETT.
Miss MARY C. MOORE.
Miss MARIAN A. HOSMER.
Miss EMMA A. COOLIDGE.

Miss SARAH ELIZABETH LANE, *Librarian.*

MUSICAL DEPARTMENT.

THOMAS REEVES.
FRANK H. KILBOURNE.
Miss FREDA BLACK.
Miss MARY L. RILEY.
Miss LUCY A. HAMMOND.
Miss JULIA H. STRONG.
Miss JENNY A. WHEATON.

Mrs. KATE RAMETTI.
C. H. HIGGINS.
EZRA M. BAGLEY.
JULIUS AKEROYD.

Music Readers.
Miss ALLIE S. KNAPP.
Miss IOLA M. CLARKE.

TUNING DEPARTMENT.
JOEL WEST SMITH, *Instructor and Manager.*
GEORGE E. HART, *Tuner.*

INDUSTRIAL DEPARTMENT.

Workrooms for Juveniles.
JOHN H. WRIGHT, *Work Master.*
Miss A. J. DILLINGHAM, *Work Mistress.*
Miss CORA L. DAVIS, *Assistant.*
THOMAS CARROLL, *Assistant.*

Workshop for Adults.
ANTHONY W. BOWDEN, *Manager.*
P. MORRILL, *Foreman.*
Miss M. A. DWELLY, *Forewoman.*
Miss ELLEN M. WHEELOCK, *Clerk.*

DOMESTIC DEPARTMENT.

Steward.
ANTHONY W. BOWDEN.

Matron.
Miss MARIA C. MOULTON.
Miss ELLA F. FORD, *Assistant.*

Housekeepers in the Cottages.
Mrs. M. A. KNOWLTON.
Mrs. L. S. SMITH.
Miss BESSIE WOOD.
Mrs. SOPHIA C. HOPKINS.

PRINTING DEPARTMENT.
DENNIS A. REARDON, ... *Manager.*
Miss ELIZABETH S. HOWE, *Printer.*
Miss MARTHA F. ROWELL,   "

Miss ELLEN B. WEBSTER, *Book-keeper.*

MEMBERS OF THE CORPORATION.

All persons who have contributed twenty-five dollars to the funds of the institution, all who have served as trustees or treasurer, and all who have been elected by special vote, are members.

Adams, John A., Providence.
Adams, Waldo, Boston.
Alden, Mrs. Sara B., Boston.
Aldrich, Mrs. Sarah, Boston.
Alger, Rev. William R., Boston.
Ames, F. L., Boston.
Ames, Miss H. A., Easton.
Ames, Oliver, Boston.
Amory, C. W., Boston.
Amory, James S., Boston.
Amory, William, Boston.
Amory, Mrs. William, Boston.
Anagnos, M., Boston.
Andrews, Francis, Boston.
Appleton, Miss Emily G., Boston.
Appleton, Mrs. William, Boston.
Apthorp, William F., Boston.
Atkins, Mrs. Elisha, Boston.
Atkinson, Edward, Boston.
Atkinson, William, Boston.
Austin, Edward, Boston.
Aylesworth, H. B., Providence.
Bacon, Edwin M., Boston.
Baldwin, William H., Boston.
Baker, Mrs. E. M., Boston.
Baker, Mrs. E. W., Dorchester.
Baker, Ezra H., Boston.

Baker, Miss M. K., Boston.
Barbour, E. D., Boston.
Barker, Joseph A., Providence.
Barstow, Amos C., Providence.
Barrows, Rev. S. J., Dorchester.
Beal, J. H., Boston.
Beard, Hon. Alanson W., Boston.
Beckwith, Miss A. G., Providence.
Beckwith, Mrs. T., Providence.
Beebe, J. A., Boston.
Bennett, Mrs. Eleanor, Billerica.
Bigelow, Mrs. E. B., Boston.
Binney, William, Providence.
Black, G. N., Boston.
Blake, James H., Boston.
Blanchard, G. D. B., Malden.
Bourn, Hon. A. O., Bristol, R. I.
Bouvé, Thomas T., Boston.
Bowditch, Mrs. E. B., Boston.
Bowditch, J. I., Boston.
Bowditch, Mrs. J. I., Boston.
Brackett, Miss Nancy, Boston.
Bradlee, F. H., Boston.
Bradlee, Mrs. F. H., Boston.
Bradlee, J. P., Boston.
Brewer, Miss C. A., Boston.
Brewer, Mrs. Mary, Boston.

ʍster, Osmyn, Boston.
ɑmer, Hon. Martin, Boston.
ɔks, Francis, Boston.
ɔks, Mrs. F. A., Boston.
ɔks, Peter C., Boston.
ɔks, Rev. Phillips, Boston.
ɔks, Shepherd, Boston.
ʍn, John A., Providence.
ʍn, Mrs. John C., Providence.
ʍne, A. Parker, Boston.
ard, W. S., Boston.
ock, Miss Julia, Providence.
dy, James J., Providence.
nett, Joseph, Boston.
ton, J. W., M. D., Flushing,
. Y.
ot, Samuel, M. D., Boston.
ot, Mrs. Samuel, Sen., Boston.
ot, W. C., Boston.
ender, Walter, Providence.
ɔenter, Charles E., Providence.
ʒer, Mrs. Helen B., West New-
n.
ʒer, J. H., Roxbury.
ʔ, Mrs. W. F., Boston.
ndler, P. W., Boston.
ndler, Theophilus P., Brook-
ıe.
ce, J. H., Valley Falls, R. I.
ce, J., Providence.
pin, E. P., Providence.
rles, Mrs. Mary C., Melrose.
ʒver, Dr. David W., Boston.
ney, Benjamin P., Boston.
ʒkering, George H., Boston.
ʒkering, Mrs. Sarah M., Joy
ılls, Pa.
ıin, Hon. William, Boston.
ɩp, William W., Boston.
ke, Mrs. Jas. Freeman, Boston.

Clarke, James W., Boston.
Clement, Edward H., Boston.
Coats, James, Providence.
Cobb, Mrs. Freeman, Boston.
Cobb, Samuel C., Boston.
Cobb, Samuel T., Boston.
Cochrane, Alexander, Boston.
Coffin, Mrs. W. E., Boston.
Colt, Samuel P., Bristol, R. I.
Conant, Mrs. Rebecca, Amherst,
N. H.
Coolidge, Dr. A., Boston.
Coolidge, J. R., Boston.
Coolidge, Mrs. J. R., Boston.
Coolidge, J. T., Boston.
Coolidge, Mrs. J. T., Boston.
Coolidge, T. Jefferson, Boston.
Corliss, George H., Providence.
Cotting, C. U., Boston.
Crane, Zenas M., Dalton.
Crosby, Joseph B., Boston.
Crosby, William S., Boston.
Cruft, Miss Annah P., Boston.
Cruft, Miss Harriet O., Boston.
Cummings, Charles A., Boston.
Cummings, Hon. John, Woburn.
Curtis, C. A., Boston.
Curtis, George S., Boston.
Curtis, Mrs. Margarette S., Boston.
Dana, Mrs. Samuel T., Boston.
Dalton, C. H., Boston.
Dalton, Mrs. C. H., Boston.
Darling, L. B., Pawtucket, R. I.
Davis, Miss A. W., Boston.
Day, Daniel E., Providence.
Deblois, Stephen G., Boston.
Denny, George P., Boston.
Devens, Rev. Samuel A., Boston.
Dexter, Mrs. F. G., Boston.
Ditson, Oliver, Boston.

Dunnell, Jacob, Pawtucket, R. I.
Dwight, John S., Boston.
Eaton, W. S., Boston.
Eliot, Dr. Samuel, Boston.
Emery, Francis F., Boston.
Emery, Isaac, Boston.
Emmons, J. L., Boston.
Emmons, Mrs. Nath'l H., Boston.
English, Jas. E., New Haven, Conn.
Endicott, Henry, Boston.
Endicott, William, Jr., Boston.
Ernst, C. W., Boston.
· Farnam, Mrs. A. G., New Haven.
Fay, H. H., Boston.
Fay, Mrs. H. H., Boston.
Fay, Miss Sarah B., Boston.
Fay, Mrs. Sarah S., Boston.
Fellows, R. J., New Haven, Conn.
Ferguson, Mrs. C. H., Dorchester.
Ferris, M. C., Boston.
Fisk, Rev. Photius, Boston.
Fiske, J. N., Boston.
Folsom, Charles F., M. D., Boston.
Forbes, J. M., Milton.
Foster, F. C., Boston.
Freeman, Miss Hattie E., Boston.
French, Jonathan, Boston.
Frothingham, A. T., Boston.
Frothingham, Rev. Fred'k, Milton.
Galloupe, C. W., Boston.
Gammell, Prof. Wm., Providence.
Gammell, Mrs. Wm., Providence.
Gardiner, Charles P., Boston.
Gardner, George, Boston.
Gardner, George A., Boston.
Gardner, Henry W., Providence.
George, Charles H., Providence.
Gill, Mrs. Frances A., Boston.
Gill, Mrs. Sarah A., Worcester.
Glidden, W. T., Boston.

Glover, A., Boston.
Glover, J. B., Boston.
Goddard, Benjamin, Brookline.
Goddard, Miss Matilda, Boston.
Goddard, Miss Rebecca, Boston.
Goddard, T. P. I., Providence.
Goddard, William, Providence.
Goff, Darius L., Pawtucket, R. I.
Goff, L. B., Pawtucket, R. I.
Gray, Mrs. Horace, Boston.
Greene, Benj. F., Central Falls, R. I.
Greene, S. H., River Point, R. I.
Greenleaf, Mrs. Jas, Charlestown.
Greenleaf, R. C., Boston.
Griffin, S. B., Springfield.
Grosvenor, William, Providence.
Grover, William O., Boston.
Guild, Mrs. S. E., Boston.
Hale, Rev. Edward E., Boston.
Hale, George S., Boston.
Hall, J. R., Boston.
Hall, Miss L. E., Hanover.
Hall, Mrs. L. M., Boston.
Hall, Miss Minna B., Longwood.
Hardy, Alpheus, Boston.
Harwood, George S., Boston.
Haskell, Edwin B., Auburndale.
Hayward, Hon. Wm. S., Providence.
Hazard, Rowland, Providence.
Heard, J. T., M. D., Boston.
Hearst, Mrs. Phebe A., San Francisco, Cal.
Hemenway, Mrs. A., Jr., Boston.
Hendricken, Rt. Rev. T. F., Providence.
Herford, Rev. Brooke, Boston.
Higginson, George, Boston.
Higginson, Henry Lee, Boston.
Hill, Hon. Hamilton A., Boston.
Hill, Mrs. T. J., Providence.

, William, Boston.
John, Boston.
r, E. W., Boston.
r, R. W., M. D., Boston.
1, Hon. W. W., Providence.
, George O., Boston.
, William A., Boston.
d, Hon. A. C., Providence.
d, Mrs. Chas. W., California.
d, Hon. Henry, Providence.
Mrs. Julia Ward, Boston.
Mrs. Virginia A., Boston.
, Miss E., Boston.
ton, Hon. H. O., Cambridge.
well, F. W., Boston.
well, H. H., Boston.
Moses, Charlestown.
, H. B., Boston.
Irs. Anna A., Providence.
n, Charles C., Boston.
n, Edward, Boston.
n, Mrs. J. B. S., Boston.
n, Patrick T., Boston.
n, Mrs. Sarah, Boston.
Mrs. Julia B. H., Boston.
n, Samuel, Boston.
Miss Ellen M., Boston.
rs. Charles H., Boston.
t, Rev. F. H., Boston.
g, Mrs. Eva D., Boston.
l, C. S., Boston.
d, Martin P., Brookline.
Mrs. Helena M., Boston.
, H. P., Boston.
r, E. W., Boston.
B. J., Boston.
ice, Abbott, Boston.
ice, Amos A., Longwood.
ice, Edward, Charlestown.
ice, James, Boston.

Lawrence, Mrs. James, Boston.
Lawrence, William, Lawrence.
Lee, Henry, Boston.
Lincoln, L. J. B., Hingham.
Linzee, J. T., Boston.
Linzee, Miss Susan I., Boston.
Lippitt, Hon. Henry, Providence.
Littell, Miss S. G., Brookline.
Little, J. L., Boston.
Littlefield, Hon. A. H., Pawtucket.
Littlefield, D. G., Pawtucket.
Lodge, Mrs. A. C., Boston.
Lodge, Henry C., Boston.
Lothrop, John, Auburndale.
Lovett, George L., Boston.
Lowell, Abbott Lawrence, Boston.
Lowell, Augustus, Boston.
Lowell, Miss A. C., Boston.
Lowell, Francis C., Boston.
Lowell, George G., Boston.
Lowell, Mrs. John, Boston.
Lowell, Miss Lucy, Boston.
Lyman, Arthur T., Boston.
Lyman, George H., M.D., Boston.
Lyman, J. P., Boston.
Lyman, Theodore, Boston.
McAuslan, John, Providence.
Mack, Thomas, Boston.
Macullar, Addison, Boston.
Marcy, Fred I., Providence.
Marston, S. W., Boston.
Mason, Miss E. F., Boston.
Mason, Miss Ida M., Boston.
Mason, I. B., Providence.
May, Miss Abby W., Boston.
May, F. W. G., Dorchester.
McCloy, J. A. Providence.
Means, Rev. J. H., D.D., Dorchester.
Merriam, Mrs. Caroline, Boston.

Merriam, Charles, Boston,
Merriam, Mrs. D., Boston.
Metcalf, Jesse, Providence.
Minot, Francis, M.D., Boston.
Minot, Mrs. G. R., Boston.
Minot, William, Boston.
Mixter, Miss Helen K., Boston.
Mixter, Miss Madelaine C., Boston.   .
Morrill, Charles J., Boston.
Morse, S. T., Boston.
Morton, Edwin, Boston.
Motley, Edward, Boston.
Moulton, Miss Maria C., Boston.
Nevins, David, Boston.
Nichols, J. Howard, Boston.
Nichols, R. P., Boston.
Nickerson, Andrew, Boston.
Nickerson, Mrs. A. T., Boston.
Nickerson, George, Jamaica Plain.
Nickerson, Miss Priscilla, Boston.
Nickerson, S. D., Boston.
Norcross, Miss Laura, Boston.
Noyes, Hon. Charles J., Boston.
O'Reilly, John Boyle, Boston.
Osgood, J. F., Boston.
Osborn, John T., Boston.
Owen, George, Providence.
Paine, Mrs. Julia B., Boston.
Paine, Robert Treat, Jr., Boston.
Palfrey, J. C., Boston.
Palmer, John S., Providence.
Parker, Mrs. E. P., Boston.
Parker, E. Francis, Boston.
Parker, Henry G., Boston.
Parker, Richard T., Boston.
Parkman, Francis, Boston.
Parkman, George F., Boston.
Parsons, Thomas, Chelsea.
Payson, S. R., Boston.

Peabody, Rev. A. P., D.D., Cambridge.
Peabody, F. H., Boston.
Peabody, O. W., Milton.
Peabody, S. E., Boston.
Peirce, Rev. Bradford K., D.D., Boston.
Perkins, A. T., Boston.
Perkins, Charles C., Boston.
Perkins, Edward N., Jamaica Plain.
Perkins, William, Boston.
Peters, Edward D., Boston.
Phillips, John C., Boston.
Pickett, John, Beverly.
Pickman, W. D., Boston.
Pickman, Mrs. W. D., Boston.
Pierce, Hon. H. L., Boston.
Pierson, Mrs. Mary E., Windsor, Conn.
Potter, Mrs. Sarah, Providence.
Pratt, Elliott W., Boston. •
Prendergast, J. M., Boston.
Preston, Jonathan, Boston.
Pulsifer, R. M., Boston.
Quincy, George Henry, Boston.
Quincy, Samuel M., Wollaston.
Reardon, Dennis A., Boston.
Rice, Hon. A. H., Boston.
Rice, Fitz James, Providence.
Richardson, George C., Boston.
Richardson, Mrs. Jeffrey, Boston.
Richardson, John, Boston.
Robbins, R. E., Boston.
Robeson, W. R , Boston.
Robinson, Henry, Reading.
Rodman, S. W., Boston.
Rodocanachi, J. M., Boston.
Rogers, Henry B., Boston.
Rogers, Jacob C., Boston.
Ropes, J. C., Boston.

Ropes, J. S., Jamaica Plain.
Rotch, Miss Anne L., Boston.
Rotch, Mrs. Benjamin S., Boston.
Rotch, Miss Edith, Boston.
Russell, Henry G., Providence.
Russell, Mrs. Henry G., Providence.
Russell, Miss Marian, Boston.
Russell, Mrs. S. S., Boston.
Saltonstall, H., Boston.
Saltonstall, Leverett, Newton.
Sanborn, Frank B., Concord.
Sayles, F. C., Pawtucket, R. I.
Sayles, W. F., Pawtucket, R. I.
Schlesinger, Barthold, Boston.
Schlesinger, Sebastian B., Boston.
Sears, David, Boston.
Sears, Mrs. David, Boston.
Sears, Mrs. Fred., Jr., Boston.
Sears, F. R., Boston.
Sears, Mrs. K. W., Boston.
Sears, Mrs. P. H., Boston.
Sears, Mrs. S. P., Boston.
Sears, W. T., Boston.
Sharpe, L., Providence.
Shaw, Mrs. G. H., Boston.
Shaw, Henry S., Boston.
Shaw, Quincy A., Boston.
Shepard, Mrs. E. A., Providence.
Sherwood, W. H., Boston.
Shimmin, C. F., Boston.
Shippen, Rev. R. R., Washington.
Sigourney, Mrs. Henry, Boston.
Sigourney, Mrs. M. B., Boston.
Slack, C. W., Boston.
Slater, H. N., Jr., Providence.
Snelling, Samuel G., Boston.
Spaulding, J. P., Boston.
Spaulding, M. D., Boston.
Spencer, Henry F., Boston.
Sprague, F. P., Boston.

Sprague, S. S., Providence.
Stanwood, Edward, Brookline.
Stearns, Charles H., Brookline.
Steere, Henry J., Providence.
Stewart, Mrs. C. B., Boston.
Stone, Joseph L., Boston.
Sturgis, Francis S., Boston.
Sturgis, J. H., Boston.
Sturgis, James, Boston.
Sullivan, Richard, Boston.
Sweetser, Mrs. Anne M., Boston.
Taggard, B. W., Boston.
Taggard, Mrs. B. W., Boston.
Thaxter, Joseph B., Hingham.
Thayer, Miss Adele G., Boston.
Thayer, Miss A. G., Andover.
Thayer, Rev. George A., Cincinnati.
Thomas, H. H., Providence.
Thorndike, Delia D., Boston.
Thorndike, Mrs. J. H., Boston.
Thorndike, S. Lothrop, Cambridge.
Thurston, Benj. F., Providence.
Tingley, S. H., Providence.
Tolman, Joseph C., Hanover.
Tingue, J. H., Seymour, Conn.
Torrey, Miss A. D., Boston.
Troup, John E., Providence.
Tucker, W. W., Boston.
Turner, Miss Abby W., Boston.
Turner, Miss Alice M., Boston.
Turner, Miss Ellen J., Boston.
Turner, Mrs. M. A., Providence.
Underwood, F. H., Boston.
Upton, George B., Boston.
Villard, Mrs. Henry, New York.
Wales, George W., Boston.
Wales, Miss Mary Ann, Boston.
Wales, Thomas B., Boston.
Ward, Rev. Julius H., Boston.
Ware, Charles E., M.D., Boston.

Ware. Mrs. Charles E.. Boston.
Warren. J. G.. Providence.
Warren. S. D.. Boston.
Warren. Mrs. Wm. W.. Boston.
Washburn, Hon. J. D., Worcester.
Weeks, A. G.. Boston.
Weeks, James H.. Boston.
Welch, E. R., Boston.
Weld, Otis E., Boston.
Weld, R. H., Boston.
Weld, Mrs. W. F.. Philadelphia.
Weld, W. G., Boston.
Wesson, J. L., Boston.
Wheeler, Nathaniel, Bridgewater, Conn.
Wheelwright, A. C., Boston.
Wheelwright, John W., Boston.
White, B. C., Boston.
White, C. J., Cambridge.
White, Charles T., Boston.
White, G. A., Boston.
Whiting, Ebenezer, Boston.
Whitman, Sarah W., Boston.

Whitney. Edward. Belmont.
Whitney. E.. Boston.
Whitney, H. A.. Boston.
Whitney, H. M., Boston.
Whitney. Mrs.. Boston.
Whitney. Miss. Boston.
Wigglesworth. Miss Ann, Boston.
Wigglesworth. Edward, M.D.. Boston.
Wigglesworth. Thomas, Boston.
Wightman. W. B.. Providence.
Wilder. Hon. Marshall P., Dorchester.
Williams, Geo. W. A.. Boston.
Winslow, Mrs. George. Roxbury.
Winsor. J. B.. Providence.
Winthrop. Hon. Robert C.. Boston.
Winthrop. Mrs. Robert C., Boston.
Wolcott, J. H., Boston.
Wolcott. Mrs. J. H.. Boston.
Woods, Henry, Paris, France.
Worthington, Roland, Roxbury.
Young, Mrs. B. L., Boston.
Young, Charles L., Boston.

SYNOPSIS OF THE PROCEEDINGS

OF THE

ANNUAL MEETING OF THE CORPORATION.

BOSTON, Oct. 8, 1884.

The annual meeting of the corporation, duly summoned, was held to-day at the institution, and was called to order by the president, Samuel Eliot, LL.D., at 3 P.M.

The proceedings of the last two meetings were read by the secretary, and declared approved.

Mr. John S. Dwight presented the report of the trustees, which was read, accepted, and ordered to be printed with that of the director, and the usual accompanying documents.

The treasurer *pro tempore*, Mr. James Sturgis, read his report, which was accepted, and ordered to be printed.

All the officers of the past year were reëlected.

The following persons were afterwards added to the list of the members of the corporation by a unanimous vote : Rev. Bradford K. Peirce, D.D., Rev. Brooke Herford, Edwin M. Bacon, J. H.

Tingue, Rev. F. H. Kasson, S. B. Griffin, James W. Clarke, and Nathaniel Wheeler.

The meeting was then dissolved, and all in attendance proceeded, with the invited guests, to visit the various departments of the school and inspect the premises.

M. ANAGNOS,
Secretary.

Commonwealth of Massachusetts.

REPORT OF THE TRUSTEES.

PERKINS INSTITUTION AND MASS. SCHOOL FOR THE BLIND,
SOUTH BOSTON, Oct. 1, 1884.

TO THE MEMBERS OF THE CORPORATION.

Gentlemen and Ladies: — By requirement of law and custom, we have the honor to present to you, and, through you, to the legislature, a brief report of the progress and condition of the institution under our charge for the financial year ending Sept. 30, 1884, — this being the fifty-third annual report.

1. No important change has been made in the manner of conducting the affairs of the institution, nor has any exceptional event of consequence occurred. The school — for this is what the institution essentially and practically is, and in no sense an "asylum" for the blind, as it is too often called — has been carried on upon the same principles and methods, under the same wise and admirable supervision, and mainly through the

same faithful and efficient corps of teachers, mostly women, as for several years past.

For fuller statements you have only to turn to the printed reports of those years.

The educational sub-committee of this board, in all their visits to the class-rooms and the weekly exhibitions, have remarked continual improvement, of a genuine and healthy sort, in all departments of the education, physical and moral, as well as intellectual. And the trustees desire hereby to congratulate you and themselves, and the whole philanthropic public, on the good providence which raised up at the right moment such a successor to the honored founder of the institution, as it enjoys in the person of its present director.

The total number of blind persons immediately connected with the institution at the end of the year was 166, of whom 132 were pupils, the rest being teachers, employés and workmen and women. Of the pupils, 66 are boys and 66 girls.

The details of the admissions and discharges will appear in the report of the director.

The applications for admission for the term just begun have been larger than ever before. The increase has been greatest in the girls' department, — to such an extent indeed, that the director has had difficulty in finding room for the accommodation of all. It is a singular fact, which may or may not admit of scientific explanation, and be reducible to rule, that this year, and for three years past, the number of girls offered has been much larger than that of boys, the contrary having always been the case before.

The general health of the inmates has been better than it was last year, though hardly up to the clean record of many years before that. In December there were several cases of diphtheria among the girls. The little patients were sent home, or to the city hospital, the cottages were thoroughly fumigated, bed-clothing disinfected, drains carefully examined by an agent of the board of health, and pronounced flawless. Two more cases, in a mild form, occurred in January, and were treated in the same way, Since then, the health of the girls has been remarkably good; and so has been that of the boys throughout the year, with the exception of one case of diphtheria, and numerous severe colds and sore throats in May and June, which rendered several of the pupils unable to perform their parts in the graduation festival.

2. COMMENCEMENT EXERCISES.

These exercises took place at Tremont Temple, on Tuesday afternoon, June 3, before an audience which completely filled the floor and galleries of the great hall, — while admission could not be granted to almost an equal crowd of later applicants; an audience representing the most intelli-

gent, earnest and philanthropic people of Boston
and the state.

The president of your corporation, **Dr.** Samuel
Eliot, who had been expected to preside, and His
Excellency Governor Robinson, who had promised
an address, were kept away by imperative engagements. Consequently there was not much speech-
making to add to the sufficient length of the
programme of the pupils' exercises, which naturally constitute the paramount interest of such an
occasion. These were excellent throughout, and
held the closest attention of the delighted audience to the very end. They were sufficiently
varied to illustrate (so far as possible in the brief
space of two hours, — and there was no time lost,
so perfect was the mechanism of all the changes —
scene-shifting, one might say) most of the important phases and branches of the education.

Short original essays, delivered by three of the
young ladies, showed clear, consistent thought,
chaste, concise expression, and a very distinct and
natural style of elocution. One young man gave
a practical exercise in physics, — experiments with
the air-pump — evincing theoretic comprehension,
dexterous manipulation, and a good lecturer's
happy way of making his point clear. This was
but one of the many specimens of this kind which
could have been produced. The examples of
ready reading with the fingers, and the exercises
in geography, were indeed wonderful to witness.

The gymnastics, calisthenics, and the military drill combined ease and accuracy of movement with attractive grace and beauty ; it all told of health and happiness, the *mens sana in corpore sano.*

. .The musical part of the exhibition, in spite of some omissions occasioned by colds among the boys, enlivened, and relieved the whole with well-rendered good selections for organ, band and solo-playing, chorus and solo singing, as well as with accompaniment for the timing and inspiring of the gymnastic and the choregraphic movements.

Kindergarten. But the most interesting feature of the programme appeared in the living practical example of the fruits of object teaching, or the kindergarten method, — that entering wedge of common sense in education, that return to nature's divine, instinctive method. These were presented by a bright and charming group of the youngest girls and boys. While their minds and fingers were busied in modelling their various devices in clay, or in simple card embroidery, etc., the time was also improved by an instructive and cogent appeal made by Mr. C. W. Ernst in behalf of the much needed fund for a kindergarten for blind children between the ages of five and nine, to save them and prepare them, before it is too late, for the more advanced tuition of the Perkins institution. Mr. Ernst set forth the duty of the state and of society to educate its blind, and give them

the equivalent of the common school education,
which is enjoyed by all seeing children as a right.
He cited the opinion of experts, that, by proper
care in this early and critical period of life, about
forty per cent. of the cases of blindness might be
cured or prevented.   The total number of the blind
in New England is not far from 5,000 — about
one blind person to every thousand inhabitants.
He dwelt on the mournful fact that, of the 50,000
blind in this country, less than 2,500 are at school,
and that *the principle of compulsory education is
not applied to those who need it most.*   He estimated
that the support of the helpless blind costs the
country some *seven and a half millions of dollars,*
in spite of the fact proved by institutions like our
own, that, with reasonable instruction, and good
moral and social influences, the blind can be made
not only happy, but self-supporting and comparatively independent. For this reason, the establishment, on a generous and broad foundation, of a
well equipped primary school, or kindergarten, for
the blind of New England is a matter of great
public urgency.

   Mr. Ernst's remarks were briefly supplemented
by the director, Mr. Anagnos, whose whole heart
is in this enterprise, who had only time to begin to
tell of the promising, but as yet very inadequate
beginning of a subscription to this end.   The trustees, before the summer adjourned, appointed a
committee of their number, who will now at once,

and in earnest, set about the work of soliciting subscriptions toward the beginning of the realization of this most important scheme of education. It had been fondly hoped that sufficient means would be raised to ensure the purchase of a place, in the neighborhood of Boston, for the planting of the nucleus of such a school this very autumn; but so far we wait in vain.

The whole matter, under all its aspects, will be fully presented in the report of the director.

To return for a moment to the commencement exercises, the number of pupils who received diplomas this time was only *three*, whereas in the year before it was *six;* the diploma being rigidly limited to those, however few, who have accomplished the whole (seven years) course of studies, to the satisfaction of all their teachers. The three graduates, this time, were girls; one of them, to whom was assigned the part of honor, the valedictory address, being colored. They go out into the world well qualified for usefulness to society, and for self-respecting self-support; openings having been already found for them either in teaching or in some industrial occupation.

3. PRINTING EMBOSSED BOOKS FOR THE BLIND.

.The work of the " Howe Memorial Press " has gone on with the usual steadiness and vigor. During the year, the following books have been added to our list of publications: — " Bible Stories

portends not only the continuance but the increase
of its usefulness, and the attainment of a higher
degree of excellence in its work.

NUMBER OF INMATES.

The total number of blind persons connected
with the institution in its various departments at
the beginning of the past year as pupils, teachers,
employés and workmen and women, was 160.
There have since been admitted, 31; 25 have been
discharged; making the present total number 166.

Of these, 145 are in the school proper, and 21 in
the workshop for adults.

The first class includes 132 boys and girls
enrolled as pupils, 10 teachers and 3 domestics.
Of the pupils, there are now 127 in attendance, 5
being temporarily absent on account of feeble
health or from various other causes.

The second class comprises 16 men and 5
women employed in the industrial department for
adults.

The number of scholars has been steadily
increasing, and the tendency to the disproportionate preponderance of the gentler sex, which was
mentioned in the last annual report, has continued
stronger than heretofore. As a consequence the
capacity of our accommodations in the girls' department was taxed during the past year to the utmost.
Nevertheless, no suitable candidate was refused
admission.

The establishment of the kindergarten may eventually lessen this pressure somewhat: but it will not remedy existing difficulties.

There are at present several applicants just of the proper age and of average intelligence, who are waiting for vacancies to occur either by graduation, or otherwise, and who are therefore losing most precious time. For these and all others who may soon present themselves, asking for the advantages of education, immediate provision should be made, and measures should at once be taken either to procure or to build an additional cottage somewhere.

HEALTH OF THE HOUSEHOLD.

The year has been favored by the continuance of many of the blessings which in past times have called for so much gratitude and thankfulness. But there has been a perceptible want in one of them, — perhaps the most important of all, — the health of the household.

At the very beginning of the term one of the pupils in the boys' department was taken ill with symptoms of typhoid fever, which he had evidently contracted at home. At the advice of our medical inspector, Dr. Homans, the patient was speedily removed to the city hospital, where he received excellent medical treatment and nursing, and whence he came out restored to health in a few weeks.

No other case of illness of any kind occurred in this department until the latter part of May, when one of the boys had the diphtheria, and a number of others were confined to bed with sore throats and with a severe influenza bordering almost on pneumonia, so that several of the pupils were not able to take part in the commencement exercises at Tremont Temple on the 3d of June. Happily they all recovered soon, and the sanitary horizon of the establishment was as cloudless as ever, before the close of the school session.

In the girls' department diphtheria in a light form invaded the household at three different times during the months of November, December, and January, and six of the younger children were attacked by it. Five of these were readily received and successfully treated at the city hospital, and one at home. They all returned to their work with a reasonable measure of strength and without any constitutional weakness resulting from the disease, and for the remainder of the year the inmates of the cottages were favored with a remarkable degree of health.

It is my pleasant duty to acknowledge in this connection the uniform courtesy and readiness with which the superintendent of the city hospital, Dr. George H. M. Rowe, and his assistants, opened their doors to such of our pupils as we deemed it necessary to remove at once from our buildings and send to them, and to express my gratitude for the friendly attention and kind care which they bestowed invariably upon each and all blind children placed under their treatment.

I fear that few of the wealthy citizens of Boston are aware that the department for contagious diseases of this hospital is one of the most important factors of public health, aiding as it does to prevent the spread of infection among the inmates of crowded tenement-houses and to check epidemics. If it were well known among the favored sons and daughters of benevolence how valuable· are its beneficent ministrations to the poor and what a great comfort and relief it often affords to many a distressed household, I doubt not that the necessary means might be easily obtained for the increase of its capacity and usefulness.

The School and its Founder.

Were a star quenched on high,
  For ages would its light,
Still travelling downward from the sky,
  Shine on our mortal sight.

So when a great man dies,
  For years beyond our ken
The light he leaves behind him lies
  Upon the paths of men.

LONGFELLOW.

A careful examination and study of the history and present condition of the institution must prove a source of pride and congratulation to its friends and patrons.

The school is the product of the last fifty-two years. During this time it has grown from small beginnings to its present proportions. Many faithful and self-sacrificing persons have devoted to it the conscientious labor of the best part of their lives, and have placed the blind under a debt of lasting gratitude. But the first and last link in this solid chain of earnest workers was the ·eminent founder of the establishment.

Dr. Howe was the king of its creation, the motive power of its advancement, the promoter of its beneficence, the director and ruler of its destinies, and the crown of its success. He tilled and prepared the ground of its organization with the vigor and skill of a sagacious husbandman, steeped the seeds of its existence in the spirit of perennial life and energy, and watched its development and growth with parental solicitude. From the day that he put his hand to the plough to that when he was stricken down, the fire burned with undiminished heat and lustre, and the ardor of his heart in the cause which he championed was as buoyant as his marvellous brain was clear.

Being a man of strong will, of cultivated tastes and lofty conscience, Dr. Howe became the inspiration of his co-laborers, — a mighty galvanic battery, as it were, which by a process of intellectual and moral induction, charged their own efforts

with electric power. These are the foremost
among the forces that mould human activity into
special phases: and the rich harvest which continues to be reaped year after year in this field of
philanthropy, is mainly and principally due to the
assiduous care with which the illustrious friend of
the blind planted the first germs of their development and advancement, to his warm zeal, his
chivalrous character, his tireless industry, and his
wisdom and proverbial broad-mindedness. For in
the words of Mazzini, the eminent Italian patriot
and agitator, "men of great genius and large heart
sow the seeds of a new degree of progress in the
world; but they bear fruit after many generations."

Dr. Howe holds a high position not only as a
pioneer, but as a permanent power in the cause of
the blind in this country, from the excellence of
his ideas, their scientific basis, their clear and
philosophic exposition, and their important practical bearing on the welfare and happiness of this
afflicted class of men. His great object was to
benefit them individually and socially, and to open
to them a career of usefulness and independence.
Like all students of human nature and of human
well-being from Socrates downwards, he realized,
as few have done more intelligently and earnestly,
that in any attempt to aid those bereft of sight, the
largest factor is thorough and liberal education,
and that in the development of this factor, science

portends not only the continuance but the increase of its usefulness, and the attainment of a higher degree of excellence in its work.

NUMBER OF INMATES.

The total number of blind persons connected with the institution in its various departments at the beginning of the past year as pupils, teachers, employés and workmen and women, was 160. There have since been admitted, 31; 25 have been discharged; making the present total number 166.

Of these, 145 are in the school proper, and 21 in the workshop for adults.

The first class includes 132 boys and girls enrolled as pupils, 10 teachers and 3 domestics. Of the pupils, there are now 127 in attendance, 5 being temporarily absent on account of feeble health or from various other causes.

The second class comprises 16 men and 5 women employed in the industrial department for adults.

The number of scholars has been steadily increasing, and the tendency to the disproportionate preponderance of the gentler sex, which was mentioned in the last annual report, has continued stronger than heretofore. As a consequence the capacity of our accommodations in the girls' department was taxed during the past year to the utmost. Nevertheless, no suitable candidate was refused admission.

from the horrors of her intellectual and moral imprisonment, Rev. John Weiss seems to think that the credentials of his mission came from on high, and speaks of the noble deed as follows: —

"Do not say that Dr. Howe was worthy to attain to immortal continuance, but that without him Laura Bridgman would nowhere ever have picked a way out of the triple-bolted dungeon of her body, in which a personal *I* languished waiting for his miracle. Dr. Howe's achievement is to us a guarantee that the Creator will not let one of His little ones perish. Laura's liberator was an incarnate word of God. In him was that impulse of creation which is continually struggling to be set free into symmetry and sanity. To every country these apostles of redemption have been furnished, for each act of whom nothing but immortality can account, as nothing else could break into this life with such an impetuous solicitation from God to us to improve His imbeciles and make His future task the easier."

Dr. Howe's deeds consecrated the very earth beneath his feet. His fame was securely chiselled on the loftiest pinnacle of the history of philanthropy. His genius was confessed in both hemispheres, and its gleaming coruscations continue to flame on the regions of ceaseless night, and to lead its victims onward and upward.

May the kindly wings of his broad and liberal spirit be forever spread over the work of his noble life and rare talents, and waft down to his successors wisdom, blessings and direction.

Early Benefactors of the Institution.

When the houses for the girls were finished and made ready for occupancy, Dr. Howe intended to dedicate each of them to the memory of one of the early and most distinguished friends and benefactors of the institution. In order to carry out his wishes and give tangible expression to his purpose, silver plates have been placed on the front doors of the four cottages, bearing the names of "Fisher," for Dr. John D. Fisher; "Brooks," for Peter C. and Edward Brooks; "May," for Samuel May; and "Oliver," for William Oliver of Dorchester.

Review of the Various Departments.

A casual visit to the institution or a brief review of the work of each department, will give an idea of its varied, extensive and beneficent operations. Hardly any mental, moral, physical or technical interest of the blind has been overlooked in the organization and administration of the establishment, every branch of which is characterized not only by thoroughness and completeness, but also by an entire absence of all stationariness and by a constant endeavor after still greater improvement.

Literary Department.

In reviewing the work performed by the school during the past year we have abundant cause to be gratified at the success which has attended it, and which is "known and read of all men."

The daily records kept by the teachers, as well as all other competent and reliable tests, show that the progress of the pupils has been commendable in every respect.

We have endeavored to adapt our methods to the requirements of the pupils, to keep pace with the demands of the time, and so to shape our course that there may be constant growth and improvement.

I can give no better proof or fairer illustration of the scientific methods of instruction which prevail in the school, and of the progressive spirit which animates those in charge of it, than that which is afforded by their own words.   To a reader or compendium of biology and natural history, which was compiled by two of our teachers from the works of Mrs. Arabella B. Buckley and of Prof. Huxley, and published during the past year under the title "Life and her Children," a third instructress, Miss Mary C. Moore, wrote a brief preface, from which I copy the following extract : —

" The value of natural science as a means of development, intellectual and moral, is incalculable. But it must be taught scientifically. Typical plants and animals should be put into the hands of the children, who must then be led to make their own careful and correct observations, their own comparisons, their own classifications, and their own deductions. So, and

prove a source of pride and congratulation to its friends and patrons.

The school is the product of the last fifty-two years. During this time it has grown from small beginnings to its present proportions. Many faithful and self-sacrificing persons have devoted to it the conscientious labor of the best part of their lives, and have placed the blind under a debt of lasting gratitude. But the first and last link in this solid chain of earnest workers' was the eminent founder of the establishment.

Dr. Howe was the king of its creation, the motive power of its advancement, the promoter of its beneficence, the director and ruler of its destinies, and the crown of its success. He tilled and prepared the ground of its organization with the vigor and skill of a sagacious husbandman, steeped the seeds of its existence in the spirit of perennial life and energy, and watched its development and growth with parental solicitude. From the day that he put his hand to the plough to that when he was stricken down, the fire burned with undiminished heat and lustre, and the ardor of his heart in the cause which he championed was as buoyant as his marvellous brain was clear.

Being a man of strong will, of cultivated tastes and lofty conscience, Dr. Howe became the inspiration of his co-laborers, — a mighty galvanic battery, as it were, which by a process of intellectual and moral induction, charged their own efforts

be gratified at the success which has attended it, and which is "known and read of all men."

The daily records kept by the teachers, as well as all other competent and reliable tests, show that the progress of the pupils has been commendable in every respect.

We have endeavored to adapt our methods to the requirements of the pupils, to keep pace with the demands of the time, and so to shape our course that there may be constant growth and improvement.

I can give no better proof or fairer illustration of the scientific methods of instruction which prevail in the school, and of the progressive spirit which animates those in charge of it, than that which is afforded by their own words. To a reader or compendium of biology and natural history, which was compiled by two of our teachers from the works of Mrs. Arabella B. Buckley and of Prof. Huxley, and published during the past year under the title "Life and her Children," a third instructress, Miss Mary C. Moore, wrote a brief preface, from which I copy the following extract : —

"The value of natural science as a means of development, intellectual and moral, is incalculable. But it must be taught scientifically. Typical plants and animals should be put into the hands of the children, who must then be led to make their own careful and correct observations, their own comparisons, their own classifications, and their own deductions. So, and

so only, will they grow into a reverent knowledge of the
life around and within them, and at the same time gather
strength to become truly ' winners in life's race.' "

While the use of text books as all-sufficient
vehicles of instruction has been persistently
avoided in our school, the practice of reading
by the touch has been encouraged by every possible means. One evening in the week has been
exclusively devoted by most of the pupils to the
perusal of works of various kinds, and their selections have covered a great range of embossed literature, and have included history, biography, poetry,
science, philosophy, and belles-lettres. The readers have been allowed to follow their inclinations,
and to make their own choice with perfect freedom, the leading motive being similar to that
enunciated in the burthen of the famous chorus in
the *Agamemnon* of Æschylus,

" Let the good prevail."

Thus the love of reading for its own sake, which
has always been cherished among the blind, is
developing into a strong habit which will follow
them through life, and afford them the means of
greater aid, solace, comfort and enjoyment.
Our library, enriched from year to year by the
choice products of the " Howe Memorial Press," is
becoming the centre of immeasurable pleasure and
inspiration to the studious pupils, and in no house-

hold can a greater appreciation of its benefits and delights be formed than in ours.

The commencement exercises of the school held in Tremont Temple on the 3d of June, were of a very high order. The large hall of the temple was filled to overflowing with an audience representative of the intelligence, the refinement and the benevolence of Boston and the neighboring towns, and several thousands of applicants were refused admission for want of room. One of the most memorable features of the occasion was the address of Mr. C. W. Ernst on the kindergarten project. Pure in diction, rich in erudition, strong in logic, and convincing in argument, it appealed to the reason and to the sense of justice rather than to the sentiments of the hearers, with irresistible force. A Greek statue could be no more simple and severe. The festival proved to be of such unusual importance, and elicited so great an interest and so many favorable comments in the community, that a full account of the proceedings, including the essays of the graduates, is given in the appendix.

Towards the close of the last school session the principal teacher in the boys' department, Miss Julia R. Gilman, presented her resignation. She was induced to take this step for the purpose of assisting her eldest sister in the establishment of a private school for young ladies, and of obtaining some recreation and rest, which in her case

Early Benefactors of the Institution.

When the houses for the girls were finished and made ready for occupancy, Dr. Howe intended to dedicate each of them to the memory of one of the early and most distinguished friends and benefactors of the institution. In order to carry out his wishes and give tangible expression to his purpose, silver plates have been placed on the front doors of the four cottages, bearing the names of "Fisher," for Dr. John D. Fisher; "Brooks," for Peter C. and Edward Brooks; "May," for Samuel May; and "Oliver," for William Oliver of Dorchester.

Review of the Various Departments.

A casual visit to the institution or a brief review of the work of each department, will give an idea of its varied, extensive and beneficent operations. Hardly any mental, moral, physical or technical interest of the blind has been overlooked in the organization and administration of the establishment, every branch of which is characterized not only by thoroughness and completeness, but also by an entire absence of all stationariness and by a constant endeavor after still greater improvement.

Literary Department.

In reviewing the work performed by the school during the past year we have abundant cause to

person of ability and experience in teaching, has
been appointed as Miss Gilman's substitute for
the current year.

About three weeks before the beginning of the
present school term, another faithful and talented
teacher, Miss Cora A. Newton, asked to be released from her engagement at the institution in
order to accept a situation at the Haverhill
training-school. I complied with her wishes very
reluctantly and with much regret. The vacancy
has been filled by the appointment of Miss Marian
A. Hosmer.

No other change has taken place in the corps of
teachers; and I am most happy to say that all of
them discharge their respective duties with hearty
zeal and exemplary fidelity. They are striving
with a determination worthy of the warmest praise
to realize the highest standard of educational
excellence, and they throw all their energy and
enthusiasm into their work and the advancement
of their pupils, cheering the industrious, sustaining the studious, rousing the inert, stimulating the
idle, encouraging the hopeful, and laboring with
all. Failure cannot possibly attend such efforts.

Music Department.

"Music alone with sudden charms can bind
The suffering sense, and calm the troubled mind."

The work of this department has been carried
on with the usual thoroughness, and with a

measure of success corresponding to the spirit of devotion on the part of those engaged in it.

The progress of the pupils both in instrumental and vocal music has been most satisfactory.

Of the ninety-four scholars who have received instruction in this department during the past year, seventy-eight have studied the pianoforte; nine, the cabinet and church organs; twenty-six, harmony; five, the violin; twenty-six, reed and brass instruments; seventy-five have practised singing in classes, and nineteen have received private lessons in vocal training. Moreover, all the advanced pupils have participated in the practical exercises of the normal teaching classes, in which they learn what are the best and most advantageous methods adopted in their profession, how to trace the difficulties which may arise in its course and to overcome them, and how to pursue their avocation with success.

Besides the practice which our advanced scholars obtain by teaching the younger ones under the supervision of their instructors, opportunities are sought and often secured for their giving music lessons to seeing children in our neighborhood. The experience gained thereby is of incalculable value to them, for it gives them a foretaste of their future profession and enables them to find out where their deficiencies will lie, and to resort for their remedy to the assistance of those who have traversed the road before them and who are familiar with its windings and its obstacles.

During the past year our supply of musical instruments has been thoroughly replenished. Twelve of the pianofortes which have been in use for a long period and have become more or less worn out, have been exchanged for new ones. Of these six were procured from the firm of Messrs. Chickering & Sons, and six from that of Mr. Henry F. Miller. They were all selected with care from large assortments, and prove to be excellent instruments in every respect. With these additions our facilities for the study and practice of music have been greatly improved, and the equipment of this department has reached a degree of completeness which is not surpassed anywhere.

Our pupils are systematically trained to avoid what is trashy and degrading, and to choose and admire what is beautiful and elevating in their art. Great stress is laid on this point, and their success is undeniable. The character of the music performed and appreciated by them is a conclusive proof of the high standard of taste which prevails among them.

For this attainment, as well as for the acquisition of artistic refinement and æsthetic culture, the development of the sense of discrimination and of the critical faculty, and the enjoyment of a great deal of pleasure, we are indebted to the continued

favors bestowed upon our students by the leading musical societies and organizations and by the distinguished artists of the city of Boston.

As in former years, the doors of the best concerts, oratorios, operas, recitals, and entertainments have been freely opened to them, and they have also been placed under renewed obligations for some excellent performances given in our own hall. For these great privileges and uncommon advantages we render our most hearty thanks and grateful acknowledgments to the generous friends and constant benefactors of the blind of New England, whose names will be printed elsewhere, and whose kindness and benevolence will be engraved in the memory and cherished in the hearts of the recipients of their liberality.

There have been three changes made in the corps of teachers and music readers of this department. Miss Annie Keith resigned her position at the close of the last school session; five or six weeks later, Miss Mary A. Proctor declined a reëlection on account of ill-health, and shortly before the reopening of the school, Miss Caroline L. Bates was advised by her physician to discontinue her work, and rest at home. All these young ladies have rendered good service to the institution, and will be missed by their pupils. Their places have been respectively filled by Miss Julia H. Strong of Auburndale, Mass., Miss Jenny A. Wheaton

of Rutland, Vt., and Miss Iola M. Clarke of
Hampton, Conn.

TUNING DEPARTMENT.

During the past year, as in previous ones, this
department has been conducted with uncommon
ability and with the most gratifying success.
Thoroughness in theoretical study and practical
training in the art of tuning in both its
scientific and mechanical bearings, has been the
mark towards which all efforts have been directed.

Indeed, nothing has been omitted, either in the
form of appliances or in that of tuition, which
could contribute to its attainment.

The contract for tuning and keeping in good
working order the pianofortes in the public schools
of Boston, — one hundred and thirty-two in
number, — has again for the eighth time been
awarded to the institution for another year, on
the same terms as heretofore. Faithful guardians
of the interests of the city, the committee on
accounts, in whose charge this matter is placed,
before coming to any decision, instituted a careful
inquiry as to the quality of the work of our tuners
and the amount of remuneration charged by them,
and, having been convinced that the instruments
are entrusted to safe hands and kept at less cost
in a far better condition than they ever were before,
they have renewed the agreement promptly and
without the least hesitation. This action is truly

beneficent to the blind of New England, and reflects
great credit on the school board. Would that all
official bodies who have access to the treasury of
Boston were as honest, fair minded, judicious and
conscientious in the discharge of their duties as
the members of this committee.

Technical Department.

The work of the technical department has been
conducted with the accustomed assiduity and
fidelity on the part of those in charge, and with
very gratifying success. No changes of any kind
have taken place in either of its two branches, and
but a few lines will suffice in review of the results
accomplished in each.

1. *Workshop for the Boys.*

The usual trades of making mattresses, seating
cane-bottomed chairs, upholstering parlor furniture,
and manufacturing brooms, have been regularly
and systematically taught in this shop, and the
pupils have been diligently trained to work
steadily, and to fit themselves for the practical
pursuits of life.

The mode of instruction employed in this department is very simple, and the advancement of its
recipients quite satisfactory.

2. Workrooms for the Girls.

Under the efficient direction of Miss Abby J. Dillingham and the assistance of Miss Cora L. Davis, uncommon activity has prevailed in these rooms, and the girls have labored with untiring diligence, and have made excellent progress in sewing and knitting, both by hand and machine, in crochetting, and in the execution of a very great variety of plain and fancy work.

The articles made by our girls for the bazaar, which they planned and carried out themselves in aid of the kindergarten for little sightless children, and for one or two smaller fairs which were held in the city for the same purpose, were in constant requisition, and the demand could hardly be supplied. A great deal of taste was displayed in the design and manufacture of these articles; and their work attracted great attention, much of it being considered very remarkable, while all of it was readily and advantageously disposed of, and received unqualified commendation.

DEPARTMENT OF PHYSICAL TRAINING.

In a complete system of education, scientifically arranged and wisely administered, the care of the physical frame is not less important than the cultivation of the brain. On the contrary, it is infinitely more so : for the operations of the mind depend wholly upon the soundness of the machin-

ery by which it manifests itself. No active intellectual life can thrive in a feeble and debilitated body. When the forecastle of a vessel sinks, the cabin must soon follow. It is impossible to preserve the leaves and blossoms of a plant when its roots are decayed.

In conformity with these views, which have been fully stated and repeatedly commented upon in previous reports, due attention has as usual been given to this branch of our scheme of instruction and training, and a system of physical exercise in the open air at proper intervals, together with regular gymnastic drill under shelter, has been carried on without interruption. The effects of the practice of this system upon the appearance, health, strength, elasticity, and endurance of the pupils are very noticeable. Many imperfections which are indicative of a stunted growth and muscular flabbiness have diminished perceptibly, gracefulness and agility have taken the place of awkwardness and clumsiness, and the groundwork upon which the temple of education can be safely built has been carefully laid.

Our scholars are required to pursue the series of exercises assigned to them with strict regularity, and only those among them are excused from spending one hour daily in the gymnasium, in whose case our medical inspector finds sufficient cause to recommend a cessation from physical exertion.

GIVE THEM LIGHT.

" Thus with the year
Seasons return ; but not to *them* returns
Day, or the sweet approach of even or morn
Or sight of vernal bloom, or summer's rose,
Or flocks or herds, or human face divine ;
But cloud instead and ever-during dark
Surrounds *them*, from the cheerful ways of men
Cut off, and for the book of knowledge fair
Presented with a universal blank
Of Nature's works, to *them* expunged and rased,
And wisdom at one entrance quite shut out."

MILTON.

This picture, conceived in the mind of one of
the most eminent victims of blindness under the
painful influence of personal experience and
tempered with the sighs of sorrow, is neither
highly colored as a whole, nor exaggerated in any
of its shades. It is true to nature and consistent
in all its features. It is a photographic portrait
of actual woes, rather than a fancy painting, in
which the reality might be idealized or travestied.
It describes forcibly and graphically the gloom,
the sadness, the privations and the intellectual
and moral disadvantages arising from the loss of
sight.

But, cogent and striking as this drawing is in
all its delineations, it can hardly be considered as
complete and adequate when applied to the case
of the little sightless children, who, oppressed by

poverty and doomed to an existence of degradation and misguided indulgence, are left to grow,
like unkempt creatures, without care, protection,
or training of any kind, and in whose behalf
repeated appeals presenting their claims to rescue
and human sympathy have been addressed to the
public; for it gives no idea of the by-ways of
ignorance and depravity in which many of them
were born, nor implies even a suggestion of the
misery, the wretchedness, the mire of vice, the
pernicious surroundings, and the deleterious atmosphere, in which they dwell and breathe and move.

Most of the unfortunate waifs never see one ray
of light. They live in ceaseless night from the
cradle to the grave. The brilliant myriads of
luminous bodies which stud the firmament, the
tints of the flowers, the plumage of the birds, the
endless varieties of foliage and scenery, the
symmetry and harmony of the visible universe,
and all the beauties of nature and excellences of
art are utterly hidden to them. Their eyes are
hopelessly closed, and no human power can open
them and restore their sight. To them all is,
and will ever be,

> " Dark, dark, dark, amid the blaze of noon,
> Irrevocably dark, total eclipse,
> Without all hope of day."

Add to this crushing pressure of the iron veil of
their calamity, the glaring want of sufficient food

and raiment and care and decent quarters, and all
the multifarious physical ills and moral monstrosi-
ties with which their environment is pregnant, and
you will have a perfect picture of their condition,
and of their sufferings and dangers. It is no
hyperbole to say that the poisonous influences to
which they are exposed not only impede healthful
development in any direction as effectually as
the iron shoe prevents the growth of a Chinese
woman's foot, but, like the blast of a frigid wind,
they freeze and kill and destroy the germinating
seeds and sprouts of all good qualities, and thus
the ground is wholly given up to weeds and tares.

But the light of truth and knowledge and honor
and love can be introduced into the heads and
hearts of these victims of affliction by means of
thorough education, and, by the aid of early and
efficient training, they can be rescued from the
very jaws of intellectual and moral darkness, and
made good, active, helpful and useful men and
women. As the primroses and violets lie in
ambush till the first warm breath of spring bids
them reveal themselves, so the minds of these
lowly waifs remain buried in the sepulchre of negligence and rust, waiting for the angel of kindness and benevolent generosity to roll off the
stone from the entrance of their prison and call
them forth to resurrection and life.

A kindergarten school, securely founded on a
sufficient endowment, wisely organized and prop-

erly conducted, will help most effectually to the accomplishment of this end.

This project, like a great mountain, is impressive from whatever side it is approached. Viewed from the heights of philanthropy, it is grand, noble, elevating; for it aims at the deliverance of scores of little blind children, who are overwhelmed by the deluge of a dreadful calamity, and are, moreover, plunged into an ocean of ills of a social, domestic and ethical nature. Considered in the light of justice and fairness, it is the embodiment of equal rights and opportunities for all members of the human family, regardless of bodily defects or imperfections, and commends itself to the judgment and sympathy of all benevolent and kind-hearted persons. Examined from the stand-point of education pure and simple, it presents its most interesting aspect, for it carries in its very roots the elements and promise of becoming an ever-burning torch, dispelling the clouds which thicken and threaten on the horizon of misfortune, and rendering its darkest sky bright.

There is no scheme of training so admirably adapted to the condition, wants, and peculiar requirements of sightless infants as that of Froebel. This wonderful system is the true starting-point on the royal road of learning. It marks the spot where we must begin to search for hidden treasures. Its philosophy is based upon the natural growth of little human beings, and is therefore as deep and

broad and high and as enduring as humanity itself.
It runs parallel with the entire educational career
of the child, the youth and the man. Its gifts and
toys, its games and amusements, its play and
merriment, are means of grace and salvation.
They give joyous employment to tiny fingers,
impart physical strength and elasticity of motion,
cheer the heart, arouse the mind and quicken its
powers, train the senses to keenness and fineness,
foster the faculty of invention, and engender habits
of observation and industry.   Through their
ministry intellectual torpor, moral sluggishness,
weak purposes, and bad tendencies and propensities are changed into a progressive forward and
upward movement, and the puny pupils, effectually
shielded from all poisonous influences, which defile
and deform the crystalline thread and the fresh
delicate bloom of the soul, grow in all things strong
and healthy and entirely free from those stains,
which, if not removed in time, would seriously
affect the course of harmonious development and
pervert its soundness.

> " A pebble on the streamlet scant
>   Has turned the course of many a river ;
> A dew-drop on the baby plant
>   Has warped the giant oak forever."

Thus the demands of equity and science blend
together in this enterprise with the iron laws of
political economy and the higher logic of the heart,
and render the foundation and endowment of a

kindergarten for sightless children of infant years
for whose care and instruction there is no provision
whatever, not a simple wish or a mere desideratum,
but a grand want and an imperative necessity.

No class of people can appreciate more thoroughly the importance of the effects of early training and of the numerous other advantages afforded
by Froebel's grand system of education, or can
estimate their value more highly than our scholars.
Those among them who have tasted the fruits of
the kindergarten even in a very small degree, have
become so infatuated with its blessings, that they
are most eager to secure them permanently for their
tiny brothers and sisters in misfortune. To this
end they have continued to labor incessantly,
unswervingly, and with profound and unabating
enthusiasm, which, in the language of Bulwer-
Lytton, "is the genius of sincerity, and truth
accomplishes no victories without it." No task
has seemed too severe to them, and no amount of
work or magnitude of difficulties could dishearten
them or diminish their zeal. Full of faith in the
goodness and grandeur of their cause, and hopeful
for its final triumph, they have shrunk from no
exertion or hard work, always conscious of the
fact, that,

> " As insect toil at last the island rears,
>   Or mushroom pillars lift the wayside stone,
> So he succeeds who truly perseveres,
>   With powers converged to noble ends alone.

With constancy through fair and foul the same,
    In growing strength our recompense we find ;
But hesitation, want of earnest aim,
    Far more than labor wearies heart and mind."

The means and measures to which our pupils
resorted for the purpose of bringing the enterprise
to the notice of the public and of enlisting the
interest of the community in its furtherance, were
many and various: but the most important among
them were the bazaar which was held in our girls'
schoolhouse on the 21st and 22d of February last;
a dramatic entertainment in which Sheridan
Knowles's play, *William Tell,* was represented by
our boys; and several concerts given in Charlestown, Allston, Milton, Bridgewater, and elsewhere.

The fair, which proved as unique in its character
as it was productive of a good harvest, was an
intuitive suggestion with our girls, and forth from
mere intention leaped the determination. For them
to resolve was to achieve. They entered upon
their work with unrivalled earnestness and with
an exemplary spirit of self-sacrifice and surrender,
but with the most modest anticipations. Fifty or
at the utmost seventy-five dollars would have been
the highest mark of their expectations. How
gratifying then was the unlooked-for result of
their patient and untiring labor. They formed
their plans, organized their committees, issued
their notices and advertisements, sent their invitations right and left for assistance, and strove in

every possible way to secure the good will and
hearty coöperation of a large class of people.
It goes without saying, that the teachers and other
officers stood steadfastly by the scholars, helping,
advising, directing and guiding them.

The pathos inspired by the sight of this group
of courageous workers was enhanced by the liveliest
and most energetic part taken in the movement by
that living monument to Dr. Howe's patience and
sagacity, Laura Bridgman.

This woman, whose touching history encircles
her with a halo which no worldly fame or brilliancy
could give, surrounded as she is by an impenetrable
wall of darkness and silence, is in all things a
living and feeling person.

> " Shut in, shut in from the noise and din
>   Of the world without to the world within,"

Laura may be likened to the snow-covered Hecla,
whose icy barriers enshroud the burning fire underneath.   Stirred up by the suffering of the poor
little sightless children, she took the success of
their cause very much to heart, and the warmth of
her interest in it had a miraculous influence upon
her whole character.   It raised her far above herself, broadened her sympathies, and led her to that
celestial ladder, which, like the vast stairway seen
by Jacob in his dream, reaches in long perspective
upward from the dungeon of seclusion and helplessness to the divine throne of goodness and joy.

In the quickness of her intellectual perceptions and
the vividness of her emotional nature, she pondered
seriously, acted energetically, worked incessantly,
and urged her friends and acquaintances to join
her in her labors. Jean Ingelow's beautiful words,

> " To serve the dear,
> The lowlier children, I am here,"

seemed as if they were written to express her feelings and purposes. To crown her endeavors,
Laura wrote *propriâ manû* the following plea to
the public, a *fac-simile* of which was reproduced
and printed in many of the leading journals of
New England: —

To. Boston, Jan. 30, 1884.
I appeal to the good
people of Boston in be-
half of the blind, and
beg them most earnest-
ly to lend a helping
hand toward the founda-
tion and endowment of

a separate kindergarten for little sightless children. They live now in darkness and gloom. Let there be light and joy for them soon.

Laura B. Bridgman.

These simple words fell among the community at large like a ball of fire, which, rolled and shaken by earnest friends, glowed with a thousand hues.

The final arrangements for the opening of the sale were completed under circumstances most favorable and auspicious, and signal were the blessings which were showered upon the efforts of its projectors. The two days of its duration were the finest in our winter calendar. Contributions flowed in generously alike from the rich and the poor, and the articles made by the girls themselves were so numerous as to fill quite a space in the rooms. Seldom has a fair in this city presented so many novel and attractive features grouped together.

No sooner were the doors of the Howe building ajar than the manifestation of genuine human goodness and of the immense public interest felt in the enterprise, became evident in the thronging crowds of friends, who came to bring the encouragement of their presence and their patronage to the enterprise. Their benevolence swept its golden circle around the little laborers. The tables were entirely depleted of their contents, and the success of the undertaking was so great as far to exceed the most sanguine expectations of its originators and ardent promoters. The net profit yielded by the fair amounted to $2,050.35.

These efforts touched the chords of the human heart throughout the community, bringing forth the sweetest music, and arousing everywhere a strong current of sympathy and a great amount of philanthropic interest. Their effect seemed to be like that of a melodious song, the refrain of which is caught and repeated in every direction. Hundreds of children as well as of grown persons warmed themselves at the fire of the enthusiasm of our girls, and learned from their fervor to cast off indifference and to participate in the cause of the little sufferers. Their tiny hands have been stretched forth in aid and have brought valuable assistance with them. Especially pathetic and marked was the zeal manifested by a number of

lame and invalid children, who, in their sad
imprisonment, were inspired by an ardent desire
to make the lives of their little blind friends more
bright. Fairs, concerts and miscellaneous entertainments, given in private drawing-rooms and
public halls and churches, have been in order for
some time past, in behalf of our enterprise, with
varied success. Even a circus was devised by
a little fellow, who announced its result in the
following charming note :

"DEAR MISS BRIDGMAN ; — Mamma read the letter in the
Christian Register, and since that we have been saving our
money. I had a circus yesterday, and raised 18 cents.
Bessie saved 75 cents. I saved $1.25. That will amount
to $2.00. Now I must close. — Yours truly,

CHAS. E. BARRY."

In numerous instances, where children denied
themselves many pleasures and enjoyments, and
even their play, in order that they might enable
the blind to taste these privileges, the spirit of
self-sacrifice was truly great, but it reached
its climax when the pupils of a charity kindergarten, on whose countenances the marks of
destitution were deeply impressed, contributed
cheerfully the very few pennies in their possession
for the purpose of helping in the efforts to extend
the light radiating from Froebel's system to the
sightless infants, whose deliverance seemed thus
to have been made the concern of the public at

large. As of old the "widow's mite" was celebrated, so to-day the children's offerings stand forth
a touching, noble monument of the power and
inherent goodness wielded by the hands of simplicity and innocence. The movement has proved
in all its phases a blessing and a benediction alike
to beneficiaries and benefactors. For the sun
which searches in the bosom of the earth for seeds
to fecundate, is also the wondrous painter who
imparts their splendor to the flowers.

The results of these efforts, rich as they were in
human kindness and sympathy and good will and
touching incidents of self-sacrifice, have not as yet,
however, placed the enterprise beyond the need of
pecuniary assistance. Thus far we have in our
treasury $25,231.63. This amount, chiefly con-
tributed from the hard earnings of people of
moderate circumstances, is not sufficient for the
purchase of suitable grounds and the erection
thereon of a cheap building. Of a permanent endowment fund, which will impart life and security
to the undertaking, there is not even a nucleus
raised. But such an institution as we propose to
establish cannot possibly exist and thrive by
depending wholly upon annual subscriptions and
occasional or casual gifts for its support. It should
rest upon a broad and solid financial foundation.
To the scanty stream of the offerings of the poor,
which can scarcely rise above the rocks and stones
of the brook-bed, should be added the mighty cur-

rent of the donations and contributions of the
affluent, brimming the river banks and rolling on
in triumph to the sea of success.

There are, no doubt, many persons, noted for
their benevolence and generosity, who, if they are
opportunely approached and properly informed of
the wants and requirements of the blind, will look
upon their case with favor and compassion, and do
their whole duty by them. In direct contrast with
these there are others, whose spirit and heart are
debased by insatiate covetousness and palsied by
selfishness and greed for the accumulation of
money, and who, enchanted and elated by the all-
absorbing music produced by the clinking of their
gold, are utterly senseless to the groans of distressed humanity. But the man or woman, who,
after becoming acquainted with the woes of little
sightless children, refuses to offer from his or her
abundance for their mitigation is unworthy to rank
among those citizens who have given Boston its
world-renowned character and glory. To such a
person the following words of Emerson can be
addressed with peculiar force and appropriateness: —

> " Oh mortal ! thy ears are stones,
>   These echoes are laden with tones,
>   Which only the pure can hear.
>   Thou canst not catch what they recite
>   Of will and fate, of want and right,
>   Of man to come, of human life,
>   Of death and fortune, growth and strife."

For a long period the project was permitted to
sail in a frail craft, and to drift along with the
current of popular favor. There were no experienced and steady hands at the helm. It was left
with our pupils and their immediate helpers to
steer it on the sea of public patronage. But no
young enterprise, however grand in its conception
and beneficent in its effects, can go on its own
feet alone. We have to furnish it with wings born
of our earnestness, our fidelity, our wisdom, and
our devotion. Unless there is behind it a strong
body of well-known and sagacious men representing its claims before the community and endeavoring to promote its interests continually, its success
is very problematic.

In view of this fact, the kindergarten scheme
was placed by the trustees in charge of a special
committee, consisting of Mr. Samuel G. Snelling
as chairman, and Messrs. Leverett Saltonstall,
Francis Brooks, and James Sturgis, with full
powers to add to the number of their members and
complete their organization.

This action of the board filled the friends of the
project with joy, and inspired them with fresh
hopes, that active measures would soon be taken
by Mr. Snelling and his associates for soliciting
contributions, and that they will strive to carry the
lamp of happiness and intelligence on to the goal
while it is burning in their hands.

I am aware that the task of raising a large sum of

money is very great, and that the forces at command are comparatively small: but I have also learned by experience, that the frosts of external obstacles and temporary hindrances dissolve as readily before the intense heat of noble resolution and moral purpose, as the snowdrifts melt away under the rays of the burning sun. Be the barriers of obstruction and the chills of indifference what they may, it is our solemn duty to press forward without a halt. Those alone serve the cause of humanity who march unflinchingly under its banner, and fight bravely in its behalf. Those who only stand and wait, may not have an opportunity to win a victory. The soldier whose heart is set on a conquest, makes no account of the perils of the battle-field, nor shuns its terrors. With the faithful and tireless worker things are easily controlled, and impossibilities are turned into possibilities. He takes hold with unrelaxed strength, and walks with a full confidence of success. If endowed with a vigorous intellect, a resolute will, and a reliable judgment, he " mounts the whirlwind and directs the storm." His earnestness grasps the cords that move the human heart. His cry, echoing in all the retreats of benevolence, arrests its attention; and, as a consequence, a new gem is added to the crown of philanthropy.

Posterity commends with admiration the perseverance of the Roman censor, who became famous, among other things, for repeating, whenever he

spoke in public, the then significant phrase,
" *Delenda est Carthago*," until, by dint of unwearied
repetition and insistence, his plan of destruction
was carried out. Much after the fashion of Cato
we must seize every opportunity, and enunciate
and reiterate in the ears of men, women and children a sentence quite as laconic as his. But ours
is not a proclamation of ruin and desolation. It is
a motto of love and charity. Instead of " *Delenda
est Carthago*," we say, " *Levanda est afflictio*," and
we must not cease rehearsing this watchword, and
emphasizing its import, until the burthen is taken
up by a friendly chorus, who will help us to fulfil
its prophecy. In other words, we should adopt all
available means, and employ all expedients calculated to arouse public sentiment in favor of our
movement. Agitation is the atmosphere of mind
and the crystallization of earnestness. It is the
marshalling of the conscience of a community to
mould its benevolence into forms which humanity
can use. It prevents injustice, stimulates fairness,
preserves harmony, and secures progress. Under
the influence of its heat and through the action of
its forces, the undisputed claims of the sightless
waifs, which are still like unrecognized fugitive
sparks in the general social atmosphere, will be
forged into a thunderbolt, which shall suffice to
dash the bulwarks of apathy to pieces, and to
demolish the ramparts of selfishness and exclusiveness. When these are removed, kind thoughts

and generous deeds will rise in their place, and pierce and dispel the dark shadows which yet hang like a murky cloud over the lives of a large part of the human family.

For the last four years Froebel's system has played so important a *rôle* in our school, and has produced such marvellous results in rescuing many of the younger pupils from the very depths of sluggishness and feeble-mindedness, into which they were gradually sinking, and in conferring substantial and lasting benefits upon all of them, that its vast and life-giving importance will undoubtedly be appreciated by those who are entrusted with the stewardship of riches, so that a kindergarten for the blind may be securely founded and adequately endowed in the near future. Of the realization of this hope I feel perfectly confident, and, as the poet says, —

"The mind I sway by, and the heart I bear,
    Shall never sag with doubt, nor shake with fear."

Fully conscious of the arduousness of the duties devolving upon the promoters of the enterprise, and of the particularly trying difficulties which stare them in the face at every step, I yet do not waver for a moment between success and failure. There is no ground of apprehension or despondency. The cause is too good and too noble to be permitted to fade away for want of support. The project is too practical and humane to be allowed

to collapse for lack of means. Its consummation
has passed the nebulous stage of uncertainty,
and assumed so tangible a form, that I can
see it with the eye of faith and hope. From
the tiny acorns· of benevolence, which have been
planted in love and kindness and watered by the
golden stream of sympathy and charity, there
cannot but grow up stately oaks, under whose
branches and thick foliage the sightless waifs of
New England will find a shelter from the storms
of misery and wretchedness, and protection from
the contagion of moral pestilences. They have
already suffered long enough for a misfortune due
to no fault of their own. Let there be an end to
their woes. Let the sum total of the ignorance
and neglect and evil and vice which shroud them
at present, be but as a dark background to a
sunny landscape in the future, where brightness
and warmth and purity and virtue will shine with
heavenly radiance : and when the poor blind
infants breathe out their sighs of deep delight
over all the joy that the kindergarten will bring,
though it be shaped into no word, it may sound
to their kind helpers and generous benefactors
like a " *Gloria in Excelsis*." However weak, and
enervated, and helpless, and almost blighted these
little soldiers may appear, give them the weapons
of character, together with the ammunition of
physical health and the drill of early education,
and cover their heads with the helmet of intelli-

gence, and their breasts with the shield of manliness, and they will hold the fort of humanity
tenaciously, and fight the battle of life successfully.

To all our fellow-citizens, but especially to those
who possess the goods of the world in abundance,
and who are light of heart and whose cup is filled
with earthly enjoyments, we most earnestly and
respectfully commend this project. To their liberality and beneficence the kindergarten for the
blind, driving away like an ever-burning taper the
darkness of affliction, will stand as a monument
in perpetuity. Sculptured marbles and bronze
statues and honorable inscriptions carved on the
front of massive and magnificent structures, will
crumble through the lapse of time and perish from
the sight and memory of mankind : but this will
endure for ever.

KINDERGARTEN EXHIBITS.

Our pupils, although busily employed with the
regular studies of the school, and with the extra
work for fairs, concerts and entertainments undertaken during the past year, found time to prepare
two exhibits. One of these was sent to the kindergarten exposition, held last summer in Madison,
Wis., during the meeting of the National Educational Association, under the direction of Prof. W.
N. Hailmann, president of the American Froebel
Institute; the other was placed in the annual fair
of the New England Mechanics' and Manufactur-

ers' Institute of this city. Both these exhibits attracted considerable attention, and were very favorably commended. A special correspondent of the "Boston Herald," from Madison, giving in its issue of the 19th of July a descriptive account of the magnificent display of the kindergarten exhibition in that city, speaks most kindly and encouragingly of the work of our children. We quote as follows from the columns of the "Herald": —

"Strange as it may seem, the finest work in clay modelling is that of scholars in the kindergarten department of the Massachusetts Institution for the Blind in South Boston. The objects represented in plastic material are almost perfection, and, in seeing the whole exhibit of this institution, the visitor can no longer doubt the value of the instruction of the blind in kindergarten methods. Some unique geometric work in the handling of problems in that subject is done by the use of pins stuck in cushions."

These words, coming as they do from an impartial judge and keen observer, bear witness to the usefulness of our infant enterprise, and add strength to the weight of the testimony in its favor.

CONCLUSION.

As the length of this report has already exceeded its reasonable limits, I feel obliged to leave out many pages of manuscript which I have already written, and among which there is a full account of the present low condition of the education of the

blind in this country, together with a brief exposition of some of the principal causes which have
produced it, and of the evils which beset the progress of many of the public institutions. This
necessity I deeply regret; but I hope to be able to
carry out my intention at some future day.

Respectfully submitted.

M. ANAGNOS.

SPECIAL REPORT OF THE DIRECTOR.

SOUTH BOSTON, Oct. 1, 1884.

TO THE TRUSTEES OF THE PERKINS INSTITUTION
AND MASSACHUSETTS SCHOOL FOR THE BLIND.

Gentlemen: — Since my communication to you with regard to the application of a portion of the income of the national subsidy fund to the purchase of books and apparatus not printed or manufactured by the American Printing House for the Blind at Louisville, Ky., two meetings of the managers of that institution have taken place, one in Louisville, and the other in St. Louis. For reasons relating partly to my work at home and partly to my health, I have not been able to comply with your directions and attend either of them personally; but I have presented the case to both of them by writing, and requested the adoption of a resolution embodying our views.

At the last of these meetings, which was held last August, the matter was discussed, and a special committee was appointed to examine the transactions of the American Printing House, but the resolution was rejected by a large majority, only three of the trustees voting in its favor.

I herewith submit to you the entire correspondence, and leave it with you to decide as to the further steps to be taken in the matter.

I have the honor to be, gentlemen,
                    Respectfully yours,

                         M. ANAGNOS.

CORRESPONDENCE.

PERKINS INSTITUTION
AND MASSACHUSETTS SCHOOL FOR THE BLIND,
SOUTH BOSTON, January 11, 1883.

DEAR SIR, — Please send by freight to this institution the following publications, issued by the American Printing House for the Blind, to be paid out of our quota of the income of the national fund : —

6 copies	Grandfather's Chair, by N. Hawthorne, .	$21 00
2 "	" " " " unbound,	5 00
6 "	Thackeray's English Humorists, . . .	21 00
2 "	" " " unbound, .	5 00
6 "	She Stoops to Conquer, etc., Goldsmith, .	18 00
2 "	" " " " " unbound,	4 00
6 "	Readings from English History, . . .	21 00
2 "	" " " " unbound, .	5 00
6 "	About Old Story-tellers, by Mitchell, . .	21 00
2 "	" " " " " " unbound, .	5 00
6 "	Chapters from a World of Wonders, . .	21 00
2 "	" " " " unbound,	5 00
6 "	Swiss Family Robinson (2 volumes), . .	42 00
2 "	" " " " " unbound,	10 00
6 "	Perry's Introduction to Political Economy, .	42 00
2 "	" " " " " unbound,	10 00
4 "	Gospel of Mark, revised version, . .	6 00
2 "	" " " " " unbound, .	1 50
2 "	Colburn's Mental Arithmetic, . . .	6 00
10 "	Classification in Zoölogy and Glossary, :	3 50
10 "	N. Y. Point Primer, ...	1 50

Carried forward, ... $274 50

Brought forward,	.	.	.	.	.	$274 50
6 copies of each of the five N. Y. Point Readers,				.	15 00
2 " unbound Picciola (2 volumes),	.	.	.	8 00

$297 50

Please also order of the Howe Memorial Press the following books, to be paid out of the amount due us under the provisions of the act of congress to promote the education of the blind : —

6 copies George Eliot's Silas Marner,	.	.	$21 00
10 " Dickens' Christmas Carol, etc.	.	30 00
10 " Children's Fairy Book,	.	.	25 00
10 " Whittier's Poems,	.	.	.	30 00
6 " Higginson's History of the U. States,	21 00
5 " Tennyson's Poems,	.	.	.	15 00
10 " Youth's Library, vol. 1st,	.	.	12 50
10 " " " " 2d,	.	.	12 50
10 " " " " 3d,	.	.	12 50
10 " " " " 4th,	.	.	12 50
10 " " " " 5th,	.	.	12 50

204 50

$502 00

I make this requisition of books not included in your own list for the following reasons : —

First. The publications issued by the Howe Memorial Press are superior to those of the American Printing House for the Blind, both in the subject-matter and in mechanical execution and durability, and better adapted to the wants and requirements of our school.

Secondly. They are more legible to the sense of touch, because, according to the testimony of experienced readers, the impression is sharper and clearer.

Thirdly. The price of books published by the Howe Memorial Press is from seventeen to twenty-five per cent., at least, lower

than that charged by the American Printing House for the
Blind. In order not to leave the least doubt on this point, I
here and now offer to reprint every one of the books on your
list in better style than they now are printed, and to furnish
them to the various institutions in the country, at a cost of
seventeen per cent. less than their present prices. A further
discount equal to the amount required for setting type and
making electrotyped plates to be made on the second edition
of every book after the first one of two hundred copies is
exhausted. Add to this the discount of fifteen per cent. below
the *actual cost* which the Howe Memorial Press allows to all
schools for the blind, and there is a difference of thirty-two
per cent., which the blind can ill afford to spare, but which
they are forced to lose for no other reason than simply to help
in establishing an absorbing and expensive monopoly at Louisville. This statement I am prepared to prove by facts and
figures at any time.

Fourthly. It is very important that the blind should have a
wider field of embossed publications from which they can select
what is best adapted to their wants than is offered to them by
your list alone, *provided* they are not compelled to pay higher
prices for them. Most of the institutions are so well supplied
with the books of your list that they have no further need of
them. Yet they are obliged to order them year after year, and
to give them away, while they are sadly in need of embossed
literature for the use of their pupils.

In view of these facts I make the above requisition, which I
hope you will not reject on mere technical grounds. The law
authorizes your printing-house to manufacture and " furnish "
books and tangible apparatus for the blind at actual cost. By
a just interpretation of the law a resolution was adopted two
years and a half ago, by which the various institutions in the
country were allowed to spend one-fifth of their quota of the
income of the national fund for the purchase of embossed
publications and apparatus not included in your own list. This

proviso, limited as was the amount, had at least the appearance of fairness, and enabled most of the schools to make a good selection of books. But you succeeded, last summer, in having it repealed, on the mere assertion that the income of the national subsidy, reduced by about fifteen hundred dollars, was not sufficient to cover the expense of the American Printing House. How could this be so ? Have you submitted to the trustees an itemized statement of receipts and expenditures, showing how much money was spent for labor, how much for stock, and when and to whom it was paid ? Have you given anywhere, and in any tangible form, the data upon which the prices set upon your publications are based ? All this is absolutely necessary, since no information whatever on any of these points can be obtained from the annual reports of the American Printing House. The abstracts or summaries therein published are extremely meagre and very general in their character. They contain no details or items. I know of no public institution in the country the financial transactions of which are set forth in so rudimentary and vague a form as are those of your printing-house. This would be a lamentable omission at all times and under any circumstances ; but it is particularly so in this case, and I for one must ask its immediate correction.

In closing these remarks permit me to assure you that I have neither the taste nor the inclination to give you the least annoyance, and that I shall be very glad to meet you half-way in any proposal of fair and equitable settlement of the matter. But if you insist upon carrying out a policy of exclusiveness, which is not only unjust but positively detrimental to the vital interests of the blind throughout the country, I shall deem it my imperative duty to submit the case to proper tribunals, leaving the whole of the responsibility with you.

I have the honor to remain, dear sir, truly yours,

M. ANAGNOS.

Mr. B. B. Huntoon, *Secretary of the American Printing House for the Blind, Louisville, Ky.*

LOUISVILLE, January 23, 1883.

DEAR MR. ANAGNOS, — Enclosed please find invoices of
books ordered by you, bill of lading of books from here, draft
to pay for books printed in Boston, blank for duplicate bill,
and blank receipts, all forwarded without prejudice, and without being considered as establishing a precedent for future
action.

I am somewhat at a loss how to answer your letter. Some
points in it are well taken. I confess our printed financial
statements are meagre; but our reports made to the general
government, and the verbal reports made at our annual meetings are so full that it never struck me before that the printed
reports might be unsatisfactory, until you called my attention
to them.

They have always been in compliance with the law, but it is
easy to make them fuller, and I think you will find them so
hereafter.

As to what you say about your own work I heartily congratulate you, not only upon your success in raising your
printing fund, but also upon the great improvement in the
character of the books you have printed. I rejoiced the more
because I thought that the result of two well-endowed printing
establishments for the blind in this country, rapidly turning
out good books for the blind, would be an incalculable good.
That gradually, as blind readers increased, and books became
more accessible, both institutions and individuals, from their
own means, would supplement governmental and other aid.

Pardon me if I cannot see that any person or any institution
is the worse off for what we have done in the American Printing House for the Blind.

As to the other remarks in your letter, it seems to me that
you mistake your premises, and so err in your conclusions.
But, as you once said to me, you and I are not the proper persons to discuss the differences between us.

Wishing you all prosperity in your kindergarten project, and in all your noble undertakings, I am yours truly,

B. B. HUNTOON.

SOUTH BOSTON, February 5, 1883.

DEAR MR. HUNTOON, — Your letter of the 23d ultimo, with the enclosed bills, blanks and draft for $204.50 (two hundred and four dollars and fifty cents) was duly received. Please accept my thanks for the same. I herewith return receipted bill in duplicate for the books ordered of the Howe Memorial Press, together with a receipt in duplicate for the amount of $520.05 (five hundred and twenty dollars and five cents) due to this institution for its quota of the income from the national fund for the year ending December 31, 1882.

I am exceedingly sorry to be obliged to say that your reply to my letter of the 11th ultimo leaves the main point entirely unsettled. I mean the question whether an arrangement may be effected whereby the schools for the blind may be enabled, through the American Printing House, to apply a reasonable portion of their share of the income of the government subsidy to the purchase of embossed publications and tangible apparatus not included in your list. I must ask for an explicit answer regarding this point. I am credibly informed by competent exponents of law that such a request can hardly be overruled under existing circumstances by the proper tribunals.

I earnestly hope that you will see the justice of the idea and adopt an equitable policy which will obviate all difficulties. If this be not possible, please then let me know your final conclusion, so that the case may be submitted to those who are competent to judge it upon its merits, and decide it definitely and permanently.

Hoping to hear from you soon, I remain, yours very truly,

M. ANAGNOS.

Mr. B. B. HUNTOON, *Secretary American Printing House for the Blind, Louisville, Ky.*

Louisville, February 17, 1883.

Dear Mr. Anagnos, — Your letter enclosing receipts was duly received.

In respect to the demands you make in your letter I can only say that I will lay your letter before our local board at their next meeting.

I may say for myself, personally, that I am in favor of anything that can conduce to the welfare of the American Printing House, and I presume you would not ask anything against its interests.

There are many things in our work here that I think you do not fully understand; but I fear that any effort on my part to explain them might increase the difficulty instead of obviating it.

I trust, however, to time, and your wise forbearance, to make things clear that now seem obscure.

Yours very truly,   B. B. HUNTOON.

South Boston, August 14, 1883.

Gentlemen, — At a meeting of the trustees of this institution, at which nine out of the twelve members of the board were present, the enclosed correspondence between Mr. B. B. Huntoon and myself was submitted and read, and the following vote was thereupon unanimously passed : —

" *Voted*, That the director be authorized to attend the meeting of the trustees of the American Printing House for the Blind at Louisville, Kentucky, and be invested with full powers to pursue such a course as he may deem necessary for the settlement of the matter of applying a portion of the income of the national fund to the purchase of embossed publications and tangible apparatus not included in the catalogue of said American Printing House for the Blind."

In compliance with this vote it was my intention to attend your meeting and submit the matter for a fair settlement. But for reasons relating to my health it is not prudent for me to take a trip to Louisville in the heat of the summer. I therefore write to request your consideration and action upon the enclosed draft of a resolution, marked No. 2.

The arguments in favor of the adoption of such a resolution are so fully stated in my letters to Mr. Huntoon that it is scarcely necessary for me to say anything further on the subject.

I have the honor to be, gentlemen, respectfully yours,

M. ANAGNOS.

To the Trustees of the American Printing House
  for the Blind, Louisville, Ky.

[No. 2.]

FORM OF RESOLUTION.

Resolved, That requisitions may be made for embossed books or tangible apparatus not printed or constructed by the American Printing House for the Blind, by any institution, not exceeding twenty-five per cent. of its money quota of the income of the subsidy fund.

Submitted by M. Anagnos.

South Boston, August 14, 1883.

DEAR MR. HUNTOON, — As I do not feel able to be present at the annual meeting of the trustees of the American Printing House for the Blind, will you be so kind as to submit to them the enclosed communication. together with the accompanying draft of a resolution, and the copies of our correspondence?

Please return the latter to me after the meeting and oblige,

Yours truly,   M. ANAGNOS.

B. B. HUNTOON, Esq , *Secretary, etc., etc., Louisville, Ky.*

Louisville, August 24, 1883.

DEAR MR. ANAGNOS, — I return herewith the copy of our correspondence, and the resolution you sent me.

The Board met on the 22d, but as only two states were represented there was no business done except the formal reëlection of officers, which is all that is usually done at the annual meeting here. Your papers were read to the board, but their consideration was postponed till the meeting next year in St. Louis.

I am sorry that your health did not permit you to pay us a visit. We would have been glad to have met you, and think you would enjoy seeing our improvements and our great exposition.

Yours very truly,   B. B. HUNTOON.

SOUTH BOSTON, August 13, 1884.

To the Trustees of the American Printing House for the Blind.

GENTLEMEN, — Permit me to submit to your consideration the enclosed correspondence, which speaks sufficiently for the subject of which it treats without any further comment on my part, and to request your action on the form of the resolution which is marked No. 2.

I have the honor to remain, gentlemen, respectfully yours,

M. ANAGNOS.

ACKNOWLEDGMENTS.

Among the pleasant duties incident to the close of the year is that of expressing our heartfelt thanks and grateful acknowledgments to the following artists, *littérateurs*, societies, proprietors, managers, editors and publishers, for concerts and various musical entertainments ; for operas, oratorios, lectures, readings, and for an excellent supply of periodicals and weekly papers, minerals and specimens of various kinds.

As I have said in previous reports, these favors are not only a source of pleasure and happiness to our pupils, but also a valuable means of æsthetic culture, of social intercourse, and of mental stimulus and improvement. So far as we know, there is no community in the world which does half so much for the gratification and improvement of its unfortunate members as that of Boston does for our pupils.

I. — Acknowledgments for Concerts and Operas in the City.

To Mr. Henry Lee Higginson we are under great and continued obligations for twenty season tickets to the public rehearsals and twelve season tickets to his series of twenty-four symphony concerts.

To Messrs. Tompkins and Hill, proprietors of the Boston Theatre, for admission of unlimited numbers to three operas.

To the late Mr. George H. Tyler, manager of the Bijou Theatre, for admission to one operetta.

To the Händel and Haydn Society, through Mr. E. B. Hagar, secretary, for tickets to two oratorios and one public rehearsal.

To the Cecilia Society, through Mr. Charles W. Stone, secretary, twenty, twenty-four and thirty-two tickets to each of three concerts.   To Mr. C. C. Perkins, for four tickets to these concerts.

To the Boylston Club, through its secretary, Mr. F. H. Radcliffe, eight tickets to each of four concerts.

To the Apollo Club, through Mr. Arthur Reed, secretary, six tickets to each of six concerts.

To the president of the Euterpe Society, Mr. C. C. Perkins, an average of six tickets to each of three concerts.

To Mr. L. C. Bailey, for an average of twenty-six tickets to the three vocal recitals given by Mr. and Mrs. Henschel.

To Mr. Arthur Foote, for twenty-three season tickets to his three concerts.

To Mr. Ernst Perabo, for ten tickets to his concert.

To Mr. H. G. Tucker, for six tickets to one concert.

To Mr. Albert F. Conant, for ten tickets to one concert.

To Miss Emma DeWitt, for fifteen tickets to one piano recital.

To Miss Etta W. Parker, for fifteen tickets to one concert.

To Dr. Eben Tourjée of the N. E. Conservatory, for tickets to various entertainments given by the society.

To Mr. L B. Marsh, for twelve season tickets to six organ recitals by Mr. George E. Whiting, in Tremont Temple.

To Mr. G. A. Foxcroft, for a generous invitation to the entertainments in the Star lecture course at the Tremont Temple.

To the Maritime Provincial Association, through its president, Mr. S. J. Peters, for thirty-seven tickets to a musical and literary entertainment.

To Dr. L. D. Packard, for twenty tickets to a concert in the Broadway M. E. Church.

To Mr. O. T. Taylor, for eight tickets to the same.

To Mr. F. Smith, for twenty tickets to a concert by his choir.

To Mr. Philip Elton's S. S. class, for admission to an entertainment in the M. E. Church.

To Rev. J. J. Lewis, for a general invitation to all entertainments held in the Broadway Universalist Church.

II. — Acknowledgments for Concerts given in our Hall.

For a series of recitals and concerts given from time to time in the music hall of the institution, we are greatly indebted to the following artists : —

To Mr. and Mrs. William H. Sherwood, assisted by his pupil, Miss Jenny Brown, pianist, and Miss Marion Osgood, violinist, for two concerts.

To Mr. John Orth, assisted by Miss Clara Nichols, and Mr. C. F. Weber, vocalist, one concert.

To Miss Culbertson, assisted by Mr. Noyes, pupils of Mr. Wm. H. Sherwood, one concert.

To Mrs. V. A. Howe, assisted by Mrs. E. C. Fenderson, Mrs. Stackpole, Miss L. B. Langley, Miss A. P. Emery, Miss Daisy Tighe, and Dr. Fenderson, reader.

To Miss McKissick, for a vocal concert.

III. — Acknowledgments for Lectures and other Entertainments.

For various lectures, readings and other entertainments, our thanks are due to the following friends : Mr. Philip Boune of Brooklyn, N. Y., Capt. S. C. Wright, Mr. S. L. Pierce, and Rev. Brooke Herford.

To Mrs. John C. Phillips, for a series of readings, given at her expense by a professional reader, in both the departments of the school.

To the managers of both the New England Institute and foreign fairs, for admitting large numbers to an afternoon entertainment at each ; and to Mr. R. M. Chase, for giving the smallest members of the school a similar pleasure at the Institute fair.

IV. — Acknowledgments for Books, Minerals, Specimens, etc.

For various books, specimens, curiosities, etc., we are indebted to the following friends : Miss Abbie Alger ; Mary M. Davidson, Kansas ; Mrs. W. C. Wendte ; Miss Fanny Eliza Webster ; Dr. T. R. Armitage, London ; Mr. Charles Fisher ; Rev. T. M. Miles ; Capt. Robert B. Forbes, Milton ; Mr. Morrison Heady, Mr. William C. Howes, C. A. W. Howland, Mrs. Pond, The Society for providing Religious Literature for the Blind, The U. S. National Museum, and The U. S. Agricultural Department.

The donations of Capt. Forbes included the model of a schooner, 26 inches long, made and fitted up by his own hands.

V. — Acknowledgments for Periodicals and Newspapers.

The editors and publishers of the following reviews, magazines, and semi-monthly and weekly papers continue to be very kind and liberal in sending us their publications gratuitously,

which are always cordially welcomed, and perused with
interest : —

The N. E Journal of Education,	. *Boston, Mass.*
The Atlantic, ...	" "
Boston Home Journal, . . .	.. ..
Youth's Companion, ...	
The Christian, ...	.. ..
The Christian Register, . . .	.. ..
The Musical Record, ...	.. ..
The Musical Herald, ...	:: ::
The Folio, ...	.. ..
Littell's Living Age, ...	.. ..
Unitarian Review, ...	.. ..
The Watchman, ...	
The Golden Rule, ...	.. ..
Zion's Herald, ...	.. ..
The Missionary Herald, . . .	" "
The Salem Register, ...	. *Salem, Mass.*
The Century, ...	*New York, N. Y.*
St. Nicholas, ...	" "
The Journal of Speculative Philosophy,	" "
Church's Musical Journal, . . .	*Cincinnati, O.*
Goodson Gazette, *Va. Inst. for Deaf-Mutes and Blind.*	
Tablet, . . *West Va.* " " " "	
Companion, . *Minnesota Institute for Deaf-Mutes.*	
Il Mentore dei Ciechi, . .	*Florence, Italy.*

I desire again to render the most hearty thanks, in behalf of
all our pupils, to the kind friends who have thus nobly remembered them. The seeds which their friendly and generous
attentions have sown have fallen on no barren ground, but will
continue to bear fruit in after years ; and the memory of many
of these delightful and instructive occasions and valuable gifts
will be retained through life.

M. ANAGNOS.

GENERAL STATEMENT OF RECEIPTS AND DISBURSEMENTS BY THE TREASURER OF THE PERKINS INSTITUTION AND MASSACHUSETTS SCHOOL FOR THE BLIND, FOR THE YEAR ENDING SEPT. 30, 1884.

I.—INCOME.

State of Massachusetts annual appropriation,	$30,000 00		
Board and tuition, State of Maine,	4,225 00		
" " of New Hampshire,	3,400 00		
" " of Vermont,	1,800 00		
" " of Rhode Island,	4,201 45		
" " of Connecticut,	4,675 00		
" " private pupils,	642 12		
		$48,943 57	
Tuning,		85 30	
Admission fees,		909 93	
Sundry small items,		188 57	
Interest on mortgage notes,	$618 75		
" on corporation notes, South Boston Railroad,	320 83		
" " Boott Cotton Mills,	1 00		
" " Children's Aid Society,		9,983 17	
" on balances N. E. T. Co.,	$300 00		
" on Ottawa & Burlington Railroad Bonds,	349 68		
" on Kansas City & Council Bluffs Bonds,	50 00		
" on Boston & Lowell Bonds,	1,080 00		
" on Chicago, Burlington & Quincy Bonds,	120 00		
" on Eastern Bonds,	299 75		
Chicago, Milwaukee & St. Paul Bonds,		2,199 43	
Dividends on stock,—			
Boston & Providence Railroad,	$240 00		
Fitchburg Railroad,	275 00		
Chicago, Burlington & Quincy Railroad,	360 00	575 00	
Rents, house 11 Oxford street, net,	$629 84		
" 3 houses on Fifth street, 1 month,	.90 00	719 84	
Sale of books in raised print,		404 06	
		$55,551 44	

I.—EXPENSES.

Maintenance,	$41,916 12	
Repairs,	8,251 96	
Expense of workshop,	712 46	
Rent of safe,	60 00	
Board of blind man,	176 73	
Expenses of boys' shop,	6 04	
Legal services,	150 00	
Expenses of printing office,	3,452 23	
Rent of office,	250 00	
		$54,975 54
Harris beneficiaries,		787 50
Taxes and insurance on houses yielding income,		158 43
Rebatement of interest on notes paid,		119 46

II.—INVESTMENTS.

Building 4 houses on Fifth street,		18,796 97
Mortgage notes,	$26,000 00	
Chicago, Burlington & Quincy Railroad, 60 shares,	7,650 00	
" " Instalments,	240 00	33,890 00
Balance Sept. 30, 1884,—		
Cash in N. E. Trust Co.,	$21,156 55	
Less amount due M. Anagnos, Director,	487 86	20,668 69

II.—Receipts, Exclusive of Income.

Legacy, Eunice M. Gridley, ...	$7,409 35	
Donations, General Fund, ...	310 00	
" Kindergarten Fund, . . .	16,998 32	
		$24,717 67

III.—Collections.

Notes collected, ...		32,500 00
Cash in N. E. Trust Co., Oct. 1, 1883, . .	$2,748 08	
" less amount due M. Anagnos, Director, .	1,120 61	
		1,627 47
		$124,396 58

$124,396 58

ANALYSIS OF THE MAINTENANCE ACCOUNT.

Meat, 26,026 lbs.,	$3,008 72
Fish, 4,056 lbs.,	199 86
Butter, 5,170 lbs.,	1,597 91
Rice, sago, etc.,	22 56
Bread, flour and meal,	1,477 56
Potatoes and other vegetables,	748 69
Fruit,	304 49
Milk, 25,520 qts.,	1,502 98
Sugar, 7,728 lbs.,	593 27
Tea and coffee, 463 lbs.,	169 67
Groceries,	732 71
Gas and oil,	482 02
Coal and wood,	2,415 23
Sundry articles of consumption,	334 10
Wages and domestic service,	4,189 05
Salaries, superintendence and instruction,	16,301 69
Outside aid,	251 63
Medicine and medical aid,	34 65
Furniture and bedding,	1,352 73
Clothing and mending,	56 04
Stable,	171 57
Musical instruments,	1,975 06
Books, stationery, etc.,	1,153 48
Construction and repairs,	1,025 88
Water taxes and insurance,	1,509 24
Travelling expenses,	65 66
Bills to be refunded,	186 94
Sundries,	52 73
	$41,916 12

EXPENSES OF THE PRINTING DEPARTMENT.

Labor,	$1,306 02
Stock,	575 52
Electrotyping,	676 98
Binding,	540 35
Type,	175 63
Machinery (repairs),	83 36
Insurance,	60 00
Cleaning, gas, etc.,	34 87
	$3,452 23

WORK DEPARTMENT, Oct. 1, 1884.

STATEMENT.

Expenditures during the year ending Sept. 30, 1884.

Salaries and wages to blind people,	$3,599 58	
" " to seeing people,	2,381 20	
Sundries for stock, rent, etc.,	10,640 72	
		$16,621 50

Receipts.

Cash received during the year for sales, rents, etc.,	15,909 04
	$712 46

Stock and Debts Due.

Stock, Oct. 1, 1883,	$7,276 51	
" Oct. 1, 1884,	$5,217 34	
Debts due,	2,004 67	
	7,222 01	
		54 50

Cost of carrying on the work department during the year,	$766 96

The following account exhibits the state of the property as embraced in the treasurer's books, September 30, 1884.

Real Estate yielding Income.		
House No. 11 Oxford street, . . .	$5,500 00	
Three houses on 5th street, South Boston,	11,472 73	
		$16,972 73
Real estate used for school purposes, .	. . .	243,824 24
Unimproved land in South Boston,	. . .	8,500 00
Mortgage notes, ...	. . .	196,000 00
South Boston Horse R.R. Co., note, .	. . .	7,500 00
Railroad Stock.		
Boston and Providence Railroad, 30 shares, value, ...	$4,920 00	
Fitchburg Railroad, 50 shares, value, .	5,600 00	
Chicago, Burlington & Quincy R R., 60 shares, value, ...	7,200 00	
		17,720 00
Railroad Bonds.		
Eastern Railroad Co. 6s, 2 at $500 each, value, $1,140, . . .	$4,560 00	
Eastern Railroad Co. 6s, 3 at $1,000 each, value, $3 420, . . .		
Boston & Lowell Railroad Co. 6s, 1 at $1,000, value, ...	1,150 00	
Chicago, Burlington & Quincy R.R. Co. 4s, 27 at $1,000, value, . . .	24,300 00	
Chicago, Milwaukee & St. Paul R.R. Co., Dubuque Division, 6s, 5 at $1,000 val.,	5,250 00	
Ottawa & Burlington R.R. Co. 6s, 5 at $1,000 value, ...	5,300 00	
Kansas City, St. Joseph & Council Bluffs Railroad Co. 7s, 5 at $1,000 value, .	5,850 00	
		46,410 00
Cash (less amount due M Anagnos, Director), ...	. . .	20,668 69
Household furniture, ...	. . .	16,320 00
Provisions and supplies, ...	. . .	890 66
Wood and coal, ...	. . .	2,718 00
Work department.—Stock and debts for same, ...	. . .	7,222 01
Amount carried forward, . . .	. . .	$584,746 33

Amount brought forward, ...			$584,746 33
Musical instruments and books, ...			17,885 00
Printing: stock and machinery, . .	$1,800 00		
Books and maps, . . .	8,500 00		
Stereotype plates, . . .	5,000 00		
			15,300 00
School furniture and apparatus.			7,700 00
Library, ...			9,900 00
Boys' shop, ...			79 80
Stable and tools, ...			988 75
			$636,599 88

The foregoing property represents the following funds and balances, and is answerable for the same.

General fund, investments, . . .	$102,632 73	
Cash, ...	799 19	
Harris fund, investments, . . .	74,720 00	
Printing " " . . .	107,250 00	
Kindergarten fund, cash, . . .	19,869 50	
		$305,271 42
Buildings, unimproved real estate and personal property in use for the school,	. . .	331,328 46
		$636,599 88

██████████████

KINDERGARTEN FUND.

LIST OF CONTRIBUTORS.

Amount acknowledged in the last report, . .	$2,855 00
Estate of Moses Day, ...	1,000 00
Miss Lucy H. Simonds, ...	10 00
Rev. A. F. Washburn, ...	10 00
Mrs. ——	5 00
Miss Clara B. Rogers, ...	3 00
Edward A. Freeman, ...	25
John Lart, ...	25
A Friend, ...	50
Two Friends, ...	2 00
Mrs. Dr. Freeman, ...	1 00
F. Freeman, ...	1 00
Walker Children, ...	1 00
A Friend to the Good Cause, ...	25 00
Joseph C. Tolman, Hanover, Mass., . . .	800 00
Little Children from Newburyport. . . .	39 00
Mrs. I. D. Harrington, ...	5 00
Miss Sarah B. Fay, ...	500 00
Lawrence Model Lodging House Fund, . . .	500 00
Mrs. J. H. Wolcott (second subscription), . .	300 00
Miss Anne Wigglesworth, ...	250 00
Mrs. Jeffrey Richardson, ...	200 00
Mrs. Susie J. Loring, ...	200 00
R. J. Fellows, New Haven, Conn., . . .	100 00

Amount carried forward, ... $6,808 00

Amount brought forward, ...	$6,808 00
Mrs. J. T. Coolidge, ...	100 00
Miss Edith Rotch, ...	100 00
T. A. W., ...	100 00
Harwood and Quincy, ...	100 00
Miss Abby W. May, ...	100 00
Mrs. Horace Gray, ...	100 00
George W. Wales, ...	100 00
Mrs. Virginia A. Howe (proceeds of concert), .	75 25
Miss Anne L. Rotch, ...	50 00
Miss A. C. Lowell, ...	50 00
Dr. S. Cabot, ...	50 00
Mrs. Wilkins Warren, ...	50 00
Mrs. Eleanor Bennett, Billerica, . . .	50 00
Edward Lawrence, Charlestown, . . .	50 00
Miss Abby W. Turner, ...	50 00
Miss Alice M. Turner, ...	50 00
Miss Ellen J. Turner, ...	50 00
Mrs. Isaac Sweetser, ...	50 00
Mrs. B. S. Rotch, ...	50 00
Miss M. A. Wales, ...	50 00
Mrs. D. Merriam, ...	50 00
Dr. J. W. Burton and Friends, Flushing, N. Y., .	50 00
Mount Everett Social and Dramatic Club, . .	50 00
Abbott Lawrence Lowell (second donation), . .	50 00
Dahlgren Post No. 2, South Boston, . . .	50 00
Mrs. Julia B. H. James, ...	50 00
Mrs. Sarah M Chickering, ...	50 00
A Friend, ...	40 00
Rev. Fred'k Frothingham, Milton, . . .	30 00
C. J. White, Cambridge, ...	30 00
Mrs. Elisha Atkins, ...	30 00
E. R. Welch, ...	25 00

Amount carried forward, . . .	$8,688 25

Amount brought forward, ...	**$8,688** 25
F. P. Sprague, ...	25 00
Miss Laura Norcross, ...	25 00
Dr. F. Minot (second donation).	25 00
Presbyterian Church, South Boston. . . .	25 00
F. W. Mackay, ...	25 00
Mrs. Phebe A. Hearst, ...	25 00
Miss Clara E. Sears, ...	20 00
Mrs. G. G. Lowell, ...	20 00
Miss Mary Larmon, ...	20 00
Mrs. James Freeman Clarke, ...	20 00
Bellingham Sunday School, Chelsea. . . .	19 72
Employés in Photo-Electric Company. . . .	17 20
Mrs. Wells, ...	10 00
Master Sumner Crosby, ...	10 00
Mr. and Mrs. Albert Lowe, Clinton. . . .	10 00
Miss Sarah A. Rollins, ...	10 00
Mrs. G. W. Hammond, ...	10 00
Ladies' Society, South Brookfield, ...	10 00
Henry M. Rogers, ...	10 00
Mrs. T. A. Davis, ...	10 00
Boston Type Foundry, ...	10 00
J. B. T., ...	10 00
H. K. Morrell, Gardiner, Maine.	10 00
Little Helpers, Unitarian S. S., Medfield, . .	9 64
Miss Sophia A. Baden, ...	5 00
Employés in Workshop of Inst. for the Blind. .	5 00
Mrs J. C. Gray, ...	5 00
William E. DeWitt, ...	5 00
W. H Reynolds, ...	3 00
Mrs. Hoyt, ...	3 00
Ellie and Walter Capron.	1 00
Willard B. Vose, ...	1 00
Amount carried forward.	**$9,102** 81

Amount brought forward, . . .	$9,102 81
Miss Lucy T. Soule, ...	1 00
A Friend, ...	1 00
Cash, ...	1 00
Cottage Place Kindergarten, ...	41
Master D. W. Merriam, ...	25
Proceeds of the Girls' Fair at South Boston, . .	2,050 35
James Coats, Providence, R. I., ...	500 00
A Friend, ...	500 00
Miss Mary Anne Wales (second donation), . .	250 00
Mrs. J. E. Lodge, ...	200 00
A Friend, ...	200 00
Miss Minna B. Hall, proceeds of concert in Long-wood, ...	176 00
C. A. Curtis, ...	100 00
W., ...	100 00
J. H. Carter, Roxbury, ...	100 00
Otis E. Weld, ...	100 00
C. W. Amory, ...	100 00
J. B. Glover, ...	100 00
The Misses C., ...	100 00
Mrs. G. Brooks, ...	100 00
E. Francis Parker, ...	100 00
Mrs. Freeman Cobb, proceeds of concert, . .	75 00
James Lawrence, ...	50 00
B. Schlesinger, ...	50 00
Mrs. B. S. Rotch (second donation), . . .	50 00
Mrs. C. B. Stewart, ...	50 00
Charles T. White, ...	50 00
Albert Glover, ...	50 00
Employés Boston Type Foundry, ...	30 35
Mrs. P. H. Sears, ...	25 00
Mrs. F. G. Dexter, ...	25 00
Amount carried forward, . .	$14,338 17

Amount brought forward, . . .	.$14,338 17
J. L. Emmons, ...	25 00
Crosbie Street S. School, Salem, ...	25 00
Sara B. Alden, ...	25 00
Henry F. Spencer, ...	25 00
In answer to Laura Bridgman's Appeal, . .	20 00
Cash, ...	20 00
Proceeds of play, " William Tell," . . .	16 75
Children of St. John's Church S. School, Sandy Hook, Conn., ...	15 40
Proceeds of concert in Allston, ...	15 20
A Friend, ...	15 00
First Parish Sunday School, East Bridgewater, .	13 00
Sunday School, Church of the Messiah, Chicago, Ill.,	12 50
Miss Sears, ...	10 00
S. M. Stewart, ...	10 00
Mrs. Otis Norcross, Jr., ...	10 00
St. Peter's Sunday School, Beverly, . . .	10 00
Through Laura Bridgman, ...	8 00
Sixth Class, Agassiz School, Cambridge, . .	6 12
H. C. Whitcomb, ...	5 90
Mrs. E. E. F. Field, Milton, ...	5 00
Mrs. Sarah M. Chickering (second donation), .	5 00
Mrs. ——	5 00
M. C., ...	5 00
Miss Mandor, ...	5 00
Bridgewater Unitarian Sunday School, . . .	4 00
Rev. Mr. Wright, ...	3 50
Philadelphia, ...	3 00
Master James S. Davis, Dorchester, . . .	2 00
Miss Pinkham's Class, Dr. Briggs's Church, Cambridgeport, ...	2 00
A Friend in Norwood, ...	2 00
Amount carried forward, . . .	.$14,667 54

Amount brought forward, . . .	.$14,667 54
Cape Cod Item, ...	1 00
A Friend, ...	1 00
Cash, ...	1 00
D. D. Tappan, ...	1 00
Laura Bridgman, ...	1 00
Miss Ida M. Mason, ...	1,000 00
Miss Nancy Brackett, ...	200 00
Mrs. James Greenleaf, Cambridge, . . .	200 00
Mrs. William Appleton, ...	200 00
Hyde Park, through Miss Florence E. Leadbetter,	130 00
Ruth N. Pearson and Minnie M. Graves, Charlestown, proceeds of Fair, ...	120 00
Dr. and Mrs. C. E. Ware, ...	100 00
Mrs. Isaac Sweetser (second donation), . .	100 00
Mrs. Frances A. Gill, ...	100 00
Mrs. Mary E. Pierson, Windsor, Conn., . .	100 00
Moses Hunt, Charlestown, ...	100 00
Proceeds of Concert in Bridgewater, . . .	100 00
Miss Anne Wigglesworth (second donation), .	100 00
Proceeds of Concert in Charlestown, . . .	74 00
Young People's Society of Christian Endeavor, Phillips Church, South Boston, ...	72 22
"Never too late to mend" Sewing Circle, . .	50 50
Mrs. J. H. Thorndike (second donation), . .	50 00
Back Bay Theatre Co., ...	50 00
Mrs. F. A. Brooks, ...	50 00
Miss S. G. Littell, ...	50 00
Through Mr. and Mrs. B. T. Johnson, Middleborough, ...	37 33
Dr. Rufus Ellis's Sunday School, ...	31 00
Miss M. L. Ware, ...	25 00
C. M. L., ...	25 00
Amount carried forward, . . .	.$17,737 59

Amount brought forward, . . .	.$17,787 59
Miss Ellen M. Jones, ...	25 00
Mrs. L. M. Hall, ...	25 00
Charles H. Stearns, ...	25 00
Mrs. Constantine V. Hutchins, ...	15 00
Mrs. Robert Swan, ...	10 00
Miss G. Lowell, ...	10 00
Mrs. C. C. Chadwick, ...	10 00
Mr. and Mrs. W. T. Piper, Cambridge, . .	10 00
Robert B. and Mary G. Stone, ...	10 00
Friends, through Miss L., ...	10 00
A. A. H., St. Paul, Minn., ...	10 00
–Miss M., ...	10 00
Through Mrs. George A. Mitchell, Hyde Park, .	10 00
Mr. and Mrs. Hamilton Morehead, Marshfield, .	10 00
Mary E. Piper, ...	5 00
E. J. Langley, ...	5 00
W. Y. Gross, ...	5 00
Lady, by E. R. Hall, ...	5 00
Mrs. Frances H. Gray, ...	5 00
Mrs. L. C. Goodwin, ...	5 00
Miss S. G. Fisher, ...	5 00
Mrs. D. N. Richards, ...	5 00
Nettie M. Bartlett, West Gardiner, . . .	5 10
Entertainment by little boys of Perkins Institution,	4 50
Sunday School, Dr. Rufus Ellis's Church (additional), ...	2 75
Anonymous, ...	2 50
Children's Fair, Bridgewater, ...	2 00
Bessie Elliot and Bertha March, Cambridge, proceeds of sale, ...	2 00
Entertainment by little girls of Perkins Institution,	1 66
Through Laura Bridgman, ...	1 00
Amount carried forward, . . .	.$17,989 10

Amount brought forward, ...$17,989 10	
Anonymous, ...	1 00
Through Miss A., ...	1 00
Hiram A. Wright, Roxbury, ...	1 00
Through Fannie E. Jackson, ...	50
Mrs. Mary L. Brown, ...	50
Sale of Kindergarten work, ...	50
Cash, ...	50
T. Jefferson Coolidge, ...	50 00
Miss Minna Wesselhoeft, ...	5 00
Ladies' Unitarian Domestic Missionary Society,	
Portsmouth, N. H., ...	25 00
Miss Isabel Merry, Newark, New Jersey, . .	5 00
Mrs. Henry Sigourney, Boston, ...	100 00
C. M. Kettell, Boston, ...	5 00
Children in Lowell, ...	5 00
Florence Sunday School, by Miss Elder, . .	11 25
Miss Martha Carter, Boston, ...	1 00
H. L., Charlestown, ...	2 00
Helping Hands Society, by Carrie T. Foster, . .	20 00
Mrs. S. K. Burgess, Boston, ...	10 00
Mrs. E. K. Storrs, Boston, ...	10 00
Faust Social Club, F. M. Dean, ...	10 70
Miss C. E. Jenks, ...	5 00
Proceeds of Dr. H. P. Bowditch's children's fair,	
Jamaica Plain, ...	44 27
G. A. White, ...	50 00
Mrs. Sarah A. Gill, Worcester, ...	500 00
Dr John H. Dix, ...	1,000 00

$19,853 32

ADDITIONAL CONTRIBUTIONS.

P. S. — Since the 30th of September, when the annual accounts of the treasurer were closed, to the 1st of December last, the following contributions were received by him : —

Amount acknowledged in the foregoing pages, .	$19,853 82
Unitarian Sunday School, New Bedford, . .	23 00
Warrenton Chapel Kindergarten, ...	3 41
Unitarian Sunday School, Dorchester, . . .	39 03
Mrs. Ferguson, proceeds of concert in Dorchester,	100 00
Mrs. Helen B. Carter, proceeds of sale, West Newton, ...	108 00
Children of Wellesley Hills Primary School, . .	2 00
Pupils of Miss Sampson's Private School, Boylston Chapel, ...	9 00
Miss Mary Brackett's infant class in Dr. Ellis's Church, ...	9 25
Poor children on Albany Street, ...	50
Fair held by four little girls, 6 North Avenue, Cambridge, ...	51 41
Eliza Blodgett and Helen Patterson, St. Johnsbury, Vermont, ...	2 00
Nimble Fingers Society, Dorchester, . . .	20 00
Entertainment by five little girls in Newtonville, .	1 50
E. W. S., ...	1 00
Little lame boy in Hartford, Conn., . . .	50
Guests of Lancaster House, through C. H. Prescott,	8 00
Sunday School class, Litchfield, Conn., . . .	5 00
Through Martin H. Smith, ...	4 75
Unitarian Sunday School, Lexington, . . .	10 00
Little lame girl in Hartford, Conn., . . .	28
Amount carried forward, . . .	$20,251 95

Amount brought forward, . . .	$20,251 95
Proceeds of fair in Swampscott by Blanche Loring and Susie Hastings, ...	110 00
Eustis P. Morgan, Saco, Me., ...	10 00
Mrs. M. C. Charles, Melrose, ...	25 00
Cash, ...	25
Miss C. F. F., ...	20 00
Lindanna Maxfield, ...	1 16
Lady from Sandwich, through Fannie Jackson, .	2 50
Sale of materials, ...	2 00
Proceeds of concert at South Abington, . .	41 88
Dennis A. Reardon, ...	30 00
Fair in Cambridgeport by Bessie Elliot, Bertha March, Marion R. Brooks, and Alice Elliot, .	34 00
Proceeds of fair, through Mrs. J. Huntington Wolcott, ...	4,602 89
Mrs. John Lowell, ...	50 00
Miss Lucy Lowell, ...	50 00
	$25,231 63

LIST OF EMBOSSED BOOKS,

Printed at the Perkins Institution and Massachusetts School for the Blind.

TITLE OF BOOK.	No. of Volumes.	Price per Volume.
Howe's Cyclopædia,	8	$4 00
Baxter's Call,	1	2 50
Book of Proverbs,	1	2 00
Book of Psalms,	1	3 00
New Testament,	4	2 50
Book of Common Prayer,	1	4 00
Hymns for the Blind,	1	2 00
Pilgrim's Progress,	1	4 00
Life of Melanchthon,	1	1 00
Natural Theology,	1	4 00
Combe's Constitution of Man,	1	4 00
Selections from the Works of Swedenborg,	1	–
Second Table of Logarithms,	1	3 00
Philosophy of Natural History,	1	3 00
"Life and her Children," or a Reader of Natural History,	1	3 00
Huxley's Science Primers, Introductory,	1	2 00
Memoir of Dr. Samuel G. Howe,	1	3 00
Cutter's Anatomy, Physiology and Hygiene,	1	3 00
Viri Romæ, new edition with additions,	1	2 00
Musical Characters used by the seeing,	1	35
Key to Braille's Musical Notation,	1	35
Guyot's Geography,	1	4 00
Scribner's Geographical Reader,	1	2 50
Dickens's Child's History of England,	2	3 00
Anderson's History of the United States,	1	2 50
Higginson's Young Folks' History of the United States,	1	3 50
Schmitz's History of Greece,	1	3 00
Schmitz's History of Rome,	1	2 50
Freeman's History of Europe,	1	2 50
An Account of the Most Celebrated Diamonds,	1	50
Extracts from British and American Literature,	2	3 00
American Prose,	2	3 00
Hawthorne's Tanglewood Tales,	2	2 00
Dickens's Old Curiosity Shop,	3	4 00
Dickens's Christmas Carol, with extracts from Pickwick,	1	3 00
The Last Days of Pompeii, by Edward Bulwer Lytton,	3	3 00
Goldsmith's Vicar of Wakefield,	1	3 00
George Eliot's Silas Marner,	1	3 50
Biographical Sketch of George Eliot,	1	25

LIST OF EMBOSSED BOOKS — *Continued.*

TITLE OF BOOK.	No. of Volumes.	Price per Volume.
Milton's Paradise Lost,	2	$3 00
Pope's Essay on Man and other Poems,	1	2 50
Shakespeare's Hamlet and Julius Cæsar,	1	4 00
Scott's Lay of the Last Minstrel and 37 other Poems,	1	3 00
Byron's Hebrew Melodies and Childe Harold,	1	3 00
Poetry of Byron, selected by Matthew Arnold,	1	3 00
Tennyson's In Memoriam and other Poems,	1	3 00
Longfellow's Evangeline,	1	2 00
Longfellow's Evangeline and other Poems,	1	3 00
Whittier's Poems,	1	3 00
Lowell's Poems,	1	3 00
Bryant's Poems,	1	3 00
Longfellow's Birthday, by J. R Anagnos,	1	25
Constitution of the United States,•	1	40
Biographical Sketches of Distinguished Persons,	1	3 00
Commemoration Ode, by H. W. Stratton,	1	10
JUVENILE BOOKS.		
Script and point alphabet sheets per hundred,	–	5 00
An Eclectic Primer,	1	40
Child's First Book,	1	40
Child's Second Book,	1	40
Child's Third Book,	1	40
Child s Fourth Book,	1	40
Child's Fifth Book,	1	40
Child's Sixth Book,	1	40
Child's Seventh Book,	1	40
Youth's Library, vol. 1st,	1	1 25
Youth's Library. vol. 2d,	1	1 25
Youth's Library. vol. 3d,	1	1 25
Youth's Library, vol. 4th,	1	1 25
Youth's Library, vol. 5th,	1	1 25
Youth's Library, vol. 6th,	1	1 25
Youth's Library, vol 7th,	1	1 25
Youth's Library. vol. 8th,	1	1 25
Children's Fairy Book. by M. Anagnos,	1	2 50
Andersen's Stories and Tales,	1	3 00
Eliot's Six Arabian Nights,	1	3 00
Lodge's Twelve Popular Tales,	1	2 00
Bible Stories in Bible language, by Emilie Poulsson,	1	3 50

N. B. The prices in the above list are set down per volume, not per set.

LIST OF APPLIANCES AND TANGIBLE APPARATUS,

Made at the Perkins Institution and Massachusetts School for the Blind.

GEOGRAPHY.

1. — *Wall-Maps.*

1. The Hemispheres, ...	size, 42 by 52 inches.
2. United States, Mexico and Canada.	" " "
3. North America, ...	" " "
4. South America, ...	" " "
5. Europe, ...	" " "
6. Asia, ...	" " "
7. Africa, ...	" " "
8. The World on Mercator's Projection,	" " "

Each $35, or the set, $280.

II. — *Dissected Maps.*

1. Eastern Hemisphere, . . .	size, 30 by 36 inches.
2. Western Hemisphere, . . .	" " "
3. North America, ...	" " "
4. United States, ...	" " "
5. South America.	" " "
6. Europe, ...	" " "
7. Asia, ...	" " "
8. Africa, ...	" " "

Each $23, or the set. $184.

These maps are considered, in point of workmanship, accuracy and distinctness of outline, durability and beauty, far superior to all thus far made in Europe or in this country.

" The New England Journal of Education" says, " They are very strong, present a fine, bright surface, and are an ornament to any school-room."

III. — *Pin-Maps.*

Cushions for pin-maps and diagrams, . . . each, $0 75

ARITHMETIC.

Ciphering-boards made of brass strips, nickel-plated, ... each, $4 25
Ciphering-types, nickel-plated, per hundred, . " 1 00

WRITING.

Grooved writing-cards, ... each, $0 05
Braille tablets, with metallic bed, . . . " 1 50
Braille French tablets, with cloth bed, . . . " 1 00
Braille new tablets, with cloth bed, . . . " 1 00
Braille Daisy tablets, ... " 5 00

TERMS OF ADMISSION.

"Candidates for admission must be over nine and under nineteen years of age, and none others shall be admitted." — *Extract from the by-laws*.

Blind children and youth between the ages above pre-scribed and of sound mind and good moral character, can be admitted to the school by paying $300 per annum. Those among them who belong to the state of Massachu-setts and whose parents or guardians are not able to pay the whole or a portion of this sum, can be admitted gratuitously by application to the governor for a warrant.

The following is a good form, though any other will do : —

" *To His Excellency the Governor.*

" SIR, — My son (or daughter, or nephew, or niece, as the case may be), named ——, and aged ——, cannot be instructed in the common schools, for want of sight. I am unable to pay for the tuition at the Perkins Institution and Massachusetts School for the Blind, and I request that your Excellency will give a warrant for free admission.
                    Very respectfully,   —— ——."

The application may be made by any relation or friend, if the parents are dead or absent.

It should be accompanied by a certificate, signed by some regular physician, in this form : —

" I certify that, in my opinion, —— —— has not sufficient vision to be taught in common schools; and that he is free from epilepsy, and from any contagious disease.
                    (Signed)   —— ——."

These papers should be done up together, and forwarded to the DIRECTOR OF THE INSTITUTION FOR THE BLIND, *South Boston, Mass.*

Blind children and youth residing in Maine, New Hampshire, Vermont, Connecticut and Rhode Island, by applying as above to the governor, or the " Secretary of State," in their respective states, can obtain warrants for free admission.

The sum of $300 above specified covers all expenses (except for clothing), namely, board, lodging, washing, tuition, and the use of books and musical instruments. The pupils must furnish their own clothing, and pay their own fares to and from the institution.

An obligation will be required from some responsible persons, that the pupil shall be kept properly supplied with decent clothing, shall be provided for during vacations, and shall be removed, without expense to the institution, whenever it may be desirable to discharge him.

The usual period of tuition is from five to seven years.

The friends of the pupils can visit them whenever they choose.

The use of tobacco, either in smoking or otherwise, is strictly prohibited in the institution.

Persons applying for admission of children must fill out certain blanks, copies of which will be forwarded to any address on application.

For further information address M. ANAGNOS, DIRECTOR, PERKINS INSTITUTION FOR THE BLIND, *South Boston, Mass.*

APPENDIX.

PROCEEDINGS

OF THE

COMMENCEMENT EXERCISES

OF THE

PERKINS INSTITUTION AND MASSACHUSETTS SCHOOL FOR THE BLIND.

COMMENCEMENT EXERCISES

OF THE

PERKINS INSTITUTION AND MASSACHUSETTS SCHOOL FOR THE BLIND.

The commencement exercises of the school were held early in June, in Tremont Temple, having been first announced by the following circular : —

PERKINS INSTITUTION AND MASS. SCHOOL FOR THE BLIND,
BOSTON, May 10, 1884.

The commencement exercises of this school will be held at Tremont Temple on Tuesday, June 3, at 3 P. M. Samuel Eliot, LL.D., will preside ; His Excellency, Governor Robinson will give a brief opening address, and Mr. C. W. Ernst will speak on the kindergarten project.

You are most cordially invited to honor the occasion with your presence.

The seats on the floor and in the first balcony of the Temple will be reserved for the choice of the members of the corporation and the friends and patrons of the institution, to whom this invitation is sent, until Saturday, May 24. Tickets are ready for delivery, and those who may be desirous of obtaining them are requested to send me a postal card indicating the number wished for. It will give me very great pleasure to forward them at once.

The seats will be reserved until 3 o'clock, punctually, when standing persons will be permitted to occupy all vacant places.

M. ANAGNOS.

No tickets are required for the Second Balcony of the Temple, to which the public are cordially invited.

A kindergarten, or primary school, is imperatively needed for little sightless children. Without it the system of education for the blind cannot be regarded complete. The attention of the generous and benevolent members of our community is most respectfully called to this project.

The total amount of the kindergarten fund on the first day of May was about $17,000. Further contributions are earnestly solicited, and will be thankfully received by

JAMES STURGIS. Treasurer pro tem.
No. 70 Kilby street, Boston.

This circular also contained the programme of exercises hereafter given. The city journals and many of the newspapers of neighboring cities and towns, then took up the word and gave it the wider utterance demanded by the increasing interest of the people in this institution.

PROGRAMME. PART I.

1. ORGAN SELECTIONS.
MISS FREDA BLACK.

2. BRIEF OPENING ADDRESS.
HIS EXCELLENCY GOVERNOR ROBINSON.

3. BAND, — March, — "British Heart," . . . *Hartner.*

4. ESSAY, — " Work."
   Miss Alice S. Holbrook.

5. SOLO FOR ALTO HORN, — " Morceau de Salon," No. 3, } *H. Painpare.*
   Christopher A. Howland.

6. EXERCISE IN PHYSICS.
   Charles T. Gleason.

7. SOLO FOR CLARINET, — " Venzano Waltz," *L. Venzano.*
   Clarence W. Basford.

8. ESSAY, — " Four Poets."
   Miss Susanna E. Sheahan.

Part II.

1. GYMNASTICS, Military Drill and Calisthenics.

2. SOLO FOR CORNET, — " Arbuckleinian Polka," *Hartmann.*
   Charles H. Prescott.

3. READING WITH THE FINGERS, — Exercise in Geography.

4. KINDERGARTEN EXERCISES.
   Remarks on the proposed Kindergarten, by Mr. C. W. Ernst.

5. DUET, — " On to the Field of Glory," — from Belisario, } *Donizetti.*
   Messrs. L. Titus and Wm. B. Hammond.

6. VALEDICTORY.
   Miss Isabella Romily.

7. CHORUS FOR FEMALE VOICES, — " Charity," *Rossini.*

8. AWARD OF DIPLOMAS.
   By Dr. Samuel Eliot.

9. CHORUS, — " O hail us ye free," — from Ernani, *Verdi.*

NAMES OF GRADUATES.

Alice S. Holbrook.   Alice M. Lowe.   Isabella Romily.

The better facilities for knowing the character of this school, afforded since holding these annual exercises in a more roomy and accessible place, has been one important means of awakening and extending the public interest; and the consequent demand for tickets was so great that the supply was exhausted several days before the festival was to take place, and hundreds (perhaps *thousands*) of applicants were unavoidably refused.

The hall was filled by an audience the character of which was an honor to the occasion. The pupils occupied nearly all the seats upon the platform, a few being reserved for the trustees, members of the corporation and other prominent gentlemen. Near the centre of the platform, among the older pupils, sat Laura Bridgman, ever an object of universal interest and wonder, and her presence awoke a deeper interest in her appeal for the kindergarten, fac-simile copies of which had been distributed through the hall and were now in the hands of the audience.

While the later arrivals were finding seats among the audience, some selections for the organ were very acceptably rendered by Miss Freda Black, and the meeting was then opened by the chairman, Mr. John S. Dwight, who made the following address: —

" It is my misfortune, as well as yours, ladies and gentlemen, that the honored president of our corporation, Dr. Samuel Eliot, is unable to be with us, and that I have to be called upon to try to seem to fill his place. I am probably selected from among my colleagues in the board of trustees, partly as representing the committee on education, but chiefly, I imagine, on the ground of age. And that shall be my fair excuse for falling back on something very near to 'total abstinence' from *speech-making*, — plenty of *that* (and of the best, I dare say) you will find provided in the programme. There, too, you will find a great variety of branches and of topics which may well surprise any one (present for the first time) to see figuring in a scheme of education for the blind. But I assure you there is no vanity in all this; no silly ambition for display. It only means that our school deals with this serious privation of its pupils in no spirit of mere sentimental charity. In the first place, it is not an '*asylum*,' as it is too often called; it is simply a *school*. And having undertaken their schooling, we think it no cruelty to them to make them perfectly aware how much they *lose*, through their infirmity, of means and opportunities and pleasures always accessible to those who see. We do not educate them on the principle that 'ignorance' (for them) 'is bliss.' On the contrary, we try to teach them *all that everybody knows*, or can and ought to know, — at least so far as practicable; teach them not only reading, writing and arithmetic, but also higher mathematics, language, literature, music, history, geography, philosophy, political economy, natural history, physical sciences, even including optics, or the laws of light and sight; and above all, the art of honest thinking and of simple, clear expression. All this on the one hand, with no neglect of physical or moral culture; while, on the other, we endeavor so to educate them as to make good their loss by more than equal gain in other faculties.

" The result you may here see in the intelligent and happy aspect which they all present; in the cheerful fervor with which they go about their studies and their work; in the ease and cleverness, the buoyancy, — I may even say, the æsthetic unity, so manifest in all their plays and their gymnastic exer-

cises; and even in the spirit and the zest, the quick perception of character and fitness, with which some of them enter
into the acting of dramas and charades.

"In short the *curriculum* is anything but fanciful or super-
ficial; it is eminently practical, — in nothing more so than in
the large share of attention which is given to *music*, which is
not only the blind man's solace, a refining, elevating influence,
and an inspirer and preserver of harmony and order in the
school (just as the electric lights are said to be the best kind
of police out of doors), but which, more generally than any
other art or craft which they can learn, enables them to earn
their living, either as teachers or performers, when they come
out into the world. The sightless can compete now with the
seeing on far more equal terms after these seven years of training so exact and thorough, of culture so liberal and many-
sided.

"This annual exhibition held for many years in the very
small hall of the institution at South Boston, and much shaded
from publicity, has been assuming larger proportions for a few
years past, and attracting wider interest and attention; so that
now it is not uncommon to hear these exercises spoken of as
our 'commencement!' The number, to be sure, who 'graduate,' or take the diploma each year, has been very small;
none can have it until they have fulfilled every requisition of
the course, — that is to say, until their teachers can pronounce
them thoroughly prepared to go out and meet the world and
take their places as useful and worthy members of society.
Last year there were *six* graduates; this year only three, and
these all of the gentler sex; and one of these, unfortunately,
is kept away by illness. For those who *do* receive it, this
diploma is ample assurance, won by thorough tests, of character and of capacity for self-supporting, good work in the
world. It carries with it, too, the hearty sympathy and God-
speed of all their teachers and companions.

"As all earnest pursuit of knowledge sooner or later teaches

us that we know almost nothing, so in all earnest *doing*, even
if we seem to reach the summit, it is only to show us that there
is yet more and greater to be done. The Perkins Institution
has reached the point where it feels the absolute necessity of a
separate provision, on a generous scale, for the introduction
of the kindergarten, —that entering wedge of common sense
in education, — for poor, sightless children of a tender age.
The want and the idea will be explained to you in the course of
the exercises, while the deft fingers of some of the smaller
children will be silently illustrating the beauty of the method
here before your eyes.

"The Perkins Institution and Massachusetts School for the
Blind originated, as you all know, in the large heart and brain
of that great philanthropist, Dr. Samuel G. Howe, of whom a
most fit monument now sits before you on this platform in the
person of Laura Bridgman who, bereft of sight and speech
and hearing, yet through the electric finger touch of friends
about her, apprehends, appreciates and feels with deepest interest and joy all that is here going on. His genius and indefatigable zeal shaped and built up the institution and left it on
a solid basis for his no less indefatigable and wise successor.
While it has owed the larger part of its financial endowment to
private munificence, notably to the late Thomas Handasyd
Perkins, it is also largely dependent on the fostering aid which
the good old state of Massachusetts has always extended to
all educational, humane and charitable institutions within her
borders; and she has shown herself no parsimonious stepmother toward this school for the blind. For years past has
the state, by act of legislature, appropriated annually $30,000
to the support of this institution. In return for this the state
is represented in its government, four of its twelve trustees
being appointed annually by the governor and council. Moreover, blind children of poorer families, or orphans, are sent to
it, under proper safeguard, without charge, as wards of the

commonwealth. The other New England states share, in their proportion, like contributions and privileges.

" Very fitly, therefore, had the chief magistrate of the commonwealth, His Excellency Governor Robinson, consented to lend us the honor of his presence here this afternoon, and make the opening address. But, unfortunately, the ' Great and General Court,' that august body that sits month after month industriously multiplying laws, having at last concluded to adjourn, has fixed upon this very day for bringing its labors to a close and keeps His Excellency a prisoner at the state house until its bills are all disposed of.

" So much the worse for *us!* But also so much the better in one view of the matter, inasmuch as you will come all the sooner to what constitutes the real and persuasive eloquence of these occasions, — that which springs from the lips and fingers of these blind pupils here before you. Such eloquence can speak for itself, perhaps, better than doctors of law or governors, however sympathetic."

The following letter from the Governor was then read: —

EXECUTIVE CHAMBER, STATE HOUSE,
BOSTON, May 30, 1884.

MY DEAR SIR : — You will remember that some time since I gave you to understand that I would be glad to accompany you to the anniversary exercises of the Perkins Institution, at 3 P.M., Tuesday, June 3. As you are probably aware, the legislature is in its closing hours, and it is extremely doubtful whether I shall be able to keep that engagement, my official duties requiring my constant presence in the executive chamber. Knowing that you will fully appreciate these circumstances, I do not hesitate to request you to release me from a definite engagement.

Very truly yours,

GEO. D. ROBINSON.

Hon. JAMES STURGIS, No. 70 St. James Ave., Boston.

The exercises commenced with Hartner's march,
"British Heart," which was played by the band
"with excellent effect and precision." The following essay was then given by Miss Holbrook, who
was commended both for "its conciseness and
argumentative sequence" and for the "exactitude
of utterance" which marked her delivery.

WORK.

BY MISS ALICE S. HOLBROOK.

He who blesses mankind by his work has reason to be proud
of that work, whatever it is.

Day after day, year after year, the miner toils in the deep
caverns of the earth. By his industry civilization makes great
strides over land and sea. The products of his labors are
present everywhere.

Long live the farmer, who ploughs, plants, reaps, tends his
flocks and herds, and by his honest toil provides food and
raiment, — sources of strength, from which all gather power
to perform their daily tasks.

If the mariner braved not the dangers of the mighty deep,
commerce would become crippled, knowledge less diffused, and
the benefits derived from the presence and thoughts of good
and wise men less universal.

Mental labor has devised better and swifter methods of
accomplishing every variety of work. The mathematician
helps to rear the lofty pile, while scientists open the book of
nature that all may read.

The pulpit, the press, and the platform exert a powerful
moral influence. Equally powerful are the smiles, the tear,
and the warm grasp of the hand to the weary one struggling
to overcome obstacles in his way. A philanthropist is too wise

even to desire the removal of obstacles, because he knows that strength is acquired by wrestling with them.

To-day calls for workers! It finds many humble, patient workers in every station making civilization a fact. The call comes to those who gratify selfish desires regardless of the ruin they bring. The call comes to the idler. "Up! rouse thyself! Shake off thy lethargy! Lo! thy brother's burden is too heavy, wilt thou not lighten it?"

As the hopes of every generation are in its children, "How shall we train the children?" is the important problem of the day. To those who have the training of youth, the call comes: Work to-day! Plant the seeds of physical, mental and moral truth. Humanity cries to every one in whatever sphere:

"Act, act, in the living present. Heart within, and God o'er head."

The pleasant tribute of several bouquets rewarded her at its close.

The solo for the alto horn, Painpare's "Morceau de Salon," played by Christopher A. Howland, was enthusiastically received by the audience, and he, too, was greeted with flowers.

The subject of the "Exercise in Physics" by Charles T. Gleason, was air-pressure, which he illustrated by several experiments, closing by exhausting the Magdeburg hemispheres and proving the truth of his previous statement by a struggle with Mr. Anagnos to wrench them apart. The exercise was watched with interest.

The solo for the clarinet was necessarily omitted on account of the illness of Clarence W. Basford,

and the first part of the programme closed with
Miss Sheahan's essay on "Four Poets."

FOUR POETS.

BY MISS SUSANNA E. SHEAHAN.

In the long list of authors who have labored during the past
fifty years, the names of Longfellow, Lowell, Whittier and
Bryant stand foremost as representatives of American literature.

In studying their writings we cannot fail to recognize the
individuality of each. Although the thought, opinion, or
object may be the same, yet there is something in the mode
of expression that seems to whisper to the careful student,
"This is Longfellow, that is Whittier."

"Death is the brother of Love, twin-brother is he, and is only
More austere to behold. With a kiss upon lips that are fading
Takes he the soul and departs, and, rocked in the arms of affection,
Places the ransomed child, new born, 'fore the face of its father."

"At that wished gate which gentle Death doth ope,
Into the boundless realm of strength and hope?"

"I cannot feel that thou art far,
Since near at need the angels are;
And when the sunset gates unbar,
Shall I not see thee waiting stand,
And, white against the evening star,
The welcome of thy beckoning hand?"

"And thou, who, o'er thy friend's low bier,
Dost shed the bitter drops like rain,
Hope that a brighter, happier sphere
Will give him to thy arms again."

The same thoughts are expressed by them all, that death is
not a separator but a uniter; that the future world is not a
place of uncertainty, but a place of strength and hope. Yet

how different are the figurative expressions of Longfellow from
the pathos and trust of Whittier; the classical phrases of
Lowell from the tender simplicity of Bryant!

Their treatment of the cause of slavery affords another
illustration of their individuality.

In all of Longfellow's poems we find that he has paid great
attention to the arrangement of verse, and his words are at
once simple and elegant. He is therefore considered by many
the most artistic of the four. The king and the beggar, the
divine and the savage, alike claim his sympathy and attention.

"Evangeline," one of his most popular poems, a description of the life and exile of the Acadian farmers, was the first
successful attempt to use the old Latin heroic metre in English
poetry. The descriptions of nature in this poem are in perfect harmony with the story, and add greatly to its pathos and
beauty.

"The Tales of a Wayside Inn" illustrate what ability
Longfellow possessed of treating a variety of subjects with
equal skill and interest. "The Song of Hiawatha" affords
beautiful examples of music in literature.

Whittier is much more impulsive than the former, and
writes, as Lowell says, "at white heats." As soon as he has
grasped the thought himself, he wishes to give it to others.
It flows from him because he cannot keep it back, and because
he is the natural poet, almost unconsciously, in verse. He
possesses a deep sense of religion, and of all that is great and
good; and his love of God and man breathes through all his
works. In the "Songs of Labor" he enters into the simplest
occupations, and finds something poetical in them all.

Lowell writes with more humor and incisiveness than any of
the others. The number of short sayings that may be quoted
on so many occasions have done much toward his popularity : —

> " They have rights who dare maintain them."
>
> " Not what we give, but what we share."

One of his finest poems is "The Vision of Sir Launfal," which contains a perfect description of a June day. "My Love," "To M. L.," "Irene," contain fine pictures of womanly character. His style is broad, comprehensive, witty and incisive, and his power of criticism is acknowledged by many to be unsurpassed.

In Bryant's writings we find more simplicity than in any of the others; and he differs from them in that he holds himself a part of all nature. The trees, flowers, streams, winds, birds and insects are alike living creatures to him, a part of the same great family of which he is a member. He talks to them as to human friends, and sees in everything about him silent lessons of love.

So great are the powers of these four poets, that the more we study them the harder it is to form a just estimate of their ability and influence; and it is only the critics of the years to come who will be able to place them according to their true merits.

Her essay was very favorably criticised by the press, and praised as "a critical analysis of rare power and discernment."

During its progress a part of the pupils had been quietly leaving the hall in little groups, and, at its close, the second part of the programme opened by their reappearance in gymnastic dress and order. First, fourteen little boys in blue flannel suits, with tri-colored breast-knots and red neckties, marched upon the platform with wooden dumb-bells, and, without word of command, performed a series of calisthenics to the music of the piano. These retired and were succeeded by nine little girls dressed in loose frocks of creamy white,

with blue sashes and caps of the same color, who
executed a different set of movements; and these,
in turn, gave place to a squad of ten young men,
commanded by Major Wright, who went through
a military drill which was intently watched by the
audience, especially the silent manual; and, as
they disappeared down one stairway, eight little
girls with silvery wands ascended the platform
from the opposite side, and performed a semi-
military drill. These exercises followed each
other in such rapid and easy sequence that, to
the eyes of the audience they formed one complete
panorama.

The illness of Charles II. Prescott necessitated
another break in the programme by the omission
of the cornet solo, " Arbuckleinian Polka."

An exercise in geography followed, in which the
teacher, showing separate models of various states
and countries, was at once answered by the pupil
giving its name and adding some geographical or
historical fact belonging to it ; after which a lad
arranged upon an easel a dissected map of Europe,
while two older girls read selections in raised type.

At the close of this exercise small tables were
placed on the platform, and a class of the youngest
boys and girls, furnished with materials for kindergarten exercises, busily worked in presence of

OUR DUTY TO THE BLIND A DUTY TO OURSELVES.

ADDRESS BY C. W. ERNST.

LADIES AND GENTLEMEN: — Your welcome presence shows you to be so well interested in our friends, the blind, as to make it entirely unnecessary on my part to arouse your sympathy or to address your pity. Moreover, other people have appealed and will appeal to your sentiments more effectually and, I am sure, more acceptably than I could. Beside that, the blind speak to-day very well for themselves. Their addresses, to which we have listened, and their interesting exercises, of which we have been grateful and delighted witnesses, plead their cause with touching eloquence, to which we all have readily responded with our applause, our sincere sympathies, and not a little of that tender emotion which dwells in this splendid audience and in every human breast. But for the present I shall bid farewell to these pleasing considerations, and in taking a somewhat sterner view of the case now in hand, permit me to address your reason rather than your sentiment, and your intellect rather than your feelings.

Though not strictly germane to the subject which Mr. Anagnos, the honored director of the Perkins Institution, desires me to lay before you, we should no longer forget that in a very large sense blindness is a preventable malady. The healing art — and in matters concerning the treatment of the human eye we may say, perhaps, medical science — has taught us, or is beginning to teach us, that what we popularly call blindness may, in very many cases, be described as a filth disease which can be prevented or removed by an early appeal to almost any one of the many excellent oculists who are now found in every great city of our country. Investigators [*] find, that of the persons now blind, about forty per cent. represent the result of simple ignorance or neglect. The census of 1880

[*] See Dr. Hugo Magnus, *Die Blindheit, Breslau*, 1883, p. 285, whose authorities are quoted.

tells us that four years ago we had 48,928 blind in the country.
Very nearly 20,000 of these are blind from causes of which
modern medicine is no longer afraid.

The lesson of this is patent. Whenever the eyes, especially
of a child and a new-born infant, are not entirely normal, the
only right thing to do is to call promptly for the assistance of a
trained oculist, — not of persons who have patent medicines
or family remedies, or undertake to cure by dogma, but of a
trained specialist who has studied modern ophthalmology.

That branch of the medical art, thanks to the great men of
our own time, is rapidly becoming an exact science, for which
the thinking people should have nothing but deep admiration
and gratitude, and the benefit of which is now accessible to
substantially all people, at least here in Boston and throughout
New England. Nevertheless we shall always have the blind
with us, and we must face the problem of which they are the
occasion.

From what is due to the blind, and far more from what
society owes to itself, the policy may be laid down that the
blind should be enabled to compete with seeing people on something like equal terms. This is not a matter of charity, but,
as Dr. Samuel G. Howe and his successor have not failed to
point out, a matter of right. In our social intercourse with
the blind it is not quite civil to remind them of what to us looks
like a defect, though to some of them a state different from
their own is scarcely imagined, much less estimated as it is by
ourselves. But the case involves rather more than mere courtesy or what the world has learned from the New Testament to
call by the sweet name of "charity." The question is one of
statute law and political economy, and I shall have failed in
my little endeavor if I do not justify our object to your sense
of right as well as to your conception of a sound public policy.

It is a fortunate circumstance that I, comparatively a stranger
to you, may reason before you and with you as to what is best
for our society, and that you solicit rather than tolerate a train

of reasoning that should bear the test of the counting-room. of our public laws and of our social polity. But Boston and New England have always listened to reason, and, when convinced by adequate arguments, have never failed to act. The result you see before you in the little people who use their pliable fingers in part for your edification, and chiefly for the purpose of showing that the blind no less than the seeing may become producers, artisans, and accomplished members of society.

The law requires that every child shall be educated at the public cost. And as the Perkins Institution is a school for all New England, I may remind you that in Massachusetts, Rhode Island and New Hampshire every child from 5 to 15 years old, in Connecticut every child from 4 to 16 years old, in Vermont every child from 5 to 20 years old, and in Maine every person from the infant age of 4 to the 21st year, is either entitled to a place in the public schools or absolutely compelled to acquire an education. If that be the law, — and a good law it is, — the blind children of New England do not ask for charity, but for their legal rights, when they or their lawful protectors ask for school accommodations. Nor would the law be wrong if it said, not that blind children may be taught, but that they shall be taught, and that the truant officer will step in if their education be neglected. It is strictly under the letter and in the spirit of our public law that we ask for a school in which the blind children of New England may learn the rudiments of knowledge, in order that later on they may attend to better advantage the higher school whose guests we are upon this occasion. It is hardly necessary to add that the Perkins Institution is neither an asylum nor an eleemosynary establishment, but simply a school somewhat like the Boston Latin school. As such it is a part of our public school system ; only, while the young people learn a little Latin and Greek in one school, they learn arts of equal usefulness in the school at South Boston.

Call it a kindergarten, or a primary school, or a preparatory school; what we urge upon your attention is that the Perkins Institution is not large enough to accommodate the blind less than nine years old, and that these young people are in need of a school, partly because they are children, and partly because they are blind. We have the law of compulsory education, let your law be executed. But I shall not hesitate to add, let your law be executed not as a matter of kindness to the blind, but as a matter of justice and right, and because there will be hard consequences if we fail to enforce the law that stands on our statute books. For it is a fundamental maxim in ethics, of which political economy is but a branch, that the evil-doer punishes himself more than he punishes the object of his act, be that act one of commission or omission.

But how can that be? Well! the answer is ready and it involves a good problem in political economy. There are in the United States, to-day, over 50,000 blind. What is the annual consumption of one blind person, if we include food, raiment, housing and the merest necessaries of life? It seems to me that $150 a year is a modest allowance. If 50,000 blind non-producers consume $150 each per year, the annual capital thus consumed is $7,500,000, or probably more than the richest state of the union raises by taxes for its own purposes. With the possible exception of New York there is no state which raises $7,500,000 a year by public taxes for its own uses. If we capitalize that sum at but four per cent. we find that our blind fellow-citizens consume the annual interest on $187,500,-000. There are not less than twelve states in the union whose total valuation respectively does not reach that sum, and I leave it to the hard-headed, gentle-hearted men in this audience to say whether or not it is expedient or sentimental, a matter of self-preservation or a mere fancy, to save a part of our national capital, the annual product of which now goes largely into unproductive consumption on the part of the blind.

The case will be very different if the blind are treated like all other people, if they are taught to support themselves, if

they are asked to produce capital instead of consuming it, and
if they are placed on terms of entire equality with ourselves.
They should vote, they should work at a trade, they should
buy and sell, they should go to church, they should go to our
places of amusement like other people. The difference between
them and ourselves, whose eyesight is as yet sound, should be
somewhat like the difference between persons who know some
foreign language and those who do not. The false difference,
as between happy people and the unfortunates, should be removed by making the blind self-reliant, self-respecting and
happy competitors in the friendly battle for all the treasures of
life. A long step will have been taken in that direction if we
join heart and hand in giving the blind children of New England a good primary school specially superintended by the
officers and teachers of the Perkins Institution whose young
pupils will now show you what may be accomplished by intelligent efforts well directed. And when you applaud these kindergarten pupils, do not omit to praise the teachers who have
taught them and you, their friends.

Mr. Anagnos added a few urgent words of the
great need of the kindergarten and his determination to effect its establishment. He said that before
autumn he hoped the trustees would purchase a
piece of real estate and that they would then start,
with a few pupils, the nucleus of the proposed
school; and that next year he hoped to bring upon
the platform some of these little children and show
the results of the work.

Now the little ones having finished their models,
held them up before the audience, telling their
names and some additional fact connected with
them. These models were of considerable variety,

ranging from simple geometric forms, wrought in clay, to a series illustrative of successive chapters of American history, and made with sticks blocks, strips of colored paper, etc. There was the ship in which John Cabot sought this country; an Indian wigwam; the Mayflower; Plymouth Pilgrim Meeting House; our flag with its stars and stripes; Bunker Hill Monument; the shackles of the slave; a statue of Lincoln; and the American eagle. Eighteen girls then formed a ring and sang a spring song, a wave song and a march.

The duet from " Belisario," " On to the Field of Glory," given by Messrs. Titus and Hammond, was remarked for having been sung " with fine intonation and the marked fidelity which distinguished all the exercises of the sightless."

Then came the valedictory, by Miss Isabella Romily, which was commended as " well written and well delivered, not the less effective that it came from the environment of a dusky skin, showing that intelligence knows not color, nor place, nor surroundings, making akin all whom the great Maker has gifted with the divine spark."

VALEDICTORY.

Before entering another field of duty, with its many paths, we pause for a moment on its margin, reluctant to bid farewell to our cherished and happy school-days and the many friends they have revealed to us.

As we retrace, in memory, the way by which we have come, we find the hopes and fears, successes and failures of school-life marvellously and closely interwoven. And we mark the obstacles that have cast their grim shadows before us, and are deeply grateful to those who have so faithfully shown us that " we rise by the things that are under our feet."

Our love and gratitude to all who have aided us are too deep for words alone ; an active and virtuous life must prove their sincerity.

To His Excellency the Governor and the legislature of Massachusetts, and to the governors and legislatures of the other New England states, we proffer our sincere thanks for their liberal support of our school.

To our trustees we extend our heartiest thanks for their never-failing interest and the zeal with which they labor to advance our cause.

Director and teachers : we shall ever be indebted to you for your faithful care and patience during these years of preparation, for which we shall endeavor to prove ourselves worthy.

Schoolmates : besides the pleasant memories of school-days, we take with us one ardent hope, in which our hearts are firmly united, — the kindergarten, — for this shall our motto continue to be, " *Orare et laborare.*"

Now must we onward to take our allotted paths. And though we cannot know what awaits us in that broad field, the future, yet may we rest assured that,

> " Behind the dim unknown
> Standeth God, within the shadow,
> Keeping watch above His own."

The chorus for female voices, " Charity," was well rendered; and the diplomas were then presented to the graduates by Mr. Dwight, who read the following address from Dr. Eliot : —

To the graduates of the day: — I had hoped, my young friends, to be present at your commencement exercises, and to perform the welcome part assigned me. But an engagement of long standing calls me from home, and I must content myself with leaving a few written words to be read to you at the moment of awarding your diplomas. These diplomas come, as you are well aware, not from me, or from any officer of administration, but from the director and teachers of the school, from those who have led you step by step along the way from your admission to your graduation. I am merely their agent in transferring the diplomas to your hands.

Let me speak, in the first place, for them. Let me tell you what they have probably already told you, that they remember all you have done to deserve these honors. They look back upon your studies, upon the difficulties you have met, the struggles to do right and be right which have marked your course, and they rejoice that this bright hour dispels all shadows as it sees you numbered among the full members, the life members as we may say, of this great institution.

Let me speak, in the next place, for the friends who have gathered here to-day. They come bringing sympathy and respect with them, yet gaining a fuller measure of both from the exercises they have attended. There is no person in this audience who cannot share your satisfaction in having reached the place at which you stand. The knowledge that you have won, the character that you have formed, the high purposes of the past and the present, claim our recognition, and you may be sure that we give it from our hearts.

I cannot stop without a word for your future. Not only your school-life rises before us, but the life yet to come, the days and years which stretch on far forward. They will be happy if our wishes can make them so. You take into them the affection of those who have taught you, the confidence of those who have administered the institution, and the good will of all acquainted with it and its work. This is a rich store for you to draw from hereafter. It is yours, you have proved yourselves worthy of it, and so long as you continue worthy, which I pray may be throughout your lives, it will never fail you. And may God himself be very near you in all you are yet to learn and to be.

Miss Lowe being absent on account of illness, was thereby prevented from receiving, in person, the diploma awarded her. The exercises closed with Verdi's chorus, "O Hail us, ye free!" sung by a full choir of the pupils, after which the audience slowly departed, many lingering to examine the educational appliances and the models made by the children.

The exercises as a whole received very favorable notices from the press. The clear enunciation of the pupils was especially remarked. The essays were characterized as "thoughtful in their nature and finished in their construction;" the vocal music, as being "very sweet and remarkable for its harmony," and the recitations, as "wonderful in accuracy;" but the gymnastics and military drill, and the exercise in geography and kindergarten work seemed to give the greatest pleasure, as well as to excite the deepest and most universal interest, and they proved a most persuasive argument for the proposed kindergarten.

MAY 26

FIFTY-FOURTH ANNUAL REPORT

OF

THE TRUSTEES

OF THE

PERKINS INSTITUTION

AND

𝕸assachusetts 𝕾chool for the 𝕭lind,

FOR THE YEAR ENDING

SEPTEMBER 30, 1885.

BOSTON:
WRIGHT & POTTER PRINTING CO., STATE PRINTERS,
18 POST OFFICE SQUARE.
1886.

FIFTY-FOURTH ANNUAL REPORT

OF

THE TRUSTEES

OF THE

PERKINS INSTITUTION

AND

Massachusetts School for the Blind,

FOR THE YEAR ENDING

SEPTEMBER 30, 1885.

BOSTON:
WRIGHT & POTTER PRINTING CO., STATE PRINTERS,
18 POST OFFICE SQUARE.
1886.

TABLE OF CONTENTS.

Commonwealth of Massachusetts.

PERKINS INSTITUTION AND MASS. SCHOOL FOR THE BLIND.
SOUTH BOSTON, Oct. 30, 1885.

To the Hon. HENRY B. PEIRCE, *Secretary of State*, Boston.

DEAR SIR : — I have the honor to transmit to you, for the use of the legislature, a copy of the fifty-fourth annual report of the trustees of this institution to the corporation thereof, together with that of the director and the usual accompanying documents.

Respectfully,

M. ANAGNOS,

Secretary.

OFFICERS OF THE CORPORATION.

1885-86.

SAMUEL ELIOT, *President.*
JOHN CUMMINGS, *Vice-President.*
EDWARD JACKSON, *Treasurer.*
M. ANAGNOS, *Secretary.*

BOARD OF TRUSTEES.

FRANCIS BROOKS.	SAMUEL M. QUINCY.
JOHN S. DWIGHT.	LEVERETT SALTONSTALL.
JOSEPH B. GLOVER.	SAMUEL G. SNELLING.
J. THEODORE HEARD, M. D.	JAMES STURGIS.
EDWARD N. PERKINS.	GEORGE W. WALES.
HENRY S. RUSSELL.	JOHN E. WETHERBEE.

STANDING COMMITTEES.
Monthly Visiting Committee.

Whose duty it is to visit and inspect the Institution at least once in each month.

1886.		1886.	
January, . . .	F. BROOKS.	July, . . .	S. M. QUINCY.
February, . . .	J S. DWIGHT.	August, . .	LEVERETT SALTONSTALL
March, ...	J. B. GLOVER.	September,.	S G. SNELLING.
April, ...	J. T. HEARD.	October,. .	JAMES STURGIS.
May, ...	E. N. PERKINS.	November,.	G. W. WALES.
June, ...	H. S. RUSSELL.	December,.	J. E. WETHERBEE.

Committee on Education.	House Committee.
J. S. DWIGHT.	E. N. PERKINS.
FRANCIS BROOKS.	G. W. WALES.
S. M. QUINCY.	FRANCIS BROOKS.

Committee on Finance.	Committee on Health.
J. B. GLOVER.	J. THEODORE HEARD, M.D.
JAMES STURGIS.	L. SALTONSTALL.
HENRY S. RUSSELL.	J. E. WETHERBEE.

Auditors of Accounts.
SAMUEL G. SNELLING.
JAMES STURGIS.

OFFICERS OF THE INSTITUTION.

DIRECTOR.
M. ANAGNOS.

MEDICAL INSPECTOR.
JOHN HOMANS, M.D.

LITERARY DEPARTMENT.

JAY M. HULBERT.

MISS ANNIE K. GIFFORD.

MISS ANNA S. LOW.

MISS JULIA A. BOYLAN.

MISS DELLA BENNETT.

MISS MARY C. MOORE.

MISS HARRIET D. BURGESS.

MISS EMMA A. COOLIDGE.

Miss SARAH ELIZABETH LANE, *Librarian.*

MUSICAL DEPARTMENT.

THOMAS REEVES.

ELMER S. HOSMER.

MISS FREDA BLACK.

MISS DELLA B. UPSON.

MISS MARY L. RILEY.

MISS JULIA H. STRONG.

LEMUEL TITUS.

MRS. KATE RAMETTI.

C. H. HIGGINS.

EZRA M. BAGLEY.

JULIUS AKEROYD.

Music Readers.

MISS ALLIE S. KNAPP.

MISS JENNY A. WHEATON.

MISS DAISY S. MONROE.

TUNING DEPARTMENT.
JOEL WEST SMITH, *Instructor and Manager.*
GEORGE E. HART, *Tuner.*

INDUSTRIAL DEPARTMENT.

Workrooms for Juveniles.

JOHN H. WRIGHT, *Work Master.*

MISS A. J. DILLINGHAM, *Work Mistress.*

MISS CORA L. DAVIS, *Assistant.*

WALTER H. FISKE, *Assistant.*

THOMAS CARROLL, *Assistant.*

Workshop for Adults.

ANTHONY W. BOWDEN, *Manager.*

PLINY MORRILL, *Foreman.*

MISS M. A. DWELLY, *Forewoman.*

MISS ELLEN M. WHEELOCK, *Clerk.*

DOMESTIC DEPARTMENT.

Steward.

ANTHONY W. BOWDEN.

Matron.

MISS MARIA C. MOULTON.

MISS ELLA F. FORD, *Assistant.*

Housekeepers in the Cottages.

MRS. M. A. KNOWLTON.

MRS. L. S. SMITH.

MISS BESSIE WOOD.

MRS. SOPHIA C. HOPKINS.

PRINTING DEPARTMENT.
DENNIS A. REARDON, ... *Manager.*
Miss ELIZABETH S. HOWE, *Printer.*
Miss MARTHA C. ALDEN,   "

Miss ELLEN B. WEBSTER, *Book keeper.*

MEMBERS OF THE CORPORATION.

All persons who have contributed twenty-five dollars to the funds of the institution, all who have served as trustees or treasurer, and all who have been elected by special vote, are members.

Adams, John A., Pawtucket, R. I.
Adams, Waldo, Boston.
Alden, Mrs. Sara B., Boston.
Aldrich, Mrs. Sarah, Boston.
Alger, Rev. William R., Boston.
Ames, F. L., Boston.
Ames, Miss H. A., Easton.
Ames, Oliver, Boston.
Amory, C. W., Boston.
Amory, James S., Boston.
Amory, William, Boston.
Amory, Mrs. William, Boston.
Anagnos, M., Boston.
Andrews, Francis, Boston.
Appleton, Miss Emily G., Boston.
Appleton, Mrs. William, Boston.
Apthorp, William F., Boston.
Atkins, Mrs. Elisha, Boston.
Atkinson, Edward, Boston.
Atkinson, William, Boston.
Austin, Edward, Boston.
Aylesworth, H. B., Providence.
Bacon, Edwin M., Boston.
Baldwin, William H., Boston.
Baker, Mrs. E. M., Boston.
Baker, Mrs. E. W., Dorchester.
Baker, Ezra H., Boston.

Baker, Miss M. K., Boston.
Barbour, E. D., Boston.
Barker, Joseph A., Providence.
Barstow, Amos C., Providence.
Barrows, Rev. S. J., Dorchester.
Beal, J. H., Boston.
Beard, Hon. Alanson W., Boston.
Beckwith, Miss A. G., Providence.
Beckwith, Mrs. T., Providence.
Beebe, J. A., Boston.
Bennett, Mrs. Eleanor, Billerica.
Bigelow, Mrs. E. B., Boston.
Bigelow, Mrs. Prescott, Boston.
Binney, William, Providence.
Black, G. N., Boston.
Blake, James H., Boston.
Blanchard, G. D. B., Malden.
Bourn, Hon. A. O., Bristol, R. I.
Bouvé, Thomas T., Boston.
Bowditch, Mrs. E. B., Boston.
Bowditch, J. I., Boston.
Bowditch, Mrs. J. I., Boston.
Brackett, Miss Nancy, Boston.
Bradlee, F. H., Boston.
Bradlee, Mrs. F. H., Boston.
Bradlee, J. P., Boston.
Brewer, Miss C. A., Boston.

Brewer, Mrs. Mary, Boston.
Brewster, Osmyn, Boston.
Brimmer, Hon. Martin, Boston.
Brooks, Francis, Boston.
Brooks, Mrs. Francis, Boston.
Brooks, Mrs. F. A., Boston.
Brooks, Peter C., Boston.
Brooks, Rev. Phillips, Boston.
Brooks, Shepherd, Boston.
Brown, John A., Providence.
Brown, Mrs. John C., Providence.
Browne, A. Parker, Boston.
Bullard, W. S., Boston.
Bullock, Miss Julia, Providence.
Bundy, James J., Providence.
Burnett, Joseph, Boston.
Burton, J. W., M. D., Flushing,
    N. Y.
Cabot, W. C., Boston.
Callender, Walter, Providence.
Carpenter, Charles E., Providence.
Carter, Mrs. Helen B., West New-
    ton.
Cary, Miss A. P., Boston.
Cary, Mrs. W. F., Boston.
Cass, Mrs. D. S., Boston.
Center, J. H., Boston.
Chandler, P. W., Boston.
Chandler, Theophilus P., Brook-
    line.
Chace, James H., Valley Falls, R. I.
Chace, Hon. Jonathan, Valley Falls,
    R. I.
Chapin, E. P., Providence.
Charles, Mrs. Mary C., Melrose.
Cheever, Dr. David W., Boston.
Cheeney, Benjamin P., Boston.
Chickering, George H., Boston.
Chickering, Mrs. Sarah M., Joy
    Mills, Pa.

Claflin, George L., Providence.
Claflin, Hon. William, Boston.
Clapp, William W., Boston.
Clarke, Mrs. Jas. Freeman, Boston.
Clarke, James W., Boston.
Clement, Edward H., Boston.
Coats, James, Providence.
Cobb, Mrs. Freeman, Boston.
Cobb, Samuel C., Boston.
Cobb, Samuel T., Boston.
Cochrane, Alexander, Boston.
Coffin, Mrs. W. E., Boston.
Colt, Samuel P., Bristol, R. I.
Comstock, Andrew, Providence.
Coolidge, Dr. A., Boston.
Coolidge, J. R., Boston.
Coolidge, Mrs. J. R., Boston.
Coolidge, J. T., Boston.
Coolidge, Mrs. J. T., Boston.
Coolidge, T. Jefferson, Boston.
Corliss, George H., Providence.
Cotting, C. U., Boston.
Crane, Zenas M., Dalton.
Crosby, Joseph B., Boston.
Crosby, William S., Boston.
Cruft, Miss Annah P., Boston.
Cruft, Miss Harriet O., Boston.
Cummings, Charles A., Boston.
Cummings, Hon. John, Woburn.
Curtis, C. A., Boston.
Curtis, George S., Boston.
Curtis, Mrs. Margarette S., Boston.
Dalton, C. H., Boston.
Dalton, Mrs. C. H., Boston.
Darling, L. B., Pawtucket, R. I.
Davis, Miss A. W., Boston.
Day, Daniel E., Providence.
Deblois, Stephen G., Boston.
Devens, Rev. Samuel A., Boston.
Dexter, Mrs. F. G., Boston.

Ditson, Oliver, Boston.
Dunnell, Jacob, Pawtucket, R. I.
Dwight, John S., Boston.
Eaton, W. S., Boston.
Eliot, Dr. Samuel, Boston.
Emery, Francis F., Boston.
Emery, Isaac, Boston.
Emmons, J. L., Boston.
Emmons, Mrs. Nath'l H., Boston.
English, James E., New Haven, Conn.
Endicott, Henry, Boston.
Endicott, William, Jr., Boston.
Ernst, C. W., Boston.
Farnam, Mrs. A. G., New Haven.
Fay, H. H., Boston.
Fay, Mrs. H. H., Boston.
Fay, Miss Sarah B., Boston.
Fay, Mrs. Sarah S., Boston.
Ferguson, Mrs. C. H., Dorchester.
Ferris, M. C., Boston.
Fisk, Rev. Photius, Boston.
Fiske, J. N., Boston.
Folsom, Charles F., M. D., Boston.
Forbes, J. M., Milton.
Foster, F. C., Boston.
Freeman, Miss Hattie E., Boston.
French, Jonathan, Boston.
Frothingham, A. T., Boston.
Frothingham, Rev. Frederick, Milton.
Gaffield, Thomas, Boston.
Galloupe, C. W., Boston.
Gammell, Prof. Wm., Providence.
Gammell, Mrs. Wm., Providence.
Gardiner, Charles P., Boston.
Gardner, George, Boston.
Gardner, George A., Boston.
Gardner, Henry W., Providence.
George, Charles H., Providence.

Gill, Mrs. Frances A., Boston.
Gill, Mrs. Sarah A., Worcester.
Glidden, W. T., Boston.
Glover, A., Boston.
Glover, J. B., Boston.
Goddard, Benjamin, Brookline.
Goddard, Miss Matilda, Boston.
Goddard, Miss Rebecca, Boston.
Goddard, T. P. I., Providence.
Goddard, William, Providence.
Goff, Darius, Pawtucket, R. I.
Goff, Darius L., Pawtucket, R. I.
Goff, Lyman B., Pawtucket, R. I.
Gray, Mrs. Horace, Boston.
Greene, Benj. F., Central Falls, R. I.
Greene, Edward A., Providence.
Greene, S. H., River Point, R. I.
Greenleaf, Mrs. Jas., Charlestown.
Greenleaf, R. C., Boston.
Griffin, S. B., Springfield.
Grosvenor, William, Providence.
Grover, William O., Boston.
Guild, Mrs. S. E., Boston.
Hale, Rev. Edward E., Boston.
Hale, George S., Boston.
Hall, J. R., Boston.
Hall, Miss L. E., Hanover.
Hall, Mrs. L. M., Boston.
Hall, Miss Minna B., Longwood.
Hardy, Alpheus, Boston.
Harwood, George S., Boston.
Haskell, Edwin B., Auburndale.
Hayward, Hon. Wm. S., Providence.
Hazard, Rowland, Providence.
Heard, J. T., M. D., Boston.
Hearst, Mrs. Phebe A., San Francisco, Cal.
Hemenway, Mrs. A., Jr., Boston.
Hendricken, Rt. Rev. T. F., Providence.

Herford, Rev. Brooke, Boston.
Higginson, George, Boston.
Higginson, Henry Lee, Boston.
Hill, Hon. Hamilton A., Boston.
Hill, Mrs. T. J., Providence.
Hilton, William, Boston.
Hodges, Dr. R. M., Boston.
Hogg, John, Boston.
Hooper, E. W., Boston.
Hoppin, Hon. W. W., Providence.
Hovey, William A., Boston.
Howard, Hon. A. C., Providence.
Howard, Mrs. Chas. W., California.
Howard, Hon. Henry, Providence.
Howe, Mrs. Julia Ward, Boston.
Howe, Mrs. Virginia A., Boston.
Howes, Miss E., Boston.
Houghton, Hon. H. O., Cambridge.
Hunnewell, F. W., Boston.
Hunnewell, H. H., Boston.
Hunt, Moses, Charlestown.
Inches, H. B., Boston.
Ives, Mrs. Anna A., Providence.
Jackson, Charles C., Boston.
Jackson, Edward, Boston.
Jackson, Mrs. J. B. S., Boston.
Jackson, Patrick T., Boston.
Jackson, Mrs. Sarah, Boston.
James, Mrs. Julia B. H., Boston.
Johnson, Samuel, Boston.
Jones, Miss Ellen M., Boston.
Joy, Mrs. Charles H., Boston.
Kasson, Rev. F. H., Boston.
Kellogg, Mrs. Eva D., Boston.
Kendall, C. S., Boston.
Kennard, Martin P., Brookline.
Kent, Mrs. Helena M., Boston.
Kidder, H. P., Boston.
Kinsley, E. W., Boston.
Lamson, Miss C. W., Dedham.

Lang, B. J., Boston.
Lawrence, Abbott, Boston.
Lawrence, Amos A., Longwood.
Lawrence, James, Boston.
Lawrence, Mrs. James, Boston.
Lawrence, William, Lawrence.
Lee, Henry, Boston.
Lincoln, L. J. B., Hingham.
Linzee, J. T., Boston.
Linzee, Miss Susan I., Boston.
Lippitt, Hon. Henry, Providence.
Littell, Miss S. G., Brookline.
Little, J. L., Boston.
Littlefield, Hon. A. H., Pawtucket.
Littlefield, D. G., Pawtucket.
Lodge, Mrs. A. C., Boston.
Lodge, Henry C., Boston.
Loring, Mrs. Susie J., Boston.
Lothrop, John, Auburndale.
Lovett, George L., Boston.
Lowell, Abbott Lawrence, Boston.
Lowell, Augustus, Boston.
Lowell, Miss A. C., Boston.
Lowell, Francis C., Boston.
Lowell, Mrs. John, Boston.
Lowell, Miss Lucy, Boston.
Lyman, Arthur T., Boston.
Lyman, George H., M. D., Boston.
Lyman, J. P., Boston.
Lyman, Theodore, Boston.
McAuslan, John, Providence.
Mack, Thomas, Boston.
Mackay, Mrs. Frances M., Cambridge.
Macullar, Addison, Boston.
Marcy, Fred. I., Providence.
Marston, S. W., Boston.
Mason, Miss E. F., Boston.
Mason, Miss Ida M., Boston.
Mason, I. B., Providence.

May, Miss Abby W., Boston.
May, F. W. G., Dorchester.
McCloy, J. A., Providence.
Means, Rev. J. H., D. D., Dorchester.
Merriam, Mrs. Caroline, Boston.
Merriam, Charles, Boston.
Merriam, Mrs. D., Boston.
Metcalf, Jesse, Providence.
Minot, Francis, M. D., Boston.
Minot, Mrs. G. R., Boston.
Minot, William, Boston.
Mixter, Miss Helen K., Boston.
Mixter, Miss Madelaine C., Boston.
Montgomery, W., Boston.
Morrill, Charles J., Boston.
Morse, S. T., Boston.
Morton, Edwin, Boston.
Motley, Edward, Boston.
Moulton, Miss Maria C., Boston.
Nevins, David, Boston.
Nichols, J. Howard, Boston.
Nichols, R. P., Boston.
Nickerson, Andrew, Boston.
Nickerson, Mrs. A. T., Boston.
Nickerson, George, Jamaica Plain.
Nickerson, Miss Priscilla, Boston.
Nickerson, S. D., Boston.
Norcross, Miss Laura, Boston.
Noyes, Hon. Charles J., Boston.
O'Reilly, John Boyle, Boston.
Osgood, J. F., Boston.
Osborn, John T., Boston.
Owen, George, Providence.
Paine, Mrs. Julia B., Boston.
Paine, Robert Treat, Boston.
Palfrey, J. C., Boston.
Palmer, John S., Providence.
Parker, Mrs. E. P., Boston.
Parker, E. Francis, Boston.

Parker, Henry G., Boston.
Parker, Richard T., Boston.
Parkman, Francis, Boston.
Parkman, George F., Boston.
Parsons, Thomas, Chelsea.
Payson, S. R., Boston.
Peabody, Rev. A. P., D. D., Cambridge.
Peabody, F. H., Boston.
Peabody, O. W., Milton.
Peabody, S. E., Boston.
Peirce, Rev. Bradford K., D. D., Boston.
Perkins, A. T., Boston.
Perkins, Charles C., Boston.
Perkins, Edward N., Jamaica Plain.
Perkins, William, Boston.
Peters, Edward D., Boston.
Pickett, John, Beverly.
Pickman, W. D., Boston.
Pickman, Mrs. W. D., Boston.
Pierce, Hon. H. L., Boston.
Pierson, Mrs. Mary E., Windsor, Conn.
Potter, Isaac M., Providence.
Potter, Mrs. Sarah, Providence.
Pratt, Elliott W., Boston.
Prendergast, J. M., Boston.
Preston, Jonathan, Boston.
Pulsifer, R. M., Boston.
Quincy, George Henry, Boston.
Quincy, Samuel M., Wollaston.
Reardon, Dennis A., Boston.
Rice, Hon. A. H., Boston.
Rice, Fitz James, Providence.
Richardson, George C., Boston.
Richardson, Mrs. Jeffrey, Boston
Richardson, John, Boston.
Robbins, R. E., Boston.
Robeson, W. R., Boston.

Robinson, Henry, Reading.
Rodman, S. W., Boston.
Rodocanachi, J. M., Boston.
Rogers, Henry B., Boston.
Rogers, Jacob C., Boston.
Ropes, J. C., Boston.
Ropes, J. S., Jamaica Plain.
Rotch, Miss Anne L., Boston.
Rotch, Mrs. Benjamin S., Boston.
Rotch, Miss Edith, Boston.
Russell, Henry G., Providence.
Russell, Mrs. Henry G., Providence.
Russell, Henry S., Boston.
Russell, Miss Marian, Boston.
Russell, Mrs. S. S., Boston.
Saltonstall, H., Boston.
Saltonstall, Leverett, Newton.
Sampson, George, Boston.
Sanborn, Frank B., Concord.
Sayles, F. C., Pawtucket, R. I.
Sayles, W. F., Pawtucket, R. I.
Schlesinger, Barthold, Boston.
Schlesinger, Sebastian B., Boston.
Sears, David, Boston.
Sears, Mrs. David, Boston.
Sears, Mrs. Fred., Jr., Boston.
Sears, F. R., Boston.
Sears, Mrs. K. W., Boston.
Sears, Mrs. P. H., Boston.
Sears, Mrs. S. P., Boston.
Sears, W. T., Boston.
Sharpe, L., Providence.
Shaw, Mrs. G. H., Boston.
Shaw, Henry S., Boston.
Shaw, Quincy A., Boston.
Shepard, Mrs. E. A., Providence.
Sherwood, W. H., Boston.
Shimmin, C. F., Boston.
Shippen, Rev. R. R., Washington.
Sigourney, Mrs. Henry, Boston.

Slater, H. N., Jr., Providence.
Snelling, Samuel G., Boston.
Spaulding, J. P., Boston.
Spaulding, M. D., Boston.
Spencer, Henry F., Boston.
Sprague, F. P., Boston.
Sprague, S. S., Providence.
Stanwood, Edward, Brookline.
Stearns, Charles H., Brookline.
Steere, Henry J., Providence.
Stewart, Mrs. C. B., Boston.
Stone, Joseph L., Boston.
Sturgis, Francis S., Boston.
Sturgis, J. H., Boston.
Sturgis, James, Boston.
Sullivan, Richard, Boston.
Sweetser, Mrs. Anne M., Boston.
Taggard, B. W., Boston.
Taggard, Mrs. B. W., Boston.
Tappan, Miss M. A., Boston.
Tappan, Mrs. William, Boston.
Thaxter, Joseph B., Hingham.
Thayer, Miss Adele G., Boston.
Thayer, Miss A. G., Andover.
Thayer, Rev. George A., Cincinnati.
Thomas, H. H., Providence.
Thorndike, Mrs. Delia D., Boston.
Thorndike, S. Lothrop, Cambridge.
Thurston, Benj. F., Providence.
Tingley, S. H., Providence.
Tolman, Joseph C., Hanover.
Torrey, Miss A. D., Boston.
Troup, John E., Providence.
Turner, Miss Abby W., Boston.
Turner, Miss Alice M., Boston.
Turner, Miss Ellen J., Boston.
Turner, Mrs. M. A., Providence.
Underwood, F. H., Boston.
Upton, George B., Boston.
Villard, Mrs. Henry, New York.

Wales, George W., Boston.
Wales, Miss Mary Ann, Boston.
Wales, Thomas B., Boston.
Ward, Rev. Julius H., Boston.
Ware, Charles E., M. D., Boston.
Ware, Mrs. Charles E., Boston.
Warren, J. G., Providence.
Warren, S. D., Boston.
Warren, Mrs. Wm. W., Boston.
Washburn, Hon. J. D., Worcester.
Weeks, A. G., Boston.
Welch, E. R., Boston.
Weld, Otis E., Boston.
Weld, R. H., Boston.
Weld, Mrs. W. F., Philadelphia.
Weld, W. G., Boston.
Wesson, J. L., Boston.
Wheeler, Nathaniel, Bridgewater, Conn.
Wheelwright, A. C., Boston.
Wheelwright, John W., Boston.
White, B. C., Boston.
White, C. J., Cambridge.
White, Charles T., Boston.
White, G. A., Boston.
Whitford, George W., Providence.

Whiting, Ebenezer, Boston.
Whitman, Sarah W., Boston.
Whitney, Edward, Belmont.
Whitney, E., Boston.
Whitney, H. A., Boston.
Whitney, H. M., Boston.
Whitney, Mrs., Boston.
Whitney, Miss, Boston.
Wigglesworth, Miss Ann, Boston.
Wigglesworth, Edward, M.D., Boston.
Wigglesworth, Thomas, Boston.
Wightman, W. B., Providence.
Wilder, Hon. Marshall P., Dorchester.
Williams, George W. A., Boston.
Winslow, Mrs. George, Roxbury.
Winsor, J. B., Providence.
Winthrop, Hon. Robert C., Boston.
Winthrop, Mrs. Robert C., Boston.
Wolcott, J. H., Boston.
Wolcott, Mrs. J. H., Boston.
Woods, Henry, Boston.
Worthington, Roland, Roxbury.
Young, Mrs. B. L., Boston.
Young, Charles L., Boston.

SYNOPSIS OF THE PROCEEDINGS

OF THE

ANNUAL MEETING OF THE CORPORATION.

SOUTH BOSTON, Oct. 14, 1885.

The annual meeting of the corporation, duly summoned, was held to-day at the institution, and was called to order by the president, Samuel Eliot, LL.D., at 3 P.M.

The proceedings of the last meeting were read by the secretary, and declared approved.

Mr. John S. Dwight presented the report of the trustees, which was read, accepted, and ordered to be printed with that of the director, and the usual accompanying documents.

The treasurer, Mr. Edward Jackson, read his report, which was accepted, and ordered to be printed.

The corporation then proceeded to ballot for officers for the ensuing year, and the following persons were unanimously re-elected: —

President — Samuel Eliot, LL.D.

Vice-President — John Cummings.

Treasurer — Edward Jackson.

Secretary — M. Anagnos.

Trustees — Joseph B. Glover, J. Theodore Heard, M. D., Edward N. Perkins, Henry S. Russell, Samuel M. Quincy, Samuel G. Snelling, James Sturgis and George W. Wales.

The meeting was then dissolved, and all in attendance proceeded, with the invited guests, to visit the various departments of the school and inspect the premises.

M. ANAGNOS,
Secretary.

Commonwealth of Massachusetts.

REPORT OF THE TRUSTEES.

PERKINS INSTITUTION AND MASS. SCHOOL FOR THE BLIND,
SOUTH BOSTON, Oct. 1, 1885.

To THE MEMBERS OF THE CORPORATION.

Gentlemen and Ladies : — We have the honor to present to you, and, through you, to the legislature of the commonwealth, the *fifty-fourth* annual report, briefly showing the progress and condition of the institution under our charge for the financial year ending Sept. 30, 1885.

1. The number of pupils keeps on steadily increasing at a moderate rate, the quarterly reports of the director presenting always very nearly the same figures. The total number of blind inmates of the institution is 172. Of these 141 are pupils, the boys outnumbering the girls by only five. The remaining 31 are teachers, workmen and employés of the institution. The number of applicants for admission this term has been larger than ever before, the accommodations, in the cottages, for

girls being taxed to their utmost capacity. Indeed of late years more girls enter, and more girls graduate, than boys.

The health of the inmates, with few and slight exceptions, has been excellent. Twice during the year there have been a few cases of measles, in a mild form, mostly among the youngest girls. The little patients were promptly placed in the city hospital, where they all recovered with the exception of one, who, while convalescing, was attacked by membranous croup of a severe form and died, much lamented by pupils and teachers. All possible care has been used during these past years to perfect the drainage and the ventilation of the several buildings, to ensure pure air and wholesome diet, and to offset sedentary class-work with frequent, timely, well regulated and attractive exercise both indoors and in the open air. The general cheerfulness and happiness of the children, both in their studies and their recreation, have done much to keep up the high standard of health.

2. The School.—

the main object of the institution — has shown better work and finer fruits than ever before,— and this is saying much. In its whole *morale* and spirit, in its methods and achievements, it has continued in the same line of steady and consistent progress and improvement — shall we say *development?* It would seem that, by long and earnest

seeking and experiment, the secret of true method
has at last been found here, and needs only to be
applied as faithfully as it has been of late years to
ensure the true reward. It consists in careful
adaptation of the schooling to the individual bent,
capacity, wants, temperament, etc., of each single
pupil; in broad field and variety of topics; in
studies, conversations, exercises that enlarge the
mind, engage the heart, build up the character, and
inspire unselfish motives with the love of knowledge, while they bring the blind practically more
and more upon a level with the seeing. In all this,
of course, *object*-teaching plays an important part,
and from the kindergarten upwards. The cabinets of mineralogy, natural history, anatomical
models, and mechanic arts, growing more and
more complete under the watchful lookout and
shrewd purveyance of the director, are doing here
almost as much for education as are the rapidly
increasing stores of books in the raised type.
Fingers are eyes for both. And the appliances
for the study of geography, in a way that impresses it wonderfully upon the memory, the
beautiful raised maps of all parts of the globe,
especially the dissecting maps (made in the institution), taken apart and reconstructed, and described without seeing, excite the admiration of all
who witness the marvellous proficiency of the average blind pupil in a branch of knowledge of which
most men are so ignorant.

For these gratifying results the pupils and
friends of the blind cannot be too grateful to the
well-selected corps of discreet, tenderly devoted,
energetic teachers, mostly women, which it has
been the rare good fortune of the school for years
past to possess. They, under the wise, paternal,
comprehensive oversight of the director, certainly
have done all that could be required of good and
faithful servants. Naturally changes in the composition of the body have occurred from year to
year; one or more, once in a little while, must
with regret be parted with, but the place has
been always soon and well supplied. The most
permanent among the teachers are, for obvious
reasons, those who themselves are blind. By
a singular fatality, owing to a concurrence of
purely personal necessities, the school opens the
new term deprived of most of the valued teachers of the past year, imposing a very difficult and
delicate task upon the director to make good their
places. This, it is believed, however, has been
done, and with the engagement, for the first time
of a male head teacher in the boys' department
where the responsibility has been growing more
and more onerous.

We do not think we overestimate the progress
that has been made. The personal observation
of members of this board, in their repeated (often
unexpected) visits to the class rooms, has never
failed to find it. The increasing eagerness of wit-

nesses from the whole neighborhood, as well as strangers from a distance, every Thursday morning, shows how attractive and impressive its manifestations have become. And, above all, the annual commencement exercises (as they have now earned the right to be called) held before an immense audience, attentive to the end of a long and varied programme, in Tremont Temple, June 2, and honored by the presence and the cheering eloquence of his Excellency, Gov. Robinson, and by the tender and inspiring words of Dr. Eliot, the president of our corporation, on presenting the diplomas to the four young lady graduates, gave as palpable, convincing proof, as any two hours' resumé of studies and acquirements can give of the sincerity, the thoroughness, the broad catholicity of culture which is helping these blind girls and boys to become useful, intelligent, true men and women. We need not rehearse the programme, which was essentially of the usual character and afforded constant pleasure and surprise. The most interesting feature of the whole was the practical illustration given by the little children of the methods of the kindergarten; modelling in clay, and embroidery, etc., at separate tables, before the eyes of all, with deft facility, and sometimes quite amusing originality of design, during the pathetic, cogent, quickening appeal of Rev. Edward A. Horton in behalf of the poor blind children, exposed from infancy to evil influences and dangers, and their right to all the counteracting good wherewith all the means and appliances of the best appointed separate kindergarten can surround them.

And this brings us to the most important event of the past year, and the most important problem, the question to be solved next in this so far advanced course of education.

3. THE KINDERGARTEN FOR THE BLIND.

The need of a special kindergarten, or preparatory infant school for little sightless children below the age of nine, to fit them to enter upon the higher course in a condition properly to avail themselves of its advantages, has long been felt to be of the first urgency. By earnest appeals in every form and on all fit occasions, by our indefatigable director especially, and by many able public orators and writers, a great interest has been awakened in the subject. Wealthy friends have contributed generously of their means. The press, both secular and religious, has in the most liberal, disinterested manner, kept the movement conspicuously before its readers. The pupils of the institution, with a tender interest in the welfare and salvation of their helpless younger brothers and sisters, have in a touching manner, clubbed together their little means and talents, musical, industrial, and social, holding fairs and giving concerts, to eke out the slowly growing fund. Even

Laura Bridgman has been instant in sympathy and delicate coöperation. Among the larger contributions were the proceeds of the fair held in the house of Mrs. J. Huntington Wolcott, amounting to $4,612.89; the munificent gift from a Boston lady of $10,000; and the subscription of $5,000 by an anonymous friend of the blind. Enough money has been raised to warrant the first step in the enterprise: the purchase, at a cost of $30,000, of the Hyde estate in Roxbury, near Jamaica Pond. It is a beautiful site of more than six acres, — large enough not only for the two cottages, school rooms and offices of the kindergarten, but even for the Perkins Institution itself, should it be found expedient at some future time to seek for it a better location than the present one. The place is central, healthy, easy of access. The work of excavation for the foundation of a new, commodious building has begun, but with slow progress on account of the immense mass of ledge to be removed. This postpones the prospect of completion and equipment into the next year. This we have called the event of the year. But it is only the first step — a most important step — toward the "consummation so devoutly to be wished." The purchase money, together with the great expense of removing the ledge, and of erecting the first building (on the most economical estimate, — the architect contributing the plans out of sympathy with "the cause"), will exhaust the last dollar of

the fund already raised, and liberal subscriptions
are still needed to put the establishment in working order and enable the school to live and to
expand. The pleasing sight of such an infant
school there, palpable and real, will, it is hoped, inspire the generous intentions of many more friends
of childhood and the blind.

4. THE FINANCES,

it will appear by the report of the treasurer, have
been wisely and economically managed. The accounts are kept in the form which is used by large
institutions and corporations. The auditors exercise careful supervision over all receipts and disbursements and scrutinize every item of expense.
The treasurer's exhibit, taking the formula of last
year's report, may be summarized as follows:—

Cash in hand Oct. 1, 1884, ...	$20,668 69
Total receipts from all sources during the year (including collections of payable notes), .	112,352 75
	$133,021 44
Total expenditure and investments, . . .	131,010 42
Balance, ...	$2,011 02

5. REPAIRS AND IMPROVEMENTS.

These have been strictly limited to what seemed
absolutely necessary for the preservation of the
buildings and the safety and comfort of the household. The sinking floor of the rotunda has been

strengthened and put in good condition. The dining room of the little boys has been thoroughly renovated; and the decayed floor and frame of a portion of the piazza have been replaced. These all relate to the main building, which is getting old.

6. PRINTING FOR THE BLIND.

Our presses have been at work with unrelaxing steadiness and vigor. The following new books have been added to our list of publications in raised type during the past year: —

1. Nine of "Emerson's Essays," with a memorial tribute by Dr. Oliver Wendell Holmes.

2. "Heidi, — a story for Children and those who love Children," translated from the German of Johanna Spyri by Mrs. Louise Brooks, in two volumes.

3. Walter Scott's "Quentin Durward" in two volumes.

4. "What Katy Did," by Susan Coolidge, — printed at the expense of one of the best friends and constant benefactors of the blind, Miss Sarah B. Fay.

5. Selections from the poetical works of Dr. Oliver Wendell Holmes, with the following dedication, written expressly by the genial author for this edition : —

"Dear friends, left darkling in the long eclipse
  That veils the noonday, — you whose finger-tips
  A meaning in these ridgy leaves can find
  Where ours go stumbling, senseless, helpless, blind,
  This wreath of verse how dare I offer you
  To whom the garden's choicest gifts are due?
  The hues of all its glowing beds are ours, —
  Shall you not claim its sweetest-smelling flowers?

Nay, those I have I bring you, — at their birth
  Life's cheerful sunshine warmed the grateful earth;
  If my rash boyhood dropped some idle seeds,
  And here and there you light on saucy weeds
  Among the fairer growths, remember still
  Song comes of grace and not of human will:
  We get a jarring note when most we try,
  Then strike the chord we know not how or why;
  Our stately verse with too aspiring art
  Oft overshoots and fails to reach the heart,
  While the rude rhyme one human throb endears
  Turns grief to smiles and softens mirth to tears.

Kindest of critics, ye whose fingers read,
  From Nature's lesson learn the poet's creed;
  The queenly tulip flaunts in robes of flame,
  The wayside seedling scarce a tint may claim,
  Yet may the lowliest leaflets that unfold
  A dew-drop fresh from heaven's own chalice hold."

6. Kingsley's Greek Heroes, in one volume.

7. Hawthorne's Scarlet Letter, in two volumes.

We have in press Shakespeare's Romeo and Juliet and King Henry Fifth.

The fruits of the "Howe Memorial Press" are multiplying and becoming more and more useful and important from year to year. They serve not only as an exhaustless source of comfort and enjoyment to many a sightless person, but as a constant invitation and incitement to study and self-culture. Among other advantages, those who employ their fingers in reading regularly, learn at the same time to spell correctly.

7. The Workshop for Adults,

while it is of great utility in furnishing employment to so many meritorious blind persons, and while the quality of its work has always proved entirely satisfactory to its patrons, still shows no improvement in its receipts. The loss is about the same as usual. Honesty and thoroughness are the governing principles in all the business transactions of the shop, and on the strength of these we ask increase of patronage.

Expenditures for the year, ...		$16,793 73
Receipts for the year, . .	$14,583 33	
Increase of stock and debts due,	. 1,817 91	
	———	16,401 24
		$392 49

Thus the cost of carrying on the workshop, over and above the receipts, has been $392.49. The loss to the treasury of the institution, compared with that of the previous year, has been decreased by $374.47.

In spite of this or any other small deductions, looking over the whole field of its educational and industrial activities, we are tempted to say, in the honest words of the director, in one of his quarterly reports to this board, —

"The institution, in all its appointments, its accommodations, its educational appliances, its facilities for thorough instruction in all branches of study, as well as in music and industrial pursuits, its wholesome discipline and high moral influence, presents a combination of advantages not surpassed if equalled by any establishment of its kind in the world."

The last word of this, as of each preceding report, must be in a sadder key.

8. Death of Members.

Since the last annual meeting of this corporation, fourteen more of its valued members have died. The list includes Mrs. Samuel Cabot, Sen., Dr. Samuel Cabot, Alfred A. Childs, Mrs. Samuel T. Dana, George P. Denny, A. B. Arnold of Providence, Dr. Robert W. Hooper, Dr. Edward Jarvis, John C. Phillips, Mrs. M. B. Sigourney, Charles W. Slack, J. H. Tingue of Seymour, Conn., Orlando Tompkins, and James H. Weeks.

Mr. Phillips had, for two years, done excellent service as a member of the board of trustees.

Dr. Jarvis, one of the genuine philanthropists of Massachusetts, was an old friend of the institution and of Dr. Howe. Twice, during the absence of the latter, he served as superintendent *pro tempore*. He was also associated with Dr. Howe in the school for feeble-minded children, and in other beneficent works. A man of singular sweetness of character, able and enlightened, he was animated by that public spirit which characterized so many of the noted men of the past and passing generation.

All which is respectfully submitted by

FRANCIS BROOKS,
JOHN S. DWIGHT,
JOSEPH B. GLOVER,
J. THEODORE HEARD,
EDWARD N. PERKINS,
HENRY S. RUSSELL,
SAMUEL M. QUINCY,
LEVERETT SALTONSTALL,
SAMUEL G. SNELLING,
JAMES STURGIS,
GEORGE W. WALES,
JOHN E. WETHERBEE,
Trustees.

THE REPORT OF THE DIRECTOR.

"'Εχθρὸν δέ μοί ἐστιν
Αὖτις αριζήλως ειρημένα μυθολογεύειν."

HOMER.

TO THE BOARD OF TRUSTEES.

Gentlemen: — Whenever I begin to write an annual report, I am instinctively reminded of the above line of the Grecian bard, which in Pope's adaptation is thus interpreted, —

" What so tedious as a twice told tale? "

Yet, in the language of Shakespeare, " custom calls me to 't" again; and I must obey its behest, and " do what it wills."

The year just closed has been very prosperous and successful in every respect. Good order and earnest endeavor have been its principal characteristics. Thorough work has been accomplished in each of the departments of the institution, and an excellent degree of progress has been attained in all.

The teachers and officers have been faithful and diligent in the discharge of their respective duti The pupils have been orderly and attentive to t work, and have made commendable advancement in their studies and other occupations. Most of them give evidence of fair mental capacity, and of aptitude for learning and improvement.

Visitors to the school, who examine its methods of instruction and training, and notice the home-like appearance of all its surroundings, bear cheerful testimony to the uncommon educational advantages afforded here, and to the air of neatness and ' harmony which pervades every part of the institution.

The citizens of Massachusetts have reason to regard this school with pleasure and pride, since its relative standing with kindred establishments and its past history and present condition, all combine to give it a high reputation and an enviable character not only on this continent, but all over the civilized world.

Good as this record is, however, there must of necessity be points where improvements could still be effected, and these should be constantly kept in view, with the determination to diminish them to the smallest number, and to reduce them to the lowest possible degree. Only the consciousness of imperfections, and the earnest desire to discover and to remedy them, lead to the highest advancement.

32

Number of Inmates.

"Heaven, yet populous, retains
Numbers sufficient to possess her realms."

MILTON.

At the beginning of the past year, the total number of blind persons connected with the institution in its various departments as pupils, teachers, employés, and workmen and women, was 166. There have since been admitted 16; 10 have been discharged, making the present total number 172.

Of these, 153 are in the school proper, and 19 in the workshop for adults.

The first class includes 141 boys and girls enrolled as pupils, 9 teachers and other officers, and 3 domestics. Of the pupils there are now 134 in attendance, 7 being temporarily absent on account of feeble health or from other causes.

The second class comprises 19 men and women, employed in the industrial department for adults.

The number of applicants for admission is steadily increasing, but our facilities for the accommodation of new pupils, especially in the girls' department, are very inadequate. In fact, they have reached their utmost limit. Every nook and corner in the four cottages has already been utilized, and, while there is no possibility of adding to their capacity, there are several eligible candidates waiting to fill any vacancies which may occur either by graduation or otherwise. This problem is becoming very serious and perplexing, and the most feasible and satisfactory solution of the difficulty would be to erect a building on our new estate in Roxbury as soon as practicable, and provide therein room and the means of instruction and training for all girls under fourteen years of age.

HEALTH OF THE HOUSEHOLD.

" My mind to me an empire is,
While grace affordeth health."

SOUTHWELL.

The past year has been marked by general good health. Of the various epidemic diseases, — which were very prevalent in the city and the neighboring towns, — only the measles invaded one of the departments of the institution, that of the girls, early in April, and eight of the pupils were taken ill with the disorder at different times. Thanks to the managers of the city hospital, most of the little patients were placed there, and received proper treatment. They all recovered and returned to their work, save one, Maud Elliott of Pretty Marsh, Maine, who, while convalescing, was attacked by membranous croup of a malignant character, and died in less than twenty-four hours after the mortal malady set in, deeply lamented both by pupils and teachers.

With this exception, the health of the household

has been exceedingly good. No accidents or cases of severe illness of any kind have occurred.

I avail myself of this opportunity again to express my hearty appreciation and grateful acknowledgments to the superintendent of the city hospital, Dr. George H. M. Rowe, and his assistants, for the readiness with which they received those of our children whom we were obliged to send to them, and for the excellent care and friendly attention which they have bestowed upon them with such unfailing kindness.

The department for contagious diseases connected with that institution is a blessing to the poor and laboring classes, and a very important factor in the general health of a city like ours, where, for the sake of economy, large numbers of people are herded together in immense tenement houses, all to breathe the same foul air, and all equally exposed to the incursion of epidemics. Besides affording the means of skilful treatment and nursing to the sufferers and great relief to many a distressed household, this department of the city hospital removes the seeds of infection from the propagating hotbeds of pestilence, thus impeding their germination, and serves to check its expansion and to prevent its spread. For these reasons the steps already taken by the proper authorities to increase the capacity of this branch of beneficence and improve its efficiency, are praiseworthy and merit public commendation. At the same time let us hope that the enterprise will soon receive due consideration from our philanthropic citizens in all its bearings, and that private munificence will not be slow in supplementing municipal appropriations and aiding to bring it to a state of completeness, both as regards the size of its accommodations and its internal arrangements for separation and isolation.

CHANGES IN THE STAFF OF ASSISTANTS.

"Life is arched with changing skies."

WM. WINTER.

The policy of this institution has ever been to select its officers and employés with sole reference to their qualifications, unbiased by any other consideration; and it has been its good fortune to retain their services for long periods. Each year there have been so few changes in the staff of assistants as to be scarcely perceptible. Thus the efficiency and usefulness of our instructors were constantly growing, since the good natural abilities and the large and varied attainments which they had originally possessed were steadily enhanced by the consummate skill which experience alone can give.

I am exceedingly sorry to report, that this chain of familiar faces was somewhat broken at the close of the last school session, and that several of its links have had to be replaced. As Longfellow expresses it,

" Nothing that is can pause or stay."

Early in the spring Miss Julia R. Gilman, who was absent on leave, notified me, that, as the continuance of her participation in the management of her sister's school was deemed indispensable, she was obliged to ask to be released from the agreement to resume her usual duties with us this autumn. Miss Olive A. Prescott, who, as a substitute, proved to be an excellent teacher and a most unselfish and tireless helper, was compelled by the sudden death of her father in June last to withdraw from our work and to stay at home and administer his affairs. Miss Etta S. Adams and Miss Frances B. Winslow resigned at the end of the term, the former to take care of an aged mother who is in feeble health; and Miss Marian A. Hosmer's connection with the institution was only temporary, and, according to previous mutual understanding, was to terminate on the first of July.

The vacancies thus created have been filled by the appointment of Mr. Jay M. Hulbert, a graduate of Dartmouth college, as principal teacher in the boys' department; Miss Annie K. Gifford and Miss Harriet D. Burgess, both graduates of the state normal school at Bridgewater; and Miss Anna S. Low, a graduate of the state normal school at Westfield. Miss Frances B. Winslow has kindly consented to continue her labors with the boys' kindergarten classes for three months, and to initiate her successor in the details of Froebel's system of training.

There have also occurred three changes in the music department. Both Mr. Frank H. Kilbourne and Miss Lucy A. Hammond have declined a reëlection, — the former to become a member of a firm for selling pianofortes in this city, and the latter to enter the matrimonial sanctum under the guidance of a sightless mentor. About ten days before the beginning of the present school term, one of the music readers, Miss Iola M. Clarke, informed us that she was ill and unable to resume her work. These places have been supplied by the engagement of Mr. Elmer S. Hosmer, a talented young man of good parts and a graduate of Brown university; Miss Della B. Upson, a graduate of the New England conservatory; and Miss Daisy S. Monroe of Waltham.

All of these new appointees give evidence of suitable qualifications, and have entered upon their allotted duties with an appreciation of their importance, which promises much usefulness in their respective positions.

Notwithstanding the unusually large number of changes which have just taken place, it affords me much pleasure to state, that the greater portion of the corps of officers still consists of tried and faithful persons, who have devoted their lives and energies to the advancement of the interests of the institution and the welfare of the blind with exemplary zeal and self-forgetfulness, and who continue to work and act, quietly and conscientiously, without the stimulus of praise, the incitement of profit, or the hope of glory. For each and all of these I would bespeak the encouragement of your confidence and support.

SCHEME OF INSTRUCTION AND TRAINING.

"Ut sementem feceris, ita metes."

CICERO.

The system of education, which has been fully described in previous reports, has been pursued with steadiness, and, in general, with satisfactory results. The main principles which enter into this plan and constitute its framework, are substantially the same as they were when adopted by the great founder of the institution, Dr. Howe; but constant improvements have been made in the methods for carrying them out.

The branches embraced in the literary department have been carefully taught and faithfully learned. The study and practice of music have continued to form an important part in the curriculum of our school. Training in the handicrafts has been as valuable an adjunct in our course of instruction as ever; and the exercises both in the gymnasium and the play-ground have been carried on with regularity and with beneficent effects to the health and strength of the participants.

The chief aim and end sought in the prosecution of this system is the complete development of the several functions and powers of the mind and body, and the efficient equipment of our pupils for the fullest and freest activity.

A brief review of the operations of each of the various departments of the institution during the past year will help the reader to form some idea of the amount and general character of the work therein performed.

Literary Department.

" Learn to live, and live to learn,
Ignorance like a fire doth burn,
Little tasks make large return."

BAYARD TAYLOR.

The object of this department is to extinguish the fire of ignorance from amidst the children and youth who come within its province, and to light in its place that of knowledge and intelligence.

The returns gathered during the past year in this field are larger than heretofore, and the amount and value of the work accomplished by both teachers and pupils is creditable to the skill and fidelity of the former and to the industry and application of the latter.

The main idea in our system of instruction has

been to proceed according to the directions pointed out by nature, and to keep constantly in view that her maxim of training is " action."

Rousseau's suggestion, that " impressions on the senses supply the first materials of knowledge," has received due attention, and teaching by means of sensible objects has been a leading feature in our school. Neither pains nor expense have been spared in increasing our facilities and enriching our collections of specimens and models for this purpose, and most satisfactory have been the results already obtained.

But even this system, — though far in advance of those in vogue, which are purely mechanical, drilling the memory to the neglect of the understanding, and cramming the mind with confusing rules and abstruse definitions without stimulating thought, — seemed to have a tendency to formality and routine. This was unmistakably the case when practised by instructors brought up in the traditions of the past, and wanting in the faculty of inventiveness. Thanks to the ingenuity and patient endeavor of some of our teachers, a new element of vital importance has been introduced, and thus a decided step forward has been taken. Several classes of the younger children have been led not only to handle tangible objects of various kinds, as our pupils have always been taught to do, examining them carefully and ascertaining their qualities and characteristics, — but to make

them. The impetus in this direction was chiefly
given by the adoption of the kindergarten plan,
and the fruits of this system in its adaptation to
the development of other studies, are clearly manifest in the geographical, botanical, zoölogical and
anatomical models, which are prepared by those of
our scholars who have been trained under the influence of Froebel's methods. These models show
conclusively, that plastic clay and other pliable
materials, used discriminatingly as a means of
illustration, and most especially as an incentive to
creative thought, will prove more valuable and
potent in the instruction of the blind than a great
portion of the rubbish which is treasured in many
a text book.

I cannot refrain from observing in this connection, that, helpful and valuable as methods, processes and all other external auxiliaries are to the
teacher, his real power lies in himself, his person-
ality, his character, his spirit and his attainments.
An earnest, vigorous person, animated by high
aims and an enthusiastic devotion to his work,
deeply in love with any subject in which he has
steeped his own soul, will awaken something akin
to his own zeal in the minds of his pupils, kindle
within them a taste for learning, arouse their dormant energies, call into exercise their dawning
faculties, impart to them of his own knowledge,
and incite them to independent research. His

method is simply his way of doing this. He does not borrow it from others; he originates it.

If, as Bacon says in one of his essays, "reading maketh a full man," the majority of our scholars manifest an upward tendency toward fulness and ripeness. They do not keep the tips of their fingers rusty or idle. On the contrary, they employ them diligently in the perusal of embossed publications of their own choice, not only on one evening of the week, which is appropriated for this purpose, but at all spare and unemployed times; and they derive much pleasure and not a little profit from the occupation. Of the character of the books which are placed in the hands of our pupils, and of the eagerness with which they seek and use them, the following statement, written by one of our teachers, Miss Mary C. Moore, will give a fair idea: —

"Subtilely but surely what we read becomes a part of our inward life and reappears in our outward acts. We read; we think; we dream; we do. Such is the sequence, and perhaps the most difficult problem for educators today to solve is: How shall young people be kept from narcotics and deadly poison in print?

"It is an immense relief to the teachers of the blind to know that their pupils are absolutely cut off for nine months of the year from the woful influence of inferior books. Our experience proves that a pure literary taste is cultivated with the greatest ease by the simple expedient of supplying the children with good books. The rapidly increasing library is the means to that long-desired end. The following may serve to illustrate this point: — When the translation of 'Heidi' (for which let all children and all lovers of children be grateful evermore) appeared, the book was read to a large class. When, a few months later, 'Heidi' was issued by the 'Howe Memorial Press,' it was eagerly reread, and children, struggling through their third and fourth readers in school, took 'Heidi' from the library for the clear delight of reading it themselves. An independent communion with the purest and best thought; — this is the gift that the printing fund has bestowed upon the blind of New England, and without doubt there is a steadily growing appreciation of the blessing.

"In the realms of literature the blind have no limitations, and ere long they will wander at will without a guide throughout her fair domains. Historians will speak to them; — scientists will show new wonders to their amazed understanding; — they will walk on the heights with philosophers; and rest in the universal truths that poets alone can teach."

The library of the institution is gradually becoming a prominent factor in its educational work, and a perennial source of learning, from which the blind of New England are able to draw wisdom and pleasure according to their several needs and capacities. Our collection of books is growing in size and improving in quality from year to year, and will be rapidly converted into a vital force available to all who are disposed to seek and enjoy its blessings.

44

Music Department.

"When griping grief the heart doth wound,
And doleful dumps the mind oppress,
Then music, with her silver sound,
With speedy help doth lend redress."

Shakespeare.

Music has continued to be taught here both in theory as a science and in practice as an art, in a thorough manner worthy of its real dignity and true value, and has been studied not merely as an accomplishment, or with a view to its usefulness as a profitable profession solely, but as a means of intellectual culture, æsthetic refinement and moral development.

The teachers have discharged their respective duties with due diligence and scrupulous care, and the results of their efforts have been very satisfactory.

The number of pupils who have received instruction in this department during the past year was ninety-four. Of these, eighty have studied the pianoforte; twelve, the cabinet and church organs; twenty-four, harmony in four separate divisions averaging six members each; six, the violin; eight, the clarinet; sixteen, brass instruments; eighty-one have practised singing in classes, of which we have five, and seventeen have received private lessons in vocal training.

The exercises of the normal teaching classes

have been carried on in a practical and most thorough manner, and twenty-one of our advanced students have participated in them with great profit.

Our band has been drilled to a high degree of efficiency, and has rendered excellent service both in and out of the institution for many years past. But instruction in brass and reed instruments is not given solely for the purpose of maintaining a group of practised players for public occasions. It aims also at the general musical culture and the individual benefit of the scholars themselves. There are several among them who are becoming quite proficient on the cornet, the clarinet and the baritone and alto horns. They are under the tuition of men who are noted in their profession both as performers and as instructors, and they have every incentive to strive to attain artistic mastery in their respective instruments, and to use them advantageously both in teaching and playing, when they leave school and are thrown upon their own resources. Efforts in this direction have in many instances been attended with most gratifying success. The method which they usually employ in learning their lessons is very simple. They copy the notes of a composition from dictation in the Braille point system of musical notation, and then they commit them to memory by means of reading them over with their fingers. Music so transcribed remains their personal property, and is carefully preserved for future reference. Thus their repertoire is ever increasing. Those of the young men, who, after graduation, wish to establish themselves at their native places or elsewhere either as workmen, tuners of pianofortes, or teachers of music, can have no better means of making themselves generally known than by being able to play an instrument acceptably in a church vestry, in a fair or in the concert hall. In fact, the demands upon our pupils for such service, even while they are still in school, are inconveniently numerous.

Our collection of musical instruments of different kinds has received several needed additions of a minor character, and one of the concert grand pianofortes, which has been in use for some time past, has been exchanged for a new one.

Besides the uncommon advantages and facilities for the study and practice of music with which our pupils are favored at the institution, they have been permitted to attend most of the best concerts given in Boston, in which the works of the great masters, Händel and Bach, Beethoven and Mendelssohn, Schumann and Chopin, and of many others of a recent date, interpreted by a complete and fine orchestra and by eminent artists and well-drilled choruses, inspire them with the sense of the highest power of music and its most sublime conceptions, and reveal to them depths and heights of elevated thought, of profound feeling, of noble aspiration and of lofty imagination.

. For these numerous and most valuable opportunities for musical culture and artistic refinement which are afforded to our scholars in so generous and munificent a spirit, our cordial thanks and grateful acknowledgments are hereby tendered to their kind friends and liberal benefactors, whose names will be given in full elsewhere.

TUNING DEPARTMENT.

" It is the lark that sings so out of tune,
 Straining harsh discords and unpleasing sharps."

SHAKESPEARE.

As the links in the chain of the industrial occupations of the blind are gradually broken one after the other by the constant invention and use of machinery and the division of labor, those avocations which still remain remunerative for them in the midst of sharpest competition, should be thoroughly cultivated and be made productive of the greatest possible good.

The art of tuning pianofortes is one of the most lucrative employments pursued by our graduates at the present time, and the department devoted to its study has continued to receive all the attention which its practical value and useful purposes merit.

The instruction given in this department has been thorough and systematic, and every facility has been afforded to its recipients for steady practice and efficient training.

48

The contract for tuning and keeping in good repair the pianofortes used in the public schools of Boston has again been renewed for another year on the same terms as the last. This is the ninth time that the work of our tuners has received so emphatic an approval and high recommendation from the committee on supplies of the school board, and we are most grateful to its members for it.

As an interesting illustration of the recognition of the value of the training conferred in our tuning department, mention may be made of the fact, that there is an increasing confidence in the work of our tuners all over New England and elsewhere, and that none of them who is honorable in his conduct, agreeable in his manners, honest in his dealings, prompt in his engagements, free from unclean habits, and industrious at all times, is wanting employment.

TECHNICAL DEPARTMENT.

> " ' Labor is worship ! ' — the robin is singing :
> ' Labor is worship ! ' — the wild bee is ringing.
> Listen ! that eloquent whisper upspringing,
>   Speaks to thy soul out of nature's great heart."
>   MRS. OSGOOD.

The importance of manual labor as the best means for the moral perfection and prosperity of the individual has been duly recognized in this institution from the date of its foundation, and instruction in handicraft has been combined organically with the whole scheme of education, and has been made

support and coalesce with all the other studies and occupations pursued in the school.

In conformity with the rules and regulations of the establishment, the pupils of both sexes have spent a part of their time in their respective work-rooms, where they have been trained by competent and faithful teachers in various mechanic arts, and a brief review of what has been accomplished in each of the two branches of the technical department of the institution seems to be in order here.

I. *Workshop for the Boys.*

Under the diligent direction and efficient supervision of Mr. John H. Wright, who, in his quiet and unostentatious way, is rendering most valuable service to the cause of the industrial and physical education of the blind, — our boys have been trained to use their hands dexterously, and have made satisfactory progress in their work.

No new trades have been introduced in this shop during the past year; but the art of mattress-making, which, compared with other mechanical employments, seems most profitable for the blind, received special attention at the beginning of the present school session. Mr. Walter H. Fiske, a young man of earnest purpose and good ability, has been engaged assistant teacher, with a view to devoting most of his time to giving instruction in this branch, new machinery has been added, the room has been enlarged, and appliances have been provided for

several apprentices to work simultaneously w
convenience and comfort.

In business, practice wisely and assiduously i
proved, is the secret of success, and this fact
are striving to impress upon the minds of our pup
at all times and in every possible way.

II. *Workrooms for the Girls.*

These rooms are most of the time hives of ind
try, and if our girls do not sing aloud " work
happiness," they show it by their activity.

Besides sewing and knitting, both by hand a
machine, they have been taught to crochet and
make hammocks, and a great variety of articles
fancy and worsted work, most of which are adva
tageously disposed of at the weekly exhibitions.

Laura Bridgman spends a part of her time eve
day with the girls, and it is very touching to s
her now threading the needle of some one with t
tip of her harmless tongue, now helping others
take up dropped stitches, and always eager to
of service to those who need assistance.

The articles sent to the exhibition, which w
held in Amsterdam, last August, in connection wi
the Vth international congress of the instructe
and friends of the blind, were among the finest ev
made by our scholars, and they did great credit
their skill and taste.

Both Miss Abby J. Dillingham, the princip
teacher, and her assistant, Miss Cora L. Davis, a

heartily devoted to the progress of their pupils, and they take a deep interest and a commendable pride in the excellence of their work. They are constantly on the alert for introducing improvements, and for opening new paths of usefulness to those who are placed under their charge.

An Indian woman has been employed during the past year to teach some of our girls the art of making fancy baskets of different sizes and shapes, with fine strips of shavings colored in various tints, and several of them have become proficient in it. This was the third attempt which we have made in this direction, and I am glad to say, that it proved quite a success. The sole obstacle to the steady and profitable practice of this handicraft by our graduates lies in the difficulty of securing a reliable and unfailing source of raw materials, which are at present under the exclusive control of the Indians.

DEPARTMENT OF PHYSICAL TRAINING.

" To be strong
Is to be happy."
LONGFELLOW.

A superstructure of intellectual achievement and moral excellence can no more be reared upon the foundations of an enervated and unsound body, than a magnificent temple or a beautiful cathedral can be securely built on shifting sands and decayed timbers.

Hence any scheme of education which pays

special attention to the training of the mind, and fails to provide properly for the necessities of the physical organism, is one-sided and faulty. It is in direct opposition to the principles of physiology. and is radically and fundamentally defective. The development produced by its means is unsymmetrical, and will not yield the best results. No matter how clever and well informed an individual may be, if his mental equipment has been acquired at the expense of his material frame, he is sadly weighted in running the race that is set before him, and disaster sooner or later is very liable to overtake him.

" The best brain," remarks Herbert Spencer, " is found of little service, if there be not enough of vital energy to work it, and hence to obtain the one by sacrificing the source of the other is now considered a folly, a folly which the eventual failure of juvenile prodigies continually illustrates."

Reason, experience and the testimony of science, all combine to show, that the training of the body and keeping it in good health and strength is a condition *sine qua non* for the sanity and growth of the indwelling mind.

But, if physical culture is so great a necessity and indispensable factor in the education of seeing persons, in that of the blind, whose infirmity is unquestionably a positive hindrance to the free and uninterrupted exercise of the muscular system, and very often undermines the bodily powers, it is demanded with tenfold force.

The importance of this fact has been fully recognized in our school, and the roots of our system of education are planted in the gymnasium, where a series of well chosen and beneficial exercises, consisting of calisthenics, military drill, swinging, vaulting, marching, climbing and the like, have been regularly pursued under the direction of experienced and competent teachers. With but few exceptions, designated by our medical inspector for good and sufficient cause, the pupils of both sexes have devoted four hours per week to physical culture by means of gymnastics.

The results of this training, blended with the effects of the exercise which they are required to take at intervals on the piazzas, the gallery, and in their daily walks, are very conspicuous in the development of bodily strength and elasticity, the power of endurance, the grace of carriage, the symmetry in growth, the vivacity in movement, and the suavity in manners of the majority of the participants.

The Kindergarten and its Prospects.

" Because the sunlight dances on the sea,
  Which smiles beneath a blue unclouded sky ;
Because the little waves break joyously
  And catch the rainbow tints that through them fly ;
Because our ship sails smoothly o'er the main,
  With snow-white canvas and a favoring breeze :
Because the hearts on board feel naught of pain,
  And tranquil days bring nights of dreamful ease ;
Because we fear no shipwreck or distress,
  And sail secure from friendly port to port, —
Shall we believe each voyage like to this,
  And, safe ourselves, give other ships no thought ? "

Le Row.

All the children who embark in the voyage of existence do not traverse the vast ocean of human life on staunch and perfect ships. Nor do they glide invariably on smiling waters beneath a blue, unclouded sky. Far from it. On the contrary, some of them sail on defective and unseaworthy vessels in the midst of frowning darkness and sullen waves, and, with tattered sails or rudder gone, and sailors disabled on the deck, are struggling with the tempest, and oftentimes in danger of becoming a hopeless wreck.

This is the case with the little sightless waifs for whom we plead. The fragile craft which bears these children, navigating under the rage of a black storm through foaming surges and breaking billows and surrounded by multifarious perils, hoisted some time ago a signal of distress, and a thrilling call for help was sent ashore. Earnest appeals on behalf of the tiny passengers were repeatedly made to the community; and their rescue became a public concern.

In order to fully understand the magnitude of the affliction of little blind children among our poorest classes, and to realize the immensity of the disadvantages arising therefrom, let us look for a moment at the educational and æsthetic benefits derived from the sense of sight, and compare them with the privations attendant upon its absence.

The chief part of all human learning is wrought early in life. Childhood is the most valuable period for formative purposes. Education is then carried on unconsciously. Curiosity impels the senses to activity, and the subsoil of the intellectual faculties is gradually cultivated. The outer world affords uncommon facilities for the best and simplest kind of schooling. In the words of Pope,—

> " Unerring nature, still divinely bright,
>   One clear, unchanged and universal light,
>   Life, force, and beauty must to all impart,
>   At once the source, and end, and test of art."

Nature is always busy with children, and keeps them in continual training. She opens before and around them a gorgeous and ever changing panorama, and from the first dawn of their intelligence they are favored with an uninterrupted series of lessons of various kinds. The radiant sunshine

glistening upon the leaves and on the impearled
gems of the morning dew, and playing in delicious
currents of warmth over the reeking earth; the
meadow spreading away under its golden flood and
rolling and rising in endless waves, bearing like
white-specked foam upon their crests a sea with here
and there a floating patch of crimson clover or
yellow haze of buttercups; the pastures clothed
with flocks; the crystalline founts springing up and
showering down amidst the clusters of the jasmine
and the rose; the forest with its copious streamlets
and majestic trees; the stately pines uplifting their
fretted summits tipped with cones ; the oaks tossing
up their broad arms with a spirit and strength that
kindles the dawning pride and purposes of the
beholder; the hills climbing green and grand to the
skies, or stretching away in distance their soft blue,
smoky caps; the ranges of lofty mountains with
their "snowy scalps pinnacled in clouds;" the fiery
volcanoes belching forth awful flames with torrents
of ashes, and sending up volumes of curled and
solemn smoke; the brooks flowing through rocky
passes and among flowery creeks and nodding ferns,
and filling the woods with light; the rivers "pouring
slantwise the long defiles," or marching calmly to
the deep through sombre leafy screens and smiling
verdant vales; the giant ocean sparkling in glee or
swelling in anger and "leaping from rock to rock
in delicious bound;" the grandeur of the heavens,
bespangled with their Pleiades and with innumer-

able other isles of light piercing through the
mellow shade and glittering like a swarm of fire-
flies tangled in a silver braid, — all these, together
with the works of art and the inventions of human
ingenuity, afford an ample field for mental development and moral culture to those who have eyes
and can see. They train their senses to keenness,
refine their taste, mould their habits, foster in them
a tendency toward the true and the natural, give
breadth and depth to the hopes and aspirations,
and strengthen the more manly qualities. Through
their silent influence the perceptions are ever at
work observing, comparing and contrasting, while
the sentiments, the imagination, the reason and the
conscience are undergoing a corresponding evolution, and a mastery is being won over every physical
power.

> " One look on nature's open face
>   Should be enough to give her grace
>   To life and thought, to bid us be
>   More like herself as day by day
>   We journey through time's highway.
>
> .　.　.　.　.　.　.　.
>
>   The nearest scene, the scene afar,
>   The twilight gleam, the twinkling star,
>   The shining of a crystal sea,
>   All these are joys whose blissful stay
>   Seems born to never fade away."

Many of the pages of this wonderful and most
instructive book of nature are blank to the blind.

They have no means of access to its treasures, no feasts over its contents. From the moment that night, the "sable goddess, from her ebon throne, in rayless majesty, stretches forth her leaden sceptre over them" and draws her sullen curtain around them, both the jewelled mantle of the sky with its countless living sapphires, which she gathers around her regal form, and the cheerful face of the young Phœbus are vanished from their view, and ever-during darkness falls precipitate over them. Their horizon is completely veiled, and they can obtain no distinct perception of the prodigious variety of objects which lie beyond the radius which can be spanned by the length of their own arms. As Thomson expresses it, —

> " At every step,
> Solemn and slow, the shadows blacker fall,
> And all is awful listening gloom around."

This barrier which exists between the mind of the blind and the outer world, aside from depriving them of one of the most prolific and unfailing sources of instruction and joy, acts as a disturbing force in the order of the development of the different intellectual and moral faculties which go to form character, undermines the vitality of their bodily organization, and renders them as weak and irresolute in thought as they are feeble and flabby in fibre. Its effects, as seen in a large number of individuals, are somewhat like those of light

coming upon a plant from one side only and causing it to grow crooked.

A system of broad and liberal education, based
upon sound scientific principles and taking cognizance of the physical peculiarities and psychological
phenomena arising from the loss of sight, is the
only means which can counteract the influences of
the privation to which the blind are subject for life,
reduce its consequences to the minimum, and enable
its victims to rise superior to fortune and win
victory from adversity itself. Without this aid,

> " Life would be a dreary load
> Along a rough and weary road."

Unfortunately this blessing does not cover the
whole ground at present. As has been repeatedly
stated in these reports, there is in New England
a large number of blind children from four to nine
years of age, who are deprived of the common
education of those who see. Their birthright to
regular and systematic instruction is wholly ignored
on account of their infirmity. There is no provision
of light to illumine their pathway and reveal to
them the many things that otherwise must lie hidden in darkness. They are allowed to grow under
the shadows of the most profound ignorance.

But, black as the landscape is, the background
is gloomier still. For most of these hapless human
beings are secluded in homes, which often are
comfortless and in some instances even vicious,

and are allowed to vegetate like untamed creatures.
From the very nature of their calamity they are
doomed to idleness and inertia. Hedged in by
their affliction and by the dangers and privations
which beset their surroundings, they are without
occupation, and have nothing to incite them to
action and to aid them in receiving impressions or
information from the outside world. They are
shrouded from infancy in a ceaseless gloom that
has settled down like night upon them. They live
in a state of the most grievous destitution and
degradation. They waste away under the rust of
neglect, and not infrequently for the want of sufficient food and raiment and proper care. Unnur-
tured, untaught and unhelped, they are fated to
grow like useless weeds in the swamps of misery
and the low lands of wretchedness.

> " Meagre their looks,
> Sharp misery hath worn them to the bones."

The tainted air which most of these unfortunate
human beings breathe in the foul tenements and
the dirty streets and filthy alleys of the larger cities,
is sapping their vitality, poisoning their blood, sow-
ing their bodies with the seeds of disease, or fostering the germination of those maladies already
planted by inheritance, and rendering them unfit to
contend in the struggle for existence. Moreover,
their environment is pregnant with a variety of
pernicious influences, which stunt their natural

growth, and produce such physical peculiarities, intellectual distortions, and moral deformities as no amount of skilful training in later years can remedy. A gradual stupefaction, which in some instances steals over their minds, ends in feeble-mindedness or hopeless imbecility. It is no hyperbole to say, that the cradle is a curse to most of these children, their life a series of troubles, their daily bread eaten in tears.

"These miseries are more than may be borne."

But there is no doubt, that in the souls of these children there are the germs of some blossoms of good and promise, which would open, if they could only find sunshine and free air to expand them. The light of truth and knowledge, of honor and love, can be introduced into the minds and hearts of these victims of affliction by means of a thorough education ; and, by the aid of early and efficient training, they can be rescued from the very jaws of intellectual and moral darkness, and made good, active, helpful and useful men and women. As the primroses and violets lie in ambush till the first warm breath of the spring bids them reveal themselves, so the minds of these lowly waifs remain buried in the sepulchre of neglect and rust, waiting for the angel of kindness and of benevolent generosity to roll off the stone from the entrance to their prison, and to call them forth to resurrection and life. Each one

████████████████████████

of them has powers within him which can be developed and brought to fruition, and it is of the utmost consequence, that they should have a fair opportunity to unfold their higher nature, and to be so trained as to become self-supporting, and to have in their own hands the means of earning an honest livelihood.

> " In each life however lowly,
> There are mighty seeds of good.
> Still we shrink from all appealing,
> With a timid, ' if we *could.*' "

In the early history of this institution, Dr. Howe used to receive some children at the tenderest age and educate them under its roof; but, owing to the rapid growth of the establishment, this practice was necessarily discontinued many years ago, and there is now no provision for them whatever, either here or elsewhere. The result is, that our school is sadly crippled for want of a prepatory department, where the sightless waifs may be kindly treated, parentally cared for, and methodically assisted to acquire under proper guidance those elementary ideas which seeing children of the same age obtain through their play and from their use of the eye in observation.

In order to supply this fundamental and indispensable step in the ladder of the education of the blind, a kindergarten school, where all the little sightless waifs can be at once removed from their dismal abodes and injurious surroundings and placed under suitable care and home-like influence, is absolutely needed and imperatively demanded.

This infant institution should be, in all its domestic arrangements and educational appointments, a complete and sunny nursery, in which the germinating faculties and budding powers of early childhood shall be skilfully drawn out and properly developed and directed into their legitimate channels of activity, — and Froebel's system of education, which is most admirably adapted to the condition, special wants and peculiar requirements of the blind, should rule supreme in this new establishment, and be the alpha and omega in its methods of training.

This wonderful system is the true starting-point on the royal road of learning, and is unapproachable as an ethical and educational agent. It is rational in its essence, broad in its principles, natural in its methods, rich in its resources, and boundless in its humanity. Through its benign influence the sombre and lowering clouds of dismal empiricism and stiff formality are lined with the silver streaks of thoughtful science and cheerful naturalness, and the tiny human beings who are fortunate enough to be placed under it grow and flourish as steadily as the plants spring up and thrive in a fertile soil under the genial warmth of the sun and the dew of heaven. By a

graduated series of plays and gifts, of exercises
and occupations, of singing and merriment, the
children are unconsciously led to observe atten-
tively, to perceive correctly, to listen intelligently,
to apprehend readily, to think spontaneously, to
acquire accurate notions of things, to express
themselves clearly, to gain bodily activity and
manual dexterity, and to cultivate a taste for
labor, an appreciation of beauty and a love for
truth and goodness, which form the groundwork
of industrial, æsthetic, and moral education. Happiness, self-reliance, helpfulness, confidence, self-
forgetfulness, improvement in health, development
of the ideas of number and form, nice discrimination, and habits of neatness and cleanliness, of
kindness and courtesy, of order and industry, all
these develop fully and freely under the kindergarten system. Here the dumb needs of the
children are met, their blind energies directed,
their unasked questions answered in anticipation,
their groping fingers clasped in a firm yet tender
hand and guided to tasks which reward the labor
of learning, and thus the pupil grows in faith and
hope as he ripens in experience and wisdom.
Here, while the senses are sharpened, the mental
faculties unfolded, and the tissues of the physical
structure invigorated, the intellect is built up high
with knowledge, the doors to productive force and
creative power are unfastened, and the moral

foundations of the character are laid deep in the heart.

Of the great and lasting benefits of the kindergarten with special reference to the case of the blind we have so ample a proof and convincing testimony in facts, that we need not waste many words. During the past five years Froebel's system has been introduced and practised in our school, and its results have been truly marvellous. Pupils whose faculties had been weakened and enervated by unwise indulgence or benumbed by the frost of privation, and who, sinking gradually into sluggishness and idiocy, were averse even to locomotion, and unable so much as to tie the strings of their shoes, have been reclaimed, and have made remarkable progress. Boys and girls who seemed entirely helpless, and had no command whatever of their hands, have been aroused to energy and activity through its ministry. Moreover, its progressive spirit has penetrated into every class-room, creeping silently into the thoughts of every teacher, and thus some of the lingering shadows of past methods have been touched by the brightness of the coming morning.

For the establishment and endowment of a separate kindergarten and primary school for little sightless children, around which cluster so many hopes and reasonable expectations for the future welfare and prosperity of the blind, a movement was inaugurated in 1882, and it has been carried on ever since with unrelaxed energy and unyielding firmness.

This enterprise, born of pure benevolence and nursed in the earnest desire of carrying the lamp of intellectual and moral light to those who are denied the splendor of heaven and the beauties of external nature, has no selfish purpose in contemplation. It aims at the deliverance of all classes of sightless children, regardless of race, color, creed or condition. Its benefits are to be extended all over New England, from the darkest and most joyless tenement houses in the city to the dreariest and most remote hamlets in the country. Its importance in a philanthropic and educational, as well as in an economic and social point of view, is too evident to need demonstration or argument. Like some towering mountain-peak, it is impressive from whatever side it is approached. Presented in its true light, developed with proper energy, maintained with unfailing perseverance, and imbued with the spirit of reliance upon its own inherent goodness and upon the fair-mindedness of the community, the project has commended itself to the feelings and to the judgment of our fellow-citizens, and has received that degree of public attention, which is a sure pledge of success. The call for aid in its furtherance was as swift in reaching many a wise head and tender heart,

"As is a wingèd messenger from heaven,
 When he bestrides the lazy, pacing clouds,
 And sails upon the bosom of the air."

The devotion of our pupils to the proposed
kindergarten has continued to be as ardent as
ever, and their zeal for the promotion of its interests and the fruition of its promise has been
truly unparalleled. They have consecrated themselves afresh solemnly to its work. They have
labored incessantly, in season and out of season,
to keep the enterprise before the public, and to
enlist the coöperation of those who have the
stewardship of riches, in its behalf. They have
omitted or left undone nothing which could be
of service to the cause of their tiny sisters and
brothers in misfortune. The difficulties in their
way seemed innumerable and almost disheartening ; but they seized upon the girdle of Hercules
with admirable alacrity. Concerts, entertainments,
exhibitions and personal appeals have been resorted
to in succession ; and there is ample proof, that
they have not failed of their purpose. Feebly as
the little fingers have struck and played on the
master-chord of beneficence, whose enchanting
music has been so often heard in our community,
they have drawn forth tones of cordiality and
good will, which encouraged and bade them continue their course unswervingly. The icicles of
indifference melted away under the rays of the
sun of earnestness and determination.

Sparks of genuine enthusiasm, thrown out from the souls of these little laborers, fell into the wide circle of the community at large, and lighted living fires in many helpful and feeling hearts. The sympathy of children and youth, as well as of grown persons, was generally aroused, and their hands were stretched forth in aid. Seldom has a movement appealed so strongly to the current of popular feeling. The poor from the rude bench of toil, the rich from their velvet cushions of ease and affluence, the strong and healthy from the field of their occupations, the lame and invalid from the depths of their imprisonment, all vied with one another for the opportunity of rendering the lives of their little blind friends more bright.

The methods adopted by all these kind helpers to raise money for the benefit of the kindergarten were both numerous and very fruitful, and they were only exceeded in touching interest by instances of self-sacrificing generosity on the part of those poor little ones who had but a "mite" to give. The exemplary readiness and pleasure with which one of our sightless girls parted with a portion of her Christmas presents in order to contribute them to the tables of the bazaar organized and carried out by her schoolmates was matched by the precious offering of a very little fellow, a pupil of the Cottage place kindergarten, who,—having attended a fair held for the benefit of our infant school and not having a single penny to bestow,—

sent his top, the only plaything of his possession, to be given to one of the younger boys of this institution. Such deeds, prompted by the instincts of true philanthropy, — which is the best leaven for the heavy dough of human selfishness, — are more than pathetic and significant; they are almost heroic, and carry in themselves the elements of a hallowed future.

> "There they stand,
> Shining in order like a living hymn
> Written in light."

It is impossible to give a detailed narrative here of the ways and means devised by the children and their coädjutors during the past year in Boston and various other cities and towns, for the purpose of obtaining substantial support for the kindergarten, as well as of the results accruing therefrom, and we must refer the reader to the accounts of the treasurer, where will be found a complete list of the names of the contributors to the fund, and of the amounts received from each and all sources.

The results of these efforts, rich as they were in sympathy and kindness and good will, and in touching incidents of self-sacrifice, were insufficient in a pecuniary point of view, however, and the prospect of investing the enterprise with a tangible form seemed rather remote. But to the steady stream of the offerings of the people of moderate circumstances, which could scarcely rise above the

rocks and stones of the brook-bed, was added the
current of a few large donations, which swelled it
in volume and increased the force and rapidity of
its course.

The proceeds of the fair held in the autumn by
Mrs. J. Huntington Wolcott in her house, amounting to $4,612.89, were the first copious spring,
which was turned into this stream of beneficence.
Under the auspices of this noble lady and most
devoted friend to the cause of the blind, Mrs.
Francis Brooks and a group of young ladies of
unbounded philanthropy and high social distinction, labored most assiduously to achieve what
proved a grand success.

A few months later a most munificent gift of
$10,000 was sent to us by a Boston lady, whose
name is withheld from the public ken in compliance with her wishes, but it will be indelibly
engraved in the hearts of scores of sightless children and their helpers. This was truly a royal
present, and all the more precious, because it was
wholly voluntary and unsought. Who shall come
after this queen of benevolence? Such an example
of princely liberality is indeed rare. But why
should it be so? Are there no others in our community, who might, with no sacrifice of comfort,
give an equal amount of money, thus following
with steady footsteps in the celestial track of generosity? Can it be true, that the sensibilities of
the great majority of the knights of wealth are so

hardened by the greed for accumulation as to render them utterly indifferent to the woes of suffering humanity? But,

" That man may last, but never lives,
  Who much receives, but nothing gives ;
  Whom none can love, whom none can thank,
  Creation's blot, creation's blank."

The receipt of the above-named donations, as well as those of Miss Ann Wigglesworth, Mrs. Sarah S. Russell, Mr. Francis Brooks, and several others, to which we cannot refer without feelings of the deepest gratitude and the most profound reverence, enabled us to come to a definite conclusion with regard to the purchase of a suitable lot of land for the establishment of the kindergarten. Honor and praise to the wisdom and foresight of all the members of the committee in charge of this project, but especially to the energy and sagacity of their indefatigable chairman, Mr. Samuel G. Snelling, — whose cordial sympathy and noble enthusiasm for the cause of the blind, are among the strongest forces in its advancement, the negotiations in this direction were conducted to a successful issue. The Hyde estate in Roxbury was secured for thirty thousand dollars, and thus the foundations of the infant institution were laid deep and broad on a solid rock.

This site comprises a tract of six acres and thirty rods of land, and is most eligible in every way. It is only three miles and a half distant from the city hall, and very accessible both by steam railroad trains and horse cars, the latter passing in front of it. The grounds are high and dry, and the entire vicinity is most healthful and desirable for the growth of such an institution as we intend planting there. Allowing sufficient space for a group of eight commodious cottages, — each separate from the others and calculated to accommodate from thirty-five to forty persons,—and also for a central or administration building, large enough to contain school and music rooms, a library and a hall, offices and a museum, workshops and a gymnasium, there will be ample room left for extensive play-grounds, court yards, flower gardens, lawns, shade trees, and the like.

As soon as we obtained possession of the property, measures were taken at once to put the premises in order, and to provide for the opening of the nucleus of a kindergarten at the earliest possible date, with a dozen or fifteen tiny pupils selected from those among the numerous and eager applicants, who are exposed to pernicious influences and must be at once rescued from the clutches of debasement and distress which surround them. As none of the three old dwelling-houses on the place was found, on thorough examination, suitable to be used as a boarding school even temporarily, it was unanimously decided by the committee to erect a new one, 86 feet long, 45 feet wide, and 3 stories

high. One of the leading architects in Boston,
Mr. Samuel D. Kelley, kindly drew a set of excellent plans and specifications, and contributed them
to the cause free of charge. Hard brick with freestone trimmings were the materials chosen for the
proposed building, and there was an earnest desire
to have it finished and ready for occupancy early
in November. To this end arrangements were
being made with all reasonable speed, and everything seemed favorable to its attainment. But
while we were about to commence operations for
the excavation of the foundation of the new structure it was discovered, that, in order to grade the
grounds and level them on the side of Day street,
a ponderous ledge would have to be removed by
blasting, and that the whole cellar of the building
would have to be carved out of the solid rock.
This unforeseen and unexpected labor could undoubtedly have been accomplished in six weeks or
two months; but its completion within such limits
would have involved an additional expense, which
was beyond our slender means. Hence we were
compelled for the sake of economy, to allow such
a length of time for the labor as would help to reduce the cost of the job. As a consequence, the
laying of the corner stone has been unavoidably
postponed until next spring. I need scarcely say
how great a disappointment this delay was to those
who take so lively an interest in the establishment

of the kindergarten; but we had to yield to th
inevitable.

"'Ανάγκα καὶ θεοὶ πείθονται."

After much discussion and careful consider:
tion of the matter, a satisfactory agreement wa
finally effected with a responsible contractor, an
the ground was broken in the latter part (
August.

Thus the first and most important step has bee
taken. The consummation of the project has passe
out of the nebulous stage of uncertainty, and enter
the domain of accomplished facts. The friends
the enterprise look forward with joyous anticipati(
to the not far distant day, when in the place whe
this massive ridge of rough and useless stone
now being demolished and carted away, educati(
will open wide her doors to those from whom tl
rays of the sun are totally shut out. She will c:
their fettered souls out from darkness and despo
dency to brightness and hope, and to the wide
fields of light. The acorns of benevolence, plant(
in love and kindness and watered by the gold(
stream of sympathy and charity, cannot but gr(
into stately oaks, under whose branches the sigl
less waifs of New England will find a shelter frc
the storms of woe and grief, and protection frc
the contagion of moral pestilences. True, o
operations so far are confined to a very narr(

compass: but, as Cicero says, the beginnings of all things are small.

"Omnium rerum principia parva sunt."

Nevertheless it is exceedingly embarrassing, that the means at command are very inadequate to carry out our plans even on so limited a scale. When the new building is finished, our treasury will be entirely depleted of its contents. There will be scarcely anything left either for furnishings, musical instruments and apparatus, or for the absolutely necessary expenses for maintenance and tuition. For an endowment fund, which will give security to the permanence of the enterprise, and will serve as a vital sap to its growth and fruition, we have not yet a penny.

But notwithstanding this lack of means, "hope should spring exulting on triumphant wing." This very stress of pecuniary perplexities, instead of causing discouragement and inertness, must lead to the development of indomitable perseverance and of that daring and self-poised cast of mind, which takes no account of existing or prospective storms, and delights in standing out from shore for deep-sea sailing. There is no ground of apprehension or despondency. The past prophesies auspiciously for the future. What has already been accomplished is an assurance, that we "shall reap a full harvest, if we faint not." After the

season of worry and anxiety will come the time of
praise and thanksgiving. There is not a shadow
of doubt as to the outcome of a movement inaugurated in mercy and carried on in faith and good
will. Far otherwise. There is an absolute certainty about it, slow though it be. We may not
rejoice over gathered crops immediately, but we
will ultimately. Wherever the sower scatters the
good seed, there the reaper's hand will be filled
with the golden sheaves. Montgomery's charming advice may be quoted in this connection with
peculiar fitness: —

> " Sow in the morn thy seed,
>   At eve hold not thy hand ;
> To doubt and fear give thou no heed,
>   Broadcast it o'er the land.
>
> .   .   .   .   .   .
>
> And duly shall appear,
>   In verdure, beauty, strength,
> The tender blade, the stalk, the ear,
>   And the full corn at length."

The significant phrase, "*action, action, and
action* again," — which was uttered by Demosthenes
as a definition of eloquence, — embodying as it does
the key to success in any undertaking, must be the
motive power and driving force in ours. We must
adhere to it with rigid pertinacity. Until the goal
is reached there should be no relaxation in our
efforts, no hesitancy in our march. Our labors
must be unremitting until the flame of earnest

interest, kindled in the souls of a large number of
men, women and children, swells into a confla-
gration and consumes all barriers and obstructions.
We should fix our eyes upon victory and never
take them off or wink until it is achieved. Agitation must be kept up and increased at any cost,
until the final triumph of our cause. All the omens
are in its favor, and no available opportunity for
its advancement should be allowed to pass
unnoticed. Success is the crown of steadfast
determination, constant endeavor, and assiduous
industry. Confidence in conquest not only rubs
off the sharp edges of hardship, but helps the
pilgrims to its shrine to go up to it in a chariot of
fire. To slacken energy and procrastinate exertion at so critical and opportune a moment as the
present, would be a serious blow to our movement.
" Forward," then, must be the watchword throughout our lines. All our forces should be marshalled
with skilful strategy, and brought to bear upon the
central point. The gods aid only those who strive
to help themselves. For the drowsy laggards
there is no prospect of hopefulness either on earth
or in heaven.

In urging the continuance of vigorous measures
in furtherance of our enterprise, I am fully conscious of the arduousness of the task devolving
upon its promoters, and of the slough of unconcern
and the brambles and briars of exclusiveness,
through which they have to fight their way. But,

be the difficulties and obstacles what they may,
our faith in the goodness and beneficence of the
kindergarten is so potent, that we do not allow
ourselves, even for an instant, to doubt about the
full supply of its wants and needs. This conviction is not the offspring of impulse, or the shadow
of the wings of a wandering imagination; nor does
it rest upon mere sentimental grounds, and dreamy
aspirations. Both reason and justice point to the
immediate accomplishment of our enterprise.
Humanity and fairness, — to say nothing about
social economy and expediency, — guarantee the
speedy realization of this fervently wished for
consummation. A large class of little children,
oppressed by poverty and burdened with one of the
severest of human calamities from no fault of their
own, are threatened with being crushed for ever
under its weight at the very threshold of their life.
They ask for a plank wherewith to be enabled to
swim across the river of affliction, to reach the
shore of self-reliance, and to enter upon a career
of activity and independence. Can it be possible,
that a community which contributes hundreds of
thousands, nay millions of dollars for the salvation
of the heathen abroad from the terrors of an unde-
finable Gehenna that is to come, will turn a deaf
ear to the pathetic prayers and thrilling entreaties
of the little sightless waifs at home for their deliverance from the actual doom and positive horrors of
intellectual and moral darkness, and let them sink

hopelessly down into the cesspools of idleness and pauperism? Will those of our citizens who possess the goods of the world in abundance be so heartless as to give no heed to the mournful calls of these tiny suppliants for mercy and their devout aspirations for redemption, and allow them to turn into moans of grief and sobs of despair? Will they be so niggardly as to withhold the pecuniary means requisite for the removal of one of the most conspicuous blots which disfigure our civilization?

I think not; at any rate, I trust not. The instincts of humanity, the promptings of benevolence, and the dictates of wisdom, all combine to induce the belief, that a ready and generous response will be given to the appeals in behalf of the kindergarten for the blind, and that this infant school will soon be sufficiently endowed and efficiently equipped, so that it may fulfil the grand object of its mission to the utmost extent, embracing in the arms of love and kindness and affectionate care all the little sightless children, and raising them from the bosom of the night of affliction to the glorious light of usefulness, dignity and blessedness.

A COLLEGE TO CROWN OUR SYSTEM OF EDUCATION.

> "Heaven is not reached by a single bound;
> But we build the ladder by which we rise
> From the lowly earth to the vaulted skies,
> And mount to the summit round by round."
>
> J. G. HOLLAND.

Of all the blessings which can be bestowed upon the blind with the view of enabling them to minister to their own wants and consequently of robbing the sting of their calamity of its sharpness, a uniform system of education, complete in itself, covering the whole ground from the lowest to the most advanced studies, is the greatest and most enduring.

This system should be broad in its aims, scientific in its methods, comprehensive in its purposes, and consistent in its parts, and should afford to all sightless children and youth of suitable age sufficient means and ample opportunities for the fullest development and most thorough training of their physical powers and mental faculties, bridging as far as possible the chasms in the course of their life caused by their infirmity and aiding them to outsoar the shadows of their affliction and to enter upon a career of activity and usefulness. Like a well planned and properly constructed stairway, the scheme of their education should have one of its ends securely resting close at the roots of the tree of knowledge, and the other reaching its highest and most fruitful branches, and it should consist of four grades, — the elementary, the secondary, the higher, and the collegiate. Two of these departments, which are to include all children between five and sixteen years of age, should be transferred to our new estate in Roxbury, where there is ample room for growth and expansion; and the other two should be located in the present premises of the institution in South Boston, and should be open only to those pupils, who are endowed with natural and acquired qualifications to enter upon the study of languages and of the higher branches of literature, science and music.

The establishment and equipment of the kindergarten will place the first round of the ladder of education on a level with the tiny feet of the very smallest sightless children. By rearranging the present school and somewhat increasing the corps of instructors, the second and third steps can be fully supplied. But even with these, the climax will not be reached. The ladder will still be imperfect. The uppermost round will still be wanting. There will be no capital on the top of the magnificent column of light which has been and is being reared by the generosity of the commonwealth and the benevolence of private citizens in behalf of the blind, until a college is founded and endowed, affording to the sightless the same or equal advantages with those which are enjoyed by the seeing. This will be the complement and crown of our system of education, the head of a completely organized body, of which only the feet, the limbs and the trunk exist at present, — the fulfilment of our most ardent hopes and highest aspirations. As soon as the kindergarten is finished and put upon a solid financial foundation, we must turn at once and concentrate our efforts to the achievement of this project, and we must not shrink from any labor or sacrifice until it is accomplished.

Wisdom as well as the best good and the most
vital interests of a large number of our fellow men
demand, that there should be no delay or hesitancy
in placing the keystone and rounding the educational arch which is erected for the benefit of the
blind.

A description of the details of the plan of the
proposed college, — which is to combine a complete
academic department with a conservatory of music,
— of the branches and languages to be taught,
of the methods of instruction and training to be
employed, and of the cabinets and collections of
specimens, models, appliances and instruments to
be obtained for illustration and practice, will be
given in due time.

GENEROUS AID FROM THE PRESS.

"I can no other answer make, but, thanks,
 And thanks; and ever oft good turns
 Are shuffled off with such uncurrent pay."
                                        SHAKESPEARE.

It is a pleasant duty to acknowledge the great
debt of deep and lasting gratitude, which the
blind of New England owe to the secular and
religious press for the most generous and efficient
aid, which it has invariably given to their cause.

The editors and proprietors of the leading newspapers published in this section of the country may
be justly classed among the principal helpers and
most active promoters of all movements in behalf

of our school and its beneficiaries. A great portion
of the response which has been given to our
appeals for funds is certainly due to their liberality
and uniform kindness. They have been ready to
aid us at all times and under any circumstances. No
matter how crowded their columns might be, or
how frequent our requests, they would find both
room and time to advocate and serve our cause.
Without the countenance and cordial support of
this powerful agency, all vital and pervasive everywhere, no project of ours could meet with signal
success. So far as we know, nowhere else in this
country does the public press take so deep and
lively an interest in the welfare of those who are
bereft of sight. Of this point the following fact
is a striking illustration.

Five young ladies, recent graduates of the New
York institution for the blind, wishing to supply a
great want in their community, have undertaken
to establish a circulating library of embossed books
for the benefit of those who are similarly afflicted
with themselves. They applied last summer for
a charter of incorporation, and when this was
granted, the newspapers of that city, with but one
exception, announced the enterprise in the fewest
possible words, without alluding to its merits or
commending its importance. But one of our
leading journals, the "Boston Daily Advertiser,"
accustomed to take notice of almost every movement regarding the education of the blind and the

amelioration of their condition, took up the subject of its own accord and without any request or suggestion from outside, and recommended the enterprise most earnestly to the favorable consideration of the public.

This is one of the very many tokens of the most generous and constant assistance which the journals of New England lend to the blind, and for which the recipients of this great and lasting benefaction and their helpers avail themselves of this opportunity to return heartfelt thanks and grateful acknowledgments.

THE INTERNATIONAL CONGRESS IN AMSTERDAM.

" Ever onward must thy soul ; —
'Tis the progress gains the goal."
SCHILLER.

The Vth international congress of the educators of the blind, which was held in Amsterdam last August, was an event of surpassing interest, showing how much progress has been recently made in most of the European institutions, and what an impetus has already been given for further advancement.

Owing to the strenuous efforts of the president, Herr J. H. Meijer, who conducted all the preliminary arrangements with great zeal and in a most thorough and systematic manner, the attendance was exceedingly large. Dutch, German, Russian, Belgian, Danish, Swedish, English, French, Greek

and Italian educators and friends of the blind
responded readily to the pressing and cordial invitations which were sent right and left, and the
gathering was decidedly cosmopolitan in its composition, and, taken as a whole, was far superior to
those which take place biennially in this country,
both in the mental calibre and erudition of its
members and in the breadth and depth of its work.
This latter fact could not be otherwise when such
profound students and eminent pedagogues as
Moldenhawer of Copenhagen, Meijer of Amsterdam, Mecker of Düren, Kull of Berlin, Wulff of
Steglitz, Heller and Binder of Vienna, Martin of
Paris, and many others of equal ability, assemble
together to discuss freely and without the interference of star-chamber committees all subjects pertaining to the education, physiology, psychology,
hygiene, scientific instruction and technical training
of the blind. Unfortunately, since the retirement
of Mr. J. Howard Hunter from the principalship of
the Ontario institution in Brantford, Canada, Mr.
A. Buckle of York is the only one among the
English-speaking superintendents on either side
of the Atlantic, who can compare favorably with
these men in intellectual acumen, force and clearness of thought, refinement of taste, ripe scholarship, and linguistic attainments.

The spirit which prevailed in the councils of the
congress and permeated its deliberations and dis-
cussions was remarkable for its catholicity and

sincerity. There seemed to be an entire absence
of the methods of wire-pulling for personal ag-
grandizement and glorification; of intrigues and
combinations for suppressing the truth and per-
verting history; of unholy alliances for deriving
mutual advantages to the detriment of the general
interests of the blind, or for appropriating the
fruits of the talents of others; of ranting and
blustering over the accomplishments of a few
sporadic cases. On the contrary, the actions and
arrangements of the managing committee were
characterized by uncommon fairness and openness,
while the leading educators of the blind evinced
both in their utterances and demeanor a degree of
unfeigned modesty, patience in research, thoroughness in knowledge and earnestness in purpose,
which enhance the beauty and value of their
achievements, and give assurance of still greater
results in the future.

> " Still streams
> Oft water fairest meadows, and the bird
> That flutters least is longest on the wing."

Among the many papers which were read and
discussed at the different meetings of the congress,
the following were of great worth and supreme
interest: "The Vicariat of the Senses," by Herr
W. J. Binder; "The Principle of Correlation in
the schools for the blind," by Herr S. Heller; "The
Instruction in Geometry in schools for the blind,"

by Herr E. Kull: "On the Printing and Bibliography for the use of the blind," by M. Emile Martin; "The development of the æsthetic element for the blind," by Herr W. Mecker, editor of the *Blindenfreund;* "The condition of blind women, — their education, and the aid which can be given them," by Herr J. Moldenhawer; and many others of great value. It is to be regretted, that an essay on the status of the question of the blind in France in 1885, prepared by M. Maurice de la Sizeranne of Paris, was not read for want of time. M. de la Sizeranne, like Signor Dante Barbi-Adriani of Florence, Italy, is a man of literary ability, and devotes his time and pen to the cause of his fellow-sufferers. He is the accomplished editor of *Valentin Haüy,* a French review of questions relating to the blind, and also the author of a most interesting work recently published and entitled, "*J. Gaudet and the Blind;* his life, his doctrines, and his writings."

The proceedings of the congress are to be published in three languages, — Dutch, German and French. They are prepared under the scrupulous care and supervision of the director of the Amsterdam institution for the blind, Herr J. H. Meijer, whose sterling character is a sufficient guarantee that they will not be allowed to suffer any surgical operations or mutilations, but that they will be a correct and honest record of what has transpired.

The exhibition of various articles illustrative of
the methods of instruction, the educational appliances and apparatus, and the technical training of
the blind, which was held in the university building in connection with the congress, occupying
four of its large lecture rooms, was one of the best
and most attractive features of the occasion. It
was divided into two sections, the pedagogic and
the industrial, and contained contributions from all
the leading schools and workshops for the blind in
Europe. It was a great pleasure and privilege to
us to join these institutions and to send an exhibit,
consisting of specimens of the work of our kindergarten classes, our industrial department and
our printing-office.

CONCLUSION.

" The end crowns all."

SHAKESPEARE.

Thus runs the record of another year, — the
fifty-fourth in the history of the institution: in one
aspect meagre and imperfect; to the deeper view,
full of promise and great hope.

In closing it, I gratefully acknowledge the cordial coöperation and efficient aid which I have
received from all the teachers and officers in the
discharge of the duties of my post. If any credit
is awarded to me for my management of the affairs
of the institution during the past or in preceding

years, I justly and frankly turn over the largest share of it to those assistants who have rendered most valuable and loyal service to the establishment.

Nor can I fail to express publicly to you my sense of gratitude for the kindness and confidence — far beyond my merits — with which the members of your board have uniformly favored me.

Respectfully submitted by

M. ANAGNOS.

ACKNOWLEDGMENTS.

Among the pleasant duties incident to the close of the year is that of expressing our heartfelt thanks and grateful acknowledgments to the following artists, *littérateurs*, societies, proprietors, managers, editors and publishers, for concerts and various musical entertainments ; for operas, oratorios, lectures, readings, and for an excellent supply of periodicals and weekly papers, minerals and specimens of various kinds.

As I have said in previous reports, these favors are not only a source of pleasure and happiness to our pupils, but also a valuable means of æsthetic culture, of social intercourse, and of mental stimulus and improvement. So far as we know, there is no community in the world which does half so much for the gratification and improvement of its unfortunate members as that of Boston does for our pupils.

I. — Acknowledgments for Concerts and Operas in the City.

To Mr. Henry Lee Higginson we are under great and continued obligations for twenty season tickets to the public rehearsals and twelve season tickets to his series of twenty-four symphony concerts.

To the same, through Mr. Charles A. Ellis, the superintendent of the Music Hall, for an average of twenty-seven tickets to each of five popular concerts.

To Messrs. Tompkins and Hill, proprietors of the Boston Theatre, for admission of unlimited numbers to seven operas.

To the Händel and Haydn society, through Mr. E. B. Hagar, secretary. for twenty tickets to the oratorio of Messiah, twenty-eight to the bi-centennial of Händel, and twenty-four to Israel in Egypt.

To the Apollo club, through its secretary, Mr. Arthur Reed, for six tickets to each of four concerts.

To Mr. G. A. Nickerson, for four tickets to one concert of the same club.

To the Boylston club, through its secretary, Mr. F. H. Ratcliffe, for eight tickets to each of five concerts.

To the Cecilia, through its secretary, Mr. Charles W. Stone, for twenty tickets to each of three concerts.

To the Euterpe, through its president, Mr. C. C. Perkins, for several tickets to their series of concerts.

To Mr. H. G. Tucker, for ten tickets to each of two concerts.

To Mr. John Orth, for ten tickets to one concert.

To Messrs. Henry F. Miller & Sons. for twenty tickets to each of two concerts by Dr. Louis Maas.

To Mr. A. F. Conant, for fifteen tickets to each of four concerts.

To Mr. E. W. Tyler, for eleven tickets to one concert by Mr. Otto Bendix.

To Miss M. Gascoigne Bullard, for twelve tickets to one concert.

To Miss Emma LeB. Kettelle, for four tickets to one concert.

To Mr. T. P. Currier, for six tickets to one concert.

To Mr. F. Dewey, for sixteen tickets to a dramatic and musical entertainment.

To Mr. Everett E. Truett, for fifty tickets to one organ concert.

To Captain Samuel C. Wright, for a large number of tickets to the Dahlgren course of entertainments.

To Mr. George H. Foxcroft, for seventy-five tickets to one concert in the Star lecture course.

To the Rev. G. A. Crawford, for tickets to a series of concerts and lectures in the Broadway Methodist Church.

. To the Rev. J. J. Lewis, for admission to a series of concerts and lectures in the Broadway Universalist Church.

To Dr. Tourjée, for twenty-five tickets to a quarterly concert of the New England Conservatory.

To Mr. Ernst Perabo, for twelve tickets to each of four lectures on music given by Prof. J. K. Paine.

To Mr. B. J. Lang, for admission of twelve persons to his lecture on mechanical appliances for aiding pianoforte technique.

To an unknown lady friend, for twenty-five tickets to a concert in aid of the free hospital for women.

II. — Acknowledgments for Concerts given in our Hall.

For a series of recitals and concerts given from time to time in the music hall of the institution, we are greatly indebted to the following artists : —

To Mr. Ernst Perabo, assisted by Miss Emma Eames, vocalist, for one concert.

To Mr. Arthur Foote, pianist, assisted by Mr. George J. Parker, vocalist, for one concert.

To Mrs. Ella Cleveland Fenderson, vocalist, assisted by Misses O'Brion and Olga Von Radecki, pianists, Mr. George J. Parker, tenor, Dr. L. B. Fenderson, reader, and Mr. John Howard, accompanist, for one concert.

To Mr. Charles H. Bond, assisted by Miss Gertrude Swayne, vocalist, Miss Lida Low, accompanist, and Miss Lizzie Gleason, reader, for one entertainment.

To Madame Marie Fries Bishop, assisted by her pupils and Mrs. Ritchings, reader, for one concert.

To Mr. Charles A. Clarke, for one pianoforte recital.

To Mrs. Virginia A. Howe and Miss Lizzie B. Langley, assisted by Mrs. H. F. Knowles, Miss Mary H. How and Mr. A. D. Saxon, vocalists, Madame Dietrich Strong, Miss Ada P.

Emery, Mr. J. Dudley Hall and Mr. Frank Smith, pianists, for one concert.

To Mrs. Freeman Cobb, assisted by Mr. Eades of Dorchester. Mr. Everett E. Truett, organist, Miss E. B. Kehew, Mrs. C. E. Wells and Mr. Frank L. Young, vocalists, Mr. Charles F. Dennée, pianist, and Mr. M. L. Bradford, Jr., flutist, for one concert.

To Mrs. William H. Sherwood, and Miss Eveline Ames, daughter of Lieutenant Governor Ames, for a fine piano concert.

III. — Acknowledgments for Lectures, Readings, and other Entertainments.

To Prof. George H. Hartwell, for one lecture.

To Mr. John S. Dwight, for reading his essays on Händel and Bach, at the musical festivals given in commemoration of the bi-centennials of these great composers by the pupils of the school.

To the managers of both the New England Institute and Mechanics' fairs, for admitting large numbers to an afternoon entertainment at each.

IV. — Acknowledgments for Books, Minerals, Specimens, etc.

For various books, specimens, curiosities, etc., we are indebted to the following friends : — Mr. J. M. Constable, Mr. Peter Corcoran, Col. H. P. Harris, Mr. George E. Hart, C. A. W. Howland, Miss R. C. Mather, Mr. Clement Ryder, Miss S. A. Wolfe, and The Society for providing Religious Literature for the Blind.

V. — Acknowledgments for Periodicals and Newspapers.

The editors and publishers of the following reviews, magazines, and semi-monthly and weekly papers continue to be very kind and liberal in sending us their publications gratuitously, which are always cordially welcomed, and perused with interest : —

The N. E. Journal of Education, . *Boston, Mass.*
The American Teacher, ... " "
The Atlantic, ...
Boston Home Journal, . . .
Youth's Companion, ...
The Christian, ...
The Christian Register, . . .
The Musical Record, ...
The Musical Herald, ...
The Folio, ...
Littell's Living Age, ...
Unitarian Review, ...
The Watchman, ...
The Golden Rule, ...
Zion's Herald, ...
The Missionary Herald, . . . " "
The Salem Register, ... *Salem, Mass.*
The Century, ... *New York, N. Y.*
St. Nicholas, ... " "
The Journal of Speculative Philosophy, "
The Christian Union, ... " "
Church's Musical Journal, . . . *Cincinnati, O.*
Goodson Gazette, *Va. Inst. for Deaf-Mutes and Blind.*
Tablet, . . . *West Va.* " " " "
Good Health, ... *Battle Creek, Mich.*
L'Amico dei Ciechi, ... *Florence, Italy.*
Valentin Haüy, a French monthly, . *Paris, France.*

I desire again to render the most hearty thanks, in behalf of all our pupils, to the kind friends who have thus nobly remembered them. The seeds which their friendly and generous attentions have sown have fallen on no barren ground, but will continue to bear fruit in after years; and the memory of many of these delightful and instructive occasions and valuable gifts will be retained through life.

M. ANAGNOS.

GENERAL STATEMENT OF RECEIPTS AND DISBURSEMENTS OF THE PERKINS INSTITUTION AND MASSACHUSETTS SCHOOL FOR THE BLIND, FOR THE YEAR ENDING SEPT. 30, 1885.

I.— INCOME.

State of Massachusetts, annual appropriation,	$30,000 00	
Board and tuition, State of New Hampshire,	3,300 00	
" " of Vermont,	2,100 00	
" " of Rhode Island,	4,579 25	
" " of Connecticut,	4,800 00	
" " private pupils,	619 56	
		$45,398 81
Tuning,		894 79
Admission fees,		92 98
Sundry small items,		318 18
Interest on mortgage notes,		10,497 50
" on South Boston Railroad note,		421 16
" on balances in N. E. Trust Co.,	$360 00	
" on Eastern Railroad bonds,	300 00	
" on Ottawa & Burlington Railroad bonds,	50 00	
" on Boston & Lowell Railroad bonds,	300 00	
" on Chicago, Milwaukee & St. Paul bonds,	300 00	
" on Kansas City, St. Jo. & Council Bluffs bonds,	350 00	
" on Chicago, Burlington & Quincy bonds,	1,050 00	
		2,410 00
Dividends, —		
Fitchburg Railroad,	$250 00	
Providence Railroad,	240 00	
Chicago, Burlington & Quincy Railroad,	516 00	
		1,006 00
Rents, 11 Oxford Street,	$160 52	
" South Boston,	953 96	
		1,114 48
" Roxbury,		195 00
Sale of books in raised print,		832 40
Sundries from the printing office,		22 28
Amount carried forward,		$63,616 08

I.— EXPENSES.

Maintenance,	$42,205 91	
Expense of men's workshop,	2,210 40	
" boys' workshop,	92	
Hire of treasurer's clerk, rent of safe and check book,	132 00	
Improvements on real estate,	508 65	
Rent of office,	250 00	
Expenses of printing office,	5,265 50	
		$50,573 38
Harris beneficiaries,		917 50
Bills to be refunded,		147 53

II.— INVESTMENT.

Real estate in Roxbury for Kindergarten,	$30,000 00	
Repairs and improvements on the same,	877 18	
		30,877 18
Real estate on Fourth street,	$5,000 00	
Repairs and improvements on the same,	360 28	
		5,360 28
Mortgage notes, Kindergarten account,	$15,000 00	
" " general account,	15,000 00	
		30,000 00
1,300 Chicago, Burlington & Quincy Railroad bonds,		12,463 75
Assessment on Fitchburg Railroad,		200 00
" C., B. & Northern Railroad,		111 00
Instalments on Chicago, Burlington & Quincy stock,		360 00
Cash balance, Sept. 30, 1885, —		
N. E. Trust Co.,	$1,597 20	
M. Anagnos,	413 82	
		2,011 02
Amount carried forward,		$133,021 44

GENERAL STATEMENT OF RECEIPTS AND DISBURSEMENTS, ETC. — Concluded.

Amount brought forward,		$63,616 08	*Amount brought forward,* $133,021 44
II — RECEIPTS, EXCLUSIVE OF INCOME.			
Legacies, General Fund, —			
Miss A. E. Gray,	$1,000 00		
Miss Gridley, balance,	82 70		
Printing Fund, balance,	500 00		
Donations, General Fund, Mrs. Susan O. Brooks,	30 00		
" Printing Fund,	10 00		
" Kindergarten Fund,	24,645 80	26,268 50	
III.—COLLECTIONS AND SALE OF STOCKS.			
Note collected,	$10,000 00		
Sale of railroad bonds,	12,468 17	22,468 17	
		20,668 69	
Cash balance, Oct. 1, 1884,		$133,021 44	$133,021 44

ANALYSIS OF THE MAINTENANCE ACCOUNT.

Meats, 28,658 lbs., ...	$2,968 69
Fish, 4,841 lbs., ...	243 54
Butter, 5,450 lbs., ...	1,490 22
Rice, sago, etc., ...	35 56
Bread, flour, meal, etc., ...	1,381 86
Potatoes and other vegetables, . . .	710 36
Fruit, ...	417 05
Milk, 26,820 qts., ...	1,469 94
Sugar, 7,373 lbs., ...	439 89
Tea and coffee, 580 lbs., ...	190 37
Groceries, ...	765 71
Gas and oil, ...	475 04
Coal and wood, ...	2,486 90
Sundry articles of consumption, . . .	437 04
Wages and domestic service, . . .	4,346 57
Salaries, superintendence and instruction, . .	16,268 79
Outside aid, ...	201 21
Medicine and medical aid, ...	15 62
Furniture and bedding, ...	2,164 36
Clothing and mending, ...	63 04
Expenses of stable, ...	434 34
Musical instruments, ...	90 63
Books, stationery, etc., ...	857 92
Construction and repairs, ...	3,216 83
Taxes and insurance, ...	653 25
Travelling expenses, ...	135 99
Board of pupil outside, ...	200 00
Sundries, ...	45 19
	$42,205 91

WORK DEPARTMENT, Oct. 1, 1885.

STATEMENT.

Salaries and wages of blind people,	.	$3,457 11
" " seeing people,	.	2,485 21
Amount paid for stock, rent and sundries,		10,851 41
		————— $16,793 73
Cash received during the year,	. . . .	14,583 33
		$2,210 40

Stock and Debts Due.

Stock on hand, Oct. 1, 1885,	. .	$6,366 48
Debts due Oct. 1, 1885,	. .	2,673 44
		$9,039 92
Stock on hand, Oct. 1, 1884,	. .	7,222 01
		————— 1,817 91
Cost for carrying on Work Department, .	.	$392 49

[*Total amount due to the institution by the workshop for investments from the first date to Sept. 30, 1885, $47,315.79.*]

Printing Fund Statement Oct. 1, 1885.

Receipts.		Expenses.	
Proportion of income of invested funds,	$5,782 86	Stock,	$1,117 63
Sale of books,	832 40	Binding,	731 65
Donations,	10 00	Electrotyping,	1,251 28
Legacy,	500 00	Wages,	1,332 07
Sundries,	22 28	Repairs,	61 08
		Type,	486 57
		Books,	42 89
		Board of printers,	200 00
		Cleaning, gas, etc.,	52 33
		Balance to be added to fund,	$5,265 50
			1,882 04
	$7,147 54		$7,147 54

Kindergarten Fund Statement Oct. 1, 1885.

Receipts.		Expenses.	
Donations,	$24,645 80	Investment, mortgage note,	$15,000 00
Rents,	195 00	Purchase of estate in Roxbury,	30,000 00
Proportion of income of invested funds,	1,030 00	Repairs, improvements and other expenses on the same,	877 17
Cash, Oct. 1, 1884,	19,869 50		
Balance due to general account,	136 87		
	$45,877 17		$45,877 17

The following account exhibits the state of the property as embraced in the books of the institution, Sept. 30, 1885:

Real Estate yielding Income.		
House No. 11 Oxford street, . . .	$5,500 00	
Three houses on Fifth street, . . .	9,900 00	
House No. 537 Fourth street, . . .	4,800 00	
Three houses, corner of Day and Perkins streets, Roxbury, ...	8,460 00	
		$28.660 00
Real estate used for school purposes, .	. . .	240,200 00
Unimproved land, South Boston, . .	. . .	8,500 00
" " Roxbury, . .	. . .	22,417 18
Mortgage notes, ...	. . .	216,000 00
South Boston Railroad Co., note, . .	. . .	7,500 00
Railroad Stock.		
Boston & Providence Railroad, 30 shares, value, ...	$5,490 00	
Fitchburg Railroad, 62 shares, value, .	5,928 00	
Chicago, Burlington & Quincy Railroad, 66 shares, value, ...	8,712 00	
		20,130 00
Railroad Bonds.		
Eastern Railroad Co. 6s, 2 at $500 each, value, $1,220, . . .		
Eastern Railroad Co. 6s, 3 at $1,000 each, value, $3,660, . . .	$4 880 00	
Boston & Lowell Railroad Co 6s, 1, .	1,000 00	
Chicago, Burlington & Quincy Railroad Co. 4s, 27 at $1,000 each, value, .	25,650 00	
Chicago, Milwaukee & St. Paul Railroad Co. 6s, 5 at $1,000 each, value, . .	4,250 00	
Chicago, Milwaukee & St. Paul Railroad Co., Dubuque Division 6s, 5 at $1,000 each, value, ...	5,550 00	
Ottawa & Burlington Railroad Co. 6s, 5 at $1,000 each, value, ...	5,500 00	
Kansas City, St Joseph & Council Bluffs R R. Co. 7s, 5 at $1,000 each, value, .	6,150 00	
		52,980 00
Amount carried forward, . .	. . .	$596,387 18

Amount brought forward, ...			$596,387 18
Cash, ...			2,011 02
Household furniture, ...			16,320 00
Provisions and supplies, ...			852 74
Wood and coal, ...			2,620 00
Work Department —Stock and debts for the same, ...			9,039 92
Musical Department, viz.:			
One large organ, ...	$5,000 00		
Four small organs, ...	450 00		
Forty-five pianos, ...	11,000 00		
Brass and reed instruments, . . .	700 00		
Violins, ...	35 00		
Musical library, ...	600 00		
		17,785 00	
Printing Department, viz.:			
Stock and machinery, ...	$2,000 00		
Books, ...	8,500 00		
Stereotype plates, ...	6,251 00		
		16,751 00	
School furniture and apparatus, . . .			7,600 00
Library of books in common type, .	$2,900 00		
" " raised type, . .	8,000 00		
		10,900 00	
Boys' shop, ...			83 00
Stable and tools, ...			688 50
			$681,038 36

The foregoing property represents the following funds and balances, and is answerable for the same.

General fund, investments, . . .	$108,485 00		
Cash, ...	2,011 02		
Harris fund, ...	80,000 00		
Printing, ...	113,325 00		
Kindergarten, investment, . . .	15,000 00		
" estate, . . .	30,877 18		
		$349,698 20	
Buildings, unimproved real estate and personal property in use for the school,			331,340 16
			$681,038 36

KINDERGARTEN FUND.

LIST OF CONTRIBUTORS.

Amount acknowledged in the last annual report, .	$25,231 63
An anonymous friend, ...	10,000 00
A friend, ...	1,000 00
The late John C. Phillips, ...	500 00
Mrs. J. R. Coolidge, ...	250 00
Mrs. D. D. Thorndike, ...	100 00
W. L., Boston, ...	100 00
Miss Madelaine C. Mixter, ...	100 00
Friend W., ...	100 00
Proceeds of Feb. 23d, including little blind girls' entertainments, ...	59 76
J. H. Center, ...	50 00
Dr. R. M. Hodges by S. N. Snelling, . . .	50 00
Mrs. Francis Brooks, ...	50 00
Thomas Gaffield, ...	50 00
Mrs. Frances M. Mackay, Cambridge, . . .	50 00
Unitarian Sunday School, Beverly, . . .	45 00
Proceeds of young ladies' entertainment at Nahant,	40 00
Additional proceeds from the blind girls' fair, .	26 10
George Sampson, ...	25 00
M. M. D., ...	25 00
G. H. Quincy, ...	25 00
Mrs. K. W. Sears, ...	25 00

Amount carried forward, ... $37,902 49

Amount brought forward, . . .	.$37,902 49
Mrs. Wm. Tappan, ...	25 00
Miss M. A. Tappan, ...	25 00
Miss Susan I. Linzee, ...	25 00
Mrs. Sarah Potter, Providence, ...	25 00
J. W. Linzee, ...	20 00
Miss Mary Parker, ...	20 00
Mrs. Hannah L. Pierce, ...	15 00
Miss E. W. Perkins, ...	13 00
Through Charlie E. Barry, ...	12 00
O. B. Frothingham, ...	10 00
A friend, ...	10 00
E. W. Clark, ...	10 00
R. Goodman, Lenox, ...	10 00
E Peaslee, Whitefield, ...	10 00
M. F. Perley, Enosburgh, Vt., . . .	10 00
Miss E. F. Faulkner, ...	10 00
Mrs. J. Sullivan Warren, ...	10 00
Dr. James J. Putnam, ...	10 00
Miss B. S. Wilder, ...	10 00
Miss E. Gertrude Decrow, ...	10 00
Mrs. V. A. Howe, proceeds of concert, . . .	9 50
Littleton Sunday School, ...	5 00
Miss S. G. Putnam, ...	5 00
J. Woodcock, Leicester.	5 00
Miss Mary P. Bacon, ...	5 00
Mrs. W. A Peabody, ...	5 00
Dr. Walter Channing, ...	5 00
A. Williams, Middleborough, England, . . .	5 00
Miss A. R. Palfrey, ...	5 00
Miss C. M. Harris, ...	5 00
C. Chenery, ...	5 00
Amount carried forward, . . .	.$38,251 99

Amount brought forward, ...	$38,251 99
A friend, ...	5 00
Sunday School First Unitarian Church, Plymouth, Mass., ...	5 25
A friend, ...	3 00
Congregational Church, Newport, N. H., . .	2 60
Children of private Kindergarten, ...	2 50
Miss Bessie Perkins, ...	2 00
Cash, ...	2 00
A reader of the "Golden Rule,"	2 00
Mrs. Jacob Smith, ...	2 00
Through Fannie Jackson, ...	1 40
Sympathizers, ...	1 00
A friend, ...	1 00
Kindergarten, B. C , ...	1 00
Miss Marcella Pendleton, ...	1 00
Proceeds of little blind girls' entertainment, . .	70
Millicent A. Hawsley, ...	50
Mrs. Sarah S. Russell, ...	1,000 00
Miss E. F. Mason, ...	500 00
Minnie T. Turner (deceased), ...	250 00
Proceeds of children's fair, Brookline, by Gertrude and Sarita Flint, Mary Crane and friends, . .	217 25
Sale of " Stardrift's Birthday Book," . . .	135 83
Proceeds of concert by the blind girls in New Haven, Conn., ...	113 00
Mrs. A. G. Farnam, New Haven, Conn., . .	100 00
First Unitarian Congregational Society, New Bedford, ...	100 00
Miss Lucy H. Symonds's Normal Class concert, .	82 75
Proceeds of concert in East Somerville, .. .	68 21
T. E. N., ...	50 00
Amount carried forward, . . .	$40,901 98

Amount brought forward, ...	.$40,901 98
F. W. Hunnewell, ...	50 00
Miss C. W. Lamson, Dedham, ...	50 00
Collected by a lady in Roxbury, ...	41 27
W. Montgomery, ...	25 00
William A. Rust, ...	20 00
Charles R. Noyes, Fort D. A. Russell, Cheyenne,	
Wy., ...	20 00
Ladies' "Frolic Club," Concord, Mass., . .	20 00
Children of Unitarian Sunday School, Dedham, .	18 00
St. Peter's Sunday School, Beverly, Mass., . .	15 00
A. and E., ...	10 00
M., Worcester, Mass., ...	10 00
Mrs. M. L. Hall, ...	10 00
Additional from Mrs. Wolcott's fair, . . .	10 00
C. T. R. and A. F. R., ...	6 00
Infant class, Congregational Church, West Gard-	
ner, Mass., ...	6 00
Miss A. M. Cudworth, East Boston, . . .	5 00
A lady in Cambridge, ...	5 00
Anonymous, ...	5 00
Mrs. Julius Eichberg, ...	5 00
Miss Ellen Guild, ...	3 56
Miss Mabel Norman, ...	3 56
Miss Susie Dalton, ...	3 56
Miss Bessie Seabury, ...	3 56
Miss Maggie Carr, ...	3 56
Miss Isabel Perkins, ...	3 56
Miss Bertha Bement, ...	3 56
Miss Ida Wilbor, ...	3 56
Miss Ethel Stockton, ...	3 56
Kindergarten at Concord, N. H., ...	3 00
Amount carried forward, . . .	.$41,268 29

Amount brought forward, . . .	.$41,268	29
J. W. French, ...	1	00
A friend, ...	1	00
Harvard Unitarian Sunday School, Charlestown,		
Easter offering, ...	439	03
Mrs. B. S. Rotch, ...	300	00
Mary E. Pierson, Windsor, ...	100	00
Miss L. E. Hall, ...	50	00
Mrs. B. L. Young, ...	50	00
Mrs. B. L. Young (income), ...	50	00
F. H. Peabody, ...	25	00
Young People's Mission Circle, Second Church,		
Dorchester, ...	25	00
Sunday School of Rev. Rufus Ellis's Church, .	22	03
Through "Aunt Patience" of the "Christian		
Union,"	20	20
Mrs. J. B. S. Jackson, ...	20	00
Miss A. P. Cary, ...	15	00
Miss Brackett's class of the First Church, . .	13	50
Miss Sallie Swan, Charlestown, ...	10	00
Mrs. E. P. Parker, ...	10	00
Miss A. P. Cary (annual), ...	10	00
Andrew H. Newell, ...	10	00
Charles H. Bond, ...	5	00
W. R. Greene, ...	5	00
Through Mrs. Howland, Providence, . . .	1	00
Frank Fuchs's "top,"		25
Francis Brooks, ...	1,000	00
Anonymous, ...	300	00
Mrs. Chickering's School, Dorchester, . . .	137	05
Children's fair in Swampscott, ...	100	65
J. T. Coolidge, ...	100	00
Amount carried forward, . . .	.$44,089	00

Amount brought forward, ...	.$44,089 00
Mrs. Prescott Bigelow, ...	100 00
Miss Abby W. May, ...	100 00
Mrs. D. S. Cass, ...	30 00
A friend, ...	25 00
Mrs. Sears, ...	25 00
Miss Wales (annual), ...	20 00
Girls in primary department of Perkins Institution,	12 71
Mrs. E. C. Drew, ...	10 00
Mrs. Robert Swan, ...	10 00
M. Brown, ...	10 00
Kindergarten children, Phenix, R. I., . . .	8 70
Children's entertainment in Swampscott, . .	7 35
Presbyterian Sunday School, Orwell, Penn., . .	5 11
Miss C. E. Jenks, ...	5 00
Unitarian Sunday School, Trenton, N. Y., . .	5 00
Children in Mrs. Bethmann's Kindergarten, . .	2 00
Seven little girl helpers, South Boston, . . .	1 25
Mrs. J. Russell Bradford, ...	1 00
Sale of Kindergarten work, ...	1 00
From the work of a C., ...	1 00

$44,469 12

We are also greatly indebted to Mrs. Delia D. Thorndike for an excellent set of parlor furniture for the kindergarten.

LIST OF EMBOSSED BOOKS,

printed at the Perkins Institution and Massachusetts School for the Blind.

TITLE OF BOOK.	No. of Volum·s.	Price per Set.
Book of Proverbs,	1	$2 00
Book of Psalms, .	1	3 00
New Testament, .	4	10 00
Book of Common Prayer,	1	4 00
Baxter's Call, .	1	2 50
Hymns for the Blind,	1	2 00
Pilgrim's Progress,	1	4 00
Natural Theology,	1	4 00
Life of Melanchthon, .	1	1 00
Selections from the Works of Swedenborg,	1	–
Biographical Sketches of Distinguished Persons,	1	3 00
Biographical Sketch of George Eliot, .	1	25
Memoir of Dr. Samuel G. Howe,	1	3 00
Howe's Cyclopædia,	8	32 00
Combe's Constitution of Man, .	1	4 00
Cutter's Anatomy, Physiology and Hygiene,	1	3 00
" Life and her Children," or a Reader of Natural History,	1	3 00
Philosophy of Natural History, .	1	3 00
Huxley's Science Primers, Introductory,	1	2 00
Anderson's History of the United States,	1	2 50
Higginson's Young Folks' History of the United States, .	1	3 50
Constitution of the United States,	1	40
Dickens's Child's History of England,	2	6 00
Freeman's History of Europe,	1	2 50
Schmitz's History of Greece,	1	3 00
Schmitz's History of Rome,	1	2 50
Guyot's Geography, .	1	4 00
Scribner's Geographical Reader, .	1	2 50
American Prose, .	2	6 00
An Account of the Most Celebrated Diamonds, .	1	50
Dickens's Christmas Carol, with extracts from Pickwick,	1	3 00
Dickens's Old Curiosity Shop,	3	12 00
Emerson's Essays,	1	3 00
Extracts from British and American Literature,	2	5 00
George Eliot's Silas Marner,	1	3 50
Goldsmith's Vicar of Wakefield, .	1	3 00
Hawthorne's Scarlet Letter,	2	5 00
Hawthorne's Tanglewood Tales,	2	4 00
Scott's Quentin Durward, .	2	6 00

LIST OF EMBOSSED BOOKS — *Continued.*

TITLE OF BOOK.	No. of Volumes.	Price per Set.
The Last Days of Pompeii, by Edward Bulwer Lytton,	3	$9 00
Bryant's Poems,	1	3 00
Byron's Hebrew Melodies and Childe Harold,	1	3 00
Poetry of Byron, selected by Matthew Arnold,	1	3 00
Holmes's Poems,	1	3 00
Longfellow's Evangeline,	1	2 00
Longfellow's Evangeline and other Poems,	1	3 00
Lowell's Poems,	1	3 00
Milton's Paradise Lost,	2	5 00
Pope's Essay on Man and other Poems,	1	2 50
Scott's Lay of the Last Minstrel and 37 other Poems,	1	3 00
Shakespeare's Hamlet and Julius Cæsar,	1	4 00
Shakespeare's King Henry Fifth,	1	2 00
Shakespeare's Romeo and Juliet,	1	2 00
Tennyson's In Memoriam and other Poems,	1	3 00
Whittier's Poems,	1	3 00
Key to Braille's Musical Notation,	1	35
Musical Characters used by the seeing.	1	35
Longfellow's Birthday, by J. R. Anagnos,	1	25
Commemoration Ode, by H. W. Stratton,	1	10

JUVENILE BOOKS.

TITLE OF BOOK.	No. of Volumes.	Price per Set.
Script and point alphabet sheets per hundred,	—	5 00
An Eclectic Primer,	1	40
Child's First Book,	1	40
Child's Second Book,	1	40
Child's Third Book,	1	40
Child's Fourth Book,	1	40
Child's Fifth Book,	1	40
Child's Sixth Book,	1	40
Child's Seventh Book,	1	40
Youth's Library, vol. 1st,	1	1 25
Youth's Library, vol. 2d,	1	1 25
Youth's Library, vol. 3d,	1	1 25
Youth's Library, vol. 4th,	1	1 25
Youth's Library, vol. 5th,	1	1 25
Youth's Library, vol. 6th,	1	1 25
Youth's Library, vol. 7th,	1	1 25
Youth's Library, vol. 8th,	1	1 25
Andersen's Stories and Tales,	1	3 00
Bible Stories in Bible Language, by Emilie Poulsson,	1	3 00
Children's Fairy Book, by M. Anagnos,	1	2 50
Eliot's Six Arabian Nights,	1	3 00
Heidi: translated from the German by Mrs. Brooks,	2	5 00
Kingsley's Greek Heroes,	1	2 50
Lodge's Twelve Popular Tales,	1	2 00
What Katy Did, by Susan Coolidge,	1	2 50

N. B. The prices in the above list are set down per SET, not per volume.

LIST OF APPLIANCES AND TANGIBLE APPARATUS,

made at the Perkins Institution and Massachusetts School for the Blind.

GEOGRAPHY.

I. — *Wall-Maps.*

1. The Hemispheres, ... size, 42 by 52 inches.
2. United States, Mexico and Canada, " " "
3. North America, ... " " "
4. South America, ... " " "
5. Europe, ... " " "
6. Asia, ... " " "
7. Africa, ... " " "
8. The World on Mercator's Projection, " " "

Each $35, or the set, $280.

II. — *Dissected Maps.*

1. Eastern Hemisphere, . . . size, 30 by 36 inches.
2. Western Hemisphere, . . . " " "
3. North America, ... " " "
4. United States, ... " " "
5. South America, ... " " "
6. Europe, ... " " "
7. Asia, ... " " "
8. Africa, ... " " "

Each $23, or the set, $184.

These maps are considered, in point of workmanship, accuracy and distinctness of outline, durability and beauty, far superior to all thus far made in Europe or in this country.

" The New England Journal of Education " says, " They are very strong, present a fine, bright surface, and are an ornament to any school-room.

III. — *Pin-Maps.*

Cushions for pin-maps and diagrams, . . . each, $0 75

ARITHMETIC.

Ciphering-boards made of brass strips, nickel-plated, ... each, $4 25

Ciphering-types, nickel-plated, per hundred, . " 1 00

WRITING.

Grooved writing-cards, ... each, $0 05

Braille tablets, with metallic bed, . . . " 1 50

Braille French tablets, with cloth bed, . . . ·· 1 00

Braille new tablets, with cloth bed, . . . ·· 1 00

Braille Daisy tablets, ... ·· 5 00

TERMS OF ADMISSION.

"Candidates for admission must be over nine and under nineteen years of age, and none others shall be admitted." — *Extract from the by-laws.*

Blind children and youth between the ages above prescribed and of sound mind and good moral character, can be admitted to the school by paying $300 per annum. Those among them who belong to the state of Massachusetts and whose parents or guardians are not able to pay the whole or a portion of this sum, can be admitted gratuitously by application to the governor for a warrant.

The following is a good form, though any other will do : —

" *To His Excellency the Governor.*

" SIR, — My son (or daughter, or nephew, or niece, as the case may be), named —, and aged —, cannot be instructed in the common schools, for want of sight. I am unable to pay for the tuition at the Perkins Institution and Massachusetts School for the Blind, and I request that your Excellency will give a warrant for free admission.
Very respectfully,   —— ——."

The application may be made by any relation or friend, if the parents are dead or absent.

It should be accompanied by a certificate, signed by some regular physician, in this form : —

" I certify that, in my opinion, —— —— has not sufficient vision to be taught in common schools ; and that he is free from epilepsy, and from any contagious disease.
(Signed)   —— ——."

These papers should be done up together, and forwarded to the DIRECTOR OF THE INSTITUTION FOR THE BLIND, *South Boston, Mass.*

Blind children and youth residing in Maine, New Hampshire, Vermont, Connecticut and Rhode Island, by applying as above to the governor, or the " Secretary of State," in their respective states, can obtain warrants for free admission.

The sum of $300 above specified covers all expenses (except for clothing), namely, board, lodging, washing, tuition, and the use of books and musical instruments. The pupils must furnish their own clothing, and pay their own fares to and from the institution.

An obligation will be required from some responsible persons, that the pupil shall be kept properly supplied with decent clothing, shall be provided for during vacations, and shall be removed, without expense to the institution, whenever it may be desirable to discharge him.

The usual period of tuition is from five to seven years.

The friends of the pupils can visit them whenever they choose.

The use of tobacco, either in smoking or otherwise, is strictly prohibited in the institution.

Persons applying for admission of children must fill out certain blanks, copies of which will be forwarded to any address on application.

For further information address M. ANAGNOS, DIRECTOR, PERKINS INSTITUTION FOR THE BLIND, *South Boston, Mass.*

APPENDIX.

PROCEEDINGS

OF THE

COMMENCEMENT EXERCISES

OF THE

Perkins Institution and Massachusetts School for the Blind.

COMMENCEMENT EXERCISES

OF THE

PERKINS INSTITUTION AND MASSACHUSETTS SCHOOL FOR THE BLIND.

The commencement exercises illustrate so well the educational methods and resources of the school, and have won for it so many valued friends, that the event deserves a full account among the records of the year. The generous comments of the press have been freely used in making up this report.

The following circular, containing the programme of exercises to be given, was sent to the friends and benefactors of the school, and was widely and kindly noticed in all the newspapers of this and neighboring cities: —

PERKINS INSTITUTION AND MASS. SCHOOL FOR THE BLIND,
BOSTON, May 11, 1885.

The commencement exercises of this school will be held at Tremont Temple on Tuesday, June 2, at 3 P. M. Samuel Eliot, LL.D., will preside; His Excellency, Governor Robinson, will give a brief opening address, and the Rev. Edward A. Horton will speak on the kindergarten project.

You are most cordially invited to honor the occasion with your presence.

The seats on the floor and in the first balcony of the Temple will be reserved for the choice of the members of the corporation, and the friends and patrons of the institution, to whom this invitation is sent, until Saturday, May 23. Tickets are ready for delivery, and those who may be desirous of obtaining them are requested to send me a postal card indicating the number wished for. It will give me very great pleasure to forward them at once.

The seats will be reserved until 3 o'clock, punctually, when standing persons will be permitted to occupy all vacant places.

No tickets are required for the second balcony of the Temple, to which the public are cordially invited.

M. ANAGNOS.

The first steps for the establishment of a kindergarten, which is imperatively needed for little sightless children, and without which the system of the education of the blind cannot be regarded as complete, have already been taken. A suitable estate has recently been secured in Roxbury, corner of Day and Perkins streets, and preparations are being made for the opening of the infant institution next autumn.

The purchase of the land and the absolutely necessary expenses for rendering the premises habitable and adapting them to the elementary wants of the kindergarten will, however, deplete the treasury of its contents entirely, and there will not be one cent left for carrying on the work. To this important fact the attention of the benevolent and philanthropic members of our community is most respectfully called. They should bear it in mind, that upon their kind consideration and generous aid the support, progress, and success of the enterprise are wholly dependent.

Both annual subscriptions for current expenses, and contributions for an endowment fund large enough to place the establishment on a permanent basis, are earnestly solicited, and will be thankfully received and duly acknowledged by

EDWARD JACKSON, *Treasurer*,

No. 178 Devonshire Street, Boston, Mass.

PROGRAMME. PART I.

1. ORGAN. Great G Minor Fugue, ... *Bach.*
   MISS FREDA BLACK.

2. BRIEF OPENING ADDRESS.
   HIS EXCELLENCY GOVERNOR ROBINSON.

3. BAND. Salutation March, ... *Wiegand.*

4. ESSAY. "Study of the Voice."
   MISS MARY E. SANFORD.

5. SOLO FOR ALTO HORN. Air and Variations, . *J. Painpare.*
   CHRISTOPHER A. HOWLAND.

6. TOPICS IN ELECTRICITY.
   WILLIAM B. PERRY.

7. READING BY THE TOUCH.
   BY FIVE LITTLE GIRLS.

8. DUET. "Quis est Homo," . . . . . . *Rossini.*
   MISSES M. E. WHEELER and C. C. ROESKE.

PART II.

1. GYMNASTICS, Military Drill and Calisthenics.

2. SOLO FOR CORNET. "Alexis Grand Fantasia," . *Hartmann.*
   CHAS. H. PRESCOTT.

3. EXERCISE IN GEOGRAPHY.
    By Four Little Boys.

4. THE KINDERGARTEN AND ITS FRUITS.
    Remarks on the Kindergarten, by Rev. E. A. Horton.

5. DUET. "The Army and Navy," . . . . . *T. Cooke.*
    Messrs. L. Titus and Wm. B. Hammond.

6. VALEDICTORY.
    Miss Susanna E. Sheahan.

7. CHORUS for Female Voices. "Down in the Dewy Dell," *Smart.*

8. AWARD OF DIPLOMAS.
    By Dr. Samuel Eliot.

9. CHORUS. "A Spring Song," . . . . . *C. Pinsuti.*

NAMES OF GRADUATES.

Cornelia C. Roeske.	Mary E. Sanford.
Susanna E. Sheahan.	Mary E. Wheeler.

Early applications for seats were presented in such numbers that nearly all were engaged before the tickets were issued, and thousands of later applicants were necessarily disappointed. So urgent were the demands, however, in some instances, that a limited number of admission tickets were issued, giving standing room to those who were willing to wait for possible vacancies among the reserved seats.

The programme as given was fully carried out, surpassing in interest as well as in execution all

that have gone before. The large auditorium of
Tremont Temple was filled to its utmost capacity
with an assembly representing the most intelligent
and influential people of Boston and the state,
"who manifested the most lively and sympathetic
interest in the remarkably successful efforts of the
pupils." The seats on the platform were nearly
filled by the scholars, the remainder being occupied
by the officers and trustees of the school, and
other friends prominent in educational and literary
circles. Among the former sat Laura Bridgman,
the world-renowned pupil of Dr. Howe, who, by
her evident interest in the festival as revealed by
her expressive face and busy fingers, attracted
much attention.

The exercises opened promptly at 3 o'clock by
a "well-executed rendering" on the organ of
Bach's "Great G Minor Fugue," by Miss Freda
Black. Dr. Samuel Eliot presided "with dignity,
ease, and with that brevity which is the soul of
wit." He came forward and said, —

"The officers and pupils of the Perkins Institution bid a
hearty welcome to their friends here assembled. We are all
aware that the connection between this school and the commonwealth has been of the closest and most important kind.
The official head of this school is in reality the Governor of the
commonwealth, and he has consented to make the opening
address. It is unnecessary for me to present him to this
audience."

OPENING ADDRESS,

By IIis Excellency Governor George D. Robinson.

Ladies and Gentlemen: — The connection, as Dr. Eliot has well said, between this school and the commonwealth is intimate. But it is because the association of the state with all educational enterprises is close. At the foundation of all our institutions lies the recognition of the fact that in the abundant and liberal education of all the people stand security and welfare. Therefore, the state has always taken it upon herself to exercise authority so far as to say to parents, "These are your children, it is true; they are members of your family, but they also are to be future inhabitants, it may be, of this commonwealth; therefore, we shall demand, in order that our state in the future may, indeed, be a commonwealth, that the children growing up to be men and women shall have an education which will fit them for the responsibilities and duties of their after life." Upon that broad principle our common school system rests; and it is placed so firmly there, so strongly sustained by reason and common sense, so abundantly guaranteed in every person's consciousness of what is right and safe, that the time is never to come in Massachusetts when it can be destroyed. [Applause.] Now, akin to that is the movement which is to have its illustration here this afternoon. If one child is to receive the benefits of public instruction, all children should have an equal opportunity. We take our information in different ways. Certain avenues of communication are open to us. They are different in degree in different persons. One person sees better than another, though each may see; another hears better than his neighbor; another's sense of touch is more delicate and apprehensive; and so on, without further illustration. Hence we seek development in different directions. One person becomes a successful musician; another one has a trained eye, with all the accomplishments that follow thereafter; and Providence, we all recognize, in some way or other, makes up in compensation ofttimes to those who may seem to lack what we prize most dearly. How often have we been touched in our tenderest sympathy, and how much we have been thrilled with joyous satisfaction to find some one that we looked upon as unfortunate come forth and stand out as a leader beyond those who seemed more blessed. [Renewed applause.]

Ladies and gentlemen, there is an adjective in the title line of the programme that introduces me, and that adjective is — "Brief opening address." [Laughter.] I have, I think, entirely fulfilled that demand. [Renewed laughter.] You came not to hear me, but others that will be far more interesting. I will add only a few words. This, you know, is the season of school life, and of the harvesting of the results of instruction. It is the season of the year, let me assure you, that keeps the Governor of the commonwealth busy (a laugh and applause), as all seasons, indeed, do, with the numerous institutions that are constantly calling for his attention. Undoubtedly in this great audience are the immediate friends of the children who sit before you. Congratulations are due to them for the abundant opportunities that are afforded for the instruction of these children. Of all the pleasant things that we meet from day to day, seldom anything appeals more strongly to me than the gathering of the older persons to witness the triumphs of the young. In this state, it is an exhibition that is witnessed on every hand. And now, while, as far as I have the right, I give you a cordial welcome, I want — and I will do it — to extend to these children my most hearty greeting. I am glad to know that they are present. I am glad to assure them that there are hundreds upon hundreds of people that not only are satisfied with seeing them, but are to be delighted with hearing them. [Applause.] I give them this testimony out of my own experience. A short time ago, on a pleasant afternoon, we all became acquainted with each other, and we will remain acquaintances as long as life lasts. I and these children stand very close together. Massachusetts gives $30,000 every year toward this institution, to assist in carrying on the enterprise. This money is well invested, and it is very properly expended. Do not think, — and correct the error if you have fallen into it, — that these children are a public charge. They are so no more than are your children or mine, now being educated in the common schools to be found in the cities and towns of the state. The state, as I said, attempts to provide education for all children; she goes further, and requires their attendance at school; she goes still another step, and says to those who are unable to take instructions in the ordinary methods in the schools: "We will not leave you in ignorance, or cast you aside as helpless, but we will make our circle broader, our institutions greater, our opportunities more numerous, so that you shall come in and study and sing, write and work, that men and women shall not know that you have not all the accomplishments which others possess." [Applause.] I thank you for your attention, I congratulate you on what is to come, and will not longer detain you from it. [Loud applause.]

Governor Robinson's address was listened to with closest attention and frequently applauded. It was spoken of by the press as a "brief but glowing speech," "thoughtful and well considered," and "very appropriate and appreciative"; and among his auditors none enjoyed it more than the members of the school, who remembered with grateful pleasure his recent visit and cheering words. At the close of his address the band played Wiegand's "Salutation March," and its "brilliant harmonics" filled the great hall.

Then followed an essay on the "Study of the
Voice" by Miss Mary E. Sanford, one of the graduates, — a young lady of color, — delivered "with
such distinctness as to be in itself an illustration
of the principles it advocated," and "in tones
which wonderfully illustrate the benefits of such
study."

STUDY OF THE VOICE.

BY MISS MARY E. SANFORD.

Singing is an art, and to be studied as such should be divided
into two distinct branches,—the technical and æsthetic. A
thorough knowledge of the technical branch is indispensable
to the student who would have an adequate understanding of
the anatomy and physiology of the most delicate and the most
perfect of all musical instruments.

A powerful voice, intellectual ability and a thorough knowledge of music, though desirable, are of themselves insufficient
to perfect a singer.

No one can hope to become a finished artist should the technical branch of study be neglected, or the æsthetic, which
treats of the beautiful in art, prematurely introduced.

To acquire a complete control over the voice in singing is a
task far more arduous and unremitting than the mastery of any
musical instrument whatever. Manufactured instruments, being
tangible and visible, appeal to the senses of touch and sight,
thus aiding the student while practising; whereas the vocal
organs are intangible and invisible, and the changes which
they undergo when engaged in the production of musical sound
can be determined only by an inner consciousness on the part
of the singer combined with concentration and determination
of mind and will. To these, the only safe guides in the pro-

duction of correct musical sounds, the careful attention of every student should be especially directed.

The four essential attributes of musical sound are pitch, timbre or quality, volume and duration. The power of the voice over these attributes varies in individuals, because of the shape, size, strength and the capacity for contraction and expansion of the organs constituting the vocal mechanism, which are the lungs, the muscles of respiration, chest, trachea, bronchi, the larynx, the pharynx, and the various organs of the mouth.

The subject which should precede all others in singing is that of respiration, or the method of breathing artistically. Until the functions of the diaphragm and other respiratory muscles are understood and their mastery acquired, true progress in singing is hopeless and a perfect development of the vocal powers impossible.

There are two grand divisions of the human voice, male and female. Each division consists of three sub-divisions or classes, those of the first being the bass, baritone and tenor; of the second, the contralto, mezzo-soprano and soprano. Each class is characterized by certain qualities peculiar to itself. The range of tones capable of being produced by a voice constitutes what is commonly called compass.

In classifying untutored voices great care should be exercised in ascertaining and analyzing the natural capabilities of each, that the voice be not forced or its development impaired.

The qualities which characterize a healthy voice are clearness, mellowness, resonance, while those characterizing an unhealthy voice are the nasal, guttural and muffled qualities.

Most persons are by nature enabled to exercise a partial control over the voice in singing; and because of this many, far too many, ignore the importance of vocal culture. While the voice is ours to do with as we will, it is, like all our powers, God-given; it is a member of the house in which we live, and should be trained with due care.

To the student striving to overcome obstacles in the pathway leading up to the heights of knowledge, whether in singing or any other art, we would say,—

> " Patiently labor thou, with firm endeavor,
> Ardently hoping on, lingering never,
> So shall thy toil bring unfailing reward."

A solo for alto horn with " Air and Variations," by J. Painparc, was then performed by Christopher A. Howland, and as its " clear notes " ceased, William B. Perry came forward, and in a brief essay presented a few " Topics in Electricity," giving a concise summary of the history of that science and illustrating his subject by experiments.

TOPICS IN ELECTRICITY.

BY WILLIAM B. PERRY.

As remote as the sixth century B. C. it was known to the ancients, that amber when rubbed with silk possessed the property of first attracting and then repelling light bodies. From the Greek word electron, the name of amber, is derived the term electricity. Pliny, soon after the beginning of the Christian era, writes of the attraction of the fingers, when briskly rubbed, for bits of straw and wood, and compares it to that of the Lydian or loadstone for iron. This, until the sixteenth century, seems to have been the extent of electrical knowledge. The theories advanced to explain the phenomena were very primitive; it was supposed by some to be a living soul that became manifest by friction. During the reign of Elizabeth, Dr. Gilbert established a number of well known principles. From this simplest beginning has grown our present knowledge, aided by such men as Franklin, Galvani, Volta and others, through whose efforts it has been converted into a mighty agent accomplishing, as it seems, almost miraculous results.

By its application to telegraphy thousands of miles have been spanned in as many seconds. By its aid we are enabled to converse with friends leagues distant as though at hand.

The electric light with its brilliant illuminating power, the microphone by which the tread of a fly becomes distinctly audible, the adoption as a motive force in the electric engine, and many other inventions all give ample proof of its incalculable worth and utility.

Electricity manifests itself in two ways—as a charge or current. The simplest manner of generating a charge is by friction. For this purpose a machine similar to this one, is used. It consists of a glass plate mounted on an axis; on each side is a rubber of chamois and an amalgam, pressed against it by a spring attached to a connecting wire or chain; opposite the rubber are a number of points connected with a metal rod terminating in a knob. The silk is to prevent the electricity from passing into the air. By turning the plate it becomes positively electrified and the rubbers negatively. From the latter the charge passes off through the conducting wire; that upon the glass acting on the metal points produces a charge in the prime conductor. If now an insulated conductor be held near the knob, it can receive a charge only equal to that of the machine; should a second conductor be separated from the first by a non-conductor, a considerable quantity can be condensed. The ordinary condenser is known as the Leyden jar. It consists of a metal cup separated from a second cup by a non-conductor, usually of glass. Holding the ball connected with the inner cup near the prime conductor of the machine, the positive electricity is repelled, giving a negative charge which neutralizes with the positive from the machine, the remaining cup positively electrified; this causes the glass to polarize and repel the positive of the outer cup which is conducted off into the earth. This operation is repeated until the jar is completely charged, when it is said to be saturated. It can then be discharged instantaneously by connecting the two cups, or by degrees, first touching the inner and then the outer cup.

The action of the electric current is well shown in the microphone. A pencil of carbon is held in loose contact between supports of the same material, that are attached to a surface sensitive to vibrations; the pencil and supports lying in the circuit of a battery and receiver; if the surface be set in vibration the pencil is disturbed and causes a change of resistance to the current, which is recorded as magnified sound at the receiver. The microphone is not very practical, but serves to illustrate one of the many applications of the electric current.

At the conclusion of the essay five little girls read "by the touch" some verses in dialogue form, and though the "piece was comparatively new to them, yet the lines were read as easily and quickly as though the pupils had been endowed with sight." Mr. Anagnos here explained that the pupils could read unfamiliar pages, even proof-sheets fresh from the press.

Miss M. E. Wheeler and Miss C. C. Roeske, two of the graduates, then sang the duet, " *Quis est Homo* " from Rossini's " Stabat Mater," which was admirably rendered and "gave evidence of musical culture."

The second part of the programme opened by the entrance upon the platform of twelve little boys in blouse suits, who performed various exercises in gymnastics with ease and precision, and as they withdrew, twelve little girls appeared, dressed

in loose, graceful frocks of creamy white, and
executed quite charmingly a series of calisthenic
movements to the music of the piano. They were
succeeded upon the stage by twelve young men,
who went through a musket drill' with and without
word of command, which "was characterized by
almost perfect military precision," and "the unity
with which the orders were carried out seemed
remarkable." "The calisthenic and military drill
was something wonderful when we remembered
that this absolute precision and freedom of movement was secured without the aid of the eye."

After a solo on the cornet, Hartmann's "Alexis
Grand Fantasia," finely performed by Charles H.
Prescott, four little boys "responded in a remarkable way to the demands made upon them in an
exercise in geography;" and the "whole of the
performance showed remarkable aptitude for both
intellectual and physical exercises, and each display of the pupils' skill evoked the warmest
applause."

The "kindergarten and its fruits" was made
the text for a "brief but very pertinent and
cogent and altogether admirable address" by the
Rev. E. A. Horton, which was also pronounced an
"eloquent appeal for the new kindergarten enterprise, presenting its demands in a manner that
was inspirational."

THE KINDERGARTEN AND ITS FRUITS.

ADDRESS BY REV. EDWARD A. HORTON.

I am glad to see the fulfilment of the wish of him who strove so hard to establish this institution. The spirit of Dr. Howe may be with us, recognizing the present guiding spirit, and blessing the efforts to carry his work on to greater triumphs through the kindergarten for the blind. It seems rather out of place for a seeing person, especially an adult, to take part in these exercises, but underneath the general surprise at the excellence of the exhibition there is a knowledge of the priceless value of this institution which I wish to speak about. There may be exhibitions in this city which are more dramatic, that will bring the tears to the eyes more readily than this: if there is I do not know what it is. I only wish that my child, endowed, as far as I know, with all her faculties, could do as much and do it as well as some who have displayed their abilities here to-day. The kindergarten, as you all know, is an aid even to those who have all their senses, and is a prerequisite for the best use of the talents. To every child the eyes are the gateway through which he receives a multitude of impressions. Unconsciously he learns a thousand things concerning what is going on around him. But a blind child is like an unfurnished room; there is nothing for him to learn by observation, and every impression must enter his mind by some other channel: there are few pictures within; few oases in the desert. The kindergarten steps in and gives to the blind child the raw materials from which he can fashion ideas and characteristics. The sightless child may claim, and with justice, too, that he is freed from the moral obligations which are expected from others, for his mind, uninstructed and neglected, is full of ungoverned impressions and is like an army or a mob, without leaders. The kindergarten steps in and marshals all his sentiments and impulses into proper moral shapes. Again, ordinary children can run and play without fear of bodily danger, thus preserving their health and strength. For the blind child there is only the folded hands which brings him into a morbid state, from which it is hard to rouse him in the future. Experiments with the blind have shown that through the delicacy of touch the highest results in science and thought can be reached, and the kindergarten early in life trains this sense of feeling. A child doomed to blindness for life is apt to be devoid of hope, and without any stimulus the mind becomes sodden, like bread without yeast. The kindergarten gives exercise to the hand and brain, and thus, through occupation, it diverts the mind from one's self. It clears the clouds of sadness away, and lets in the sunshine. This is no sentimental idea; it is practical, for the kindergarten utilizes the child's love of play, which is perfectly natural, and takes away the gloom that inevitably settles over unoccupied hours. It also brings the child, early in life, into contact with men and women, and his love for those who have instructed him is developed into a desire to teach others later on. This instruction leads to the acquiring of a means of support, and when it is remembered that one person out of every thousand is blind and likely to be an expense to the community, it will be seen that it is a matter of political economy to educate the blind to a self-supporting condition early in life. The funds of this institution are getting low, and if the people of Boston do not go a little farther and give a little more money, it will be a cause of regret to them for several reasons. The little ones cannot be properly cared for; they will grow up in ignorance, and become helpless dependents, instead of self-respecting members of the community. If they are placed in the advanced classes of the institution it is not only an injury to themselves but to the others. They must have their own school. We do not want to have this school, which is second to none in the world, run behindhand; it should be carried forward to its last stage.

Shall Massachusetts be behind Saxony? Shall not the creative influence of Froebel give light to the blind, revealing a new heaven and a new earth? May this institution, through you and its other friends, obtain its wished for kindergarten.

While this appeal was being presented it was supplemented and enforced by some twelve young pupils, six boys and as many girls, who illustrated in the presence of the audience some of the fruits of their own kindergarten training. From the class in physiology one made the model of a heart; another, the human spinal column. A boy from the class in zoölogy moulded the form of a large turtle with its articulations; another, polyps at work on a coral reef. Pupils from the botany class made the stem, root and leaf of a plant, describing the changes which the leaf undergoes. Little fellows who had studied geography modelled in clay from memory very good representations of the valley of the Nile, and North America with its capes and crannies; and a very little girl exhibited a book as her work and named it "Heidi" in honor of her favorite story book. Thus they gave " very effective illustrations of their object lessons, demonstrating better than any formal address the possibility and propriety of such a preliminary school" as the necessities of the young blind demand. Mr. Anagnos here added a few words emphasizing the importance of this method of training, showing its value in the progressive

studies of the school, and exhibiting as proof
some beautiful specimens of handiwork made by
the young girls, to be sent to an international exhibition in Holland, held in connection with the
fifth European congress of the educators of the
blind.

Messrs. L. Titus and William B. Hammond then
gave a duet, "The Army and Navy," which was
sung in a very spirited manner.

The valedictory followed, given by Miss S. E.
Sheahan, which was delivered in a clear, expressive voice, and "gave evidence of intellectual
ability."

VALEDICTORY.

BY MISS SUSANNA E. SHEAHAN.

Before saying a final "Good-bye" to our school days, we
linger for a moment to consider what education really is, and
how far it prepares us for the active duties of life.

Living as we do in an age when education is universal and
in a country where institutions of learning rise on every side,
and hundreds of young men and young women receive diplomas
every year, it is necessary that we should understand the meaning and object of education in its grandest and broadest sense.
For it is only when we appreciate the fact that education is
something more than the completion of a certain course of
study, something higher and nobler than mere intellectuality,
that we are qualified to take our stand among the useful and
happy members of society.

Intellect, culture, knowledge and opportunities are but step-
ping stones to the grand object of education, which is character. It is character that leads us out of ourselves to the great

■■■■■■■■■■■■■■■■■■■■■■■■■■

world beyond ; it is character that makes a man forget himself
and his own sorrows in alleviating the afflictions of others, and
enables him to enjoy the greatest happiness when doing the
greatest good to humanity.

Talent may win admiration, intellect dazzle, knowledge
attract attention ; but it is only the careful and conscientious
study that brings with it self-denial, perseverance, quickness
in thought and action, earnestness in performance, that can
teach us how to live.

To educate is to unfold the whole nature of man, to lift him
up to all that is highest and best ; and this is the work of a
lifetime.

The success of the past and the future is not to be estimated
by the height that is reached, but by the obstacles that have
been overcome. That only is education which teaches us to
use faithfully the talents that have been entrusted to our keeping ; — to advance day by day in knowledge and strength,
year by year in wisdom and perfection, until we are worthy to
receive the reward, " Well done, good and faithful servant."

To his Excellency the Governor and the legislature of Massachusetts, and to the corresponding representatives of the
several New England states, we return our thanks for their
generous support of our school.

To our trustees we are deeply grateful for their constant interest in all that concerns our welfare.

Director, teachers and matrons, words are weak to-day to
express the gratitude we feel, and we rejoice in the thought
that it is in our power to prove ourselves worthy in the future
of all that has been done for us in the past.

Schoolmates, though the long happy years that we have
spent together are now ended, yet our love for our school and
our interest in that beautiful garden so soon to be prepared for
the little ones will ever serve to keep us firmly united.

Classmates, our school work is over, and duty calls us to a

new field of action. Bravely, hopefully, let us obey her voice and —

> " Through weal or woe
> Where'er we go,
> Be this our high endeavor, —
> Some good to do,
> Some service true,
> That shall endure forever."

The chorus for female voices, "Down in the Dewy Dell," was rendered with fine effect, after which the four graduates received their diplomas from the hands of Dr. Eliot, who presented them in a very touching and impressive speech, and dwelt upon the blessing which "comes from an effort to live up to our ideals," closing with the beautiful benediction, "through your lives may new streams of holiness come into the world."

The exercises closed with Pinsuti's "Spring Song," given by a full chorus of pupils, and the whole entertainment occupied but two hours and a half. It was pronounced "one of the most satisfactory that has ever been given by the institution, and reflected the highest credit on its methods of instruction."

Comments of the Press.

The proceedings of the festival were fully reported and most favorably commented upon both
by the secular and religious press, and the attention of the public was earnestly called to the work
of the institution and its present wants and future
needs. Of the numerous articles, which appeared
in the editorial columns of leading newspapers on
the occasion of our commencement exercises, we
copy the following: —

The commencement exercises of the Perkins Institution
for the Blind, held yesterday at Tremont Temple, bring again
to notice the high rank which has been attained in Massachusetts through the agency of this institution in the care and
instruction of the sightless. The enthusiastic remarks of the
governor were quite aside from the perfunctory address common on such occasions. The notable feature of the day was,
however, the attention which was paid, both in the exhibition
and in the addresses, to the new movement to provide kindergarten instruction for the blind. Already results have been
achieved, and were exhibited yesterday, which illustrate the
peculiar fitness of the inductive method for the teaching of
blind children. The training of sense perceptions should

proceed even more expeditiously, relatively speaking, with this class, so peculiarly sensitive, than with children at large. It is not, therefore, impossible that the work now being done, and to be undertaken when the new kindergarten for the blind shall be established in Roxbury, may not only render these people useful and self dependent, but may contribute important suggestions to the growing science of sense training. — *Boston Daily Advertiser*, June 3.

Among the most interesting of the educational anniversaries that are held in this State are the commencement exercises of the Perkins Institute and Massachusetts School for the Blind; and those held at Tremont Temple last Tuesday afternoon surpassed in some respects any former commencement of this school, showing the constant advance that is being made in proficiency under the faithful superintendence of Mr. Anagnos. The Temple was crowded with an audience who manifested the most lively and sympathetic interest in the remarkably successful efforts of the pupils. The music by the band, the vocal and instrumental solos and duets, the essays, the reading by touch, the gymnastics, military drill and calisthenics, the exercises in geography, were all such as to reflect the highest credit upon the school and the pupils; and not the least interesting and important were the kindergarten illustrations by several of the younger pupils, in connection with which Rev. E. A. Horton made an eloquent appeal for the new kindergarten enterprise, presenting its demands in a manner that was inspirational. A brief and very appropriate opening address was made by Gov. Robinson. Dr. Samuel Eliot presided and presented diplomas to four graduates.—*Boston Home Journal*, June 6.

THE KINDERGARTEN FOR THE BLIND.

The commencement exercises of the Perkins Institution for the Blind touch a tender chord in the life of the Boston public, and are always awaited with eagerness, but it is more and more evident that the Perkins Institution is like what Harvard University would be if it had no preparatory schools. The blind children from 4 to 9 years of age are exempt from the common education of other youth of their own age; they are alone in homes which are often comfortless; they are without occupation and have nothing to aid them in receiving impressions from the outside world; and, without some preparatory school, there are comparatively few who will receive proper training when their minds crave most eagerly something to work upon. The result is that the South Boston institution is sadly crippled for want of a preparatory school, a kindergarten, where the pupils may be assisted by themselves in acquiring those elementary ideas which other children obtain through their play and their use of the eye in observation. The more people give their attention to this matter, the more important does a kindergarten institution become as a preparatory school for the blind. It is announced that so much interest is felt in this work that the trustees of the Perkins Institution have already secured a suitable estate in Roxbury for the beginning of the school, and that it will probably be opened in the autumn. This is good news, and the work here required is so much larger than that which is done at South Boston, and is yet so intimately connected with it as preparatory to it, that those who feel an interest in the older institution are almost sure to be the helpers in the new undertaking. It is a very interesting field that the kindergarten opens out to the blind children, and it is also strictly in the line of their proper education. No one who witnessed yesterday the work of the little kindergartners at Tremont Temple could fail to see what delight the children have in manipulating clay, and this was but a specimen-brick, so to speak, of the kind of instruction which the kindergarten system offers to these unfortunate children. Mr. Anagnos has not only succeeded to Dr. Howe's great ability as the head of the Perkins Institution, but, in pushing forward the kindergarten scheme to a point where it is possible to make a suitable beginning, has more than justified the hopes of those who made him Dr. Howe's successor. The good work now almost begun will not be allowed to stop. When Boston takes hold of a great charity, it never withdraws its hand, and in creating and endowing a kindergarten for the blind it supplements an enterprise that has carried the praise of our city to the ends of the earth—*Boston Herald*, June 3.

EDUCATION FOR THE BLIND.

The commencement exercises of the Perkins Institution and Massachusetts School for the Blind, held in Tremont Temple on Tuesday afternoon (June 2), more than justified the increasing, deepening interest and sympathy with which the annual return of this occasion is looked forward to by thousands of our citizens, especially by those who not only have a tender feeling for those deprived of the advantages which all seeing persons share in the struggle for life and happiness and usefulness, but who, in a patriotic spirit, believe in the equal right of sightless children to all the education which the state, for its own preservation, feels itself bound to provide for all its future fathers, mothers, citizens, and helpers.

This admirable school has proved, and is more and more signally proving, year by year, what solid, beautiful results can be accomplished in this field, which once appeared so hopeless. The great work begun fifty-three years ago by Dr. Howe goes on with what seems an ever self-renewing energy and ever fresh surprises of improvement, under the whole-souled devotion, watchful care and wisdom, and one is tempted to say philanthropic *genius* even, of his successor, Mr. Anagnos. This week's exhibition of the educational methods and resources and astonishing results surpassed all that have gone before. The lesson, of course, was carried home to the hearts of the audience chiefly by the pupils themselves, through the happy and intelligent aspect which they all presented, the look of love and innocence and joy, and of fond reverence for their teachers; through their aptness at reading with their fingers; their well-considered, well-expressed answers to questions in geography and literature and science; their excellent, short original addresses; their music of band, choruses and solo singing, true in intonation, refined and spirited in style and expression; the military drill of the older boys, remarkable for the precision of every movement, and the gymnastic and calisthenic exercises of the younger girls and boys, which had an æsthetic quality of culture besides the mere athletic.

Most interesting of all, very naturally, were the instances of kindergarten training, in which children below the age of nine modelled curious things from clay before the eyes of the audience, showing how work and play (and even art) may be and should be made *one* in the earliest years of education.

While this was going on, a brief but very pertinent and cogent and altogether admirable address was made by the Rev. E. A. Horton, showing how indispensable, as preparation for the more advanced schooling of the blind, is the separate kindergarten to keep their young hope and faculties alive and active, and save their tender minds and bodies from becoming "sodden." The director supplemented these remarks by holding some of the products which the young fingers had twined or moulded in the school, and with the cheering announcement that a fine estate of over six acres has at last been purchased by the trustees for a kindergarten, of which a beginning will, it is hoped, be made next fall. The purchase and first outlay will exhaust the funds so far contributed;

and the friends of the blind, no doubt, will see to it that the enterprise shall not languish for lack of further means.

. The opening words of the president of the corporation, Samuel Eliot, LL.D., and the brief but glowing speech of Gov. Robinson, fully indorsing the duty of the commonwealth to its blind as well as to its seeing children, made a deep impression. Still more so the touching, simple eloquence and fervor with which President Eliot addressed the four girl graduates (Misses Cornelia C. Roeske, Susanna E. Sheahan, Mary E. Sanford, and Mary E. Wheeler), on presenting them with their diplomas, to bear witness to the world that they go forth qualified to be self-supporting, useful members of society, educated both intellectually and morally above the need of what is commonly called charity. — *The Christian Register*, June 11.

LETTER FROM MR. WILLIAM CHAPIN.

In connection with the comments of the public press we cannot refrain from publishing the following letter from the venerable principal of the Pennsylvania Institution for the Blind in Philadelphia, Mr. William Chapin, who has labored in this field of beneficence with signal devotion and self-forgetfulness for forty-five years, and than whom no living man in this country can speak with more authority upon all subjects relating to the education and welfare of the blind: —

PENNSYLVANIA INSTITUTION FOR THE INSTRUCTION OF THE BLIND.

PHILADELPHIA, June, 1885.

My DEAR MR. ANAGNOS. — I have read with much interest the grand success of your commencement exercises, as given in the three papers you sent me ; and owe you an apology for not acknowledging your invitation cards. We are only now concluding our public examinations, and preparing for our final exercises on Wednesday. We cannot awaken the interest here which surrounds you in Boston. Your Governor's address was appropriate and beautiful, with an expression of tender sympathy for the blind, which could not in the least wound their self-respect. Your public papers also show a noble interest in your work, and impress the public with a pride in your institution which is rarely shown elsewhere.

But in this, I must not overlook the *master hand* that inspires this feeling in the Boston community, — even the energy of its present Director, on whom the mantle of *Howe* has fallen so kindly.

We graduate this year about 21. We have made some interesting advances in kindergarten, — admitting children at an earlier age than formerly, for that purpose.

I write in some haste, and beg you will present my kind regards to Mrs. Anagnos, and accept for yourself my admiration for your success.

WILLIAM CHAPIN.

M. ANAGNOS, ESQ.

FIFTY-FIFTH ANNUAL REPORT

OF

THE TRUSTEES

OF THE

PERKINS INSTITUTION

AND

Massachusetts School for the Blind,

FOR THE YEAR ENDING

SEPTEMBER 30, 1886.

BOSTON:
WRIGHT & POTTER PRINTING CO., STATE PRINTERS,
18 POST OFFICE SQUARE.
1887.

TABLE OF CONTENTS.

Commonwealth of Massachusetts.

PERKINS INSTITUTION AND MASS. SCHOOL FOR THE BLIND,
SOUTH BOSTON, Oct. 30, 1886.

To the Hon. HENRY B. PEIRCE, *Secretary of State*, Boston.

DEAR SIR : — I have the honor to transmit to you, for the use of the legislature, a copy of the fifty-fifth annual report of the trustees of this institution to the corporation thereof, together with that of the director and the usual accompanying documents.

Respectfully,

M. ANAGNOS,

Secretary.

BOARD OF TRUSTEES.

FREDERICK L. AMES.	EDWARD N. PERKINS.
FRANCIS BROOKS.	SAMUEL M. QUINCY.
JOHN S. DWIGHT.	HENRY S. RUSSELL.
JOSEPH B. GLOVER.	JAMES STURGIS.
J. THEODORE HEARD, M. D.	THOMAS F. TEMPLE.
ANDREW P. PEABODY, D. D.	GEORGE W. WALES.

STANDING COMMITTEES.

Monthly Visiting Committee,

whose duty it is to visit and inspect the Institution at least once in each mo

1887.		1887.	
January,	F. L. AMES.	July,	EDWARD N. P
February,	F. BROOKS.	August,	S. M. QUINCY
March,	J. S. DWIGHT.	September,	H. S. RUSSEL
April,	J. B. GLOVER.	October,	JAMES STURGI
May,	J. T. HEARD.	November,	T. F. TEMPLE
June,	A. P. PEABODY.	December,	G. W. WALES

Committee on Education.	House Committee.
J. S. DWIGHT.	E. N. PERKINS.
FRANCIS BROOKS.	G. W. WALES.
S. M. QUINCY.	FRANCIS BROOKS.

Committee on Finance.	Committee on Health
J. B. GLOVER.	J. THEODORE HEARD
JAMES STURGIS.	F. L. AMES.
HENRY S. RUSSELL.	T. F. TEMPLE.

OFFICERS OF THE INSTITUTION.

DIRECTOR.
M. ANAGNOS.

MEDICAL INSPECTOR.
JOHN HOMANS, M. D.

LITERARY DEPARTMENT.

JAY M. HULBERT.	Miss DELLA BENNETT.
Miss ANNIE K. GIFFORD.	Miss HARRIET D. BURGESS.
Miss SARAH J. WHALEN.	Miss FANNY S. MARRETT.
Miss JULIA A. BOYLAN.	Miss EMMA A. COOLIDGE.

Miss SARAH ELIZABETH LANE, *Librarian.*

MUSIC DEPARTMENT.

THOMAS REEVES.	CARL BAERMANN.
ELMER S. HOSMER.	GEORGE J. PARKER.
Miss FREDA BLACK.	JULIUS AKEROYD.
Miss DELLA B. UPSON.	
Miss MARY L. RILEY.	**Music Readers.**
Miss JULIA H. STRONG.	
LEMUEL TITUS.	Miss ALLIE S. KNAPP.
THOMAS LEVERETT.	Miss JENNY A. WHEATON.
LORENZO WHITE.	Miss DAISY S. MONROE.

TUNING DEPARTMENT.
JOEL WEST SMITH, *Instructor and Manager.*
GEORGE E. HART, *Tuner.*

INDUSTRIAL DEPARTMENT.

Workrooms for Juveniles.	Workshop for Adults.
JOHN H. WRIGHT, *Work Master.*	ANTHONY W. BOWDEN, *Manager.*
Miss A. J. DILLINGHAM, *Work Mistress.*	PLINY MORRILL, *Foreman.*
Miss CORA L. DAVIS, *Assistant.*	Miss M. A. DWELLY, *Forewoman.*
EUGENE C. HOWARD, *Assistant.*	Miss ELLEN M. WHEELOCK, *Clerk.*
THOMAS CARROLL, *Assistant.*	

DOMESTIC DEPARTMENT.

Steward.	Housekeepers in the Cottages.
ANTHONY W. BOWDEN.	Mrs. M. A. KNOWLTON.
	Mrs. L. S. SMITH.
Matron.	Miss BESSIE WOOD.
Miss MARIA C. MOULTON.	Mrs. SOPHIA C. HOPKINS.
Miss ELLA F. FORD, *Assistant.*	

PRINTING DEPARTMENT.
DENNIS A. REARDON, ... *Manager.*
Miss ELIZABETH S. HOWE, *Printer.*
Miss MARTHA C. ALDEN, "

Miss ELLEN B. WEBSTER, *Book keeper.*

All persons who have contributed twenty-five dol
the funds of the institution, all who have served as t
or treasurer, and all who have been elected by specia
are members.

Adams, John A., Pawtucket, R I.
Adams, Waldo, Boston.
Alcott, Miss Louisa M., Concord.
Alden, Mrs. Sara B., Boston.
Aldrich, Miss Mary Jane, Boston.
Aldrich, Mrs. Sarah, Boston.
Alger, Rev. William R., Boston.
Ames, F. L., Boston.
Ames, Miss H. A., Easton.
Ames, Oliver, Boston.
Amory, C. W., Boston.
Amory, James S., Boston.
Amory, William, Boston.
Amory, Mrs William, Boston.
Anagnos, M., Boston.
Andrews, Francis, Boston.
Appleton, Miss Emily G., Boston.
Appleton, Mrs. William, Boston.
Apthorp, William F., Boston
Atkins, Mrs. Elisha, Boston.
Atkinson, Edward, Boston.
Atkinson, William, Boston.
Austin, Edward, Boston.
Aylesworth, H. B., Providence.
Bacon, Edwin M., Boston.
Balch, E V Boston

Ballard, Miss E., Boston.
Baker, Mrs. E. M , Boston.
Baker, Mrs. E. J. W., Dorc
Baker, Ezra H., Boston.
Baker, Miss M K., Boston.
Barbour, E. D., Boston.
Barker, Joseph A , Provide
Barstow, Amos C., Provide
Barrows, Rev. S. J., Dorch
Beal, J. H., Boston.
Beard, Hon. Alanson W., E
Beckwith, Miss A. G., Pro
Beckwith, Mrs. T., Provide
Beebe, J. A., Boston.
Bennett, Mrs. Eleanor, Bill
Bigelow, Mrs. E. B., Bosto
Bigelow, Mrs. Prescott, Bo
Binney, William, Providen
Black, G. N., Boston.
Blake, James H., Boston.
Blanchard, G. D. B., Malde
Bourn, Hon. A. O., Bristol,
Bouvé, Thomas T., Boston.
Bowditch, Mrs. E. B., Bost
Bowditch, Dr. H. P., Jamaic
Bowditch J I Boston

Brackett, Mrs. Henry, Boston.
Brackett, Miss Nancy, Boston.
Bradlee, F. H., Boston.
Bradlee, J. P., Boston.
Brewer, Miss C. A., Boston.
Brewer, Mrs. Mary, Boston.
Brewster, Osmyn, Boston.
Brimmer, Hon. Martin, Boston.
Brooks, Francis, Boston.
Brooks, Mrs. Francis, Boston.
Brooks, Mrs. F. A., Boston.
Brooks, Peter C., Boston.
Brooks, Rev. Phillips, Boston.
Brooks, Shepherd, Boston.
Brown, John A., Providence.
Brown, Mrs John C., Providence.
Browne, A. Parker, Boston.
Bullard, W. S., Boston.
Bullock, Miss Julia, Providence.
Bundy, James J., Providence.
Burnett, Joseph, Boston.
Burton, J W., M. D., Flushing, N. Y.
Cabot, W. C., Boston.
Callender, Walter, Providence.
Carpenter, Charles E., Providence.
Carter, Mrs. Helen B., West Newton.
Cary, Miss A. P., Boston.
Cary, Miss Ellen G., Boston.
Cary, Mrs. W. F., Boston.
Cass, Mrs. D. S., Boston.
Center, J. H., Boston.
Chandler, P. W., Boston.
Chandler, Theophilus P., Brookline.
Chace, James II, Valley Falls, R. I.
Chace, Hon. Jonathan, Valley Falls, R. I.
Chamberlin, E. D., Boston.
Chapin, E. P., Providence.
Charles, Mrs. Mary C., Melrose.
Cheever, Dr. David W., Boston
Cheeney, Benjamin P., Boston.
Chickering, George II., Boston.

Chickering, Mrs. Sarah M., Joy Mills, Pa.
Claflin, Hon. William, Boston.
Clapp, William W., Boston.
Clarke, Mrs. Jas. Freeman, Boston.
Clarke, James W., Boston.
Clement, Edward H., Boston.
Coats, James, Providence.
Cobb, Mrs. Freeman, Boston.
Cobb, Samuel C., Boston.
Cobb, Samuel T., Boston.
Cochrane, Alexander, Boston.
Coffin, Mrs. W. E., Boston
Colt, Samuel P., Bristol, R. I.
Comstock, Andrew, Providence.
Coolidge, Dr. A., Boston.
Coolidge, J R., Boston.
Coolidge, Mrs. J. R, Boston.
Coolidge, J. Templeman, Boston.
Coolidge, Mrs. J. Templeman, Boston.
Coolidge, T. Jefferson, Boston.
Corliss, George H., Providence.
Cotting, C. U., Boston.
Crane, Zenas M., Dalton.
Crocker, Mrs. U. H., Boston.
Crosby, Joseph B, Boston.
Crosby, William S, Boston
Cruft, Miss Annah P., Boston.
Cruft, Miss Harriet O., Boston.
Cummings, Charles A, Boston.
Cummings, Hon. John, Woburn.
Curtis, C. A., Boston.
Curtis, George S, Boston.
Curtis, Mrs. Margarette S., Boston.
Dalton, C H., Boston.
Dalton, Mrs. C. H., Boston.
Darling Hon. L. B, Pawtucket, R I.
Davis, Miss A. W., Boston.
Davis, Mrs. Nancy S., Fitchburg.
Day, Daniel E., Providence.
Dean, Hon. Benjamin, South Boston.
Deblois, Stephen G., Boston.
Devens, Rev. Samuel A., Boston.

Endicott, Henry, Boston.
Endicott, William, Jr , Boston.
Ernst, C. W., Boston.
Farnam, Mrs. A. G., New Haven.
Fay, H. H., Boston.
Fay, Mrs. H. H., Boston.
Fay, Miss Sarah B., Boston.
Fay, Mrs. Sarah S., Boston.
Ferguson, Mrs. C. H., Dorchester.
Ferris, M. C., Boston.
Field, Mrs. Nancy M., Monson.
Fisk, Rev. Photius, Boston.
Fiske, J. N., Boston.
Folsom, Charles F., M.D., Boston.
Forbes, J. M., Milton.
Foster, F. C., Boston.
Freeman, Miss Hattie E., Boston.
French, Jonathan, Boston.
Frothingham, A. T., Boston.
Frothingham, Rev. Frederick, Milton.
Gaffield, Thomas, Boston.
Galloupe, C. W., Boston.
Gammell, Prof Wm., Providence.
Gammell, Mrs. Wm., Providence.
Gardiner, Charles P., Boston.
Gardner, George, Boston.
Gardner, George A , Boston.
Gardner, Henry W., Providence.
Gardner, Mrs John L., Boston.
George, Charles H., Providence.
Gill, Mrs. Frances A., Boston.
Gill, Mrs. Sarah A. W.

Greene, Edward A., Provi
Greene, S. H., River Point.
Greenleaf, Mrs Jas., Char
Greenleaf, R. C., Boston.
Griffin, S. B., Springfield.
Grosvenor, William, Provi
Grover, William O., Bostol
Guild, Mrs. S. E., Boston.
Hale, Rev. Edward E., Bos
Hale, George S., Boston.
Hall, J. R., Boston.
Hall, Miss L. E., Hanover.
Hall, Mrs. L. M., Boston
Hall, Miss Minna B., Long
Hardy, Alpheus, Boston.
Harwood, George S., Bosto
Haskell, Edwin B., Auburn
Hayward, Hon.Wm.S., Prov
Hazard, Rowland, Provider
Heard, J. T., M.D., Boston.
Hearst, Mrs. Phebe A., Sa
cisco, Cal.
Hemenway, Mrs. A., Jr., Bo
Herford, Rev. Brooke, Bost
Higginson, George, Boston
Higginson, Henry Lee, Bos
Hill, Hon. Hamilton A., Bo
Hill, J. E. R , Boston.
Hill, Mrs. T. J., Providence
Hilton, William, Boston.
Hodges, Dr. R. M., Boston.
Hogg, John, Boston.

Hoppin, Hon. W. W., Providence.
Hovey, William A , Boston.
Howard, Hon. A. C., Boston
Howard, Mrs Chas. W., California.
Howard, Hon. Henry, Providence.
Howe, Mrs. Julia Ward, Boston.
Howe, Mrs. Virginia A., Boston.
Howes, Miss E., Boston.
Houghton, Hon H. O , Cambridge.
Hunnewell, F. W., Boston.
Hunnewell, H. H., Boston.
Hunt, Moses, Charlestown.
Inches, H. B., Boston.
Ives, Mrs Anna A., Providence.
Jackson, Charles C., Boston.
Jackson, Edward, Boston.
Jackson, Mrs. J. B. S., Boston.
Jackson, Patrick T., Boston.
Jackson, Mrs. Sarah, Boston.
James, Mrs. Clitheroe Dean, South Boston.
James, Mrs. Julia B. H., Boston.
Johnson, Samuel, Boston.
Jones, Miss Ellen M., Boston.
Joy, Mrs. Charles H., Boston.
Kasson, Rev. F. H , Boston.
Kellogg, Mrs. Eva D., Boston.
Kendall, C. S., Boston.
Kennard, Martin P., Brookline.
Kent, Mrs. Helena M., Boston.
Kinsley, E W., Boston.
Lamson, Miss C. W., Dedham.
Lang, B J., Boston.
Lawrence, Abbott, Boston.
Lawrence, James, Groton.
Lawrence, William, Lawrence.
Lee, Henry, Boston.
Lincoln, L. J. B., Hingham.
Linzee, J. T., Boston.
Linzee, Miss Susan I., Boston.
Lippitt, Hon. Henry, Providence.
Littell, Miss S G., Brookline.
Little, J. L., Boston.
Littlefield, Hon. A. H., Pawtucket.
Littlefield, D. G., Pawtucket.

Lodge, Mrs. A. C., Boston.
Lodge, Henry C., Boston.
Loring, Mrs. Susie J , Boston.
Lothrop, John, Auburndale.
Lovett, George L., Boston.
Lowell, Abbott Lawrence, Boston.
Lowell, Augustus, Boston.
Lowell, Miss A. C., Boston.
Lowell, Francis C., Boston.
Lowell, Mrs. G. G., Boston.
Lowell, Mrs. John, Boston.
Lowell, Miss Lucy, Boston.
Lyman, Arthur T., Boston.
Lyman, George H., M.D., Boston.
Lyman, J. P., Boston.
Lyman, Theodore, Boston.
McAuslan, John, Providence.
Mack, Thomas, Boston.
Mackay, Mrs. Frances M., Cambridge.
Macullar, Addison, Boston.
Marcy, Fred. I., Providence.
Marston, S. W , Boston.
Mason, Miss E. F., Boston.
Mason, Miss Ida M , Boston.
Mason, I. B., Providence.
May, Miss Abby W., Boston.
May, F. W. G , Dorchester.
McCloy, J. A., Providence.
Means, Rev. J. H., D D., Dorchester.
Merriam, Mrs Caroline, Boston.
Merriam, Charles, Boston.
Merriam, Mrs D., Boston.
Metcalf, Jesse, Providence.
Minot, Francis, M.D., Boston.
Minot, Mrs. G. R., Boston.
Minot, William, Boston.
Mixter, Miss Helen K., Boston.
Mixter, Miss Madelaine C., Boston
Montgomery, W., Boston.
Morrill, Charles J., Boston.
Morse, S. T., Boston.
Morton, Edwin, Boston.
Motley, Edward, Boston.

Moulton, Miss Maria C., Boston.
Nevins, David, Boston.
Nichols, J Howard, Boston.
Nichols, R. C., Boston.
Nickerson, Andrew, Boston.
Nickerson, Mrs. A. T., Boston.
Nickerson, George, Jamaica Plain.
Nickerson, Miss Priscilla, Boston.
Nickerson, S. D., Boston.
Norcross, Miss Laura, Boston.
Noyes, Hon. Charles J., Boston.
O'Reilly, John Boyle, Boston.
Osgood, J. F., Boston.
Osborn, John T., Boston.
Owen, George, Providence.
Paine, Mrs. Julia B., Boston.
Paine, Robert Treat, Boston.
Palfrey, J. C., Boston.
Palmer, John S., Providence.
Parker, Mrs. E. P., Boston.
Parker, E. Francis, Boston.
Parker, Henry G., Boston.
Parker, Richard T., Boston.
Parkinson, Mrs. J., Boston.
Parkman, Francis, Boston.
Parkman, George F., Boston.
Parsons, Thomas, Chelsea.
Payson, S. R., Boston.
Peabody, Rev. A. P., D.D., Cambridge.
Peabody, F. H., Boston.
Peabody, O W., Milton.
Peabody, S. E., Boston.
Pearson, Miss Abby W., Boston.
Peirce, Rev. Bradford K., D.D., Boston.
Perkins, A. T., Boston.
Perkins, Edward N., Jamaica Plain.
Perkins, William, Boston.
Peters, Edward D., Boston.
Pickett, John, Beverly.
Pickman, W. D., Boston.
Pickman, Mrs. W. D., Boston.
Pierce, Hon. H. L , Boston.

Pierson, Mrs. Mary E., Windsor, Conn.
Potter, Isaac M., Providence.
Potter, Mrs. Sarah, Providence.
Pratt, Elliott W., Boston.
Prendergast, J. M., Boston.
Preston, Jonathan, Boston.
Pulsifer, R. M., Boston.
Quincy, George Henry, Boston.
Quincy, Samuel M., Wollaston.
Reardon, Dennis A., Boston.
Rice, Hon. A. H , Boston.
Rice, Fitz James, Providence.
Richardson, Mrs. Jeffrey, Boston.
Richardson, John, Boston.
Richardson, Mrs. M. R., Boston.
Robbins, R. E., Boston.
Robeson, W. R., Boston.
Robinson, Henry, Reading.
Rodman, S. W., Boston.
Rodocanachi, J. M., Boston.
Rogers, Henry B., Boston.
Rogers, Jacob C., Boston.
Ropes, J. C., Boston.
Ropes, J. S., Jamaica Plain.
Rotch, Miss Anne L., Boston.
Rotch, Mrs. Benjamin S., Boston.
Rotch, Miss Edith, Boston.
Russell, Henry G., Providence.
Russell, Mrs. Henry G., Providence.
Russell, Henry S., Boston.
Russell, Miss Marian, Boston.
Russell, Mrs. S. S., Boston.
Saltonstall, H., Boston.
Saltonstall, Hon. Leverett, Newton.
Sampson, George, Boston.
Sanborn, Frank B., Concord.
Sayles, F. C., Pawtucket, R. I.
Sayles, W. F , Pawtucket, R. I.
Schlesinger, Barthold, Boston.
Schlesinger, Sebastian B., Boston.
Sears, David, Boston.
Sears, Mrs. David, Boston.
Sears, Mrs. Fred., Jr., Boston.
Sears, F. R., Boston.

Sears, Mrs. K. W., Boston.
Sears, Mrs. P. H., Boston.
Sears, Mrs. S. P., Boston.
Sears, W. T., Boston.
Sharpe, L., Providence.
Shaw, Mrs. G. H., Boston.
Shaw, Henry S., Boston.
Shaw, Quincy A., Boston.
Shepard, Mrs. E. A., Providence.
Sherwood, W. H , Boston.
Shimmin, C. F., Boston.
Shippen, Rev. R. R., Washington.
Sigourney, Mrs. Henry, Boston.
Slater, H. N., Jr., Providence.
Snelling, Samuel G., Boston.
Spaulding, J. P., Boston.
Spaulding, M. D., Boston.
Spencer, Henry F., Boston.
Sprague, F. P., Boston.
Sprague, S. S., Providence.
Stanwood, Edward, Brookline.
Stearns, Charles H., Brookline.
Steere, Henry J., Providence.
Stewart, Mrs. C. B., Boston.
Stone, Joseph L., Boston.
Sturgis, Francis S., Boston.
Sturgis, J. H., Boston.
Sturgis, James, Boston.
Sullivan, Richard, Boston.
Swan, Mrs. Robert, Boston.
Sweetser, Mrs. Anne M., Boston.
Taggard, B. W., Boston.
Taggard, Mrs. B. W., Boston.
Tappan, Miss M. A., Boston.
Tappan, Mrs. William, Boston.
Temple, Thomas F., Boston.
Thaxter, Joseph B., Hingham.
Thayer, Miss Adele G., Boston.
Thayer, Miss A. G., Andover.
Thayer, Rev. George A., Cincinnati.
Thomas, H. H., Providence.
Thorndike, Mrs. Delia D., Boston.
Thorndike, S Lothrop, Cambridge.
Thurston, Benj. F., Providence.
Tilden, Mrs. M. Louise, Milton.

Tingley, S. H., Providence.
Tolman, Joseph C., Hanover.
Torrey, Miss A. D., Boston.
Troup, John E., Providence.
Turner, Miss Abby W., Boston.
Turner, Miss Alice M., Boston.
Turner, Miss Ellen J., Boston.
Turner, Mrs. M. A., Providence.
Underwood, F. H., Boston.
Upton, George B., Boston.
Villard, Mrs. Henry, New York.
Wales, George W., Boston.
Wales, Miss Mary Ann, Boston.
Wales, Thomas B., Boston.
Ward, Rev. Julius H., Boston.
Ware, Charles E., M.D., Boston
Ware, Mrs. Charles E., Boston.
Ware, Miss M. L., Boston.
Warren, J. G., Providence.
Warren, S. D., Boston.
Warren, Mrs. Wm. W., Boston.
Washburn, Hon. J D., Worcester.
Weeks, A. G., Boston.
Welch, E. R , Boston.
Weld, Otis E., Boston.
Weld, R. H., Boston.
Weld, Mrs. W. F., Philadelphia.
Weld, W. G , Boston.
Wesson, J. L., Boston.
Wheeler, Nathaniel, Bridgewater, Conn.
Wheelwright, A. C., Boston.
Wheelwright, John W., Boston.
White, B. C., Boston.
White, C. J., Cambridge.
White, Charles T., Boston.
White, G. A., Boston.
White, Joseph A., Framingham.
Whitford, George W , Providence
Whiting, Ebenezer, Boston.
Whitman, Sarah W., Boston.
Whitney, Edward, Belmont.
Whitney, E., Boston.
Whitney, H. A., Boston.
Whitney, H. M., Boston.

Whitney, Mrs., Boston.
Whitney, Miss, Boston.
Wigglesworth, Miss Ann, Boston.
Wigglesworth, Edward, M.D., Boston.
Wigglesworth, Thomas, Boston.
Wightman, W. B., Providence.
Wilder, Hon. Marshall P., Dorchester.
Williams, George W. A., Boston.
Winslow, Mrs. George, Roxbury.

Winsor, J. B., Providence.
Winthrop, Hon. Robert C., Boston.
Winthrop, Mrs. Robert C., Boston.
Winthrop, Mrs. Thomas L., Boston.
Wolcott, J. H., Boston.
Wolcott, Mrs. J. H., Boston.
Woods, Henry, Boston.
Worthington, Roland, Roxbury.
Young, Mrs. B. L., Boston.
Young, Charles L., Boston.

SYNOPSIS OF THE PROCEEDINGS

ANNUAL MEETING OF THE CORPORATION.

SOUTH BOSTON, Oct. 13, 1886.

The annual meeting of the corporation, duly summoned, was held today at the institution, and was called to order by the president, Samuel Eliot, LL.D., at 3 P.M.

The proceedings of the last meeting were read by the secretary, and declared approved.

Mr. John S. Dwight presented the report of the trustees, which was read, accepted, and ordered to be printed with that of the director, and the usual accompanying documents.

The treasurer, Mr. Edward Jackson, read his report, which was accepted, and ordered to be printed.

The suggestions of the auditors of the treasurer's accounts with regard to changes to be made in some of the details of keeping the books of the institution, were read and discussed, and the matter was referred to a special committee, consisting of Messrs. S. Lothrop Thorndike, Joseph B. Glover and James Sturgis, with full powers.

The corporation then proceeded to ballot for officers for the ensuing year, and the following persons were unanimously elected : —

President — Samuel Eliot, LL.D.

Vice-President — John Cummings.

Treasurer — Edward Jackson.

Secretary — M. Anagnos.

Trustees — Joseph B. Glover, J. Theodore Heard, M. D., Andrew P. Peabody, D. D., Edward N. Perkins, Henry S. Russell, Samuel M. Quincy, James Sturgis and George W. Wales.

The meeting was then dissolved, and all in attendance proceeded, with the invited guests, to visit the various departments of the school and inspect the premises.

M. ANAGNOS,

Secretary.

REPORT OF THE TRUSTEES.

PERKINS INSTITUTION AND MASS. SCHOOL FOR THE BLIND,
SOUTH BOSTON, Oct. 1, 1886.

TO THE MEMBERS OF THE CORPORATION.

Gentlemen and ladies: — We respectfully present to you, and, through you, to the legislature of Massachusetts, the *fifty-fifth* annual report, showing the progress and condition of the institution under our charge for the financial year ending Sept. 30, 1886.

Fuller details are appended in the report of the director.

1. The year has been very prosperous, the number of pupils increasing rapidly, indeed to such an extent that all the buildings are almost overcrowded.

The health of the household has been exceedingly good. During the summer vacation one of the pupils died, in the country, of malarial fever, which he contracted the previous year in his native place in Rhode Island. Also, one of the first ten pupils of Dr. Howe, Miss Caroline A. Sawyer, for many years the faithful janitress of the main building of the institution, died from the effects of an accident, at the age of 66 years.

The total number of blind persons connected with the institution is 180 ; of these 146 are pupils, and 34 teachers, workmen and employés. A year before, the pupils numbered 141. The number of applicants for admission this . term has been larger than ever.

2. THE SCHOOL —

which is the main object of the institution — continues to improve upon its methods, or, at least, to carry them out more thoroughly, and with more and more satisfactory results. It seems unnecessary to repeat, in only stronger words, what was said in our last year's report of the many-sidedness and wisdom of the plan of education — physical, intellectual and moral ; of its careful adaptation to each individual bent, capacity and temperament, as well as to the whole idea of perfect womanhood and manhood ; of the excellence of the instruction in every department of a very comprehensive curriculum of studies, each gaining zest by the continual relief from all monotony of subjects and of exercises ; or of the marked fidelity and patience of a superior and successful corps of teachers. Every intelligent, right-minded visitor of the school rooms must have been convinced of this.

3. Commencement Exercises.

But the most interesting and persuasive demonstrations have appeared in the annual commencement exercises of the graduating classes, which have been held for several years in the presence of the whole school, and of overflowing and enthusiastic audiences — never more so than at the last occasion of the kind, at Tremont Temple, June 1, of the present year. We let the *Christian Register* (June 10) describe it.

"The sympathy was partly of delight and ever fresh surprise, partly, too, of sadness. But the sadness seemed to be wholly on the part of tender-hearted listeners and spectators, and, to a great extent, superfluous, imaginative, and not at all on that of the bright-looking objects of the sympathy. They, older or younger, appeared too happy in the many-sided exercise of all their faculties, both intellectual and physical and moral, and in the delightful consciousness of a continually widening progressive culture, all pervaded by a rhythmical, æsthetic sense and spirit even to realize their deprivation of the sense of sight. Somehow, their whole bodies seemed to see ; else, how could they find their way, with such unerring accuracy, through all the complicated evolutions of their gymnastic exercises and the military drill, never overstepping dangerous limits, and marching off the platform with free step, heads erect, without once stumbling on the stairs?

"Dr. Samuel Eliot, president of the corporation, presided with his usual grace and tact, first introducing Governor Robinson, who expressed a warm appreciation of the school and what it had accomplished. (Before this, however, Händel's Fifth Concerto had been finely played upon the organ by one of the graduating pupils, Mr. Charles H. Prescott. It was too good to be made a mere accompaniment to all the talk and bustle of a crowd coming in.)

"Next, the band of the pupils (brass, with clarinets) gave a spirited performance of the 'Bridal Chorus,' with introduction, from 'Lohengrin.' Then, a young lady graduate, Miss Evalyn A. Tatreau, in a clear voice and good accent, spoke briefly of the 'Laws of Mechanics,' which she illustrated by the sewing-machine before her; and no one was any the less convinced of her thorough acquaintance with the instrument, or of her skill in using it, by the slight difficulty which she had in threading the needle, owing to nervousness and to the fact that the machine was a new one, brought there for good looks. A double quartet for male voices — a hunting chorus — was sung with fine effect. It was from a manuscript opera by Mr. H. Strachauer, of which the libretto, founded on Campbell's short ballad of 'Glenara,' was one of the last literary works of Julia R. Anagnos, the gifted and lamented wife of the director of the institution.

"This was followed by the always remarkable exercise in geography, — this time by four little boys, whose sure and rapid recognition and description and replacing of different countries, taken from dissecting maps, called forth continual applause; and then specimens of reading by the touch by two girls, one of whom, very young, a pupil only since September, showed wonderful aptitude, including a very clear and eloquent delivery in her simple way. A solo for the clarinet, quite a difficult and varied cavatina, played with fine, smooth tone and artistic phrasing by Clarence W. Basford, brought Part I. to a close.

"Without a pause, Part II. followed (for great care was taken this time to keep the exercises within a reasonable length, and so successfully that scarcely any left the hall so long as anything remained upon the programme). It was ushered in with martial music on the piano, when a brave squad of noble youths marched in, clad in simple uniform, and went through the manual of musket-handling and all the common military movements with perfect promptness and precision. Their 'colonel' and instructor had great reason to be proud of them. There were also dumb-bell exercises by a fine-looking set of young boys, all with good heads and good physique, all bright and animated, which showed a unity of time and movement which it would seem hardly possible to teach to pupils without sight. Girls followed (in tasteful, simple uniform, as were the boys; and this æsthetic phase of the business both parties seemed to enjoy as keenly as if they had their eyes) in very graceful rhythmic exercises, with long silvered tubes or wands.

"And then came the most interesting part of all. Before eight little tables sat six little boys and six little girls, who modelled figures (a windmill, a lighthouse, the beacon on old Beacon Hill, a ship, a pen, etc.), illustrating 'Early Boston in Clay.' The charm and quaintness of the show, the quick, bright way in which each little one held up and explained his work, drew laughter even to tears. And, meanwhile, a most eloquent, persuasive appeal in behalf of the kindergarten school for little sightless children, of a tenderer age than these, was addressed to the audience by Hon. Leverett Saltonstall. Then, if ever, were the sympathies of twenty-five hundred people warmed to a pitch that would respond to any such appeal. What if the benevolent-looking trustees on the platform had been provided with contribution-boxes, and had walked round canvassing the crowd in person? Would they not have reaped a harvest? For that would have been striking while the iron was hot.

"After a fine duo for two cornets, beautifully executed by C. H. Prescott and C. T. Gleason, came the only address by a graduate, the valedictory, by Miss Annie M. Sullivan, of which we have not room to say a tithe of what we would. It was in an altogether earnest, sincere, thoughtful spirit, full of wise suggestions, and spoken in tones that vibrated with true feeling and with genuine refinement; a fit prelude to the touching, wise remarks of Dr. Eliot, before presenting the diplomas to the eight graduates of the day, whose names are: Alice Viola Carleton, Lillie May Fletcher, Charles Timothy Gleason, Charles Harrison Prescott, Daniel Scott, Annie Mansfield Sullivan, Evalyn Annie Tatreau and Arthur Leon Warren. God crown their honest aspirations with success!

"Another extract from 'Glenara,' a brilliant finale sung in chorus by all the voices, worthily closed the memorable exhibition of the ways in which the blind are taught to see, and with an inner sight that more than makes up for the loss of any single outward sense."

4. TEACHERS AND OFFICERS.

With two exceptions, the services of all the officers and teachers have been re-engaged for the coming year. The school loses two teachers in Miss Anna S. Low and Miss Mary C. Moore. The former resigned in May, to accept a more lucrative position elsewhere; while the latter was obliged to retire from the work of the school — it is hoped only temporarily — by utter need of rest and recreation after the arduous labors of nine consecutive years. Both of these vacancies have been filled.

5. POST-GRADUATE COURSE.

The success of the school is so far most encouraging. Yet, in the opinion of the director, founded on the best of reasons, our educational ladder is still incomplete. Two most important rounds, the lowest and the uppermost, are wanting. The kindergarten is intended to supply the one. The other may be called a *post-graduate course*, for the advantage of deserving graduates of our school, who have shown a marked talent and a capacity for higher attainment in some important branch of study or of art, — say music. We would secure for them such " finishing lessons " as would outrun the period of our school course, and enable them to enjoy the lessons, counsels and examples of the most distinguished masters and professors within reach in each department. This board has already authorized the taking of the first steps, in a tentative and gradual way, beginning modestly, for the organization of such a course. It is confidently hoped that wealthy friends of education and the blind, will be found willing and happy to endow a few *scholarships* with this view. It is not a mere desideratum, but an absolute necessity, in order to complete the system of the education of the blind.

We have the pleasure to add, that the eminent artist, Prof. Carl Baermann, has, after careful examination of their capacities, consented to give lessons to two of last year's graduates on the pianoforte.

6. The Kindergarten for the Blind.

This is by no means yet an outworn subject of appeal. Newspapers, public halls and private parlors, and indeed the minds and sympathies of the most charitable and thoughtful of the whole community, have for several years been full of it. Much has certainly been given, and much done, towards the realization of the plan. Still the need continues. Great interest has been manifested by old and young, by rich and poor, and even by the children. At a children's fair in Swampscott, a few months since, the sum of $672.66 was obtained for the cause. And the blind children of our school, eagerly, in many humble ways, have clubbed together their small means, giving concerts, holding fairs, to do their part for the salvation and fair education of their sightless younger brothers and sisters, so that they may not be past recovery, both morally and mentally, before they have attained the age that fits them to become pupils of this institution. During the last winter and spring, several most attractive entertainments were given at large private houses, by a number of our foremost authors and musical artists, by which the project was brought to the direct notice of the more favored and benevolent of our community. The result pecuniarily was very handsome ($915.00).

As the case now stands, the new building (first of a contemplated group of several), on the beautiful grounds secured at Roxbury, is rapidly reaching completion, and will be ready for occupancy in about three months. But the funds so liberally subscribed for the purchase of the land

and for the building are entirely exhausted; and a
debt of about $12,000 will be incurred for finishing
and furnishing the house, and for the employment
of a corps of teachers and attendants.

The infant school will be organized about the
first of January with a dozen or fifteen little pupils;
and there is not a penny left in our treasury for its
support! Funds are absolutely needed for carrying on the work whose importance, desirableness
and absolute necessity are fully conceded, and
whose promise is enthusiastically hailed by all
good men and women who have the interests of
education and the young at heart. If the enterprise, which has been so sanctioned by the general
God-speed, and which has striven upward to so
promising a height of realization, shall now, after
all, be allowed to fail for want of the material
means which so abound in many rich and kindly
hands, there will be much time lost before there
will be the courage to begin anew to climb up
from the bottom of the mountain. So far the effort
has succeeded well; but it must be *crowned* with
success. The kindergarten for the blind must be
made an accomplished fact, beyond the possibility
of any further doubt or drawback. We must all
put our hands to the wheel *now* — now that the
chance is good — and lift it to the height of safe
and permanent accomplishment.

7. The Finances

are in a healthy condition. Strict economy is practised, and careful oversight in the matter of expenses is exercised by the auditors.

Grateful acknowledgments are due both to Judge Chas. Allen for including our school in the list of the institutions which he designated as the recipients of certain funds left by the late Mrs. Valeria G. Stone, to be applied to charitable purposes, and to the trustees of the estate, Rev. William H. Wilcox, D. D., and Hon. Alpheus Hardy, for paying our share ($5,000) to our treasurer at once.

The treasurer's exhibit may be summarized as follows: —

Cash on hand Oct. 1, 1885, ...	$2,056 55
Total receipts from all sources during the year (including collections of payable notes), .	136,176 56
	$138,233 11
Total expenditures and investments, . . .	101,905 66
Balance, ...	$36,327 45

8. Printing for the Blind.

The work has continued with its accustomed vigor. Among the books issued in raised type during the past year are Sir Walter Scott's "Talisman" in two volumes; a complete edition of the New Testament, in three volumes; and the first two volumes of Charles Dickens's "David Copperfield."

Improvements are constantly making in the printing office, and a new press has been built for it, which gives better satisfaction than any other machine of the kind.

9. THE WORKSHOP FOR ADULTS.

The results here are about the same as in the preceding year. The department is not self-supporting. Nor does it afford sufficient employment for a large number of blind persons who are eager to earn their bread by the sweat of their brow. It is not pleasant to have to make the same report, substantially, year after year. Success is certainly deserved. The work is warranted to be very satisfactory, both as regards material and labor. An increase of patronage is again most earnestly solicited.

10. DEATH OF MEMBERS.

During the past year, as in almost every year, this corporation has suffered serious losses in its list of members. Among those who have been removed from us by death we have to count such honored names as Henry P. Kidder, Hon. Amos A. Lawrence, and Charles C. Perkins, all of Boston; also Mrs. Frederic H. Bradlee, George L. Claflin, Providence; Mrs. Rebecca Conant, Amherst, N. H., Jacob Dunnell, Pawtucket, R. I., R. J. Fellows, New Haven, Conn., Benjamin F.

Greene, Central Falls, R. I., Rt. Rev. T. F. Hendricken, Providence, Edward Lawrence, Charlestown, George C. Richardson, William W. Tucker, and John E. Wetherbee.

But the irreparable loss which comes immediately home to the school, the institution, and to all of us, — particularly to the school, and to its teachers and its pupils personally, — is that of one who grew up with this school, and who gave her energies and her rich resources of mind and character to its advancement and to the welfare of the blind, — the oldest child and daughter of its noble founder, — the admirable wife, and the best human inspiration and support of Dr. Howe's successor in the arduous work, which he still carries on with all his heroic zeal and energy in spite of this bereavement, as if she yet, invisibly, were with him. From her childhood her sympathies were irresistibly drawn to her father's philanthropic enterprise; and she became year by year, though not officially, a more and more valuable assistant. She inherited philanthropy, and in her hands the talents were increased. She not only contributed to the instruction, teaching languages, reading choicest literature to classes of the pupils, conversing with them, and in a very quickening way, on serious and improving topics; but she was in an important sense the confidential friend of many of the girls particularly, and also of the boys. They derived high aim, direction and encouragement from her.

She did all she could to make their life here happy,
employing to this end those rare social gifts which
she had enriched, refined, enlarged by an unremitting process of self-culture in the least selfish
sense. Hers was a large and generous nature.
Her love of truth amounted to a passion. Her
sympathies were very broad and catholic. And
she was honored and beloved in life, as she is
now lamented, by all who came within her sphere.

All which is respectfully submitted by

FREDERICK L. AMES,
FRANCIS BROOKS,
JOHN S. DWIGHT,
JOSEPH B. GLOVER,
J. THEODORE HEARD,
ANDREW P. PEABODY,
EDWARD N. PERKINS,
SAMUEL M. QUINCY,
HENRY S. RUSSELL,
JAMES STURGIS,
THOMAS F. TEMPLE,
GEORGE W. WALES,

Trustees.

THE REPORT OF THE DIRECTOR.

" Though varying wishes, hopes and fears,
  Fever'd the progress of these years,
  Yet now, days, weeks and months but seem
  The recollection of a dream."

SCOTT.

To the Board of Trustees.

Gentlemen : — In conformity with a regulation of your board, which requires of the director an annual account of the condition and progress of the school, and of the advancement of its objects, and the administration of its internal concerns, I have the honor to submit the following report : —

During the past year a high degree of success has been attained in every department of the institution.

The usual course of physical training, of literary studies, of music, and of handicrafts, has been pursued uninterruptedly, and has borne good fruit.

A spirit of marked devotion to the objects for which the establishment was founded, has animated the teachers and officers in the discharge of their respective duties, and perfect freedom from friction has prevailed in the management of the affairs of the household.

The pupils have pursued their studies and occupations with diligence and faithful industry, have exhibited commendable deference and obedience towards those who have had the care of them, and have shown much harmony and good will in their intercourse with each other.

The school has been preparing the youth of both sexes to free themselves from the incubus of dependence, which weighs so heavily upon them, and to vindicate that capacity for perfect development, which is their birth-right, in common with all other classes of children.

The continuance of public esteem has been proved by the increasing number of visitors, and the friends of the establishment have manifested in various ways their interest in its beneficiaries and their confidence in its management.

There has scarcely ever been a time when the institution had larger and more pressing work to do in behalf of the blind of New England, and it should be strengthened and enabled to go forward, not only unincumbered, but with increased energy and resources. Its graduates have gained a place in the regard of the community which promises a yet more prosperous and beneficent future.

Number of Inmates.

"And better thence again, and better still,
In infinite progression."

Thomson.

On the 1st of October, 1885, the total number of
blind persons connected with the institution in its
various departments as pupils, teachers, employés,
and workmen and women, was 172. Since then,
30 have been admitted and 22 have been discharged, making the present total number 180.

Of these, 158 are in the school proper and 22
in the workshop for adults.

The first class includes 146 boys and girls,
enrolled as pupils, 10 teachers and other officers,
and 2 domestics. Of the pupils there are now 141
in attendance, 5 being temporarily absent on account of ill-health or from other causes.

The number in actual attendance has been
greater than ever before; it is indeed larger than
would be desirable in institutions organized upon
the usual plan. In ours the evil effects of the congregation of so many defectives are less perceptible, because they are divided into five distinct
families, live in separate dwellings, and come together in classes only for purposes of instruction,
as ordinary children go to day school.

There has been a steady increase of applicants
for admission during the past year, and I am sorry
to say that, although the cottages for girls are

crowded to their utmost capacity, there are still several eligible candidates waiting to fill any vacancies which may soon occur, and that it will not be very long ere the boys' department will be in the same predicament.

The problem of procuring sufficient accommodations for all children of suitable age, so that we may be able to receive them readily and without loss of valuable time, is more serious and perplexing now than ever before, and demands speedy solution. Considering the matter in all its present bearings and future prospects, I cannot but think that the most feasible and satisfactory way to overcome the difficulty would be to erect a building, or buildings, on our new estate in Roxbury without delay, and provide therein room and the means of instruction and training for all girls and boys who are under fourteen years of age.

HEALTH OF THE HOUSEHOLD.

" From toil he wins his spirits light,
  From busy day the peaceful night ;
  Rich, from the very want of wealth,
  In heaven's best treasures, peace and health."

GRAY.

The measure of health with which this school has been always blessed, and which has been frequently mentioned in former reports as remarkable and as a cause of devout thankfulness, has been enjoyed during the past year to its fullest extent.

No epidemic or contagious disease of an alarming kind has prevailed among the members of the household, and no death has invaded our circle in the institution itself; yet, to use the words of the poet,

" We cannot hold destruction's hand,"

and we have to record a sad instance of mortality which has occurred during the summer vacation in the country. A much-prized pupil was sent out of town as soon as the school term closed, at the expense of a most benevolent lady, with the hope that the tone of his debilitated system might be restored under good care and healthful surroundings. James H. Gallan, one of the beneficiaries from the state of Rhode Island, died in South Chelmsford of intermittent malarial fever, which he contracted about a year ago in Pawtucket — the place of his residence — and from which he suffered more or less ever after. He was a lad of considerable parts, but with a constitution lacking in strength and vitality. His amiable disposition, modest demeanor, goodness of heart, correct deportment and manly aspirations had endeared him to all with whom he had come in contact, and his loss was severely felt by both teachers and scholars.

Not less affecting was the end of Miss Caroline

Augusta Sawyer, one of the earliest pupils of the institution, whose familiar footstep and voice ceased very suddenly to be heard within its walls. On Friday, March 19th, she complained of feeling ill, but could not be persuaded to stay in her chamber. She went to breakfast as usual that morning, and as she came out from the dining-room, fell fainting in the entrance hall and fractured a hip bone. The following day she was removed by Dr. Homans to the Massachusetts General Hospital for treatment, where she passed away peacefully on Tuesday, March 23d. Her death was the direct result of the accident. Miss Sawyer was born in Sterling, Mass., Aug. 2, 1819. On the 18th of March, 1833, she joined the little group of nine sightless children whom Dr. Howe had just gathered under the roof of his father's house in Pleasant street as the nucleus of the school. After graduating, she continued to serve the establishment, in her humble way, with great zeal, striking fidelity, inimitable loyalty and exemplary honesty. She was a person of uncommon sincerity and marked individuality. Pure-minded, clear-headed, straightforward, intelligent in conversation, diligent in her work, vivacious in temper and wonderfully simple in manner, she was regarded with great affection by a large circle of friends and acquaintances. Beneath her silver locks was thriving a golden heart. Within her frail frame was nourished an upright conscience

From her time-worn features radiated a smile so
full of tenderness and genial sympathy that it was
more contagious than the laugh of youth. Her
good old age was like the evergreens of the forest
that tower above the sheeting snows in the midst
of winter frosts; though bending with their load
of icicles, they are yet robed in a foliage that
never fades. Miss Sawyer was most happy and
joyous in the performance of her duties under the
roof of the institution. Of the many fine qualities
which adorned her character, her profound gratitude for the educational advantages provided for
the blind and the true filial love which she entertained toward their illustrious benefactor, were the
noblest. Her heart was filled with delight at
every new improvement or increase of opportunities and facilities for the instruction and training
of sightless children, and the kindergarten project
was uppermost in her feelings and thoughts. The
fiftieth anniversary of her connection with the
establishment was celebrated three years ago in a
most fitting manner. Cordial congratulations and
numerous tokens of appreciation and good will
were presented to her on the occasion by relatives,
friends and associates, and she received them with
becoming modesty and child-like pleasure. Miss
Sawyer's death was deeply lamented by many persons who were warmly attached to her; but to
none could it have caused so sharp a pain as it did
to me. Coming immediately after the dreadful

blow which had fallen upon me so suddenly — a blow that deprived me of the most precious treasure which I possessed on earth — it left a terrible impression upon my mind, and I cannot ever think of the sad events which have come to pass in rapid succession without recalling to memory the following well-known lines of Moore, which seem to bear upon my case with peculiar fitness : —

> " When I remember all
>   The friends, so link'd together
> I've seen around me fall,
>   Like leaves in wintry weather ;
>
> I feel like one who treads alone
>   Some banquet-hall deserted,
> Whose lights are fled, whose garlands dead,
>   And all but he departed."

AIM OF THE EDUCATION OF THE BLIND.

" The fair mind in the fair body will be the fairest and love-liest of all sights to him who has the seeing eyes."

PLATO.

Of all the nations of antiquity the Greeks occupy the most prominent position in the history of peda-gogy. They held a very exalted idea of manly excellence, and aimed at the attainment of a high degree of development. " To produce harmony and symmetry and grace in every faculty of mind and body, was their notion of education," says Charles Kingsley; and his statement is fully confirmed by the writings of the two most mighty philosophers the world has ever seen. Plato and Aristotle have thrown into relief this conception and urged its realization. The Athenian law-giver, Solon, has placed physical and intellectual training upon the same footing. These were made parts of a whole system, inseparable from each other. The children were required to attend by turns the school for gymnastics and that for grammar. The mind was considered, however, as the seat of the higher aspirations, and its cultivation received due attention not only in the *academia* and the *lyceum*, but everywhere. It was indeed in the *palaestra* that Socrates found his readiest hearers, and dispensed his abstrusest lore. Can we imagine a dialogue such as the *Theaetetus* or *Phaedo* being held in a cricket-ground with the players waiting for their innings?

Above all other races, the Greeks strove to produce a strong and beautiful nature by lopping and pruning and trimming the branches which it sends out on all sides into the circumambient air: and they achieved unparalleled success; and placed the civilized world under great and permanent obligations. The higher spiritual life and æsthetic refinement of all nations have been nurtured under their influence. Though the stream of culture has broadened and deepened since the glory of the Hellenic republics waned, receiving in particular the mighty tributaries of modern science and invention, it must yet trace its origin to the renowned cities of Athens and Sparta. They have left us a rich heritage in the domains of thought and government. They have transmitted to us the records of heroic deeds of patriotism that have never been surpassed. In architecture and sculpture they have furnished models and inspiration for all time; and in the most important departments of literature, — in poetry, history, oratory and philosophy, — they have produced works of exalted genius and perpetual worth. No doubt many are the causes which have contributed to the fertile growth of such extraordinary fruits; but the principal among them may be justly ascribed to the pedagogy of the Greeks, whose ideal sprang from a passion for beauty and harmony, and a joyous sense of well-being.

As of old, so in the present age the end of education is complete human development. This is attained by leading the several sides of a child's nature to a harmonious realization of their highest possibilities. The finished result is a noble manhood and womanhood, whose elements are a healthy body, a clear and well-informed intellect, sensibilities quickly susceptible to every right feeling, and a steady will, the volitions of which are determined by reason and an enlightened conscience.

The foundation upon which the weight of modern education rests, is the doctrine of inter-dependence of body and mind, — the creed, that to work the latter is also to set in action a number of the organs of the former; that "not a feeling can arise, not a thought pass, without a set of concurring processes of the physical frame." This belief is the child of the scientific spirit embodied in the new physiology and psychology, and was engendered through the labors of Harvey and Haller, Müller and Weber, Helmholtz and Wundt. Prof. Huxley gives utterance to the views of a large circle of scientific thinkers when he says: "That man, I think, has had a liberal education who has been trained in his youth that his body is the ready servant of his will, and does with ease and pleasure all the work it is capable of; whose intellect is a clear, cold logic-engine, with all its parts of equal strength, and in smooth working order, ready, like a steam-engine, to be turned to any kind of work, and spin the gossamers as well as forge the anchors of the mind; whose mind is stored with a knowledge of the great and fundamental truths of nature, and of the laws of her operations; one who, no stunted ascetic, is full of life and fire, but whose passions are trained to come to heel by a vigorous will, the servant of a tender conscience; who has learned to love all beauty, whether of nature or of art, to hate all vileness, and to respect others as himself."

In its essential principles, the education of the blind does not differ from that of the seeing. It is the same both in theory and practice. It aims at developing a strong intellect in a healthy frame, improving and counteracting so far as possible such physical imperfections and psychological peculiarities as arise from the void of sight; at building in their minds a new dome of thought high enough to enable them to supersede all material obstructions, and to open to them new vistas of intellectual joy and moral excellence; and at imparting to them that special training and practical knowledge, which are required for the performance of the various labors and duties of life.

A cursory review of what has been accomplished in the various departments of the institution during the past year will show, that physical, intellectual, moral, æsthetic and technical education have been marching abreast, and that high motives and noble aspirations have been kindled and fostered in the pupils as the impelling force to arouse to self-activity, thus enabling them to conquer the difficulties and surmount the obstacles that lie in their path and hinder their progress.

DEPARTMENT OF PHYSICAL CULTURE.

> " To cure the mind's wrong bias, spleen,
> Some recommend the bowling green,
> Some hilly walks, — all, exercise ;
> Fling but a stone, the giant dies."
>
> GREEN.

That physical culture constitutes the foundation upon which an efficient system of education should be based, and that too much attention can scarcely be bestowed upon it, a few words will suffice to prove.

A sound and vigorous body is indispensable to a healthy and powerful mind. It is the main instrument in all achievements of great importance and supreme value. It is to the intellectual faculties and ethical nature what the roots, the trunk and the branches of a tree are to its leaves, blossoms and fruit, — the source of their development, as well as the *sine qua non* condition on which it depends.

For reasons relating partly to the sedentary habits and sluggish inactivity which the loss of sight superinduces in its victims, but mainly to the organic diseases which destroy or impair the visual sense, the blind as a class are poor in stamina and inferior in physique. Compared with seeing children and youth, they lack vitality and endurance. The fine animal, which Emerson considers as the first requisite in every efficient man, seems to have become extinct in their ranks. It is very rare to find among them a person with an erect frame, a well developed thorax, and that clear, glowing countenance, which is not only an essential ingredient of beauty, but a sure sign of health.

On the other hand, puny forms, pale faces, nerveless looks, lateral curvatures of the spine, crooked backs, projecting necks, uncouth habits of reeling backward and forward, hollow chests and slouching shoulders abound among them. Nor do these physical blemishes and peculiarities exist without corresponding intellectual imperfections. Indolence, inertia, want of mental alertness and concentration, laxity of memory, restiveness under discipline, weariness of study, as well as numberless moral evils, are quite often allied to them.

But these and numerous other ills of a similar kind are not merely accidental nor simply the result of ignorance and neglect. As a general rule they are visible symptoms of some latent disorder or constitutional weakness. They can be traced to physical causes. In some instances, they indicate unerringly, that the nervous force is at a low ebb, and that debility and insidious scrofulous affections are at work, consuming the vitality and sapping the foundations of the material organism.

Hence it is of prime importance, that these defects should be remedied so far as possible, and the machine put in good working order before we can reasonably hope to render the brain a garden of knowledge and the heart a nursery of goodness and noble aspirations. In order to make thorough scholars, efficient musicians, skilful mechanics, nay, men and women fitted for life, and able to perform its ordinary duties, we must first and above all build securely the pedestal upon which the statue of their education and professional training is to be raised. Without this, all attempts to pursue

" Paths of renown and climb ascents of fame "

will prove abortive. No one can scale the lofty
summits of Helicon and seek admission to the
abodes of Apollo and the muses without being
endowed with a sound body, clad in beauty and
strength,

" With health in every vein,
And reason throned upon his brow."

It is no more possible to nurture high thoughts,
fine taste and great inspirations in an enervated
and sickly frame, than it is to make fair plants
grow and thrive in a stony and barren ground.

In view of these facts, and in compliance with
the principles which lie at the foundation of our
scheme of education, physical culture has continued to constitute an integral part of the work of
our school, and has received unswerving attention.

During the past year our gymnasium has been
refitted and provided with a variety of new apparatus, which not only add to its attractions, but
increase its efficiency.

The course of bodily training therein pursued
has been prosecuted with uncommon energy, and
no pains have been spared on the part of those in
charge to improve and systematize a regular, intelligent, and, to some degree, scientific series of exercises, consisting of free gymnastics, calisthenics
and military drill. These exercises are calculated

to enlarge and strengthen the various muscles of the trunk, neck, arms and legs; to expand the chest so as to facilitate the play of the lungs; to render the joints supple, and to impart to the pupils grace, ease, and steadiness of carriage, combined with vigor, elasticity and quickness of movement.

Experience and daily observation enable me to state, that the favorable results of a strict adherence to our system of physical training are strikingly noticeable in the health and symmetrical growth, as well as in the appearance, gait, manners and disposition of our pupils.

Thus our efforts in this direction have met with their legitimate reward.

I take sincere pleasure in availing myself of this opportunity to acknowledge publicly, that the good work already accomplished in this department is a living and lasting monument to the industry, devotion, patience, ingenuity and judicious efforts of both Col. John H. Wright and Miss Della Bennett. Their trust in the salutary effects of physical culture is unwearying, and it would be scarcely possible to find two more earnest and faithful laborers in the circle of its promoters than they are.

But beneficent and valuable as gymnastics and calisthenics under shelter are, exercise taken out of doors in the blaze of broad day is infinitely more so. Everything that grows requires this light of day. The esculent that sprouts in the cellar has

no vigor, no greenness, no flavor: it needs the
and the sunshine to give it these. Fishes that ;
found in the pools of caves, where the beams
the gold lamp of heaven never penetrate, ;
destitute of eyesight. It is the light and warn
of the sun that cheer, embellish and bless.

Blind children more than all others should
made to spend a part of every hour in the open ;
They should be urged to join in sports on 1
play-ground in all kinds of weather. In the woi
of Horace, —

> " They must sharp cold and scorching heat despise,
>   And most tempt danger where most danger lies."

If we would make them hardy and fearless, '
must require them to go abroad as often as pos
ble, and amuse themselves together in playing;
defying wind and weather, romping in the fine d
snow, —

> " Smoothing and twirling the hoary locks of winter."

Instead of keeping them in the house all day ne
steam-pipes and heaters, we must let them face t
keen edge of a north wind, when the mercury
near or below zero; and, instead of minding a liti
shivering and complaining when they return, che
up their spirits and send them out again. In th
way we will teach them, that they are not born t
live in a nursery, nor to brood over the radiator,

but to range abroad, as free as the snow and the air, and to gain warmth from exercise. As Humphrey says, the youth who turns not back from the howling wintry blast, nor withers under the blaze of summer, nor magnifies "mole-hills into mountains," but whose daring mind, exulting, scales the eagle's airy crag, that youth is ready to undertake anything that is prudent and lawful within the range of possibility. Who would think of planting the mountain oak in a greenhouse, or of rearing the cedar of Lebanon in a lady's flower-pot? Who does not know, that in order to attain their mighty strength and majestic forms, these trees must freely enjoy the rain and the sunshine, and must feel the rocking of the tempest?

LITERARY DEPARTMENT.

" As the uncultured prairie bears a harvest
  Heavy and rank, yet worthless to the world, —
  So mind and heart, uncultured, run to waste ;
  The noblest natures serving but to show
  A denser growth of passion's deadly fruit."

MRS. HALE.

Although unable to chronicle any uncommon event or special measure of improvement in this department, I can say with truth, that its rightful purposes have been prosecuted with a fair degree of success.

The school is a sort of intellectual gymnasium, where the muscles of the mind and the tissues of

the brain are thoroughly and systematically exer
cised and developed.

The various studies included in our curricului
have been selected with much care and due delib
eration, and are pursued not as ends but as mean
of mental discipline.

All methods which tend to inflate the pupil
vanity, and to give them an over-estimate of thei
attainments, have been studiously avoided as harm
ful and injurious.

As often as occasion has seemed to require it
the subsoil plough of reform has been pushed s
deep as to turn up the weeds of empiricism by th
roots. But no changes of any kind have ever beer
effected for the sake of novelty or from a flippan
pride in being in the van of progress.

Efficiency and thoroughness have been held t
be of paramount importance, and they have no
been allowed to suffer from any consideration
The pupils have not been taught in great masse
by machine methods. They have been divide
into small classes and have received a certai
amount of individual instruction in a simple an
natural way. The fossilized spelling-books, th
antiquated geographies, the obsolete grammars
and all that endless hash of *à priori* deduction
and of confused statements and misty definitions
with which the minds of children are invariably
nauseated, have been gradually discarded and sup-
planted by the methods of Pestalozzi and Froebel.

The change has proved to be very wholesome, and the influence of a diet of *things* prescribed by the former in the place of words, and a little vigorous practice of *doing* in lieu of empty talking, induced by the system of the latter, have been truly magical.

Miss Mary C. Moore, formerly one of the leading teachers in the girls' department, has prepared at my request the brief statement given below. This is a clearer exposition and affords a better description than any that I can write, of the scientific and objective methods of instruction which prevail to a very great extent in our school, as well as of the adaptation of the kindergarten system to the development of several studies. It tells also of the introduction of an element of vital importance, — that of training the pupils to make from plastic materials many of the models and tangible illustrations which are used in class work. As these innovations had their origin and growth in the department where Miss Moore taught, she is specially qualified to speak about them. Here are her words: —

"About six years ago, a regular course of instruction in natural science was instituted in the girls' department of this school, and now we may say it is fairly established.

The work in the kindergarten classes trains the children to habits of observation, and furnishes them with material whereby they can represent forms of life. On leaving the kindergarten the first subject in order is zoölogy, afterward

comes botany, and later physiology. With some knowledge o
life in general, the pupil is ready to study that most intricate
and wonderful organism, the human body, and to be led to
draw up for himself a code of laws upon which his health,
usefulness and happiness largely depend.

The work in zoölogy begins with the vertebrates, on the
principle that the mind goes naturally from the known to the
unknown. Stuffed specimens of the higher vertebrates are
good practicable subjects for the study of the exterior appearance of such animals.

Some of the internal organs can easily be discerned by
touch, when a fresh specimen has been carefully prepared by
the teacher. Thanks to the new art of tanning animals, the
relation of the parts will hereafter be detected very easily by
touch; meanwhile models and clay are useful. Of course
there is no difficulty whatever with skeletons.

When the class is ready for the invertebrates more difficulties present themselves; yet with great care and patience
on the part of the pupil, and a judicious selection of specimens
on the part of the teacher, our children have been able to find
the leading characteristics of a large number of types, indeed
of nearly all above the protozoa.

At times when a microscope is indispensable to the seeing
student, the instructor may give directions for modelling the
magnified object in clay. I remember an insect copied in clay
by direction of the teacher from a drawing. A block was
made first, and upon it were placed little models of the different parts of the insect, greatly enlarged, but nearly correct
as to form and absolutely right as to position.

This is but a single instance. The children are required to
make models from direction or 'memory very often, and no
second bidding is necessary, for they delight in exercising
their power to *do*, and in thus learning by *doing*.

The instruction in botany proceeds on the same general
principles as those which govern the work in zoölogy. Speci-

mens are placed in the hands of the student for observation, and he describes what he finds in language, written and spoken, and in clay. The morphology of the parts of a flower can be represented very prettily and the subject much simplified by use of clay.

It is really wonderful how many delicate things our pupils are able to observe themselves! Fingers, lips, and tongue are used unsparingly. In the spring, the children keep close watch of the very few representatives of the vegetable kingdom that our little patch of ground affords, and happy is the little girl who finds the first chick-weed blossom.

Physiology has been a favorite subject, and I doubt not, that its popularity is due principally to the thorough preparation for its study, given in the kindergarten, botany and zoölogy classes.

The plan of work is this : — Attention is called throughout the course to the body as a living organism. The anatomy of an organ or system of organs is studied with models, of which the institution has a beautiful and abundant supply. The relation of structure to function is always brought out, and when simple experiments demonstrating the working of any parts are requisite, they are performed, first by the teacher and afterwards, if practicable, by the pupil. From their knowledge of anatomy and physiology the scholars are led to formulate laws of health.

Throughout this course, clay is used freely. We know that a girl understands the articulation of the skull and vertebral column when she can take a bit of clay and show it.

Other branches of natural science are taught in the same way. I may say in passing, that one of the members of a class in physics made from memory a model of a steam-engine in which all the essential parts were shown.

Too much stress cannot be laid on the value of manual training; for blind children, contrary to the suppositions of people who are not acquainted with them, keep their hands idle until they have been taught to use them, and many are obliged to overcome a dislike for handling things or be forever dependent on what A, B or C may choose to tell them.

Natural science gives just this training in a very pleasant way, and it would be invaluable for that alone if for nothing else. But it does much more. It places its students in communion with nature that humbly and reverently they may learn of her.

In the gradual evolution of the science course there have been many things to learn, and we might have been struggling in the dark till this day had we not been blessed with a most generous and efficient friend, Prof. Alpheus Hyatt; for from him and from his teachings the very life of the work has come.

We regard what has been done as an earnest of better things to be, when the kindergarten shall have given to little children such elementary training as will fit them for more advanced work in the institution.

A profound faith in the divine light within the human soul is an essential qualification for a teacher of the blind. There are especial limitations undoubtedly, but it is not for us to say what can and what cannot be done by any human being. Our duty is to give these children every opportunity to develop all their powers. The results are beyond our ken."

But efficient and productive of excellent results as our system of instruction and training is in other respects, its most significant feature is its positive and constructive tendency in relation to the development of character. Character, character, always character! To this we pay close and unremitting attention, for it is "higher than intellect" and a sort of life-preserver. It is the keynote to a useful and successful career. *All*

attainments, endeavors and hopes, unless they
be sustained and nourished by it, will be but as
the baseless fabric of a vision. George Washington considered the character of an honest man as
the "most enviable of all titles." Milton observed,
that "he that has light within his own clear breast,
may sit in the centre and enjoy bright day." Pope
said, that "worth makes the man, and want of it
the fellow;" and in the words of Shakespeare,—

" Good name, in man and woman,
    Is the immediate jewel of their souls."

At the end of the last term one of the most
talented teachers ever employed in the institution, Miss Mary C. Moore, expressed the wish that
she might not be considered as a candidate for
reëlection, provided her retirement would not
cause any inconvenience in our arrangements.
She was induced to take this step for the purpose
of obtaining some rest and recreation, which, in
the case of so earnest and conscientious a worker,
were much needed. The request seemed so just
and reasonable, and was presented in such a considerate manner, that it was granted in the same
spirit in which it was made.

Miss Moore is a person of marked abilities.
She possesses rare qualities of both head and
heart. The pages of these reports bear testimony
to her literary culture and professional attain-

ments. Those who know her well cannot fail to
appreciate fully her merit, and to be deeply impressed with the graces of her character and the
charm of her virtues. Fidelity to principle, refined modesty, loyal devotion to the cause of the
blind, cheerful readiness to sacrifice herself in
the interest of her pupils and associates, gentle
urbanity, serene dignity, generous recognition of
what is good and honorable in others, kindness
towards all and malice towards none, these are the
principal ornaments that adorn her noble life.
In parting with so admirable an assistant we cannot help feeling the separation very keenly; but,
at the same time, we are pleased to be able to
cherish the thought, that our loss is a great gain
to a child with imperfect sight, whose education
has been entrusted to her, and who is as near and
dear to us as any that we have under our immediate charge.

To supply the vacancies left in the corps of
teachers by the resignation of Miss Moore and
that of Miss Anna S. Low, which was accepted
last June, we have engaged the services of Miss
Sarah J. Whalen of Rochester, N. Y., and Miss
Fanny S. Marrett of Standish, Maine. Both these
new appointees have entered upon their duties
with an earnest appreciation of their importance,
and are eager to succeed in the sphere of their
ministrations.

MUSIC DEPARTMENT.

" Oh ! thou, whose soft bewitching lyre
   Can lull the sting of pain to rest ;
Oh ! thou, whose warbling notes inspire
   The pensive muse with visions blest ;
Sweet music ! let thy melting airs
   Soften my sorrows, and soothe my cares !

Sweet music ! when thy notes we hear,
   Some dear remembrance oft they bring
Of friends beloved no longer near,
   And days that flew on rapture's wing ;
Hours of delight that long are past,
   And dreams of joy too bright to last ! "

The work assigned to this department has been carried forward very successfully, and it affords me great pleasure to be able to give a most favorable account of its condition.

The number of pupils who received instruction in music during the past year was one hundred and thirteen. Of these, eighty-eight studied the pianoforte ; ten, the cabinet and church organs ; six, the violin ; seven, the clarinet ; one, the flute ; nineteen, brass instruments ; eighty-one, practised singing in classes, of which we have five ; twenty-five received private lessons in vocal training ; and thirty-eight studied harmony, divided into seven separate classes, averaging five members each.

When the pupil first begins the study of music, he receives simple instructions in theory as well as in the practice of instruments, so that step by step his mind is led onward, almost imperceptibly, into the marvels of harmony and composition.

The means and facilities afforded by the institution for the best musical instruction, and the ample opportunities it offers for practice, can hardly be surpassed anywhere. Yet, cognizant of the fact that the standard of music is advancing very rapidly throughout the country, and that the success of those of our students who intend making it their profession for life depends in no small measure upon the thoroughness of their equipment, we strive to improve the department dedicated to this art in every possible way, and to keep it in the line of progress.

A new parlor grand pianoforte has been recently procured, and our collection of musical instruments of different kinds has been replenished and received several needed additions.

Besides the uncommon advantages which our students enjoy at the institution itself, they are most liberally favored with external opportunities of a high order for the cultivation and refinement of their musical taste and the development of their artistic sense. Through the unfailing kindness and boundless generosity of the leading musical societies of Boston, of the proprietors of theatres, the managers of public entertainments, and also of the most eminent musicians of the city — whose names will be given in *full* elsewhere — our scholars have been permitted to attend the finest concerts, rehearsals, operas, oratorios, recitals, and the like, and have also been delighted with many excellent performances given in our own hall.

The advantages afforded by music are fully appreciated by the pupils, and they apply themselves to it with great zeal; but their progress is very unequal. "*Non omnia possunt omnes.*" As there are those among them who have a rare aptitude for the art and advance rapidly in it, so there are others, who, destitute of the wings of talent, make slow acquisitions by hard labor. But in the latter cases the gain, when attained, is more valuable perhaps than in the former.

We avail ourselves of every possible opportunity to impress upon the minds of both teachers and students of this department the important fact, that a complete musical education includes not only the necessary qualifications in the art itself, but also a high degree of physical, intellectual and moral culture. These are among the indispensable factors that go to make up a true artist. Nothing of permanent value can be accomplished without them. How can a pianist or a singer attain distinction in his specialty without healthy and well-formed hands and vocal organs? How can the works of Händel and Bach, of Beethoven and Mendelssohn, of Chopin and Schumann, be

satisfactorily interpreted by an imbecile in matters
of thought, imagination and judgment? How
can the subject of harmony be fully understood
by one not conversant with the science of sound
and with the evolution and history of music?
How is it possible to obtain a perfect technique—
vocal, manual, or pedal — without the knowledge
of anatomy, or to explore the labyrinth of emotions, sensibilities, sensations and sentiments without the guidance of mental philosophy? Supreme
excellence in art is one of the choicest flowers
which grow and thrive in the fertile soil of harmonious development. Hence, as Goethe expresses it, let us look up to the " sublime business,
the cultivation of all the faculties."

> "Zum erhabenen Geschäfte
> Zu der Bildung aller Kräfte."

TUNING DEPARTMENT.

> " For now to sorrow I must tune my song."
> MILTON.

One of the main objects of our system of education is to enable the recipients of its benefits to
become active members of human society, imbued
with a sense of dignity and armed for the struggle
of life.

The results of the past year, as well as those of
the preceding ones justify us in affirming, that the

tuning department is contributing its full share to this end.

The course of instruction and training therein pursued is full and systematic. It embraces both the principles and practice of the art of tuning.

The rooms devoted to this department are supplied with models of actions furnished by the leading manufacturers in the country, and with the necessary apparatus, appliances, tools and implements. This equipment affords ample means and facilities for the study of musical acoustics and the development of mechanical aptitude.

Our system of training is broad, practical and efficient. First the scholars receive regular and progressive lessons in the theory of scales, harmonics, beats and temperaments. Then, aided by the use of models and the dissection of old instruments, they acquire a thorough knowledge of the construction of the pianoforte and of all its parts and the details of the workings of its internal mechanism. Finally they are taught to do all the minor repairs, such as replacing broken strings, adjusting the hammers when they are out of position, regulating the jacks, mending fractured stems or putting new ones in their stead, and the like.

I have repeatedly stated in my previous reports, that the blind develop, in consequence of their deprivation, a remarkable power of distinguishing the pitch and quality of sounds; that, as a result of this ability, they acquire great proficiency in the art of tuning pianofortes; that in this calling they labor under no disadvantage whatsoever, and therefore are exceedingly successful; and that their work is in many respects more thoroughly and satisfactorily done than that of most of their seeing competitors. I desire to repeat the assertion here with all the emphasis which proceeds from full conviction; for it does not rest upon mere à priori reasoning, but is warranted by experience gathered in the field of observation and confirmed by an array of undisputed facts. The increased patronage which is extended to our tuners by some. of the very best and most intelligent families of Boston and the neighboring towns, and the unqualified recommendations with which many of the leading music teachers and prominent artists favor our work, are not the least proofs of its excellence.

The institution owns an assortment of forty-six, grand, square and upright pianofortes, which are in constant use every day from morning until evening. Our advanced students in tuning are entrusted with the care of these instruments. In keeping them in good working order, they have a fair opportunity to gain sufficient confidence and experience in their art before undertaking to exercise it outside.

But our graduates must bear it in mind always, that their business standing in the community or

their career of usefulness is not determined solely
by superior qualifications in their chosen calling
and complete mastery of its details. Far from it.
On the contrary, their worth is often estimated by
their conduct, discretion, tact, general intelligence
and personal appearance. To be rude, coarse, uncouth or overbearing, is an insuperable bar to their
advancement. Hence, in addition to high professional attainments, a tidy dress, habits of neatness,
polite manners, sensible conversation, and sterling
honesty in all dealings are indispensable to the
success of a tuner. To him no less than to a
music teacher the following words of Emerson
may be applied with peculiar force: —

> " What boots it thy virtue,
> What profit thy parts,
> While one thing thou lackest —
> The art of all arts?
> The only credentials,
> Passport to success,
> Opens castle and parlor,
> Address, man, address."

The friends of the blind will be glad to know
that the contract giving the pianofortes of the
public schools of Boston, 134 in number, into the
charge of the tuners of this institution, has been
renewed for another year on the same terms as the
last. This is the tenth time, that the work of the
blind has received the unanimous verdict of " well

done" from the committee on supplies of the school board, and we render heartfelt thanks and grateful acknowledgments to its members therefor.

The total receipts for tuning during the past year amount to $1,900.

To Messrs. Hook and Hastings we are greatly indebted for the gift of a model of the action of a full-sized pipe organ, by means of which our scholars are able to obtain an accurate knowledge of the complicated mechanism of this instrument.

TECHNICAL DEPARTMENT.

" Μοχθεῖν βροτοῖσιν αναγκη."

EURIPIDES.

Work is of inestimable value to mankind. It is the sire of wealth and the comrade of virtue. Its praises have been sung alike in verse and prose, and its worth as a source of human happiness and as the solid foundation of general prosperity and social safety and progress is almost universally admitted.

Euripides, the last of the illustrious trio of the tragic poets of Athens, says, that " toil is a necessity for all men," and the experience of the world bears testimony to the verity of his words. Carlyle observes, that " labor, wide as the earth, has its summit in heaven." Horace remarks, that nature gives nothing to mortals without it : —

" Nibil sine magno
Vita labore dedit mortalibus."

According to a Greek proverb, "love of toil is
the father of glory." Virgil declares, that work
conquers everything : —

" Labor omnia vincit ; "

and Pictet considers the industry of the hands as
the best means for the moral perfection of the
individual.

Manual training as a means of development has
attracted the attention of the great thinkers,
philosophers and teachers of every age and
nation. Bacon and Comenius, Milton and Hecker,
Semler and Pestalozzi, Fellenberg and Froebel,
were all stout champions thereof. Both Locke
and Pitt advocated ardently the establishment of
work schools as the best means of counteracting
the spread of pauperism in England. Instruction
in the mechanic arts found a most influential sup-
porter in Kant; and the scheme of national education, proposed by Fichte when Germany was
prostrate after the conquest by Napoleon, combined labor with learning.

The importance of handicraft is fully recognized
in this institution; and the employment of the
body as well as of the mind is a very essential
part of the education of our pupils. The experi-

satisfactorily interpreted by an imbecile in matters of thought, imagination and judgment? How can the subject of harmony be fully understood by one not conversant with the science of sound and with the evolution and history of music? How is it possible to obtain a perfect technique — vocal, manual, or pedal — without the knowledge of anatomy, or to explore the labyrinth of emotions, sensibilities, sensations and sentiments without the guidance of mental philosophy? Supreme excellence in art is one of the choicest flowers which grow and thrive in the fertile soil of harmonious development. Hence, as Goethe expresses it, let us look up to the " sublime business, the cultivation of all the faculties."

"Zum erhabenen Geschäfte
Zu der Bildung aller Kräfte."

TUNING DEPARTMENT.

" For now to sorrow I must tune my song."

MILTON.

One of the main objects of our system of education is to enable the recipients of its benefits to become active members of human society, imbued with a sense of dignity and armed for the struggle of life.

The results of the past year, as well as those of the preceding ones justify us in affirming, that the tensive use of machinery and the division of labor, is contracting, instead of expanding, year by year. Moreover, the state of the market is so uncertain, and the competition in all industrial products so sharp, that some of our graduates find it very difficult, if not utterly impossible, to work advantageously at the trades, to which they bestowed special attention while at school. To these, as well as to all others who are determined to depend upon their own exertions for their living, but whose experience in their chosen profession is rather discouraging, and suggests the necessity of seeking new resources, I would say, —

> " Go and toil in any vineyard,
>   Do not fear to do and dare ;
> If you want a field of labor,
>   You can find it anywhere."

In place of Mr. Walter H. Fiske, who resigned voluntarily last summer, Mr. Eugene C. Howard, a young man of modest mien, but of strict honesty and veracity and of good mechanical ability, has been appointed instructor in mattress-making and upholstery, and I take great pleasure in reporting that he has proved to be a very desirable acquisition to our staff of assistants.

of this ability, they acquire great proficiency in
the art of tuning pianofortes; that in this calling
they labor under no disadvantage whatsoever, and
therefore are exceedingly successful; and that
their work is in many respects more thoroughly
and satisfactorily done than that of most of their
seeing competitors. I desire to repeat the assertion here with all the emphasis which proceeds
from full conviction; for it does not rest upon
mere *à priori* reasoning, but is warranted by experience gathered in the field of observation and
confirmed by an array of undisputed facts. The
increased patronage which is extended to our
tuners by some. of the very best and most intelligent families of Boston and the neighboring
towns, and the unqualified recommendations with
which many of the leading music teachers and
prominent artists favor our work, are not the least
proofs of its excellence.

The institution owns an assortment of forty-six,
grand, square and upright pianofortes, which are
in constant use every day from morning until
evening. Our advanced students in tuning are
entrusted with the care of these instruments. In
keeping them in good working order, they have
a fair opportunity to gain sufficient confidence and
experience in their art before undertaking to exercise it outside.

But our graduates must bear it in mind always,
that their business standing in the community or

suspend operations in this branch of industry, which seemed to be quite promising both in an educational and a business point of view.

In addition to the special and efficient training which our girls receive daily in the workrooms, they are brought up to believe in the dignity of labor and in the thorough mastery of manual and domestic occupations, which are invariably considered as an essential part of their education. Moreover, those entrusted with their instruction and care do not confine their ministrations to the limits of their specific duties. They extend their influence over the formation of the morals and manners of the scholars, and with the usual lessons in literature, music, handicraft and house economy,

> "Sweetness, truth and every grace
> With time and use are wont to teach."

The cottage plan, which is in full operation in the girls' department of our school, affords excellent opportunities for this end. Here fifteen or sixteen pupils sit at the same table and form one circle in family affairs with their teachers and other officers, who are four in number. The close and beautiful relationship that is thus brought about by the tie of domestic and social duties performed in common, and by enjoyments shared with one another, has a most powerful influence.

Workshops for Blind Adults.

"True industry doth kindle honour's fire."

SHAKESPEARE.

The cause of the blind has taken strong hold on the hearts of the American people, and it will never be abandoned or neglected. It is deeply rooted in the letter and .spirit of the fundamental laws of the different states, and draws the sap of its vitality from a wide-spread sense of justice and fairness. It is as much a matter of certainty, that sufficient provision will be made by the public for the education of de-:fective children as for the instruction of the most favored class.

When we recall to mind, that fifty-seven years .ago the good Dr. John Fisher and a small group of sympathizing friends had obtained an .act of incorporation from the legislature of Massachusetts for the foundation of the first school for the blind in America, but that for several years they could not raise the necessary funds for organizing and putting it into opera-tion, and then reflect that this continent is now dotted over through its length and breadth with establishments of this kind, there is surely reason for rejoicing.

These institutions are founded upon the solid rock of equity and not upon the piers of pity or charity. They derive the means of their support from unfailing sources, and constitute important links in the magnificent chain of public education, which encircles and binds together and solidifies the great republic. They have aimed at the attainment of practical results, and have aided the recipients of their advantages to rise above the clouds of ignorance and superstition, and to breathe the air of independence on the heights of activity and social equality. Through the agency of these establishments a great change has been wrought in the general condition of the blind, and a sense of dignity and manliness, arising from consciousness of ability to support themselves, is prevalent among them. Hence the feeling of helplessness and the fear of dependence no longer make the pathway of life dreary to every sightless person.

With all this success and progress, however, there is still a certain proportion of blind adults who cannot maintain themselves by their unassisted labor, and who are tottering under the heavy burden of their affliction. Besides the aged and the infirm, this class embraces those who are trained to diligence and skill and are eager to earn their living by the sweat of their brow, but who are not able to obtain employment or to carry on business; it also includes those who are deprived of the sense of sight by accident or disease at an age when they are no longer fit subjects to be educated at schools for children and youth.

ment has been faithfully tried for more than fifty
years, and the result has been uniformly favorable.
We find that intellectual improvement, instead of
being retarded, is decidedly aided by manual
training. Resolution and all the preparatives for
vigorous and successful application to study are
gained. Habits of industry and thrift are formed.
Cheerfulness and health are promoted. The
tedium of the schoolroom is relieved. Manual
dexterity and bodily elasticity are secured. Valuable mechanical knowledge is attained; and in
many cases a trade has been acquired, whereby a
livelihood might be obtained.

The work in both branches of this department
has been conducted with marked earnestness and
fidelity, and with equally satisfactory results in
each case.

I. Workshop for the Boys.

This shop is designed to impart fitting general
training in various crafts, and to prepare the
pupils to pursue one or more of the mechanic arts
successfully.

Seating cane-bottomed chairs, manufacturing
brooms, making mattresses and upholstering parlor furniture have been taught, and lessons in
practical prudence and in the conduct of actual
business have been given.

Confessedly the number of manual employments
for the blind is very limited, and owing to the ex-

or mind, or disposed to subsist on the bread of
charity and to shun the active occupations of
life. The motto, "independence through industry," should not only be inscribed in large letters
over the entrance of such institutions, but should
also constitute the animus of their organization.
Of establishments for eager and willing workers
there is evident and imperative need: while there
is none for special almshouses for idle paupers
which would serve merely as receptacles, where
the good and the bad, the vicious and the virtuous, the irrepressible beggars and the self-
respecting laborers would have to be mixed up
together. The springs of the beneficence of these
latter institutions are congealed by the demoraliz-
ing influences inherent in their nature. The flaw
in them is their tendency to do away with all in-
ducement and necessity for industry. Being nests
of indolent drones rather than hives of diligent
workers, they are prolific of evils of every description. They put a premium on idleness and
improvidence. They relax natural ties, dissolve
the amenities of kinship and affection, paralyze
all motives of self-respect, remove all incentives
to activity, and tend to harden, brutalize and
degrade their beneficiaries. In other words, they
crush the spirit while they seem to aid the
body. The defective material which is so closely
massed in them is very apt to produce immoral
fermentation, out of which spring petty social

II. *Workrooms for the Girls.*

Good as the condition of these rooms has
always been, it never was better than now. A
spirit of refreshing activity pervades the atmosphere, and neatness and order are noticeable in
every direction.

Both Miss Abby J. Dillingham, the principal
teacher, and Miss Cora L. Davis, her assistant,
are deeply interested in the progress of the
pupils and are tireless in endeavoring to enlarge
the sphere of their usefulness.

The girls are carefully and patiently instructed
in the mysteries of stitching, hemming, darning,
plain sewing and knitting, both by hand and
machine. Those among them who are thoroughly
grounded in these elementary branches, are occupied with fine needle and machine work, as well
as with crocheting, and making hammocks and
a great variety of articles of fancy and worsted
work, all of which are easily and profitably disposed of at the weekly exhibitions.

Several of the pupils have been taught the
art of making fancy baskets of different shapes,
sizes and colors, and have become very proficient
in it; but I regret to say that the raw material
for this work, — consisting of long strips of shavings of hard wood, — are under the exclusive
control of the Indians, and that our supply has
already been cut off. Thus we are compelled to

cided to incorporate the school for the young
blind with the asylum of *Quinze - Vingts*, Haüy,
the "apostle of the blind," considered the association of his pupils with the degraded and depraved men and women who lived in that retreat,
as the greatest of all the calamities that befell
them.

> " By nature's laws, immutable and just,
> Enjoyment stops where indolence begins;
> And purposeless, to-morrow, borrowing sloth,
> Itself heaps on its shoulders loads of woe,
> Too heavy to be borne."

With these facts before us, it is neither unjust nor unkind to state, that for persons who
are willing to enter such institutions and to live
in an atmosphere of demoralization and in a state
of inertia, the ordinary town and county poor-
houses, with all their imperfections and disadvantages, are much preferable to almshouses intended
for a special class. The evils arising from the congregation of a large number of persons similarly
afflicted with a common bodily infirmity are, at
any rate, not found in the former.

Active occupation and opportunity to be useful constitute the sum and substance of the
happiness of the blind; and efforts in their
behalf should be concentrated in the direction
of opening fields to them, wherein they can
exercise their skill and develop a power that

Workshops for Blind Adults.

"True industry doth kindle honour's fire."

SHAKESPEARE.

The cause of the blind has taken strong hold on the hearts of the American people, and it will never be abandoned or neglected. It is deeply rooted in the letter and .spirit of the fundamental laws of the different states, and draws the sap of its vitality from a wide-spread sense of justice and fairness. It is as much a matter of certainty, that sufficient provision will be made by the public for the education of defective children as for the instruction of the most favored class.

When we recall to mind, that fifty-seven years ago the good Dr. John Fisher and a small group of sympathizing friends had obtained an act of incorporation from the legislature of Massachusetts for the foundation of the first school for the blind in America, but that for several years they could not raise the necessary funds for organizing and putting it into operation, and then reflect that this continent is now dotted over through its length and breadth with establishments of this kind, there is surely reason for rejoicing.

These institutions are founded upon the solid rock of equity and not upon the piers of pity or charity. They derive the means of their sup-

cided to incorporate the school for the young blind with the asylum of *Quinze - Vingts*, Haüy, the " apostle of the blind," considered the association of his pupils with the degraded and depraved men and women who lived in that retreat as the greatest of all the calamities that befell them.

> " By nature's laws, immutable and just,
> Enjoyment stops where indolence begins;
> And purposeless, to-morrow, borrowing sloth,
> Itself heaps on its shoulders loads of woe,
> Too heavy to be borne."

With these facts before us, it is neither unjust nor unkind to state, that for persons who are willing to enter such institutions and to live in an atmosphere of demoralization and in a state of inertia, the ordinary town and county poorhouses, with all their imperfections and disadvantages, are much preferable to almshouses intended for a special class. The evils arising from the congregation of a large number of persons similarly afflicted with a common bodily infirmity are, at any rate, not found in the former.

Active occupation and opportunity to be useful constitute the sum and substance of the happiness of the blind; and efforts in their behalf should be concentrated in the direction of opening fields to them, wherein they can exercise their skill and develop a power that will enable them to minister to the wants of the world and receive the means of their sustenance in return for their labor.

Workshops then and not asylums are needed for the relief of the blind. It is this kind of institution that will lessen the darkness which is set in their path. It is within the walls of such a one that they will find employment for their hands, and comfort for their hearts, and not in vast almshouses built for their benefit, where there will be no work for them to do, no hope for them to cherish, and scarcely anything to reconcile them to life.

There is a serious question, however, as to whether those who are employed in these workshops should be kept under the care and guardianship of the institutions, should be provided with board and lodgings in common establishments, and their expenses covered wholly or in part by their earnings; or whether they should be treated as other grown-up people are, that is, paid in cash all they can earn and left to the wholesome responsibility of taking care of themselves.

Individual opinions, influenced by economy and other side issues, are conflicting on this point; but both reason and experience are unquestionably in favor of the latter plan, which has in itself the great merit of leaving the blind to their own self-control and of making them as far as possible independent. This scheme, viewed from whatever side, is much simpler and more natural than the other. It is less ostentatious. It dispenses with a great deal of the show and parade of a public eleëmosynary institution, and with much of the complexity and perplexity of its management. It has nothing in its organiza-. tion or its internal arrangements that would tend to create an atmosphere of pauperism, or to sow the seeds of dissatisfaction and grumbling, or to foster the germination of the very evils which it seeks to remedy. Moreover, it relieves the blind in some measure from the disagreeable consciousness of dependence and of being subject to particular observation as members of an asylum; it enables them to feel that they are coming together not to eat charity soup at a common table, but to do their day's work. Thus by means of this plan the great moral evil of having a large community of infirm persons living without the wholesome influence of the social and family circle, would be effectually obviated. They would be scattered about in private houses. In some instances they would be with their kith and kin. In all cases they would keep up relations with seeing people; they would be still of the world. They would not consider the workshop as their home. They would be thrown more completely upon their own exertions, and learn to go alone.

vices. Witness the *Quinze-Vingts*, or retreat
for "fifteen score" of blind persons in Paris,
and the asylum for about the same number at
Naples, both of which are marked by the worst
features of such establishments. The inmates
are not obliged to work, and no steady employment is provided for them. In the words of
Thomson, —

> " Their only labor is to kill the time,
> And labor dire it is and weary woe."

Helping themselves to the means of subsistence
furnished by the public, and no longer spurred
to action by the feeling or fear of hunger,
they cease all exertion and become parasites on
the industry of others. They associate but little
with seeing persons. They have few relations
and sympathies with the world. They form an
unnatural community of infirm adults, and consequently a morbid, most undesirable and un-
lovely spirit pervades that community. All the
moral disadvantages arising from blindness are
increased and intensified in their midst to a
deplorable extent, and the ethical atmosphere is
most unpropitious to the growth of generous
and manly virtue. Thus the unfortunate inmates
become clannish to the last degree. They are extremely suspicious of seeing persons. They are
unamiable, unhappy and not infrequently vicious.
When the consular government of France de-

Secondly. — They should be located in large cities, so that their industrial products or manufactures may find a ready market, and their business character be developed and sustained through the patronage and encouragement of the community. This fact is so important in itself, that it outweighs all apparent and real advantages which a farm in the country might offer.

Thirdly. — The management of these institutions should not be hitched to the chariot of a party or religious denomination, and their organization should be such as to keep them entirely free from political influence and favoritism, or from ecclesiastical bias and taint. For this purpose the establishments should be placed by law under the absolute and exclusive control of corporations or associations, consisting of the most benevolent, high-minded and public-spirited citizens, who should be invested with full powers to elect annually a board of five or seven trustees and to add to their own membership from time to time. No remuneration of any kind should be allowed either to the members and officers of the corporation or to the trustees.

Fourthly. — The capacity of these workshops should not exceed the limits required for the accommodation of all eligible applicants residing within a reasonable distance from them, and the means for their support should not be supplied from the state or city treasury, but should be raised by free gifts and voluntary contributions from benevolent men and women.

Fifthly.—Inducements sufficient to make them willing to undertake the direction of the affairs of these establishments should be offered to men of high character, culture, executive ability, and more than average intelligence and physical strength ; and reasonable freedom should be granted to them in shaping their policy and in selecting their assistants and subordinates.

Sixthly.—If it is necessary for these institutions to provide homes for some of the apprentices while they are learning their trades, and who in consequence have no means for their own support, then it would be by far the best plan to board them in the neighborhood of the workshop for a strictly limited period of time, and not to bring them together under one roof.

Seventhly.—It should be not only the policy, but the duty and business of these institutions to encourage all blind persons who can work quietly at home to do so, providing employment for them, furnishing them with stock at wholesale cost, and disposing of their produce at the best possible market price.

Lastly.—Instead of spending large sums of money for the purchase of grounds and for vast piles of bricks and mortar, these institutions should have a permanent fund invested, the interest of which should be devoted to eking out

the wages of men and women who can earn
nearly but not quite enough to support themselves.

Want of time and strength has rendered it
impossible for me to treat this most important
subject . *in extenso* and to elaborate it in all
its bearings; but the above sketch, imperfect
though it be, contains the main principles upon
which supplementary institutions should be organized. In endeavoring to solve so serious a
problem, affecting the general welfare and the
social and moral standing of a whole class of
people, we must not be influenced in our deci-
sions by the distressing condition of a few individuals, whose lack of industry and of mental
and bodily strength renders them pitiable objects
of compassion. As a matter of course. people of
this sort are inclined to live on charity in any
place regardless of its character, and to accept
assistance in whatever form it is given to them.
But the great majority of the blind, especially
those who were born and brought up in this
country, are deeply imbued with that spirit of
freedom and independence which is the legitimate outcome of its institutions, and therefore.
shrink from the thought of receiving alms or of
being gathered together and cared for in large
poorhouses. They are disposed to struggle resolutely and against fearful odds for an honest
livelihood. They ask only for the means of earn-

ing a crust and of obtaining a corner in which to eat it; and to this end they are eager to work hard, and early and late.

In bringing these remarks to a close I cannot refrain from stating, that, in dealing with questions relating to the ameioration of the present condition of the blind and to their future welfare, we must never depart from the following cardinal principles: —

First. — Instead of congregating them together. thus making of them a class apart, we should conform to the sound principle of dispersing them as much as possible through general society, mingling them with others and subjecting them to the ordinary influences of life.

Secondly. — There should be a strict and absolute separation of sexes whether in schools or in workshops. Surely, little need be said to prove the necessity of this. A marked hereditary tendency to any physical infirmity is more than liable to transmission. Science and statistics leave not a shadow of doubt on this point. This being true, it is a stern moral duty to use every precaution against a perpetuation of such tendency through successive generations. Marriage in cases where one of the parties has such hereditary predisposition is generally unwise, often far from right; intermarriage between two persons so predisposed is invariably wrong, very wrong. This consideration should decide the matter and

lead to the adoption of measures which will
secure the separation of the sexes, not by fences
and walls alone, but by a distance of several
miles, if possible. I am aware that this is a most
unpopular doctrine to preach; it is an odious
one to enforce in practice : but no one fully impressed with respect for the immutable laws of
nature, can hesitate between thus incurring un-
deserved odium and permitting the existence of
a system, which an enlightened posterity will no
doubt condemn as an abomination.

Respectfully submitted by

M. ANAGNOS.

raised by free gifts and voluntary contributions from benevolent men and women.

Fifthly.— Inducements sufficient to make them willing to undertake the direction of the affairs of these establishments should be offered to men of high character, culture, executive ability, and more than average intelligence and physical strength ; and reasonable freedom should be granted to them in shaping their policy and in selecting their assistants and subordinates.

Sixthly.—If it is necessary for these institutions to provide homes for some of the apprentices while they are learning their trades, and who in consequence have no means for their own support, then it would be by far the best plan to board them in the neighborhood of the workshop for a strictly limited period of time, and not to bring them together under one roof.

Seventhly.— It should be not only the policy, but the duty and business of these institutions to encourage all blind persons who can work quietly at home to do so, providing employment for them, furnishing them with stock at wholesale cost, and disposing of their produce at the best possible market price.

Lastly.— Instead of spending large sums of money for the purchase of grounds and for vast piles of bricks and mortar, these institutions should have a permanent fund invested, the interest of which should be devoted to eking *out*

To Mr. Eugene Tompkins, proprietor, and Mr. Henry A. McGlenen, manager of the Boston Theatre, for a pass admitting parties of about fifty in number to ten operas.

To the Händel and Haydn Society, through its secretary, Mr. E. B. Hagar, for twenty-eight tickets to the oratorio of Elijah.

To the Apollo Club, through its secretary, Mr. Arthur Reed, for six tickets to each of six concerts. To an anonymous friend for two tickets to the same.

To the Boylston Club, through its secretary, Mr. F. H. Ratcliffe, for eight tickets to each of six concerts.

To the Cecilia, through its secretary, Mr. Charles W. Stone, for twenty tickets to each of four concerts.

To the late Mr. C. C. Perkins, for five tickets ; and to anonymous friends for ten tickets to the same.

To the Euterpe, through its president, the late Mr. C. C Perkins, for an average of six tickets to each of four concerts. To an anonymous friend for three tickets to the same.

To Madame Helen Hopekirk, for a pass to six pianoforte recitals.

To Mr. Arthur Foote, for six tickets to one recital.

To Mr. Charles A. Ellis, for a pass to Mr. Carl Faelten's three pianoforte recitals.

To Mr. John A. Preston, for twelve tickets to one pianoforte recital.

To Mr. Charles A. Clark, for twenty-eight tickets to one pianoforte recital.

To Mrs. Julia Ward Howe, for two tickets to August Hylsted's concert.

To Frau Anna Steiniger-Clark, for ten tickets to each of six Beethoven concerts.

To Miss Annie M. Keith, for four tickets to one pianoforte recital.

To Miss Anna M. Dunlap, for eight tickets to one concert.

ing a crust and of obtaining a corner in which
to eat it; and to this end they are eager to
work hard, and early and late.

In bringing these remarks to a close I cannot
refrain from stating, that, in dealing with questions relating to the ame ioration of the present
condition of the blind and to their future welfare, we must never depart from the following
cardinal principles:—

First.—Instead of congregating them together,
thus making of them a class apart, we should
conform to the sound principle of dispersing
them as much as possible through general society, mingling them with others and subjecting
them to the ordinary influences of life.

Secondly.—There should be a strict and absolute separation of sexes whether in schools or in
workshops. Surely, little need be said to prove
the necessity of this. A marked hereditary tendency to any physical infirmity is more than liable to transmission. Science and statistics leave
not a shadow of doubt on this point. This being
true, it is a stern moral duty to use every precaution against a perpetuation of such tendency
through successive generations. Marriage in
cases where one of the parties has such hereditary predisposition is generally unwise, often far
from right; intermarriage between two persons
so predisposed is invariably wrong, very wrong.
This consideration should decide the matter and

IV. — Acknowledgments for Periodicals and Newspapers.

The editors and publishers of the following reviews, magazines, and semi-monthly and weekly papers continue to be very kind and liberal in sending us their publications gratuitously, which are always cordially welcomed and perused with interest : —

The N. E. Journal of Education, .	. *Boston, Mass.*
The Atlantic, ...	. " "
Boston Home Journal, . . .	. .. ..
Youth's Companion, . . .	. .. ..
Our Dumb Animals, . . .	. .. ..
The Christian, ...	. .. ..
The Christian Register, . .	. .. ..
The Musical Record, . . .	. .. ..
The Musical Herald, . . .	. .. ..
The Folio, ...	. .. ..
Littell's Living Age, . . .	. .. ..
Unitarian Review, ...	. ..
The Watchman, ...	. ..
The Golden Rule, ...	. " "
Zion's Herald, ' . . .	. .. ..
The Missionary Herald, . .	. .. ..
The Well-Spring, ...	. " "
The Salem Register, . . .	. *Salem, Mass.*
The Century, ...	. *New York, N. Y.*
St. Nicholas, ...	. " "
The Journal of Speculative Philosophy,	.
The Christian Union, . . .	. " "
Church's Musical Journal, . .	. *Cincinnati, O.*
Goodson Gazette, .	*Va. Inst. for Deaf-Mutes and Blind.*
Tablet, . . .	*West Va.* " " " "
Good Health, ...	. *Battle Creek, Mich.*
L'Amico dei Ciechi, . . .	. *Florence, Italy.*
Valentin Haüy, a French monthly, .	. *Paris, France.*

ACKNOWLEDGMENTS.

Among the pleasant duties incident to the close of the year is that of expressing our heartfelt thanks and grateful acknowledgments to the following artists, *littérateurs*, societies, proprietors, managers, editors and publishers, for concerts and various musical entertainments; for operas, oratorios, lectures, readings, and for an excellent supply of periodicals and weekly papers, minerals and specimens of various kinds.

As I have said in previous reports, these favors are not only a source of pleasure and happiness to our pupils, but also a valuable means of æsthetic culture, of social intercourse, and of mental stimulus and improvement. So far as we know, there is no community in the world which does half so much for the gratification and improvement of its unfortunate members as that of Boston does for our pupils.

I. — Acknowledgments for Concerts and Operas in the City.

To Mr. Henry Lee Higginson we are under great and continued obligations for thirty-two season tickets to the series of twenty-four symphony concerts, and for forty season tickets to a series of four popular symphony concerts.

To an anonymous lady friend for three tickets to one popular symphony concert.

EDWARD JACKSON, *Treasurer, in account with the* PERKINS INSTITUTION AND MASSACHUSETTS SCHOOL FOR THE BLIND.

For the financial year ending October 1, 1886.

RECEIPTS.			EXPENDITURES.		
1885.					
Oct. 1, by balance on hand,		$2,056 55			
1886.					
Income from invested funds for the year,	$18,039 62		To General Fund, paid drafts in favor of M. Anagnos,		$55,500 00
State of Massachusetts,	30,000 00		" Printing " " "		5,519 95
" of New Hampshire,	3,000 00		" " M. Anagnos, balance due Oct. 1, 1886,		41 53
" of Vermont,	2,100 00		" Kindergarten Fund, drafts in favor of M. Anagnos,		20,027 18
" of Rhode Island,	6,175 00		" General Fund, Treasurer for clerk hire,		150 00
" of Connecticut,	4,650 00		" " discount on check,		25
" of Maine (two years),	9,350 00		" " balance of assessments on $500 bond		
Legacy from Valeria G. Stone,	5,000 00		5 per cent, 3 shares of Chicago,		
" " Mary Elizabeth Davis for Printing Fund,	400 00		Burlington & Northern R.R.,		444 00
General Fund, received of M. Anagnos,	7,979 87		" " bought 5,000 of Chicago, Burlington		
" " of unexpended balance,	610 02		& Northern R.R. 5 per cent.		
Printing Fund, Miss Fay, to print "What Katy Did,"	481 00		bonds,		5,218 75
" " Miss Howes, to print "The Deacon's Week,"	20 00		Harris Fund, mortgage on 226 Newbury street trans-		
" " M. Anagnos, sale of books,	840 14		ferred from Kindergarten Fund,		15,000 00
" " unexpended balance of draft,	57 47		Balance on hand Oct. 1, 1886,		36,327 45
Kindergarten Fund, collections during the year,	16,128 39				
" " M. Anagnos, unexpended balance,	3,246 85				
" " mortgage on 226 Newbury street transferred to Harris Fund,	15,000 00				
Harris Fund, H. W Muzzey, mortgage collected in full,	9,000 00				
" " collected on account of House of Angel Guardian mortgage,	4,000 00	136,176 56			
Total,		$138,233 11	Total,		$138,233 11

Boston, Oct. 13, 1886

EDWARD JACKSON, *Treasurer.*

To Mr. F. J. Campbell, for an average of seventy-five tickets to two concerts.

To Dr. E. Tourjée, for tickets to the quarterly concerts of the New England Conservatory.

To the ladies of the First Baptist Church, for forty tickets to one concert in Association Hall.

To the St. John's M. E. Church, for a general invitation to their concerts and lectures.

To Rev. J. J. Lewis, pastor of the Broadway Universalist Church, for a general invitation to their concerts and lectures.

II. — *Acknowledgments for Concerts, Lectures and Readings given in our Hall.*

For a series of recitals, concerts and readings given from time to time in the music hall of the institution, we are greatly indebted to the following artists : —

To Dr. L. J. Fenderson, reader, Mrs. Ella Cleveland Fenderson, vocalist, assisted by Mr. George J. Parker and others, for one concert.

To Mr. Southwick, for one reading.

To Mr. E. B. Perry, for one pianoforte recital.

To Mr. Charles A. Clark, assisted by Miss Marion Osgood, violinist, for one concert.

To Mrs. William H. Sherwood, for one pianoforte recital.

To Miss C. Culbertson, for one pianoforte recital.

To Mr. Charles A. Bond, assisted by Miss Alta Pease and others, for one concert,

To Capt. C. A. Jackson, for one lecture.

III. — *Acknowledgments for Books, Minerals, Specimens, etc.*

For various books, specimens, curiosities, etc., we are indebted to the following friends : —

To Hon. Spencer F. Baird, Mr. Clement Ryder, Mrs. L. M. Prescott and the society for providing religious literature for the blind.

GENERAL STATEMENT OF RECEIPTS AND DISBURSEMENTS, ETC. — Concluded.

Amount brought forward,	. . . . .	$82,228 53	*Amount brought forward,*	. . . . .	$77,283 04
II.—RECEIPTS, EXCLUSIVE OF INCOME.			II.—INVESTMENTS.		
From Legacies, General Fund, Mrs Valeria G. Stone,	$5,000 00		Assessments on Chicago, Burlington & Northern R.R.,	$444 00	
" Printing Fund, Miss M. E. Davis,	400 00		Five Chicago, Burlington & Northern R.R. bonds,	5,218 75	5,662 75
" Donations, General Fund,	6 30				
" " Printing Fund,	501 00		Cash balance Oct 1, 1886,	.	36,327 45
" " Kindergarten Fund,	16,126 39				
		22,033 69			
III.—COLLECTIONS AND SALE OF STOCKS.					
From notes collected,	. . . . .	13,000 00			
Cash balance Oct. 1, 1885,	. . . . .	2,011 02			
Total, ...	.	$119,273 24	Total, ...	.	$119,273 24

I desire again to render the most hearty thanks, in behalf of all our pupils, to the kind friends who have thus nobly remembered them. The seeds which their friendly and generous attentions have sown have fallen on no barren ground, but will continue to bear fruit in after years; and the memory of many of these delightful and instructive occasions and valuable gifts will be retained through life.

M. ANAGNOS.

GENERAL STATEMENT OF RECEIPTS AND DISBURSEMENTS, ETC. — Concluded.

Amount brought forward,	. . . . .			$92,228 53	
II.—RECEIPTS, EXCLUSIVE OF INCOME.					
From Legacies, General Fund, Mrs Valeria G. Stone,		$5,000 00			
" Printing Fund, Miss M. E. Davis,		400 00			
Donations, General Fund,		6 30			
" Printing Fund,		501 00			
" Kindergarten Fund,		16,126 39			
				22,033 69	
III.—COLLECTIONS AND SALE OF STOCKS.					
From notes collected,	. . . .			13,000 00	
Cash balance Oct. 1, 1885,	. . .			2,011 02	
Total, . . .				**$119,273 24**	

Amount brought forward,	. . . . .		$77,283 04
II.—INVESTMENTS.			
Assessments on Chicago, Burlington & Northern R.R.,		$444 00	
Five Chicago, Burlington & Northern R.R. bonds,		5,218 75	
			5,662 75
Cash balance Oct 1, 1886,	. .		36,327 45
Total, . . .			**$119,273 24**

GENERAL STATEMENT OF RECEIPTS AND DISBURSEMENTS OF THE PERKINS INSTITUTION AND MASSACHUSETTS SCHOOL FOR THE BLIND FOR THE YEAR ENDING SEPTEMBER 30, 1886.

I.—INCOME.

State of Massachusetts, annual appropriation,	$30,000 00		
Board and tuition, State of Maine (two years),	9,450 00		
" " of New Hampshire,	3,600 00		
" " of Vermont,	2,100 00		
" " of Connecticut,	4,650 00		
" " of Rhode Island,	5,175 00		
" " private pupils,	835 96	$56,210 96	
From tuning,		1,900 00	
admission fees,		84 35	
boys' shop,		34 00	
sundry small items,		671 58	
Interest on mortgage notes,		11,174 99	
" South Boston Railroad note,		412 50	
" balances in N. E. Trust Co.,		252 34	
" Ottawa & Burlington Railroad bonds,	240 00		
" Eastern Railroad bonds,	300 00		
" Boston & Lowell Railroad bonds,	50 00		
" Chicago, Milwaukee & St. Paul bonds,	300 00		
" KansasCity,St.Jo.&CouncilBluffs bds,	350 00		
" Chicago, Burlington & Quincy bonds,	1,080 00		
" Chicago,Burlington&Northern bonds,	5 98	2,325 98	
" dividends, Fitchburg Railroad,	290 00		
" Providence Railroad,	240 00		
" Chicago,Burlington&Quincy Railroad,	528 00	1,028 00	
" rents, 11 Oxford street,	448 73		
" North Boston,	1,550 00		
" Roxbury,	824 58		
" work department, men's shop,		2,846 31	
sale of books in embossed print,		4,447 73	
		840 14	
Amount carried forward,		$82,298 53	

II.—EXPENSES.

Maintenance,	$43,813 23	
Work department, men's shop,	2,714 38	
Tuning department,	963 90	
Hire of treasurer's clerk and collection of check,	150 25	
Taxes, insurance and repairs on property from which income is received,	738 94	
Rent of office,	250 00	
Expenses of printing office,	5,402 48	$54,033 18
Harris beneficiaries,		937 50
Kindergarten grading and building,		21,903 15
Bills to be refunded,		359 21
Amount carried forward,		$77,233 04

WORK DEPARTMENT, Oct. 1, 1886.

STATEMENT.

Amount due Perkins Institution from first date, .		$49,133 70
Amount of receipts over expenditures for the year 1886, ...		1,733 35
		$47,400 35

Cash received during the year 1886, . . .			$16,968 24
Salaries and wages paid blind people, .	$3,461 72		
" " seeing people,	2,438 95		
Amount paid for stock, rents and sundries,	9,334 22		
		15,234 89	
		$1,733 35	
Stock on hand Oct. 1, 1885, . .	$9,039 92		
" " Oct. 1, 1886, $5,501 62			
Debts due Oct. 1, 1886, . 1,925 76			
	7,427 38		
		1,612 54	
		$120 81	

PRINTING FUND STATEMENT OCT. 1, 1886.

Receipts.		Expenses.		
Proportion of income of invested funds,	$5,182 75	Labor,	$1,832 29	
Sale of books,	840 14	Stock,	159 72	
Donations,	501 00	Machinery,	1,163 73	
Legacy,	400 00	Electrotyping,	1,356 20	
		Binding,	485 25	
		Type,	91 38	
		Books,	106 58	
		Board of printers,	200 00	
		Cleaning, gas, freight, etc.,	67 33	5,462 48
		Balance to be added to fund,		2,411 41
	$7,873 89			$7,873 89

KINDERGARTEN FUND STATEMENT OCT. 1, 1886.

Receipts.		Expenses.		
Proportion of income of invested funds,	$1,152 80	Building and grading,	$21,903 15	
Donations,	16,126 39	Due general fund, Oct., 1885,	136 88	22,040 03
Sale of investment,	15,000 00	Balance,		10,239 16
	$32,279 19			$32,279 19

The following account exhibits the state of the property as embraced in the books of the institution, Sept. 30, 1886 :

Real Estate yielding Income.		
House No. 11 Oxford street, . . .	$5,500 00	
Three houses on Fifth street, . . .	9,000 00	
House No. 537 Fourth street, .	4,500 00	
Three houses, corner Day and Perkins streets, Roxbury, ...	8,460 00	
Real estate used for school purposes, So.		$27,460 00
Boston, ...	. .	240,200 00
Real estate used for school purposes, Roxbury, ...	. .	44,320 33
Unimproved land in So Boston, . .	. .	8,500 00
Mortgage notes, ...	. .	203,000 00
So. Boston R. R. Co., note, . . .		7,500 00
Railroad Stock.		
Boston & Providence, 30 shares, value, .	$5,490 00	
Fitchburg, 52 shares, value, . .	7,280 00	
Chicago, Burlington & Quincy, value, .	10,000 00	
Chicago, Burlington & Northern, value,	250 00	
		23,020 00
Railroad Bonds.		
Eastern R. R. 6s, 4 at $1000, value, .	$5,400 00	
Boston & Lowell, 5s, 1, "	1,000 00	
Chicago, Burlington & Quincy, 4s, 27 at $1,000, value, ...	27,000 00	
Chicago, Burlington & Northern, 5s, 5 at $1,000, value, ...	5,500 00	
Chicago, Milwaukee & St. Paul, 6s, 5 at $1,000, value, ...	6,000 00	
Ottawa & Burlington, 6s, 5 at $1,000, value, ...	5,500 00	
Kansas City, St. Joseph & Council Bluffs, 7s, 5 at $1,000, ...	6,150 00	
		56,550 00
Cash, ...	. ,	36,327 45
Household furniture, ...	. .	15,000 00
Provisions and supplies, ...	. .	968 04
Wood and coal, ...	. .	2,222 00
Work Department.		
Stock and bills, ...	. .	7,427 38
Musical Department, viz.:		
One large organ, ...	$5,000 00	
Four small organs, ...	450 00	
Forty-five pianos, ...	11,000 00	
Brass instruments, ...	700 00	
Violins, ...	35 00	
Musical library, ...	600 00	
		17,785 00
Amount carried forward, . .	. .	$690,280 20

Printing Fund Statement Oct. 1, 1886.

Receipts.			Expenses.		
Proportion of income of invested funds,	$5,132 75		Labor,	$1,832 29	
Sale of books,	840 14		Stock,	159 72	
Donations,	501 00		Machinery,	1,163 73	
Legacy,	400 00		Electrotyping,	1,356 20	
			Binding,	485 25	
			Type,	91 38	
			Books,	106 58	
			Board of printers,	200 00	
			Cleaning, gas, freight, etc.,	67 33	
			Balance to be added to fund,	5,462 48	2,411 41
	$7,873 89				$7,873 89

Kindergarten Fund Statement Oct. 1, 1886.

Receipts.			Expenses.		
Proportion of income of invested funds,	$1,152 80		Building and grading,	$21,903 15	
Donations,	16,126 39		Due general fund, Oct., 1885,	136 88	
Sale of investment,	15,000 00		Balance,	22,040 03	10,239 16
	$32,279 19				$32,279 19

KINDERGARTEN FUND.

List of Contributors.
From September 30, 1885, to October 1, 1886.

Amount acknowledged in the last annual report,	$44,469 12
Henry B. Rogers,	1,000 00
A friend,	1,000 00
Shepherd Brooks,	500 00
Mrs. J. H. Wolcott (fourth contribution),	300 00
Miss Louisa M. Alcott,	125 00
Dr. Samuel Eliot,	100 00
Miss Mary Jane Aldrich,	100 00
Mrs. M. R. Richardson,	100 00
Miss Abby W. May (third contribution),	100 00
A Christmas offering,	100 00
C. W. Amory (second contribution),	100 00
R. T. Parker,	100 00
J. N. Fiske,	100 00
W.,	100 00
Proceeds of fair held by Miss Bacon and her Sunday-school class of First Religious Society, Roxbury,	80 00
Amos A. Lawrence,	50 00
Mrs. G. G. Lowell (second contribution),	50 00
Danbury, Conn., through Nellie Hancock,	41 00
G. H. Quincy (second contribution),	25 00
Mrs. W. F. Weld,	25 00
Miss Laura Norcross (second contribution),	25 00
Amount carried forward,	$48,590 12

Amount brought forward, ...		$690,280 20
Printing Department, viz.:		
Stock and machinery, ...	$2,800 00	
Books, ...	9,400 00	
Stereotype plates, ...	7,607 00	
		19,807 00
School furniture and apparatus, ...		7,900 00
Library of books in common type, .	$2,900 00	
" " raised type, . .	9,000 00	
		11,900 00
Boys' shop, ...	. . .	118 75
Stable and tools, ...	. . .	804 17
		$730,810 12

The foregoing property represents the following funds and balances and is answerable for the same.

General fund, investments, real estate, .	$19,000	
General fund, investments, stocks and mortgages, ...	96,745	
		$115,745 00
General fund, cash, ...	. . .	23,676 88
Harris fund, investments, . . .	. . .	80,000 00
Printing fund, investments, . . .	. . .	113,325 00
" " cash, ...	. . .	2,411 41
Kindergarten fund, real estate yielding income, ...	. . .	8,460 00
Kindergarten fund, cash, ...	. . .	10,239 16
		$353,857 45
Buildings, unimproved real estate and personal property, in use for the institution, So. Boston, ...	. . .	332,632 34
Buildings, unimproved real estate and personal property, in use for the institution, Roxbury, ...	. . .	44,320 33
		$730,810 12
Total amount of property belonging to Kindergarten, ...	. . .	$63,019 49
Total amount of property belonging to Institution proper, . . .	. . .	667,790 63
		$730,810 12

Amount brought forward, ...$52,047 30

H. Bradlee Fenno, Edward N. Fenno, jr., Thomas
   G. Stevenson, R. H. Stevenson, jr., and George
   H. Blake, ... 50 55
J. R. Hall, ... 50 00
E. P., ... 50 00
Miss Ellen G. Cary, ... 50 00
F. V. Balch, ... 50 00
T. E. U., ... 50 00
Mrs. J. B. S. Jackson, for current expenses (third
   contribution), ... 50 00
Mrs. Nancy M. Field, Monson, Mass., . . . 50 00
Mrs. J. Parkinson, ... 25 00
Mrs. Horace Gray (second contribution), . . 25 00
Mrs. S. E. Guild, ... 25 00
Miss Lucy Lowell ($10 annual, second contribu-
   tion), ... 25 00
Miss Abby W. Pearson, ... 25 00
E. D. Chamberlin, ... 25 00
William Montgomery (second contribution), . . 25 00
L. W. D., ... 25 00
M. M. D., ... 25 00
H., ... 25 00
Mrs. Mason's Sunday-school class, Harvard Church,
   Brookline, ... 25 00
Mrs. Mary C. Charles (second contribution), . 25 00
Harvard Sunday-school Infant class, Brookline, . 12 00
H. W., ... 10 00
Mrs. C. C. Chadwick (second contribution), . . 10 00
Children of Boylston Chapel private school (second
   contribution), ... 8 00
George Whitney, ... 5 00
Lewis B. Bailey, ... 5 00

Amount carried forward, ...$52,797 85

Amount brought forward, . . .	.$48,590	12
R. Sullivan (second contribution), . . .	25	00
Miss A. D. Torrey, ...	20	00
S., ...	20	00
Children of Misses Garland and Weston's kindergarten, ...	17	37
Mrs. C. P. Curtis, ...	15	00
Sunday-school class Dr. Briggs' church, Cambridgeport, ...	12	00
Through Miss C. B. Rogers, ...	10	00
Mrs. Julia Ward Howe, ...	10	00
Sunday School First Congregational Church, Danvers, ...	10	00
Miss C. Wood, ...	10	00
Sunday School Unitarian Church, Littleton, Mass.,	7	00
Mrs. E. Pickering, ...	5	00
Sunday School St. James Church, ...	3	00
Entertainment by little boys of Perkins Institution,	2	45
A friend of the little ones, ...	2	00
Through Laura Bridgman, ...	1	50
A friend, ...	1	00
Through M. L., ...	1	00
Sunday-school teacher, San Diego, Cal., . .	1	00
Through Miss L. D. Swinerton, ...	1	00
Through J. V., ...		50
Miss Mary Ann Wales (third contribution), . .	1,000	00
Mrs. Porter, proceeds of three entertainments, .	915	00
Mrs. William Appleton (second contribution), .	500	00
Mrs. Gardner Brewer, ...	500	00
Mrs. Francis Brooks, profits on sale of "Heidi," .	192	05
Cash, ...	100	00
Proceeds of pupils' exhibitions at Perkins Institution, Feb. 22, ...	75	31
Amount carried forward, . . .	.$52,047	30

Amount brought forward, ...$60,358	20
Benjamin Dean, ...	25 00
Mrs. E. Wigglesworth, ...	20 00
Unitarian Sunday School, First Parish, Beverly, .	15 00
From sale of " Star Drifts," through Miss M. H. Hill, ...	14 73
South Congregational Church, South Framingham,	12 00
Phenix, R. I., Kindergarten (second contribution),	10 84
Mrs. F. H. Swan, ...	10 00
Mrs. Robert Swan (third contribution), . .	10 00
Mrs. R. M. White, ...	10 00
Mrs. Annie W. Sweetser's Kindergarten, West Newton, ...	10 00
A friend, through J. S. D., ...	10 00
Proceeds of fair by Carrie B. Phippen and Edith M. Colburn, ...	9 75
Miss Brackett's infant class, in the First Church (third contribution), ...	9 50
Henrietta Heinzen and Miriam Tower, . . .	7 50
Miss Harriet S. Parsons, ...	5 50
Cash, ...	5 00
Mrs. K. A. Baxter, ...	5 00
J. R. Corthell, ...	5 00
Mrs. E. E. Pratt, ...	5 00
Through Laura Bridgman, ...	5 00
Mrs. J. H. Meredith, ...	5 00
Miss Lucy H. Symonds' Kindergarten, . . .	3 07
Florence Stanley and Grace Clapp, . . .	3 00
Through Miss B., ...	2 25
Mrs. E. I. Welch, Lyndon, Vt., ...	2 00
William E. Howarth, ...	2 00
A member of the Second Congregational Church, Dorchester, ...	2 00
Amount carried forward, ...$60,582	34

██

98

Amount brought forward, ...$52,797	85
Mrs. Chickering's School at Dorchester, additional,	1 00
Mrs. D. Wallis Morrison, New Rochelle, N.Y., .	1 00
A sympathizer, ...	1 00
Three little girls, ...	30
A friend, ...	5,000 00
Proceeds of children's fair at Swampscott, . .	672 66
The Misses Worthington, part proceeds of a fair held by them, ...	388 88
Mrs. J. H. Wolcott (fifth contribution), . .	300 00
Mrs. J. Templeman Coolidge (second contribution), ...	200 00
Mrs. Francis Brooks, sale of " Heidi," . . .	200 00
William Perkins, ...	100 00
Mrs. Henry Brackett, ...	100 00
Mrs. John L. Gardner, in memory of Mrs. J. R. Anagnos, ...	100 00
Mrs. Nancy S. Davis and Mrs. M. Louise Tilden, in memory of Miss Caroline A. Sawyer, . .	100 00
Proceeds of pupils' concerts in Vermont, . .	60 00
First Congregational Society in New Bedford, .	50 00
C. M. L., ...	50 00
Henry Whitney Bellows, Katy Putnam Peabody, Robert Peabody Bellows, Ellen Derby Bellows, and Mary Derby Peabody, ...	44 06
Third Congregational Church, Cambridge, . .	32 85
Six young girls, through Mrs. Margaret F. King, .	30 00
Children of Miss Perkins' Kindergarten, Amherst, Mass., ...	28 60
Mrs. U. H. Crocker, ...	25 00
Miss E. Ballard, ...	25 00
Mrs. Edward J. Holmes, ...	25 00
Mrs. Clitheroe Dean James, ...	25 00
Amount carried forward, ...$60,358	20

LIST OF EMBOSSED BOOKS,

PRINTED AT THE PERKINS INSTITUTION AND MASSACHUSETTS
SCHOOL FOR THE BLIND.

TITLE OF BOOK.	No. of Volumes.	Price per Set.
Book of Proverbs,	1	$2 00
Book of Psalms,	1	3 00
New Testament,	3	7 50
Book of Common Prayer,	1	4 00
Baxter's Call,	1	2 50
Hymns for the Blind,	1	2 00
Pilgrim's Progress,	1	4 00
Natural Theology,	1	4 00
Life of Melanchthon,	1	1 00
Selections from the Works of Swedenborg,	1	–
Biographical Sketches of Distinguished Persons,	1	3 00
Biographical Sketch of George Eliot,	1	25
Memoir of Dr. Samuel G. Howe,	1	3 00
Howe's Cyclopædia,	8	32 00
Combe's Constitution of Man,	1	4 00
Cutter's Anatomy, Physiology and Hygiene,	1	3 00
" Life and her Children," or a Reader of Natural History,	1	3 00
Philosophy of Natural History,	1	3 00
Geometrical Diagrams,	1	1 00
Huxley's Science Primers, Introductory,	1	2 00
Higginson's Young Folks' History of the United States,	1	3 50
Constitution of the United States,	1	40
Dickens's Child's History of England,	2	6 00
Freeman's History of Europe,	1	2 50
Schmitz's History of Greece,	1	3 00
Schmitz's History of Rome,	1	2 50
Guyot's Geography,	1	4 00
Scribner's Geographical Reader,	1	2 50
American Prose,	2	6 00
Most Celebrated Diamonds, by Julia R. Anagnos,	1	50
Dickens's Christmas Carol, with Extracts from Pickwick,	1	3 00
Dickens's David Copperfield, 1st and 2d vols.,	–	6 00
" " " 3d and 4th vols. in press,	–	–
Dickens's Old Curiosity Shop,	3	12 00
Emerson's Essays,	1	3 00
Extracts from British and American Literature,	2	5 00
George Eliot's Silas Marner,	1	3 50
Goldsmith's Vicar of Wakefield,	1	3 00
Hawthorne's Scarlet Letter,	2	5 00
Hawthorne's Tanglewood Tales,	2	4 00
Scott's Quentin Durward,	2	6 00
Scott's Talisman,	2	6 00
The Deacon's Week,	1	25
The Last Days of Pompeii, by Edward Bulwer Lytton,	3	9 00
Bryant's Poems,	1	3 00
Byron's Hebrew Melodies and Childe Harold,	1	3 00
Poetry of Byron, selected by Matthew Arnold,	1	3 00

Amount brought forward, ...	.$60,582	34
Brookfield Sunday School, through Miss S. M. M.,	2	00
Mrs. J. C. Roberts, ...	2	00
Minnie Tupper and Fanny Johnson, . . .	1	34
Mrs. Holbrook's Sunday-school class, First Church,	1	25
Miss Baxter, ...	1	00
School at Beverly, ...	1	00
Cash, ...	1	00
Little children of Miss Gray's and Miss Gordon's Kindergarten, Cortes street, ...	1	00
Miss Sallie Wilbur, Acushnet, Mass., . . .	1	00
Florence Kindergarten, ...		60
Cash, ...		50
Mrs. Bethmann's Kindergarten (second contribution), ...		48
Total, ...	.$60,595	51

We are also indebted to Miss Sarah E. Nickerson for a steel engraving for the kindergarten.

All contributors to the fund are respectfully requested to peruse the above list, and to report either to EDWARD JACKSON, *treasurer, No. 178 Devonshire street, Boston, or to the director,* M. ANAGNOS, *South Boston, any omissions or inaccuracies which they may find in it.*

LIST OF APPLIANCES AND TANGIBLE APPARATUS,

MADE AT THE PERKINS INSTITUTION AND MASSACHUSETTS
SCHOOL FOR THE BLIND.

_____

GEOGRAPHY.

I. — *Wall Maps.*

1. The Hemispheres, ... size, 42 by 52 inches.
2. United States, Mexico and Canada, " " "
3. North America, ... " " "
4. South America, ... " " "
5. Europe, ... " " "
6. Asia, ... " " "
7. Africa, ... " " "
8. The World on Mercator's Projection, " " "

Each $35, or the set, $280.

II. — *Dissected Maps.*

1. Eastern Hemisphere, . . . size, 30 by 36 inches.
2. Western Hemisphere, . . . " " "
3. North America, ... " " "
4. United States, ... " " "
5. South America, ... " " "
6. Europe, ... " " "
7. Asia, ... " " "
8. Africa, ... " " "

Each $23, or the set, $184.

These maps are considered, in point of workmanship, accuracy and distinctness of outline, durability and beauty, far superior to all thus far made in Europe or in this country.

"The New England Journal of Education" says, "They are
very strong, present a fine, bright surface, and are an ornament to any school-room."

III. — Pin-Maps.

Cushions for pin-maps and diagrams, . . . each, $0 75

ARITHMETIC.

Ciphering-boards made of brass strips, nickel-
plated, ... each, $4 25
Ciphering-types, nickel-plated, per hundred, . " 1 00

WRITING.

Grooved writing-cards, ... each, $0 05
Braille tablets, with metallic bed, . . . " 1 50
Braille French tablets, with cloth bed, . . " 1 00
Braille new tablets, with cloth bed, . . . " 1 00
Braille Daisy tablets, ... 5 00

· TERMS OF ADMISSION.

"Candidates for admission must be over nine and under nineteen years of age, and none others shall be admitted."— *Extract from the by-laws*.

Blind children and youth between the ages above prescribed and of sound mind and good moral character, can be admitted to the school by paying $300 per annum. Those among them who belong to the state of Massachusetts and whose parents or guardians are not able to pay the whole or a portion of this sum, can be admitted gratuitously by application to the governor for a warrant.

The following is a good form, though any other will do : —

" *To His Excellency, the Governor.*

" Sir: — My son (or daughter, or nephew, or niece, as the case may be), named —— and aged ——, cannot be instructed in the common schools, for want of sight. I am unable to pay for the tuition at the Perkins Institution and Massachusetts School for the Blind, and I request that your Excellency will give a warrant for free admission. Very respectfully, —— ——."

The application may be made by any relation or friend, if the parents are dead or absent.

It should be accompanied by a certificate, signed by some regular physician, in this form : —

" I certify that, in my opinion, —— —— has not sufficient vision to be taught in common schools; and that he is free from epilepsy, and from any contagious disease.

(Signed) —— ——."

These papers should be done up together, and forwarded to the DIRECTOR OF THE INSTITUTION FOR THE BLIND, *South Boston, Mass.*

Blind children and youth residing in Maine, New Hampshire, Vermont, Connecticut and Rhode Island, by applying as above to the governor, or the "Secretary of State," in their respective states, can obtain warrants for free admission.

The sum of $300 above specified covers all expenses (except for clothing), namely, board, lodging, washing, tuition, and the use of books and musical instruments. The pupils must furnish their own clothing, and pay their own fares to and from the institution.

An obligation will be required from some responsible persons, that the pupil shall be kept properly supplied with decent clothing, shall be provided for during vacations, and shall be removed, without expense to the institution, whenever it may be desirable to discharge him.

The usual period of tuition is from five to seven years.

The friends of the pupils can visit them whenever they choose.

The use of tobacco, either in smoking or otherwise, is strictly prohibited in the institution.

Persons applying for admission of children must fill out certain blanks, copies of which will be forwarded to any address on application.

For further information address M. ANAGNOS, DIRECTOR, PERKINS INSTITUTION FOR THE BLIND, *South Boston, Mass.*

APPENDIX.

PROCEEDINGS

OF THE

COMMENCEMENT EXERCISES

OF THE

PERKINS INSTITUTION AND MASSACHUSETTS
SCHOOL FOR THE BLIND.

COMMENCEMENT EXERCISES

OF THE

PERKINS INSTITUTION AND MASSACHUSETTS SCHOOL FOR THE BLIND.

" Invest me with a graduate's gown,
'Midst shouts of all beholders,
My head with ample square-cap crown,
And deck with hood my shoulders."

SMART.

The greatest event in the yearly history of the Perkins Institution occurs on its commencement day. A year of hard study, of earnest endeavor, opening with a dim outlook and leading along a somewhat misty pathway, has at length been crowned with success as, on the fairest of June days, the school publicly presents a brief *résume* of its work and receives the kindly plaudits and congratulations of its benefactors and friends.

In compiling this report of the exercises, we have culled freely from the very full accounts given by the press.

The following circular, announcing the programme to be given, and including a concise statement relative to the kindergarten enterprise, — which now claims an equal interest with the school proper, — was fully and favorably noted in all the prominent newspapers of the city : —

PERKINS INSTITUTION AND MASS. SCHOOL FOR THE BLIND,
BOSTON, May 10, 1886.

The commencement exercises of this school will be held at Tremont Temple, on Tuesday, June 1, at 3 P. M. Samuel

mportant fact the attention of the benevolent and philanthropic members of our community is most respectfully called. They should bear it in mind, that upon their kind consideration and generous aid the support, progress and success of the enterprise are wholly dependent.

Both annual subscriptions for current expenses, and contributions for an endowment fund large enough to place the establishment on a permanent basis, are earnestly solicited, and will be thankfully received and duly acknowledged by

EDWARD JACKSON, *Treasurer,*

No 178 Devonshire street, Boston, Mass.

PROGRAMME.

PART I.

1. ORGAN. Fifth Concerto, ... *Handel.*
   CHARLES H. PRESCOTT.

2. BRIEF OPENING ADDRESS.
   HIS EXCELLENCY GOVERNOR ROBINSON.

3. BAND. "Lohengrin." Introduction and Bridal Chorus,
   Wagner, arr. by J. B. Claus.

4. LAWS OF MECHANICS, Illustrated by Sewing Machine.
   MISS EVALYN A. TATREAU.

5. DOUBLE QUARTETTE for Male Voices, from "Glenara,"
   H. Strachauer.
   [Libretto by JULIA R. ANAGNOS.]

6. EXERCISE IN GEOGRAPHY.
   BY FOUR LITTLE BOYS.

7. READING BY THE TOUCH.
   JULIA ROESKE AND M. EUNICE FRENCH.

8. SOLO FOR CLARINET. Cavatina, op. 82, . . *M. Bergson.*
   CLARENCE W. BASFORD.

Eliot, LL. D., will preside; His Excellency, Governor Robinson, will give a brief opening address, and the Hon. Leverett Saltonstall will speak on the kindergarten project.

You are most cordially invited to honor the occasion with your presence.

The seats on the floor and in the first balcony of the Temple will be reserved for the choice of the members of the corporation, and the friends and patrons of the institution, to whom this invitation is sent, until Saturday, May 22. Tickets are ready for delivery, and those who may be desirous of obtaining them are requested to send me a postal card indicating the number wished for. It will give me very great pleasure to forward them at once.

The seats will be reserved until 3 o'clock, punctually, when standing persons will be permitted to occupy all vacant places.

No tickets are required for the second balcony of the Temple, to which the public are cordially invited.

M. ANAGNOS.

The second step for the establishment of a kindergarten, — which is most imperatively needed for little sightless children, and without which the system of the education of the blind has no solid foundation to rest upon, — has already been taken. A new, commodious brick building, large enough to accommodate from thirty-five to forty persons, is in the process of erection on the estate purchased last year in Roxbury, corner of Day and Perkins streets, and preparations are being made for the opening of the infant institution next autumn.

The funds in the treasury will be entirely exhausted, however, when the walls and the roof of the new structure are completed, and there will be not one cent left either for finishing its interior and providing the necessary furniture and domestic appliances, or for carrying on the work. To this

The programme promised a feast of exceptional interest in the fulness and variety of its musical and literary
numbers, interspersed with other brief exercises of the
usual pleasing character.

Among the distinguished persons who occupied seats
upon the platform were His Excellency, Governor Robinson, Hon. Leverett Saltonstall, Mrs. Julia Ward Howe,
widow of Dr. S. G. Howe, founder of the school, trustees and others. The pupils, officers and teachers were
also seated on the platform, and prominent among them
was Laura Bridgman, whose finger conversation with a
friend at her side attracted constant attention.

The first number on the programme was an organ selection, Händel's "Fifth Concerto," rendered "with fine
technical skill and expression" by one of the graduates,
Charles H. Prescott. This was given as an introductory
while the audience were assembling.

Dr. Samuel Eliot presided "with his usual grace and
tact," and opened the exercises in the following words : —

Ladies and gentlemen : — In behalf of the teachers and
pupils of the Perkins Institution and Massachusetts School for
the Blind, I welcome you to these graduating exercises. They
will begin with an address from one who needs no introduction ; but there may be some here who are not aware that he
is the real official head of the institution, in virtue of his
position as governor of the state, to whose wise liberality and
long-continued devotion this school owes much of what, under
the providence of God, it has been enabled to accomplish
in the fifty-odd years of its existence. I present to you His
Excellency, Governor Robinson.

OPENING ADDRESS.

BY HIS EXCELLENCY, GOVERNOR GEORGE D. ROBINSON.

Ladies and gentlemen: — There was a peculiar and sad significance in the opening remarks of Dr. Eliot, wholly unintentional on his part, in the fact that he brings me forward to take the first part in the *graduating* exercises. Of course that indicates that I am pretty nearly through. I *am*, but I do not like to be reminded of it. I better like the title on the first page of the programme, "Commencement Exercises." *Commencement* is rather more agreeable than *graduation* to one who is in politics. I should say, however, that I find. in this last year of my service, renewed delight in coming here; not alone in standing before you, ladies and gentlemen. and welcoming you, in behalf of the commonwealth, to this delightful and instructive entertainment, for I find still greater pleasure in standing before the pupils of the institution, and giving them today my heartiest wishes. I am glad to see them all here. Their faces are not at all unfamiliar to me, because it has been my pleasure to make them a recent visit at their school, and there to see more of them than we have opportunity for on an occasion like this.

Few institutions in our commonwealth command such cordial attention as the Perkins Institution. In fact. if you observe the writings of those who have come here from foreign lands to visit us, to examine America and her works, you scarcely find one who has not given his testimony about this school. For more than fifty years have people come and gone. bearing tribute to its excellence and its influence. Our own people perhaps do not fully appreciate it. It is not an unusual thing for ourselves to be less acquainted with what lies next to our doors, than is the stranger who visits us. We are less inclined to visit the great fields of renown in our immediate vicinity, than are those who come here for a brief period. and look about to find what will interest and instruct them. So undoubtedly in proportion to the number of people the Perkins Institution receives as visitors, many are strangers to the state of Massachusetts. There is nothing peculiar in this institution, marking it as outside the educational developments of the state. We have our schools all over the commonwealth, — to such a degree are the people interested in the education and advancement of every child. Therefore it is to be expected, in the present time, that new appliances, new facilities, better opportunities, will be provided for this institution, as well as for all the others. The great advance made in the methods of teaching in the schools throughout this state is within the easy remembrance of many of us. The older men and women now present will run back in quick recollection to the days of their boyhood and girlhood, — to the small number of schools, to the imperfect methods and limited opportunities; and, comparing those privileges with these which are afforded today, they will see wherein, in every possible way, we have given extraordinary effort and encouragement in this direction.

Coming to the front of the platform, the thought passed through my mind: What a variety of scenes I have witnessed in this hall; how many different audiences have I stood before, to say the few or the many words. One day it is the graduation of the Boston Latin School, with the boys' exercises in elocution; another day it is to hear a great orator; another day it is to engage in some festival; another day, to welcome people from all parts of the country, gathered here in fraternal intercourse; and so on without limit; but none of these occasions are more pleasing and interesting than this which brings us here today.

In order to develop most carefully the method of instruction pursued in a school like this, it is found that earlier attempts must be made with the children,— that we should begin with the little ones, and give them facilities which are readily afforded, for children in general, in the primary schools.

OPENING ADDRESS.

BY HIS EXCELLENCY, GOVERNOR GEORGE D. ROBINSON.

Ladies and gentlemen: — There was a peculiar and sad significance in the opening remarks of Dr. Eliot, wholly unintentional on his part, in the fact that he brings me forward to take the first part in the *graduating* exercises. Of course that indicates that I am pretty nearly through. I *am*, but I do not like to be reminded of it. I better like the title on the first page of the programme, "Commencement Exercises." *Commencement* is rather more agreeable than *graduation* to one who is in politics. I should say, however, that I find, in this last year of my service, renewed delight in coming here; not alone in standing before you, ladies and gentlemen, and welcoming you, in behalf of the commonwealth, to this delightful and instructive entertainment, for I find still greater pleasure in standing before the pupils of the institution, and giving them today my heartiest wishes. I am glad to see them all here. Their faces are not at all unfamiliar to me, because it has been my pleasure to make them a recent visit at their school, and there to see more of them than we have opportunity for on an occasion like this.

Few institutions in our commonwealth command such cordial attention as the Perkins Institution. In fact, if you observe the writings of those who have come here from foreign lands to visit us, to examine America and her works, you scarcely find one who has not given his testimony about this school. For more than fifty years have people come and gone, bearing tribute to its excellence and its influence. Our own people perhaps do not fully appreciate it. It is not an unusual thing for ourselves to be less acquainted with what lies next to our doors, than is the stranger who visits us. We are less inclined to visit the great fields of renown in our immediate vicinity, than are those who come here for a brief period, and look about to find what will interest and instruct

The "Laws of Mechanics, illustrated by the Sewing Machine," was a brief, practical essay, given by one of the young lady graduates, Miss Evalyn A. Tatreau, an earnest and diligent student, whose skilful handling of her text, as well as of the instrument, gave but a small proof of her attainments in the various branches of study pursued during her residence at the school. The brief time allowed for the exposition of the subject made it necessary to condense her statements into the following concise form : —

LAWS OF MECHANICS.

ILLUSTRATED BY THE SEWING MACHINE.

BY MISS EVALYN A. TATREAU.

Standing as we do today in the midst of the great results which have been achieved through the constant and untiring labor of man, can we look back over the centuries that have passed since his first appearance on the earth and imagine a period of time more brilliantly illuminated by grand and noble works? The oldest implements that have been found in connection with man, are of stone, such as hatchets and arrowheads. Implements of this kind in a later age were found polished, showing one step in advance. Very rude this may seem to people living in the nineteenth century ; yet it was one drop in the great sea of discoveries and inventions which today marks the physical, moral and intellectual growth of the race.

Although the resources of man are great yet they are limited. Force he cannot create ; that is of divine origin alone. But by scientific reasoning and planning, together with the labor of his hands, he has constructed objects which concentrate and distribute force. In this way his mental force is transformed into physical.

Now a limit of age is fixed, and children are only taken into this institution after they have passed that limit. How much better it would be if at once, at the ordinary school age, blind children could be put under instruction, given the advantages of development and culture, trained in little ways, taught by the simplest system, until they should attain a greater advance, when they can enter this institution and take its enlarged course. I understand that a gentleman who has given special attention to this matter, — who is announced in the programme, — will speak more particularly on this question ; and I hope, if the effort is made, in Boston and vicinity, to collect the necessary means to establish this kindergarten addition to the resources of the institution, it will meet with that ready and hearty response which always characterizes the efforts of Boston and her people in good works of this kind. It is an institution which receives constantly the support, in large measure. of the state, and that support is most heartily accorded.

Dr. Eliot responded happily that Governor Robinson "deserved to receive the highest political degree to which ne might aspire, and should then be made a perpetual under-graduate." The address of His Excellency was delivered with the earnestness and warmth of feeling which characterize all his utterances, and called forth frequent applause, expressive of a hearty response to his inspiring words. The assurance of his deep interest in the school, personal as well as official, was warmly and gratefully appreciated by all its members.

Following this address the brass band with clarinets gave a "spirited performance" of the "Introduction and Bridal Chorus" from "Lohengrin," executed with remarkable facility.

"Reading by the touch," which followed, was pronounced a "truly wonderful" performance, as given by Julia Roeske and Eunice French. The first, a tiny little girl, read some juvenile verses about "a pin" with a clearness and *naïveté* of expression that caught the fancy of the audience at once; and "showed wonderful aptitude," in view of the fact that she had been a pupil at the school since last September only. Eunice French read with fine expression and intelligence an enjoyable selection from the "Autocrat of the Breakfast Table."

A "solo for clarinet," quite a difficult cavatina, was played "with fine expression and skill" by Clarence W. Basford, and this closed the first part of the programme.

The second part opened with the appearance of sixteen boys, dressed in uniform, who gave a series of dumb-bell exercises with remarkable precision, and "showed a unity of time and movement which it would seem hardly possible to teach to pupils without sight." The sound of their retreating footsteps gave the signal to another set of actors who appeared in the form of eleven little girls, attired in white, and carrying silvery wands with which they performed various rhythmic exercises, "exhibiting grace of motion and an adaptation to physical development," and guided wholly in their movements by the notes of a piano played by a young pupil. A squad of twelve young men succeeded them upon the stage, advancing with military step and bearing, and clad in simple uniform. They went through the manual of arms and other military exercises with "promptness, exactness and perfect unison of movement."

The chorus for female voices, Molloy's "Song of the Triton," was then given in a manner that showed "well-trained voices of rare power and sweetness."

is gained in proportion to the '
band-wheel the force is sent :
the needle and part to the sl

The practical value of '
that of the complicated
great amount of force i

Miss Tatreau's ·
siastic applause, .
At its close, J
from " Glena·
very patheti·
production
whose lo·
and ev·
numbe
with
par

'g
ustratec
re it could
ade an excell
tines; another, a
tes River; and a thi
oined in 1652. The li
scribed very good repre:
n objects of interest; a win
ll, the Boston stone, the bea
the State House, and a ship in
might have immigrated. A tiny g
h she had manufactured, as a liken
l by the first white inhabitant of Boston.
the companion of the solitude and aid to th
Rev. William Blackstone. The story of (
sletter printed in 1704 was told in connect
odel of a printing press; and the difficult task
very small spinning wheel was successfully ac
by the skilful and industrious fingers of anothe
explained that the Boston ladies used to spin

The concentration and distribution of force we see plainly illustrated in the sewing machine, by means of a rod which connects the treadle with the large wheel. The force which I apply in a vertical direction is carried and concentrated in this wheel. A connection is made between the large and small wheels by the use of a band; through this connection velocity is gained in proportion to the size of the wheels. From the band-wheel the force is sent in two directions, part going to the needle and part to the shuttle lever.

The practical value of the simplest machinery far exceeds that of the complicated, as in all complicated machinery a great amount of force is expended in overcoming friction.

Miss Tatreau's performance was received with enthusiastic applause, and was very generously commended. At its close, Dr. Eliot announced the double quartette from " Glenara," prefacing it with the remark that " a very pathetic as well as artistic interest attaches to this production, as the libretto was written by Mrs. Anagnos, whose loss by death during the past year every inmate and every friend of the institution deplores." This number consisted of a hunting chorus, and was rendered with " fine effect" by eight male voices with piano accompaniment arranged for two performers.

"One of the most interesting numbers on the programme" was then given, — an exercise in geography, " characteristic of this school," — by four little boys, one of whom put together very rapidly and accurately a dissected map of South America; while the others " showed great facility" in recognizing by size and outline, as well as giving facts concerning the various countries represented by the different sections of the maps examined by their small fingers.

"Reading by the touch," which followed, was pronounced a "truly wonderful" performance, as given by Julia Roeske and Eunice French. The first, a tiny little girl, read some juvenile verses about "a pin" with a clearness and *naïveté* of expression that caught the fancy of the audience at once; and "showed wonderful aptitude," in view of the fact that she had been a pupil at the school since last September only. Eunice French read with fine expression and intelligence an enjoyable selection from the "Autocrat of the Breakfast Table."

A "solo for clarinet," quite a difficult cavatina, was played "with fine expression and skill" by Clarence W. Basford, and this closed the first part of the programme.

The second part opened with the appearance of sixteen boys, dressed in uniform, who gave a series of dumb-bell exercises with remarkable precision, and "showed a unity of time and movement which it would seem hardly possible to teach to pupils without sight." The sound of their retreating footsteps gave the signal to another set of actors who appeared in the form of eleven little girls, attired in white, and carrying silvery wands with which they performed various rhythmic exercises, "exhibiting grace of motion and an adaptation to physical development," and guided wholly in their movements by the notes of a piano played by a young pupil. A squad of twelve young men succeeded them upon the stage, advancing with military step and bearing, and clad in simple uniform. They went through the manual of arms and other military exercises with "promptness, exactness and perfect unison of movement."

The chorus for female voices, Molloy's "Song of the Triton," was then given in a manner that showed "well-trained voices of rare power and sweetness."

WORK OF THE KINDERGARTEN CLASSES.

The most "unique" and "telling" feature of the commencement exercises was presented by six small boys and an equal number of girls, who took their places upon the stage in front of tables prepared for them. Each one then modelled different forms representing "Early Boston in Clay," thus giving a charming illustrated recitation in the history of this noble city before it could boast of a printing press. One little girl made an excellent map of Boston and described its outlines; another, an Indian canoe for crossing the Charles River; and a third modelled a pine tree shilling coined in 1652. The little boys also exhibited and described very good representations of several well-known objects of interest; a windmill like that on Copp's hill, the Boston stone, the beacon, lighthouse, dome of the State House, and a ship in which the first settlers might have immigrated. A tiny girl held up a pen which she had manufactured, as a likeness of the one used by the first white inhabitant of Boston, and which was the companion of the solitude and aid to the study of the Rev. William Blackstone. The story of the Boston Newsletter printed in 1704 was told in connection with a model of a printing press; and the difficult task of making a very small spinning wheel was successfully accomplished by the skilful and industrious fingers of another girl, who explained that the Boston ladies used to spin and make their own cloth instead of buying it from England. Altogether the work of these little ones was so well performed as to prove "an unanswerable argument in favor of the kindergarten," and added intensely to the interest created in its behalf. "Although smiles and praise were everywhere accorded the workers on the platform,

many an eye was wet, and many a heart warm with the
desire to aid their little neglected brothers and sisters in
misfortune." While this work was in progress the
audience listened to a most eloquent, persuasive appeal
in behalf of the kindergarten, by the Hon. Leverett
Saltonstall, who strongly reënforced the impressions made
by the children, — the speaker and his subject having
been first introduced to the audience by Dr. Eliot with
the following appropriate words : —

Everyone is aware that steps have been taken, over and over
again, within the past three or four years, towards the establishment of a kindergarten department in the Massachusetts
School for the Blind, and probably everyone is aware of the
great necessity for such an addition. But if there are any
minds at all in doubt on the subject, if anybody here questions
the propriety of the course which the government of this
institution has adopted and is still following, I am sure their
doubts will yield, and all will become clear to them, as they
listen to the Honorable Leverett Saltonstall, who has kindly
consented to address you on this subject.

ADDRESS ON THE KINDERGARTEN.

BY HON. LEVERETT SALTONSTALL.

Ladies and gentlemen: — I am asked for a few words about
the proposed kindergarten. I feel that I know little on the
subject, but am thankful to contribute my small efforts toward
the accomplishment of this admirable design.

What form of human affliction calls for our sympathy more
than blindness? — especially at this lovely season when God
has unfolded before his children the wonders of his creation,
appealing to their hearts through all their senses, but especially
through that of sight, and calling upon them for gratitude and
praise, through every delicate leaf and flower which bursts

from the dry twig, through sun and moon and stars, blue sky
and fleecy cloud, through bird and insect, ocean, river, lake
and mountain, through unnumbered forms of beauty and of
grace, which adorn all nature, but more than all, through the
form and expression of those we love and who love us. When
then we think of those who are deprived of sight, how can
our hearts but be filled with tenderest sympathy?

Think! you who are thus blest with the power to enjoy this
feast which is daily spread before you, from the moment when
you open your eyes to behold the glorious light of day, till
you close them to rest, never a moment but you are experienc-
ing the wondrous blessing of sight.

How, then, can we better estimate our obligation, to aid
those of our human brotherhood who are deprived of sight,
than by thus summing its blessings and by thinking what the
loss of it would be to ourselves?

Having once been a trustee of the Perkins Institution, I
cannot but feel the deepest interest in its admirable work.
Already famous among similar institutions, it needs only
larger endowments and more commodious buildings to spring
to the front, and to take the lead.

Fortunate is it in having at its head one who seems to
have received from his friend and instructor, the late Dr.
Howe, the genius, the heart and the will to carry on the great
work which he bequeathed him. Were he not present, I
should say more, far more of Mr. Anagnos, of his gentle care
and devotion, his self-sacrificing zeal in the cause of the
blind. His enthusiasm and confidence in his cause remind me
of the same qualities in the late Professor Agassiz, in the
cause of science, — both of foreign birth, — the one from the
Swiss Republic, that Alpine nursery of freedom; the other,
from the classic land of Greece, in his noble career and
exalted endeavors, showing that this little kingdom can send
to the young republic those who, in the cause of philanthropy,
are worthiest successors to her scholars, poets, statesmen and
philosophers of old.

You are aware that young children are not admitted to the institution, and that it is for these little ones that Mr. Anagnos wishes to found the kindergarten ; for the reason that it is during these tender years that so much can be done to develop the child, and so much of neglect, and far worse, oftentimes of brutal treatment can be avoided ; that so much work has now to be devoted to undoing what has been badly done, that the little child, while at its most plastic age, may be, under kind and skilful teachers, and, like the clay which their little hands are now moulding with such intelligence [referring to the children at work on the platform], that they may be taken in hand before their faculties have become hardened and benumbed from neglect.

It is during these early years that the affections as well as the faculties, if rightly directed, are made to bear fruit. And what must be the life of those who have known nothing but neglect, who have been left to sit in idleness and to feel themselves cut off from all the pleasures and pursuits of childhood? How difficult the task to mould into gentle, happy, useful men and women, the children who have been thus treated ! Seeing this daily, and becoming more and more impressed with the necessity of overcoming this terrible obstacle in their education, our wise teacher, with his warm heart, conceived the design of founding the kindergarten for the blind.

The money thus far obtained through the zeal which he has kindled in others has been found sufficient for the purchase of a beautiful lot in Roxbury, and for the erection of a plain but substantial building, the lot being large enough to admit of others as they may be required.

But here the project is stopped for the present for want of funds. This cannot, however, long be so. Men and women will rise up who will be fired with the desire to do something to assist this good man in carrying out his noble scheme. Our interest cannot but be enlisted for it, as we look at these little ones, so earnest and so intelligent in their work, and, indeed, by all that we see and hear at these touching exercises.

Think of what was formerly the fate of the blind, and of the constantly increasing facilities for their education, so that now their resources and accomplishments are sufficient to render them self-supporting and useful members of society.

Through the zeal of gentle, affectionate and devoted teachers, as well as the generosity of those who have provided the means to enable them to annually add to their library (an inestimable fund), the blind are made in great measure to receive their sight, and even the little children seem through their intelligence to have worked in clay, as the Saviour did, a miracle; for I am quite sure that few children blessed with vision could evince more intelligence and skill than they.

Shall we, then, aid Mr. Anagnos in this noble work? Let all who feel their hearts touched by what they see and hear today, try to strengthen his hands, and before another year the kindergarten will be built and equipped, shedding its blessings on fifty or more little blind children who are now unhappily wasting their precious years in pitiful darkness.

A grand duo for two cornets from " Fliege du Vöglein," was then " beautifully executed " by two of the graduates, C. H. Prescott and C. T. Gleason. This was followed by the valedictory of Miss Annie M. Sullivan, who " acquitted herself of the always touching duty of farewell with a felicity of thought and tender grace of expression that raised her efforts far above conventionality."

VALEDICTORY.

BY MISS ANNIE M. SULLIVAN.

Today we are standing face to face with the great problem of life.

We have spent yèars in the endeavor to acquire the moral and intellectual discipline, by which we are enabled to distinguish truth from falsehood, receive higher and broader views of duty, and apply general principles to the diversified details of life. And now we are going out into the busy world, to take our share in life's burdens, and do our little to make that world better, wiser and happier.

We shall be most likely to succeed in this, if we obey the great law of our being. God has placed us here to grow, to expand, to progress. To a certain extent our growth is unconscious. We receive impressions and arrive at conclusions without any effort on our part; but we also have the power of controlling the course of our lives. We can educate ourselves; we can, by thought and perseverance, develop all the powers and capacities entrusted to us, and build for ourselves true and noble characters. Because we can, we must. It is a duty we owe to ourselves, to our country and to God.

All the wondrous physical, intellectual and moral endowments, with which man is blessed, will, by inevitable law, become useless, unless he uses and improves them. The muscles must be used, or they become unserviceable. The memory, understanding and judgment must be used, or they become feeble and inactive If a love for truth and beauty and goodness is not cultivated, the mind loses the strength which comes from truth, the refinement which comes from beauty, and the happiness which comes from goodness.

Self-culture is a benefit, not only to the individual, but also to mankind. Every man who improves himself is aiding the progress of society, and every one who stands still, holds it back. The advancement of society always has its commencement in the individual soul. It is by battling with the circumstances, temptations and failures of the world, that the individual reaches his highest possibilities.

The search for knowledge, begun in school, must be continued through life in order to give symmetrical self-culture.

For the abundant opportunities which have been afforded to us for broad self-improvement we are deeply grateful.

We thank His Excellency, the Governor, and the legislature of Massachusetts, and the governors and legislatures of the several New England states, for the most generous and efficient aid they have given our school.

We thank our trustees for the zeal and invariable interest which they have shown in all that concerns our well-being.

Director, teachers and matrons: we enter life's battle-field determined to prove our gratitude to you, by lives devoted to duty, true in thought and deed to the noble principles you have taught us.

Schoolmates: though the dear happy years we have spent together are over, yet the ties of friendship, and an enduring love and reverence for our school, and the sacred memory of her whom God has called from her labor of love to be an unseen but constant inspiration to us through life, are bonds of union that time and absence will only strengthen.

Fellow-graduates: duty bids us go forth into active life. Let us go cheerfully, hopefully, and earnestly, and set ourselves to find our especial part. When we have found it, willingly and faithfully perform it; for every obstacle we overcome, every success we achieve tends to bring man closer to God and make life more as he would have it.

The high thoughts, noble purposes and grateful feelings animating the hearts of the young graduates, — whose early-darkened childhood had brightened into happy, hopeful youth under the fostering care of the school, — thus found fitting and true expression in the words of one of their number, to whom the highest encomiums were lavishly awarded. It was pronounced "a beautifully original production, and the speaker's tender reference to the late Mrs. Anagnos as one who had been a cheering light to the pupils' hearts, and whose spirit would be ever present with them in memory's vision, was received with a sympathetic silence that could be felt by all, and many were moved to tears."

The graduates then came forward, eight in number, and received their diplomas from the hands of Dr. Eliot, who presented them with the following remarks : —

My dear young friends: — After the words that you have just heard from your associate, it is not necessary for me to enlarge upon what she has so well expressed. I am sure you have listened to her with very deep feeling, and that what you have heard will be helpful to you as you go on through life. Without saying more to you in the way of advice, I wish it were in my power to bring anything to you in the way of encouragement, as you stand this afternoon before me, and before this great audience, which has been gathered in profound interest and sympathy for your present and your future. I am sure that the opportunities and privileges which you have enjoyed in the Massachusetts School for the Blind have been of the utmost value to you ; and that the training which is unseen but which reaches far out into the visible world, and makes itself felt in all your communion with your fellow-beings, has had the first place in the education which is now brought, not to a close, but to a period in which one phase of it is over and another phase begins. You remember those lovely lines which Mrs. Wordsworth wrote, and which her husband put into one of his poems, where she speaks of

" That inward eye,
Which is the bliss of solitude."

It is the bliss of society also, the bliss of life, and with it you see, we all see, into the great realities of spiritual existence. There is a place waiting for you, for each one of you. mong your fellow-men and fellow-women; and you are needed by them just as much, and in the same proportion, as they are needed by you. As you take the place which God has prepared for you, and which this school has enabled you to fill. you will find, day by day, that there are duties and responsibilities which no other man and no other woman can fulfil but just yourselves.

I have been very much interested, within a few months, in reading a book which I hope you will read, the Life of Fawcett, the English statesman, who died a year or two ago, after a long service of consummate usefulness to his country. He was blind from the age of twenty-five, when an accident suddenly cut him off from sight forever in this world; and this book tells us of his heroism at that moment, how he determined, within ten minutes after the accident, that it should make no difference in his plans of life. True to his resolution, he went on from stage to stage, a professor in the university, a member of parliament, until he became a minister of the crown, the highest dignity to which the political Englishman aspires. He had some great disadvantages. Having become blind when he was twenty-five years old, he lacked the early opportunities for training which you have had, and which quicken your senses to activity and keenness of perception; and he never gained, as long as he lived, that dexterity which you have acquired, and which you have practised before our eyes this very afternoon; but he had a keen sense of enjoyment in life, and that feeling of dependence upon God, and upon God's will, which strengthened and enlightened him. He always said one and the same thing, whenever he spoke to the blind: "Do what you can, and act as if you were not blind. Take courage and help yourselves." To those who could see, he was as continually saying with regard to their treatment of him and those situated like him : " Don't patronize, but help us to be independent."

You have been trained to this independence ; and all I can say is : May you have the courage to go on and prove it. Never forget, though this terminates your connection with the school as pupils, that you can be its members and helpers in ways you have never had a chance to be until now. Every school, every college in the country counts upon its graduates as its best supporters, to stand by it through good report and evil report, through prosperity and adversity, and this school counts upon you to do the same. It has hosts of friends, but the friends whom it has are continually passing away. Those who have been closest to it are taken from it, and the places that have known them know them no more ; but the places which are waiting to know you, will know you, I trust, through long years of happiness and usefulness ; and may your usefulness never be nearer to you, or your happiness dearer to you than as they connect themselves with this school. The training you have had here is to perfect itself hereafter and to grow brighter and brighter to the end.

And now, as I give you these diplomas, though it is my hand which places them in yours, and my voice that calls your name, it is not from me, but from your faithful director and his faithful staff of teachers that they come.

The exercises closed with a grand chorus by all the voices, giving another selection from " Glenara," which was chosen by the school, and presented as one more public tribute in which all might join, to the memory of her who had ever been to them " a sunny presence that it needed no retina to perceive."

The performances throughout " were of an intensely interesting character," and though similar ones are repeated year by year, " there has been nothing worn out,

but something ever new in the emphasis of these appeals."
"The enthusiasm of the public on the festival days of the
blind youth is unfailing, and the applause, repeated again
and again, was the warmest assurance that could be given
of a very real interest in the work of the institution."

COMMENTS OF THE PRESS.

The proceedings of the festival were fully reported and
most favorably commented upon both by the secular and
religious press, and the attention of the public was
earnestly called to the work of the institution and its
present wants and future needs. Of the numerous articles, which appeared in the editorial columns of leading
newspapers on the occasion of our commencement exercises, we copy the following, including one on the kindergarten project : —

BLIND KINDERGARTNERS.

As often as the closing of the year brings the pupils of the
Perkins Institution for the Blind to Tremont Temple, the sympathy with this work gathers an eager and enthusiastic audience
to witness their exercises and express interest in their doings.
Recently, the little kindergartners have added their contributions to the occasion, and yesterday quite outdid themselves
in illustrating the early history of Boston in figures and
designs made from clay. The dozen children who thus displayed their ability to teach history in object lessons suggest
what may be done through the same method when applied to
the younger children who are now neglected in their homes,
because no adequate provision is made for them in institutions
for the blind. These children, from three to five years of
age, need to have their minds brightened and quickened in

these earliest years, and the uplifting of the blind can never reach a high degree of attainment until the kindergarten for the young, which Mr. Anagnos has designed, and the trustees of the institution have approved, has been completed and endowed. It is this work which makes its constant appeal, and which yesterday put its claims eloquently forward in the suggestive exercises in which the children of the Perkins Institution engaged, and in the admirable address of Mr. Leverett Saltonstall. Where is the $15,000 which will enable this projected institution to reach the point where it can begin its operations? — *Boston Herald*, June 2.

One of the most interesting educational anniversary occasions that occur in our city is the commencement of the Perkins Institution and Massachusetts School for the Blind. The exercises for the school year just closed took place in Tremont Temple last Tuesday afternoon, in the presence of a thoroughly sympathetic audience that completely filled the Temple. These occasions are always of a very high order of merit and fraught with pathetic interest, as well as being the cause of wonder and admiration at the perfection to which the instruction of the blind has been brought, and this year was no exception; in some respects the exercises were remarkably interesting, the pupils acquitting themselves in a manner to call out the most hearty enthusiasm from the audience. Dr. Samuel Eliot, president of the corporation, presided, and when he announced the double quartette from "Glenara" — which was beautifully sung by male pupils — he said that a very pathetic as well as artistic interest attaches to this production, as the libretto was written by Mrs. Anagnos, whose loss by death during the past year every inmate and every friend of the institution deplores. The work of a class of the smallest children in the kindergarten line, who modelled in clay several designs suggestive of incidents in the history of

Boston, in the presence of the audience, was a peculiarly interesting feature, and was an unanswerable argument in favor of the kindergarten department which is now being inaugurated, and which it is earnestly hoped will not be allowed to languish for want of funds. During the modelling work, Collector Saltonstall was introduced by Dr. Eliot, and made an eloquent and appreciative address, in the course of which he paid a warm tribute to the qualities of Mr. Anagnos, and said that he was worthy to come from the classic land of Greece. He closed with an urgent appeal for sympathy and support toward the project of the kindergarten school, which was an outgrowth of Mr. Anagnos' heart and zeal and was calculated to give to the work of training the blind children here a completeness scarcely to be found elsewhere in the world. Before the opening of the exercises by the pupils, Dr. Eliot asked Governor Robinson to speak, and he responded in his accustomed manner, paying a glowing tribute to the management and work of the institution. The valedictory, by Miss Annie M. Sullivan, was worthy of special mention, for its felicity of thought and grace of expression. It was emphatically a beautifully original production, and the speaker's tender reference to the late Mrs. Anagnos as one who had been a cheering light to the pupils' hearts, and whose spirit would be ever present with them in memory's vision, was received with a sympathetic silence that could be felt by all, while tears freely rolled down many faces. Dr. Eliot made a feeling and worthy response to this address, and then distributed the diplomas to the following graduates: Alice Viola Carleton, Lillie May Fletcher, Charles Timothy Gleason, Charles Harrison Prescott, Daniel Scott, Annie Mansfield Sullivan, Evalyn Annie Tatreau, Arthur Leon Warren. The exercises closed with the singing of the chorus finale from " Glenara." — *Boston Home Journal*, June 5.

No public exercise held in the city is more attractive than the annual exhibition of the Perkins Institution for the Blind. The repetition of these services for over half a century seems rather to increase than to diminish the interest. Tremont Temple was crowded last Tuesday by an eager and sympathetic company. On the stage, as usual, neatly dressed, sat the pupils — girls and boys, and young ladies and young men. They were as bright and alive to all the incidents of the hour as any of the spectators, giving little evidence of the veil upon their vision except by the motionless gaze in one direction, and when called to enter upon some exercise. Mrs. Julia Ward Howe, so well-known in the literary world, widow of the first director and founder of the institution, was upon the stage. Her dark dress recalled the late sudden and sad decease of her daughter, Mrs. Anagnos, the beloved wife and inspiring companion in his work of the present director of the school. Just behind her, in busy conversation with her hands with her friend, sat Laura Bridgman, the wonderful monument of painstaking, persistent and successful Christian philanthropy in reaching and quickening the mind when nearly every outward sense was closed. The fine brass band of the institution gave admirably performed pieces of music before and during the services. Samuel Eliot, LL. D., president of the corporation, presided, and introduced Governor Robinson in a graceful short address. The Governor is always happy on such occasions. He was playful, sympathetic and suggestive, heartily appreciative of the importance and success of the work accomplished in the school, and earnest in his appeal to the benevolent for the early and generous endowment of the kindergarten branch, now in construction. The exercises of the pupils, the excellent essays of two of the graduates, the illustrations of school work in geography, and of finger reading from the raised-letter volumes, the singing and instrumental music, the calisthenic and military drill, and finally the apt and amusing work of the younger pupils in clay, with their illustrated recitations on the early history of Boston — all met with the warmest expressions of appreciation on the part of the audience. Hon. Leverett Saltonstall made an animated address in advocacy of the new movement to receive these rayless children at an earlier age, and to bestow upon them the advantages of the kindergarten training. Many little fellows and their sisters, lonely enough at home while their companions are at school or at play, are awaiting the opening of this school with eager expectation. Certainly their sympathizing parents and friends are awaiting with impatient interest for the opportunities to be afforded to their afflicted children. The community is now so widely alive to this important undertaking that we cannot doubt but it will at once receive adequate funds for its completion and ample endowment. Four young gentlemen and four young ladies, having completed the course of study at the institution, were graduated, and received at the hands of Dr. Eliot, with tender and appropriate words of encouragement and congratulation, their diplomas. — *Zion's Herald*, June 9.

LIGHT FOR THE BLIND.

"There is a time to every purpose under the heaven," and the friends of blind children think the time to carry out their purpose of endowing a kindergarten is at hand.

The subject of establishing a kindergarten for the blind children of New England has been before the public for a year or two; and we have frequently alluded to it in these columns, besides printing the *fac simile* of the appeal in its behalf by Laura Bridgman. Other journals have been earnest in their endeavors to help on so good a cause; and, by fairs and entertainments, many friends have materially aided in starting this work. Among the large contributions was the sum of more than $4,000 from the proceeds of a fair held in the house of Mrs. J. H. Wolcott. Two generous hearts contributed $5,000 and $10,000 each; and these gifts were supplemented by smaller sums raised, by means of concerts chiefly, by the pupils of the Perkins Institution for the Blind. In all, enough was raised to begin the enterprise. An estate of six acres in Roxbury was bought, which will afford room not only for the school-rooms and cottages of the kindergarten, but even for the Perkins Institution itself, should the time ever come when the trustees desire to move that school from its hill overlooking the sea to a less crowded quarter.

We have good Scripture authority for saying that a house ought to be founded on a rock, and the new buildings in Roxbury will have that merit; but, unhappily, there proved to be too much rock. In attempting to build, it was found that an " immense mass of ledge" had to be removed. Every property owner who has had occasion to lay gas, water, and sewer pipes through rock-ribbed streets and grounds knows what an addition to the cost of the work these stony barriers make. It was never more manifest than in this case.

The trustees, twelve well-known business men, were ready to obey the advice given in Proverbs, " Prepare thy work without and make it fit for thyself in the field; and *afterward* build thine house." They made ready the field, hoping to finish the house last fall. But the ledge was more than their match, with the limited funds at their command.

St. Luke asks a very pertinent question about architecture: " Which of you, intending to build, . . . sitteth not down first and counteth the cost, whether he have sufficient to finish it? Lest haply, after he hath laid the foundation, and is not able to finish it, all that behold it begin to mock him, saying, This man began to build and was not able to finish."

The friends of the new enterprise did count the cost. The rocks were all blown out on paper before the first fuse was lighted; and it looked very much as though, after they had laid the foundation, they might not be able to finish their modest structure. But by careful husbanding of their resources and by the generosity of the architect, **Mr. S. D. Kelley,** who contributed plans and specifications, the trustees will be able to finish one building. It will, however, be a good deal like the house that Jack built, — empty, except a bag of malt and a rat, — unless the treasury, which will then be also empty, is refilled. Mr. Anagnos says : —

" There will be scarcely anything left, either for furnishings, musical instruments and apparatus, or for the absolutely necessary expenses for maintenance and tuition. For an endowment fund, which will give security to the permanence of the enterprise and will serve as a vital sap to its growth and fruition, we have not yet a penny."

The trustees, over their own names, invite aid to complete this work, saying with confidence. —

" The pleasing sight of such an infant institution, palpable and real, will, it is hoped, inspire the generous intentions of many more friends of childhood and the blind."

They state the necessity for such continued aid most cogently : —

" The purchase money, together with the great expense of removing the ledge and of erecting the first building, will *exhaust the last dollar of the fund already raised;* and liberal subscriptions are still needed to put the establishment in working order and enable the school to live and to expand."

It seems as though all that were necessary to secure the money was to state the need. The thought of little blind children growing up in eternal night all over this fair New England is pitiful. If science cannot restore to them the light of day, generosity can at least pour a flood of sunshine into their hearts and minds. Formerly there was the excuse that there was no channel through which to give aid to them. The opportunity is here. He doubles his gift who gives promptly.
— *Christian Register,* January 28, 1886.

Lightning Source UK Ltd.
Milton Keynes UK
UKHW020630051218
333473UK00010B/221/P

9 780266 058526